Router Security Strateg

Securing IP Network Traffic Planes

Gregg Schudel, CCIE No. 9591
David J. Smith, CCIE No. 1986

Cisco Press

Cisco Press
800 East 96th Street
Indianapolis, Indiana 46240 USA

Router Security Strategies:

Securing IP Network Traffic Planes

Gregg Schudel, CCIE No. 9591

David J. Smith, CCIE No. 1986

Copyright © 2008 Cisco Systems, Inc.

Cisco Press logo is a trademark of Cisco Systems, Inc.

Published by:
Cisco Press
800 East 96th Street
Indianapolis, IN 46240 USA

Printed in the United States of America

First Printing   December 2007

Library of Congress Cataloging-in-Publication Data:

Schudel, Gregg.

  Router security strategies : securing IP network traffic planes /
Gregg Schudel, David J. Smith.

       p. cm.

  ISBN 978-1-58705-336-8 (pbk.)

  1. Routers (Computer networks)—Security measures. 2. Computer networks—Security measures.
3. TCP/IP (Computer network protocol)—Security measures. I. Smith, David J., CCIE. II. Title.

  TK5105.543.S38 2007

  005.8—dc22

2007042606
ISBN-13: 978-1-58705-336-8
ISBN-10: 1-58705-336-5

Warning and Disclaimer

This book is designed to provide information about strategies for securing IP network traffic planes. Every effort has been made to make this book as complete and as accurate as possible, but no warranty or fitness is implied.

The information is provided on an "as is" basis. The authors, Cisco Press, and Cisco Systems, Inc. shall have neither liability nor responsibility to any person or entity with respect to any loss or damages arising from the information contained in this book or from the use of the discs or programs that may accompany it.

The opinions expressed in this book belong to the authors and are not necessarily those of Cisco Systems, Inc.

Trademark Acknowledgments

All terms mentioned in this book that are known to be trademarks or service marks have been appropriately capitalized. Cisco Press or Cisco Systems, Inc., cannot attest to the accuracy of this information. Use of a term in this book should not be regarded as affecting the validity of any trademark or service mark.

Feedback Information

At Cisco Press, our goal is to create in-depth technical books of the highest quality and value. Each book is crafted with care and precision, undergoing rigorous development that involves the unique expertise of members from the professional technical community.

Readers' feedback is a natural continuation of this process. If you have any comments regarding how we could improve the quality of this book, or otherwise alter it to better suit your needs, you can contact us through e-mail at feedback@ciscopress.com. Please make sure to include the book title and ISBN in your message.

We greatly appreciate your assistance.

Corporate and Government Sales

The publisher offers excellent discounts on this book when ordered in quantity for bulk purchases or special sales, which may include electronic versions and/or custom covers and content particular to your business, training goals, marketing focus, and branding interests. For more information, please contact:

U.S. Corporate and Government Sales   1-800-382-3419   corpsales@pearsontechgroup.com

For sales outside the United States please contact: **International Sales**   international@pearsoned.com

Publisher	Paul Boger
Associate Publisher	Dave Dusthimer
Cisco Representative	Anthony Wolfenden
Cisco Press Program Manager	Jeff Brady
Executive Editor	Brett Bartow
Managing Editor	Patrick Kanouse
Development Editor	Eric Stewart
Project Editor	San Dee Phillips/Jennifer Gallant
Copy Editor	Bill McManus
Technical Editors	Marcelo Silva, Vaughn Suazo
Editorial Assistant	Vanessa Evans
Book Designer	Louisa Adair
Composition	ICC Macmillan Inc.
Indexer	WordWise Publishing Services, LLC
Proofreader	Molly Proue

CISCO

Americas Headquarters	Asia Pacific Headquarters	Europe Headquarters
Cisco Systems, Inc.	Cisco Systems, Inc.	Cisco Systems International BV
170 West Tasman Drive	168 Robinson Road	Haarlerbergpark
San Jose, CA 95134-1706	#28-01 Capital Tower	Haarlerbergweg 13-19
USA	Singapore 068912	1101 CH Amsterdam
www.cisco.com	www.cisco.com	The Netherlands
Tel: 408 526-4000	Tel: +65 6317 7777	www-europe.cisco.com
800 553-NETS (6387)	Fax: +65 6317 7799	Tel: +31 0 800 020 0791
Fax: 408 527-0883		Fax: +31 0 20 357 1100

Cisco has more than 200 offices worldwide. Addresses, phone numbers, and fax numbers are listed on the Cisco Website at www.cisco.com/go/offices.

©2007 Cisco Systems, Inc. All rights reserved. CCVP, the Cisco logo, and the Cisco Square Bridge logo are trademarks of Cisco Systems, Inc.; Changing the Way We Work, Live, Play, and Learn is a service mark of Cisco Systems, Inc.; and Access Registrar, Aironet, BPX, Catalyst, CCDA, CCDP, CCIE, CCIP, CCNA, CCNP, CCSP, Cisco, the Cisco Certified Internetwork Expert logo, Cisco IOS, Cisco Press, Cisco Systems, Cisco Systems Capital, the Cisco Systems logo, Cisco Unity, Enterprise/Solver, EtherChannel, EtherFast, EtherSwitch, Fast Step, Follow Me Browsing, FormShare, GigaDrive, GigaStack, HomeLink, Internet Quotient, IOS, IP/TV, iQ Expertise, the iQ logo, iQ Net Readiness Scorecard, iQuick Study, LightStream, Linksys, MeetingPlace, MGX, Networking Academy, Network Registrar, Packet, PIX, ProConnect, RateMUX, ScriptShare, SMARTnet, StackWise, The Fastest Way to Increase Your Internet Quotient, and TransPath are registered trademarks of Cisco Systems, Inc. and/or its affiliates in the United States and certain other countries.

All other trademarks mentioned in this document or Website are the property of their respective owners. The use of the word partner does not imply a partnership relationship between Cisco and any other company. (0609R)

About the Authors

Gregg Schudel, CCIE No. 9591 (Security), joined Cisco in 2000 as a consulting system engineer supporting the U.S. Service Provider Organization. Gregg focuses on IP core network and services security architectures and technology for inter-exchange carriers, web services providers, and mobile providers. Gregg is also part of a team of Corporate and Field resources focused on driving Cisco Service Provider Security Strategy. Prior to joining Cisco, Gregg worked for many years with BBN Technologies, where he supported network security research and development, most notably in conjunction with DARPA and other federal agencies involved in security research.

Gregg holds an MS in engineering from George Washington University, and a BS in engineering from Florida Institute of Technology. Gregg can be contacted through e-mail at gschudel@cisco.com.

David J. Smith, CCIE No. 1986 (Routing and Switching), joined Cisco in 1995 and is a consulting system engineer supporting the Service Provider Organization. Since 1999 David has focused on service provider IP core and edge architectures, including IP routing, MPLS technologies, QoS, infrastructure security, and network telemetry. Between 1995 and 1999, David supported enterprise customers designing campus and global WANs. Prior to joining Cisco, David worked at Bellcore developing systems software and experimental ATM switches.

David holds an MS in information networking from Carnegie Mellon University, and a BS in computer engineering from Lehigh University. David can be contacted through e-mail at dasmith@cisco.com.

About the Technical Reviewers

Marcelo I. Silva, M.S., is a technical marketing engineer for the Service Provider Technology Group (SPTG) at Cisco. Marcelo is a 19-year veteran of the technology field with experiences in academia and the high-tech industry. Prior to Cisco, Marcelo was an independent systems consultant and full-time lecturer at the University of Maryland, Baltimore County. His career at Cisco began in 2000, working directly with large U.S. service provider customers designing IP/MPLS core and edge networks. Marcelo's primary responsibility at Cisco today as a technical marketing engineer (TME) requires him to travel the world advising services provider customers on the deployment of Cisco's high-end routers: Cisco 12000 Series (GSR) and Cisco CRS-1 Carrier Routing System. Marcelo has an MS in information systems from the University of Maryland, and lives in Waterloo, Belgium with his wife Adriana and son Gabriel.

Vaughn Suazo, CCIE No. 5109 (Routing and Switching, Security), is a consulting systems engineer for Wireline Emerging Providers at Cisco. Vaughn is a 17-year veteran of the technology field with experience in server technologies, LAN/WAN networking, and network security. His career at Cisco began in 1999, working directly with service provider customers on technology areas such as core and edge IP network architectures, MPLS applications, network security, and IP services. Vaughn's primary responsibility at Cisco today is as a consulting systems engineer (CSE) for service provider customers, specializing in service provider security and data center technologies and solutions. Vaughn lives in Oklahoma City, Oklahoma with his wife Terri and two children, and enjoys golfing in his leisure time.

Dedications

To my best friend and beautiful wife, Carol, for her love and encouragement, and for allowing me to commit precious time away from our family to write this book. To my awesome boys, Alex and Gary, for their patience and understanding, and for their energy and enthusiasm that keeps me motivated.

Thanks to my co-author, David Smith, for gratefully accepting my challenge, and for bringing his knowledge and experience to this project.

—Gregg

I dedicate this book to my loving wife, Vickie, and my wonderful children, Harry, Devon, and Edward, whom have made my dreams come true. Thank you for all of your support and inspiration during the writing of this book. I also dedicate this book to my mother and late father, whose sacrifices have afforded my brothers and me great opportunities. Finally, to my co-author, Gregg Schudel, for considering me for this special project. It was an opportunity of a lifetime and I am forever grateful.

—David

Acknowledgments

This book benefited from the efforts of all Cisco engineers who share our dedication and passion for understanding and furthering IP network security. Among them, there are a few to whom we are particularly grateful. To Barry Greene, for his constant innovations, tireless leadership, and dedication to SP security. Without his efforts, many of these IP traffic plane security concepts would not have been developed. Also, to Michael Behringer, for his constant encouragement, and for always providing sound advice on our many technical questions. And to Roland Dobbins, Ryan McDowell, Jason Bos, Rajiv Raghunarayan, Darrel Lewis, Paul Quinn, Sean Donelan, and Dave Lapin, for always making themselves available to consult on the most detailed of questions.

We gratefully thank our extraordinary technical reviewers, Marcelo Silva and Vaughn Suazo, for their thorough critiques and feedback. Thanks also to John Stuppi and Ilker Temir for providing their invaluable reviews as well as to Russell Smoak for his leadership. We also thank Dan Hamilton, Don Heidrich, Chris Metz, Vaughn Suazo, and Andrew Whitaker for reviewing our original proposal and providing valuable suggestions. We also give special thanks to John Stewart, Cisco Systems Vice President and Chief Security Officer, for taking time from his very busy schedule to write the foreword of our book, as well as for his unique leadership in the areas of both security and network operations.

We would like to thank our managers, Jerry Marsh and Jim Steinhardt, for their tremendous support throughout this project.

Finally, special thanks go to Cisco Press and our production team: Brett Bartow (Executive Editor), Eric Stewart (Development Editor), San Dee Phillips (Senior Project Editor), Jennifer Gallant (Project Editor), and Bill McManus (Copy Editor). Thanks also to Andrew Cupp (Development Editor) for the valuable editorial assistance. Thank you for working with us to make this book a reality.

This Book Is Safari Enabled

The Safari® Enabled icon on the cover of your favorite technology book means the book is available through Safari Bookshelf. When you buy this book, you get free access to the online edition for 45 days.

Safari Bookshelf is an electronic reference library that lets you easily search thousands of technical books, find code samples, download chapters, and access technical information whenever and wherever you need it.

To gain 45-day Safari Enabled access to this book:

- Go to http://www.ciscopress.com/safarienabled.

- Complete the brief registration form.

- Enter the coupon code 4NE7-N9TF-PHL8-DTFR-9X38.

If you have difficulty registering on Safari Bookshelf or accessing the online edition, please e-mail customer-service@safaribooksonline.com.

Contents at a Glance

Contents

Icons Used in This Book

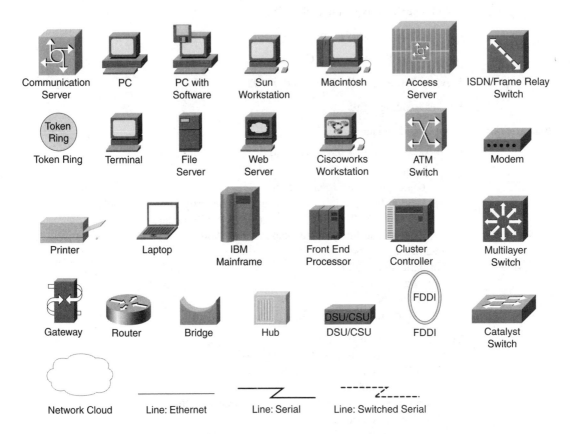

Command Syntax Conventions

The conventions used to present command syntax in this book are the same conventions used in the IOS Command Reference. The Command Reference describes these conventions as follows:

- **Boldface** indicates commands and keywords that are entered literally as shown. In actual configuration examples and output (not general command syntax), boldface indicates commands that are manually input by the user (such as a **show** command).
- *Italics* indicate arguments for which you supply actual values.
- Vertical bars (l) separate alternative, mutually exclusive elements.
- Square brackets [ ] indicate optional elements.
- Braces { } indicate a required choice.
- Braces within brackets [{ }] indicate a required choice within an optional element.

Foreword

In the past 20 years, networks moved from archane (ARPANET) to everywhere (wireless hotspots), and with that adoption came its use in health care systems, airplanes, commerce, video communications, telephony, storage, and interactive sports just to name a few.

Networking went from the data center, to the service provider, to our neighborhoods, to our homes. To say that network security is an "important topic" is such an understatement, to me, because it fails to call out the disparity between host security—where many dollars are spent—to network security—where little is spent. How is that possible given how vital networks are today, and why is this happening?

Instead of answering that question here, embrace for a moment that network security is essential because networks are now essential. To that end, the knowledge about what threats and attacks against network devices already exist, required configuration techniques for networking devices to best counter those threats and attacks, and real-life examples on how this increases resiliency in your network are included here from which to learn.

The bulk of Gregg's and David's book splits its time between data, management, and services plane security—explaining the what, then the why, and then the how for each traffic plane. Securing all four traffic planes are necessary to secure a network device and, therefore, a network built with many such devices. Focusing on all four, which are considerably different from one another, is the only way to do it right.

If you do nothing else as a result, after reading this book ask yourself—when protecting data, have I protected my increasingly data-rich, services-rich, and capability-rich network which I now rely upon? Experience has taught each one of us that defense-in-depth and defense-in-breadth are both the strongest techniques. Your network is multi-device, multi-layer deep, and nearly ubiquitious in its reach—it already plays the key role in protecting your network. Make sure it is successful; after all...

...we're all connected.

John Stewart

Vice President and Chief Security Officer

Cisco

Introduction

The networking world is evolving at an ever-increasing pace. The rapid displacement of legacy, purpose-built networks based on time-division multiplexing (TDM), Frame Relay, and Asynchronous Transfer Mode (ATM) technologies to ubiquitous Internet Protocol (IP) packet-based networks capable of supporting converged network services is well under way. Service providers can no longer afford to deploy multiple networks, each built to support a single application or service such as voice, business-class data, or Internet traffic. The cost of deploying and operating multiple networks in this business model is not financially sustainable. In addition, customer demand for integrated services and applications, as well as new services and applications, means service delivery velocity is a critical requirement of modern network architectures. Leading wireline and wireless service providers worldwide are already migrating legacy network services onto IP core networks to take advantage of the bandwidth efficiencies and scalability offered by IP networks, and their ability to enable rapid expansion into new service markets.

Building and operating IP network infrastructures to meet the same carrier-class requirements that customers demand, while carrying multiple, diverse services that have different bandwidth, jitter, and latency requirements, is a challenging task. Single-purpose networks were designed and built to support specific, tightly controlled operational characteristics. Carrying Internet traffic, voice traffic, cellular traffic, and private (VPN) business traffic over a common IP backbone has significant implications for both network design and network security. The loss of integrity through a network attack, for example, in any one of the traffic services can potentially disrupt the entire "common network," causing an impact to the entire revenue base. Further, enterprises are increasingly dependent upon IP networking for business operations.

Fundamentally, all networks have essentially two kinds of packets: *data packets*, which belong to customers and carry customer traffic, and *control and management packets*, which belong to the network and are used to create and operate the network. One of the strengths of the IP protocol is that all packets traverse a "common pipe" (or are "in-band"). Networking professionals coming from the legacy TDM/ATM network world may be unfamiliar with the concept of a common pipe for data and control plane traffic, as these legacy systems separate data channels from "out-of-band" control channels. Misunderstanding and trepidation often exist about how data packets and control packets can be segmented and secured in a common network.

Even though IP networks carry all packets in-band, it is possible and, now more than ever, critical to distinguish between the various types of packets being transported. Separating traffic into data, control, management, and services planes (referred to as traffic planes) and properly segmenting and protecting these traffic planes are required tasks to secure today's highly converged IP networks. This book is the first to cover IP network traffic plane separation and security in a formal and thorough manner.

Goals and Methods

The goal of this book is to familiarize you with concepts, benefits, and implementation details for segmenting and securing IP network traffic planes. This includes a review of the many threats facing IP networks and the many techniques available to mitigate the risks. Defense in depth and breadth strategies are also reviewed to highlight the interactions between various IP traffic plane security techniques. Detailed analyses at the operational level of IP networks from the perspective of each of the data, control, management, and services planes form the basis for the security principles and configuration examples described herein. Case studies further illustrate how optimizing the selection of IP traffic plane protection measures using defense in depth and breadth principles provides an effective security strategy.

Who Should Read This Book?

This book was written for network engineers, and network operations and security staff of organizations who deploy and/or maintain IP and IP/MPLS networks. The primary audience includes those engineers who are engaged in day-to-day design, engineering, and operations of IP networks. Subscribers of a service based on IP or IP/MPLS will benefit from this book as well. The secondary audience includes those with less network-centric backgrounds who wish to understand the issues and requirements of IP network traffic plane separation and security. This book also provides great insight into the technical interworkings and operations of IP routers that both senior and less-experienced network professionals can benefit from.

How This Book Is Organized

For those readers who are new to IP network security concepts, especially the concepts of separation and protection of IP traffic planes, this book should be read cover to cover. If you are already familiar with IP networks, protocols, network design, and operations, you may refer to specific sections of interest. This book is divided into four general parts, which are described next.

Part I, "IP Network and Traffic Plane Security Fundamentals," provides a basic overview of the IP protocol, the operations of IP networks, and the operations of routers and routing hardware and software. It is in this section that the concepts of IP traffic segmentation and security are introduced. At the end of this section, casual readers will understand, at a high level, what IP traffic plane separation and protection entails. This section includes the following chapters:

- **Chapter 1, "Internet Protocol Operations Fundamentals":** Discusses the fundamentals of the IP protocol, and looks at the operational aspects of IP networks from the perspective of the routing and switching hardware and software. It is in this context that the concept of IP network traffic planes is introduced.

- **Chapter 2, "Threat Models for IP Networks":** Lays out threat models for routing and switching environments within each IP network traffic plane. By reviewing threats in this manner, you learn why IP traffic planes must be protected and from what types of attacks.

- **Chapter 3, "IP Network Traffic Plane Security Concepts":** Provides a broad overview of each IP traffic plane, and how defense in depth and breadth strategies are used to provide robust network security.

Part II, "Security Techniques for Protecting IP Traffic Planes," provides the in-depth, working details that serious networking professional can use to actually implement IP traffic plane separation and protection strategies. For less-experienced network professionals, this section provides great insight into the technical operations of IP routers. This section includes the following chapters:

- **Chapter 4, "IP Data Plane Security":** Focuses on the data plane and associated security mechanisms. The data plane is the logical entity containing all user traffic generated by hosts, clients, servers, and applications that use the network as transport only.

- **Chapter 5, "IP Control Plane Security":** Focuses on the control plane and associated security mechanisms. The control plane is the logical entity associated with routing protocol processes and functions used to create and maintain the necessary intelligence about the operational state of the network, including forwarding topologies.

- **Chapter 6, "IP Management Plane Security":** Focuses on the management plane and associated security mechanisms. The management plane is the logical entity that describes the traffic used to access, manage, and monitor all of the network elements for provisioning, maintenance, and monitoring functions.

- **Chapter 7, "IP Services Plane Security":** Focuses on the services plane and associated security mechanisms. The services plane is the logical entity that includes user traffic that receives dedicated network-based services requiring special handling beyond traditional forwarding to apply or enforce the intended policies for various service types.

Part III, "Case Studies," provides case studies for two different network types: the enterprise network, and the service provider network. These case studies are used to further illustrate how the individual components discussed in detail in Part II are integrated into a comprehensive IP network traffic plane separation and protection plan. This section includes the following chapters:

- **Chapter 8, "Enterprise Network Case Studies":** Uses two basic enterprise network situations—the Internet-based IPsec VPN design, and the MPLS VPN design—to illustrate the application of IP network traffic plane separation and protection concepts for enterprises. These cases studies focus on the Internet edge router and customer edge (CE) router, respectively, to present the IP traffic plane security concepts.

- **Chapter 9, "Service Provider Network Case Studies":** Uses the same topologies from the two case studies of Chapter 8, but presents them from the service provider network perspective. In this chapter, two provider edge router configurations are studied—one for the Internet-based IPsec VPN design case, and one for the MPLS VPN case—to illustrate the application of IP network traffic plane separation and protection concepts for service providers.

Part IV, "Appendixes," supplements many of the discussions in the body of the book by providing handy references that should be useful not only during the course of reading the book, but also in day-to-day work. The following appendixes are provided:

- **Appendix A, "Answers to Chapter Review Questions":** Provides answers to the chapter review questions.

- **Appendix B, "IP Protocol Headers":** Covers the header format for several common IP network protocols, and describes the security implications and abuse potential for each header field.

- **Appendix C, "Cisco IOS to IOS XR Security Transition":** Provides a one-for-one mapping between common IOS 12.0S security-related configuration commands and their respective IOS XR counterparts.

- **Appendix D, "Security Incident Handling":** Provides a short overview of security incident handling techniques, and a list of common security incident handling organizations.

PART I

IP Network and Traffic Plane Security Fundamentals

In this chapter, you will learn about the following:

- IP networking concepts
- IP protocol operation concepts
- IP traffic plane concepts
- Router packet processing and forwarding concepts
- Router architecture concepts

CHAPTER 1

Internet Protocol Operations Fundamentals

This chapter builds the foundation for the remainder of the book by introducing the concepts and terminology critical to understanding IP traffic plane security. Basic IP network concepts and IP protocol operations are reviewed, including the various packet types found in the network and how these packets apply to different IP traffic planes. Then, packet processing and forwarding mechanisms used by routers are reviewed. Special attention is given to how various packet types within each traffic plane affect forwarding mechanisms. Finally, various router hardware architectures are reviewed, again highlighting how router performance and network security are affected by the IP traffic planes.

IP Network Concepts

Internet Protocol (IP) and IP/Multiprotocol Label Switching (IP/MPLS) packet-based networks capable of supporting converged network services are rapidly replacing purpose-built networks based on time-division multiplexing (TDM), Frame Relay, Asynchronous Transfer Mode (ATM) and other legacy technologies. Service providers worldwide are deploying IP/MPLS core networks to realize the efficiencies and scalability offered by IP networks, and their ability to enable rapid expansion into new service markets. Enterprises are also taking advantage of the end-to-end, any-to-any connectivity model of IP to drive business-changing profit models through infrastructure and operational efficiency improvements, as well as to capture e-commerce opportunities.

Building and operating IP network infrastructures for converged services is a balancing act. Meeting the carrier-class requirements that customers demand, while supporting multiple, diverse services that have distinct bandwidth, jitter, and latency requirements, is a challenging task. Legacy, single-purpose networks were designed and built with specific, tightly controlled operational characteristics to support a single service. Hence, the (typically) single service each network supported usually worked flawlessly. This was relatively easy to achieve because these networks catered to a single application/service that was tightly controlled. Carrying Internet traffic, voice and video traffic, cellular traffic, and private (VPN) business traffic over a common IP backbone has significant implications for both network design and network operations. Disruptions in any one of these traffic services may potentially disrupt any of the other services, or the wider network. Thus, the importance of network security in converged networks is magnified.

NOTE   The traditional focus areas of network security include *confidentiality*, *integrity*, and *availability* (CIA), in varying degrees, depending on network functions. As network convergence has taken hold, the importance of each of these areas changes.

Availability, for example, is no longer simply a binary "up/down" or "on/off" function, but must now consider other issues such as network latency caused by congestion and processing delays. For example, consider the effects of malicious traffic, or even changes in the traffic patterns of one service, say Internet data. This might cause congestion that affects another service such as Voice over IP (VoIP) traffic traversing the same core routers but in a different *services plane* (as will be defined later in this chapter). Because one of the prime motives for converging disparate services and networks onto a single IP core is to gain capital and operating expenditure (CapEx and OpEx) efficiencies, this perturbation in availability may lead to a disruption in the entire revenue model if high-value services cannot be supported adequately. This is the basis for developing a different way of thinking about IP network security, one modeled around the IP traffic plane concept.

The concept of IP network traffic planes is best introduced by first considering the features that distinguish IP networks from other network types:

- IP networks carry all packets in a common *pipe*. Fundamentally, all networks have essentially two kinds of packets:

    — *Data packets* that belong to users and carry user or application traffic

    — *Control packets* that belong to the network and are used to dynamically build and operate the network

    One of the strengths of the IP protocol is that all packets are carried in a *common pipe* (also referred to as "in-band"). Legacy networks typically relied on separate channels for data and control traffic. IP does not segment traffic into separate channels. As the subject of this book implies, classifying different traffic types is the first step in segmenting and securing an IP network. Each of these tasks—traffic classification, segmentation, and control—is essential for IP network security.

- IP networks provide any-to-any and end-to-end connectivity by nature. In its simplest form, a router provides destination-based forwarding of IP packets. If a router has a destination prefix in its forwarding table, it will forward the packet toward its final destination. Hence, routing (and more specifically, what prefixes are in the forwarding table of the router) is one of the most important, but often overlooked, components of IP network security.

    For example, using a *default route* often has significant implications for network security. The ubiquitous nature of IP, along with its any-to-any, end-to-end operational characteristics, provides inherent flexibility and scalability at unprecedented levels. This is at the same time both a positive and a negative aspect of IP networking. On the positive side, this provides instant global connectivity, which enables innovation and constant evolution. On the negative side, however, this global connectivity also provides unparalleled opportunities for misuse and abuse through these same networks. (In the physical world, one must be proximate to the scene to carry out a crime. This is not the case in the cyber world. Also, one person can do significant damage in the cyber world—in other words, there is a force-multiplier—which the physical world does not offer.)

- IP networks use open standards defined by the IETF; access to the protocol standards is freely available to everyone. These standards are independent from any specific computer hardware or operating system. This openness encourages and drives innovation of new applications and services that run over IP networks. This leads to several challenges as well, however. It is often difficult for networks to keep pace with rapidly changing demands. Supporting new applications and services may present challenging new flow characteristics. A few examples include:

  - Asymmetric vs. symmetric upstream/downstream bandwidth with peer-to-peer networking

  - Increases in absolute bandwidth utilization and unicast vs. multicast packet types with video services

  - Tolerance to variations in delay and jitter characteristics for voice services

  In addition, networks must be resilient enough to account for abuse, either from misuse, misconfigurations, obfuscation, or outright maliciousness.

These concepts are the driving factors behind this book. In today's IP networks, it is critical to distinguish between the various traffic types, segment them into various IP traffic planes, and incorporate mechanisms to control their influences on the wider network.

Two broad network categories are highlighted in this book to provide a context for demonstrating the concepts of IP network traffic plane separation: the *enterprise network* and the *service provider network*. Although there are similarities between them, the significant differences between them are useful for demonstrating IP traffic plane security concepts and techniques covered in detail in later chapters. The following description of these network types is provided as an overview, simply to introduce the concepts of IP traffic planes. This is not intended as a design primer for enterprise or service provider networks.

Enterprise Networks

Enterprise networks form a large, broad class distinguished by their architectural details and typical traffic flows. Enterprises often build networks to satisfy four goals:

- To interconnect internal users and applications to each other

- To provide internal users with access to remote sites within the same organization (administrative domain) and, most likely, to the wider Internet as well

- To connect external users (Internet) to publicly advertised resources under control of the organization (for example, a web site)

- To connect external partners (extranet) to segmented business resources (nonpublic) under the control of the organization

Enterprise networks may be small, medium, or large, and undoubtedly have many internal variations. Yet they also have many common characteristics, including:

- A well-defined architecture, typically following the hierarchical three-layer model of core, distribution, and access layers. Here, the core layer provides the high-speed switching backbone for the network, as well as connectivity to the wide-area network, which may consist of the public Internet, an IP VPN, or a private IP network. The distribution layer connects the core and access layers, and often provides a policy-enforcement point for the network. The access layer provides user and server access to local segments of the network. In smaller networks, these three layers are often consolidated.

- A well-defined edge that serves as the demarcation for distinguishing *enterprise side* and *provider side* (or private and public) from the perspective of both ownership and capital property. It is clear in most cases who owns the devices in a network, what these devices are responsible for, and who is authorized to access these particular devices and services.

- A well-defined set of IP protocols, including an Interior Gateway Protocol (IGP) for dynamic routing (such as Open Shortest Path First [OSPF]), network management protocols (such as Simple Network Management Protocol [SNMP], syslog, FTP, and so forth), and other IP protocols supporting enterprise client/server applications and other internal functions.

- A well-defined traffic flow running across the network edge (inside-to-outside and outside-to-inside), and traffic flows running exclusively within the interior of the network. The edge almost always serves as a security boundary, and presents an opportunity to constrain traffic flows crossing this boundary based upon defined security policies. Internal traffic flows stay entirely within the enterprise network. Enterprise networks should never have transit traffic flows—that is, packets that ingress the network edge should never have destination addresses that are not part of the enterprise network address space, and hence would simply flow back out of the network.

Figure 1-1 illustrates a common, enterprise network architecture.

These characteristics provide the basis for securing IP traffic planes in enterprise networks, as you will learn in more detail in later sections. In addition, a detailed case study on securing IP traffic planes in enterprise networks is provided in Chapter 8, "Enterprise Network Case Study."

Figure 1-1   *Conceptual Enterprise Network Architecture*

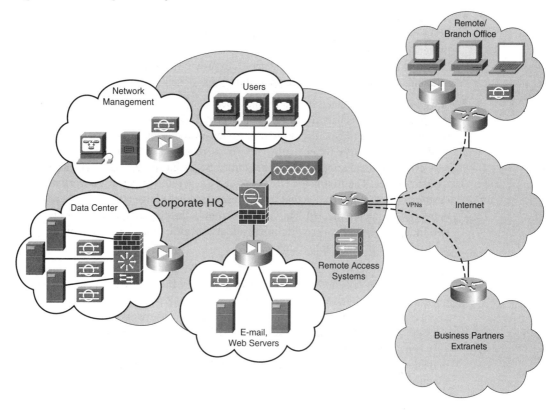

Service Provider Networks

Service provider networks also form a large, broad class distinguished by their architectural details and typical traffic flows. Service provider networks are built for profit. That is, the network is the revenue generator (or facilitates the revenue generation). In order to create revenues, service providers build networks for the following reasons:

- To provide *transit* traffic capacity for their own (enterprise) customers for access to other directly attached (enterprise) customer sites, and to all publicly advertised address space (in other words, the Internet)

- To provide traffic capacity and access by external users to content and services directly hosted by the service provider

- To provide *internal* traffic capacity for other converged services owned by the service provider to take advantage of the IP core network

In general, SP networks have the following characteristics:

- A well-defined architecture, typically consisting of edge and core routers. The scope of the network usually reaches regional, national, or even global scale, with "points of presence" (PoP) located in strategic locations. The network architecture is built with hardware and physical plant redundancies to provide high availability and fault tolerance. Network capacities support the largest of scales.

- A well-defined edge that is the demarcation between *provider* and *customer* networking equipment. It is clear in most cases who owns all devices, what these devices are responsible for, and who is authorized to access all particular devices and services. While this is also true for enterprise networks, there are some differences as to how service providers distinguish their networks. Service provider networks have two types of edges. The first is the edge between the service provider network and its customers' networks. The second is the peering edge, the edge where service provider networks are interconnected. This adds different IP traffic plane complexities because two independent networks with independent IP traffic planes are interconnected. Security is particularly important here.

- A well-defined set of IP protocols, including an IGP, and numerous Border Gateway Protocol (BGP) sessions. The IGP runs completely internal to the network and generally never contains customer IP addresses. BGP generally runs between the service provider and enterprise networks, and peering networks, and contains a publicly addressable IP address space. For IP VPNs, an IGP or BGP may be used between customer and service provider. Other IP protocols supporting network management (such as SNMP, syslog, FTP, and so forth), billing, and other internal functions are also defined.

Figure 1-2 illustrates a common, service provider network architecture.

It is interesting to compare service provider networks with enterprise networks because their traffic flows are very different. In many regards, they can be viewed as opposites of one another.

First, enterprise networks almost always present a *hard* edge to the Internet, where nothing is allowed to cross unless it is either return traffic from internally generated traffic, or tightly controlled externally originated traffic destined to well-defined publicly exposed services. Service providers, on the other hand, are just the opposite. They build their networks to allow all traffic to cross their edge almost without impediment. The edge is designed to be wide open—everything crosses unless it is explicitly forbidden from crossing.

Second, enterprise networks also are built for traffic either to stay completely within the network or to reach the core (interior) of the network. To control this traffic flow, enterprises almost always use stateful devices such as firewalls to control any external traffic flows. Service provider networks, on the other hand, again, are just the opposite. External, customer traffic should never reach any of the core (interior) devices or network elements. Instead, traffic is expected to *transit* the network—that is, it is expected to be destined to other locations outside the service provider network. In addition, due to the great volume of traffic and the myriad of entrance and exit points found in service provider networks, stateful traffic devices such as firewalls and intrusion protection systems are rarely deployed for transit traffic. The job of the service provider is to forward packets toward their ultimate destination as quickly as possible.

Figure 1-2   *Conceptual Service Provider Network Architecture*

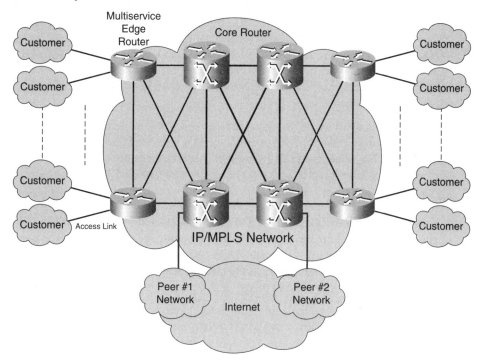

These characteristics provide the basis for securing IP traffic planes in service provider networks, as you will learn in more detail in later sections. In addition, a detailed case study on securing IP traffic planes in service provider networks is provided in Chapter 9, "Service Provider Network Case Studies."

Why is the network design so important? Mainly because the way a network is built—from its topology, to the addressing plan, to the hardware selections—greatly influences how well (or easily) it can be secured. As you will learn, the network design provides the basis from which IP traffic planes can be defined and how they can be secured. Before IP traffic planes can be discussed, however, a quick review of IP protocol operations is required.

IP Protocol Operations

Fundamentally, all networks have essentially two kinds of packets—*data packets*, which belong to the customer and carry customer application traffic, and *control packets*, which belong to the network and carry network operational and routing protocol traffic. Of course, further refinement within each of these broad categories is necessary to understand the full complexities of IP network design and protocol operation. But for the moment, this simplified view with just these two traffic types helps illustrate the concepts.

Legacy networks such as Private Line, ISDN, Frame Relay, and ATM use separate control channels and data channels for the purpose of segmenting and carrying these two traffic types. ISDN, for example, uses the delta channel (or D channel) to construct and maintain the network, and the bearer channel (or B channel) to carry customer traffic. Frame Relay uses one control virtual circuit (VC) for the construction and management of all data VCs, and data VCs to carry customer traffic. This hard separation of control traffic from customer data traffic, coupled with a closed, controlled user community, leads to reasonably secure network environments.

While these networks were not immune from attack, the malicious knowledge necessary to actually attack these networks was not well known. In addition, there was no "global reachability" as is the case in IP. Because the network elements were not easily accessible by customer traffic, direct attacks were not easily accomplished. Most security issues were related to misconfigurations, and service disruptions were related to network element hardware or software flaws or basic provisioning (often human) errors. These same attributes also led to inflexibilities and inefficiencies that prevent these networks from surviving in today's anywhere, anytime global communications world. IP is dominating the networking world due to the simplicity and efficiency resulting largely from its connectionless, any-to-any nature, its open, standards-based architecture, and its universal support over any link-layer technology.

The Internet Protocol technically refers in full to the Transmission Control Protocol/ Internet Protocol (TCP/IP) suite. The TCP/IP protocol suite divides the complex task of host-to-host internetworking into layers of abstraction, with each layer representing a function performed when data is transferred between cooperating applications across an internetworking environment. A layer does not typically define a single protocol, but rather a data communications function performed by any number of protocols that could operate at that layer. Every protocol communicates with a peer of the same protocol in the equivalent layer on a remote system. Each protocol is concerned with communicating only to its peer and does not concern itself with the layer above or below, except to the extent that data must be passed between the layers on a single device. The Open System Interconnection (OSI) seven-layer reference model is commonly used to describe the structure and function of the layers used in IP protocol data communications, although for TCP/IP the mapping to seven layers is not exact. The OSI seven-layer model is illustrated in Figure 1-3.

Figure 1-3   *TCP/IP 7-Layer Model*

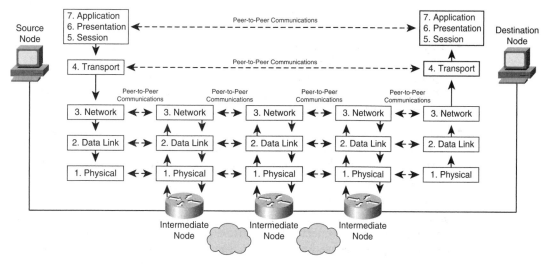

The key features of the seven layers in this model, and their mapping to the TCP/IP protocol suite, are as follows:

- **Layer 7—application layer:** Defines the user (application) process interface for communications and data-transfer services. A very common example of an application layer protocol is HTTP for user applications. Some network control applications also operate at this layer.

- **Layer 6—presentation layer:** Provides data format translation services between dissimilar systems. MIME encoding, data compression, data encryption, and similar data manipulations are described as performing at this layer.

- **Layer 5—session layer:** Manages the establishment and termination of user sessions, including connections between the local and remote applications. TCP uses this layer to provide certain session management functions.

- **Layer 4—transport layer:** Manages end-to-end sessions between local and remote endpoints in the network. Examples include the connection-oriented, reliable, and sequential segment delivery mechanisms with error recovery and flow control provided by TCP, and the connectionless packet delivery mechanisms provided by User Datagram Protocol (UDP).

- **Layer 3—network layer:** Provides the mechanisms for routing variable-length packets between network devices. This layer also provides the mechanisms to maintain the quality of service (QoS) requested by the transport layer, perform data segment fragmentation and reassembly (when required), and report packet delivery and network errors. The IP protocol operates at this layer. Other protocols such as Internet Message Control Protocol (ICMP) and Address Resolution Protocol (ARP) are often described as operating at this layer as well.

- **Layer 2—data link layer:** Provides the mechanisms for transferring frames between adjacent network entities, and may detect and correct frame transmission errors. Although the most common example is Ethernet, other well-known examples include High-Level Data Link Control (HDLC), Point-to-Point Protocol (PPP), and the legacy protocols FDDI and Token Ring.

- **Layer 1—physical layer:** Defines the physical medium over which data is sent between network devices as voltages or light pulses. It includes optical power and electrical voltage levels, cable mechanical characteristics such as layout of pins, and other cable specifications.

As shown in Figure 1-3, each layer plays a role in the process of transporting data across the network. Not every layer is processed by each device along the network, however. In addition, not every protocol operates from end to end. Some are meant for user applications, and these do typically operate from end to end. However, certain protocols are meant for network operations. These may operate in an end-to-end manner, where the endpoints are the network elements themselves, or they may operate in a point-to-point manner between adjacent devices. As you will learn in more detail later, this layering, and the function and operation of the various protocols, is critically important in developing IP traffic plane security strategies.

The fundamental protocols of the TCP/IP protocol suite include:

- IP—Layer 3
- TCP—Layer 4
- UDP—Layer 4
- ICMP—Layer 3

IP is a network layer (Layer 3) protocol that contains addressing information and some control information that enables packets to be routed to their final destination. Along with TCP, IP represents the heart of the Internet protocols. As noted earlier, TCP provides connection-oriented transport (Layer 4) services for applications. UDP is also a transport (Layer 4) service, but unlike TCP, UDP provides connectionless transport. ICMP is a control protocol that works alongside IP at the network layer to provide error control and maintenance functions. Of course, many other protocols are relevant in the TCP/IP world, and there are numerous references that describe their uses and operations. Several excellent resources are listed in the "Further Reading" section at the end of this chapter.

Numerous applications (Layer 7) take advantage of the transport (Layer 4) services of TCP and UDP. Some common examples include the following:

- **Hypertext Transfer Protocol (HTTP):** A client/server application that uses TCP for transport to retrieve HTML pages.

- **Domain Name Service (DNS):** A name-to-address translation application that uses both TCP and UDP transport.

- **Telnet:** A virtual terminal application that uses TCP for transport.

- **File Transport Protocol (FTP):** A file transfer application that uses TCP for transport.

- **Trivial File Transfer Protocol (TFTP):** A file transfer application that uses UDP for transport.

- **Network Time Protocol (NTP):** An application that synchronizes time with a time source and uses UDP for transport.

- **Border Gateway Protocol (BGP):** An exterior gateway routing protocol that uses TCP for transport. BGP is used to exchange routing information for the Internet and is the protocol used between service providers.

Because IP is a connectionless protocol, it forwards data in self-contained routable units known as datagrams or packets. Each packet includes an IP header (built by the end station during encapsulation) that contains information (such as source and destination addresses) that is used by routers when making forwarding and policy decisions. The existence of this IP header is why, in a connectionless networking environment, there is no need (as there would be in the legacy networks previously mentioned) for prior setup of an end-to-end path between the source and destination before data transmission is initiated.

The IP packet header normally requires 20 bytes to specify the data necessary to route the packet. The IP header is capable, however, of allowing further optional information to be added to invoke specialized services during packet transit. With certain exceptions, IP options are not normally used. (You will learn much more about IP options and their impact on IP traffic plane security later in this section.) The IP header is shown in Figure 1-4.

Figure 1-4   *IP Packet Header Layer 3*

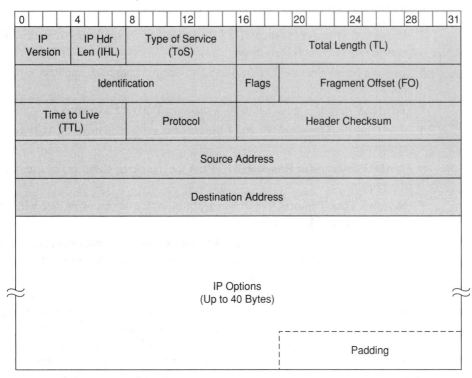

The header fields shown in Figure 1-4 include the following:

- **IP Version:** Indicates the version of IP used by the packet. A value of 4 indicates IP version 4, which is the most prevalent version in use today. A value of 6 indicates the newer IP version 6, which is beginning to become more widely deployed (and likely will dominate IPv4 in the future).

- **IP Header Length:** Indicates the header length in 32-bit words. Typical IPv4 packets with a header length of 20 bytes have a value of 5, meaning five 32-bit (4-byte) words. Recall that the IPv4 header is not a fixed length. It has a minimum length of 20 bytes (an IP Header Length value of 5), but when IP options are included, a maximum length of up to 60 bytes (a value of 15, or 0x0F) may be indicated.

Note   Historically, the variable-length header size of IPv4 packets has always been problematic, for routing and security reasons. It is worth noting that IPv6 has a fixed-length header size of 40 bytes and there is no corresponding Header Length field. The simplified IPv6 fixed-length header is intended to speed processing and resolve many of the security issues associated with IPv4 header options.

- **Type of Service (ToS):** Specifies how an upper-layer protocol would like packets to be queued and processed by network elements as they are forwarded through the network (if so configured). This is usually set to zero (0), but may be assigned a different value to indicate another level of importance.

- **Total Length:** Specifies the length, in bytes, of the entire IP packet, including the data and IP header.

- **Identification:** Contains an integer that identifies the current datagram. This field is used during reassembly of fragmented datagrams.

- **Flags:** Consists of a 3-bit field, the two low-order (least-significant) bits of which control fragmentation. The high-order (first) bit is not used and must be set to 0. The middle (second) "Don't Fragment" (DF) bit specifies whether the packet is permitted to be fragmented (0 = fragmentation permitted, 1 = fragmentation not permitted). The low-order (third) "More Fragments" (MF) bit specifies whether the packet is the last fragment in a series of fragmented packets (set to 1 for all fragments except the last one, telling the end station which fragment is the last).

- **Fragment Offset:** Provides the position (offset), in bytes, of the fragment's data relative to the start of the data in the original datagram, which allows the destination IP process to properly reconstruct the original datagram.

- **Time to Live (TTL):** Specifies the maximum number of links (also known as "hops") that the packet may be routed over. This counter is decremented by one by each router that processes the packet while forwarding it toward its destination. When the TTL value reaches 0, the datagram is discarded. This prevents packets from looping endlessly, as would otherwise occur during accidental routing loops, for example.

- **Protocol:** Indicates which upper-layer protocol receives incoming packets after IP processing is complete. Normally, this indicates the type of payload being carried by IP. For example, a value of 1 indicates IP is carrying an ICMP packet, 6 indicates a TCP segment, and 17 indicates that a UDP packet is being carried by IP.

- **Header Checksum:** A 1's-compliment hash, inserted by the sender and updated by each router that modifies the packet while forwarding it toward its destination (which essentially means every router because, at a minimum, the TTL value is modified at each hop). The header checksum is used to detect errors that may be introduced into the packet as it traverses the network. Packets with an invalid checksum are required to be discarded by any receiving node in the network.

- **Source Address:** Specifies the unique IP address of the sending node (the originator of the IP packet).

- **Destination Address:** Specifies the unique IP address of the receiving node (the final destination of the packet).

- **IP Options:** Allows IP to support various options, such as timestamp, record route, and strict source route. IP options are not normally used.

The data carried by the IP packet, including any additional upper-layer header information (such as from TCP or UDP, for example), follows this IP header. A more detailed look at the protocol headers for IP, TCP, UDP, and ICMP is included in Appendix B, "IP Protocol Headers." Appendix B also provides a short discussion on how some of these header values are manipulated for malicious intent and what the security implications may be.

NOTE   Network security specialists must be extremely well-versed in IP protocol header structures, options, operations, and manipulations. This knowledge is required to understand and mitigate the potential threats against an IP network. Threats are reviewed in Chapter 2, "Threat Models for IP Networks," and techniques to mitigate risks of attack are reviewed in Section II. Many excellent references cover IP protocol operations in significant detail. One excellent source of information is *TCP/IP Illustrated, Volume 1*. This and other references are listed in the "Further Reading" section at the end of this chapter.

IP forwarding is based on the destination address in the IP header, and routers are the devices that perform destination-based forwarding in IP networks. IP options also influence routing. A router is a network device that forwards packets downstream to a target destination. It makes its forwarding decisions based on its knowledge of both directly connected networks and networks discovered via routing protocol operations with other routers. A router may consist of many network interfaces that provide connectivity to other network entities, including routers, hosts, network segments, and so forth. As you learned at the beginning of this section, all networks have essentially two kinds of packets, data packets and control packets. You also learned that IP networking carries both kinds of packets in a common *pipe* (in other words, "in-band"). Thus, a router must look at every single packet entering an interface and decide what type of packet it is—data or control—and apply the appropriate processes to each packet based on this determination. Understanding the details of how routers perform this operation is a key concept in separating and securing IP network traffic planes.

Data packets belong to the customer and carry customer application traffic. Control packets belong to the network and carry network operational and management traffic. Control packets are used by various router functions to create and maintain the necessary intelligence about the state of the network and a router's interfaces. IP routing protocols provide the framework for gathering this intelligence. Data packets are processed and forwarded by the router using the intelligence and network state created by the control packets. Both functions must be accomplished by every router in the network, and in a coordinated manner. Even though IP networks carry all packets in-band, it is still possible, and perhaps even more critical than ever, to distinguish between the various types of packets being transported by the network.

So how does a router decide what kind of packet it is receiving—essentially, whether it is a data packet or a control packet? In general, this determination is made at the outset by looking at the destination address in the IP header. That is, if the destination address of the packet is meant to terminate on the router itself—every device on the network has at least one IP address of its own—then it is most likely a control packet. If the destination address of the packet is meant to be forwarded out one of the router's interfaces toward an external destination (from the perspective of an individual router), then the local router treats it as a data plane packet (although it may be a control packet for another downstream router.) Why this matters is that routers are optimized to forward data packets. Control packets, under normal circumstances, form a small percentage of the packets handled by the router. How routers process various packet types is discussed in the IP Traffic Concepts section in this chapter. As you will learn, these processing differences have often profound implications on network security. Chapter 2 discusses these concepts in greater detail.

IP Traffic Concepts

You just learned that IP is connectionless, and that IP encapsulates data in self-contained routable units known as packets. Each packet includes an IP header that contains information (such as source and destination addresses) that is used by routers when making forwarding decisions. You also saw how IP transmits everything in-band. Control and data packets arrive on a common interface and are handled by the same router, but for obviously different purposes. Finally, you learned that, in a simplified way, routers process each packet based on its destination address. From the perspective of any single router, if a packet has a destination of the router itself, it is most likely a control packet, and if the destination is somewhere else in the network, it is treated as a data packet and forwarded. Of course, this is a very simplified view of IP network operations. Achieving a full understanding of how IP traffic plane separation and control impacts IP network security requires a deeper investigation of network and router operations.

As illustrated in Figure 1-5, a single router participates in a larger network environment, possibly even the Internet. Thus, individual routers, by themselves, may or may not understand the full *context* of each IP packet they are processing (in other words, in which IP traffic plane the packet belongs). What is relevant from each router's perspective, at the very moment it is processing any individual packet, is the IP *traffic type* it is seeing. The concept of *traffic planes* is a logical one, not a physical one. The concept of *traffic type* is a real one, and is the focus of this section.

How routers actually process different packet types must be fully understand. Why do routers process some packets differently from others? What are the security implications resulting from differences? These are the concepts that require a more in-depth understanding for the three broad categories: transit, receive, and exception packets.

Figure 1-5   *IP Networking Perspective*

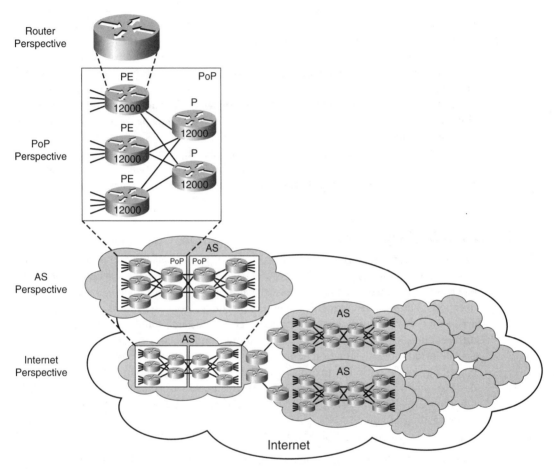

Transit IP Packets

IP networks are built to forward packets between end hosts. What a router does, primarily, is take packets in one interface, look at the destination field in the IP header, look for a match with a destination network in the routing table (built by the control plane!), and forward the packet out the appropriate interface that gets the packet one hop closer to its final destination.

In the case of transit packets, the destination network is somewhere *off* the router. That is, the IP address is not owned by the *particular router* processing the packet, but rather is somewhere else in the network. The destination could be on a directly attached subnet

(LAN), or it could be many downstream hops away. The key is that the packet is not destined *to* this router but, more accurately, *through* this router. Hence, when a router sees a transit packet, the decision it makes is to forward the packet out one of its interfaces. Routers typically use specialized forwarding hardware and algorithms to accomplish this forwarding function as quickly as possible. Additional details on router forwarding architectures are discussed in the "General IP Router Architecture Types" section of this chapter.

You should note that there is no explicit or implicit statement here about what *IP traffic plane* these transit packets are part of. From the perspective of a single router, transit packets may be of any IP traffic plane, as you will see shortly. Consider the example of a management session between a Secure Shell (SSH) client in the network operations center (NOC) and a router in the core of the network. The management session packets traverse many routers on their way to the destination router. Hence, they are transit packets according to every router along the path, until they reach the final core router. On that final router, they are no longer transit packets but are *receive* or *receive-adjacency* packets. (See the following section.) Yet, as you will learn shortly, it is clear from a logical perspective that these packets are all part of the *management plane* from a traffic plane perspective.

Receive-Adjacency IP Packets

IP packets that arrive at a router and that are destined to an IP address *owned* by that router itself as the final destination are called *receive-adjacency* packets.

NOTE   The term *receive packet*, or *receive-adjacency packet*, comes from nomenclature used by the adjacency table created by the Cisco Express Forwarding (CEF) forwarding mechanism. When CEF builds its adjacency table, it lists IP addresses for interfaces (both physical and logical) that are owned by the router as "receive." Another term used in some documentation is "for-us" packets. CEF is discussed in more detail later in this section.

When a router sees receive-adjacency packets, the destination address of the packet is always something that the router itself owns. It could be the IP address of a physical interface or of a logical interface such as a *loopback* interface or *tunnel* interface. These packets could have arrived from a host on a directly connected LAN, or they could have arrived after traversing several or many upstream routers to get to this final router. Either way, the decision the router makes when it sees receive-adjacency packets is very different from the one it makes for transit packets. With receive-adjacency packets, the router cannot engage any specialized forwarding hardware; the router must process the packet itself, using its own local CPU resources.

<table>
<tr><td>**NOTE**</td><td>The term often used in documentation to describe moving a packet from the normal, high-speed forwarding path to the router's own CPU for local processing is *punt*. For example, you may read that some types of packets are *"punted to the CPU for processing."* This terminology will be used in this book as well.</td></tr>
</table>

Although it may seem that all receive packets are control packets, this is not the case. As with transit packets, many kinds of packets potentially fall into the receive category. Receive packets generally include traffic in the *control*, *management*, and *services planes*.

The most important concept to understand with receive packets is that the router must treat them differently from transit packets. Usually, this implies that the router is using different hardware and/or software to process these packets and, nearly always, that the speed of processing is much slower than for transit packets. How receive and transit packet processing interactions affect the overall performance of the router, and the implications this has on network security, is one of the main reasons why IP traffic plane segmentation and control is so critical.

Exception IP and Non-IP Packets

In the preceding two sections, you learned about two different traffic types, transit and receive. Traffic in the transit family includes packets that the router forwards on toward some final destination, typically using some high-speed forwarding mechanism. Traffic in the receive family includes packets that the router must process itself locally. Interestingly, these two traffic types do not cover all cases in IP networks. Two other traffic types also seen by routers include the catch-all group known as *exception IP packets*, and the *non-IP packets* group.

Exception IP packets include transit or receive IP packets that have some exceptional characteristic about them and that cannot be handled by normal processing by the router. Non-IP packets are basically just that—packets that are not part of the IP protocol. These typically are used by the routers themselves to construct and maintain the network. Why exception IP and non-IP traffic types are so important is that routers process these packets in a different way from how they process normal transit or receive packets. These packets are important because each has the potential to impact the network. They can move data, they can help build routing tables, and they can control routers. These all potentially have security implications. Several examples will help illustrate this point.

Exception IP Packets

An example of an exception IP packet is as follows: An IP packet arrives at the router, and it is determined to be a transit packet (in other words, the router wants to forward it downstream). However, the TTL field in the IP header has a value of 1. Because the router is required to decrement the TTL field prior to forwarding the packet, the resultant value would be 0. The IP networking protocol requires that packets with TTL = 0 must be dropped. In addition, an ICMP error message must be generated and sent back to the originator of the packet to inform them that the packet was dropped. The specific ICMP error message is the "time exceeded in transit" message, or ICMP Type 11, Code 0. (See Appendix B for complete details on ICMP error messages.) The exception condition here is due to the fact that the router must alter its normal transit packet processing to drop the expired packet and generate and send the correct ICMP message back to the source of the original packet. This exception process requires the router to expend additional resources it would otherwise not expend, simply to forward the packet.

Other examples include: IP packets containing options in their header field, IP packets requiring fragmentation, and IP multicast packets used to create state. There are other exceptions as well, and these vary between router platforms.

Non-IP Packets

The other group of exception packets includes non-IP packets. In general, there are two groups of non-IP packets that routers may need to process. The first group includes the Layer 2 packets that are generated by the routers themselves to construct and maintain the network. Examples of packets of this type include:

- **Layer 2 keepalives:** Cisco HDLC, Frame Relay, ATM Operation, Administration, and Maintenance (OAM), and other Layer 2 protocols typically send periodic L2 messages to convey interface up/down status between devices.

- **Link Control Protocol (LCP):** LCP is an integral part of PPP and Multilink PPP (MLP), and provides automatic configuration of the interfaces such as setting datagram size, escaped characters, and magic numbers, and selecting (optional) authentication. LCP can also detect a looped-back link and other common misconfigurations, and terminate the link.

- **Cisco Discovery Protocol (CDP):** CDP is a proprietary protocol that transmits router hardware, software, and interface status information between adjacent routers via multicast Layer 2 frames.

The preceding examples use purely Layer 2 frames, which are handled as exceptions by the router (punted and handled by the router CPU).

NOTE   All of the Layer 2 packets just described are local packets, meaning point-to-point packets that are processed by the local router CPU. This distinguishes them from Layer 2 packets that are tunneled (for example, AToM, VPLS, and L2TPv3).

The other group of non-IP packets includes all Layer 3 "non-IP" packets that may be configured to run on the router concurrently with IP.

Examples of non-IP Layer 3 protocols include:

- **Intermediate System-to-Intermediate System (IS-IS):** An IGP used by many large service providers to maintain routing information within their own network administrative domain (instead of OSPF) to support reachability between BGP next-hops. IS-IS operates at Layer 3 like IP, but is a separate protocol that was originally developed by the International Organization for Standardization (ISO) as a routing protocol for Connectionless Network Protocol (CLNP) as part of Connectionless Network Services (CLNS). It was later extended to support IP routing, and is referred to as Integrated IS-IS.

- **Address Resolution Protocol (ARP):** Used by hosts to find the corresponding Layer 2 (hardware) address to an IP network (Layer 3) address.

- **Multiprotocol Label Switching (MPLS):** A data-carrying mechanism that emulates some of the properties of a circuit-switched network. MPLS is generally considered to operate between the traditional definitions of Layer 2 and Layer 3 protocols.

Other examples of non-IP Layer 3 protocols include: Novell Corporation's Internetwork Packet Exchange (IPX) and Apple Corporation's AppleTalk protocol.

As you have just seen, four distinct traffic types must be handled by routers: transit traffic, receive traffic, exception IP traffic, and non-IP traffic. The primary reason these four types of traffic are described separately here is that routers process these packets in different ways. Router vendors, such as Cisco, build hardware and software to handle all types of traffic within acceptable performance bounds appropriate for a given cost structure. At the same time, network architects and operators must be aware of the interactions between these four traffic types and understand the effects each may have on router and network performance and availability. For example, certain denial-of-service (DoS) attacks may be based on the purposeful manipulation of IP protocol exception packets. Routers and network infrastructure must be designed and built to efficiently forward "normal" traffic, while at the same time handle exception traffic and mitigate attack traffic without adverse impact.

IP Traffic Planes

Sufficient background has been covered to now fully explore the concepts of *IP traffic planes*. What types of IP traffic planes are there? Why should network traffic be segmented into IP traffic planes? What types of traffic are found in each traffic plane? These are the questions answered here.

Traffic *planes* are *logical* separations used to classify traffic based on the function it performs in the network. This approach is used for several reasons. First, it provides a consistent basis from which security policies can be developed. Second, it provides the basis for transforming these security policies into actual network control functions that can be implemented on various network elements.

As you saw in the previous discussion, depending on where a router is in the network, it will have a different perspective on what type of packet it is processing (transit vs. receive, for example). However, whether a packet is transit or receive does not automatically give any indication as to the function each packet is ultimately supporting. It is the concept of IP traffic planes that provide this end-to-end framework. Packets in each traffic plane have certain requirements that must be enforced, regardless of where they are within the network. Four distinct IP traffic planes are defined: the data plane, the control plane, the management plane, and the services plane. Each has its own distinctive characteristics, and its own security requirements. The four IP traffic planes are described in detail next.

Data Plane

The data plane is the logical entity containing all "customer" application traffic. In this context, customer traffic refers to traffic generated by hosts, clients, servers, and applications that are intended to use the network as transport only. Thus, data plane traffic should never have destination IP addresses that belong to any networking devices (routers, switches), but rather should be sourced from and destined to other devices, such as PCs and servers, that are supported by the network. The primary job of the router in the case of the data plane is simply to forward these packets downstream as quickly as possible. Figure 1-6 illustrates the basic concepts of the data plane.

Figure 1-6 *Data Plane*

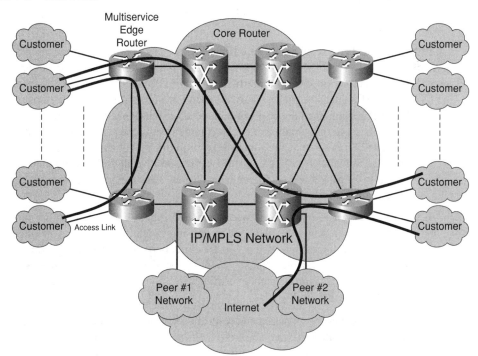

Networks are built and operated to support data plane traffic. Without the data plane, there is no need for a network. First and foremost, the data plane must be "available." As you will see shortly, the data plane depends on the control plane and, to a certain extent, the management plane. Thus, interdependencies exist between these planes and they must be considered. In addition, there may be a "confidentiality" requirement, which may be satisfied via data separation (as would be provided by Frame Relay or MPLS VPNs, for example) or encryption. This is discussed further in the "Services Plane" section.

Data plane traffic always includes transit packets. Under normal conditions, transit traffic should account for a large percentage of all data plane traffic. This is precisely why routers often use specialized forwarding hardware and algorithms to accomplish this forwarding function as quickly as possible. That does not imply that all transit packets belong to the data plane, or that the data plane consists only of transit packets. There are exceptions, and in this case, routers may be required to perform some additional work to forward certain data plane packets. Hence, the data plane may also include certain (transit) exception packets. When this occurs, additional router resources are required to forward data plane traffic. Two examples will help clarify this point:

- **Example 1:** A packet enters the router's interface, and the router determines that it is a transit packet that needs to be delivered to a host on a directly connected Ethernet LAN segment. However, the router does not have an ARP entry for the destination IP address. In this case, the router must use its control plane to "ARP" for the destination MAC address. Once the MAC address has been obtained, the packet (and all subsequent packets destined to this IP address) can be forwarded directly without further "exceptions."

- **Example 2:** A packet enters an interface on the router that has a maximum transmission unit (MTU) of 1500 bytes. The router determines that the transit packet should be forwarded out an interface with an MTU of 1300 bytes. This requires the router to fragment the packet. Thus, the router must determine whether this is allowable by first checking the DF (Don't Fragment) bit in the IP header (see Figure 1-4). If the DF bit is set to 0, the packet must be fragmented by the router and then forwarded. If the DF bit is set to 1, the router must drop the packet and then generate an error message of ICMP Type 3, Code 4 (Fragmentation Needed, Don't Fragment Set) and send it to the packet source. Either event causes additional router processing resources to be consumed.

As you can see even with just these two examples, legitimate data plane traffic can impact the performance of a router or a network by causing exception conditions that the router must fulfill through special processing. Most security books describe methods for protecting data plane traffic from various attacks. There is also the need to protect the router and network from data plane traffic under exception conditions. An effective data plane security policy must accomplish both goals.

Data plane traffic must be separated and controlled to protect the router and network against many threats. These threats can come from legitimate traffic and malicious traffic, and the data plane security policy must be prepared for either case. When the router or network performance is impacted, does it matter whether malicious traffic or legitimate traffic caused the problem? Not to the other users of the network. Thus, data plane security must ensure the delivery of customer traffic, and ensure that customer traffic, whether legitimate, malformed, or malicious, does not interfere with the proper operation of the network. Chapter 2 provides additional discussion on some of the threats to the data plane. Chapter 4, "Data Plane Security," provides detailed descriptions of the current best practices for securing the data plane.

Control Plane

The control plane is the logical entity associated with routing processes and functions used to create and maintain the necessary intelligence about the state of the network and a router's interfaces. The control plane includes network protocols, such as routing, signaling, and link-state protocols, that are used for communication between network elements, and other control protocols that are used to build network services. Thus, the control plane is *how* the network gets dynamically built, and provides the mechanisms for routers to understand forwarding topologies and the operational state of the network. Without the control plane, no other traffic planes would function. Figure 1-7 illustrates the basic concepts of the control plane.

Figure 1-7   *Control Plane Example*

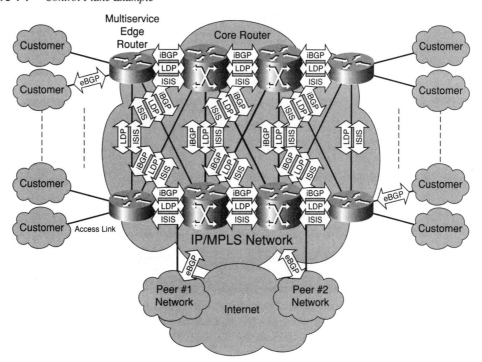

The control plane always includes receive packets. Receive packets are both generated and consumed by various control processes running on the router. These may include Layer 3 packets for routing protocol processes such as OSPF and BGP, or for other processes that maintain the forwarding state such as Protocol Independent Multicast (PIM), Label Distribution Protocol (LDP), and Hot Standby Routing Protocol (HSRP).

The control plane also includes transit packets. For example, multihop eBGP packets traverse several intermediate routers between peers, and thus have transit characteristics from the perspective of the intermediate routers along their path. These eBGP packets are not destined for processes running on the intermediate routers, yet they are undoubtedly part of the control plane for the overall network. Other examples include mechanisms such as OSPF virtual-link and Resource Reservation Protocol (RSVP). ICMP is the part of the control plane that typically generates messages in response to errors in IP datagrams or for diagnostic or routing purposes.

The control plane also includes certain Layer 3 non-IP packets, such as the routing protocol IS-IS, and ARP, and the Layer 2 packets such as Layer 2 keepalives, CDP, ATM OAM, and PPP LCP frames.

NOTE   The control plane is typically associated with packets generated by the network elements themselves. End users typically do not interact with the control plane. The *ICMP ping* application is one exception where a control plane protocol may be directly employed by end users. The ping application allows end users to directly interact with the control plane to determine network reachability information.

Securing the control plane is critical to both router and network operations. If the control plane is compromised, nothing can be guaranteed about the state of the network. Compromises in the control plane may adversely affect the data plane, management plane, and services plane. This could lead to the following:

- **Service disruption:** Data not being delivered
- **Unintended routing:** Data traversing adversary networks for packet sniffing, rogue DNS use, and Trojan/malware insertion, for example
- **Management integrity issues:** Billing, service theft, and so forth

How exposed the control plane is depends greatly on the device location and reachability. For example, routers on the edge of a service provider (SP) network are more exposed than those deep within the SP core simply because they are directly adjacent to uncontrolled customer and peering networks. Enterprise routers also have similar points of increased risk at the Internet edge. Certain Layer 2 vulnerabilities exist as well. These issues and others are described in Chapter 2. In addition, Chapter 5, "Control Plane Security," provides detailed descriptions of the current best practices for securing the control plane.

Management Plane

The management plane is the logical entity that describes the traffic used to access, manage, and monitor all of the network elements. The management plane supports all required provisioning, maintenance, and monitoring functions for the network. Like the other IP traffic planes, management plane traffic is handled in-band with all other IP traffic. Most service providers and many large enterprises also build separate, out-of-band (OOB) management networks to provide alternate reachability when the primary in-band IP path is not reachable. These basic management plane concepts are illustrated in Figure 1-8.

Figure 1-8 *Management Plane Example*

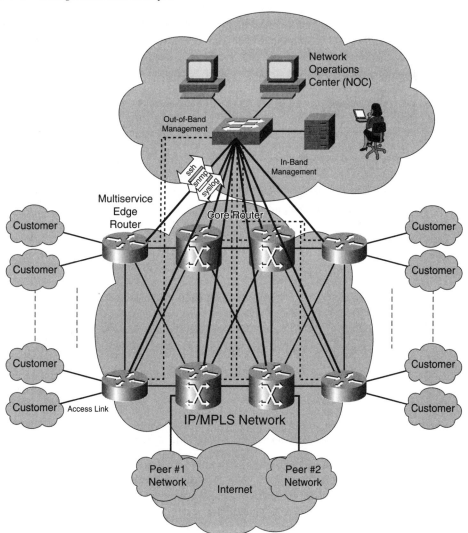

The management plane always includes receive packets. Receive packets are both generated and consumed by various management processes running on the router. As you might imagine, traffic such as SSH (please do not use Telnet!), FTP, TFTP, SNMP, syslog, TACACS+ and RADIUS, DNS, NetFlow, ROMMON, and other management protocols that the NOC staff and monitoring applications use is included in the management plane. In addition, from the perspective of some routers, transit packets will also be part of the management plane. Depending on where the management servers and network operations staff are located, all of the preceding management protocols appear as transit packets to intermediate devices and as receive packets to the destination devices. However, management plane traffic typically remains wholly "internal" to the network and should cross only certain interfaces of the router. Further details on this topic are covered in the case studies presented in Chapters 8 and 9. The management plane should rarely include IP exception packets (MPLS OAM using the Router Alert IP options is one exception). It may however, include non-IP exception packets. CDP is a Layer 2–based protocol that allows Cisco routers and switches to dynamically discover one another.

Securing the management plane is just as critical for proper router and network operations as securing the control plane. A compromised management plane inevitably leads to unauthorized access, potentially permitting an attacker to further compromise the IP traffic planes by adding routes, modifying traffic flows, or simply filtering transit packets. Attackers have repeatedly demonstrated their ability to compromise routers when weak passwords, unencrypted management access (for example, Telnet), or other weak management plane security mechanisms are used. Remember, access to routers is like getting the "keys to the kingdom!" Additional discussions on some of the threats to the management plane are provided in Chapter 2, and Chapter 6, "Management Plane Security," provides detailed descriptions of the current best practices for securing the management plane.

Services Plane

Network convergence leads to multiple services of differing characteristics running over a common IP network core. Where this is the case, these can be treated within a "services plane" so that appropriate handling can be applied consistently throughout the network. The services plane is the logical entity that includes customer traffic receiving dedicated network-based services such as VPN tunneling (MPLS, IPsec, and Secure Sockets Layer [SSL]), private-to-public interfacing (Network Address Translation [NAT], firewall, and intrusion detection and prevention system [IDS/IPS]), QoS (voice and video), and many others. These basic services plane concepts are illustrated in Figure 1-9.

Services plane traffic is essentially "customer" traffic, like data plane traffic, but with one major difference. The services plane includes traffic that is intended to have specialized network-based functions applied, and to have consistent handling applied end to end. Data plane traffic, on the other hand, typically receives only native IP delivery support. Because different kinds of services may be represented, different polices may need to be created and enforced when working with the services plane.

Figure 1-9   *Services Plane Example*

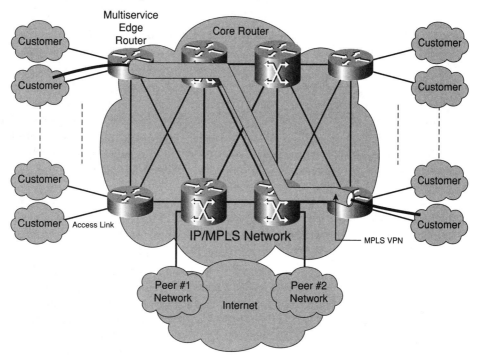

Services plane traffic is generally "transit" traffic. But routers and other forwarding devices typically use special handling to apply or enforce the intended policies for various service types. That is, services plane traffic may be processed in a very different manner from regular data plane traffic. The following examples help illustrate this point:

- Encrypted tunnels using SSL or IPsec. Internal redirection to specialized cryptographic hardware, may be required to support SSL or IPsec VPNs. This often creates additional CPU and switching overhead for certain devices. Service encapsulation in tunnels often changes the nature of the traffic from transit to receive as packets now terminate on the network devices for decapsulation. This too can impact the processing operations of certain devices.

- Routing separation using MPLS VPN. Routers participating in MPLS VPN services must maintain virtual routing and forwarding (VRF) instances for each customer. This requires additional memory, and can create additional packet overhead due to encapsulation that may result in fragmentation.

- Network-based security via firewalls, intrusion protection systems (IPS), and similar systems. The application of network-based security services oftentimes impacts the traffic-flow characteristics of the network. Firewalls and IPS typically require symmetric traffic-flows (egress traffic following the same path as the ingress traffic). Symmetric traffic flows are not inherent to IP and must be artificially enforced.

- Network-based service-level agreements (SLA) via QoS: QoS provides virtual class of service (CoS) networks using a single physical network. The application of QoS polices impacts other, non-QoS traffic due to modifications in packet-forwarding mechanisms as latency and jitter budgets are enforced.

Because services planes often "overlay" (Layer 7) application flows on the foundation of lower layers, services planes often add to the control plane and management plane burdens. For example, MPLS VPNs (RFC 4364) add control plane mechanisms to BGP for routing separation, and LDP and RSVP for forwarding path computation. IPsec VPNs add Internet Key Exchange (IKE) mechanisms to the control plane for encryption key generation, and tunnel creation and maintenance. Additional support in the management plane is also required. Tunnel management for IPsec VPNs requires interfacing with each router involved in the service delivery. Similarly, MPLS OAM is required for end-to-end label switch path verification. Other services add different control plane and management plane burdens.

Securing the services plane is critical to ensure stable and reliable traffic delivery of specialized traffic flows. In some cases, this may be straightforward. Encapsulating user-generated IP traffic within a common service header allows for a simplified security approach. Policies need to look only for the type of service, not at the individual user traffic using the service (as in the data plane case). In some cases, this encapsulation may add protections to the core network, because the relatively "untrusted" user traffic can be isolated in a service wrapper and cannot touch the network infrastructure. For example, MPLS VPNs separate per-customer routing functions and network infrastructure routing functions. Dependencies between the services plane and the control plane and management plane add complexities that must be considered carefully. Chapter 2 provides additional discussion on some of the threats to the services plane, and Chapter 7 provides detailed descriptions of the current best practices for securing the services plane.

IP Router Packet Processing Concepts

The last topics to be discussed in this introductory chapter are those of router software and hardware architectures. This will tie together all of the preceding concepts, and illustrate why IP traffic plane separation and control is so vital to the stability, performance, and operation of IP networks.

Routers are built to forward packets, whether in the data plane or services plane, as efficiently as possible. These same routers must also build and maintain the network through the control plane and management plane. The concept of IP traffic planes is a "logical" one, and provides a framework within which to develop and enforce specific security requirements. As illustrated in Figure 1-5 earlier in the chapter, IP traffic plane security concepts can be viewed from the Internet perspective down to the individual router perspective. Where is traffic originated and where is it destined? Where are the network boundaries and what traffic should be crossing those boundaries? Which IP addresses should be included and advertised in various routing protocols? These and many more questions are discussed and answered in the following chapters.

One of the most important areas in this process, and the reason for the perspective view previously shown in Figure 1-5, is that individual routers handle the actual packets in the network. At the end of the day, these devices can only act in an autonomous manner consistent with their hardware, software, and configurations. Understanding how an individual router handles each packet type reaching its interfaces, and the resources it must expend to process these packets, is a key concept in IP traffic plane security.

Although this section focuses specifically on Cisco routers, these concepts are by no means exclusive to Cisco platforms. Every network device that "touches" a packet has a hardware and software architecture that is designed to process a packet, determine what exactly it is required to do with the packet, and then apply some policy to the packet. The term "policy" in this context means any operation applied to the packet, generally including: forward/drop, shape/rate-limit, recolor, duplicate, and tunnel/encapsulate.

A router's primary purpose is to forward packets from one network interface to another. Each network interface represents either a directly connected segment containing hosts and servers, or the connection to another routing device toward the next hop along the downstream path to the ultimate destination of the packet. In the most basic sense, the Layer 3 decision process of an IP router includes the following steps:

1 A packet comes into an interface.

2 The IP header checksum is recomputed and compared to validate the packet integrity. If it does not compare, the packet is dropped.

3 If it does compare correctly, the IP header TTL is decremented and the checksum is recomputed (because the header data changes with the new TTL value).

4 The new TTL value is checked to ensure that it is greater than 0. If it is not, the packet is dropped and an ICMP Type 11 message (time exceeded) is generated and sent back to the packet source.

5 If the TTL value is valid (>=1), a forwarding lookup is done using the destination address. That destination could be to somewhere beyond the router (a transit packet) or to the router itself (receive packet). If a match does not exist, the packet is dropped and an ICMP destination unreachable (type 3) is generated.

6 If a match is found, appropriate Layer 2 encapsulation information is prepared, and the packet is forwarded out the appropriate interface (transit). In the case of a "receive" destination, the packet is punted to the router CPU for handling.

This process is illustrated in Figure 1-10.

Figure 1-10 *Simple IP Forwarding Example*

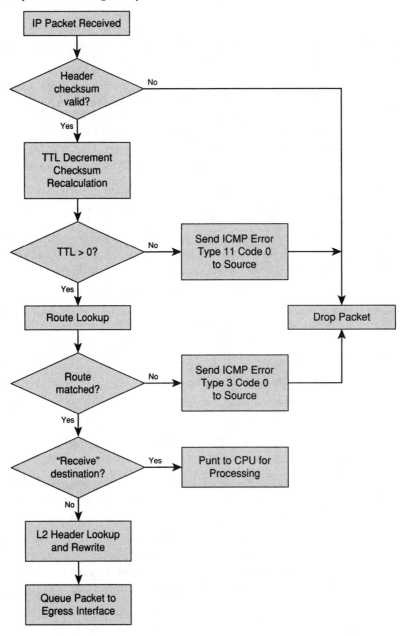

Of course, the actual packet processing flow can be significantly more complex than this as memory, I/O hardware, IP packet variations, configured polices, and many other factors affect packet processing. Normally, the great majority of all packets in the network are related to the data plane and services plane. Control plane and management plane traffic make up a small portion of overall network traffic. Exception cases exist where data plane packets may require additional control plane resources, or where packets cannot be handled by the normal packet-forwarding mechanisms. In general, routers handle transit, receive, and exception packets in different ways. As you may imagine, routers are optimized to process transit traffic with the most efficiency and speed. But it is how a router handles receive and exception cases that gives you a full understanding of the performance envelop (and vulnerabilities or attack vectors) of the router.

Most Cisco routers use Cisco IOS Software to perform packet-switching functions. (IOS XR is available on high-end routing platforms, including CRS-1 and XR 12000, and was developed for the carrier class requirements of service providers.) When IOS was first developed, only a single switching mechanism existed. This method, known as *process switching*, was very simple and not very efficient. As network speeds and the demand for higher performance grew, enhancements were made to Cisco IOS Software that provided improved methods of switching. Specialized hardware components were also developed and incorporated into certain routers to improve forwarding performance. Today, Cisco routers are available that switch between thousands of packets per second (Kpps) to hundreds of millions of packets per second (Mpps). Dedicated hardware-based forwarding engines, mainly implemented as application-specific integrated circuits (ASIC), are necessary to achieve the highest forwarding rates. Other parameters, such as I/O memory speed and bus performance, can have a big impact on switching performance. The challenge is to create the highest possible switching performance within the limits of available ASIC, CPU, I/O bus, and memory technology and cost. The switching method used by various Cisco routers to achieve these rates depends on the specific routing platforms.

In general, three switching methods are available in Cisco IOS today:

- **Process switching:** Packets are processed and forwarded directly by the router CPU.
- **Fast switching:** Packets are forwarded in the CPU interrupt, using cache entries created by process switching.
- **Cisco Express Forwarding (CEF):** Packets are forwarded using a precomputed and very well-optimized version of the routing table.

Each of these three switching methods is reviewed in general detail next. The intent of this review is not to describe all the optimizations and mechanisms used by each in forwarding packets. Many excellent references cover these aspects already. Check the "Further Reading" section at the end of this chapter for specific recommendations. The intent is to investigate how these three switching methods deal with packets in the various IP traffic planes, and to see what impact this has on router performance and, hence, network stability and security.

Process Switching

The oldest and most basic switching mode is process switching, also referred to as "slow path" switching. Process switching refers to switching packets by queuing them to the CPU on the route processor and then having the CPU make the forwarding decisions, all at the process level. The term "route processor" is used to describe the module that contains the CPU, system software, and most of the memory components that are used by the router to forward packets. In the process switching model, every packet-switching request is queued alongside all other applications and serviced, in turn, by the software running on the CPU on the route processor.

Figure 1-11 illustrates the steps, listed next, involved in forwarding packets by process switching:

1 Process switching begins when the network interface hardware receives the packet and transfers it into I/O memory. This causes the network interface hardware to interrupt the CPU, alerting it to the ingress packet waiting in I/O memory requiring processing. IOS updates its inbound packet counters.

2 The IOS software inspects the packet header information (encapsulation type, network layer header, and so on), determines that it is an IP packet, and places it on the input queue for the appropriate switching process.

3 The CPU performs a route lookup (Layer 3). Upon finding a match, the CPU retrieves the next-hop address from the routing table (Layer 3) and the Media Access Control (MAC) address (Layer 2) associated with this next-hop address from the ARP cache, and builds the new header. The CPU then queues the packet on the outbound network interface.

4 The outbound network interface hardware senses the buffered packet, dequeues it from I/O memory, and transmits it on to the network. It then interrupts the main processor to indicate that the packet has been transmitted. IOS then updates its outbound packet counters and frees the space in I/O memory formerly occupied by the packet.

You may already recognize that, although straightforward, process switching has many deficiencies in terms of performance as a switching method. First, each and every packet is switched according to the process described in the preceding list. Any subsequent packets belonging to the same flow are also switched using the exact same switching process. In this basic scheme, no mechanisms are available to recognize that subsequent packets may be part of an already-established flow, and that Layer 3 route-lookups and Layer 2 MAC lookups have previously been performed. Second, because process switching requires a routing table lookup for every packet, as the size of the routing table grows, so does the time required to perform any lookup (and hence the total switching time). Recursive routes require additional lookups in the routing table, further increasing the length of the lookup time.

Figure 1-11 *Illustration of Process Switching*

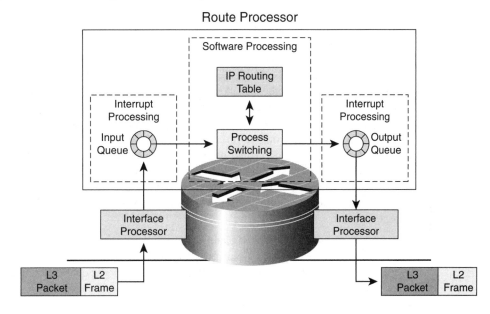

From an IP traffic plane perspective, it should be clear that process switching performs identical functions, initially, for every packet in any IP traffic plane, regardless of the packet type, because each and every packet must be processed by the CPU. Depending on the traffic plane and packet type, however, once IOS inspects the packet header, it determines which software process to hand the packet off to. At this point, additional processing is generally required for certain packets, possibly affecting overall router performance.

- **Data plane:** Data plane packets with transit destinations are handled by process-switching operations exactly as Figure 1-11 illustrates. Because the CPU has finite clock cycles available for switching packets, computing routes, and performing all other functions it is required to, forwarding performance is limited by CPU utilization and can vary. There is also an upper limit on packet forwarding that is a maximum number of packets per second (pps), regardless of interface bandwidth values. This concept is explored further in Chapter 2. Additional processing is required to handle data plane exception packets as well. For example, TTL = 0 packets must be dropped and an ICMP error message must be generated and transmitted back to the originator. Packets with IP options may also require additional processing to handle the header option. When the ratio of exception packets becomes large in comparison to normal transit packets, forwarding performance may be impacted. Thus, controlling the impact of data plane exception packets in particular will be critical in protecting router resources. Chapter 4 explores these concepts in detail.

- **Control plane:** Control plane packets with transit destinations are processed exactly like data plane transit packets. Control plane packets with receive destinations and non-IP exception packets (for example, Layer 2 keepalives, IS-IS, and so forth) also follow the same initial process-switching operations illustrated in Figure 1-11. However, once packet identification determines these are receive or non-IP packets, they are handed off to different software elements in the CPU, and additional resources are consumed to fully process these packets. For example, frequent routing protocol updates (as may occur when interfaces are flapping) will cause routing advertisements and path recomputations and result in temporarily high CPU utilization. High CPU utilization may result in dropped traffic in the data plane if the router is unable to service forwarding requests. Proper network design should minimize routing instabilities. For process-switching platforms, it is critical to prevent spoofed and other malicious packets from impacting the control plane, potentially consuming router resources and disrupting overall network stability. Chapter 5 explores these concepts in detail.

- **Management plane:** Management plane packets with transit destinations are processed exactly like data plane transit packets. Management plane packets with receive destinations also follow the same initial process-switching operations described for the control plane. However, once packet identification determines these are receive packets, they are handed off to software elements in the CPU that are responsible for the appropriate network management service. Management plane traffic typically does not contain IP exception packets (MPLS OAM using the Router Alert IP options is one exception), but may contain non-IP (Layer 2) exception packets (generally in the form of CDP packets). In general, management plane traffic should have little impact on CPU performance. It is possible that some management actions, such as conducting frequent SNMP polling or turning on debug operations, or the use of NetFlow may cause high CPU utilization. Carefully defined *acceptable use* policies for production networks should prevent unintentional CPU impacts. However, because management plane traffic is handled directly by the CPU, the opportunity for abuse makes it critical that management plane security be implemented. Chapter 6 explores these concepts in detail.

- **Services plane:** Services plane packets follow the same initial process-switching operations illustrated in Figure 1-11. However, services plane packets generally require special processing by the router. Examples include performing encapsulation functions (for example, GRE, IPsec, or MPLS VPN) or performing some QoS or policy routing function. This requires services plane packets to be handled by different software elements in the CPU, incurring additional, possibly heavy, CPU resources. In general, process switching services plane packets can have a large impact on CPU utilization. The main concern then is to protect the integrity of the services plane by preventing spoofed or malicious packets from impacting the CPU. Chapter 7 explores these concepts in detail.

Although process switching contains the least amount of performance optimizations and can consume large amounts of CPU resources, it does have the advantage of being platform-independent, making it universally available across all Cisco IOS–based products. Still, from a performance perspective, process switching leaves a lot to be desired. You may have noticed in the process-switching flow illustrated in Figure 1-11 that three key pieces of information are required to switch any packet:

- **Destination network reachability:** A route must exist in the forwarding table for the destination address.

- **Egress interface:** If a route exists, the IP address of the next hop toward the destination must be known.

- **Next-hop Layer 2 address:** The Layer 2 (for example, MAC) address of the next hop must also be known.

This information is determined for each packet forwarded by process switching, even if the previous packet required the exact same information. In most IP networks, flows normally consist of multiple packets. What if the results of one of these lookups, essentially reachability/interface/MAC combinations, were temporarily saved in a small table? Could substantial reductions in forwarding time be achieved for most of the incoming packets? This is the idea behind fast switching in IOS.

Fast Switching

Fast switching is a software enhancement to process switching that speeds the performance of packets using the forwarding path. You may also see this referred to as "fast cache switching." Fast switching uses a route cache to store information about packet flows. The route cache is consulted first in each forwarding attempt, instead of using the more expensive, process switching lookup procedures described in the previous section.

Figure 1-12 illustrates the steps, listed next, involved in forwarding packets by fast switching:

1 Fast switching begins exactly like process switching. First, the network interface hardware receives the packet and transfers it into I/O memory. The network interface interrupts the CPU, alerting it to the ingress packet waiting in I/O memory for processing. IOS updates its inbound packet counters.

2 The IOS interrupt software inspects the packet header information (encapsulation type, network layer header, and so forth) and determines that it is an IP packet. Instead of placing the packet on the input queue for CPU processing, however, the interrupt software consults the fast cache for an entry matching the destination address. If an entry exists, the interrupt software retrieves the Layer 2 (MAC) and outbound interface information out of the fast cache and builds the new Layer 2 header. Finally, the interrupt software alerts the outbound interface.

3 Like process switching again, the outbound network interface hardware senses the packet, dequeues it from I/O memory, and transmits it on to the network.

Figure 1-12 *Illustration of Fast Switching*

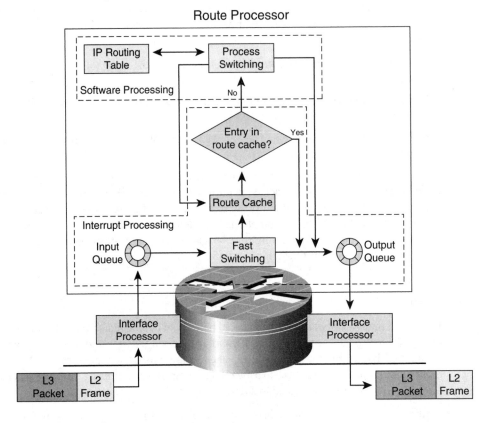

Note that if the destination address is not found in the cache, the router reverts to process switching to forward the packet using the procedures described in the preceding section. One difference, however, is that when fast switching is enabled, after process switching completes, a new entry is made in the fast cache (route cache) for future use. That is, the first packet of any new flow is always process switched. Subsequent packets are fast switched.

Fast switching separates the expensive CPU-based routing procedures from the relatively simple, interrupt-process driven forwarding procedures. This is why fast switching is often referred to as a "route once, forward many" process. Fast switching cache entries are created and deleted dynamically. A new cache entry is created when the first packet to a given destination is process switched and the **ip route-cache** command is enabled on the *output* interface. A route cache entry can be deleted when it has not been used for some time (idle timeout), and under certain low-memory conditions.

In addition to performing high-speed IP forwarding, fast switching implements many other features at the interrupt level. For example, infrastructure access control lists (iACL), policy routing, and IP multicast routing are all supported in fast switching. Not all features are supported by fast switching, however, and it may need to be disabled. (Disabling fast switching causes the router to fall back to process switching.) For example, you may need to disable fast switching when debugging and packet-level tracing are required.

Like process switching, fast switching is platform-independent and is used on all native Cisco routers. In Cisco IOS, fast switching is enabled by default. You can verify that fast switching is enabled and view the routes that are currently in the fast switching cache. As you can see in Example 1-1, the interface Serial4/1 has fast switching enabled. Example 1-2 shows the contents of the fast-switching cache. As you can see, each entry includes the destination prefix, age that the prefix has been in the cache, egress interface, and next-hop layer IP address.

Example 1-1   *Verifying that Fast Switching Is Enabled*

```
R1# show ip interface Serial4/1
Serial4/1 is up, line protocol is up
  Internet address is 10.0.0.1/30
  Broadcast address is 255.255.255.255
  Address determined by non-volatile memory
  MTU is 4470 bytes
  Helper address is not set
  Directed broadcast forwarding is disabled
  Outgoing access list is not set
  Inbound  access list is not set
  Proxy ARP is enabled
  Security level is default
  Split horizon is enabled
  ICMP redirects are always sent
  ICMP unreachables are always sent
  ICMP mask replies are never sent
  IP fast switching is enabled
  IP fast switching on the same interface is enabled
  IP Flow switching is disabled
  IP CEF switching is enabled
  IP Fast switching turbo vector
  IP Normal CEF switching turbo vector
  IP multicast fast switching is enabled
  IP multicast distributed fast switching is disabled
  IP route-cache flags are Fast, CEF
  Router Discovery is disabled
  IP output packet accounting is disabled
  IP access violation accounting is disabled
  TCP/IP header compression is disabled
  RTP/IP header compression is disabled
  Probe proxy name replies are disabled
  Policy routing is disabled
  Network address translation is disabled
  WCCP Redirect outbound is disabled
  WCCP Redirect inbound is disabled
  WCCP Redirect exclude is disabled
  BGP Policy Mapping is disabled
```

Example 1-2 *Viewing the Current Contents of the Fast-Switching Cache*

```
R1# show ip cache
IP routing cache 3 entries, 480 bytes
   4088 adds, 4085 invalidates, 0 refcounts
Minimum invalidation interval 2 seconds, maximum interval 5 seconds,
   quiet interval 3 seconds, threshold 0 requests
Invalidation rate 0 in last second, 0 in last 3 seconds
Last full cache invalidation occurred 8w0d ago

Prefix/Length           Age          Interface        Next Hop
10.1.1.10/32            8w0d         Serial0/0        10.1.1.10
10.1.1.128/30           00:00:10     Serial0/2        172.17.2.2
10.1.1.132/30           00:10:04     Serial0/1        172.17.1.2

R1#
```

From an IP traffic plane perspective, it should be clear that fast switching is mainly meant to accelerate the forwarding of data plane traffic. This works well in higher-speed networks when the packets are simple, data plane packets. However, not all features or packets can be fast switched. When this is the case, forwarding reverts to process switching, which adversely impacts router performance. This makes it all the more critical to classify traffic planes and to protect the router resources as network speeds increase and routers see higher packet rates (pps). When traffic fits the normal, fast switching profile, the router should perform well. However, if the traffic changes (for example, under malicious conditions) and process switching is required, the router could experience resource exhaustion and impact the overall network conditions. Let's take a look at each traffic plane again from the perspective of fast switching:

- **Data plane:** Fast switching operations were developed to speed delivery of data plane traffic, as Figure 1-12 illustrates. Packets will be fast switched when the destination is transit and a cache entry already exists. When a cache entry does not exist, for example, for the first packet of each new flow, process switching must be used to determine the next hop and Layer 2 header details. Preventing spoofed or malicious packets from abusing the data plane will keep the router CPU and fast cache memory from being abused. As with process switching, additional processing is required to handle data plane IP exception packets as well. For example, TTL = 0 packets must be dropped and an ICMP error message must be generated and transmitted back to the originator. Packets with IP options may also require additional processing to fulfill the invoked option. When the ratio of exception packets becomes large in comparison to normal transit packets, router resources can be exhausted, potentially affecting network stability. These and other concepts are explored further in Chapter 2. Chapter 4 explores in detail the concepts for protecting the data plane.

- **Control plane:** Control plane packets with transit destinations are fast switched exactly like data plane transit packets. Control plane packets with receive destinations and non-IP exception packets (for example, Layer 2 keepalives, IS-IS, and so on) follow the same initial fast-switching operations illustrated in Figure 1-12. However, once packet identification determines these are receive or non-IP packets, they are handed off to the CPU for processing by the appropriate software elements, and additional resources are consumed to fully process these packets. Thus, regardless of the switching method invoked, receive and non-IP control plane packets must be processed by the CPU, potentially causing high CPU utilization. High CPU utilization can result in dropped traffic if the router is unable to service forwarding requests. It is critical to prevent spoofed and other malicious packets from impacting the control plane, potentially consuming router resources and disrupting overall network stability. Chapter 5 explores these concepts in detail.

- **Management plane:** Management plane packets with transit destinations are fast switched exactly like data plane transit packets. Management plane packets with receive destinations follow the same initial fast-switching operations described for the control plane. Once these packets are identified, they are handed off to software elements in the CPU responsible for the appropriate network management service. Management plane traffic should not contain IP exception packets (again, MPLS OAM being one exception), but may contain non-IP (Layer 2) exception packets (generally in the form of CDP packets). Under normal circumstances, management plane traffic should have little impact on CPU performance. It is possible that some management actions, such as conducting frequent SNMP polling or turning on debug operations, or the use of NetFlow may cause high CPU utilization. Because management plane traffic is handled directly by the CPU, the opportunity for abuse makes it critical that management plane security be implemented. Chapter 6 explores these concepts in detail.

- **Services plane:** Services plane packets follow the same initial fast switching operations illustrated in Figure 1-12. However, services plane packets generally require special processing by the router. Examples include performing encapsulation functions (for example, GRE, IPsec, or MPLS VPN), or performing some QoS or policy routing function. Some of these operations can be handled by fast switching and some cannot. For example, policy routing is handled by fast switching, while GRE encapsulation is not. When packets cannot be handled by fast switching, forwarding reverts to process switching because these packets must be handled by software elements in the CPU. When this occurs, services plane packets can have a large impact on CPU utilization. The main concern then is to protect the integrity of the services plane by preventing spoofed or malicious packets from impacting the CPU. Chapter 7 explores these concepts in detail.

The growth of the Internet has led Internet core routers to support large routing tables and to provide high packet-switching speeds. Even though fast switching was a major improvement over process switching, it still has deficiencies:

- Fast switching cache entries are created on demand. The first packet of a new flow needs to be process switched to build the cache entry. This is not scalable when the network has to process switch a considerable amount of traffic for which there are no cache entries. This is especially true for BGP-learned routes because they specify only next-hop addresses, not interfaces, requiring recursive route lookups.

- Fast switching cache entries are destination based, which is also not scalable because core routers contain a large number of destination addresses. The memory size used to hold the route cache is limited, so as the table size grows, the potential for cache memory overflow increases. In addition, as the depth of the cache increases, so does the lookup time, resulting in performance degradation.

- Fast switching does not support per-packet load sharing among parallel routes. If per-packet load sharing is needed, fast switching must be disabled and process switching must be used, resulting in performance degradation.

In addition, the "one CPU does everything" approach was also found to no longer be adequate for high-speed forwarding. New high-end Cisco routers were developed to support a large number of high-speed network interfaces, and to distribute the forwarding process directly to the line cards. As a solution for these and other issues, Cisco developed a new switching method—Cisco Express Forwarding (CEF). CEF not only addresses the performance issues associated with fast switching, but also was developed with this new generation of "distributed" forwarding platforms in mind as well.

Cisco Express Forwarding

CEF, like fast switching, uses cache entries to perform its switching operation entirely during a route processor interrupt interval (for CPU-based platforms). As you recall, fast switching depends on process switching for the first packet to any given destination in order to build its cache table. CEF removes this demand-based mechanism and dependence on process switching to build its cache. Instead, the CEF table is pre-built directly from the routing table, and the adjacency table is pre-built directly from the ARP cache. These CEF structures are pre-built, before any packets are switched. It is never necessary to process switch any packet to get a cache entry built. Once the CEF tables are built, the CPU on the route processor is *never* directly involved in forwarding packets again (although it may be required to perform memory management and other housekeeping functions). In addition, pre-building the CEF structures greatly improves the forwarding performance on routers with large routing tables. Note that CEF switching is often referred to as "fast path" switching.

There are two major structures maintained by CEF:

- Forwarding Information Base (FIB)
- Adjacency table

Forwarding Information Base

The FIB is a specially constructed version of the routing table that is stored in a multiway tree data structure (256-way MTrie) that is optimized for consistent, high-speed lookups (with some router and IOS dependence). Destination lookups are done on a whole-byte basis; thus it takes only a maximum of four lookups (8-8-8-8) to find a route for any specific destination.

The FIB is completely resolved and contains all routes present in the main routing table. It is always kept synchronized. When routing or topology changes occur in the network, the IP routing table is updated, and those changes are reflected in the FIB. Because there is one-to-one agreement between FIB entries and routing table entries, the FIB contains all known routes and eliminates the need for the route cache maintenance associated with fast switching.

Special "receive" FIB entries are installed for destination addresses owned by the router itself. These include addresses assigned to physical interfaces, loopback interfaces, tunnel interfaces, reserved multicast addresses from the 224.0.0.0/8 address range, and certain broadcast addresses. Packets with destination addresses matching "receive" entries are handled identically by CEF, and simply queued for local delivery.

Each FIB entry also contains one or more links to the entries in the adjacency table, making it possible to support equal-cost or multipath load balancing.

Adjacency Table

The adjacency table contains information necessary for encapsulation of the packets that must be sent to given next-hop network devices. CEF considers next-hop devices to be neighbors if they are directly connected via a shared IP subnet.

Each adjacency entry stores pre-computed frame headers used when forwarding a packet using a FIB entry referencing the corresponding adjacency entry. The adjacency table is populated as adjacencies are discovered. Each time an adjacency entry is created, such as through the ARP protocol, a link-layer header for that adjacent node is pre-computed and stored in the adjacency table.

Routes might have more than one path per entry, making it possible to use CEF to switch packets while load balancing across multiple paths.

In addition to next-hop interface adjacencies (in other words host-route adjacencies), certain exception condition adjacencies exist to expedite switching for nonstandard conditions. These include, among others: punt adjacencies for handling features that are not supported in CEF (such as IP options), and "drop" adjacencies for prefixes referencing the Null0 interface. (Packets forwarded to Null0 are dropped, making an effective, efficient form of access filtering. Null0 will be discussed further in Section II).

Example 1-3 shows the output of the **show adjacency** command, displaying adjacency table information. Example 1-4 shows the output of the **show ip cef command**, displaying a list of prefixes that are CEF switched.

Example 1-3 *Displaying CEF Adjacency Table Information*

```
R1# show adjacency
Protocol Interface            Address
IP       Serial4/0            point2point(7)
IP       Tunnel0              point2point(6)
```
continues

Example 1-3   *Displaying CEF Adjacency Table Information (Continued)*

```
IP          POS5/0.1                point2point(9)
IP          POS5/0.2                point2point(5)
IP          FastEthernet0/2         10.82.69.1(11)
IP          FastEthernet0/2         10.82.69.82(5)
IP          FastEthernet0/2         10.82.69.103(5)
IP          FastEthernet0/2         10.82.69.220(5)
R1#
```

Example 1-4   *Displaying CEF FIB Table Information*

```
R1# show ip cef
Prefix                   Next Hop            Interface
0.0.0.0/0                12.0.0.2            Serial4/1
0.0.0.0/32               receive
10.0.0.0/8               10.82.69.1          FastEthernet0/0
10.82.69.0/24            attached            FastEthernet0/0
10.82.69.0/32            receive
10.82.69.1/32            10.82.69.1          FastEthernet0/0
10.82.69.82/32           10.82.69.82         FastEthernet0/0
10.82.69.121/32          receive
10.82.69.220/32          10.82.69.220        FastEthernet0/0
10.82.69.255/32          receive
172.0.0.0/30             attached            Serial4/1
172.0.0.0/32             receive
172.0.0.1/32             receive
172.0.0.3/32             receive
172.12.12.0/24           attached            Loopback12
172.12.12.0/32           receive
172.12.12.12/32          receive
172.12.12.255/32         receive
192.168.100.0/24         172.0.0.2           Serial4/1
224.0.0.0/4              drop
224.0.0.0/24             receive
R1#
```

CEF Operation

CEF switching is enabled globally using the **ip cef** global configuration mode command, after which CEF switching is enabled on all CEF-capable interfaces by default. CEF can be enabled or disabled on a per-interface basis. CEF must be enabled on the ingress interface (whereas fast switching is enabled on the egress interface) to CEF switch packets, because CEF makes the forwarding decision on ingress. Use the interface configuration mode command **ip route-cache cef** to enable CEF, or the **no** version of the same command to disable CEF on the ingress interface.

A distributed version of CEF is available for the 7500, 7600, and Cisco 12000 routers. On the Cisco 12000 GSR, CEF is enabled by default and in fact is the only version of switching available on that platform although multiple forwarding paths exist within the router architecture.

Each time a packet is received on a CEF-enabled interface, the CEF process forwards the packet, as illustrated in Figure 1-13 and explained next:

1 CEF switching begins exactly like the other switching methods. First, the network interface hardware receives the packet and transfers it into I/O memory. The network interface interrupts the CPU, alerting it to the ingress packet waiting in I/O memory for processing. IOS updates its inbound packet counters.

2 The IOS interrupt software inspects the packet header information (encapsulation type, network layer header, and so forth) and determines that it is an IP packet. Instead of placing the packet on the input queue for CPU processing, however, the interrupt software consults the FIB for an entry matching the destination address. If an entry exists, the interrupt software retrieves the pre-built Layer 2 header information from the adjacency table, and builds the packet for forwarding. Finally, the interrupt software alerts the outbound interface.

3 The outbound network interface hardware senses the packet, dequeues it from I/O memory, and transmits it on to the network.

4 If the destination address is not found in the FIB, instead of reverting to fast switching and then process switching, CEF simply drops the packet which causes a CPU hit for the resultant ICMP destination unreachable (type 3) generation. Fast switching has no visibility into the routing table. It depends on process switching to build the fast cache on the fly. Thus, fast switching can never assume that if a destination prefix does not exist in the cache, the packet has an unreachable destination. CEF, however, pre-builds the FIB based on the routing table. Thus, if no entry exists in the FIB, then a valid destination prefix never will be found, regardless of switching mechanisms. This is one of the best features of CEF; no processor load is expended for unresolved destinations.

Figure 1-13 *Illustration of CEF Switching*

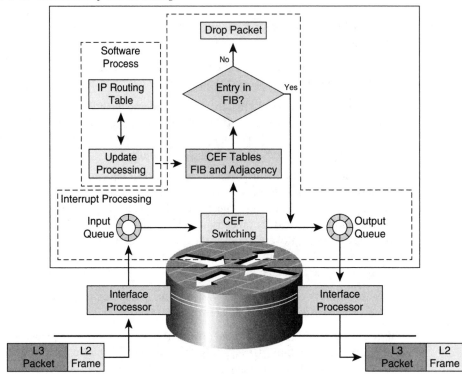

From an IP traffic plane perspective, CEF switching primarily not only helps accelerate the forwarding of transit data plane traffic, but also performs consistent operations for many other packet types. This is exactly what is needed for building and running higher-speed networks with high packet rates. All traffic planes and packet types exist in any network, not to mention malicious packets. All of these packet types must be handled within the network, but not all of these packets can be CEF switched. When this is the case, routers must invoke alternate processing functions, often impacting performance. It is most critical in networks to classify traffic planes and protect router resources. Let's take a look at each traffic plane again from the perspective of CEF switching:

- **Data plane:** CEF switching operations were developed to speed delivery of data plane transit traffic. These packets will be CEF switched when a FIB entry exists and will be dropped when a FIB entry does not exist. Dropping packets with unresolved destinations gives CEF a tremendous advantage over other switching methods because no CPU involvement is necessary simply to drop these packets. You should be aware, however, that dropping these packets does cause the generation of an ICMP unreachable error message. On most routers, ICMP packets are generated by the CPU. Thus, even with CEF switching, some CPU impacts can be seen when high rates of ICMP unreachable messages are generated. As you will learn in Chapter 4, ICMP unreachable message generation can be rate-limited or disabled. Preventing spoofed or malicious packets from abusing the data plane will also help protect router and network resources. As with other switching methods, additional processing is required to handle data plane exception packets as well. For example, TTL = 0 packets must be dropped and reply ICMP error messages must be generated and transmitted. Packets with IP options may also require additional processing to satisfy the invoked option. CEF does use special adjacencies to switch these types of packets to the appropriate handlers, which means the CPU is not involved in the switching portion of the operation. Nonetheless, the CPU may be required to process these packets after CEF. When the ratio of exception packets becomes large in comparison to normal transit packets, router resources can be taxed, potentially affecting network stability. These and other concepts are explored further in Chapter 2. Chapter 4 explores in detail the concepts for protecting the data plane.

- **Control plane:** Control plane packets with transit destinations are CEF switched exactly like data plane transit packets. Control plane packets with receive destinations and non-IP exception packets (for example, Layer 2 keepalives, IS-IS, and so on) are switched by special adjacencies in CEF to the CPU for processing. Additional resources are consumed to fully process these packets. Thus, regardless of the switching method invoked, receive and non-IP control plane packets must be processed by the CPU, potentially causing high CPU utilization. High CPU utilization could affect the synchronization of CEF tables (for example, when routing table updates must be computed), resulting in dropped traffic. It is critical to prevent spoofed and other malicious packets from impacting the control plane, potentially consuming router resources and disrupting overall network stability. Chapter 5 explores these concepts in detail.

- **Management plane:** Management plane packets with transit destinations are CEF switched exactly like data plane transit packets. Management plane packets with receive destinations are switched by special adjacencies in CEF to the CPU for processing. Additional resources are consumed to fully process these packets and provide the appropriate network management service. Management plane traffic should not contain IP exception packets (again, MPLS OAM being one exception), but may contain non-IP (Layer 2) exception packets (generally in the form of CDP packets). Under normal circumstances, management plane traffic should have little impact on CPU performance. It is possible that some management actions, such as conducting frequent SNMP polling or turning on debug operations, or the use of NetFlow may cause high CPU utilization. High CPU utilization could affect the synchronization of CEF tables (for example, when routing table updates must be computed), resulting in dropped traffic. Because management plane traffic is handled directly by the CPU, the opportunity for abuse makes it critical that management plane security be implemented. Chapter 6 explores these concepts in detail.

- **Services plane:** Services plane packets generally require special processing by the router. Examples include things like performing some encapsulation function (for example, GRE, IPsec, or MPLS VPN), or performing some QoS or policy routing function. Some of these operations can be handled by CEF switching and some cannot. If a feature or encapsulation is not supported in CEF, the packet is passed to the next switching level (for most routers this would be fast switching), which tries to switch the packet by using its cache. If it cannot be switched at the interrupt level, the packet is placed into the IP processing queue for direct CPU handling. CEF fails to switch packets only because of unsupported features. When this occurs, services plane packets may have a large impact on CPU utilization. The main concern then is to protect the integrity of the services plane by preventing spoofed or malicious packets from impacting the CPU. Chapter 7 explores these concepts in detail.

General IP Router Architecture Types

Now that the main switching methods available in IOS today have been reviewed, and the impact of various IP traffic planes on their operation and performance has been described, it is worth looking at the various hardware architectures used in Cisco routers. Although most Cisco routers implement all of the switching methods described in the previous section, some do not. In addition, hardware variations lead to different performance levels for each of the IP traffic planes. Thus, it is important to understand the performance envelop for each platform inserted in the network. This section gives special attention to the way in which malicious traffic can affect router hardware architectures.

Increases in performance and the demand for integrated services have driven substantial changes in router hardware. Most Cisco routers use only one active route processor, even if more than one is installed. Thus, processing is done in one central location. Some routers incorporate specialized ASIC hardware to accelerate switching performance. Still others use distributed hardware architectures to achieve the highest forwarding rates.

The following sections provide general overviews of the basic hardware architectures used by Cisco routers today. These architectures are covered in sufficient detail to provide a good understanding of how various IP traffic planes impact their performance. Many excellent references provide much deeper insights into router architectures. Check the "Further Reading" section at the end of this chapter for specific recommendations.

Centralized CPU-Based Architectures

The architecture used by the original Cisco routers, and several generations of enterprise-class routers that have followed, is the centralized CPU-based design. Routers in this category that you will find in service today include the 800, 1600, 1700, 2500, 2600, 3600,

RPM-PR, and 3700 series models. The long-lived 7200 series and the newer 1800, 2800, and 3800 series Integrated Services Routers (ISR) also use a centralized CPU-based architecture.

Centralized CPU-based architectures rely on a single CPU to perform all functions required by the router. This includes such functions as the following:

- Supporting all networking functions, such as running and maintaining routing protocols and cache states, link states, interfaces and global counters, error packet (ICMP) generation, and other network control functions

- Supporting all packet forwarding and processing functions, including applying all services such as access lists, NAT, QoS, and so on as might be applied to packets during the forwarding process

- Supporting all housekeeping functions, such as servicing configuration and management functions, including command-line configuration, SNMP and syslog support, and other device management functions

All of these (and other) functions are handled within Cisco IOS Software. Cisco IOS is a monolithic operating system; all software modules are statically compiled and linked at build time, operating in a run-to-completion model within a single address space. In this kind of model, faults in one function can cause disruptions in other functions. In the previous section you learned about three different kinds of switching methods, each of which has different levels of interaction and, hence, impact on the CPU.

A typical centralized CPU-based architecture is shown in Figure 1-14. Advances in bus architecture, memory size and speed, and CPU processor performance and the addition of specialty, task-oriented chipsets have led to improvements in overall router performance. However, even with these advances and additions, centralized CPU-based devices will always be limited in overall performance given the processing constraints of the CPU-based architecture.

As illustrated in Figure 1-14, the central CPU provides support for router maintenance (CLI, management functions, and so on), for running the routing protocols, and for computing the FIB and adjacency tables described in the previous section. The FIB and adjacency table information is stored in memory attached to the CPU. All packets transiting the router (in other words, that ingress and egress through various interfaces) are processed within the CPU interrupt process if CEF is capable of switching the packet. Packets that cannot be handled by CEF are punted (switched out of the fast path) for direct handling by the CPU in software processing (slow path). Packets in this group include all receive packets, which under normal conditions means control plane, management plane traffic, plus all exception IP and non-IP packets.

Routers in this category are still quite adequate for most small to medium-sized enterprise locations where low bandwidth but rich, integrated service requirements are found. These routers represent an excellent trade-off between acceptable performance, application of integrated services, and cost. Their lack of capacity for high-speed service delivery and dense aggregation solutions means that other architectures must be explored.

Figure 1-14 *Centralized CPU-Based Router Architecture*

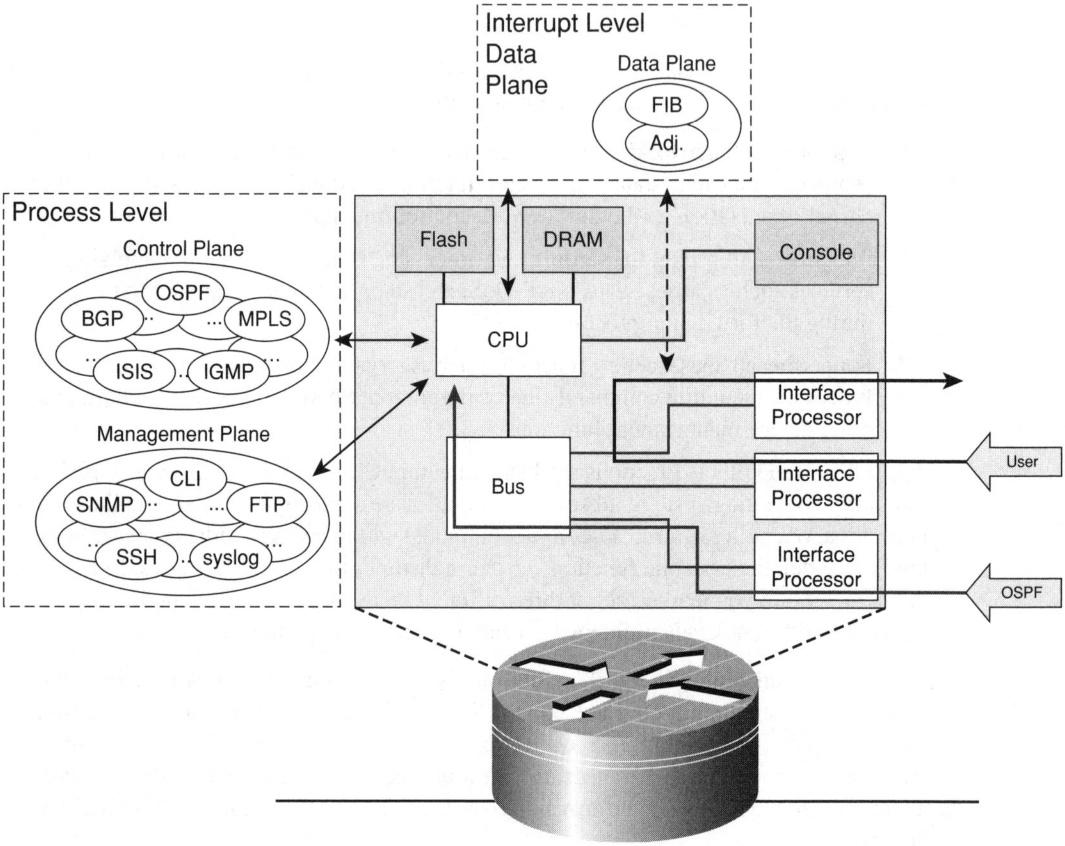

Centralized ASIC-Based Architectures

As network demands increased, CPU-based architectures alone were unable to provide acceptable performance levels. To overcome this shortcoming, modern centralized CPU-based platforms began to include forwarding ASICs in the architecture in order to offload some processing duties from the CPU and improve upon overall device performance. This category of devices includes the ubiquitous Catalyst 6500 switch family, the Cisco 7600 router family, the Cisco 7300 and RPM-XF PXF-based routers, and the Cisco 10000 Edge Services Router (ESR) family. You will most frequently find these devices in large-scale aggregation environments (such as at the service provider network edge), and medium- to large-scale enterprise and data center environments where large numbers of flows and high switching rates are common.

Retaining the centralized architecture makes sense when trading off cost, complexity, and performance. Of course, the single CPU still performs many of the functions described in the preceding section, such as supporting all networking and housekeeping functions. The ASIC incorporated into the architecture provides the ability to apply very complex operations, such as access control lists (ACL), QoS, policy routing, and so on while maintaining very high-performance forwarding rates. A typical centralized ASIC-based architecture is shown in Figure 1-15, which illustrates at a high level the Cisco 10000 ESR forwarding architecture.

The Cisco 10000 ESR forwarding functions shown in Figure 1-15 are carried out in the Performance Routing Engine (PRE). The PRE includes a central CPU to support router maintenance (CLI, management functions, ICMP, and so on) and to run the routing protocols and compute the FIB and adjacency tables. Once the CPU builds these FIB and adjacency tables, this information is pushed into the Parallel Express Forwarding (PXF) ASIC structure. All packets transiting the router (in other words, that ingress and egress through various line cards) are processed by the PXF. The CPU is not involved in forwarding packets. If other services are configured, such as the application of ACLs, QoS, policy routing, and so on, they are also configured and applied in the PXF ASIC structures.

Certain packets and features cannot be processed within ASIC architectures. These packets are punted to the supporting CPU for full processing. Packets falling into this group include all receive packets, which essentially means all control plane and management plane packets, and all exception packets. ASICs are designed to perform high-speed operations on a well-defined set of packets. Buffers, memory allocations, and data operations are designed for typical packets with 20-byte IP headers, for example. Packets that include IP options in the header exceed the 20-byte limit, and thus cannot be handled in the ASIC. Packets like these are punted to the CPU for handling in the slow path, meaning their processing speed is much slower. Because the ASIC is forwarding packets independently from the CPU, some amount of punts will not impact the overall platform throughput for normal, transit traffic. However, when the rate of exceptions becomes large, forwarding performance may be impacted.

IP traffic plane security must be developed with an understanding of how forwarding is accomplished in this centralized ASIC-based architecture, including a detailed understanding of how exception packets affect the performance *envelop* for the platform. The mechanisms for securing each traffic plane are covered in detail in Section II.

The centralized ASIC-based architecture offers excellent trade-offs between performance, application of integrated services, and cost. Routers in this category are well suited for their intended environments. Yet they are not adequate when the very highest throughputs are required. The centralized nature of any platform limits forwarding rates to the speed of the single forwarding engine. To achieve even faster forwarding rates, different architectures must be used, specifically distributed architectures.

Figure 1-15 *Centralized ASIC-Based Router Architecture*

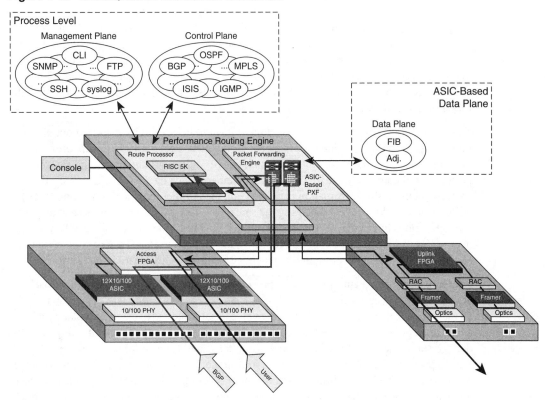

NOTE   Centralized ASIC-based routers may have higher performance than certain distributed
CPU-based routers.

Distributed CPU-Based Architectures

Routers used in large-scale networks require not only high packet-forwarding performance,
but also high port densities. High port densities reduce the overall hardware costs, as well
as the operational costs because fewer devices need to be managed. These demands have
constantly driven router architectures to keep pace. Two approaches can be taken to increase
the forwarding speed of a router. The first, which you just learned about, is to retain the
centralized processing approach but increase the CPU speed or add hardware-based (ASIC)
high-speed forwarding engines. This architecture runs into limitations at some point in both
maximum packet-forwarding rates and port density.

The other approach breaks the router into discrete line cards, each capable of supporting a number of network interfaces, and "distributing" the processing and forwarding functions out to each line card. In the earlier section on CEF switching, you learned that CEF pre-computes the FIB and adjacency tables, and then populates the forwarding engine with these tables. You can see how CEF is ideally suited for a distributed architecture where each line card has the intelligence to forward packets as they ingress the router. In this case, each line card is capable of switching packets, bringing the switching function as close to the packet ingress point as possible. The other component required to complete the distributed architecture is a high-speed bus or "switching fabric" to connect the line cards into what logically appears to the routing domain as a single router. Early distributed architecture systems used CPU-based forwarding engines. These early distributed CPU-based devices include the Cisco 7500 series routers and early Cisco 12000 Gigabit Switch Router (GSR) family line cards (in other words, Engine 0 and Engine 1). Figure 1-16 shows the Cisco 7500 router to illustrate the basics of the distributed CPU-based architecture.

Figure 1-16 *Distributed CPU-Based Router Architecture*

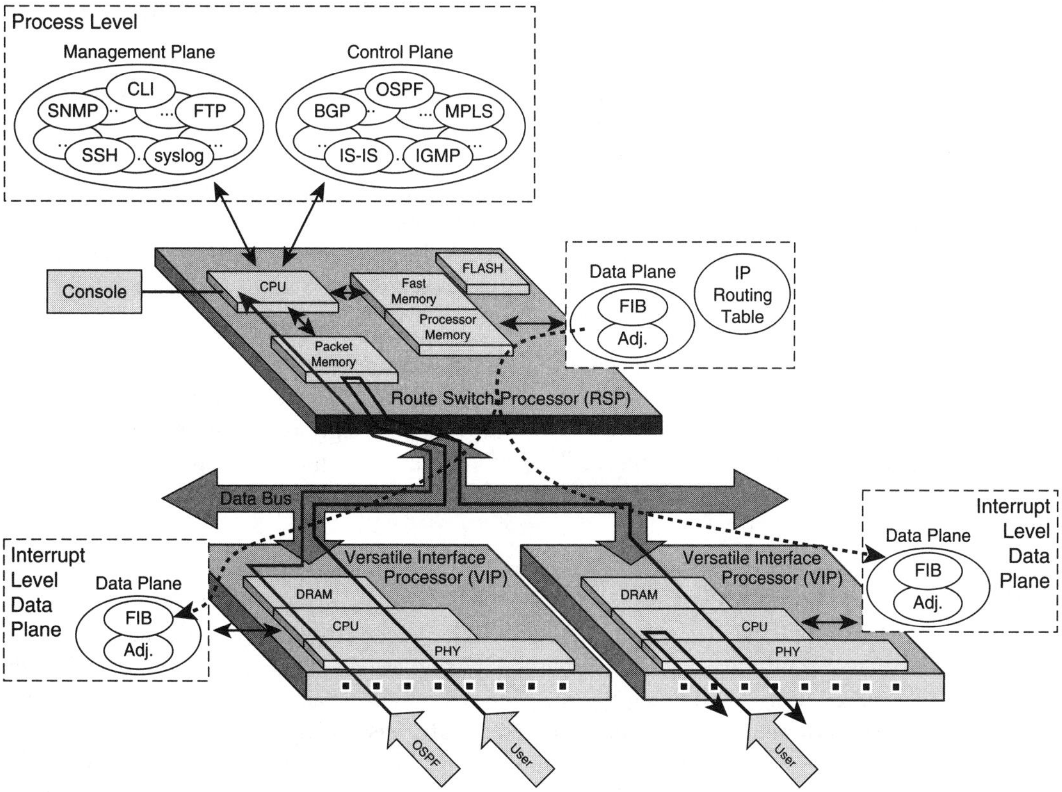

As illustrated in Figure 1-16, the Cisco 7500 router includes a central CPU, referred to as the Route Switch Processor (RSP), which performs all networking and housekeeping functions, such as maintaining routing protocols, interface keepalives, and so forth. Thus, all control plane and management plane traffic is handled by the RSP. The 7500 also includes multiple Versatile Interface Processors (VIP) with port adapters (PA). Using port adapters not only provides high port density but also adds flexibility in interface type through modularity. Distributed switching is supported in VIPs by their own CPUs, RAM, and packet memory. Each VIP runs a specialized IOS image. Two data transfer buses provide packet transfer capabilities between VIPs (line cards) and the RSP to support high-speed forwarding. When a PA receives a packet, it copies the packet into the shared memory on the VIP and then sends an interrupt to the VIP CPU. The VIP CPU performs a CEF lookup, and then rewrites the packet header. If the egress port is on the same VIP, the packet is switched directly. If the egress port is on a different VIP, the RSP is not required for packet processing but does spend CPU time as a bus arbiter for inter-processor communication while moving packets across the bus. VIPs can support very complex operations, such as ACLs, QoS, policy routing, encryption, compression, queuing, IP multicasting, tunneling, fragmentation, and more. Some of these are supported in CEF; others require the other switching methods.

In general, the RSP is not directly involved in forwarding packets. There are exceptions, however, just as with other router architectures. Of course, control, management, and supported services plane traffic are always punted to the RSP for direct handling. Other exceptions occur under various memory constraints, and when processing packets with specific features such as IP options, TTL expirations, and so on. Too many or inappropriate packets punting to the RSP can jeopardize the status of the entire platform. Thus, IP traffic plane security must provide the mechanisms to control how various packets affect the performance *envelop* of the platform.

Distributed CPU-based architectures were the first routers in this category and were the original routers used within high-speed core networks. Many of these routers are still in use today. The logical follow-on to these CPU-based designs is the current state of the art, distributed ASIC-based architecture. Distributed hardware designs are required to achieve the feature-rich, high-speed forwarding required in today's networks.

Distributed ASIC-Based Architectures

Modern large-scale routers designed for very high-speed networks must operate with truly distributed forwarding engines capable of applying features at line rate. As you learned with centralized ASIC-based architectures, ASICs provide this capability by offloading forwarding functions from the CPU. In the centralized ASIC-based architecture, the limitations on performance were due to the use of a single ASIC for forwarding. To increase the overall platform forwarding capacity, the ASIC concept is extended into the distributed environment. In distributed ASIC-based platforms, each line card has its own forwarding ASIC that operates independently from all other line cards. In addition, by using modular line cards, high port densities and flexibility in interface type can be achieved. The Cisco 12000 family was the first to use the fully distributed ASIC-based architecture, followed by the Cisco 7600. Recently, the Carrier Routing System (CRS-1) became the latest addition to the Cisco family of fully modular and distributed ASIC-based routing systems.

To illustrate at a high level how distributed ASIC-based architectures function, review the Cisco 12000 diagram shown in Figure 1-17.

Figure 1-17 *Distributed ASIC-Based Router Architecture*

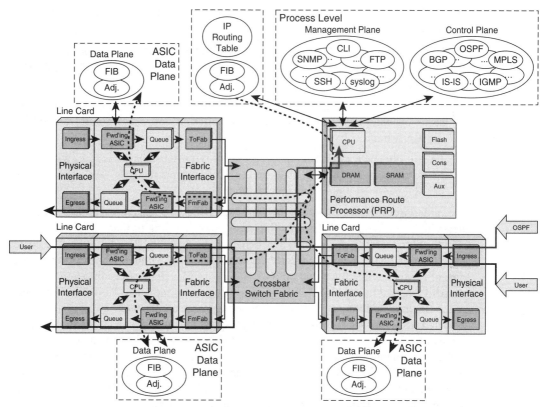

The Cisco 12000 includes one active main route processor, the most current version of which is the Performance Route Processor 2 (PRP). Redundant PRPs may be used but only one is active and acts as the primary. The PRP is critical to the proper operation of the whole chassis. It performs network routing protocol processing to compute FIB and adjacency table updates and distributes updates to the CEF tables stored locally on each line card. The PRP also performs general maintenance and housekeeping functions, such as system diagnostics, command-line console support, and software maintenance and monitoring of line cards. The Cisco 12000 crossbar switch fabric provides synchronized gigabit speed interconnections for the line cards and the PRP. The switch fabric is the main data path for packets that are sent between line cards, and between line cards and the PRP. Modular line cards provide the high port-density interfaces to the router. The packet-forwarding functions are performed by each line card, using a copy of the forwarding tables computed by the PRP and distributed to each line card in the system. Each line card performs an independent destination address lookup for each datagram received using its own local copy of the forwarding table. This determines the egress line card that will handle the packet, which is then switched across the switch fabric to the egress line card.

Modular line cards give flexibility to the GSR platform. Each line card contains three discrete sections:

- **Physical Layer Interface Module (PLIM) section:** Terminates the physical connections, providing the media-dependent ATM, Packet-over-SONET (POS), Fast Ethernet, and Gigabit Ethernet interfaces.

- **Layer 3 Switching Engine section:** Provides the actual forwarding hardware. This section handles Layer 3 lookups, rewrites, buffering, congestion control, and other support features.

- **Fabric Interface section:** Prepares packets for transmission across the switching fabric to the egress line card. It takes care of fabric grant requests, fabric queuing, and per-slot multicast replication, among other things.

Line cards are classified by their "engine type," referring to the generation of the forwarding engine included on the card. The first line cards, known as Engine 0 and Engine 1, are CPU-based forwarding engines and thus behave like other CPU-based routers. The next generation, Engine 2, included an early version of an ASIC within the line card to offload some of the forwarding functions from the line card CPU. Higher-speed versions with true ASIC support followed in the Engine 4 and Engine 4+ line cards. The newest line cards are the Engine 3 and Engine 5 families. These line cards use the latest generation of dedicated ASICs, which incorporate very high-speed memory known as Ternary Content Addressable Memory (TCAM) that enables all features such as the application of ACLs, QoS, policy routing, and so forth to be performed simultaneously, while maintaining high-performance forwarding. The programmability of the ASIC allows them to support feature enhancements rather easily, as well. The Engine 3 line card, also known as the IP Services Engine, is shown in Figure 1-17 to illustrate this type of distributed ASIC-based router architecture.

On the GSR, line cards are responsible for making all packet-forwarding decisions. Because the FIB is predefined and loaded on each line card, each line card has all of the information necessary to forward any packet. If the destination address is not in the FIB, the packet is simply discarded. Distributed CEF (dCEF) is the only switching method available, and fast switching and process switching are not available as fallbacks for unresolved destinations (there are not any). There are, of course, receive packets and the exception packets to consider as well, however. Packets with a "receive" adjacency are punted to the PRP for handling. These are mainly control plane and all management plane packets, which are all handled by the PRP. Other exception packets, such as TTL expires, ICMP echo requests, IP options, and so on, are handled in various ways. Some of these packets are capable of being handled directly by the line card CPU. Technically, although still considered a punt because the line card ASIC does not support processing these packets, they are still capable of being handled locally, thus protecting the RP from unnecessary packet processing. ICMP unreachable generation, for example, is handled directly by the line card CPU. Other exception packets can be handled only by the PRP. Too many or inappropriate packets punting to either the line card CPU or the PRP can be detrimental to the platform. Again, IP traffic plane security mechanisms must be provided to control how various packets affect the platform.

The newest router in the Cisco family, the CRS-1, requires its own discussion here, as it brings both evolutionary and revolutionary changes to previous router technologies. Four key elements define these architectural advances, including: 40-Gbps line cards, advanced Route Processors, a service-intelligent switch fabric, and Cisco IOS XR Software. Some of these elements are illustrated in Figure 1-18 and described next.

Figure 1-18 *CRS-1 Router Architecture and 40-Gbps Line Card*

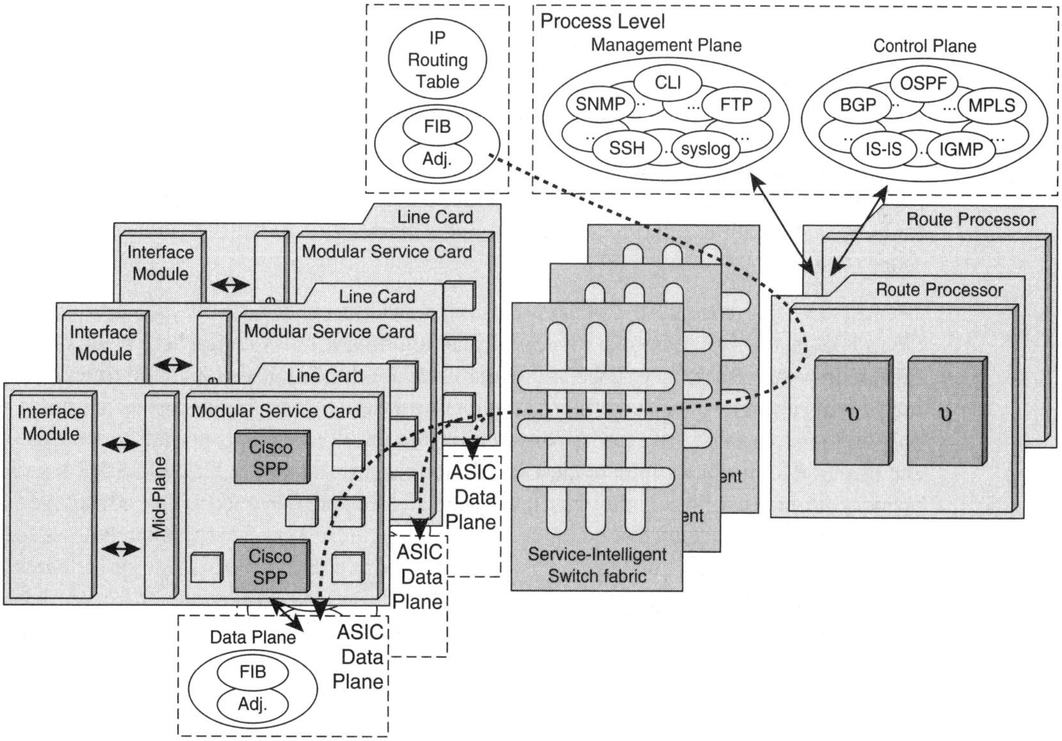

NOTE   This is not meant to be a detailed review of the CRS-1. Such a task requires a book in itself. Additional citations to relevant CRS-1 and IOS XR documents are given in the "Further Reading" section at the end of this chapter.

The first key feature illustrated in Figure 1-18 is the new 40-Gbps line card design. Each line card is separated by a midplane into two main components: the interface module (IM) and the modular services card (MSC). The IM provides the physical connections to the network, including Layer 1 and 2 functions (POS and Gigabit Ethernet). The MSC is the high-performance Layer 3 forwarding engine and is equipped with two high-performance Cisco Silicon Packet Processor (SPP) 40-Gbps ASIC devices, one for ingress and one for egress packet handling. You may also see the SPP referred to as the Packet Switching Engine (PSE) ASIC in Cisco documentation and in the output of certain router commands. Each Cisco CRS-1 line card maintains a distinct copy of the adjacency table and forwarding information databases, enabling maximum scalability and performance.

The second key feature involves the Route Processors (RP). Unlike previous routers that can have only a single active route processor, even if multiple devices are included for redundancy, the CRS-1 is able to use multiple active RPs to execute control plane features, system management, and accounting functions. Allowing multiple route processors also provides service separation capabilities through control plane (routing) segmentation, providing simplified migration paths for network convergence.

The third key feature, the service-intelligent switch fabric, provides the communications path between line cards. In brief, the switch fabric is designed with separate priority queues for unicast and multicast traffic and control plane messages. Further details are outside the scope of this book.

The last key feature for CRS-1 is the use of the new Cisco IOS XR Software. Traditional Cisco IOS is a modular, cooperative, multitasking operating system where processes execute in a shared memory space and feature sets are defined at system build time. IOS implements a single-stage forwarding architecture where forwarding decisions are made only on ingress ports or line cards. This architecture provides the appropriate performance and resource footprint for the broadest set of platforms and markets. Cisco IOS XR uses a memory-protected, micro-kernel-based software architecture designed to take advantage of the multi-CPU architecture found in the CRS-1. This micro-kernel architecture allows for maximum resource usage, no resource bottlenecks, and excellent control plane performance. Processes such as routing and signaling protocols can run on a single route processor or be distributed over multiple route processors. In addition, IOS XR implements a two-stage forwarding architecture where forwarding decisions are made on both the ingress and egress line cards, providing tremendous performance and scaling advantages. (The ingress line card FIB simply has destination addresses paired with the outgoing line card only. There is no binding to Layer 2 addresses at this point. The egress line card does a second lookup to determine Layer 2 header details.)

NOTE   The Cisco 12000 GSR is also able to run Cisco IOS XR Software with appropriate route
processor and line card hardware installed.

It is worth noting that the CLI is different for IOS XR as compared with the traditional IOS
CLI. In addition, the feature set available within IOS XR, including many of the security
mechanisms, is also different than with traditional IOS. To aid in this transition, Appendix
C provides a side-by-side comparison of the main security features found in the IOS version
12.0(32)S against the IOS XR equivalent features where applicable.

The CRS-1 must handle receive packets and exception packets, as any IP router is required
to do. In a similar manner as the ASIC-based line cards for GSR, CRS-1 line cards are
capable of handling certain packets within their SPP ASIC or local line card CPU. Receive
packets in the control plane and management plane are punted to the RP for handling.
Certain exception packets can be handled locally, while others can be handled only by the
RP. Unlike traditional IOS, the IOS XR Software provides automatic mechanisms, such as
dynamic control plane protection, for handing these packets to prevent resource abuse.
Other unique mechanisms and the more familiar ones can also be used to secure IP traffic
planes. Detailed descriptions of some of these mechanisms are covered in later chapters as
appropriate.

NOTE   Many excellent references cover in more detail the significant Cisco router architectures.
One such reference, *Inside Cisco IOS Software Architecture*, provides excellent coverage
of the Cisco 7500 and Cisco 12000 GSR. A list of suggested references is provided in the
"Further Reading" section at the end of this chapter.

In summary, the following can be stated about all the router architectures described in this
chapter:

- Data plane packet handling depends on the switching mode enabled and the router
  architecture. Despite the switching mode, however:
  - IP options are always process switched (or handled in the slow path in the
    case of the GSR).
  - TTL expiry packets are always process switched path (or handled in the
    slow path in the case of the GSR).
  - The first packet of a multicast stream is always punted to create the
    multicast routing state on the route processor (see Chapter 2).
- Control plane and management plane packets are always handled by the CPU on the
  route processor within the software slow path.

— ICMP replies may be handled on distributed line cards, but always by a CPU and never by an ASIC.

- Services plane packets impact routers in varying ways. The specific router architecture must be considered to determine their overall impact.

Summary

This chapter introduced the concepts of IP traffic planes and their relationship to IP protocol and IP network operations. IP traffic planes were segmented into four logical groups:

- **Data plane:** User and customer traffic
- **Control plane:** Routing protocol and other router state traffic
- **Management plane:** Network operations traffic
- **Services plane:** Customer or application traffic with specialized traffic handling requirements

The basics of IP network forwarding architectures were then reviewed, with specific focus placed on how each of the IP traffic planes interact with these forwarding concepts. Finally, router hardware architecture and packet processing concepts were reviewed to illustrate how IP traffic planes can impact various platforms through resource abuse, and why IP traffic plane security is so vital for network stability and operations.

Review Questions

1 Name three distinguishing characteristics of the IP protocol.

2 What are the main challenges when services are converged on a common IP core network?

3 Name the four distinct types of packets seen by a router, and give an example of each.

4 Identify the three common switching methods used by Cisco routers when forwarding IP packets.

5 True or False: Data plane traffic includes all customer traffic that is subject to the standard forwarding process and includes only transit IP packets.

6 True or False: Control plane traffic typically includes packets generated by network elements themselves.

7 What are the main functions supported by the management plane?

8 How does the forwarding of services plane traffic differ from data plane traffic?

9 Identify the four basic router architecture types.

Further Reading

Bollapragada, V., C. Murphy, and R. White. *Inside Cisco IOS Software Architecture*. Cisco Press, 2000. ISBN: 1-57870-181-3.

Stevens, W. Richard. *TCP/IP Illustrated, Volume 1*. Addison-Wesley Professional, 1993. ISBN: 0-20163-346-9.

"Cisco 12000 Series Internet Router Architecture: Line Card Design." Cisco Tech Note. (Doc. ID: 47242.) http://www.cisco.com/en/US/partner/products/hw/routers/ps167/products_tech_note09186a00801e1dbd.shtml.

"Cisco 12000 Series Internet Router Architecture: Packet Switching." Cisco Tech Note. (Doc. ID: 47320.) http://www.cisco.com/en/US/partner/products/hw/routers/ps167/products_tech_note09186a00801e1dc1.shtml.

"Cisco Catalyst 6500 Supervisor Engine 32 Architecture." Cisco white paper. http://www.cisco.com/en/US/products/hw/switches/ps708/products_white_paper0900aecd803e508c.shtml.

"Cisco CRS-1 Carrier Routing System Security Application Note." Cisco white paper. http://www.cisco.com/en/US/products/ps5763/products_white_paper09186a008022d5ec.shtml.

"IP Services Engine Line Cards." Cisco Documentation. http://www.cisco.com/univercd/cc/td/doc/product/software/ios120/120newft/120limit/120s/120s19/ise.htm.

"Parallel Express Forwarding on the Cisco 10000 Series." Cisco white paper. http://www.cisco.com/en/US/partner/products/hw/routers/ps133/products_white_paper09186a008008902a.shtml.

"Switching Path." Section in "Performance Tuning Basics." Cisco Tech Note. (Doc. ID: 12809.) http://www.cisco.com/warp/public/63/tuning.html.

"Tracing a Packet from Network Ingress to Egress, or 'The Life of a Packet.'" Cisco Tech Note. (Doc. ID: 13713.) http://www.cisco.com/warp/public/105/42.html.

In this chapter, you will learn about the following:

- Threats against IP network infrastructures
- Threats against Layer 2 switched Ethernet network infrastructures
- Threats against IP VPN network infrastructures

CHAPTER 2

Threat Models for IP Networks

Knowledge of the threats against IP, Layer 2 switched Ethernet, and IP VPN network infrastructures will allow you to gain a firmer understanding of the vulnerabilities and risks associated with your network. Without a thorough understanding of the many threats, you cannot take the necessary steps to implement an effective security solution. Network design techniques to mitigate the risks are presented in Part II, "Security Techniques for Protecting IP Traffic Planes."

Threats Against IP Network Infrastructures

IP networks and the Internet deliver a wide variety of services to consumers, businesses, and governments alike. As a result, businesses and governments are realizing unprecedented increases in productivity and effectiveness. Similarly, the Internet is changing the way individuals work, live, play, and learn. With the increased dependence on IP networks and the Internet, the potential exposure to and impact of network-based security attacks also increases. Given this trend, as a network or security operator (or both), you need to ensure that your IP network and services remain available and, in some cases, that the confidentiality and integrity of the information transmitted remains intact.

As IP networks continue to evolve, so do attack methods and threat models. IP networks and the wider Internet have experienced a paradigm shift from one of implicit trust to one of pervasive distrust. As a result, no packet can be trusted, and each packet must earn its trust through the network's ability to classify and enforce policy. There are many forces that threaten IP infrastructures, including both natural disasters and man-made threats. Both must be considered in terms of capabilities and intent.

Natural disasters, such as earthquakes and hurricanes, are potentially significant threats. They generally strike without warning and can have devastating effects on IP infrastructures and facilities. Although a natural disaster has no intent to threaten an area, it certainly has the capability to damage and destroy.

Man-made threats may include human errors such as router misconfiguration, poor network design, or construction workers accidentally cutting through a fiber-optic cable with a backhoe. Software defects are also a significant threat because they may provide a potential attack vector or may result in the inadvertent loss of network resources such that an intended service can no longer be provided. Although not the result of malice, these threats may significantly impact the operations of an IP network and may often appear at first glance to be a malicious attack.

Conversely, a hacker, on the other hand, might have the intent to attack but not necessarily the capability to accomplish the intended act. Malicious attacks against IP infrastructures are a significant and growing threat. Many service providers (SPs) use Cisco NetFlow in conjunction with traffic anomaly detection systems, and they indicate that security attacks are an increasing part of everyday network operations. Further, the profile of an attacker has changed from mostly script-kiddies and geeks with a craze for notoriety to professional hackers interested in financial profit, espionage, and revenge. The clear distinction between human errors and malicious attacks is *intent*. Regardless of intent, at the end of the day and from a user's perspective, an outage is an outage. Thus, protection against both intentional and unintentional threats must be considered. Although the target and purpose of attacks vary widely, they each aim to exploit a weakness or vulnerability within the target system. Hosts are the preferred target for worms and viruses, and compromised hosts are often used as attack launch points. Everything is a potential target, and network infrastructure such as IP routers and Ethernet switches, network services such as DNS, DHCP, and NTP, and network bandwidth (capacity) are now becoming high-value targets.

Attacks may have additional consequences beyond the intended target. This is referred to as *collateral damage* and demonstrates why IP traffic plane security is so critical. Within an SP network, for example, a denial-of-service (DoS) attack against one customer may trigger collateral damage that adversely affects other customers attached to the same provider edge (PE) router. Collateral damage must also be considered as a threat when evaluating vulnerabilities and mitigation techniques.

In this chapter, you will learn about the potential threats against and vulnerabilities of IP and Layer 2 Ethernet networks, as well as threats against the two most widely deployed IP VPN technologies. Techniques to mitigate these threats are reviewed in Part II. This chapter also assumes that the network is physically secure. Network-based security measures become ineffective if physical security has been breached.

Resource Exhaustion Attacks

Resource exhaustion attacks are a form of DoS attack.

Denial-of-Service Attack

A denial-of-service (DoS) attack aims to make the target unavailable for its intended service. Such attacks are often launched using a set of distributed systems or hosts, hence the term distributed DoS (DDoS). In this book, DoS refers to both distributed and nondistributed DoS attacks.

By targeting IP routers, a miscreant may adversely affect the integrity and availability of the network infrastructure, including end-to-end IP connectivity. This section reviews various DoS techniques used to attack IP routers and the specific router resource(s) commonly targeted. However, as outlined in Chapter 1, "Internet Protocol Operations Fundamentals," router architectures vary widely from router to router; hence, platform-specific performance and scale limits relating to DoS resistance are not included in this discussion and must be considered independently per individual routing platform.

Direct Attacks

If a miscreant has IP reachability to a router or other network device, they can target it, as illustrated in Figure 2-1.

Figure 2-1   *Direct DoS Attack*

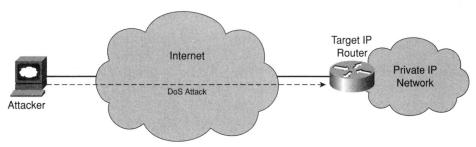

Direct attacks using packet floods are not very complex and consist only of a large volume of attack traffic addressed directly to the target router.

IP Reachability

IP host A has reachability to IP host B when it can source an IP packet destined to B and B receives and processes the packets. Such packets are neither discarded along the path from A to B nor filtered through a security policy by B once received. IP reachability is also independent of physical connectivity (in other words, local versus remote connectivity).

The characteristics and traffic profile of the packet flood required to successfully leverage a DoS attack against the target router depend upon the router's configuration, performance, and scale limits, which vary among router platforms, as previously stated. Generally, directed packet flood attacks are intended to exhaust router resources with attack traffic. If the attack is successful, the integrity and availability of the targeted router may be adversely affected and, if repeated, the result might be a sustained DoS condition. Router resources that are commonly affected by packet flood attacks include the following:

- **CPU:** The CPU implements the control and management plane tasks within an IP router. In some cases, they may also be used for data plane forwarding and services plane functions. Because CPU generally serve as master controllers of the router, packet flood attacks aim to saturate them with attack traffic, causing high CPU utilization. Under these conditions, the CPU may not be able to adequately process legitimate control and management plane traffic, resulting in a DoS condition.

- **Packet memory:** Packet buffering is necessary during router packet processing and applies to each of the IP traffic planes and to both the receive and transmit directions. Packet buffers may fill up if the packet enqueuing rate exceeds the buffer drain rate. Once a particular memory buffer is full, any new packets may be discarded until a free memory buffer is made available. When a router's packet buffers are exhausted, legitimate traffic is discarded, which may result in a DoS condition.

Note   Although routers serve as hosts for IP control, management, and services plane traffic, they are not optimized to process this "receive" traffic. For example, they have a limited number of IP reassembly buffers for processing IP fragments. Hence, packet flood attacks using IP fragments may saturate a router's IP reassembly buffers, causing legitimate IP fragments to be discarded. IP reassembly is also CPU intensive. Therefore, it is considered a network design and security best practice to avoid IP fragmentation and reassembly entirely within IP routers. This topic is further discussed in Chapter 7, "Services Plane Security." Further information on IP fragmentation and reassembly is specified in RFC 791.

- **Network bandwidth:** IP network topologies and architectures vary significantly from network to network. While IP routers make path forwarding decisions between sources and destinations, traffic is transported using OSI Layer 2 (L2) and Layer 1 (L1) technologies, including, but not limited to, Ethernet, Frame Relay, ATM, Serial, and POS. Although some of these L2/L1 technologies may support significant traffic capacities—for example, 10-Gbps Ethernet and 40-Gbps (OC-768c) POS—the vast majority of WAN links deployed have much lower capacity. Serial NxDS0, T1/E1, and DS-3/E-3 links are not uncommon. A packet flood attack may be engineered to saturate a network link, affecting legitimate traffic forwarding across that link and resulting in a DoS condition.

- **Route memory:** The primary purpose of a router is to provide IP reachability and traffic forwarding between known IP prefixes (or routes). The size of IP routing tables vary significantly among networks and routers. The size of the global Internet routing table, which makes use of classless interdomain routing (CIDR) aggregation, consists of greater than 200,000 IP prefixes. A router's routing table, known as the Routing Information Base (RIB), and its associated forwarding table (FIB or CEF table) have bounded sizes. Advertising nonexistent destination prefixes or, alternatively, many longer (more-specific) prefixes versus a single aggregate prefix can exhaust the available routing table capacity. When this de-aggregation occurs, any new IP prefixes cannot be installed within the RIB, preventing IP reachability to those new prefixes.

- **VTY lines:** The router virtual terminal (VTY) lines provide remote in-band management access, including Telnet and SSH connectivity. An attack may open all configured vty lines and prevent remote management (CLI) access to the router. Loss of remote in-band access also makes troubleshooting and mitigating attacks very difficult. One typical form of this attack is the basic TCP SYN flood, which is discussed later, in the section "TCP Protocol Attacks."

Directed packet flood attacks may be devised to target one specific IP traffic plane or network protocol (or both). A specific attack profile may be required due to IP reachability—for example, to bypass access control lists (ACL) or to ensure that the target processes the attack packets. If the target router receives attack traffic for a protocol it does not have enabled, it may simply discard the traffic with no adverse impact. One protocol that is common and integral to the IP protocol and traffic planes is ICMP (RFC 792). ICMP processing is software intensive and is commonly handled by the router CPU(s). ICMP Message Reply Types 3, 4, 5, 11, and 12, for example, require that the original packet's IP header and 64 bits of its original payload be included within the ICMP reply. Hence, packets that require ICMP handling are generally punted from the CEF fast path to the process-level slow path for processing. For this reason, ICMP is a commonly used attack vector for resource exhaustion attacks. Examples of ICMP-based resource exhaustion attacks include flooding the target with any of the following ICMP request packets:

- ICMP Echo Request (Message Type 8)
- ICMP Timestamp Request (Message Type 13)
- ICMP Information Request (Message Type 15)
- ICMP Address Mask Request (Message Type 17, defined in RFC 950, Appendix I)

For each of the preceding ICMP requests, the router may respond with the corresponding ICMP reply, including:

- ICMP Echo Reply (Message Type 0)
- ICMP Timestamp Reply (Message Type 14)
- ICMP Information Reply (Message Type 16)
- ICMP Address Mask Reply (Message Type 18, defined in RFC 950, Appendix I)

A significant volume of received ICMP requests and sourced ICMP replies may adversely affect the CPU, packet memory, and network bandwidth of the target, potentially resulting in a DoS condition. Some ICMP messages are processed by routers by default, while others are not, and configuration commands may allow you to change the default behavior. Because router configurations vary from network to network, directed packet flood attack profiles also vary significantly, and an attack profile that may successfully cause denial of service on one target may have no impact on another target.

Given the simplicity and potentially significant impact of directed packet flood attacks, mitigation techniques are commonly deployed to prevent IP reachability of untrusted sources to IP routers. These techniques are considered a best common practice (BCP) and are reviewed in detail in Part II. The one common characteristic of a successful directed packet flood attack is IP reachability to the target (and, of course, resource exhaustion by the target). A variety of other resource exhaustion attack techniques are available to target IP routers even without direct IP reachability. These are reviewed in the following section.

Transit Attacks

Directed packet flood attacks use IP packets with a destination address of the target router. Transit packet flood attacks do not specify the target router as the IP destination address, but rather use crafted packets to trigger a DoS condition on an intermediate IP router in the forwarding path of the packet's specified destination. That is, the intermediate router is the "target" of the attack, as illustrated in Figure 2-2.

Figure 2-2 *Transit DoS Attack*

Transit DoS techniques do not require IP reachability to the target; only IP reachability to the destination is required, with the target intermediate router being part of the forwarding path to the destination. Further, these attacks may be sourced from and destined to legitimate destination hosts, enabling the attack traffic to masquerade as legitimate transit traffic even though it is crafted to attack intermediate IP routers along the forwarding path between the source(s) and destination(s). Once again, if an attack is successful, the integrity and availability of the targeted routers may be adversely affected and, if repeated, may result in a sustained DoS condition. Several attacks using these techniques are described next: transit ICMP attacks, transit IP options attacks, and transit multicast attacks.

Transit ICMP Attacks

Given that ICMP is an integral part of the IP protocol, as previously described, it is often used to launch DoS attacks against IP infrastructure. In addition to the direct attacks outlined in the previous section, ICMP has been used to attack intermediate routers when direct IP reachability is not available. Transit ICMP attacks use crafted packet floods that result in significant ICMP handling on intermediate routers—the true targets of the attack. Such ICMP attack techniques targeting intermediate IP routers include:

- **TTL expiry attack:** This attack uses crafted transit IP packets timed to expire on the targeted intermediate router(s). As outlined in Chapter 1, the IP header of each IP packet includes a Time to Live (TTL) field that maintains the maximum lifetime of a packet. Each IP router that receives the packet decrements the IP TTL before processing and forwarding the packet downstream. After being decremented, if the TTL = 0, the router considers the packet expired and discards it. Further, per RFC 792, the router must signal to the packet source using ICMP Message Type 11 that the packet was discarded in transit due to an expired TTL. When flooded with a significant volume of TTL expiring transit packets, an intermediate router may be adversely impacted, potentially resulting in a DoS condition.

- **IP unreachable attack:** This attack uses a crafted packet flood that consists of IP packets that knowingly do not have IP reachability to the destination. Reachability may be prevented by an ACL filter, for example, or simply may result from the lack of a route to the destination within the FIB/CEF table. (Of course, the sender would be using a "default route" to source the packet in the first place.) If an intermediate router is unable to forward the packet, it will discard the packet and signal back to the source using the appropriate ICMP message. Typical ICMP messages in this case include: Destination Unreachable–Administratively Prohibited (Type 3, Code 13) when ACL filters are employed, or Destination Unreachable–Network Unreachable (Type 3, Code 0) when a destination IP route is not found. Again, because ICMP handling is often done within the CPU of the router, a flood of such packets may trigger a DoS condition. Note that this form of attack can also be used within a direct attack that targets a router directly using a closed protocol or TCP/UDP port, which would result in the ICMP Destination Unreachable–Protocol Unreachable (Type 3, Code 2) reply. Further, ICMP Destination Unreachable replies may provide useful network reconnaissance information, such as whether an IP (destination) host or network is "administratively" prohibited (ACL filtered) or simply unreachable (no route available). Network reconnaissance attacks are discussed further in the "Malicious Network Reconnaissance" section below.

- **Other ICMP transit attacks:** Both transit ICMP attacks outlined in the preceding bullets exploit ICMP reply message handling on intermediate routers. ICMP TTL Exceeded and ICMP Unreachable are only two specific examples. Similar attacks can be crafted for other ICMP reply messages. For example, ICMP Redirect (Message Type 5) and ICMP Parameter Problem reply messages can be used in similar attacks.

NOTE   For more information on ICMP and the different message types refer to RFC 792 and RFC 950 and the ICMP parameters documented at http://www.iana.org/assignments/icmp-parameters. Additional information on the ICMP protocol, headers, and potential attack vectors is provided in Appendix B, "IP Protocol Headers." Attackers may attempt to exploit these ICMP attack vectors to trigger a DoS condition on a router for which they do not have direct IP reachability.

Transit IP Options Attacks

The IP header provides for various IP options as specified in RFC 791. Unlike IPv6 extension headers, IPv4 options are not widely used; most of them are deprecated by other higher-layer protocols and enhancements. IP protocols that do use IP option headers include:

- IGMPv2 (RFC 2236) and IGMPv3 (RFC 3376)
- MPLS Label Switched Path (LSP) Ping and Traceroute (RFC 4379)
- DVMRP (RFC 1075)
- RSVP (RFC 2205)
- MPLS TE (RFC 2702 and RFC 3209)

Given their limited deployment and complex processing requirements resulting from the variable-sized IP header, routers do not support CEF fast path forwarding of IP options packets. As a result, packets with IP options are punted to the Cisco IOS process-level slow path for data plane forwarding. As outlined in Chapter 1, the process-level slow path has much lower forwarding capacity than the CEF fast path, which, in general, can support full interface capacity (or line rate). Further, the process-level slow path (in other words, CPU) is also shared with the IP control, management, and, optionally, services planes. Thus, a flood of IP options packets may saturate the process-level slow path and strain router resources, potentially affecting other IP traffic planes and resulting in a DoS condition. These may be legitimate IP packets with legitimate sources and destinations, so even in the case of legitimate traffic, a DoS condition may result if proper protection mechanisms are not applied.

Slow path and fast path packet processing capacity varies by platform and configuration. In general, however, packets that include IP option headers require process-level slow path forwarding. Packets with IP options are not the only case where process-level slow path forwarding may be required. Specific IP multicast packets must also be forwarded in the process-level slow path. These IP multicast packets are discussed in the next section.

A separate class of attacks using IP options takes advantage of the strict and loose source-routing capability. In general, an attacker cannot influence the forwarding path taken by packets to a given destination. Thus, the ability to target specific intermediate routers is limited. IP options, however, provide for strict and loose source routing (RFC 791) whereby the source IP host is able to specify an explicit route it wishes the packet to traverse through the network. In order for this path to be honored, this feature must be enabled on each router along the path within the IP network. This IP option provides greater control to the attacker by allowing them to specify forwarding paths through the network, which can then be used to attack specific intermediate routers. IP source routing is enabled by default within Cisco IOS. It is common to disable IP source routing because it provides little benefit. Only DVMRP (RFC 1075) tunnels use loose source-route IP options. Alternatively, IP routing attacks are another approach to manipulate packet forwarding and are reviewed in the "Routing Protocol Threats" section below.

Transit Multicast Attacks

IP routing and forwarding operations for IP multicast packets are vastly different than for IP unicast packets. With unicast routing, traffic flows are forwarded through the network along a single path from source to destination. Further, unicast routing considers only the destination address when making its forwarding decision; it does not consider the source address.

With multicast forwarding, the source is sending traffic to an arbitrary *group of hosts* that is represented by a multicast group (destination) address. Multicast-enabled routers must determine which direction is the upstream direction (toward the source) and which is the downstream direction(s) (toward the receiver(s)). Forwarding paths between senders and receivers are maintained using a multicast distribution tree (MDT) per multicast group and, optionally, per source. These are referred to as (*, G) shared and (S, G) source trees, respectively, which are both represented within the multicast forwarding table illustrated in Example 2-1.

Example 2-1 *IOS Sample Output from the* **show ip mroute** *Command*

```
Router# show ip mroute

IP Multicast Routing Table
Flags: D - Dense, S - Sparse, B - Bidir Group, s - SSM Group, C - Connected,
       L - Local, P - Pruned, R - RP-bit set, F - Register flag,
       T - SPT-bit set, J - Join SPT, M - MSDP created entry,
       X - Proxy Join Timer Running, A - Candidate for MSDP Advertisement,
       U - URD, I - Received Source Specific Host Report, Z - Multicast Tunnel,
       Y - Joined MDT-data group, y - Sending to MDT-data group
Timers: Uptime/Expires
Interface state: Interface, Next-Hop, State/Mode
```

continues

Example 2-1 *IOS Sample Output from the* **show ip mroute** *Command (Continued)*

```
(*, 224.0.255.3), uptime 5:29:15, RP is 192.168.37.2, flags: SC
  Incoming interface: Tunnel0, RPF neighbor 10.3.35.1, Dvmrp
  Outgoing interface list:
    Ethernet0, Forward/Sparse, 5:29:15/0:02:57

(192.168.46.0/24, 224.0.255.3), uptime 5:29:15, expires 0:02:59, flags: C
  Incoming interface: Tunnel0, RPF neighbor 10.3.35.1
  Outgoing interface list:
    Ethernet0, Forward/Sparse, 5:29:15/0:02:57
```

MDTs are created through IP routing protocols, such as PIM, as well as on-demand via sourced multicast traffic flows. When a router discovers a new multicast source, it creates state within its multicast forwarding table (in other words, mroute) and either builds or joins an MDT for the associated multicast group. Depending upon the multicast routing protocol deployed, state creation may require that the first data plane packet of each multicast traffic flow be punted to the IOS process-level for multicast control plane processing. Once the mroute forwarding entry is created, any subsequent packets within the flow will be CEF (fast path) switched through the router as opposed to slow path processed.

Hence, multicast-based attacks may attempt to exploit this behavior using many different IP sources and multicast groups to purposefully cause each attack packet to punt to the process-level control plane. Excessive multicast state creation processing may adversely affect router resources, triggering a DoS condition. Such attacks not only require multicast to be enabled on the router or network, but also require valid receivers in order to build the required MDT. Without these, any multicast traffic received may be silently discarded at the input router interface. For more multicast information, refer to the Cisco IOS Software IP Multicast Groups home page at ftp://ftpeng.cisco.com/ipmulticast/html/ipmulticast.html.

Reflection Attacks

A reflection attack is another form of DoS attack in that the source IP address of the attack packets is spoofed to match that of the intended target. The attack then transmits a flood of protocol request messages to innocent IP hosts (or broadcast addresses), which become *reflectors*. These reflectors simply respond to the spoofed request messages, flooding the unsuspecting victim. Using this technique, a large number of reflectors can be harnessed to collectively attack a target, as illustrated in Figure 2-3.

Spoofed addresses and the use of many reflectors also make attack traceback much more difficult. Further, if the attack is distributed among many reflectors, the reflectors may not notice any adverse impact associated with the attack, whereas an attack launched via a single reflector would be noticed. Because the reflector is only required to reply to the spoofed request, any bidirectional or client/server IP protocol may be used to launch such an attack. The following are examples of reflection attacks, reported by CERT, that have used different protocols. Spoofing attacks are further discussed in the next section.

- Spoofed UDP echo requests (http://www.cert.org/advisories/CA-1996-01.html)
- Spoofed TCP SYN flooding (http://www.cert.org/advisories/CA-1996-21.html)
- Spoofed ICMP echo requests (http://www.cert.org/advisories/CA-1998-01.html)
- Spoofed DNS (Domain Name Service) queries (http://www.cert.org/incident_notes/IN-2000-04.html)

Figure 2-3   *Reflection DoS Attack*

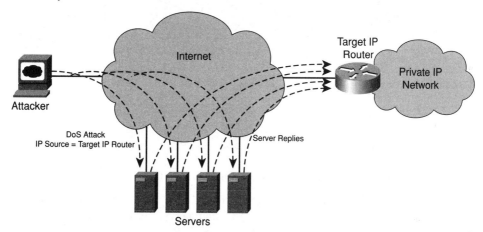

Spoofing Attacks

A spoofing attack uses packets that masquerade themselves with false data, typically the source IP address, to exploit a trusted relationship. In this way, these packets appear as if they were generated by a trusted source and, thereby, gain unauthorized privileges to a destination host or network. This enables them to target otherwise unreachable destinations (for example, bypass ACL filtering rules), intercept and manipulate data, and launch further attacks against the IP infrastructure. Given the potential impact, and the operational challenges of detecting, tracing, and mitigating these types of attacks, spoofed source attacks remain a significant threat. All of the attacks outlined in this chapter may employ spoofing techniques. Source IP address spoofing is often used to hide an attacker's identity, to bypass authentication or poorly written ACL filters, or to prevent effective attack mitigation. Conversely, other forms of attack require advanced spoofing of both IP and upper-layer protocol parameters to successfully attack a target.

The man-in-the-middle (MiTM) attack is a well-known spoofing attack whereby the attacker intercepts a legitimate communication between two trusted hosts. The attacker then attempts to control the flow of communication, as illustrated in Figure 2-4, either to read the information being exchanged or to manipulate the information exchanged, without either participating host's knowledge. This can be achieved if the attacker is able to spoof itself as one of the trusted hosts. Alternatively, routing protocol attacks (see "Routing Protocol Threats" later in the chapter) may be used to redirect traffic flows.

Figure 2-4 *Man-in-the-Middle Attack*

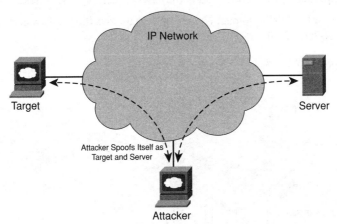

IP addresses that are commonly used within spoofing attacks include:

- **Bogon address:** A source address within the reserved IP address space that has not yet been allocated or delegated by the Internet Assigned Numbers Authority (IANA) or a delegated Regional Internet Registry (RIR).

- **Martian address ("packets from Mars"):** A source address that does not correspond to a destination prefix within the local IP routing table.

- **Private network address:** A source address that uses address space reserved by RFC 1918, RFC 3330, and RFC 3927. Private addresses are not routed within the public Internet.

The next section discusses specific TCP attacks that require advanced spoofing techniques. Techniques to mitigate spoofing attacks are reviewed in Part II.

Transport Protocol Attacks

The Internet Protocol (OSI Layer 3) provides connectionless, best-effort delivery of packets to the destination as well as fragmentation and reassembly of packets in support of network links with different maximum transmission unit (MTU) sizes. The transport layer (OSI Layer 4) provides transmission handling between host applications and the IP infrastructure, which may include connection establishment, buffering, flow control, and retransmissions. The two primary IP transport protocols in use today are User Data Protocol (UDP) and Transmission Control Protocol (TCP), defined in RFC 768 and RFC 793, respectively.

UDP is a connectionless transport layer protocol that provides no reliability, flow control, or error-recovery functions between host applications. Conversely, TCP is a connection-oriented transport layer protocol that does provide end-to-end reliable transmission, flow control, and error-recovery functions. Both are widely used by protocols within each of the IP traffic planes, as illustrated in Figure 2-5.

Figure 2-5 *Example TCP- and UDP–Based IP Traffic Plane Protocols*

Transport Protocol	IP Traffic Planes		
	Data Plane	Control Plane	Management Plane
TCP	• HTTP • SMTP	• BGP • DNS (Zone Transfer) • MPLS LDP (Label Distribution)	• Telnet • SSH • FTP • TACACS +
UDP	• NFS • VoIP • IPTV	• RIP • HSRP • DHCP • DNS (Record Lookups) • MPLS LDP (Peer Discovery)	• TFTP • SNMP • Syslog • RADIUS • NTP

UDP and TCP also provide for multiplexing numerous simultaneous application layer conversations over a single connection between hosts. As highlighted in Chapter 1, depending on which router is processing the packets, IP control, management, and services plane packets may appear as "transit" packets rather than "receive" packets. On intermediate routers along the downstream path, for example, these packets are treated as transit packets. Only the source and destination IP routers view ingress control, management, or services plane traffic as receive packets. This is an important distinction and is illustrated in Figure 2-6, which shows the different receive and transit treatment between IP edge and MPLS core routers, respectively. Because the core router is configured for MPLS, it is not required to run BGP. Internal BGP traffic between IP edge routers is handled as transit traffic by the core router.

Figure 2-6 *Example Receive Versus Transit Control Plane Treatment*

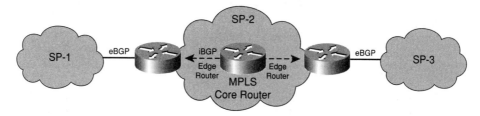

As transport layer protocols that provide transmission handling for upper-layer applications, UDP and TCP are both subject to threats such as the following:

- Attacks that hijack established sessions in order to capitalize on any previous authentication measures, enabling eavesdropping and false data injection

- DoS attacks that aim to prevent upper-layer communications between hosts

Given the fundamental differences between UDP and TCP, however, attack techniques vary significantly. Several of the more important threats against both the UDP and TCP protocols are reviewed in the following two sections. One challenge with transport protocol attacks is that they are often more difficult to detect than general DoS resource saturation attacks.

UDP Protocol Attacks

Attacking a UDP session is not highly complex because UDP itself has no authentication and is connectionless (in other words, no connection state is maintained between UDP peers). Injecting false data requires application awareness because application protocols generally apply their own authentication and integrity checks before accepting data. The potential threats against IP routing and control plane services protocols that rely on UDP for IP transport are reviewed in the "Routing Protocol Threats" and "Other IP Control Plane Threats" sections, respectively.

Launching a DoS attack against a UDP session can be achieved without application awareness. However, knowledge of the source and destination UDP port numbers, and the source and destination IP addresses, is generally required and more effective. This information is often necessary to successfully pass UDP integrity checks on the target host or target specific open UDP services. One well-known attack targets the Internet Key Exchange (IKE) protocol. IKEv1 uses UDP for transport when it performs mutual authentication and establishes security associations (SA) for IPsec. By flooding the IKE receiver with numerous bogus IKE initiation requests, the IKE resource may become depleted (in a similar way, the TCP SYN flood depletes server resources, as described in the next section). When this occurs, VPN termination devices may not allow legitimate VPN connection requests or may drop already established connections during rekeying. (IPsec VPNs are discussed further in the "IPsec VPN Threat Models" section below. Additional information on UDP, its header format, and potential security issues is provided in Appendix B.)

TCP Protocol Attacks

TCP is vastly different from UDP in that it provides connection-oriented reliable delivery of a traffic flow (RFC 793). TCP uses a number of control flags to manage the connection state, and 32-bit sequence and acknowledgment numbers to make certain that no packets are lost in transit and that the payload data is delivered to higher layers in the protocol stack at the receiving end in the correct order. TCP hosts process packets only if their sequence numbers fall within a range of unacknowledged sequence numbers defined by a "sliding window." A TCP "reset" attack, for example, attempts to insert a TCP connection reset (RST) packet within an active TCP session by guessing a sequence number within this sliding window range in hopes of bringing down the connection.

TCP is widely used by upper-layer protocols within each of the IP traffic planes when reliable delivery is required. With or without application awareness, an attack must first successfully pass the integrity checks of TCP in order to target an established connection. Passing these checks requires spoofing source and destination IP addresses, source and destination port numbers, and the TCP sequence number. Successfully spoofing these 5-tuples enables an attacker to target an established TCP connection.

Whereas source and destination IP addresses may be relatively easy to determine and spoof, spoofing the source TCP port is often a matter of guessing. The destination TCP port is usually well known for all standard services (for example, port 23 for Telnet, port 80 for HTTP). Recent research has shown that spoofing the sequence number is easier than previously believed, as the spoofed sequence number does not have to be an exact match, but rather must simply fall within the advertised window. This significantly decreases the effort required by an attacker: the larger the window, the easier it is to manipulate the connection. If the sequence number is outside of the advertised window, or if any of the other 4-tuples are invalid, the target (receiver) should simply discard the attack packet.

Two broad families of TCP attacks generally take advantage of spoofing a TCP packet. The first is the MiTM attack (outlined earlier in the section "Spoofing Attacks"), whereby an attacker intercepts packets exchanged between the targeted hosts to learn the 5-tuples required for spoofing. With this information, the attacker might forge spoofed packets that will pass the TCP integrity checks and, thereby, allow the attacker to insert itself as a proxy between the two target hosts. This is done by resetting the original connection and then re-establishing two new connections using new sequence and acknowledgement numbers with both sides of the original connection. The second technique involves blind attacks where the attacker is not able to intercept packets between the targeted hosts. As a result, the attacker must guess the 5-tuples in order to spoof the TCP connection. If the sequence number can be compromised, attack traffic can be sent to the target.

NOTE   In the past, TCP hosts used simple and predictable techniques for generating initial sequence numbers. This made TCP connections more susceptible to blind attacks. Random sequence number generation is more commonly implemented within TCP stacks today, making blind attacks more difficult.

Whereas spoofing the 5-tuples is required for attacking established TCP connections, TCP hosts may also be targeted with DoS attacks that aim to exhaust system resources. Some of the common DoS threats against TCP are as follows:

- **SYN flood attacks:** TCP SYN floods are a type of resource saturation (DoS) attack in which the attacker sends many spoofed TCP connection requests at the target. The spoofed TCP connection requests consist of TCP packets having random source addresses and the SYN flag set that signals initial sequence number synchronization. In response, the target allocates local system resources for each spoofed request. The TCP three-way handshake is never completed for any of the requests, forcing the target's TCP stack to maintain system resources for each outstanding connection request indefinitely. TCP stacks generally support a finite number of open connection requests. If the target receives connection requests at a higher rate than the rate at which open connection requests expire, system resources on the target may become exhausted. This prevents any valid new connection requests from being established, effectively creating a DoS condition on the target. Each TCP stack is, of course, implemented differently, and mechanisms have been integrated into many TCP stacks to protect against and minimize the impact of TCP SYN and other resource exhaustion attacks. However, these mechanisms do not make them impervious to such attacks. Note, because an SYN flood attack is not targeting an existing TCP connection, sequence number spoofing is not required. Figure 2-7 illustrates the fundamentals of the TCP SYN flood attack.

Figure 2-7 *TCP SYN Flood Attack*

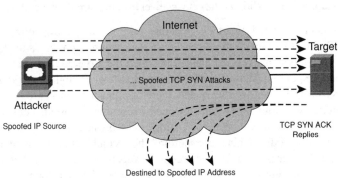

- **RST attacks:** If an attacker is able to spoof the 5-tuples (as outlined earlier in the section), including the TCP sequence number, it is possible to *reset* an established TCP connection by sending a packet to the target with the RST or synchronize (SYN) flag set. The resulting impact on specific upper-layer protocols may vary. However, if this attack is sustained, it will result in a DoS condition. RST attacks can also be used to hijack TCP sessions, as described next.

- **Session hijacking:** TCP session hijacks are intended to take control of an existing TCP connection, enabling the attacker to inject false data or eavesdrop on the connection. Figure 2-8 illustrates the fundamentals of a TCP session hijacking.

Figure 2-8   *TCP Session Hijacking*

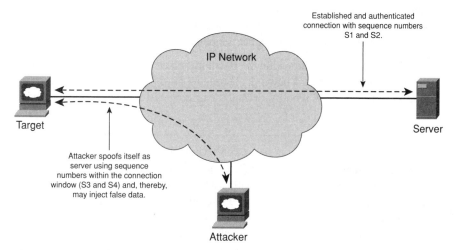

- **ICMP attacks against TCP:** TCP is subject to ICMP attacks that may cause TCP connection resets or reduce the throughput of existing connections. One interesting example involves the use of ICMP Type 3, Code 4 (Fragmentation Needed and Do Not Fragment Bit Set) error messages. TCP maintains state for established connections as outlined in the "TCP Protocol Attacks" section above. One parameter considered is the end-to-end path MTU. Certain upper-layer applications take advantage of TCP's ability to use ICMP Type 3, Code 4 messages (which include a "suggested" MTU size) to optimize the size of transmitted packets. In this case, if an attacker can spoof an ICMP Type 3, Code 4 message targeting one end of an established TCP connection, the connection can be convinced that it should "decrease" its transmitted packet size, perhaps even down to some absurdly small value. To successfully complete such an attack, the attacker must spoof the 5-tuples of the TCP connection within the ICMP payload, because the target must correlate the spoofed ICMP packet to an existing connection.

Additional information on TCP, its header format, and potential security issues is provided in Appendix B.

This section outlined attacks specific to the UDP and TCP transport protocols. All network protocols, however, are potential attack targets. In the next section, you will see how attacks against IP routing protocols and IP control plane services in general can affect the network.

Routing Protocol Threats

A number of routing protocols are available; BGP, OSPF, IS-IS, RIPv2, and EIGRP are the most widely deployed. Each routing protocol has its own advantages and limitations. Selecting a routing protocol depends on many factors, including convergence speed, scalability, feature support, topology support, operation and maintenance, and a number of other factors that are outside the scope of this book. While several Interior Gateway Protocols (IGP) are available, BGP is the industry standard for interdomain Internet routing. Therefore, a large-scale BGP protocol attack has the potential to affect the wider Internet.

Routing protocols operate within the IP control plane and are often used as a starting point for a leveraged attack on a network. Through a routing protocol attack, an attacker can disrupt traffic or, more broadly, disrupt the routing system forwarding the traffic.

Routing System

A routing system is a collection of (IP) routers that build neighbor relationships and adjacencies to reliably exchange routing data, including destination and topology information. Information is exchanged through routing protocols that have well-defined semantics and state machines. Using these relationships and routing protocols, the routing system identifies loop-free paths through the network.

Routing protocol attacks are designed to do the following:

- Destroy the router's or network's ability to perform routing tasks
- Prevent new routing protocol peering and disrupt current peering
- Redirect traffic flows to inject false information, alter existing information, or remove valid information for the purposes of corrupting user data

BGP uses TCP as its transport protocol and, thus, attacks against BGP often involve the same or similar attack vectors previously described for TCP. In general, the most common are the TCP connection reset (RST) attack and the MiTM data-insertion attack. DoS attacks directly against BGP are also plausible; however, although a flood of BGP traffic may adversely impact an IP router, this is not considered a true BGP attack but rather a resource exhaustion DoS attack.

Routing protocols may also be used to attack a target by exhausting the routing table capacity, thus affecting a router's ability to perform routing tasks, including packet forwarding and routing protocol peering. A more subtle attack is one that exploits a software implementation vulnerability—for example, using a malformed packet, which results in a routing protocol state machine violation and, consequently, a peering session failure.

Malformed Packet

A malformed packet conforms neither to the IETF Internet Protocol specifications nor to applicable vendor-proprietary protocol formats. The error may exist within the TCP/IP header or within the upper-layer protocol header—for example, ICMP, BGP, OSPF, and so on. Malformed packets are illegal and should be discarded upon receipt.

Given IP reachability, an attacker may disrupt a routing protocol peering session using the transport protocol attacks previously outlined. After all, routing protocols are simply seen by UDP and TCP as upper-layer applications.

Other routing protocol peering sessions that do not rely on TCP or UDP may also be attacked. To attack these routing protocol peering sessions, an attacker may transmit a crafted routing protocol packet from a spoofed source, thereby forcing a peering session or adjacency failure. In OSPF, for example, this can be (theoretically) achieved by spoofing an OSPF hello to the all routers address (224.0.0.5) with an empty neighbor list. Similarly with EIGRP, this can be (theoretically) achieved by sending an EIGRP update to the all routers address (224.0.0.10) with the INIT bit set. Similar attacks can be launched against the other routing protocols as well.

Attacks that cause a routing session between two routers to be torn down result in all routes advertised between these two peers to be withdrawn. When this occurs, and before the routing protocol state can be rebuilt, all of the traffic destined to prefixes whose routes have been removed is either rerouted (if an alternate path exists) or discarded (if no alternate path exists). Rerouted traffic may also introduce some congestion along these alternate paths.

Attackers may also attempt to insert bogus route updates into the routing protocol to cause traffic redirection. One purpose of this attack is to cause a routing loop, resulting in a large-scale network outage and effectively "blackholing" traffic and disrupting communications. A second purpose might be to cause traffic redirection onto insecure networks where the attacker may eavesdrop on conversations and manipulate packet content. This involves attacking the information carried within the protocol with false routing, rather than attacking the protocol peering itself. Such attacks are potentially feasible using any one of the following techniques:

- The attacker may compromise a trusted router attached to the target network, using its trusted status to inject false routing information. For more information on unauthorized access attacks, see the upcoming section "Unauthorized Access Attacks."

- The attacker may compromise a link between two routers, and inject false data or modify data in transit. In certain topologies, this may be achieved using a MiTM attack, as outlined earlier in the "Spoofing Attacks" section.

- The attacker may spoof a valid peer and advertise false data such as invalid prefixes, invalid next hops, and invalid AS PATHs. This may be achieved using a blind spoofing attack. Further, injecting false routes may only require a single spoofed update message.

Routing protocol attacks are not specific to unicast routing protocols. Multicast routing protocols may also be targeted.

Other IP Control Plane Threats

Although routing protocols enable the IP control plane to dynamically build a forwarding path supporting the IP data plane between sources and destinations, hosts may not participate in the network until they are assigned an IP address. Similarly, a host may not communicate with other *named* hosts without first resolving host names into IP addresses. These essential network parameters may be assigned statically, or handled dynamically via other IP control plane applications, specifically, the Dynamic Host Configuration Protocol (DHCP) and Domain Name Service (DNS) protocols. Due to the high administrative overhead in managing these parameters through static configurations, most IP networks use DHCP and DNS.

The Network Time Protocol (NTP) is also widely deployed within IP networks to provide a clock source and synchronized timekeeping between distributed time servers and network elements. Accurate timekeeping is critically important for correlating network events (including security incidents) during troubleshooting and for quantifying network performance (including packet delay and jitter).

Threats against these IP control plane protocols include:

- **DoS attacks:** Because all of these protocols are UDP based, they are subject to many of the DoS, spoofing, and UDP attacks previously outlined. DoS attacks against these specific protocols also include:

  — **DoS attacks against the DHCP server:** This attack intends to prevent clients from acquiring an IP address and other DHCP-supplied parameters, such as default gateway, IP subnet, DNS server addresses, and so on. This attack can affect hosts as they initially connect to the network, or hosts renewing DHCP leases as they expire. In this event, affected hosts lose network connectivity. DHCP servers may also be subject to resource-starvation DoS attacks where the target DHCP server is flooded with many bogus DHCP requests, each having a unique MAC address. If successful, this attack may exhaust the DHCP server address pool, preventing valid hosts from acquiring an IP address and network connectivity.

  — **DoS attacks against the DNS server:** This attack attempts to prevent clients from translating destination host names to IP addresses, thereby affecting application connectivity. DNS (and DHCP) servers may also be leveraged for reflection attacks because they reply to any received request—legitimate or spoofed!

  — **DoS attacks against the NTP server:** This attack attempts to prevent synchronized timekeeping among network elements, thereby affecting network event correlation and troubleshooting and network SLA measurements.

- **Spoofed attacks:** If an attacker is able to masquerade as a DHCP, DNS, or NTP server, the following threats exist:

  — Advertisement of spoofed IP gateway information to DHCP clients enables the attacker to intercept traffic flows, facilitating MiTM attacks, eavesdropping, and the injection of false data. Information gathered from intercepted packets (for example, passwords) may also enable further attacks. The advertisement of bogus DHCP information may also prevent clients from communicating to the network, triggering a DoS condition.

— Advertisement of spoofed DNS name records (in other words, "A records") enables the attacker to redirect traffic flows to the destination of their choice, facilitating MiTM attacks, eavesdropping, the injection of false data, and the distribution of Trojans, malware, and password/keystroke loggers. Consider the following scenario. By default, when you enter an IOS command within user or privileged (enable) EXEC mode and the command is not recognized by the IOS command interpreter, the router considers the invalid command as the host name of another device that you are attempting to connect to, for example, via Telnet or SSH. Therefore, the IOS router tries to resolve the unrecognized command into an IP address by performing an IP domain lookup via DNS. If no specific domain name server (DNS) has been explicitly configured, the router will issue a local DNS broadcast for the unrecognized command to be translated into an IP address. Such broadcasts could be used by a local attacker to gain unauthorized access to the IOS router by spoofing a DNS reply with its own IP address. The attacker will then receive the unintentional connection request and proxy it back to the router as a new inbound connection. If you enter commands or a password through this connection they will be captured by the attacker. This issue was reported to Cisco by Stephen Dugan and Jose Avila. Techniques to mitigate the risk of this threat are described in Chapter 6. Similarly to DHCP, the advertisement of bogus DNS records may also prevent clients from communicating to legitimate network resources, triggering a DoS condition. In recursive resolution environments, cache poisoning (whereby cached entries within a DNS server are deliberately contaminated) is used to cause the spoofed DNS records.

— Advertisement of spoofed NTP server messages may adversely affect timekeeping within a network, affecting network event correlation and troubleshooting, as well as network SLA measurements if applicable.

In addition to the DoS and spoofing attacks discussed, IP control plane services are also subject to unauthorized access attacks. Unauthorized access attacks are reviewed next, followed by software vulnerabilities and network reconnaissance attacks.

Unauthorized Access Attacks

IP management plane attacks that attempt to gain access to unauthorized systems and networks have long existed. These attacks pose a very serious threat. Security policies and tools often protect against external threats but not internal ones. If an attacker gains unauthorized EXEC-level CLI (command-line interface) access to a router, some of the potential threats include:

• Disabling the router (DoS) by disabling interfaces or protocols (or both)

- Changing security policies to permit further attacks, deny legitimate traffic, or disable logging, monitoring, tracing, and accounting capabilities so any other attacks go undetected

- Exposing usernames and passwords, SNMP read/write communities, protocol authentication keys (for example, MD5 passwords), and IPsec/IKE shared secrets

- Accessing network topology and IP addressing information (network reconnaissance), as well as router security and routing policies

Some of the techniques commonly used to gain unauthorized access include:

- **Social engineering:** A technique that manipulates people to acquire confidential information (for example, passwords).

- **Physical security breeches:** If physical security is compromised, other higher-layer security mechanisms may become ineffective. For example, publicly known mechanisms are available to recover passwords when physical access is available (refer to http://www.cisco.com/warp/public/474/).

- **Password cracking:** A variety of techniques, including brute force and dictionary attacks that attempt to guess an authentication password.

- **Cyber attacks:** Attempts to capture passwords or bypass authentication mechanisms through malware programs, phishing, packet sniffing, cryptanalysis, or software vulnerabilities. Software vulnerabilities are discussed further in the next section.

These techniques may be applied against any one of the available router configuration, protocol authentication, or encryption methods if IP reachability is available. Typical access points include:

- Privileged EXEC-level CLI access via enable secret, enable password, or username password

- Console CLI access via console password

- Telnet or SSH access via vty password

- Routing protocol authentication via MD5 hash

- IPsec/SSL VPN tunnel access via encryption keys

- SNMP MIB object access via SNMP read and write communities

- HTTP access via password

- FTP access via password, if FTP server is enabled

To mitigate the risk of management plane attacks, security policies often implement multiple layers of protection. In Chapter 3, "IP Network Traffic Plane Security Concepts," you will learn about the principles of defense in depth and breadth, and how the distinction between network "core" and "edge" locations can aid in the development of appropriate security policies. Chapter 6 reviews security techniques available to protect the IP management plane.

Software Vulnerabilities

Software products inevitably have software defects; IP routers are no exception. In some instances, an IP router software defect may represent a security vulnerability that, if exploited, may compromise the confidentiality, integrity and availability of the router and IP data plane traffic. Or, the software vulnerability may affect the IP management plane, allowing an attacker to bypass authentication mechanisms, for example, and gain unauthorized access to the router. The potential threat and impact of a given vulnerability depends not only on the specific defect but also on the methods required to exploit the defect. For example, a vulnerability that can be exploited only locally (for example, a Layer 2 Ethernet attack, as reviewed in the upcoming section "Threats Against Layer 2 Network Infrastructures") has limited exposure compared to vulnerabilities that can be exploited remotely via the wider Internet. Similarly, some vulnerabilities may be easily exploited via a single malformed packet, whereas others may require complex tools and advanced skills to exploit.

The potential impact of an exploit is also independent of risk factors and must be considered separately. That is, an attack that is "low risk but high impact" may be more critical than an attack that is "high risk but low impact." The classic ping of death (PoD) attack illustrates an exploit of a known software vulnerability. The PoD attack sends a fragmented ICMP ping (echo) packet that, when reassembled, exceeds the maximum 65,535-byte limitations of IP. (This is possible due to the way fragmentation relies on an offset value in each fragment to determine where the individual fragment goes upon reassembly. Thus, on the last fragment, it is possible to combine a valid offset with a suitable fragment size such that [offset + size] > 65,535.) In older IP stacks, receiving a PoD packet would often crash the target host (due to a buffer overflow) and provided an almost trivial ability to perform a DoS attack. Most TCP/IP stack implementations have been corrected to prevent this type of attack.

Cisco IOS Software has had software vulnerabilities as well. Some of these have been discovered internally during development testing; others have been discovered in the field. However vulnerabilities are discovered, they are always resolved and disclosed by Cisco in a public forum. Published Cisco security advisories and responses are available at http://www.cisco.com/go/psirt. Some of the more well-known IOS vulnerabilities are reported in the following Cisco Security Advisories:

- "Cisco IOS Interface Blocked by IPv4 Packets"
  http://www.cisco.com/warp/public/707/cisco-sa-20030717-blocked.shtml

- "TCP Vulnerabilities in Multiple IOS-Based Cisco Products"
  http://www.cisco.com/warp/public/707/cisco-sa-20040420-tcp-ios.shtml

- "IPv6 Crafted Packet Vulnerability" http://www.cisco.com/warp/public/707/cisco-sa-20050729-ipv6.shtml

- "Crafted ICMP Messages Can Cause Denial of Service"
  http://www.cisco.com/warp/public/707/cisco-sa-20050412-icmp.shtml

Cisco publishes this information so that customers and partners are able to take the necessary actions, if any, to protect their networks. Attackers also have access to this same information and may use it to launch attacks. Deploying up-to-date software versions that include fixes for disclosed security vulnerabilities is highly recommended. Further, Cisco follows a responsible disclosure process for communicating product vulnerabilities with customers and partners. The Cisco Security Vulnerability Policy is available at http://www.cisco.com/en/US/products/products_security_vulnerability_policy.html. For more information on security incident handling, refer to Appendix D, "Security Incident Handling."

Malicious Network Reconnaissance

Reconnaissance is the process of gathering information about a target. Network reconnaissance is considered malicious when it is conducted in preparation for an attack; malicious reconnaissance is normally considered the first phase of an attack and precedes the actual attack. Collecting intelligence about a target enables the attacker to identify specific security weaknesses that may be exploited as part of a future attack. Information that may be of interest and collected during network reconnaissance often includes:

- IP router platform hardware types and specific software versions deployed

- IP addressing schemes and reachable devices

- Network topology, protocols, forwarding paths, and path MTUs

- Host or router operating system and specific versions deployed via responses and/or banners received for Telnet, FTP, TCP/IP, and ICMP host queries, or scanning (for example, Nmap OS fingerprinting)

- Network services deployed (for example, DNS, DHCP, and NTP) and versions

- Usernames, passwords, and router configurations

- Remote access servers and extranet connectivity

- Network filtering capabilities (for example, ACLs, firewalls, IPS, and so on)

- Unprotected files, hosts, and network infrastructure

- Network and host monitoring systems (for example, IDS/IPS, anomaly detection systems, and so on)

Similar methods as outlined above in the "Unauthorized Access Attacks" section may be used to conduct network reconnaissance, including social engineering, physical security breaches, password cracking, and cyber attacks. Public information and information obtained via network scanning (for example, IP ping sweeps and port scans, IP traceroute, ICMP information requests, Cisco Discovery Protocol (CDP), SNMP MIBs, file retrieval via TFTP/FTP, remote login via Telnet, etc.) is also commonly used to gather intelligence about a potential target. Publicly available information may include:

- Internet DNS and BGP tools that provide IP address resolution, IP prefixes, and ASN information (for example, route servers, dig/nslookup, whois, and so on)

- Vendor product and software documentation
- Security vulnerabilities and software defects (for example, Cisco security advisories and Cisco CCO BugToolkit)

This is by no means a complete list, but does provide some insight into the many different methods used by attackers to conduct network reconnaissance.

Threats Against Layer 2 Network Infrastructures

Ethernet switches are widely deployed within enterprise and SP network infrastructures. Ethernet is also increasingly being deployed within consumer networks as it is commonly integrated in DSL/cable modems. Metro-Ethernet and Ethernet WAN (for example, VPLS, VPWS, and MPLS VPN) services are also increasing in deployment and are expected to replace traditional Frame Relay and ATM aggregation networks. Given this fact, Ethernet switches are increasingly being seen as good launch points for leveraged attacks.

Ethernet switches that incorporate Layer 3 functions are subject to the same IP threats outlined in the "Threats Against IP Network Infrastructures" section above. Ethernet switches are also subject to other, unique network attacks. Although IP and Ethernet operate at different layers of the OSI protocol stack, an attack within the Ethernet link layer (Layer 2) may adversely impact IP traffic planes. Because Ethernet frames are not IP routable, Ethernet attacks, in general, must be launched locally. That is, these attacks must be launched by devices connected directly to the specific Ethernet segment. However, given the increasing deployment of Metro-Ethernet and Layer 2 Ethernet WAN services, remote attacks are feasible. This section reviews specific threats against Layer 2 Ethernet infrastructures, including both native Layer 2 Ethernet switches and multilayer Ethernet switches. Additional information on mitigating the risk of these threats is provided in Part II. Note that physical security is also not considered here because it is considered out of scope.

CAM Table Overflow Attacks

Ethernet switches maintain content-addressable memory (CAM) lookup tables to dynamically track the MAC addresses for hosts connected to the physical switch ports, as well as associated VLAN parameters. CAM tables are populated by a dynamic source MAC address learning process. As the switch receives a frame on a switch port, it creates a CAM table entry that includes the source MAC address, switch port and VLAN parameters associated with the received frame, and a timestamp. If a duplicate entry already exists, the switch resets the timestamp. If the entry already exists but is associated with a different switch port or VLAN, the entry is updated based on the most recently received port or VLAN information and timestamp.

The CAM table is populated based on source MAC address information of received frames; CAM table forwarding lookups use the destination MAC address of received frames to determine the output port. In this way, the switch simply forwards the frame out the known port indicated by the CAM table instead of broadcasting the frame out of every switch port within the associated VLAN. When the destination MAC address is not present within the CAM table, the frame is broadcast out of every switch port within the associated VLAN. Broadcasting frames reduces available network capacity and increases the risk of broadcast storms and bridging loops.

Similar to IP route memories, CAM tables also have a fixed size. Once the CAM table on the switch is full, no new MAC address entries can be added. Only after the timestamps of entries expire will free space become available. Knowing this, an attacker may attempt to flood the network with bogus traffic sourced from many different spoofed MAC addresses in order to overflow the CAM tables of all Ethernet switches within the domain. Periodically repeating the attack prevents the bogus CAM table entries from expiring. This may result in legitimate traffic (with no associated CAM table entries) being broadcast out every switch port within the associated VLAN, greatly increasing the risk of broadcast storms and bridging loops. This attack may also be used to facilitate eavesdropping on traffic flows as frames are broadcast out of every switch port, facilitating packet capture, as illustrated in Figure 2-9.

Figure 2-9 *CAM Table Overflow Attacks*

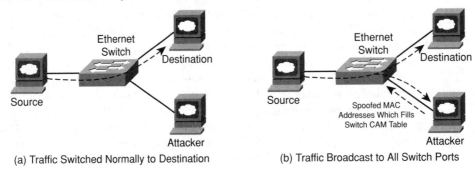

(a) Traffic Switched Normally to Destination   (b) Traffic Broadcast to All Switch Ports

MAC Spoofing Attacks

The CAM table overflow attack is predicated on MAC address spoofing as well as the attacker having local connectivity to the same Ethernet infrastructure as the target. While the CAM table overflow attack may facilitate eavesdropping on traffic flows, MAC spoofing may also be used to intercept traffic flows and modify payload information. This is possible using the following techniques:

- With local connectivity to the same Ethernet infrastructure as the target host, an attacker may spoof the target's MAC address. The Ethernet switch will then reprogram the CAM table entry for the target MAC address with the attacker's switch port. The attacker may now intercept frames destined to the target. Of course, when the target transmits a new frame, the CAM table will be reprogrammed with the correct switch port. An attacker may use this technique to modify intercepted frames and retransmit them to the target. Intercepting traffic flows in this way is very difficult given the synchronized timing required by the attacker to control the switch's CAM table entry of the target. Nevertheless, intercepting a limited number of frames may be sufficient to capture a username and password, for example, which may then be used to gain unauthorized access. This technique may also be used to prevent IP connectivity with spoofed destinations and, thereby, trigger a DoS condition.

- With local connectivity to the same Ethernet infrastructure as the target host, an attacker may use ARP spoofing to intercept IP traffic flows. ARP (Address Resolution Protocol) provides a mechanism to resolve a MAC address to an IP address in order to provide IP connectivity within a Layer 2 broadcast domain. Using ARP, an IP host dynamically learns the MAC address for the destination IP address or the corresponding default gateway so that the proper Layer 2 frame can be built for the Layer 2 next-hop destination. Unsolicited ARP replies (known as gratuitous ARPs, or GARPs) are used to proactively advertise MAC and IP address bindings and may be transmitted without an initial ARP request. Using an unsolicited ARP reply (or GARP), an attacker may falsely advertise a spoofed IP address. Unsolicited ARP replies are not authenticated and, by default, will overwrite the MAC and IP address bindings maintained within the target's ARP cache. Thus, using ARP spoofing, an attacker can intercept traffic flows destined to the spoofed address.

These techniques may also be used by an attacker to launch MiTM attacks, facilitating eavesdropping or the insertion of false application data. Further, these techniques may also be used to launch a DoS attack against the target and prevent IP connectivity with spoofed destinations, as illustrated in Figure 2-10.

Figure 2-10 *ARP Spoofing Attacks*

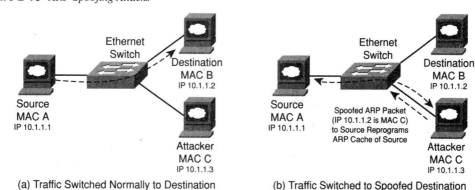

(a) Traffic Switched Normally to Destination   (b) Traffic Switched to Spoofed Destination

VLAN Hopping Attacks

VLAN hopping attacks are malicious schemes that enable an attacker on one VLAN to obtain unauthorized access to hosts on other VLANs within the same switched Ethernet domain. This is possible using the following techniques:

- **Switch spoofing:** Switch spoofing attacks may be launched from switch ports enabled for dynamic trunking. Switch spoofing requires an attacker to masquerade as a switch, and transmit spoofed trunked packets, which may result in the switch port being reconfigured as a VLAN trunk port. If the port is compromised and becomes a VLAN trunk port, an attacker may gain unauthorized membership to all VLANs within the switched domain, allowing attacks to be launched against other VLANs simply by transmitting spoofed 802.1Q or Cisco ISL tagged frames. Further, because the attacker appears as a valid switch with a trunk port, they may be able to both receive and transmit traffic with any IP device that is reachable through any VLAN configured on the compromised trunk port, as illustrated in Figure 2-11.

Figure 2-11 *Switch Spoofing Attack*

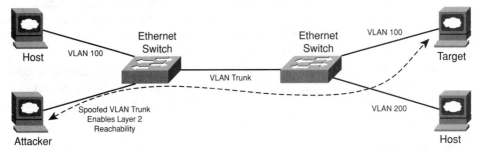

- **Double tagging:** Double tagging attacks transmit (attack) frames with two 802.1Q headers in an attempt to forward frames to another VLAN. VLAN tagging rules are defined by Cisco ISL or IEEE 802.1Q. ISL is a Cisco proprietary VLAN encapsulation format. The 802.1Q VLAN encapsulation format was defined by the IEEE standards organization. Unlike the Cisco ISL protocol, IEEE 802.1Q defines a native VLAN for backward compatibility, enabling 802.1Q-capable 802.3 ports to communicate with non-802.1Q-capable 802.3 ports directly by sending and receiving untagged traffic. The native VLAN is not explicitly associated to any VLAN tag on an 802.1Q link and is used for all untagged traffic received on any 802.1Q-capable port. Although the native VLAN provides backward compatibility, it may be used as an attack vector because frames associated with the native VLAN are not tagged when transmitted over any 802.1Q trunk within the switched domain. Consider the following scenario, illustrated in Figure 2-12:

Figure 2-12 *Double 802.1Q Encapsulation Attack*

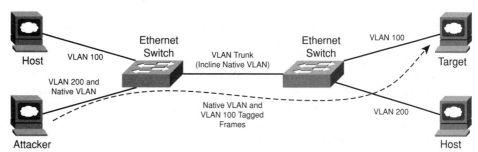

If the switch port through which an attacker has network connectivity is configured with the VLAN that is also used as the native VLAN on 802.1Q trunk ports within the switched domain, the attacker may be able to use double-encapsulated 802.1Q packets to hop across VLANs and launch attacks against other VLANs. This is made possible due to native 802.1Q VLAN handling within the switched domain. The switch that first receives the double-tagged frame first strips the outer 802.1Q tag off the frame and broadcasts it out ports also configured with the native VLAN. The frame is broadcast because the destination MAC is not known to the native VLAN. This results in the downstream switch receiving the frame with a single 802.1Q tag. The downstream switch then forwards the packet based on the original inner 802.1Q VLAN identifier of the frame. As illustrated in Figure 2-12, this enables an attacker to hop across and launch attacks against other VLANs. As previously noted, this technique works only if the attacker switch port is configured as part of the native VLAN. Further, this provides connectivity only from the attacker to other VLANs and not vice versa, because any attempt by the target to send traffic back to the attacker will be blocked by the non-native VLAN configuration of the target's switch port.

Private VLAN Attacks

Private VLANs (PVLAN) provide Layer 2 isolation of hosts within the same VLAN and IP subnet. This is useful in situations where you need to prevent direct connectivity between hosts without placing the hosts into different IP subnets. PVLANs are often used to isolate traffic between customers within an SP server farm, for example, and reduces the consumption of IP addresses and subnets.

PVLANs work by limiting communication among switch ports within the same VLAN. Isolated switch ports within a VLAN may communicate only with promiscuous switch ports. Community switch ports may communicate only with promiscuous switch ports, as well as other ports belonging to the same community. Promiscuous switch ports may communicate with any switch port and typically connect to the default gateway IP router. By using the default gateway as a proxy, a miscreant may bypass the access restrictions of a PVLAN, facilitating attacks against isolated host(s). Using this technique, an attacker launches an attack against the target using the target's IP address as the IP destination, but using the default gateway router's MAC address. Upon receipt of the attack frames, the IP router simply reroutes the Ethernet encapsulated IP packets to the target's MAC address, as llustrated in Figure 2-13. This is feasible only if the attacker specifically sets the destination MAC address of the attack frames. Otherwise, the default gateway router, by default, will not respond to ARP requests issued by the attacker because it is on the same IP subnet as the target. The default gateway assumes the two hosts have direct connectivity and is not aware that PVLANs keep them isolated. Therefore, any attempt by the target to send traffic back to the attacker will be blocked by the PVLAN configuration. Hence, this technique only allows for unidirectional traffic flow but does enable an attacker to bypass PVLAN configurations and launch attacks against isolated hosts.

Figure 2-13 *Private VLAN Attack*

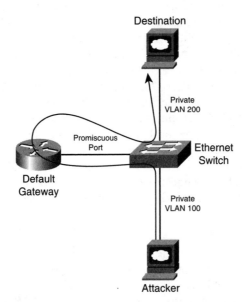

STP Attacks

IP routing protocols are used within the IP control plane to determine forwarding paths between IP sources and destinations. The Spanning Tree Protocol (STP) serves as the control plane within Layer 2 Ethernet networks. STP prevents the creation of bridging loops within a redundant or multipath Layer 2 Ethernet network. STP achieves this by selecting one switch as a root bridge and building a loop-free path to all devices within the Layer 2 network. STP selects one forwarding path between each device and the root bridge. Redundant paths are placed in a blocked stated and may be activated only in the event that the active path fails. If an attacker spoofs STP Bridge Protocol Data Unit (BPDU) messages, the attacker may trigger STP recalculations and the reselection of the root bridge. In the event the attacker is dual-homed and elected as the root bridge, it may be able to insert itself within the forwarding path between two hosts, as illustrated in Figure 2-14. This would enable eavesdropping and the injection of false data through MiTM attacks. Further, the attacker may also introduce bridging loops, triggering a DoS condition.

Figure 2-14 *Spanning Tree Protocol Attack*

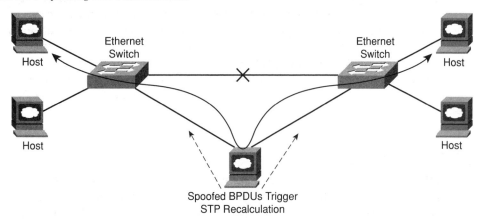

VTP Attacks

Similar to the spoofed STP attack, an attacker may also spoof VLAN Trunking Protocol (VTP) advertisements. VTP is a Cisco proprietary Layer 2 messaging protocol that enables network operators to centrally manage VLAN configurations within a switched Ethernet domain. As VLANs are added, deleted, or renamed, VTP propagates these configuration changes to each switch within the VTP domain. VLAN trunk ports, for example, are automatically reconfigured based on the VTP advertisements. This greatly simplifies the configuration process of the switched network. If an attacker spoofs VTP advertisements, they may be able to add, delete, or rename VLANs within the VTP domain. This may result in bridging loops and STP recalculations, both of which may trigger a DoS condition. Further, the attacker may reconfigure the VTP domain to gain unauthorized access to specific VLANs.

Threats Against IP VPN Network Infrastructures

Virtual Private Networks (VPN) offer an alternative to deploying a private network for tying together geographically dispersed corporate networks, offices, and employees with mission-critical business applications. By not having to maintain a private network, businesses can realize significant cost savings through the use of a shared VPN infrastructure. VPNs also offer rich connectivity options, often leveraging the ubiquity of the Internet to provide connectivity from anywhere.

VPNs are often categorized as either remote-access VPNs or site-to-site VPNs. Remote-access VPNs provide mobile workers with secure access to the corporate network, whereas site-to-site VPNs provide secure connectivity between branch and corporate offices. VPNs are further categorized as Layer 2 (L2) VPNs or Layer 3 (L3) VPNs based on where they operate within the OSI reference model. There is no single best choice among the available VPN technologies. The optimal VPN architecture depends on the business requirements. In fact, many businesses are best served by some combination of several VPN technologies. Common to each VPN technology, however, is the promise of secure connectivity. This section reviews the threats and security vulnerabilities against the two most widely deployed network-based L3 VPN technologies: Multiprotocol Label Switching (MPLS) and IP Security (IPsec).

MPLS VPN Threat Models

MPLS is typically offered as a site-to-site VPN service from an SP, mainly as a replacement for traditional Frame Relay or ATM networks. The SP offers business customers IP VPN connectivity between customer sites across a shared IP infrastructure. Not only is the SP IP network shared among MPLS VPN customers but it may also be shared by SP customers of other services, including, for example, Internet transit and Layer 2 VPNs. Although the SP IP network is shared, addressing and routing separation is assured between customer VPNs, and between VPNs and the SP global IP routing table. This is inherently achieved through the use of the following mechanisms, as defined by RFC 4364 (which obsoletes RFC 2547) and illustrated in Figure 2-15:

- VPN-IPv4 addressing to ensure unique addressing and routing separation between VPNs

- Virtual routing and forwarding instances (VRF) to associate VPNs to physical (or logical) interfaces on provider edge (PE) routers

- Multiprotocol BGP to exchange VPN routing information between PE routers

Figure 2-15 *MPLS VPN Architecture*

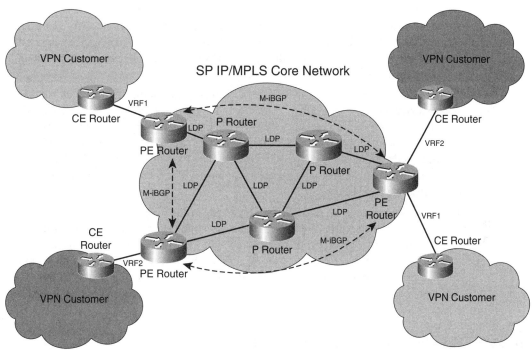

The privacy of an MPLS VPN is, therefore, similar to the privacy provided by traditional Layer 2 WAN infrastructures such as Frame Relay and ATM. The preceding mechanisms provide a secure boundary around and within each MPLS VPN. With no VPN or customer site in common, communication between different VPN or Internet customer sites via the SP network is not possible. RFC 4364 also categorizes the different roles of IP routers within the MPLS VPN architecture as follows:

- **Customer edge (CE) routers:** CE routers are logically part of a customer VPN. Each MPLS VPN site must contain one or more CE routers. Each CE router is connected, via some sort of Layer 2 network link, to one or more provider edge routers. CE routers (with the exception of carrier-supporting-carrier models, discussed further in the "Threats Against the Inter-Provider Edge" section below) use only IP routing (not MPLS) and carry only IP prefixes of the associated the VPN.

- **Provider edge (PE) routers:** PE routers are logically part of the SP's network and peer at Layer 3 with both directly connected CE routers and SP core (P) routers. PE routers represent the edge of the SP IP network and carry both SP core IP prefixes as part of the global IP routing table and customer IP prefixes associated with attached customer VPNs. PE routers use both IP and MPLS for route propagation and packet forwarding with core (P) routers and use only IP with CE routers (except for carrier-supporting-carrier models per the "Threats Against the Inter-Provider Edge" section below). PE routers distribute VPN prefix information to other PE routers using M-BGP. Therefore, as part of the MPLS VPN service, the SP participates in and manages customer routing information.

- **Provider (P) routers:** P routers are also logically part of the SP's network but do not peer or connect to CE routers. P routers represent the core of the SP network and connect to PE routers and other P routers only. P routers carry only SP core IP prefixes as part of the global IP routing table and have no knowledge of customer VPNs. P routers do not need to run M-BGP because they have no customer VPN knowledge. Conversely, P and PE routers share a common IGP and forward customer traffic as MPLS labeled packets.

Unlike an Internet service, an MPLS VPN service is considered trusted—hence, often few or no security measures are applied. The remaining sections review the specific threats and security vulnerabilities against each of the MPLS VPN router categories previously outlined. Note that all of the IP and Layer 2 threats previously outlined apply, in the event an attacker gains IP or Ethernet connectivity, respectively, within the customer VPN.

Threats Against the Customer Edge

Given the IP addressing and routing separation provided by MPLS VPNs, the CE router is only reachable from within the assigned customer VPN. Therefore, by default, the CE router is not susceptible to attacks sourced from outside the customer VPN. The CE router is subject to attacks only in the following scenarios:

- **Internal threats:** Attacks sourced from inside the customer VPN, including the IP and Layer 2 Ethernet threats previously outlined. Also, if an attacker is able to compromise the SP network infrastructure and gain unauthorized access, they may be able to execute PE and P router configuration changes, enabling unauthorized connectivity to the customer VPN and CE router, thereby facilitating internal attacks.

- **External threats:** Attacks sourced from outside the customer VPN. This includes attacks launched through extranet or Internet connections, which, if configured, may provide external IP reachability to the customer VPN or CE router. If the customer VPN does not include extranet or Internet connectivity, this threat does not apply. A management VPN (or extranet) is often used by the SP for management of SP managed CE routers. This enables external reachability between the SP network operations center (NOC) and managed CE routers. However, because external connectivity is provided only to the SP NOC that provides the MPLS VPN service, its trust level is the same as the underlying MPLS VPN service. Hence, only if the SP NOC or network infrastructure is compromised may an attacker gain external IP reachability to the CE router through the management VPN. Of course, if the SP NOC or network infrastructure is compromised, the attacker may be able to launch a much wider attack against the SP network, affecting many customers and services. For more information on the management VPN, refer to Chapter 6, "Management Plane Security."

- **Multi-access broadcast network threats:** As outlined in the "MPLS VPN Threat Models" section above, CE and PE routers are connected via a Layer 2 network link. If this link is a multi-access Layer 2 technology such as an Ethernet switch, then each configured customer VPN must be represented by a distinct VLAN and IP subnet. Otherwise, the CE is subject to spoofed IP attacks (as is the PE). Irrespective, the attacks outlined in the "Threats Against Layer 2 Network Infrastructures" section above may also apply.

Techniques to mitigate the risk of the preceding threats are recommended, as reviewed in Part II.

Threats Against the Provider Edge

PE routers associate physical (or logical) interfaces to customer VPNs using VRFs. VRFs are statically assigned to interfaces and cannot be modified without PE router reconfiguration. Techniques are available for the PE router to dynamically select a VRF (or VPN) based on the IP source address of traffic received from the CE router or through policy-based routing (PBR); however, these are not generally recommended for site-to-site MPLS VPN services, given the threat of spoofed IP attacks, and hence are not widely deployed. Using a static VRF configuration provides complete separation between VPNs, and between VPNs and the SP global IP routing table.

VPN customer packets cannot travel outside of the assigned VPN unless the SP VPN policies explicitly allow for it. Conversely, external packets cannot be injected inside the VPN unless explicitly allowed. RFC 3032 and IETF draft-ietf-mpls-icmp-07 specify the interaction between MPLS and ICMP, and allow for core (P) router generated ICMP messages to be sent to a source IP host within a customer VPN as required, for example, ICMP Time Exceeded (Type 11) and ICMP Destination Unreachable (Type 3) due to "Fragmentation Needed and Don't Fragment was Set" (Code 4).

With the exception of carrier-supporting-carrier configurations detailed in the "Threats Against the Inter-Provider Edge" section below, all MPLS labeled packets received on a VRF interface or a native IP interface (for example, PE-CE) not enabled for MPLS will be discarded. This prevents an attacker from injecting unauthorized packets into the VPN through the use of spoofed MPLS labels. MPLS VPNs also prevent against external attempts to hijack customer VPN routes. If a malicious or compromised CE router advertises to a PE router an IPv4 route tagged with an illegal route target (RT), the PE router will strip the illegal RT off and only advertise the PE-configured export RT list when converted to a VPN prefix and advertised within M-iBGP. Similar attempts to hijack a VPN prefix through eBGP on a native IP external interface also do not pose a risk, because these BGP prefixes use separate subsequent address family identifiers (SAFI). In summary, only a misconfiguration or software vulnerability would allow illegal VPN packets or prefixes to leak into a VPN.

Although the PE router provides routing and address separation between VPNs, it is also reachable by its IP address within each configured VPN. This makes it vulnerable to internal IP attacks sourced from within a VPN. If an Ethernet switch is used to connect the PE router with CE routers, then the Layer 2 Ethernet threats may also apply. Further, given that a PE router aggregates many customers and VPNs, an attack against the PE within one VPN may adversely affect other VPN customers. This is due to the PE router sharing its resources, including CPU, memory, and internal (uplink) interface bandwidth, among the different customer VPNs. Hence, withstanding internal attacks and unauthorized access to the SP network infrastructure, the impact of collateral damage is the most significant threat against MPLS VPNs.

The risk of this threat may increase if the PE router also delivers Internet transit services. In this scenario, an Internet attack against the PE router (or an attached Internet transit customer) may trigger collateral damage within the PE router, thereby adversely affecting VPN customers attached to the same PE router. Collateral damage may cause packet loss, which may then trigger Layer 2 or Layer 3 protocol timeouts. In this event, affected interfaces and routing protocols may fail, resulting in loss of VPN connectivity. Hence, although an MPLS VPN assures routing and addressing separation between VPNs, and between VPNs and the SP global IP routing table, collateral damage remains a very real threat. Techniques to mitigate the risk of collateral damage are available and are reviewed in Part II. Additional threats against the PE router include:

- **MPLS VPN protocol threats:** The MPLS VPN architecture makes use of M-BGP routing on PE routers for VPN route propagation, and LDP on PE and core (P) routers for MPLS label switch path (LSP) establishment between ingress and egress PE routers. MPLS forwarding follows the best paths selected by IP routing except when MPLS traffic engineering (TE) is used. Both M-BGP and LDP are used within the SP IP network only (except inter-provider VPNs per the "Threats Against the Inter-Provider Edge" section below). While M-BGP uses only TCP for IP transport, LDP uses UDP for peer discovery and TCP for distribution of label bindings. PE and CE routers may exchange customer prefixes using a dynamic routing protocol or static routes. Cisco IOS supports BGP, OSPF, RIPv2, and EIGRP on MPLS VPN (PE-CE) interfaces. Hence, from a control plane perspective, PE routers are subject to the same routing and transport protocol threats as outlined in the "Routing Protocol Threats" and "Transport Protocol Attacks" sections above, however, such attacks only affect the customer VPN from which they are sourced. MPLS VPNs may also be deployed using IP transport as opposed to MPLS. Instead of using the MPLS LDP label to reach the M-BGP next hop, an IP tunnel may be used. With IP tunnels, MPLS labels are still allocated and exchanged via M-iBGP for VPN prefixes and, again, used only by the PE routers. MPLS VPNs using IP tunneling are specified in RFC 4023. Security considerations of MPLS VPNs using IP tunnels are outside the scope of this book. For more information on this topic, refer to Section 8 of RFC 4032.

- **IP fragmentation and reassembly threats:** MPLS VPN PE routers impose an 8-byte MPLS header on all nonlocal transit traffic received from connected CE routers. Locally switched transit traffic does not require an MPLS header because the traffic remains local to the PE router and does not transit a core (P) router. Local traffic applies when two or more customer sites within the same VPN are connected to the same PE router. Nevertheless, the addition of the 8-byte MPLS header may result in IP fragmentation of transit VPN traffic. If IP fragmentation is required, a flood of transit VPN traffic may adversely affect the ingress PE router that handles IP fragmentation within its process-level (CPU) slow path. For unicast traffic, any PE fragmented IP packets will be reassembled by the destination address specified in the fragmented packets; hence, only the ingress PE is affected. Conversely, for multicast VPN (MVPN) traffic, which is encapsulated within a 24-byte GRE point-to-multipoint tunnel header (per IETF draft-rosen-vpn-mcast-08.txt) and not within an MPLS header, the egress PE may be required to reassemble the fragmented MVPN (GRE) packets because the tunnel endpoint or destination address is the egress PE. As outlined in the "Resource Exhaustion Attacks" section above, IP routers have a limited number of IP fragment reassembly buffers. Further, fragment reassembly is very CPU intensive. If PE routers are required to fragment VPN traffic or reassemble MVPN traffic, they may be used as an attack vector. Techniques are available to mitigate this risk, as reviewed in Part II. Given the different tunnel header encapsulations used for unicast and multicast VPN traffic (in other words, 8 versus 24 bytes), mitigating unicast fragmentation does not necessarily mitigate the threat of MVPN fragmentation and reassembly.

Threats Against the Provider Core

Excluding the PE router, the SP infrastructure is inherently hidden from MPLS VPN customers given VPN routing separation. Consequently, it is not possible for a VPN customer to launch direct attacks against core (P) routers due to the absence of IP reachability. Nevertheless, core (P) routers remain susceptible to the following transit attacks:

- **TTL expiry attacks:** The default behavior within Cisco IOS copies the IP TTL value (after receive processing) into the MPLS TTL field of any imposed labels. Per RFC 3032, the MPLS TTL field works similarly to the IP TTL in that it is decremented for each MPLS router hop. Note that the encapsulated IP TTL is not decremented by MPLS routers except on the ultimate hop popping (UHP) router, per IETF draft-ietf-mpls-icmp-07. Given the IOS default behavior of propagating the IP TTL into the MPLS TTL, it is possible for VPN customer packets to TTL expire on a core (P) router. In this event, the core (P) router discards the expired packet and generates an ICMP TTL expiry to the original source of the packet using the techniques specified in RFC 3032. By crafting VPN packets to TTL expire within the SP core, an attacker may adversely affect a core (P) router. A sustained attack may trigger a DoS condition.

> **Note** Within an MPLS network, ultimate hop popping (UHP) occurs when
> the *last* router along an MPLS label switch path (LSP) pops the
> MPLS label stack and forwards the encapsulated IP packet
> downstream. Within an MPLS VPN network, UHP occurs at the
> egress PE router. Conversely, penultimate hop popping (PHP) occurs
> when the *next to the last* router along an MPLS label switch path
> (LSP) pops the MPLS label stack and forwards the encapsulated IP
> packet downstream. PHP applies to native MPLS (not MPLS VPN)
> networks. The next to the last router along the MPLS LSP within a
> native MPLS network is referred to as the PHP router.

- **IP options attacks:** As detailed in the "Transit IP Options Attacks" section above, IP
  option packets are normally punted into the router process-level (CPU) slow path for
  data plane forwarding and, hence, may be used to attack transit (or intermediate)
  routers. VPN customer traffic with IP options are MPLS encapsulated at the ingress
  PE and forwarded downstream across the SP core. Core (P) routers forward packets
  based upon the MPLS label and do not consider the IP options header. RFC 3032
  defines a *Router Alert Label*, which is analogous to the *Router Alert* IP option header.
  Therefore, MPLS labeled packets having the Router Alert Label as the top label
  will be handled within the IOS process-level (CPU) slow path of the core (P) router.
  A sustained flood of MPLS packets having the Router Alert Label at the top of the
  MPLS label stack may adversely affect core (P) routers. MPLS VPN PE routers
  running Cisco IOS do not impose the Router Alert Label onto the MPLS label stack
  for any transit VPN customer IP packets, including those having the Router Alert IP
  option header. This eliminates the threat of IP options attacks sourced within an
  MPLS VPN against core (P) routers. However, there is no IETF standard specifying
  IP option processing in MPLS networks. Therefore, different MPLS VPN PE routers
  may function differently with respect to MPLS encapsulation of IP option packets,
  which may introduce such an attack vector against core (P) routers. Note that VPN
  packets with IP Source Route option header will be MPLS label switched across the
  SP network provided the IP addresses specified within the Source Route option header
  are valid within the associated customer VPN routing table. If not, such packets will
  be discarded at the ingress PE.

- **Attacks against SLAs:** Because MPLS VPNs are primarily used for business services,
  traffic classes such as the following with differentiated levels of service (QoS) and
  service-level agreements (SLA) are commonly offered to VPN customers:

  - **Real-time:** Targets applications such as VoIP. It offers low delay, jitter, and
    packet loss. Traffic associated with this class is marked with Class Selector
    DSCP value 5 (0x101).

— **Business Data:** Targets delay-sensitive data applications that are bursty in nature. This class also has a bounded delay, jitter, and loss. Traffic associated with this class is marked with Class Selector DSCP value 4 (0x100).

— **Best Effort:** Represents all traffic not classified as Real-time or Business Data. Delay and jitter characteristics are not specified for this class. Traffic associated with this class is marked with Class Selector DSCP value 0 (0x000).

With IP QoS mechanisms being more commonly deployed within SP networks in support of IP VPN SLAs, recoloring uniformly across the edge is necessary to prevent low-priority traffic from being treated with high priority within the SP network. This applies not only to VPN services but to all services using the shared SP infrastructure. If, for example, best-effort Internet traffic is not recolored at the network edge, it may get improperly classified within the SP network's high-priority traffic classes, including Real-time and Business Data per the preceding examples. This may affect the SP's ability to satisfy SLAs offered to VPN customers. Without packet recoloring at the network edge, attackers may craft packet QoS markings to launch attacks against high-priority traffic classes or steal high-priority services when not entitled to it. For more information on QoS as a security technique, refer to Chapter 4, "Data Plane Security." Protecting QoS services is also discussed in Chapter 7.

Threats Against the Inter-Provider Edge

There are two primary components of the inter-provider MPLS VPN architecture: Carrier Supporting Carrier (CsC) and Inter-AS VPNs. CsC is a hierarchical VPN model that enables downstream service providers (DSP), or customer carriers, to interconnect their geographically dispersed IP or MPLS networks over an upstream SP's MPLS VPN backbone. This eliminates the need for customer carriers to build and maintain their own private MPLS backbone.

Inter-AS is a peer-to-peer model that enables customer VPNs to be extended through multiple provider or multidomain networks. Using Inter-AS VPN techniques, SPs peer with one another and offer end-to-end VPN connectivity over extended geographical locations for those VPN customers who may be out of reach for a single SP. The threats against both of these inter-provider VPN technologies are described next.

Carrier Supporting Carrier Threats

Within the CsC model, customer carriers (or DSPs) may offer Internet or MPLS VPN services, or both, to their customers. The challenge in supporting this model with native MPLS VPNs is the potential number of IP prefixes that must be carried within the associated VRF table on the PE routers. Because the customer carrier is itself an SP, it may carry both the IP prefixes of its own VPN customers and the global Internet routing table if it offers Internet transit services. This potential volume of prefixes would limit the number of customers that may be supported on the PE router because VPN routes is one of the limiting factors in scaling the PE router. The CsC model reduces the number of routes carried within the CsC-PE VRF table by enabling MPLS on the CsC-PE to CsC-CE link between the backbone carrier (CsC-PE) and customer carrier (CsC-CE), as illustrated in Figure 2-16. Applying MPLS on this link eliminates the need for the customer carrier to advertise its external IP and VPN prefixes to the backbone carrier. In this way, the CsC-PE VRF table only carries the internal IP prefixes of the customer carrier.

Within this CsC model, the CsC-PE router is not receiving IP packets from the CsC-PE but rather MPLS labeled IP packets. Label distribution between the CsC-CE and CsC-PE may be done through either MPLS LDP (RFC 3036) or BGP+Labels (RFC 3107). Using only BGP, the CsC control plane operates similarly to native MPLS VPNs. MPLS LDP provides an alternate control plane protocol for label distribution between the CsC-CE and CsC-PE. From a security perspective, the CsC-PE is subject to the same threats as outlined in the "Threats Against the Provider Edge" section above. Similarly, the CsC-CE is subject to the same threats as outlined in the "Threats Against the Customer Edge" section above. The customer carrier (or DSP) is itself an SP and, hence, the CsC-CE is also a core (P) router from the perspective of the DSP's customers. The potential threats against the CsC-CE as a customer carrier core (P) router depends upon whether the DSP offers Internet transit or MPLS VPN services or both. The threats associated with both of these scenarios were described in the "Threats Against IP Network Infrastructures" and "Threats Against the Provider Core" sections above.

Despite the CsC-CE forwarding and receiving MPLS labeled data plane IP packets to and from the CsC-PE router, the CsC-PE assures routing and addressing separation of the customer carrier VPN using the same techniques outlined in the "MPLS VPN Threat Models" section above including VPN-IPv4 addressing, VRF instances, and M-iBGP. The CsC-PEs also implement an automatic MPLS label spoofing avoidance mechanism that prevents the CsC-CE from using spoofed MPLS labels to transmit unauthorized packets into another customer VPN. MPLS packets with spoofed labels that are associated with another customer VPN are automatically discarded upon ingress of the CsC-PE. This is possible because, within Cisco IOS, the labels distributed from the CsC-PE to the CsC-CE using either LDP or RFC 3107 (BGP) are VRF-aware. Hence, CsC provides addressing and routing separation between VPNs equivalent to native MPLS VPNs.

Figure 2-16 *Carrier Supporting Carrier MPLS VPN Model*

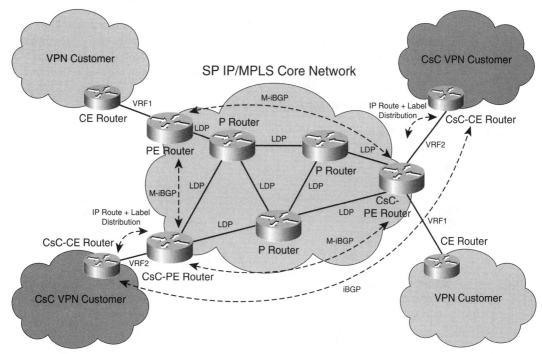

Inter-AS VPN Threats

As outlined at the start of the "Threats Against the Inter-Provider Edge" section, Inter-AS VPNs are intended to expand a single customer VPN through multiple provider networks. Section 10 of RFC 4364 outlines several techniques to achieve this, which are widely known within the industry as options (a), (b), and (c). Each has trade-offs in terms of scalability, security, and service awareness. The following list reviews the security threats associated with each option and assumes that the interconnection between MPLS VPN networks is under the control of different SPs—hence, untrusted. Conversely, if both networks are within the control of one SP, then the security threats outlined may not apply because the interconnect may be considered trusted.

- **Option (a):** Within option (a), the ASBR router of each SP network effectively operates as a PE router. Each ASBR, however, sees the peer ASBR as a CE router. A physical (or logical) interface is used for each VPN that requires inter-provider connectivity. Each interface is then configured with the associated VRF and eBGP routing. This is also applied on both ends of the link, which results in back-to-back (or peer-to-peer) VRFs, as illustrated in Figure 2-17. The IP control and data planes of this model are identical to that of native MPLS VPNs. Hence, this model introduces no additional threats. Each SP network operates independently (no shared IGP) and only IP reachability between Inter-AS VPN sites is exchanged. SPs have no reachability into each other's core networks. The most significant potential threat remains collateral damage and operator misconfiguration. However, the use of distinct interfaces per Inter-AS VPN facilitates resource management within the ASBR per VPN, which may limit any impact of collateral damage.

Figure 2-17 *Inter-AS Option (a): Back-to-Back VRFs*

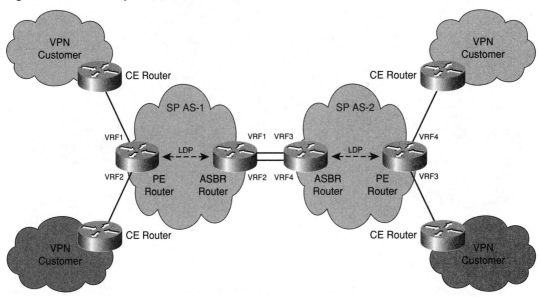

- **Option (b):** Within option (b), the ASBR routers use a single M-eBGP session to exchange all Inter-AS customer VPN prefixes over a single interface between SPs, as illustrated in Figure 2-18. Although this improves ASBR scaling, it prevents resource management within the ASBR per VPN. Hence, there is a much greater risk with option (b) for one Inter-AS VPN to adversely impact connectivity of another. Also, because no VRF configurations are applied on the ASBR, MPLS label spoofing avoidance checks similar to CsC cannot be applied. Thus, routing and address separation between Inter-AS VPNs depends entirely on the peer SP, because VPN label spoofing avoidance techniques are not available with option (b). Given this set of issues, this model is deemed insecure for Inter-AS VPN connectivity between different SPs.

Figure 2-18 *Inter-AS VPN Option (b): M-eBGP*

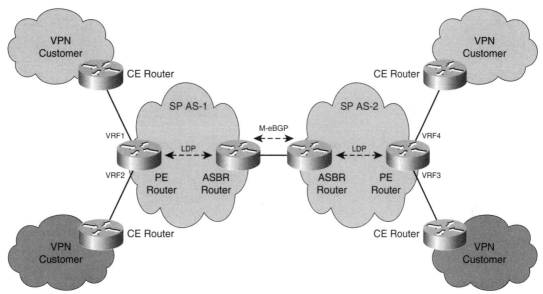

- **Option (c):** Within option (c), the ASBR routers exchange only PE /32 loopback addresses and associated label information using either MPLS LDP or BGP+Labels (RFC 3107). VPN prefixes are then exchanged between route reflectors within each AS using multihop M-eBGP, as illustrated in Figure 2-19. This option requires IP reachability between each SP's route reflectors (RR), which exposes not only the RRs but also the core networks of each peer to one another. Similar to option (b), because no VRF configurations are applied on the ASBR, MPLS label spoofing avoidance checks similar to CsC cannot be applied. Thus, routing and address separation between Inter-AS VPNs depends entirely on the peer SP, because VPN label spoofing avoidance techniques are also not available with option (c). Given this set of issues, this model is deemed insecure for Inter-AS VPN connectivity between different SPs.

Although MPLS VPNs provide addressing and routing separation between VPNs similar to FR and ATM VPNs, they do not provide cryptographic privacy. The next section reviews IPsec and the threats against IPsec VPNs. Note that the MPLS VPN architecture is compatible with the use of cryptography on a CE-CE basis, if that is desired.

Figure 2-19 *Inter-AS VPN Option (c): Multihop M-eBGP*

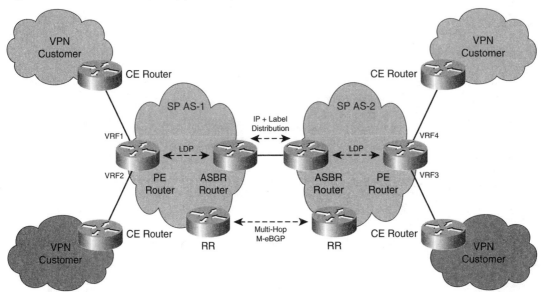

IPsec VPN Threat Models

IPsec is an alternative to MPLS VPNs for site-to-site VPN connectivity. Similar to MPLS VPNs, IPsec VPNs also operate at the network layer and are transparent to upper-layer applications. Conversely, IPsec VPNs are most often deployed as CPE-based Layer 3 VPNs, whereas MPLS VPNs are an SP edge (PE) network-based Layer 3 VPN solution. IPsec VPNs are often chosen instead of MPLS VPNs in cases where end-to-end data encryption is required. Unlike MPLS VPNs, IPsec provides mechanisms for data encryption, integrity, origin authentication, and replay protection.

Further, IPsec also supports remote-access VPNs for mobile workers. Because MPLS VPNs do not directly support a remote-access function, the termination of an IPsec tunnel into an MPLS VPN is available within Cisco IOS today and enables remote access into an MPLS VPN. The MPLS VPN architecture may also be augmented with IPsec when data encryption is required.

The IPsec protocol is based on a suite of IETF open standards developed to protect IP traffic as it travels across the Internet or a shared IP infrastructure. This is achieved using a combination of network protocols, including:

- **Internet Key Exchange (IKE):** Defined by RFC 2409, IKE provides a framework for negotiation of security parameters and establishment of authentication keys. IKEv2 is defined in RFC 4306.

- **Encapsulating Security Payload (ESP):** Defined by RFC 2406, ESP provides a framework for encrypting, authenticating, and securing the integrity of data.

- **Authentication Header (AH):** Defined by RFC 2402, AH provides a framework for authenticating and securing the integrity of data (without confidentiality, because no encryption is provided).

ESP supports symmetric encryption algorithms, including standard 56-bit Data Encryption Standard (DES), the more secure Triple DES (3DES), and the newest and most secure, Advanced Encryption Standard (AES). IPsec uses the IKE protocol to establish secure communication channels, or SAs, between network devices. These SAs are used as a control channel through which IKE negotiates the encryption and authentication methods, and generates shared keys for the encryption algorithms on behalf of the IPsec data plane. The IKE protocol also provides the primary authentication mechanism for IPsec, verifying the identity of the remote system before negotiating the encryption algorithm and keys. The AH protocol verifies the integrity and authenticates the origin of IPsec packets. It can also protect against reply attacks by detecting aged or duplicate packets.

As outlined previously and illustrated in Figure 2-20, IPsec is suitable for both site-to-site and remote-access VPNs. For site-to-site IPsec VPN connectivity, an IPsec-enabled VPN router or firewall will manage IPsec sessions with remote VPN sites. Conversely, for remote-access IPsec VPN connectivity, the mobile-user devices must run IPsec VPN client software. This client software initiates and manages IPsec sessions with the head-end device(s) at the central site(s).

IPsec is a highly complex protocol suite. Attacks against cryptography algorithms, such as brute force attacks for the purposes of data compromise or data insertion, are beyond the scope of this book. IPsec remains, however, subject to other forms of attack, as outlined here:

- **Reconnaissance attacks:** Similar to other protocols, IPsec reconnaissance attacks may be conducted against IP reachable addresses to locate IPsec gateways. Once known, other attacks may be launched against these devices. The most common approach is to port-scan for UDP port 500, the default port used by the IKE protocol in support of IPsec. Tools such as ike-scan may be used during this process, instead of standard protocol scanners, to perform OS fingerprinting on the IPsec implementation down to a vendor, and perhaps even the software version. This information can then be used to find known vulnerabilities against the specific platform and software version. For more information on ike-scan refer to http://www.nta-monitor.com/tools/ike-scan/.

Figure 2-20 *IPsec VPNs*

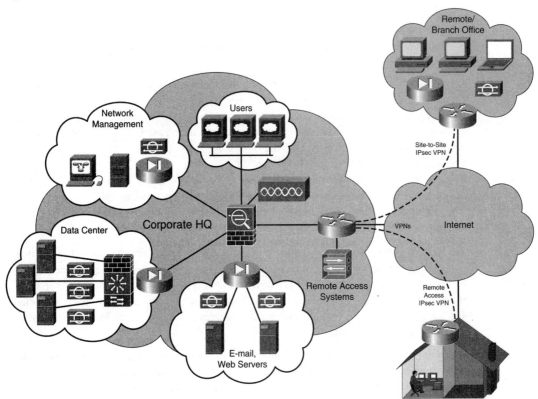

- **DoS attacks:** IP reachability to the IPsec tunnel endpoints is required for session establishment and VPN connectivity. Attackers may use these public addresses to launch DoS attacks against the IPsec devices, including routers, firewalls, and IP hosts. A direct attack simply involves flooding the IPsec gateway with spoofed packets that may consume limited resources. IPsec devices usually handle encryption in specialized hardware accelerators, but other ancillary processes are handled directly within the device CPU. An indirect attack against IPsec might attempt to disrupt the IKE control plane, which uses UDP for transport. A well-known attack against IKEv1 involves flooding the IPsec gateway with numerous bogus IKE initiation requests, causing IKE resources to become depleted (in a similar way that a TCP SYN flood depletes server resources). When this occurs, legitimate VPN connection requests cannot be serviced, and already-established connections may be dropped during rekeying. Further, because IPsec (and IKE) depend on IP reachability, orthogonal attacks against the routing protocol infrastructure may impact the ability of both IPsec and IKE to function correctly.

- **Software vulnerabilities:** Similarly, attackers may use these public addresses to exploit known software vulnerabilities within IPsec code, or the underlying OS, to create a DoS condition. IPsec is complex, and it is not inconceivable that anomalous permutations in header fields or crafted packets could potentially result in a DoS condition.

- **Split tunneling threats:** Split tunneling occurs by configuration, when a remote-access client is permitted to exchange traffic simultaneously with both the shared (public) network and the internal (private) network without first placing all of the network traffic inside the VPN tunnel. This provides an opportunity for attackers on the shared network to compromise the remote computer and use it to gain network access to the internal network.

- **Unauthorized access attacks:** If the IPsec router, firewall, or host is compromised, an attacker may launch a variety of attacks. For example, if digital certificates are used, it should be possible to modify the clock on the IPsec gateway so that it believes all of the certificates are expired, potentially causing a DoS condition. (In theory, this should also be possible through NTP.) If compromised, an attacker may also be able to learn the shared secrets, encryption keys, or digital certificates applied to the IPsec tunnel, potentially allowing access to data within the tunnel via an MiTM attack. Further, if compromised, an attacker may be able to modify the routing configuration to eavesdrop or modify data before it is transmitted through the encrypted tunnel. Default user accounts and passwords are often a good starting point. Software vulnerabilities may provide unauthorized access as well.

The preceding attacks are, for the most part, IPsec-specific. Attacks against unencrypted segments, such as the IP and Layer 2 Ethernet threats described in the "Threats Against IP Network Infrastructures" and "Threats Against Layer 2 Network Infrastructures" sections above, may adversely affect or compromise the data transmitted via the IPsec tunnel. Collateral damage should always be considered as a potential attack vector against any security mechanism, especially when it is as robust as IPsec. The most efficient way to attack IPsec may not be to attack it directly, but rather to attack the surrounding, less-secure infrastructure.

Summary

This chapter reviewed the many threat vectors that exist against IP networks and against Layer 2 Ethernet switches as well as network-based IP VPN protocols. In Part II, you will learn about the techniques that you can apply to mitigate these threats. It is of benefit for everyone (except attackers) to make the Internet and private IP networks as robust and as secure as possible. Security is one of the prime enablers of the new Internet economy. Without security, development of peer-to-peer, business-to-business, and real-time interactions will be impeded.

Review Questions

1 Name the seven layers identified by the OSI reference model, and briefly describe the function of each layer.

Note For more information on the OSI reference model, refer to *Internetworking Terms and Acronyms* on Cisco.com: http://www.cisco.com/en/US/tech/tk1330/tsd_technology_support_technical_reference_chapter09186a00807598b4.html#wp998586.

---

2 Name two types of Layer 2 Ethernet attacks, and briefly describe why these attacks must be locally sourced.

3 Name a widely available computer network tool that may be used to determine intermediate routers along the forwarding path taken by packets transiting an IP network. Briefly describe how this tool works.

4 Identify a search technique that is often used by attackers to discover network hosts, and briefly describe the value it provides.

5 Describe the difference between a crafted IP packet and a malformed IP packet.

6 Identify three different DoS attack approaches, and briefly describe how each functions.

7 When a DoS attack adversely impacts users and network components beyond the intended target, this is referred to as?

8 What MPLS VPN mechanism is used to associate an IP VPN to a physical (or logical) IP interface on a PE router?

9 Which Layer 3 IP VPN technology supports both remote-access VPNs and site-to-site VPNs?

10 Name three primary reasons for an attacker to use spoofed IP source addresses?

Further Reading

Behringer, M., and M. Morrow. *MPLS VPN Security.* Cisco Press, 2005. ISBN: 1-58705-183-4.

Bellovin, S. "A Look Back at 'Security Problems within the TCP/IP Protocol.'" *20th Annual Computer Security Applications Conference.* (Dec. 2004): 229-249. http://www.cs.columbia.edu/~smb/papers/acsac-ipext.pdf.

Bellovin, S. "Routing Threats." Columbia University, April 10, 2006. http://72.14.209.104/search?q=cache:cLj6O5bgUNQJ: www.cs.columbia.edu/~smb/talks/routesec-arin.ps+routing+ security+attacks&hl=en&gl=us&ct=clnk&cd=10.

Bellovin, S. "Towards a TCP Security Option." draft-bellovin-tcpsec-00. IETF, Oct. 15, 2006.

Clark, D. "Vulnerability's of IPsec: A Discussion of Possible Weaknesses in IPsec Implementation and Protocols." SANS Institute, March 14, 2002. http://www.sans.org/reading_room/whitepapers/vpns/ 760.php?portal=a207e10e552a50dba6f2fd8079afd772.

Dubrawsky, I. "Safe Layer 2 Security In-depth – Version 2." Cisco white paper. March 2004. http://www.cisco.com/warp/public/cc/so/cuso/epso/sqfr/sfblu_wp.pdf.

Fang, L. *Security Framework for Provider-Provisioned Virtual Private Networks (PPVPNs).* RFC 4111. IETF, July 2005. http://www.ietf.org/rfc/rfc4111.txt.

Gont, F. "Increasing the Payload of ICMP Error Messages." draft-gont-icmp-payload-00. IETF, Aug. 2, 2004. http://tools.ietf.org/html/draft-gont-icmp-payload-00.

Gont, F. "ICMP Attacks Against TCP." draft-ietf-tcpm-icmp-attacks-01. IETF, Oct. 23, 2006. http://www3.tools.ietf.org/html/draft-ietf-tcpm-icmp-attacks-01.

Greene, B. R., and P. Smith. *ISP Essentials.* Cisco Press, 2002. ISBN: 1-58705-041-2.

Halpern, J., S. Convery, and R. Saville. "SAFE: VPN IPsec Virtual Private Networks in Depth." Cisco white paper. March 2004. http://www.cisco.com/warp/public/cc/so/neso/sqso/safr/savpn_wp.pdf.

Householder, A., and B. King. "Securing an Internet Name Server." CERT/CC, Aug. 2002. http://www.cert.org/archive/pdf/dns.pdf.

Lam, K., D. LeBlanc, and B. Smith. *Assessing Network Security.* Microsoft Press, 2004. ISBN: 0-73562-033-4.

Longstaff, T. A., J. T. Ellis, S. V. Hernan, H. F. Lipson, R. D. McMillan, L. H. Pesante, and D. Simmel. "Security of the Internet." CERT/CC, Aug. 2002. http://www.cert.org/ encyc_article/tocencyc.html.

May, C., J. Hammerstein, J. Mattson, and K. Rush. "Defense in Depth: Foundations for Secure and Resilient IT Enterprises." CERT/CC, Sept. 2006. http://www.cert.org/archive/pdf/Defense_in_Depth092106.pdf.

Ramaiah, A., R. Stewart, and M. Dalal. "Improving TCP's Robustness to Blind In-Window Attacks." draft-ietf-tcpm-tcpsecure-06. IETF, Nov. 7, 2006. http://tools.ietf.org/html/draft-ietf-tcpm-tcpsecure-06.

Retana, A. "Routing Protocols Security." Cisco Systems. Cisco Networkers 2005. Las Vegas. June 19, 2005.

Singh, B., and S. S. Sofat. "Future of Internet Security – IPSec." SecurityDocs.com, Jan. 26, 2005. http://www.securitydocs.com/library/2926.

Tanase, M. "IP Spoofing: An Introduction." SecurityFocus, March 11, 2003. http://www.securityfocus.com/infocus/1674.

Touch, J. "Defending TCP Against Spoofing Attacks." draft-ietf-tcpm-tcp-antispoof-04. IETF, May 15, 2006. http://tools.ietf.org/html/draft-ietf-tcpm-tcp-antispoof-04.

Tulloch, M. "DHCP Server Security (Part 1)." WindowSecurity.com, Oct. 27, 2006. http://www.windowsecurity.com/articles/DHCP-Security-Part1.html.

Tulloch, M. "DHCP Server Security (Part 2)." WindowSecurity.com. Oct. 27, 2006. http://www.windowsecurity.com/articles/DHCP-Security-Part2.html.

Watson, P. A. "Slipping in the Window: TCP Reset Attacks." OSVDB, Dec. 25, 2003. http://osvdb.org/reference/SlippingInTheWindow_v1.0.doc.

White, R., A. Retana, and D. Slice. *Optimal Routing Design*. Cisco Press, 2005. ISBN: 1-58705-187-7.

Willman, M. "NTP Security." GIAG, Aug. 2002. http://www.giac.org/certified_professionals/practicals/gsec/2115.php.

"ICMP Parameters." IANA. http://www.iana.org/assignments/icmp-parameters.

"IP Parameters." IANA. http://www.iana.org/assignments/ip-parameters.

"Managed VPN – Comparison of MPLS, IPSec, and SSL Architectures." Cisco white paper. http://www.cisco.com/en/US/netsol/ns465/networking_solutions_white_paper0900aecd801b1b0f.shtml.

"Network Security Policy: Best Practices White Paper." (Doc. ID: 13601.) Cisco white paper. http://www.cisco.com/warp/public/126/secpol.html.

"Securing IP Multicast Services in Triple-Play and Mobile Networks." Cisco white paper. http://www.cisco.com/en/US/products/ps6552/ products_white_paper0900aecd80557fd4.shtml.

"VLAN Security White Paper." Cisco white paper. http://www.cisco.com/en/US/products/hw/switches/ps708/ products_white_paper09186a008013159f.shtml.

"VPN Architectures—Comparing MPLS and IPSec." Cisco white paper. http://www.cisco.com/en/US/netsol/ns341/ns121/ns193/ networking_solutions_white_paper09186a008009d67f.shtml.

In this chapter, you will learn about the following:

- The principles of defense in depth and breadth, and how these principles apply to IP network traffic plane security

- IP network element interface concepts and how these apply to IP network traffic plane security

- IP network edge and core security concepts, how these differ for enterprise and SP environments, and how these apply to IP network traffic plane security

CHAPTER 3

IP Network Traffic Plane Security Concepts

IP traffic plane concepts provide the mechanisms from which comprehensive IP network security strategies can be implemented. Before discussing detailed security techniques and implementations for each of the four IP network traffic planes, which occur in Chapters 4 through 7, it is useful to look at how cohesive, integrated security policies based on IP network traffic plane concepts can be developed. The first important concept is that of defense in depth and breadth, and specifically, how the principles of defense in depth and breadth apply to IP traffic plane security. The next concept involves the special relationships between the network edge and core and the ability to classify packets and enforce security policies.

Principles of Defense in Depth and Breadth

The concepts of "defense in depth" or, more appropriately, "defense in depth and breadth" are often used by network security professionals to operationalize "layered defense" techniques for protecting network assets. Defense in depth became popularized in the late 1990s under research conducted by military and intelligence organizations as well as by various universities. Knowing that the concepts of defense in depth were formalized in a military environment aids in the understanding of how these techniques arose. Military strategies are typically defined to counter specific adversaries, weapons, and objectives. In the networking world, these concepts were adopted for cyber adversaries under certain attack scenarios and led to the development of various defensive strategies.

Initially, defense in depth applied multiple *layers* of defense technologies—including network-based techniques such as access lists and encryption, security appliances such as firewalls and intrusion detection systems (IDS), and software programs such as antivirus, host-based intrusion detection, and personal firewalls—throughout an enterprise network to protect sensitive information and business-critical resources. In theory, greater security is provided by forcing the attacker to penetrate these multiple layers, devices, or software elements, often of different implementations (for example, a hardware-based firewall and then a software-based personal firewall), such that if one layer is compromised, secondary layers are available to mitigate the attack. This approach is predicated on the expectation that adding multiple layers increases the difficulty and skills required to successfully attack the target. Defense in depth was later expanded to encompass more than hardware and software systems by incorporating personnel and operational requirements as well.

Defense in depth is often illustrated through the use of analogies taken from the physical world and then (oftentimes inappropriately) extended to the cyber world. One of the most popular examples describes a high-security facility with fences (perhaps multiple, separated by some distance), locked doors, guards inside the doors, and video surveillance cameras. Although this seems appealing as an analogy, these physical concepts do not necessarily translate well in the cyber world. Most obvious of course is the *physical* aspect of the analogy. IP reachability and connectivity to the Internet means that anyone with a networked personal computer (PC) located anywhere in the world can target any other Internet-connected device. Conversely, in the real world, you must be physically proximate to the target to attack it. Less obvious, perhaps, is the "asymmetry" afforded attackers in the cyber world. A single PC or a single person who has organized a "zombie army" of compromised PCs (that is, a roBOT NETwork or botnet as it is commonly referred to) may cause great damage with little or no active involvement of others or expenditures of funds. In the real world, a single person is limited in destructive capability and generally requires the active cooperation of others to launch a large-scale attack.

Perhaps least translatable is the notion of *spectrum*. In the physical world, visible, thermal, acoustic, and seismic sensors, all guarding the same valuable object, provide the ability to measure parameters in different spectra, which improves the protection capabilities over a single spectrum sensor. In the networking world, most security revolves around scrutinizing and controlling IP packets. It is often difficult to find a measurable analog to spectrum in the cyber world. Monitoring parameters such as CPU and memory utilization of devices and enforcing application behaviors may be useful for detecting (and preventing) some types of attack. Finally, it is not often that a protection mechanism in the physical world actually becomes a liability to defense, but this happens often in the cyber world, specifically with respect to DoS attacks. (This concept is discussed in more detail in the "What Are Defensive Layers" section.)

Understanding Defense in Depth and Breadth Concepts

When properly understood and implemented, defense in depth and breadth techniques are very useful for constructing and deploying network security policies from an IP network traffic plane perspective. This requires a clear understanding of the most important defense in depth and breadth concepts. This can be accomplished by addressing the following questions in the context of IP network traffic planes:

- What needs to be protected?
- What are defensive layers?
- What is the operational envelope of the network?
- What is your organization's operational model?

Let's look at these important questions separately.

What Needs to Be Protected?

Determining what needs to be protected is not necessarily as straightforward as it seems. Some organizations may need to protect assets such as trade (or military) secrets and other intellectual property. Others need to protect e-commerce site access (which could be bandwidth or server resources or both), credit card or customer databases, and health care records. Service providers (SP), on the other hand, often have very different needs because their value is in the network and services they provide. Ensuring network and service availability is paramount for SPs, so they need to protect network assets, including IP routers, switches, VoIP gateways, security appliances, and other network assets such as DNS servers, Internet peering links, and billing servers.

As is most often the case, you will need to expend some effort to deploy security measures, and when they are deployed, you will incur a level of administrative overhead and operational inconvenience, and may also find that there is an impact to network performance. Not everything can be protected equally, and you will need to make trade-offs that fully consider the risk and the cost of applying the security measures needed to mitigate the risk to acceptable levels.

In addition, orthogonal linkages between high-value assets and peripheral or relatively obscure services or devices may expose vulnerabilities that enable indirect attacks. These indirect attacks can cause substantially the same kind of impacts against a target that has only been protected against direct attack. DNS is a classic example from the e-commerce world. You may expend significant resources and money protecting your web servers but give little consideration to the DNS servers, leaving them vulnerable to any number of malicious attacks. Without DNS, the availability of the web site that itself was the primary focus of your security efforts will be severely impacted. ARP tables and routing tables are good examples of control plane elements that are often attacked not for the direct impact but for the indirect, collateral damage effects that these attacks cause on surrounding systems.

In summary, the key concepts when determining what needs to be protected are:

- Understand where the value is in the network and how this translates to the primary services and devices that must be protected.

- Understand the interrelationships between various network services and devices and how each may be leveraged to indirectly target the high-value resource.

What Are Defensive Layers?

Defense in depth and breadth describes the use of multiple *layers*, which are often implemented as distinct devices such as routers, firewalls, and intrusion protection systems (IPS), or as software such as antivirus or personal firewall applications. In most cases, this granularity is too coarse, because within each of these devices or applications themselves, multiple operations may be considered as providing some layer of protection. When considering a router, for example, packets ingressing an interface are affected by a number of hard-coded and configurable processes both before and after the routing function occurs. Figure 3-1 illustrates the typical packet processing "order of operation" that Cisco IOS routers employ. (Some variations in feature ordering may occur in specific router platforms and IOS software releases.)

Figure 3-1 *Cisco IOS Feature Order of Operations*

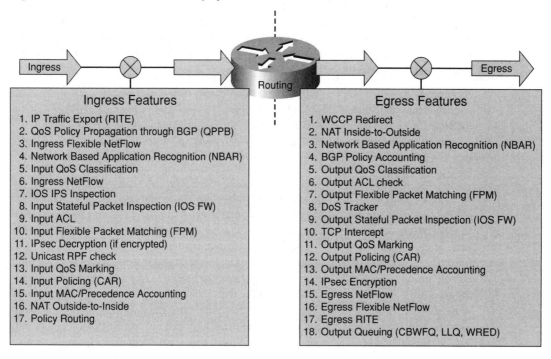

Each of these features, when implemented, must be considered as a *layer* because each may potentially impact the forwarding of the packet (permit, deny, rate-limit, mark/color), and in fact each operation may impact the performance of the router (CPU and memory, throughput, and so on). It is also important to note that each upstream layer may also have an impact on the effectiveness and performance of other downstream layers in the overall system.

Layers are selected to protect against specific attack vectors. By considering each feature as an individual layer rather than considering the entire device as a layer, you can clearly distinguish the purpose that each layer fulfils. This enables you to develop a security architecture that addresses both depth and breadth aspects, as required. But what are these concepts of depth and breadth? Depth and breadth can be described as follows:

- Depth—When considering a single service, if one layer is added to protect against a particular attack vector, and then a second layer is added to protect against the same attack vector, the second layer provides *depth* against that specific attack vector. Depth is generally used to provide redundant layers such that if one is compromised, the target remains protected by the secondary layers. An example of depth principles would be using a router-based ACL to permit traffic only to TCP port 80 of a web server, and then deploying a host-based ACL on the web server that also restricts inbound traffic to only TCP port 80.

- Breadth—When considering a single service, if one layer is added to protect against one specific attack vector that could compromise the service, and then a second layer is added to protect against a completely different attack vector against that same service, these layers are considered as providing *breadth* for attacks against that service. For example, consider the BGP service. One layer might configure MD5 authentication on each BGP peer to mitigate the risk of router advertisement spoofing. Adding an edge ACL to permit only valid BGP peers from communicating protects the BGP service from the separate and distinct attack vector by preventing non-BGP peers from reaching the service. (For more information on ACLs and MD5 authentication, refer to Chapter 4, "Data Plane Security," and Chapter 5, "Control Plane Security," respectively.)

When combined, defense in depth and breadth aim to mitigate as many potential attack vectors as practical, while at the same time providing backup protection if any one defensive layer is compromised.

A single layer may also provide protection against multiple attack vectors. When viewed from an IP network traffic plane perspective, a single layer may be effective in protecting (or have an impact on) multiple traffic planes. In IOS, for example, features such as interface ACLs and Unicast Reverse Path Forwarding (uRPF) affect every packet ingressing an interface and therefore have an impact on all four traffic planes. Other features such as Control Plane Policing (CoPP) or Receive ACLs (rACL) apply to punted traffic only and therefore affect only control plane and management plane traffic. (For more information on ACLs and uRPF, refer to Chapter 4. For more information on CoPP and rACL, refer to Chapter 5.)

It is critical to note that simply adding more layers is not always beneficial. Each layer, although intended to provide protection against a specific attack vector, may also *enable* additional attack vectors that previously did not exist without that layer having been deployed. That is, adding a protection layer against an attack vector in one domain may also *create* a new attack vector that may be exploitable in another domain. Stateful security devices such as firewalls and IPS systems often have this effect when improperly sized for different attack conditions, potentially enabling a DoS attack vector where one previously did not exist. The entire *system* must be considered when developing a layered strategy.

In addition, adding one type of security layer may negate the effectiveness of another type of security layer. For example, encryption is often added to provide confidentiality and integrity protection for data traversing unsecured networks. However, this same encryption layer negates the effectiveness (against certain attack vectors) of intrusion detection and protection systems (IDS/IPS) by making payload inspection impossible.

In summary, the key concepts regarding defensive layers are as follows:

- Understand which layers are available per device.
- Understand what attack vectors each layer is effective against.

- Understand how adding layers impacts each IP network traffic plane.
- Understand how layers can be combined to provide *depth* and *breadth* as a system.
- Understand the implications and interactions each layer has on other layers and the system as a whole.

Chapters 4 through 7 provide details on how different techniques may provide distinct layers of protection for each of the IP traffic planes.

What Is the Operational Envelope of the Network?

All network devices have certain performance characteristics that can be measured in terms of parameters such as bits per second of throughput, packets per second of forwarding, transactions per second of application processing, and so on as might be relevant to a particular device. For most network devices, performance characteristics are impacted not only by the type and number of features that are enabled, but also by the type and quantity of network traffic being processed. These performance characteristics then define the operational envelope of the device. The combination of devices within a network topology in aggregate implies that the overall system also has an operational envelope. Whereas it is necessary to understand the operational envelope for your devices and the overall network under ideal or normal operating conditions, knowing these operational envelopes is especially crucial under attack conditions.

In Chapter 1, "Internet Protocol Operations Fundamentals," you learned that the forwarding functions of a router may be implemented in hardware (fast path) or software (slow path). This is also true of the security features. All devices, security and otherwise, have performance limits. Each feature enabled on a device may potentially have some impact on its performance. Depending on the feature and its implementation method (hardware or software), this impact may be negligible or significant to the operational envelop of the device. This is one reason why the previous section stressed that enabling a feature (layer) for protection may actually produce adverse effects or enable a new attack surface that makes the overall system more susceptible to attack. In addition, enabling a particular security feature on one type of device (or router platform) may have a far different impact than enabling the same type of feature on a different type of device (or router platform).

Oftentimes, network security architectures are developed where certain features are enabled full-time to create a security baseline, and then additional features are enabled dynamically, under attack conditions. For example, an SP may enable on-the-fly (in reaction to an attack) an ACL on the interface serving the customer under attack. In this scenario, two conditions are occurring simultaneously, both of which may have an impact on the operational envelop of the device or network. First, an attack condition is underway. Thus, the packet rate, packet size, or packet characteristics (for example fragments, IP header options, and so on) may be much different from what they are under normal conditions. Second, the addition of the ACL may change the device performance. This is why it is critical to understand the operational envelop of your devices and networks when specific features are enabled, and under normal and attack conditions. At some point, under certain conditions, every device can reach some resource exhaustion state. It is critical to understand how each device behaves when certain features are enabled under adverse conditions. This is why it is critical to understand the operational envelop of your devices and networks when specific features are enabled, and under both normal and attack conditions. For DoS attacks in particular, the most destructive approach possible is often used.

In summary, the key concepts in determining the operational envelope of the network are as follows:

- Understand the base operational envelop of the device.

- Understand how enabling each defensive layer impacts the operational envelope, especially under adverse conditions.

What Is Your Organization's Operational Model?

An organization's operational model can help or hinder network security efforts. In many enterprise organizations, for example, the network staff and the security staff belong to separate groups. The network staff typically focuses on the routers and switches and has a good understanding of routing protocols such as OSPF, EIGRP, and BGP. Conversely, the security staff typically focuses on things such as firewalls and IDS/IPS devices, mail filters, and antivirus software. The security staff typically has limited hands-on knowledge of router operations and routing protocols (especially BGP), but rather is more familiar with end-station operating systems, servers, and some applications and the configuration and monitoring of their security systems.

When these operational impediments occur, the potential synergy that must exist between routing and security is often lost. For example, a good IP addressing plan and routing scheme can greatly enhance the ability of the security staff to efficiently configure firewall rules. Avoiding the use of default routes also enhances security. Many other examples exist.

In summary, the key concept here is to understand that networking and security operations must be coordinated and that a team approach will maximize the effectiveness of both groups. After all, both groups have a vested interest in network availability, which is directly linked with network security.

IP Network Traffic Planes: Defense in Depth and Breadth

From a defense in depth and breadth perspective, many features are available to protect each IP traffic plane and its protocols. Which specific features you select will depend on many aspects. Defense in depth and breadth should be considered when selecting these mechanisms to ensure that the important attack vectors are adequately covered (breadth), redundant mechanisms are applied where appropriate (depth), and interdependencies between components are considered to mitigate the risk of one attack vector leveraging some component to indirectly target another component (depth and breadth). In addition, the mechanisms selected must be supportable from an architectural standpoint and an operational standpoint. Chapters 4 through 7 provide detailed descriptions of many protection mechanisms available for each IP traffic plane. In order to provide some context for the mechanisms detailed in those chapters, each IP traffic plane is briefly described in turn from a defense in depth and breadth perspective.

Data Plane

As you learned in Chapter 1, the data plane contains *customer* application traffic generated by hosts, clients, servers, and applications that use the network as transport. Thus, data plane traffic should never have source or destination IP addresses that belong to any network elements such as routers and switches, but rather should be sourced from and destined to end devices such as PCs and servers. Network elements are optimized to forward data plane traffic as quickly as possible. As you learned in Chapter 2, many types of attacks attempt to use data plane traffic to indirectly influence other IP traffic planes (most often the control plane) to disrupt network operations. Data plane packets with IP header options, low TTL values, or spoofed source IP addresses belonging to the control plane are examples of where this may occur.

From a defense in depth and breadth perspective, the primary role of selecting protection mechanisms is to ensure that these data plane packets stay within the data plane and, further, are forwarded downstream only if authorized. Chapter 4 provides detailed descriptions of many mechanisms that may be used to protect the data plane, each with its own benefits and drawbacks.

Control Plane

The control plane is described in Chapter 1 as the logical entity associated with router processes and functions used to create and maintain the necessary intelligence about the state of the network and a router's interfaces. The control plane includes network protocols, such as routing, signaling, and link-state protocols that are used to build and maintain the operational state of the network, and provide IP connectivity between IP hosts.

Control plane traffic is generated and processed by network elements such as switches and routers. Thus, the source and destination IP addresses (for Layer 3 control plane packets) should correspond to the addresses of the network elements themselves. As described in Chapter 1, control plane packets are ultimately processed as *receive-adjacency* traffic by participating network elements and thus are processed by *slow path* mechanisms (for example, the IOS process level). Under normal operating conditions, the load placed on the network element by control plane traffic is relatively small. However, as you learned in Chapter 2, attacks may target the control plane, either directly or indirectly, to disrupt network element operations. If the network element CPU is busy processing bogus packets, resources may be unavailable for processing legitimate control plane traffic. Control plane failures may then prevent IP reachability within the data, management, and services planes.

From a defense in depth and breadth perspective, the primary goal for selecting protection mechanisms for the control plane is to ensure that the IOS process level resources, as well as slow path and receive-adjacency resources, are available for use by legitimate control plane functions. This is accomplished by doing the following:

- Ensuring the integrity of the control plane such that only legitimate control plane traffic is processed by the network element

- Ensuring that other IP traffic plane packets that may use the slow path (such as exception data plane packets, as described in the preceding section) do not overwhelm the IOS process level resources

Chapter 5 provides detailed descriptions of many different security techniques available to protect the control plane.

The control plane is unique in that it is at the same time both something that must be itself *protected* and something that facilitates protection of other IP traffic planes. That is, from a defense in depth and breadth perspective, there are control plane–based security techniques that are quite important for protecting the data plane, management plane, and services plane. Full details of these and many other control plane security techniques are described in detail in Chapters 4 and 5.

Management Plane

The management plane is the logical entity that describes the traffic used to access, manage, and monitor all of the network elements. The management plane supports all required provisioning, maintenance, and monitoring functions for the network. Like all other IP traffic planes, management plane traffic can be handled in-band with all other IP traffic. But, unlike other IP traffic planes, the management plane also has the capability to be carried via a separate out-of-band (OOB) management network to provide alternate reachability in the event that the primary in-band IP management path is not available. OOB management access is typically available through a console port or auxiliary port, or, depending on the device, a separate management Ethernet port. Each of these OOB access methods has its own security requirements, and defense in depth and breadth can be applied here as well.

Management plane traffic is both generated and consumed by network elements such as switches and routers and by servers running provisioning and monitoring applications, billing systems, security alerting systems, and other management applications. Thus, the source and destination IP addresses should correspond to the addresses of the network elements themselves, and a select range of trusted management devices. As described in Chapter 1, management plane packets ultimately are processed as receive-adjacency traffic by destination network elements, similar to control plane packets. Thus, management plane traffic is processed at the IOS process level, like control plane traffic, when these packets arrive at the network element itself. As you learned in Chapter 2, attacks may target the management plane for reconnaissance purposes, to gain unauthorized access to a device, or to disrupt network element operations. If the network element CPU is busy processing bogus packets, resources may be unavailable for processing legitimate management plane traffic.

From a defense in depth and breadth perspective, protection mechanisms selected for the management plane must prevent unauthorized access and ensure that the IOS process level, as well as slow path and receive-adjacency resources are available for use by legitimate management plane functions. Some of the same mechanisms that are useful for the data plane and control plane are also useful for the management plane. Additional features are available to provide depth and breadth to the overall protection scheme that are specific to the management plane. Chapter 6, "Management Plane Security," provides detailed descriptions of many security techniques available to protect the management plane.

Services Plane

Network convergence has led to multiple services of differing characteristics, running over a common IP network core. The services plane is the logical entity that enables network-based services and includes all traffic requiring dedicated network-based services, such as IP VPNs (for example, MPLS, IPsec), private-to-public interfacing (NAT, firewall, and IDS/IPS), QoS (voice and video), and many others. Services plane traffic generally requires high-touch traffic handling and as a result often introduces greater network complexity.

Services plane traffic is generally created by customer-based clients, servers, and applications that use the network as transport and thus would normally appear as *transit* traffic to the routers. Because of the specialized services being applied, however, routers and other forwarding devices typically use dedicated hardware or forwarding mechanisms to handle services plane traffic. That is, services plane traffic may be processed in a very different manner from regular data plane traffic, or even control or management plane traffic. For example, IPsec VPNs require high-speed encryption and decryption services, which are usually performed in dedicated hardware optimized for this purpose.

From a defense in depth and breadth perspective, then, the primary goal for selecting protection mechanisms for services plane traffic is to ensure that the specialized resources are available for use by legitimate services plane traffic. This is accomplished by doing the following:

- Ensuring the integrity of the services plane such that only legitimate traffic is allowed within specific service types
- Ensuring that one service type does not impact any other service type
- Ensuring that other IP traffic planes do not impact services plane traffic

Chapter 7, "Services Plane Security," provides detailed descriptions of security techniques available to protect the services plane.

The services plane also can have unique requirements. When services are delivered (for example, MPLS VPN services), potential attack vectors may exist against the traffic within the service itself as well as against the delivery of the service. Hence, security techniques both within the services plane and in protection of the services plane are required to fully mitigate the risk of attacks against the service. These types of considerations are among those discussed in Chapter 7.

Network Interface Types

In a perfect world, network elements would operate in ideal conditions and simply be required to forward well-behaved data and services plane packets through a network built and managed by optimized control and management planes. Unfortunately, this is not a perfect world and network elements must operate in more hostile and unpredictable environments where network attacks (intentional), misconfigurations (unintentional), and software and hardware failures stress the real-world operational environment. From a security perspective, this means that you must take proactive steps to make the network elements themselves more resilient to these events. In total, network elements include devices such as routers, LAN switches, wireless access points, firewalls, IDS/IPS components, load balancers, deep packet inspection components, web servers, clients, and anything else that forwards, inspects, generates, or processes IP packets within any one of the IP traffic planes. This book focuses on routers as an example of the type of considerations that are necessary from a defense in depth and breadth perspective to properly secure an IP network and the individual network elements.

A router must be able to forward well-behaved packets and gracefully handle harmful packets. Cisco routers and IOS software have both evolved over time to include more built-in and configurable security functions that allow these devices to be protected in the operational environment. Some of these capabilities are platform dependent, while others are generic across all IOS routers. Further, some of the platform-dependent capabilities are designed for particular router architectures (central versus distributed processing, for example). From a defense in depth and breadth standpoint, it is essential to understand both the performance envelop of the platform and the operating environment. Both of these are critical for developing appropriate security strategies.

For routers, externally sourced packets can *physically* enter a router only through physical network interfaces. Physical interfaces are those that include a data link layer with an associated link-layer encapsulation. However, other types of *interfaces* exist on routers as well. These, of course, are the logical interface types. Although logical interfaces do not have a data link layer, they are real in the sense that they are IP reachable, keep track of associated packet statistics, may have certain features that can be applied to them, including security features, and packets that logically use these interfaces can be impacted by these features.

From a defense in depth and breadth perspective, all interface types, both physical and logical, must be considered in order to develop an overall security strategy. With this in mind, it makes sense to fully categorize these interfaces. For physical interfaces, three types exist: external, internal, and OOB interfaces. For logical interfaces, four types exist:

loopback, null0, services, and receive interfaces. Each of these interface types is illustrated in Figure 3-2.

Figure 3-2   *External, Internal, Out-of-Band, Loopback, Null0, Service, and Receive Interfaces*

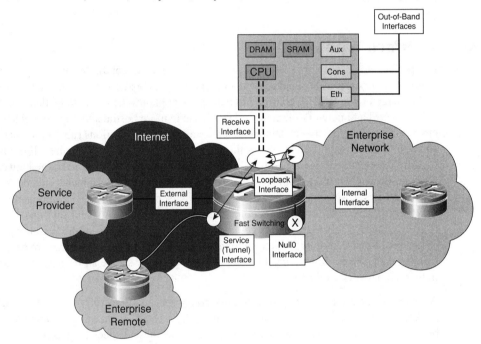

Not all of these types of interfaces need be present or configured in every router. However, recognizing which types do exist and understanding how each differs from the other allows for the most appropriate security strategies to be developed. Each of these interface types are described next in turn.

Physical Interfaces

Physical interfaces include the types external, internal, and out-of-band. Each of these is described next. Note that physical interfaces include those with any number of IP subinterfaces such as FR DLCIs, ATM VCs and Ethernet VLANs encapsulations as well as when multiple physical interfaces are bonded into a single IP interface (for example, MLPPP link bundling). In all cases, defense in depth and breadth concepts must be applied to each distinct IP interface.

External Interfaces

Security practitioners who work with firewalls and other security devices have always understood the concept of external and internal interfaces (or inside and outside, as they are often called). Data-link interfaces on routers may be considered as external or internal based on the trust relationship of connected devices. Routers that provide connectivity between two (or more) different administrative domains will have (at least) one interface in each domain. From the perspective of the administrator of the router, the connection to the uncontrolled domain is considered to be an external (or outside) interface. Routers such as these are also referred to as border or edge routers. For enterprises, this is commonly found at the Internet boundary, but could just as easily be representative of a router (or switch) that connects different organizations within a single company, or an extranet connection. For SPs, this describes essentially every edge router in the network.

Interfaces designated as external provide the first and typically the best opportunity to describe the traffic that should be crossing this untrusted boundary (both ingress and egress), in such terms as expected source and destination address ranges, traffic types, rates, and others. That is, it should be possible to describe the appropriate traffic according to each IP traffic plane that should be seen at each external interface. For example, external interfaces may be expected to see only data plane traffic and a small subset of control plane traffic. Taking this approach allows you to define customized traffic policies that are most effective for your network topology, traffic behavior, and organizational mission. Figure 3-3 illustrates this concept.

Figure 3-3 *IP Traffic Plane Relationships to Router Interfaces*

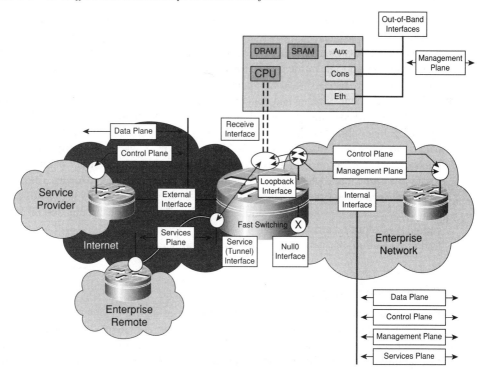

As you can see in Figure 3-3, classifying packets within their respective IP traffic planes helps to establish the security policies that will be carried throughout the network. What traffic types should be seen in the data plane? Similarly, what protocols are used within the control plane and management plane? Should there be any control plane or management plane traffic on the external interface? Can these specific traffic types be filtered with ACLs or rate limiting, or is another technique required? What other security techniques are available to be applied to external interfaces, and do these techniques affect transit or receive traffic or both?

Internal Interfaces

Referring to Figure 3-2 again, from the perspective of the administrator of a router, connections to routers within the same domain are considered to be internal (or inside) interfaces. For enterprises, the Internet boundary (or edge) router has at least one internal interface and one external interface. The internal interfaces only connect to routers within a single organization. For SPs, internal interfaces represent the backbone uplinks on every edge router in the network, plus all interfaces of core routers within the SP infrastructure that provide connectivity between border routers. Core routers are unique in that all data-link interfaces in the router are internal interfaces. Routers with all internal interfaces may also be found in enterprise networks.

When an interface is distinguished as internal, it defines the frame of reference for traffic crossing this trusted interface boundary, again in terms such as expected source and destination address ranges, traffic types, rates, and others. Thus, it should be possible to describe the appropriate traffic according to each IP traffic plane that should be seen at each internal interface. As illustrated in Figure 3-3, internal interfaces see not only data plane traffic, but also control plane and management plane traffic, and may see services plane traffic as well. Classifying packets relative to the IP traffic planes helps to establish the optimal policies and identify the appropriate security features necessary to implement a defense in depth and breadth security architecture. Note, however, that just because an interface is defined as internal does not mean traffic entering the interface is trusted. Nor is it safe to assume that routers with only internal interfaces are secure. As described in Chapter 2, many attack methods target core routers using transit attacks such as TTL expiry and reflection attacks using source address spoofing. Just because a router should not see a certain type of traffic arriving via an internal interface does not mean it will not see this traffic. Protection mechanisms are still required on internal interfaces.

Out-of-Band Interfaces

Finally, routers and other network elements usually contain OOB interfaces for management purposes. Unlike the other IP traffic planes, the management plane has the capability to be carried via a separate OOB management network to provide alternate reachability in the event the primary in-band IP (management plane) path is lost. OOB access is typically available through a console port, auxiliary port, and, depending on the device, a dedicated management Ethernet port. As illustrated in Figure 3-2, these special OOB interfaces typically have direct access to the route processor. Hence, these interface types have their own special security requirements.

As illustrated in Figure 3-3, OOB interfaces should only see management plane traffic. In addition, this management plane traffic should be within a well-defined range of source addresses, protocols, and applications—for example, OOB interfaces should never receive traffic from external sources. As previously noted, because receive-adjacency management plane traffic is processed at the IOS process level, and because the management plane is critical to the proper operation of the network, from a defense in depth and breadth perspective, protection mechanisms must be applied to both in-band and OOB management plane traffic.

Logical Interfaces

Whether explicitly configured or not, all network elements have certain logical interfaces. In general, four types of logical interfaces exist on IOS routers: loopback, null0, services, and receive interfaces. Depending on the device, these logical interfaces may be configurable to one degree or another. Only if configured, are some installed within the local CEF table as receive adjacencies or IP next hops. It is important to realize that these interfaces exist in network devices, and that they must be accounted for in the overall network security architecture. It is also important to realize that these interfaces have specialized security requirements. In some cases, they may also be used to enable other security mechanisms that are useful in protecting IP traffic planes. These aspects are discussed in detail in Chapters 4 through 7. Each of these logical interface types are described next.

Loopback Interfaces

IOS supports the configuration of loopback interfaces, which are virtual interfaces defined in software only with no associated data link layer physical interface. Because it is a logical instantiation versus a physical one, a loopback interface is *always up* and thus it is considered a best practice to tie control and management plane protocols such as OSPF, BGP, IS-IS, SNMP, NTP, SSH and others to loopback interfaces. This concept is illustrated in Figure 3-3. Also as illustrated in Figure 3-3, when used for control plane and management plane functions, loopback interfaces are tied to the receive path and, hence, packets destined to these interfaces are always processed at the IOS process level on the route processor.

From a defense in depth and breadth standpoint, it is appropriate to enable or disable certain features on loopback interfaces to protect the route processor. Loopback interfaces are also used as endpoints for some services plane traffic, and may be used in conjunction with tunnel interfaces for this purpose as well.

Null0 Interface

IOS also supports a null0 interface. Like the loopback interface, the null0 interface is also a virtual interface that is *always up*, but unlike the loopback, it can never forward or encapsulate traffic. This null0 interface is always defined and installed within the CEF table. Its purpose is to provide within the CEF (fast path) forwarding process a mechanism to discard unwanted packets. As you will see in Chapters 4 and 5, many control plane–based security mechanisms take advantage of the null0 interface in this regard. The null0 interface cannot be assigned an IP address and only one feature can be modified on the null0 interface—whether ICMP Destination Unreachable (Type 3) messages are generated for discarded packets.

Services Interfaces

Services interfaces include tunnel interfaces, dynamic virtual tunnel interfaces, and other services-oriented logical interfaces. Unlike loopback and null0 logical interfaces, however, services interfaces *do* provide the mechanisms to encapsulate specific packets inside of a configured transport protocol such as IP-in-IP, GRE, or IPsec. In this way, instantiations such as tunnel interfaces provide a convenient logical interface on which to configure services without being tied to any specific data link layer physical interface. This allows the creation of highly available network architectures that use routing to control data forwarding paths in the case where any physical interface may go down. When used in this manner, and as illustrated in Figure 3-3, tunnel encapsulation and decapsulation operations may or may not require slow path processing at the IOS process level within the route processor. In addition, tunneled packets may bypass other configured security mechanisms, thus potentially requiring the addition of other security features to provide defense in depth and breadth security.

Receive Interface

In Chapter 1, you were introduced to the concepts of receive-adjacencies and receive packets. Receive-adjacencies are associated with the IP addresses that a router considers as belonging to itself. In some cases, these are the IP addresses that you configure on data link layer physical (external and internal) and logical (loopback and tunnel) interfaces. In other cases, these are packets destined to certain reserved IP addresses within broadcast and multicast ranges. Also as described in Chapter 1, exception conditions may also cause data plane packets to be punted for handling at the IOS process level (route processor) instead of by fast path forwarding mechanisms (interrupt process or ASIC hardware). In router architectures, this is often considered logically as the *receive interface* to the IOS process level on the route processor. Considering this as a receive interface provides a logical context within the defense in depth and breadth framework to define the appropriate protection schemes necessary to ensure that the IOS process level, as well as slow path and receive-adjacency resources are available for legitimate uses.

Network Edge Security Concepts

The ability to classify packets by IP traffic plane helps define and enforce security policies. You can achieve improved clarity and accuracy during the classification process by considering the point in the network at which packets are observed. That is, the location of packet classification allows more intelligence to be applied when identifying good and bad traffic. In general, two distinctions are made regarding location: edge and core. Chapter 1 briefly introduced the concepts of the network edge and core, and how these differ for enterprise and SP networks. The "Network Interface Types" section earlier in this chapter introduced the concept of external and internal interfaces, which are directly related to edge and core concepts. This section extends this discussion by looking more closely at network edge and core concepts.

The network edge is your first, and sometimes best, opportunity to make decisions about trusted and untrusted packets (classification), and to apply appropriate policies. In general, both ingress and egress perspectives are important, but for different reasons. On ingress, you want to deny bad traffic and permit only good traffic. Obviously, the main question is how to determine good traffic from bad. Of course, the goal of applying security policies to ingress traffic is to protect from attack the network infrastructure itself and downstream devices and services. On egress, the same considerations should be made. On egress, bad traffic should be denied and only good traffic should be permitted to exit your network. There are several goals for egress policies, one being preventing infected or zombie internal hosts from causing damage to other internal and external networks. Once interfaces are categorized and classifications are made, policies may be applied such as: permit, deny, rate limit, recolor, tunnel, count, or others as required. Of course, distinct policies at the edge for ingress and egress traffic flows may also be applied.

Different types of networks have different definitions of trust and different security requirements. As briefly discussed in Chapter 1, and as you will see next, very different security requirements may exist even for similar networks but with differing network edge types. The Internet edge looks very different from the perspective of an enterprise than it does from the perspective of an SP, for example. These security requirements and resulting policies determine in large part just how robust the entire network is against attacks. Two types of network edges are reviewed here: the Internet edge, and the MPLS VPN edge. (Other types exist, such as the Layer 2 Ethernet edge.)

Internet Edge

The Internet edge is always the most vulnerable of any of the network edge types. Enterprises have little control over what traffic reaches their Internet edge. SPs even have limited control as well. The only guaranteed control is the one you apply to packets as they cross this Internet edge boundary. IP packets can be sourced from anywhere and carry anything as a payload. They may be legitimate, of course, or they may have malicious intentions. There may be a single malformed or crafted packet destined to one IP address, or a flood of millions of packets per second targeting a single destination IP address. Thus, the decisions made about ingress packets at the Internet edge are the most critical to overall network security. Service providers and enterprises have vastly different security policies at the Internet edge. These can be summarized as follows:

- As introduced in Chapter 1, enterprises typically have well-defined traffic flows traversing the Internet edge from inside-to-outside and outside-to-inside. (Internal traffic flows that stay entirely within the enterprise network are not discussed here.) Also, enterprise networks should never see transit traffic; that is, packets ingressing the Internet edge should never have destination IP addresses that are not part of the enterprise network address space. This gives enterprises the opportunity to deploy well-defined security policies at the Internet edge. Generally the approach is "everything is denied unless explicitly permitted."

- Also as introduced in Chapter 1, SPs have quite different traffic flows at their Internet edge as compared with enterprises. First, it is worth identifying just exactly where the *Internet edge* is for SPs. For enterprises, the Internet edge is easily identifiable; it is simply their WAN connection to their SP(s). However, for SPs, their Internet edge represents all external interface Internet connections including peering interconnects, transit customer access links, and any upstream or downstream SP interconnects. These are the boundaries where SPs apply their Internet edge security policies. And in just the opposite manner as an enterprise, an SP should only see transit traffic (with the exception of some control plane and possibly management plane traffic) at these edge boundaries. This also gives the SP the opportunity to deploy well-defined security policies at their Internet edge. Generally the approach is "everything is permitted unless explicitly denied."

In looking at the most basic perspective, the Internet edge policies for enterprises and SPs are opposites from one another. The enterprise Internet edge appears as a hard boundary where nothing is permitted unless it is either return traffic from internally generated traffic, or tightly controlled externally originated traffic destined to well-defined publicly exposed services. SPs, on the other hand, build networks to *allow* all transit traffic to cross their Internet edge without impediment. The SP edge is designed to be generally wide open and everything is permitted except for a few explicitly forbidden destinations belonging to the SP infrastructure. These differences in philosophy are illustrated in Figure 3-4.

Chapters 4 through 7 describe in detail the many security techniques that may be used on the Internet edge to mitigate the risk of attacks. The case studies in Chapters 8 and 9 present additional details on how these and other features may be deployed and how they complement one another.

Figure 3-4 *Internet Edge Security Policy Comparisons for Enterprise and Service Provider Networks*

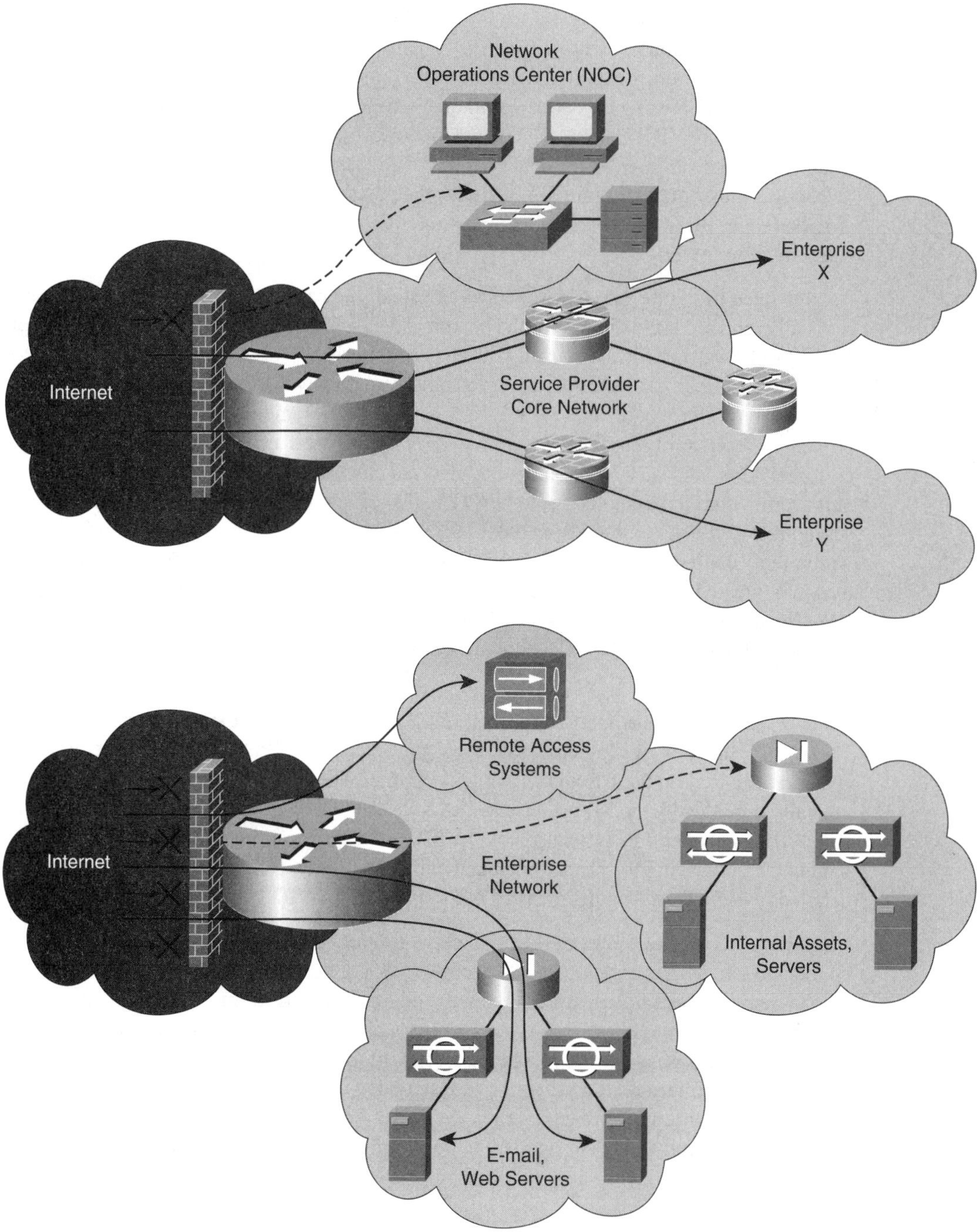

MPLS VPN Edge

Multiprotocol Label Switching (MPLS) Virtual Private Networks (VPN) provide addressing and routing separation to create virtual IP VPN networks, typically as replacements for classic SP-based Frame Relay or ATM-based networks. MPLS-based Layer 3 VPNs combine Multiprotocol BGP using extended community attributes and VPN address families, LDP (RFC 3036) or RSVP-TE (RFC 3209) for label distribution, and router support for Virtual Routing and Forwarding (VRF) instances to create these virtual IP networks. The MPLS VPN edge, illustrated in Figure 3-5, includes the portion of the network encompassing the provider edge (PE) router(s), the customer edge (CE) router(s), and the CE-PE links between these routers.

As illustrated in Figure 3-5, CE routers sit physically at each customer premises location (typically) and are logically part of the customer VPN. CE routers use only IP routing (not MPLS) to forward traffic associated with the customer's VPN network. IP traffic destined to remote customer VPN sites is forwarded downstream toward the PE routers, exactly like any other IP router would. The MPLS VPN functions implemented on the PE routers provide IP reachability to remote customer VPN sites as well as isolation between different customer VPNs. As such, CE routers and internal customer VPN networks are reachable only from within the assigned customer VPN. Therefore, by default, CE routers are not susceptible to attacks sourced from outside the assigned VPN. Internal attacks sourced from within the VPN remain possible just as with any enterprise or SP network. For example, a malware infected host within one customer VPN site may attack other hosts within the same VPN (locally or remotely connected). Thus, security mechanisms appropriate for internal deployment within the enterprise network remain appropriate, even for managed MPLS VPN–based services.

Each CE router is connected to one or more PE routers via some data link layer interface. This CE-PE link belongs logically to the assigned customer VPN as well, and includes the IP addresses used on the CE and associated PE interfaces. These interface addresses are typically provided by the SP, because MPLS VPNs are often offered as a managed service, and the management functions used by the SP network operations center (NOC) require unique CE addressing for proper management connectivity. Refer to Chapter 6 for a detailed review of the Management VPN used for MPLS VPNs.

PE routers are logically part of the SP's network and peer at Layer 3 with both directly connected CE routers and SP core (P) routers. SP core (P) routers are not directly reachable by VPN customer traffic given the addressing and routing separation provided by RFC 4364, although indirect attacks are plausible. However, PE routers (the PE side of each CE-PE link) are often reachable from within a customer VPN and thus must be protected from internal attacks. In the Internet edge case, CE routers may be attacked from the wider Internet if reachable via the wider Internet. In the general MPLS VPN case, however, each VPN is logically isolated from one another as well as from the global

Internet routing table. Thus, CE and PE routers are only susceptible to attacks sourced from inside a customer VPN. Note, even though CE and PE routers are reachable internally within the configured customer VPN(s), it is not possible for a host in one VPN to directly attack the CE router or PE router interfaces associated with another customer VPN given the isolation provided by RFC 4364. However, an attack against the PE from within one customer VPN may have an adverse impact on other VPNs configured on the same PE if the attack is able to disrupt a shared PE resource such as CPU, packet memory, and so forth. This is referred to as collateral damage, as described in Chapter 2, and is considered the most significant threat against MPLS VPNs.

Figure 3-5   *Conceptual MPLS VPN Network Topology*

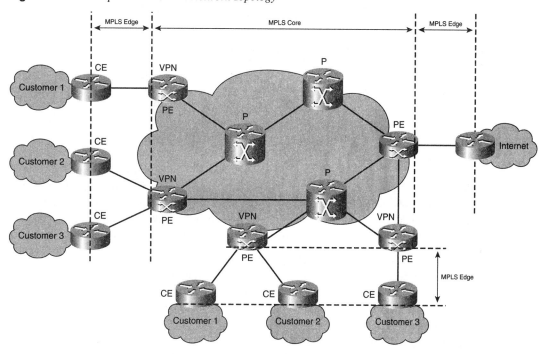

Thus, similar to the Internet edge, SPs may also consider deploying security mechanisms on MPLS VPN PE routers to protect their own infrastructure from attack. Although not generally susceptible to Internet-based attacks, internal attacks sourced from inside a customer VPN may adversely affect other VPN customers as outlined previously in this chapter. Chapter 7 describes the security techniques applicable to MPLS VPN networks.

NOTE	Additional security policies must be applied by SPs in support of inter-provider MPLS VPNs. The two primary architectures are Carrier Supporting Carrier (CsC) and Inter-AS VPNs, and techniques available to mitigate the risk of attacks via these inter-provider MPLS VPN interfaces are described in Chapter 7. Additional details on these topics are also provided in the Cisco Press book entitled *MPLS VPN Security* (listed in the "Further Reading" section).

Network Core Security Concepts

The network core is the trusted domain of a single organization. It includes network devices that typically only have internal (trusted) interfaces that are wholly within and controlled by a single group or administrative domain. For enterprises and SPs alike, with rare exceptions, external IP traffic should never be destined to core network infrastructure. Generally, the only packets destined to these devices should be internal control plane and management plane traffic generated by other network elements or management stations also within the same administrative domain. A well-designed network edge security policy may greatly limit the exposure of the network core to attacks. Even so, human error, misconfigurations, change management, and exception cases dictate that core security mechanisms must be defined and deployed in support of defense in depth and breadth principles. Such core policies help to mitigate the risk if edge policies are inadvertently bypassed.

The primary role of security in the core is to protect the core, not to apply policy to mitigate transit attacks within the data plane. Such attacks should be filtered at the network edge to mitigate the risk of transit attack traffic from adversely affecting transit authorized traffic. Further, anti-spoofing protection mechanisms need to be deployed at the edge; otherwise, it is not possible to accurately verify IP source addresses, which increases the risk of IP spoofing attacks. Nevertheless, control and management plane security policies are applied in support of the defense in depth and breadth strategy to protect the core in the event that edge policies are bypassed.

Just as with the network edge, different types of IP core networks exist. This section considers two types of network cores: an IP core and an MPLS VPN core. Although there are some similarities, each type has its own distinct security requirements, based on attack types and risks present in each network.

IP Core

IP core networks of enterprise and SPs have some basic similarities, but also some distinguishing characteristics. The most obvious similarity is the ability of all IP core networks to route IP packets (as compared with Layer 2 Ethernet switching and MPLS forwarding core networks). Packets are forwarded based on the destination address in the IP header and the matching prefix entry or entries installed in the CEF forwarding table. Having correct routing information is fundamental to a secure IP core network, and this is achieved by maintaining the integrity of the control plane.

The most obvious difference between enterprise and SP core networks involves transit traffic. Enterprise core networks do not carry transit traffic. They are closed private networks and interconnect with SP networks for Internet and/or VPN access (via MPLS, IPsec, Frame Relay, or ATM VPN services). SPs, on the other hand, are purpose-built transit networks. How this impacts the security of core networks may not be obvious, but the implications with respect to routing protocols and security may be quite substantial. These can be summarized as follows:

- IP networks use an Interior Gateway Protocol (IGP) to dynamically learn and provide reachability to internal prefixes. The dominant IGPs in use today are OSPF and EIGRP for enterprises, and OSPF and IS-IS for SPs. Enterprises often only run an IGP, and thus all the prefixes contained in the forwarding tables on all network devices (routers and Layer 3 switches) are from the IGP, connected interfaces, and static routes (if any), and all packet forwarding decisions are made using these prefixes. SPs, on the other hand, use the IGP only to carry prefixes associated with the internal network infrastructure. That is, no customer or Internet prefixes are carried in the IGP and thus no transit traffic packet forwarding decisions are made exclusively based on IGP-learned prefixes (other than for IP load balancing). Transit customer and Internet peer prefixes are only carried in BGP, for which the IGP provides reachability information between BGP border (or edge) routers.

- Service providers and larger enterprises, especially those with multiple Internet connections to different SPs (multi-homing) also require BGP for reachability to external IP prefixes. In these networks, the core is typically configured either as a full-mesh iBGP network (or uses some BGP scalability scheme such as route reflectors). In addition, these networks are typically default-route free because they have the full Internet routing table.

The main idea here, then, is that the focus of security in the network core is on protecting the control plane and management plane, as everything else follows from this. Control plane and management plane protocols and applications are well known, and may be unique to each network. Mechanisms must also be deployed that prevent data plane and services plane traffic from impacting the control plane and management plane. As previously described, exception data plane traffic (for example, TTL expiry, IP header options, and so on) may adversely impact network devices in the core of the network. Finally, internally based attack mechanisms and paths cannot be ignored. For example, malware infected hosts may flood the core from the inside, potentially leading to serious network disruptions. This is especially true in enterprise networks where default routes are used, because all destination IP addresses are then considered valid from a routing perspective (hence, nothing is dropped for lack of a route), and stateful control is only enabled at the enterprise edge. Appropriate security techniques are discussed in detail in Chapters 4 through 7 and in the case studies in Chapters 8 and 9.

MPLS VPN Core

Referring to Figure 3-5 once again, you can see that MPLS VPN core routers only have internal interfaces wholly within a single administrative domain. These are known as *provider* (P) routers or *intermediate* label switch routers (LSR). MPLS core routers perform label switching to forward customer traffic within the services plane. Even so, all MPLS routers rely on the underlying IGP routing protocol(s) to construct the label forwarding information base (LFIB). From the perspective of the MPLS core routers, therefore, only internal control plane and management plane traffic generated by MPLS network elements or management stations should be seen within the IP core control and management planes. MPLS core routers receive customer traffic as labeled packets only. Recall that the MPLS edge (PE) routers receive customer IP packets and apply the appropriate labels to switch these packets across the MPLS core.

The addressing and routing isolation provided by RFC 4364, makes MPLS core (P) routers hidden to MPLS VPN customers. Consequently, it is not possible for a VPN customer to launch direct attacks against core (P) routers because they have no IP reachability. Nevertheless, core (P) routers remain susceptible to, and must be protected against, transit attacks. Of course, if the MPLS core also provides Internet services, then both MPLS VPN and IP security techniques must be considered to prevent Internet-based attacks against the network core infrastructure from impacting MPLS operations.

The MPLS core control plane and management plane must be protected as well. MPLS VPNs depend on proper label distribution, which is generally done using M-BGP for customer prefix label distribution and LDP for IGP prefix label distribution. The typical implementation includes M-BGP routing on MPLS edge (PE) routers for VPN route propagation, and LDP on PE and MPLS core (P) routers for MPLS label switched path (LSP) establishment between ingress and egress PE routers based upon the IGP protocol best paths. While M-BGP uses only TCP for IP transport, LDP uses UDP for peer discovery and TCP for transport of LDP messages.

The main ideas for the MPLS VPN core are as follows:

- PE isolates the core from direct attack, but still must be protected from transit attacks.

- The MPLS core uses IP protocols for the control plane and management plane and these should be protected just like in the IP core case.

- When the MPLS core also provides Internet transit services, both MPLS VPN and IP security techniques must be considered to prevent Internet-based attacks against the network core infrastructure from impacting MPLS operations.

Additional details are provided in Chapters 4 through 7 and in the case studies in Chapters 8 and 9. In addition, the Cisco Press book entitled *MPLS VPN Security* covers these topics in thorough detail.

Summary

This chapter introduced the concepts of defense in depth and breadth as applied to IP traffic plane security. You learned how defense in depth is used to provide multiple layers against a single attack vector, whereas defense in breadth is used to address distinct attack vectors. You also learned that enabling each individual security technique must be well understood because each may potentially impact the overall network performance and operational envelope. Therefore, it is important to understand the impact of all security techniques during both normal operating conditions and attack conditions. You also learned that when multiple mechanisms are enabled, they may interact, either directly or indirectly, in ways that may not be readily apparent. Understanding these interactions and interdependencies allows for a more robust and resilient system design.

The ability to classify packets by IP traffic plane helps define and enforce security policies, and that improved clarity and accuracy may be achieved by considering location during the classification process. The concepts of physical and logical interfaces were introduced, as well as network edge and core concepts. The edge is the first opportunity to make decisions that affect the security of the network as a whole. This was described in the context of two network edge types, the Internet edge and the MPLS VPN edge. Finally, network cores for both IP networks and MPLS VPN networks were reviewed, including the need for control and management plane security policies to mitigate the risk of core attacks if edge security policies are bypassed.

Review Questions

1 Briefly describe the meaning of *depth* as referred to by the concept of defense in depth and breadth as applied to network security.

2 Briefly describe the meaning of *breadth* as referred to by the concept of defense in depth and breadth in network security.

3 True or False: Adding additional layers of defense always improves the overall security of the network.

4 True or False: To protect a service, protection may be required both within the services plane and in protection of the services plane to fully mitigate the risk of attacks against a service.

5 Which of the following interfaces are defined as logical interfaces?

  a Loopback interface

  b Receive interface

  c Out-of-band (OOB) interface

  d Null0 interface

  e Tunnel interface

6 True or False: In an enterprise environment, the IGP carries all network reachability information, including user address space and network infrastructure address space.

7 Briefly describe how the security policies for the enterprise edge and SP Internet edge differ.

8 True or False: In an SP default route-free core, transit traffic can never impact the internal network interfaces.

9 True or False: In an MPLS VPN core network, PE routers isolate the core P routers from direct attack by hiding core addresses from customer traffic through VRF separation.

Further Reading

Behringer, M. H., and M. J. Morrow. *MPLS VPN Security.* Cisco Press, 2005. ISBN: 1-58705-183-4.

Greene, B. R., and D. McPherson. "ISP Security: Deploying and Using Sinkholes." NANOG 28. Salt Lake City, Utah. June 2003. http://www.nanog.org/mtg-0306/sink.html.

McDowell, R. "Implications of Securing Backbone Router Infrastructure." NANOG 31. San Francisco. May 4, 2004. http://www.nanog.org/mtg-0405/mcdowell.html.

Meyer, D. A. "Complexity and Service Provider Networks in the 21st Century." SANOG V. Dhaka, Bangladesh. Feb. 5, 2005. http://www.sanog.org/resources/sanog5-dave-keynote.pdf.

Schudel, G. W., and B J. Wood. "Adversary Work Factor as a Metric for Information Assurance." Proceedings of the New Security Paradigms Workshop. Ballycotton, County Cork, Ireland. Sept. 19, 2000. ISBN: 1-58113-260-3. http://www.csl.sri.com/~bjwood/nspw_wood_v1e.pdf.

"Internet Exchanges/Internet Exchange Points/BGP Peering Points/IXP." BGP4AS. http://www.bgp4.as/internet-exchanges.

"NAT Order of Operation." (Doc. ID: 6209.) Cisco Tech Note. http://www.cisco.com/warp/public/556/5.html.

"The Team Cymru Bogon Reference Page." Team Cymru. http://www.cymru.com/Bogons/index.html.

PART II

Security Techniques for Protecting IP Traffic Planes

In this chapter, you will learn about the following:

- Data plane techniques to protect the network edge and core, including the different router interface types

- Techniques to protect the network and to mitigate network attacks within the data plane by using control plane techniques

- Layer 2 Ethernet techniques to protect switched Ethernet LANs

CHAPTER 4

IP Data Plane Security

Chapter 2, "Threat Models for IP Networks," reviewed the many threats facing IP networks and Layer 2 Ethernet and IP VPN networks. This chapter describes security measures available within the data plane to protect against those IP network threats. Chapters 5 through 7 will review techniques to secure and mitigate attacks within the IP control, management, and services planes, respectively.

Data plane security requires that all packets going into (and in many cases, going out of) a network be inspected and subject to policy control. When a packet arrives at a router, the router must do *something* with the packet. IP routing dictates that the packet either be forwarded (if a destination route exists) or be dropped (if no route exists). Hence, a routing decision is the *first* and most basic form of classification and policy enforcement applied to data plane traffic. And yet, little effort is typically placed on the impact of routing on security. In this chapter, you will learn how IP routing techniques may be used to support data plane security. Of course, given the pervasive deployment of IP networks and the wider Internet, and the broad range of threats against those networks (as described in Chapter 2), more rigorous controls and filtering are required, and are described in this chapter.

As outlined in Chapter 3, "IP Network Traffic Plane Security Concepts," no single technology (or technique) makes an effective security solution. Conversely, redundant vertical layers might only increase complexity and not enhance network security. A defense in depth and breadth strategy provides an effective approach for deploying complementary techniques to mitigate the risk of security attacks. The optimal techniques will vary by organization and depend on network topology, product mix, traffic behavior, operational complexity, and organizational mission. The following sections review data plane techniques that should be considered for deployment to mitigate the risk of security attacks.

Interface ACL Techniques

IP access control lists (ACL) are the most widely deployed IP data plane security technique. Typically, they are also the first line of defense both in securing a network and in reacting to an attack. IP ACLs perform packet filtering to control which packets may flow through the specific point of implementation. Such control aims to restrict network access to authorized traffic flows only. Just what constitutes *authorized* traffic depends on the network type and function, and where in the network the ACL is being implemented. These issues were discussed in Chapter 3 where, for example, Internet edge comparisons for SP and enterprise ACLs were described. Proper classification is critical to making correct *permit* or *deny* decisions. Exactly *where* an ACL is implemented (in other words, in which interface and in what direction) provides a frame of reference for the ACL construction.

The application of interface ACLs is not limited to the IP data plane. Because this mechanism is implemented on the interface of the router, it sees all packets that ingress or egress the interface (depending upon which direction the policy is applied). Hence, control, management, and services plane security policies may also take advantage of interface ACLs to filter unauthorized traffic flows and to restrict the content of traffic flows. For more information on the application of other ACL types within the IP control, management, and services planes, refer to Chapters 5 through 7, respectively. Within the data plane, interface ACLs have a variety of applications, including but not limited to the following:

- Filter incoming packets on an interface by using the **ip access-group** {*access-list-number*} **in** IOS interface configuration command

- Filter outgoing packets on an interface by using the **ip access-group** {*access-list-number*} **out** IOS interface configuration command

- Classify traffic for advanced features, such as:

    — QoS, using the **match access-group** {*access-list-number*} IOS Modular QoS CLI (MQC) configuration command

    — Policy-based routing (PBR), using the **match ip address** {*access-list-number*} IOS route-map configuration command

    — uRPF ACL bypass, using the **ip verify unicast source reachable-via** {**rx|any**} {*access-list-number*} IOS interface configuration command

    — MPLS VPN selection based on IP source address, using the **ip vrf select source** IOS interface configuration command

- Trigger dial-on-demand routing (DDR) calls by using the **dialer-list** {*access-list-number*} IOS global configuration command

- Perform informational logging of packets by using the **log** keyword within IOS ACL CLI syntax

As discussed in detail in Chapter 3, in the context of network security, the most logical place to apply interface ACL policies is on the network edge, where unauthorized traffic is generally first encountered. After all, you cannot always control what traffic is headed toward your network. However, you can control what traffic is allowed to enter your network by using ingress policy decisions applied on the network edge. In this regard, the following interface ACL types are typically found on the network edge and are important for securing the IP data plane:

- **Infrastructure ACLs (iACL):** iACLs prevent unauthorized external traffic from gaining IP reachability to internal network infrastructure. iACLs increase network security by mitigating the risk of directed attacks against the network infrastructure. SPs commonly deploy iACLs, for example, to prevent external attacks against SP infrastructure. Similarly, enterprises commonly deploy iACLs to limit external access to only specific IP networks such as web and mail servers within a DMZ (demilitarized zone). iACLs are considered a network security best practice and should be deployed as a permanent network security feature. Of course, they should be updated as applicable in conjunction with any future network and topology changes. The content and construction of iACLs is highly dependent on the network type and function. In general, however, iACLs are constructed based on source and destination IP addresses, because infrastructure IP addresses, including trusted sources and destinations, should be well known. The Cisco white paper "Protecting Your Core: Infrastructure Protection Access Control Lists" (see the "Further Reading" section) presents guidelines and recommended deployment techniques for iACLs.

- **Transit ACLs (tACL):** tACLs explicitly permit only required and authorized traffic to transit the IP network. Any traffic not explicitly permitted is discarded at the network edge. tACLs increase network security by mitigating the risk of transit attacks against downstream network infrastructure and IP hosts. Unlike iACLs, which concentrate their filtering based on source and destination IP addresses (and Layer 4 transport protocols and ports), tACLs rarely include IP addresses. Instead, tACLs filter based on packet types, such as IP fragments or IP headers option, and restricted protocols. For example, tACLs may filter unauthorized peer-to-peer (P2P) protocols and packets with IP headers option at the network edge. (Techniques to mitigate IP options–based attacks are described further in the "IP Options Techniques" section later in the chapter.) tACLs may also be used to filter traffic flows that would normally expire at an intermediate router along the forwarding path toward the downstream. Such packets are often crafted for DoS attacks, as outlined in Chapter 2. Consider the illustration in Figure 4-1.

Figure 4-1   *TTL Expiry DoS Attack Example*

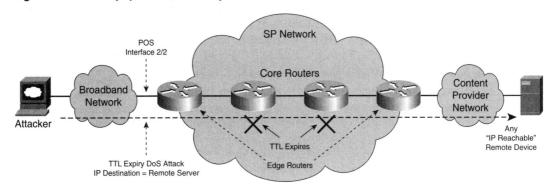

A tACL may be applied on ingress interface POS2/2 such that any packets with a TTL value less than or equal to 4 are discarded. In this way, the risk of TTL expiry attacks against the SP network infrastructure may be mitigated. tACLs are also considered a network security best practice and should be deployed as a permanent network security feature. Similarly, tACLs should also be updated in conjunction with any applicable network changes. tACLs protect both the router where the ACL is configured and other downstream devices. tACLs are also useful for incident response, to filter attack traffic before it reaches the intended target. Further information about tACLs is available in the Cisco white paper "Transit Access Control Lists: Filtering at Your Network Edge" (see the "Further Reading" section).

- **Antispoofing ACLs:** Antispoofing ACLs explicitly permit traffic based on authorized source IP addresses only. Any traffic sourced from outside the explicitly permitted IP address range is dropped at the network edge. Antispoofing ACLs increase network security by mitigating the risk of spoofed attacks, including reflection attacks. SPs, for example, generally filter the traffic of Internet transit customers that is sourced from outside of the customer assigned IP address space, including but not limited to traffic that spoofs internal network infrastructure addresses of the SP network. Other commonly spoofed IP addresses include bogons, Martians, and private network addresses. These are further described in the "Loose uRPF" section later in the chapter. Unicast Reverse Path Forwarding (uRPF) provides an alternate technique for antispoofing protection and is described in the next section, "Unicast RPF Techniques." Antispoofing protection also facilitates source address traceback during incident response of active attacks. For more information on antispoofing protection, refer to RFC 2827 (BCP 38).

- **Classification ACLs:** Classification ACLs provide a method for determining the characteristics of network traffic by adding instrumentation to the network. This is particularly useful during incident response so that the profile of an attack (for example, IP addresses, IP protocol, and TCP/UDP port numbers) may be determined. Classification ACL entries may take the form of either *permit* or *deny*—there is no requirement to perform packet filtering but rather simply to serve as an informational logging mechanism. Classification ACLs generally provide per-ACE (access control entry) counters and, optionally, logging of packets via the ACE **log** keyword. Using this information, you may determine the type of traffic used within an attack. An iACL, tACL, or antispoofing ACL may then be applied to mitigate the attack.

ACL policies are applied at the interface level; however, a single ACL policy may be shared among many IP router interfaces. ACLs may be applied on ingress or egress, and operate as a sequential list consisting of at least one **permit** statement (enabling some traffic to flow) and possibly one or more **deny** statements.

TIP   Depending on the ACL type and its application, you will find that the actual policy construction of the ACL will follow one of two forms: deny a few specific things and permit everything else, as in the case of an SP tACL, or permit a few specific things and deny everything else, as in the case of most enterprise edge security ACL configurations. Remember that an *implicit deny* is always appended to the end of an IOS ACL. Rather than allowing the implicit deny to terminate the ACL or adding a single **deny ip any any** statement in its place (or the comparable **permit ip any any** for tACLs), try incorporating the ideas of the classification ACL at the end of your security ACL. In the deny case, you may build a very granular set of deny rules for different protocols and port ranges (for example, **deny tcp any any eq 80**, and so on), terminated with a concluding **deny ip any any** entry. In this way, when you issue the **show access-list** IOS command, the ACE counter values will give an indication of how much traffic is being denied, and for which protocols and ports. The permit case would be constructed in a similar manner, but with **permit** statements instead of the **deny** statements.

Applying ACLs on an interface may (or may not) adversely impact the forwarding performance associated with that interface, line card, or routing platform. Performance impacts, if any, depend on several factors:

- **IP router platform:** As discussed in Chapter 1, "Internet Protocol Operations Fundamentals," routers generally fall into software-based and hardware-based categories. Within these categories, centralized and distributed architectures may be found. The impact of enabling ACLs on software-based routers is generally far greater than the impact of enabling ACLs on hardware-based routers. Hardware-based platforms generally include dedicated ASICs for ACL processing (and other features) to be performed at full line rate. The depth of the ACL (number of ACEs) may also affect feature performance. Therefore, when constructing ACLs, it is best to organize the most likely hits to occur early in the list.

- **ACL feature selection:** Enabling certain ACL features may potentially impact the overall forwarding rate of the platform. For example, using the **log** keyword requires slow path processing of packets in order to copy packet attributes to the log buffer. That is, even in hardware-based routers, the **log** keyword changes the packet processing path and performance of matching packets to that of the slow path. Thus, use this feature with discretion. For more information on ACL logging, refer to the Cisco white paper referenced in the "Further Reading" section.

Understanding the performance characteristics of any ACL implementation, especially under DoS attack conditions (such as a high rate of small packets), is particularly important in the context of network security. Network attacks often increase the resource load on affected routers. Although a security ACL may be able to mitigate an attack by filtering unauthorized traffic, it may also degrade the overall performance of the router itself. Nevertheless, ACLs are a very useful tool for mitigating attacks. You simply need to be aware, prior to their deployment, of any potential ACL engineering limits and impacts associated with your IP router platforms.

IOS supports a single ACL per interface, per direction. That is, you may configure only one ingress ACL per interface and one egress ACL per interface. Given this restriction, the iACL, tACL, antispoofing ACL, and classification ACL policies are often combined into a single ACL policy. Infrastructure and antispoofing ACLs are generally static and rarely modified as compared to transit and classification ACLs, which are more often used for incident response and attack mitigation and, hence, are modified more frequently. Given these differences, you may consider a modular approach to ACL design and deployment, which entails the following:

- **Layered ACL architecture:** This involves distributing each ACL component among distinct network components (for example, routers and router interfaces). Consider the illustration shown in Figure 4-2.

Figure 4-2 *Layered ACL Architecture*

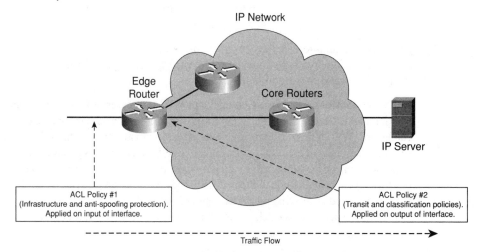

Rather than combine each of the four ACL types into a single policy, you may define the passive and reactive ACL functions in two distinct policies. In this way, the passive ACL functions, such as infrastructure and antispoofing ACL entries, are not disrupted when modifications to the transit and classification ACL entries are being made. This mitigates the risk of a change within the reactive transit or classification ACL policies from adversely affecting the passive infrastructure or antispoofing ACL policies. Further, this distributed, layered ACL policy may also provide performance gains, in terms of both deployment speed (distinct passive and reactive ACL policies simplify policy changes compared to a single larger policy) and processing speed (reduced-length ACL).

- **Policy-based routing:** PBR may be used as a technique for implementing ACL modularity and for augmenting the IOS restriction of only a single ACL per interface direction. PBR may use ACL policies for packet classification. This allows the passive and reactive ACL functions to be defined within two distinct policies, similar to the layered ACL architecture outlined in the preceding bullet. The configuration in Example 4-1 illustrates how PBR may be used to modularize ACL filtering. Similar to ACLs, PBR can have a different performance depending on the router platform and policy configuration.

Example 4-1 *PBR ACL Modularization Configuration Example*

```
interface pos1/1
  encapsulation ppp
  ip address 209.165.200.225 255.255.255.224
  ip policy route-map anti-spoof-acl
  ip access-group 196 in
!
access-list 195 permit ip 10.0.0.0 0.255.255.255 any
access-list 195 permit ip 127.0.0.0 0.255.255.255 any
access-list 195 permit ip 192.168.0.0 0.0.255.255 any
access-list 195 permit ip 224.0.0.0 15.255.255.255 any
access-list 195 permit ip 172.16.0.0 0.15.255.255 any
access-list 196 permit ip any any fragments log
access-list 196 permit ip any any
!
route-map anti-spoof-acl permit 10
  match ip address 195
  set interface Null0
```

Using the PBR configuration illustrated in Example 4-1, ingress packets received on POS1/1 that match the antispoofing policy defined by ACL 195 are redirected toward the Null0 interface and silently discarded. Note that unauthorized packets must be *permitted* within the PBR referenced ACL policy in order for them to match the policy and be discarded. Conversely, authorized packets should be denied within ACL policy 195. Packets denied by ACL 195 are not subjected to the PBR filtering policy since ACL 195 is used for PBR classification only. This is orthogonal to ACL policies applied directly to an interface such as the classification ACL policy 196. ACL policy 196 is applied to all IPv4 packets received on interface POS1/1. To see how many (unauthorized) packets are filtered by the PBR policy, use the **show route-map** command, as illustrated in Example 4-2.

Example 4-2 *Sample IOS* **show** *Output for PBR Filtering*

```
Router> show route-map anti-spoof-acl
route-map anti-spoof-acl, permit, sequence 10
  Match clauses:
    ip address (access-lists): 195
  Set clauses:
    interface Null0
  Policy routing matches: 1000 packets, 1500000 bytes
Router>
```

Similar to the layered ACL architecture technique outlined earlier in this list, this PBR technique may be used to ensure that the passive ACL functions, such as infrastructure and antispoofing ACL entries, are not tampered with when modifications to the transit and classification ACL entries are being made. This mitigates the risk of a change within the reactive transit or classification ACL policies adversely affecting the passive infrastructure or antispoofing ACL policies. Again, prior to deployment of this technique, you should understand any potential engineering limits and performance impacts associated with deploying PBR on your IP router platforms.

- **QoS:** Similar to PBR, QoS may also be used as a technique for implementing ACL modularity and for working around the IOS limit of supporting only a single ACL per interface direction. IOS MQC may also use ACL policies for packet classification. This allows the passive and reactive ACL functions to be defined within two distinct policies, similar to the layered ACL architecture and PBR techniques outlined in this list. The configuration in Example 4-3 illustrates how MQC may be used to modularize ACL filtering.

Example 4-3 *QoS-Based ACL Modularization Configuration Example*

```
class-map acl-195
  match access-group 195
!
policy-map anti-spoof-acl
  class acl-195
    police 10000 conform-action drop exceed-action drop
!
interface pos1/1
  encapsulation ppp
  ip address 209.165.200.225 255.255.255.224
  service-policy input anti-spoof-acl
  ip access-group 196 in
!
access-list 195 permit ip 10.0.0.0 0.255.255.255 any
access-list 195 permit ip 127.0.0.0 0.255.255.255 any
access-list 195 permit ip 192.168.0.0 0.0.255.255 any
access-list 195 permit ip 224.0.0.0 15.255.255.255 any
access-list 195 permit ip 172.16.0.0 0.15.255.255 any
access-list 196 permit ip any any fragments log
access-list 196 permit ip any any
```

The MQC configuration works similarly to the PBR configuration previously outlined, with the exception that instead of redirecting spoofed packets to Null0 via PBR, MQC effectively polices those packets to a rate of 0 bits per second via the **conform drop exceed drop** MQC policer actions. Packets denied by ACL 195 are not subjected to the MQC filtering policy since ACL 195 is used for MQC classification only. To see how many (unauthorized) packets are filtered by the MQC policy, use the **show policy interface** command, as illustrated in Example 4-4.

Example 4-4   *Sample IOS* **show** *Output for MQC Filtering*

```
Router> show policy interface pos1/1
POS0/0

  Service-policy input: anti-spoof-acl

    Class-map: acl-195 (match-all)
      1000 packets, 1500000 bytes
      5 minute offered rate 5000 bps, drop rate 5000 bps
      Match: access-group 195
      police:
          cir 100000000 bps, bc 1500 bytes
        conformed 1000 packets, 1500000 bytes; actions:
          drop
        exceeded 0 packets, 0 bytes; actions:
          drop
        conformed 10000000 bps, exceed 0 bps
```

Similar to the layered ACL architecture and PBR techniques outlined earlier in this list, this QoS technique may be used to ensure that the passive ACL functions, such as infrastructure and antispoofing ACL entries, are not tampered with when modifications to the transit and classification ACL entries are being made. This mitigates the risk of a change within the reactive transit or classification ACL policies from adversely affecting the passive infrastructure or antispoofing ACL policies. You should understand any potential QoS/MQC engineering limits and performance impacts associated with the applicable IP router platforms prior to deployment of this technique.

The preceding techniques provide you with the flexibility to respond to known and unknown threats in a scalable and low service-impacting manner using modular ACLs. Although ACLs provide strong protection against network attacks, they are limited in a number of ways:

- IP ACLs have specific predefined header fields available for classification criteria. Exactly which header fields are available is a function of the IOS release train, and the ACL type (standard, extended, or named). Thus, any flexibility in terms of classification granularity is strictly a function of these predefined header parameters. Many security attacks hide within well-known TCP/UDP port numbers (such as TCP port 80 for HTTP), making it difficult to filter attack traffic without adversely affecting legitimate traffic when limited to the predefined ACL fields. To improve classification granularity, later versions of certain IOS software incorporate a new feature called Flexible Packet Matching (FPM), which allows for user-specified bit-offset matches anywhere within an IP packet header and some portion of its payload. FPM is described in detail in the "Flexible Packet Matching" section later in the chapter.

(Consult the ACL configuration guide or command reference for your Cisco IOS release train for full details on available ACL header classification parameters. Consult the Cisco Feature Navigator at http://www.cisco.com/go/fn to determine the availability of FPM.) Alternatively, IOS NBAR (Network Based Application Recognition) provides intelligent traffic classification and policy functions. NBAR is outside the scope of this book. For more information on NBAR, refer to the "Further Reading" section.

- ACLs may become lengthy and complex, making them operationally difficult to maintain. The layered ACL architecture, including the use of the PBR and QoS techniques outlined in the previous list, may help to reduce this complexity. However, implementing antispoofing protection generally requires customized, per-interface specific antispoofing ACL configurations. Managing these policies across many network edge routers with many external interfaces is very challenging and a daunting problem that SPs face. Similarly, changes within the network topology and new prefix assignments may require changes within the ACL policies. Managing the number of ACL changes and distinct policies, and the complexity of the individual ACL policy rules (or ACEs) themselves, results in a high cost of ownership.

ACLs continue to be one of the mainstays of any network security policy and form an essential layer in the defense in depth and breadth paradigm.

Unicast RPF Techniques

Unicast Reverse Path Forwarding (uRPF) is an alternative technique for filtering ingress packets that lack a verifiable source IP address, such as spoofed IP source addresses. As mentioned in the previous section, such packets should be filtered at the network edge to mitigate the potential threat of spoofed attacks, including reflection attacks. Further, in mitigating the risk of spoofed attacks, IP source traceback of nonspoofed attacks is simplified. Although ingress ACLs may be configured to provide equivalent antispoofing protection, ingress ACL policies are static and require reconfiguration to reflect changing network conditions, including topology changes and new prefix assignments. uRPF was developed specifically to address the scaling and operational expense issues of providing antispoofing filtering of ingress packets using ACLs alone.

When uRPF is enabled on an interface, the router examines all ingress packets on that interface to verify that the source IP address is reachable and, optionally, reachable via the ingress interface. This *reverse path* check is accomplished by looking for the existence of a prefix within the Forwarding Information Base (FIB) that matches the source IP address and, optionally, the ingress interface. As you learned in Chapter 1, Cisco Express Forwarding (CEF) generates the FIB automatically through dynamic IP routing protocols and static routes. Because uRPF uses the FIB to validate source IP addresses, it is capable of dynamically adapting to changes in network topology and IP prefix changes because these are automatically captured by the FIB through routing protocol changes. This enables uRPF to maintain conformance with ingress security policies without reconfiguration, unlike antispoofing ACLs, as described in the previous section, "Interface ACL Techniques." Obviously, CEF must be enabled on the router for uRPF to function.

NOTE   In addition to antispoofing protection on a per-interface basis, uRPF also provides the mechanisms that enable the global DoS mitigation technique known as source-based remotely triggered black hole (RTBH) filtering (described in detail in the "Remotely Triggered Black Hole Filtering" section later in the chapter).

Even though uRPF provides antispoofing protection (and source-based RTBH filtering) and conceivably negates the need for antispoofing ACLs, it may still be applied on an interface in conjunction with other ACL types such as iACL, tACL, and classification ACLs, as described in the previous section. It is also worth pointing out that even in cases where both uRPF and an antispoofing ACL are deployed simultaneously, uRPF adds an extra layer of protection by dynamically covering any holes that may exist in the antispoofing ACLs between the time network topologies change and the (static) antispoofing ACLs may be updated.

uRPF operates in several different modes and has several configuration options, but each mode provides source address–based ingress packet filtering. The differences between each of the uRPF techniques are described next.

Strict uRPF

Strict mode uRPF (also referred to as version 1 or uRPFv1) verifies whether the ingress interface of a received packet is the router's best path back toward the source IP address of the packet. If true, the packet is routed downstream to the IP next hop associated with the longest prefix match within the FIB as normal. Otherwise, if no FIB entry matches the source address or if the ingress interface is not a best path toward the source address, the packet is considered spoofed and is silently discarded. Both of these scenarios are illustrated in Figure 4-3.

Note that for topologies where multiple paths to an IP destination prefix may be installed within the FIB table, all *equal-cost* best paths are considered valid and used within the uRPFv1 check. Also, if the source IP address of an incoming packet is resolved within the FIB to a Null0 interface adjacency, the packet is automatically discarded. The Null0 interface is treated as an invalid interface by uRPF, and as you will see later, it is this mechanism within uRPF that enables source-based RTBH filtering.

The IOS CLI syntax for strict mode uRPF is

```
ip verify unicast source reachable-via rx [allow-default] [allow-self-ping] {list}
```

Figure 4-3 *Strict uRPF Source Address Verification Example*

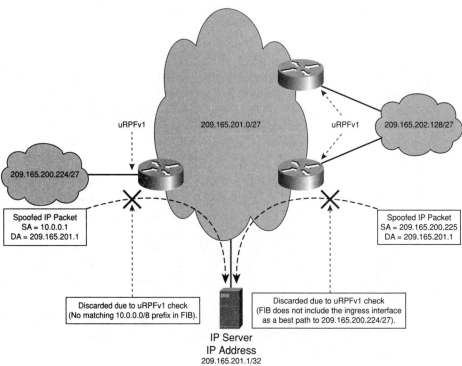

In this case, the **rx** parameter, meaning *receive interface*, is the key to configuring strict mode uRPF. This command is applied within IOS interface configuration mode. The optional parameters allow for the following:

- **allow-default:** Allows the use of the default route for uRPF verification. Normally, source IP addresses found to match only a default route are discarded. That is, a default route is not normally considered valid for uRPF verification. By specifying the **allow-default** optional keyword, this behavior is overridden and packets with source IP addresses found to match the default route are permitted. You should be aware that the effectiveness of uRPF is substantially reduced when a default route is deployed.

- **allow-self-ping:** Allows a router to ping its own interface(s). Without this option, all packets sourced by the local router and destined to a local router interface enabled for uRPF will fail the uRPF verification check. That is, self-pinging is not allowed by default. This makes troubleshooting and some management tasks difficult. This option should be used with caution, however, and it is recommended that it only be enabled when required (for example, during troubleshooting). When this option is configured, it enables a potential DoS attack vector by allowing an attacker to transmit crafted packets destined to the local router that spoof one of the router's local addresses. Note that the name used for the keyword (**allow-self-ping**) is somewhat of a misnomer as it is not exclusively tied to ping (ICMP Echo) packets. In fact, *all* protocols are affected, because uRPF simply performs a Layer 3 check against the source IP address and has no Layer 4 awareness.

- **list:** Specifies a standard or extended numbered IP ACL to be checked only if a received packet fails the uRPF check. When an ingress packet fails the uRPF verification check, it is then compared against the ACL, if configured, to determine whether the packet should be forwarded (matches a **permit** statement in the ACL) or dropped (matches a **deny** statement in the ACL). If no ACL is configured and the packet fails the uRPF check, the packet is dropped. This feature is used mainly for the purpose of allowing *exception* packets to be *saved* from a failed uRPF check. A deny ACL is also useful for logging discarded packets. The {*list*} option is not available in all IOS versions and across all router platforms.

NOTE	In addition to the configurable {*list*} option just described, uRPF has a built-in bypass mechanism that *saves* DHCPDISCOVER messages (that is, IP source address of 0.0.0.0 IP destination address of 255.255.255.255) from being discarded. Otherwise, uRPF would prevent a networked host from dynamically acquiring an IP address and other DHCP-supplied parameters, such as default gateway, IP subnet, DNS server addresses, and so on. Note also that implementations of uRPF in older versions of IOS did not include these bypass mechanisms. It is always best practice to check your version of IOS prior to implementation.

uRPFv1 works well for networks where IP routing is symmetrical (in other words, where the ingress and egress directions of a bidirectional traffic flow deterministically follow the same forwarding path). For networks with multiple paths between sources and destinations where IP routing path selection may result in asymmetrical forwarding paths, uRPFv1 may result in the discarding of legitimate traffic flows, as illustrated in Figure 4-4.

Nevertheless, uRPFv1 may still be effective in multihomed situations, provided that optional BGP attributes, such as weight and local preference, are used to achieve symmetric routing, as illustrated in Figure 4-5.

Figure 4-4 *Strict uRPF Example Within Multihomed Network Topologies*

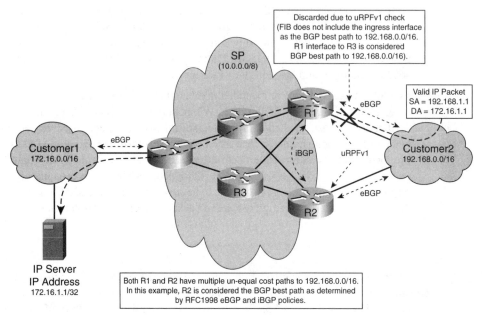

Figure 4-5 *Strict uRPF Example Using Cisco IOS BGP Weight Attribute Within Multihomed Topologies*

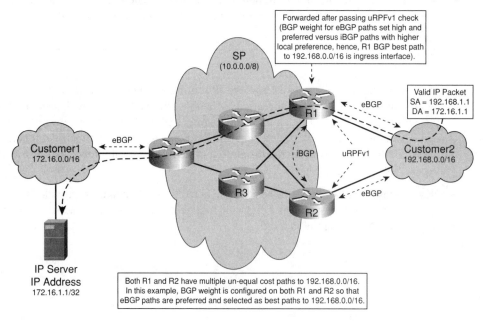

One caveat with this approach is that when manipulating the BGP path selection in this way, the customer routing policy may be inadvertently changed. As illustrated in Figure 4-4, Customer2 may prepend its eBGP update to R1 using RFC 1998 techniques, indicating the preferred return path to 192.168.0.0/16 should always be via R2 (versus R1 or multipath load balancing). SP BGP policies then force R1 to select the iBGP path via R2 versus its eBGP path. If the SP configures BGP weight on R1 to allow transit traffic sent from Customer2 through R1 to pass the ingress uRPFv1 check, traffic from any other SP customers directly connected to R1 will use R1, and not R2, to reach 192.168.0.0/16. This changes Customer2's routing policy as previously caveated.

To view uRPF drop statistics, you may use the **show ip interface** command, as illustrated in Example 4-5. This command reports the number of uRPF drops for the associated interface. Alternatively, you may use the **show ip traffic** command to view the total number of uRPF drops on the router across all interfaces.

Example 4-5   *Sample IOS* **show** *Output Reporting uRPF Drops*

```
Router> show ip interface pos 1/1 | begin IP verify
              IP verify source reachable-via RX
              1000 verification drops
              0 suppressed verification drops
Router>
```

Loose uRPF

Loose mode uRPF (also referred to as version 2 or uRPFv2) simply verifies whether the source address of a received packet matches a prefix within the CEF/FIB table with *any* valid interface. Unlike uRPFv1, uRPFv2 does not verify whether the ingress interface of a received packet is the router's best path back toward the IP source address of the packet. Instead, uRPFv2 only verifies that the source address of a received packet is a valid prefix within the FIB and has a valid interface adjacency (in other words, not Null0). If true, the packet is routed downstream to the IP next hop associated with the longest prefix match within the FIB as normal. Otherwise, if the source address does not match a valid prefix within the FIB, or if the source address matches a valid prefix that is associated with a Null0 interface adjacency, the packet is silently discarded. Loose uRPF is illustrated in Figure 4-6.

Because uRPFv2 does not verify the ingress interface, uRPFv2 works well in network topologies with multiple paths between sources and destinations where IP routing is asymmetric. However, because any source address that matches a prefix within the IP routing table is considered valid, uRPFv2 is generally only effective in filtering spoofed packets that use one of the following types of IP source addresses (as outlined in Chapter 2):

- **Bogon address:** A source address within the reserved IP address space that has not yet been allocated or delegated by the Internet Assigned Numbers Authority (IANA) or a delegated Regional Internet Registry (RIR). Such address blocks are also referred to as *dark address space*.

- **Martian address ("packets from Mars"):** A source address that does not correspond to a destination prefix within the local routing table.

- **Private network address:** A source address that uses address space reserved by RFC 1918, RFC 3330, and RFC 3927. These private addresses are not routed within the public Internet.

Figure 4-6 *Loose uRPF Source Address Verification Example*

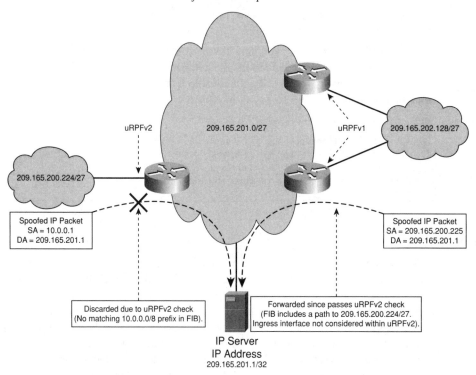

uRPFv2 does not filter packets that spoof valid network addresses. However, uRPFv2 does mitigate attacks using bogon, Martian, and private network addresses, making it reasonably useful at peering edges (unless your organization uses private addressing within its network infrastructure, in which case uRPFv2 will not be able to filter packets with spoofed private addresses). One of the most useful reasons for deploying uRPFv2 is that it enables the ability to mitigate DoS attacks through the source-based RTBH filtering technique. All versions of uRPF consider the Null0 interface as invalid, so if the source IP address of an incoming packet is resolved to a Null0 interface adjacency, the packet is automatically discarded. This makes source-based RTBH filtering an effective network-wide incident response tool. For more information, refer to the "Remotely Triggered Black Hole Filtering" section later in the chapter.

The IOS CLI syntax for loose mode uRPF is

```
ip verify unicast source reachable-via any [allow-default] [allow-self-ping] {list}
```

In this case, the **any** parameter, meaning *any interface*, is the key to configuring loose mode uRPF. This command is applied within IOS interface configuration mode. The optional parameters shown are identical to those described for uRPFv1.

VRF Mode uRPF

The newest implementation of uRPF is VRF (Virtual Routing and Forwarding) mode (also referred to as version 3 or uRPFv3). uRPFv3 operates similarly to loose mode uRPF (uRPFv2), but instead of verifying the IP source address of received packets against the router's global FIB, uRPFv3 performs its source address verification checks against the FIB table associated with a defined VRF. Normally, VRFs enable routing and addressing separation between IP VPNs as defined for MPLS VPNs in RFC 4364. In the context of MPLS VPNs, the VRFs contain IP prefixes learned from within the VPN (in other words, learned through interfaces configured for IP VRF forwarding). These prefixes, which are never found in the global table, are carried in Multiprotocol BGP (MBGP) VRFs only, and are referred to as VPNv4 prefixes. In the context of uRPFv3, however, the VRFs may be populated only with prefixes contained in the global BGP table, and not with VPNv4 prefixes carried in MBGP VRF tables. uRPFv3 is not dependent upon MPLS in any way, and MPLS does not need to be configured for uRPFv3 to operate.

NOTE   uRPFv3 should not be confused with applying uRPF (any version) to an interface for which IP VRF forwarding has been enabled, as would be the case on an MPLS VPN PE router. That is, uRPFv1, v2, or v3 may be enabled on an interface that has also been placed in an MPLS VPN (via the **ip vrf forwarding** {*name*} interface configuration command). In the case of uRPFv1 or v2, source IP address verification will be performed against the FIB associated with the interface VRF instance rather than against the global FIB. In the case of uRPFv3, the source IP address verification will be performed against the FIB associated with the uRPFv3 designated VRF rather than against the FIB associated with the interface, albeit global FIB or VRF-specific FIB.

---

uRPFv3 supports two modes of operation, as illustrated in Figure 4-7: permit mode, which may be thought of as a *white list* mode, and deny mode, which may be thought of as a *black list* mode.

Figure 4-7 *VRF Mode uRPF Source Address Verification Example*

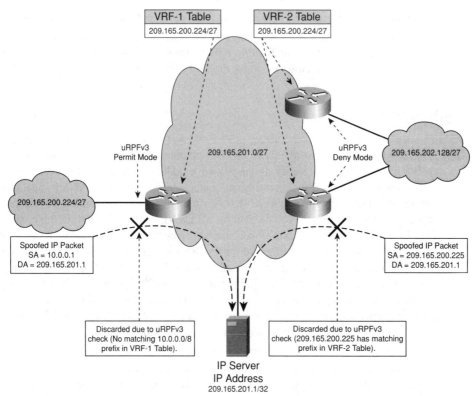

In permit mode, the defined VRF is populated (via BGP) with permitted IP prefixes. When a packet is received on an interface configured for uRPFv3 permit mode, the packet source address is verified against the FIB generated by CEF for the defined VRF. If the source address matches a prefix within the FIB of the defined VRF, the packet is forwarded. If the source address does not match a prefix in the FIB for the defined VRF, it is silently discarded. In deny mode, the defined VRF is populated (via BGP) with unauthorized IP prefixes. When a packet is received on an interface configured for uRPFv3 deny mode, the packet source address is verified against the FIB of the defined VRF. If the source address matches a prefix within the FIB of the defined VRF, the packet is silently discarded. If the source address does not match a prefix in the FIB for the defined VRF, it is permitted.

uRPFv3 permit mode was originally designed to give SPs an automated way to enforce peering (transit) agreements with downstream, smaller providers. In such cases, the idea is that the smaller downstream providers should be sourcing IP packets only from an agreed-upon IP prefix range or ranges. Prior to uRPFv3, enforcement would require that static interface ACLs be built to permit specific source address ranges. With uRPFv3, this may be automated by using the eBGP session to import these prefixes into a VRF that is used by uRPFv3 in permit mode for accomplishing this enforcement task.

The configuration illustrated in Example 4-6 shows how uRPFv3 may be configured using permit mode for peering policy enforcement. All prefixes received from Customer1 via eBGP are marked with the community 600:100, and then imported into the Customer1-VRF table. The source address of each IP packet received on interfaces POS1/1 will then be verified against the FIB generated by CEF for the Customer1-VRF table. If a longest prefix match exists within the Customer1-VRF FIB with a valid interface adjacency (in other words, not Null0), the packet will be forwarded downstream to the IP next hop. Otherwise, the packet will be silently discarded. Because the Customer1-VRF table is populated with the IP prefixes advertised from Customer1 via eBGP, any packets sourced from an IP address outside of those advertised prefixes will be silently discarded.

Example 4-6 *uRPFv3 Permit Mode Illustration*

```
ip vrf Customer1-VRF
 rd 600:1
 import ipv4 unicast 100 map permittedPrefixes
!
interface pos1/1
  description external link to customer1
  encapsulation ppp
  ip address 10.9.1.2 255.255.255.252
  ip verify unicast vrf Customer1-VRF permit
!
router bgp <asn1>
  no synchronization
  network 10.9.1.0 mask 255.255.255.252
  neighbor 10.9.1.1 remote-as <asn2>
  neighbor 10.9.1.1 route-map allowPrefix in
  no auto-summary
!
  address-family ipv4 vrf Customer1-VRF
  no synchronization
  exit-address-family
!
ip bgp-community new-format
ip community-list 99 permit 600:100
!
ip prefix-list eBGPinterface seq 5 permit 10.9.1.0/30
!
route-map allowPrefix permit 10
 set community 600:100
!
route-map permittedPrefixes permit 10
 match community 99
!
route-map permittedPrefixes permit 20
 match ip address prefix-list eBGPinterface
```

As illustrated in Example 4-6, uRPFv3 permit mode provides peering enforcement that dynamically adapts to BGP routing protocol changes, and supports multipath topologies. In addition to the current IOS IPv4 VRF table limit of five IPv4 VRF instances per router, you also need to be aware of the potential memory scale impacts of uRPFv3 due to uRPFv3-related prefixes being maintained in both the global IP routing table and the VRF table. The configuration in Example 4-6 takes advantage of the BGP *import* feature in Cisco IOS. You can find the full details of this feature and its uses in "BGP Support for IP Prefix Import from Global Table into a VRF Table," referenced in the "Further Reading" section.

NOTE	Cisco IOS currently supports a maximum of five IPv4 VRF instances per router that may be created to import IPv4 prefixes from the global routing table. This restriction applies to IPv4 VRF instances only and not to VPNv4 VRF tables that are used for MPLS VPNs.

uRPFv3 deny mode is designed to provide an automated way to explicitly block packets with specific source addresses. This is useful not only for filtering bogon, Martian, and private network addresses, but also for filtering external packets that spoof an internal infrastructure source address. Attackers may spoof internal infrastructure source addresses to exploit a trust relationship and, thereby, attack internal network resources. The uRPFv3 deny mode configuration is much the same as that shown in Example 4-6, with one exception. As illustrated in Example 4-6 above, uRPFv3 permit mode imports prefixes directly from the global BGP table. However, because infrastructure addresses are not (typically) carried in BGP, and bogon, Martian, and private network addresses also are not available in the global BGP table, you cannot populate the VRF to be used within uRPFv3 deny mode using the import feature directly on the routers for which it is intended. Thus, a separate router (or other BGP speaking device, such as a Linux platform running quagga or zebra for example) is required to populate the VRF.

Many security operation centers maintain a "trigger router" for deploying other network-wide security mechanisms such as RTBH (see the "Remotely Triggered Black Hole Filtering" section later in the chapter), and this makes an ideal place to create the routes used for uRPFv3 deny mode. In deny mode, then, the source address of each IP packet received on an external interface, such as POS1/1 in Example 4-6, will be verified against the prefixes in the bogon/infrastructure VRF table. If a longest prefix match exists within the Customer1-VRF table with either a valid interface adjacency or Null0 adjacency, the packet will be silently discarded. Otherwise, the packet will be forwarded downstream to the IP next hop.

Feasible uRPF

Feasible uRPF is an extension of strict uRPF whereby all known paths (active and inactive) will be considered during the source address check. As previously outlined for strict uRPF, BGP techniques are required to make strict uRPF work in networks with multiple paths between sources and destinations and asymmetric routing. Feasible uRPF eliminates the need for BGP techniques, however, it installs all known paths (including best paths and inactive paths) into the RIB and FIB which may result in significant route scale issues on the configured router. Consider the large number of paths available within a SP router carrying the full Internet routing table. With feasible uRPF, all known paths are considered during the uRPF check, not only the selected best paths. This results in feasible uRPF verifying whether the ingress interface of a received packet is simply a *known* path toward the IP source address of the packet (versus a *best* path with uRPFv1). If true, the packet is routed downstream to the IP next hop associated with the longest prefix match within the FIB. Otherwise, if the ingress interface is not a known path toward the source address, the packet is considered spoofed and is silently discarded. Feasible uRPF is illustrated in Figure 4-8. Compare Figure 4-8 with Figure 4-4 strict uRPF within multihomed network topologies.

Figure 4-8   *Feasible uRPF Source Address Verification Example*

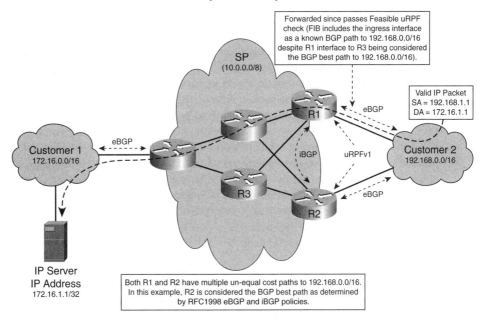

Similar to the other uRPF modes, if the source IP address of an incoming packet is resolved to a Null0 interface adjacency, the packet is automatically dropped. The Null0 interface is treated as an invalid interface within uRPF. Feasible uRPF is not supported within IOS at the time of this writing. For further information on feasible uRPF, refer to RFC 3704 (BCP 84).

Flexible Packet Matching

ACLs are the most widely deployed security tool for network protection and incident response. As noted in the earlier "Interface ACL Techniques" section, however, IP ACLs use specific predefined header fields for classification criteria. This is usually acceptable for developing security policies for traffic enforcement, but falls short for active attack mitigation cases. Attack traffic often hides within common protocols and port numbers (for example, HTTP port 80) requiring payload matching for filtering. In these cases, the offending packets are best characterized by subtle or very specific identifying features within Layer 3 or Layer 4 header fields that are not available within the predefined ACL syntax rules, or within some portion of the actual packet payload. When the required granularity for classification is unavailable, the alternative of filtering all traffic destined to the target (as opposed to filtering only attack traffic) is often all that remains, and which may be more detrimental than the attack itself.

FPM is a flexible Layers 2–7 stateless classification mechanism that was specifically developed to address the challenges and shortcomings of ACLs, as described in the "Interface ACL Techniques" section. FPM is considered the next generation of ACL technology within IOS, and provides the policy language and mechanisms to develop fully customized packet filters, including the ability to match on arbitrary bits within the packet header and payload. In this way, FPM removes the constraints of using predefined fields that previously limited packet inspection as outlined previously.

Using FPM, you may configure packet-matching criteria for any or all fields in a packet's header and for bit patterns, that you may also define, at arbitrary offsets within the packet's headers or payload. The only constraint is that FPM policies are capable of inspection only within the first 256 bytes of the packet. Nevertheless, this allows the characteristics of an attack (source port, packet size, byte string) to be uniquely matched and a configurable action, such as drop, count, or log, to be taken. The offset or depth at which to begin matching can be specified in terms of absolute bit offsets or referenced from defined locations within the packet. Using these locations is dependent upon loading one or several protocol header description files (PHDF). Cisco provides PHDFs for well-known, established protocols such as Ethernet, IP, TCP, and UDP. However, because PHDFs are written in XML, you may also create your own customized PHDFs to describe the format of any packet. You would write these PHDFs off-box with any text editor and then copy them to the target router and load them.

FPM rules may be provisioned by using IOS CLI or by creating them off-box in XML and loading them. Regardless of method, the procedures essentially involve defining the traffic classes and then defining the actions (policies). When using CLI, FPM is configured using a syntax analogous to MQC, including class maps to describe the traffic to be filtered, policy maps to define the action to be taken for filtered traffic, and service policies to attach the filter and action to an interface.

Example 4-7 provides a sample FPM configuration that is meant to classify and drop packets generated by the computer worm *SQL Slammer*. In this example, the PHDF files for IP and UDP are loaded to allow offsets to be specified in terms of header fields (such as *destination port*) rather than absolute offsets. Next, match criteria are defined within the class maps, first to look for UDP packets and secondly to look for packets matching the Slammer-specific attributes, including a UDP destination port of 1434 (eq 0x59A), an IP packet length of exactly 404 bytes (eq 0x194), and a bit pattern of 0x04011010 beginning 224 bytes from the start of the IP header. Finally, the service policy **fpm-policy** is created to combine these classification criteria with a policy action that drops any matching packets (that is, SQL Slammer). This service policy is then applied to the Gigabit Ethernet 0/1 interface.

Example 4-7 *FPM Configuration Illustration*

```
load protocol disk0:ip.phdf
load protocol disk0:udp.phdf
!
class-map type stack match-all ip-udp
 description "match UDP over IP packets"
 match field ip protocol eq 0x11 next udp
!
class-map type access-control match-all slammer
 description "match on slammer packets"
 match field udp dest-port eq 0x59A
 match field ip length eq 0x194
 match start l3-start offset 224 size 4 eq 0x04011010
!
policy-map type access-control fpm-udp-policy
 description "policy for UDP based attacks"
 class slammer
  drop
!
policy-map type access-control fpm-policy
 description "drop worms and malicious attacks"
 class ip-udp
   service-policy fpm-udp-policy
!
interface GigabitEthernet 0/1
 service-policy type access-control input fpm-policy
```

As Example 4-7 illustrates, FPM enables you to specify powerful custom pattern matching deep within the packet header or payload to block viruses, worms, and attacks while minimizing inadvertent filtering of legitimate network traffic. FPM is stateless, like ACLs, providing a rapid and scaleable security tool for mitigating attacks at the network edge. Additional information about FPM, including XML configuration guides, is located at http://www.cisco.com/en/US/products/ps6723/prod_white_papers_list.html.

QoS Techniques

Quality of service (QoS) is generally thought of exclusively in the context of IP differentiated services, which, of course, is its primary use. Although many operators generally agree that QoS is required at the network edge in support of differentiated services due to lower-bandwidth network links and subsequently higher serialization delay, the merits and necessity of deploying QoS within the network core are often debated. Overprovisioning and traffic engineering of network capacity to avoid congestion events is argued to be an equivalent solution (albeit more costly in terms of network capital expense, but arguably less costly in terms of operational expense). Although both solutions may be engineered to achieve tight service-level agreement (SLA) capabilities, the QoS solution reduces the risk of collateral damage often caused by DoS attacks, thereby providing greater network resilience. This is achieved by using the intelligent packet scheduling and discard techniques described in this section, including queuing, recoloring, and, optionally, rate limiting. Although many other important QoS techniques are available, such as shaping and RED/WRED, the applicable techniques from a security perspective are reviewed next.

Queuing

Queuing provides bandwidth isolation between traffic classes. A variety of queuing algorithms are available, such as Priority Queuing, Custom Queuing, Weighted Fair Queuing (WFQ), Class-Based WFQ, and Modified Deficit Round Robin (MDRR). Queuing support varies among IP router platforms. Nevertheless, each algorithm aims to isolate traffic classes from one another and provide bandwidth guarantees per class.

Through QoS and queuing, you may isolate IP control and management plane traffic from data plane traffic. This may help prevent critical control and management protocols from being adversely affected by data plane DoS attacks. Attacks within the control and management planes may be mitigated using the techniques described in Chapter 5, "Control Plane Security," and Chapter 6, "Management Plane Security," respectively. Further, QoS and queuing also facilitate isolation within the data plane among different IP services. In a combined Internet and IP (MPLS) VPN backbone, for example, QoS enables VPN traffic to be isolated and unaffected by DoS attacks within the Internet data and services planes. If a link fails and subsequent loss of bandwidth occurs, queuing also provides service isolation between traffic types, to avoid fate sharing.

Queuing may also be configured to provide priority treatment of one traffic class over other traffic classes. For example, high-priority traffic classes such as real-time VoIP services and control and management plane protocols may be prioritized above low-priority best-effort data plane traffic. Queuing also enables minimum (or relative) bandwidth guarantees per traffic class. In this way, for example, control and management plane traffic may be assured a configurable percentage of a network link's capacity. The CLI shown in Example 4-8 illustrates the use of the Cisco MQC to assign a minimum bandwidth guarantee of 25 percent of a POS link's capacity to control and management plane traffic.

Example 4-8 *IP Queuing Policy Example*

```
policy-map foo
  class control-n-mgmt-planes
    bandwidth percent 25
  class data-plane
    bandwidth percent 75

interface pos1/1
 service-policy output foo
```

Such a QoS policy minimizes the risk of attacks within the data plane from adversely affecting the control and management planes. It may also reduce the risk of collateral damage, as described in Chapter 2, whereby a transit attack within the data plane causes routing protocol failures and, thereby, loss of IP reachability to and from other IP networks connected to the affected router.

IP QoS Packet Coloring (Marking)

Before packets may be enqueued within a queuing system, they must be classified. QoS packet classification may use a wide variety of parameters, including but not limited to those listed in Table 4-1.

Table 4-1 *QoS Packet Classification Parameters*

MQC Classification Parameter	Represents
match ip precedence	The IP precedence, per RFC 791
match ip dscp	The IP DSCP (differentiated services code point), per RFC 2474
match vlan	The IEEE 802.1Q VLAN that the IP packet was transmitted or received on
match dlci	The Frame Relay DLCI (data-link connection identifier) that the IP packet was transmitted or received on
match access-group	An IP standard or extended ACL (see "Interface ACL Techniques" earlier in this chapter)
match qos-group	An IOS internal QoS group identifier that may be set using any of the other MQC classification parameters as well as through QoS Policy Propagation on BGP (see "BGP Policy Enforcement Using QPPB" later in this chapter)
match mpls experimental	The MPLS Experimental (EXP) field value of an MPLS labeled packet (for more information on this field, refer to Chapter 7 and Appendix B)

IP precedence and DSCP values are specifically defined for IP QoS purposes. Hence, most IP QoS deployments classify packets using either the IP precedence or IP DSCP values.

Packet coloring simply refers to setting the QoS classification identifier (for example, IP DSCP) according to each packet's assigned traffic class as it ingresses the network. IP precedence is actively used on the Internet, and routing protocol traffic is set with IP precedence 6 and DSCP 48. Consider the following traffic classes that are commonly defined within differentiated services–based IP QoS architectures:

- **IP precedence (or class Selector DSCP) value 6:** IP control plane protocols, including, for example, BGP, OSPF, RIP, PIM, IGMP, HSRP, and MPLS LDP.

- **IP precedence (or class Selector DSCP) value 5:** Real-time data plane traffic class that supports applications such as Voice over IP (VoIP). It offers low delay, jitter, and packet loss.

- **IP precedence (or class Selector DSCP) value 0:** Best-effort data plane traffic class that defines no minimum requirements for packet delay, jitter, or loss.

For proper QoS handling, the IP precedence value associated with each packet must be set correctly. Otherwise, packets associated with one traffic class may be incorrectly enqueued within another traffic class queue, which prevents isolation between the different traffic classes (as outlined in the preceding "Queuing" section) and thereby enables low-priority traffic to adversely affect high-priority traffic. Using the traffic classes defined in the preceding list as an example, an attacker may attempt to launch a DoS attack against VoIP and control plane traffic by flooding the network with traffic marked as IP precedence values 5 and 6, respectively. Note that the attack traffic may be legitimate best-effort, transit traffic (that is, not malicious). However, because it is simply marked with IP precedence value 5 or 6, it is mistakenly serviced from the VoIP or control plane queues instead of the lower-priority best-effort traffic queue. A flood of such traffic may exhaust the real-time and control plane queues, resulting in increase packet drops, control protocol timeouts, and routing protocol failures. If routing protocols fail, IP reachability may be lost, resulting in a DoS condition. Similarly, packet drops within the real-time queue may adversely affect VoIP applications. Hence, to ensure proper packet classification downstream, packet coloring upstream or at the network edge is required. In this way, traffic isolation can be maintained between low- and high-priority traffic classes and between IP services (for example, Internet and IP VPNs).

IP QoS mechanisms are increasingly being deployed within SP backbones in support of differentiated services and to reduce the risk of collateral damage often caused by transit DoS attacks. QoS requires that packets be classified and colored. However, many SPs want to avoid modifying customer traffic QoS markings, because these packets may be marked in a manner appropriate for some application relevant to the customer's internal environment. In this case, SPs may provide QoS transparency such that the customer marking is maintained end to end. IP QoS transparency is only supported if the SP tunnels traffic across its core using, for example, MPLS. If the SP tunnels customer traffic through MPLS, there is no need to recolor customer QoS markings at the edge because the customer

QoS markings are hidden when transiting the SP network. Therefore, the SP only needs to ensure that the tunnel header (for example, MPLS) is appropriately marked.

There are several different versions of QoS transparency. These are well defined within the RFC 3270 MPLS DiffServ tunneling specification. Note, however, that if traffic is not tunneled and the SP does not recolor customer QoS values at the network edge, isolation between traffic classes and services within the SP core cannot be assured. This may provide a potential DoS attack vector, as described previously.

The MQC policy shown in Example 4-9 illustrates re-marking the IP DSCP of all packets received on interface POS 1/1 to a value of 0. This prevents external transit traffic from entering a downstream *control-n-mgmt-planes* traffic queue defined in Example 4-8 above.

Example 4-9   *IP QoS Packet Recoloring Example*

```
policy-map edge-coloring
    class-default
      set ip dscp 0

interface pos1/1
  service-policy input edge-coloring
```

Based upon the queuing and recoloring configurations illustrated in Examples 4-8 and 4-9, transit traffic will be isolated from the network core control and management planes. This mitigates the risk of DoS attacks that aim to bypass QoS classification policies.

Rate Limiting

Traffic rate limiting (or policing) is a QoS technique used to discard or recolor packets that do not conform to an SLA or traffic rate. IOS rate limiting may be configured using either committed access rate (CAR) or MQC policing. MQC is the recommended CLI syntax, as it allows you to define a traffic class independently of QoS policies.

Although ACLs enable you to permit or deny a traffic flow, rate limiting permits a traffic flow up to a configurable maximum rate. From a security perspective, this may be useful for allowing a traffic flow to pass while limiting its potential impact on the network and destination. In the past, for example, many SPs responded to increasing P2P traffic volumes by rate limiting it to limit the amount of network capacity it may utilize. Rate limiting drove P2P software providers to use a combination of encryption and port number changes, including the use of port 80 (HTTP) to masquerade P2P flows as regular HTTP traffic and, thereby, bypass these mechanisms. Nevertheless, rate limiting remains a useful security tool for bounding the maximum transmission rates of traffic flows.

Consider the MQC configuration illustrated in Example 4-10. In this example, the MQC configuration rate limits ICMP Echo Requests (pings) and TCP SYN packets received on interface POS 1/1. An ACL is used for packet classification and separate MQC policers are used for ICMP Echo Requests versus TCP SYN packets. Rate limiting such as this may be configured against any identifiable traffic flow and may be applied on ingress or egress of an interface.

Example 4-10 *MQC-Based Rate Limiting Example*

```
class-map icmp-pings
  match access-group 102
class-map tcp-syns
  match access-group 103
!
policy-map police-policy
  class icmp-pings
    police <rate> conform-action transmit exceed-action drop
  class tcp-syns
    police <rate> conform-action transmit exceed-action drop
!
interface pos1/1
 service-policy input police-policy
!
access-list 102 permit icmp any any echo
access-list 103 deny tcp any any established
access-list 103 permit tcp any any
```

As stated previously, rate limiting is useful for allowing a traffic flow to pass while limiting its potential impact on network resources. IP routers are increasingly using predefined rate limiters to protect the router from exception traffic flows and DoS attacks. Predefined rate limiters vary between IP router platforms and between the IP traffic planes. Rate limiting within the IP control plane using Control Plane Policing (CoPP) is described in Chapter 5. Also, before applying a rate limiter, you should first consider whether it may actually introduce a potential attack vector. If, for example, a rate limiter is applied on an interface to limit the maximum transmission rate of a given traffic flow, an attacker may flood the interface with spoofed traffic such that the legitimate traffic flow is considered above the maximum permitted transmission rate of the rate limiter and, thereby, discarded. To minimize the risk of this threat, a granular rate limiter should be used wherever possible, as opposed to a coarse rate limiter.

IP Options Techniques

As described in Chapter 2, the IP packet header provides for various IP options as specified in RFC 791. IP options are used to enable control functions within the IP data plane that are required in some specific situations but not necessary for most common IP communications. Typical IP headers option include provisions for timestamps, security, and special routing. IP packets may or may not use IP headers option—they are optional—but IP header option handling mechanisms must be implemented by all IP protocol stacks (hosts and routers).

As you learned in Chapter 1, packets with IP headers option are punted to the IOS process level slow path (CPU) for data plane forwarding due to their variable length and complex processing requirements. Further, given that the IOS process level is shared with the IP control, management, and, optionally, services planes, a flood of IP option packets may easily saturate the IOS process level, triggering a DoS condition. As described in Chapter 2, these may be valid transit IP packets with legitimate sources and destinations, so even in the case of legitimate transit traffic, a DoS-like condition may exist if proper precautions are not taken.

IP headers option are not widely used in general-purpose IP networks. The functions provided by many of these options are deprecated by other, higher-layer protocols and enhancements. Of course, there are still IP protocols that cannot function without certain options. At the time of this writing, the IP protocols that (legitimately) make use of IP headers option include IGMPv2 (RFC 2236), IGMPv3 (RFC 3376), DVMRP (RFC 1075), and RSVP (RFC 2205). When these protocols and features are required, IP headers option must be allowed and processed accordingly. However, given the limited legitimate requirements for packets with IP headers option and the potentially disruptive impact they may have on network infrastructure, when options are not required, you should consider discarding them or at least limiting their ability to impact the network. Techniques available to mitigate the risk of IP options–based DoS attacks are reviewed next.

Disable IP Source Routing

IP source routing is enabled by default within IOS. When IP source routing is enabled, IOS is able to process IP packets with source-routing headers option. As described in Chapter 2, there are two problems with this. First, this introduces a potential DoS vulnerability against IP routers due to the slow path processing that is required. Second, this allows an attacker to specify the packet-forwarding path that should be taken to a given destination, enabling targeted attacks against downstream routers. Security best practices require IP source routing to be disabled. Disabling IP source routing via the global IOS command **no ip source-route** effectively mitigates the risk of attacks relating to packets with source-routing headers option. Of the protocols listed in the previous paragraph that use IP options, only DVMRP uses source-routing headers option.

IP Options Selective Drop

By default, all IPv4 packets (transit and receive) containing headers option are punted to the IOS process level for processing. As described previously, this is due to the variable-length nature of IP headers option, and the hardware and software forwarding optimizations built into modern routers to expedite normal IPv4 packets having 20-byte headers. IPv4 supports a maximum of 32 different option types (due to the 5-bit Type field in the option header), not all of which are currently assigned. The currently specified options, including source routing, are described at http://www.iana.org/assignments/ip-parameters. IP source routing is the only header option that allows a source to specify the forwarding path, but all other options remain as potential DoS threats to IP routers due to the need for IOS process level processing as just outlined. To mitigate the risk of all IP header option packet types, the global IOS command **ip options drop** (referred to as the IP Options Selective Drop feature) may be configured.

The IOS IP Options Selective Drop feature operates in two modes:

- **Drop mode:** For all IOS routers supporting this feature, when **ip options drop** is configured, all IP packets (transit and receive) containing options are punted to the IOS process level and then immediately (and silently) discarded. Drop mode is configured using the global IOS command **ip options drop** and affects all ingress IPv4 packets on all interfaces. Note that on Cisco 12000 (GSR) series routers, these actions occur on the distributed line card CPU and not on the central Route Processor (RP). Even though the punt to the IOS process level is still required, impact on the CPU is much smaller than that of fully processing the packet. In addition, because drop mode discards packets from the network, it relieves downstream routers and hosts from the load of IP option packets as well. This effectively mitigates the risk of IP options–based DoS attacks.

- **Ignore mode:** Because the Cisco 12000 (GSR) series is a distributed routing platform, two different mechanisms are used for processing IP option packets, depending on the option type. By default, all IP packets (transit and receive) containing the Router Alert IP header option are punted all the way to the RP for process level handling. All other IP option types are punted only to the distributed line card CPU for handling. Thus, an additional mode was added to the IP Options Selective Drop mechanism to protect the 12000 RP. On Cisco 12000 series routers only, the global IOS command **ip options ignore** may be configured. When **ip options ignore** is configured, all transit IP options packets are punted to the distributed line card CPU (slow path) for processing, but the options portion of the header is ignored (not processed). This includes transit packets with the Router Alert IP option header, and thus the 12000 RP is spared from handling any IP options packets. All receive IPv4 options packets are processed as they normally would be by the Cisco 12000 series routers. That is, IP packets with headers option are punted to the RP for handling (because they are CEF receive adjacencies). In addition, all transit packets with headers option are forwarded downstream but the IP headers option are ignored. Note that transit IP options packets still require slow path (distributed line card CPU) processing because other features requiring access to the Layer 4 information (such as ACLs) may be invoked. When IP options are included, the Layer 4 offset is variable and, thus, cannot be handled in hardware.

As you can see, **ip options drop** provides an effective solution to mitigate the risk of IP options–based DoS attacks. The operational costs are minimal due to the single, global configuration command. However, the scope of the command is global (not per interface), and there is still a small impact on performance because packets with IP headers option are still punted to the IOS process level before they are silently discarded. For Cisco 12000 series environments in which some IP option packets are required, protecting the RP through **ip options ignore** may be sufficient. Alternatively, ACLs may also be used to filter IP option packets on select interfaces, as described in the next section.

NOTE	When using the **ip options drop** or **ip options ignore** global configuration command, IP header option processing is modified as just described. To restore the default behavior, you must issue the global configuration command **no ip options**. Do not confuse the syntax of this command to imply that IP options will not be processed. That is not what this command does. This is simply the way in which configuration commands are removed from within IOS configurations.

ACL Support for Filtering IP Options

In certain versions of Cisco IOS, named, extended ACLs may also be used to filter IP packets with headers option. The use of ACLs provides for more granular control than the globally configured **ip options drop** mechanism. For one thing, the ACL technique may be applied on a per-interface basis rather than on a global basis. In addition, ACL keywords allow for filtering specific header option types, as opposed to discarding all IP packets containing any headers option. As an example, consider the ACL configuration illustrated in Example 4-11. This example configuration shows the named, extended ACL called *filter-options* that has been constructed to discard all IP packets having a strict source route (SSR), loose source route (LSR), or timestamp header option. The named, extended filter-options ACL is then applied to interface POS1/1 to filter packets received on this interface (inbound direction).

Example 4-11   *Filtering IPv4 Packets Containing Specific Options Using ACLs*

```
ip access-list extended filter-options
  10 deny ip any any option ssr
  20 deny ip any any option lsr
  30 deny ip any any option timestamp
  40 permit ip any any
!
interface POS1/1
  access-group filter-options in
```

The ACL used in Example 4-11 only includes ACEs for dropping specific IP header option types. In practice, these ACEs would most likely be combined with other ACEs used to support infrastructure, transit, antispoofing, or classification ACLs, as described in the "Interface ACL Techniques" section earlier in the chapter. Additional details on filtering IP options using ACLs can be found in "ACL Support for Filtering IP Options" (see the "Further Reading" section).

Control Plane Policing

Control Plane Policing (CoPP) is an IOS security technique that is used to protect the control and management planes of an IP router and, optionally, the services planes. This feature is described in detail in Chapter 5.

As you learned in Chapter 1, a small group of transit IP packets, called *exception* packets, must also be punted to the IOS process level for forwarding. IP packets with headers option were discussed in the previous section as one example, but a few others exist as well. CoPP is mentioned in this chapter because it may also be used to protect an IP router from these exception IP packets, such as a flood of IP packets with the Router Alert header option. All IP packets with a Router Alert option are punted to the IOS process level for handling, irrespective of being transit or receive adjacency packets. This makes them subject to CoPP policies that may be configured to limit the impact on the IOS process level against a flood or DoS attack crafted with Router Alert option packets. CoPP is described in detail in Chapter 5.

ICMP Data Plane Mitigation Techniques

As discussed in Chapter 2, ICMP is commonly used as an attack vector for data plane DoS attacks. One reason for this is that ICMP processing is often handled at the IOS process level (CPU) of IP routers, and hence, can be leveraged directly from the data plane to attack the same router components that support the control plane.

By default, IOS software enables certain ICMP processing functions in accordance with IETF standards. These default configurations may not conform to security best practices or to security policies you may have for your network. To reduce the impact of ICMP-related data plane DoS attacks within IP network environments, IOS includes interface configuration commands to disable many of these ICMP handling features. These ICMP mitigation techniques are discussed next:

- **no ip unreachables:** Disables the interface from generating ICMP Destination Unreachable (Type 3) messages, thereby reducing the impact of certain ICMP-based DoS attacks on the router CPU. This command is applied within IOS interface configuration mode. The command **ip unreachables** is used to restore the ability to generate ICMP Destination Unreachables, which is the default behavior within IOS. The **no ip unreachables** command applies to all types of ICMP Unreachable messages as defined by http://www.iana.org/assignments/icmp-parameters. (ICMP Destination Unreachables are also covered in Appendix B.) ICMP Destination Unreachable messages are often generated by network edge routers and default gateways as a result of ACL filtering or IP routing table inconsistencies (in other words, lack of a prefix match within the IP routing table for the destination address of a received packet). However, as described in Appendix B, other than a few management applications (such as traceroute), very few applications actually use ICMP Destination Unreachable messages. One exception is Path MTU Discovery (PMTUD), which relies upon ICMP Destination Unreachable (Type 3), Fragmentation Needed and Don't Fragment was Set (Code 4) messages for proper operation. Disabling IP Destination Unreachable generation will prevent these ICMP Type 3, Code 4 messages, potentially breaking PMTUD. Generally, this would only be true in cases where interface MTU values were inconsistent across a router's interfaces. (IP fragmentation and interface MTUs are discussed further in Chapter 7.) Therefore, the logical place to apply **no ip unreachables** to mitigate the risk of ICMP Unreachable DoS attacks is at the network edge, where ingress filtering and IP routing table inconsistencies generally occur and where the router CPU could potentially be externally attacked by causing excessive ICMP Unreachable message generation. Further, the network edge and core should be engineered to avoid IP fragmentation such that applying **no ip unreachables** at the network edge does not break PMTUD. Example 4-12 illustrates the Cisco IOS CLI used to disable the generation of ICMP Unreachable messages on an Ethernet interface.

Example 4-12   *Configuration for* **no ip unreachables** *Interface Command*

```
interface Ethernet 0
  no ip unreachables
```

You should be aware that some versions of IOS also provide the ability to rate limit the generation of ICMP Destination Unreachable messages to limit their impact on the IOS process level. IOS maintains two timers per interface: one for general Destination Unreachable messages, and one for Fragmentation Needed and Don't Fragment was Set Destination Unreachable messages. Both share the same time limits and defaults. The default value for both timers is one ICMP Destination Unreachable message per 500 ms. Default values may be changed using the **ip icmp rate-limit unreachable** global configuration command. In this way, using the default values, only two ICMP Destination Unreachables will be sent per second per interface (assuming **ip unreachables** is enabled). Note that the **ip icmp rate-limit unreachable** and **no ip unreachable** commands apply only to ICMP Destination Unreachable messages. These commands have no effect on other ICMP message types (for example, Type 11, Time Exceeded).

- **no ip redirects:** Disables the interface from generating ICMP Redirect (ICMP Type 5) messages when it is forced to send an IP packet through the same interface on which it was received, and the subnet or network of the source IP address is on the same subnet or network of the next-hop IP address in the Redirect message per RFC 792. This command is applied within IOS interface configuration mode, and applies only to ICMP Redirect messages. By default, Cisco IOS interfaces generate ICMP Redirect messages. Thus, the interface command **no ip redirects** is required to change this default behavior. Most ICMP Redirects are generated in shared LAN environments by network edge routers, specifically default gateways because IP hosts and default gateways typically do not exchange routing protocol information and because ICMP Redirects are generated only if the source of the original packet is directly connected. An IP host's statically or DHCP assigned default gateway may not provide the best path to a remote destination. In these scenarios, the default gateway forwards the packet but also generates an ICMP Redirect to the source IP host. Therefore, the logical place to apply the **no ip redirects** command to mitigate the risk of ICMP Redirect attacks is on router interfaces that do not provide default gateway services via a shared LAN. Disabling ICMP redirects on shared LAN default gateway router interfaces is also an option and is often considered a best practice to prevent the generation of ICMP redirect messages from impacting the IOS process level. Example 4-13 illustrates the Cisco IOS CLI used to disable the generation of ICMP Redirect messages on an Ethernet interface.

Example 4-13 *Configuration for* **no ip redirects** *Interface Command*

```
interface Ethernet 0
  no ip redirects
```

Note More information on the generation of ICMP Redirect messages may be found in the Cisco.com document "When Are ICMP Redirects Sent?" (see the "Further Reading" section).

- **IP packet with parameter problem:** Per RFC 792, if an IP router receives a packet with an IP header problem and discards the packet, it must generate an ICMP Parameter Problem (Type 12) message. These are only sent if the IP packet is discarded. The default behavior within IOS is to generate such ICMP Parameter Problem messages, and there is no CLI to disable this behavior. CoPP may be used to limit the impact of DoS attacks using IP packets with parameter problems. (For further information on CoPP, refer to Chapter 5.) Note that such attacks generally apply only to first-hop (default gateway) routers, because they would first encounter and discard such malformed packets rather than forward them downstream. Hence, default gateway routers are most susceptible to this specific attack.

- **IP packet with expired TTL:** Per RFC 792, if an IP router receives a packet with a TTL value of 1 or 0, the packet must be discarded and an ICMP Time Exceeded (Type 11) message must be generated and sent to the original source. The default behavior within IOS is to generate such ICMP Time Exceeded messages, and there is no CLI available to disable it. However, other techniques are available to mitigate the risk of TTL expiry–based DoS attacks, including:

  — ACL filtering of IP TTL. For further information, refer to the "Interface ACL Techniques" section earlier in the chapter.

  — CoPP. For further information, refer to Chapter 5.

  — Disabling IP TTL to MPLS TTL propagation within MPLS networks. For further information, refer to Chapter 7.

Because ICMP packets often bridge the data plane and control plane, you should put extra effort into understanding their use and misuse and methods to control their generation. As described previously, both data plane and control plane security techniques are often used for these purposes. Techniques to mitigate the risk of attacks using ICMP protocol packets are discussed in Chapter 5.

Disabling IP Directed Broadcasts

An IP directed broadcast is an IP packet whose destination address is a valid broadcast address for an IP subnet (or network) that is one or more router hops from the source address. Intermediate routers that are not directly connected to the destination subnet forward IP directed broadcasts in the same way as unicast IP packets. However, when a directed broadcast packet reaches the ultimate hop router that is directly connected to the destination subnet, it is broadcast to every IP device attached to that subnet using the Layer 2 link-layer broadcast address. This is consistent with the IP broadcast address 255.255.255.255/32, however, IP directed broadcasts allow IP broadcasts to be remotely transmitted versus remaining local to the directly connected network. Each IP router (and device) listens for the IP broadcast address of its own subnet and handles such packets as a CEF receive adjacency.

IP directed broadcasts, and specifically ICMP directed broadcasts, have been used to launch DoS attacks (see, for example, "CERT Advisory CA-1998-01 Smurf IP Denial-of-Service Attacks," at http://www.cert.org/advisories/CA-1998-01.html). As a result, and given the limited legitimate uses of IP directed broadcasts, IOS changed the default interface configuration to **no ip directed-broadcast**, which disables IP directed broadcasting. When disabled for an interface, directed broadcasts destined for the associated IP subnet to which that interface is attached will be discarded, rather than being broadcast. This command only affects the final transmission of the directed broadcast on the egress interface of the ultimate hop router. It does not affect the transit unicast routing of IP directed broadcasts along the forwarding path to the ultimate hop router. Alternatively, an ACL may be configured to filter unauthorized directed broadcasts. In this way, only directed broadcasts that are permitted by the ACL will be forwarded; all other directed broadcasts will be discarded.

For those IP networks or specific subnets that may require IP directed broadcasts, it may be enabled by applying the **ip directed-broadcast** command within IOS interface configuration mode. When enabled, ACLs are recommended to limit the scope of IP directed broadcasts. For example, only devices associated with trusted (or internal) IP subnets may be permitted to transmit IP directed broadcasts. Conversely, IP directed broadcasts sourced from untrusted (or external) IP subnets should be filtered. Antispoofing techniques, including ACLs and uRPF, may be used to mitigate the risk of spoofed IP directed broadcasts. If IP directed broadcast support has been enabled and you want to disable this functionality, use the **no ip directed-broadcast** IOS interface configuration command.

IP Sanity Checks

IP routers perform integrity checks on received packets, including verification of the IP checksum and the IP header format, including options fields. If a router discards a packet due to a header parameter problem, the router may signal that to the packet source via an ICMP Parameter Problem message (Type 12) indicating the error condition. Within the control plane, routers also perform integrity checks to validate routing protocol advertisements received. Such integrity checks are often specified within the IETF protocol specifications and state machines. OSPF advertisements received, for example, are not accepted at the IP process level per Section 8.2 of RFC 2328 until a variety of integrity checks are performed against both the IP and OSPF packet headers. Other control plane protocols have their own distinct integrity checks, given the inherent differences among them, including transport layer protocol checks. TCP-based protocols, for example, verify packet sequence numbers before accepting packets associated with established sessions. Conversely, Generalized TTL Security Mechanism (GTSM) is an IP integrity check that is protocol independent and helps to reduce the risk of spoofed attacks. For more information on GTSM, refer to Chapter 5.

To reduce the risk of spoofed and broadcast attacks, high-end Cisco routers have integrated additional IP sanity checks within the data plane to filter illegal packets having

- IP source address equal to IANA reserved IP multicast address 224.0.0.0/4
- IP source address equal to the IANA reserved host loopback address 127.0.0.0/8
- IP source address equal to the all 1s broadcast address 255.255.255.255/32
- IP destination address equal to the all 0s network address 0.0.0.0/32

The preceding packet types are illegal and are discarded with no ICMP messages generated. Although support is limited to high-end Cisco routers such as the Cisco 12000 series, it is recommended that you add similar checks to interface ACL policies as illustrated in the Example 4-14 configuration.

Example 4-14   *IP Sanity Check Access List Illustration*

```
interface pos1/1
  access-group 100 in

access-list 100 deny ip 224.0.0.0 31.255.255.255 any
access-list 100 deny ip 127.0.0.0 0.255.255.255 any
access-list 100 deny ip 255.255.255.255 0.0.0.0 any
access-list 100 deny ip any 0.0.0.0 0.0.0.0
access-list 100 permit ip any any
```

You should consider filtering other illegal IP address combinations within your ACL policies as defined within RFC 3330.

BGP Policy Enforcement Using QPPB

As outlined within the "Interface ACL Techniques" section earlier in the chapter, interface ACLs provide static policies within the data plane to filter IP traffic flows. Hence, ACLs work well when traffic filtering policies are generally static. For those applications where traffic filtering policies change frequently, ACLs are often too difficult and costly to manually maintain. Enforcement of Internet peering agreements is one such application where SPs often consider the cost of manually maintaining ingress ACL policies to be too significant compared to the risk of Internet peers violating established agreements. As a result, many SPs simply rely upon control plane techniques to enforce peering agreements. Control plane–based techniques, however, only affect routing protocol policies and do not mitigate the risk of an Internet peer using IP routing tricks to bypass control plane techniques and, thereby, steal bandwidth in violation of peering agreements. Consider the network topology illustrated in Figure 4-9.

Figure 4-9   *Internet Peering Policy Violation*

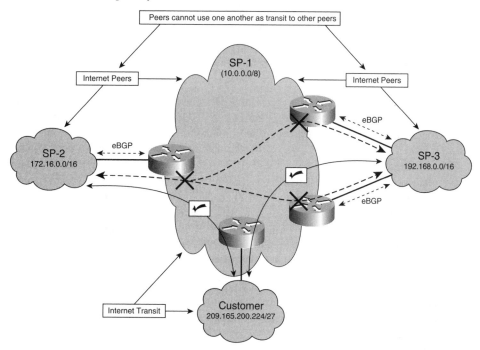

SP-2 and SP-3 are both Internet peers of SP-1. As a result, SP-1 and SP-2 exchange only their customer IP prefixes with one another via eBGP, as do SP-1 and SP-3. Because SP-2 and SP-3 only peer with SP-1 (either settlement-free or settlement-based) and do not purchase Internet transit services from SP-1, from the perspective of SP-1, there should be no IP reachability between SP-2 and SP-3. That is, SP-2 and SP-3 should not be using SP-1 as transit to reach each other's prefixes.

In general, Internet peering between SPs provides IP reachability to each other's customer prefixes (not downstream peer prefixes). Per Figure 4-9, traffic between 172.16.0.0/16 and 192.168.0.0/16 networks should not transit SP-1. Otherwise, such traffic flows between SP-2 and SP-3 would effectively be stealing bandwidth from SP-1. Conversely, SP-1 customer prefixes (for example, 209.165.200.224/27) have full IP reachability to and from both SP-2 and SP-3 prefixes because SP-1 has established peering agreements with both SP-2 and SP-3. If SP-2 desires IP reachability to SP-3 prefixes, and vice versa, SP-2 and SP-3 should either peer with one another directly or purchase Internet transit services from SP-1. Although the benefit for SP-1 in peering with both SP-2 and SP-3 is IP reachability to their respective customer prefixes, in general, there is no benefit for SP-1 in providing free transit services between SP-2 and SP-3. If SP-2 and SP-3 do not purchase SP-1 transit services and remain SP-1 peers, any transit traffic transferred between SP-2 and SP-3 via SP-1 is considered to be in violation of the SP-1 peering agreements. Although this may be considered a business dispute between Internet peers, such traffic may adversely affect (paying) transit customers of SP-1 in terms of packet delay, loss, and jitter. Hence, SP-1 needs to protect its (paying) transit customers and well-behaved (conforming) peers and mitigate the risk of Internet peers stealing bandwidth in violation of established peering agreements.

Typically, SP-1 prevents IP reachability between SP-2 and SP-3 solely through BGP routing policies (in other words, control plane). BGP route maps and prefix filters control route advertisements and prevent the propagation of SP-2 and SP-3 customer prefixes between one another. In this way, SP-2 does not learn SP-3 customer prefixes via eBGP, and vice versa. If, however, SP-2 or SP-3 plays routing tricks to bypass these control plane policies, such as using SP-1 as a default route, then SP-1 may forward unauthorized transit traffic between SP-2 and SP-3, because the BGP techniques just outlined do not apply within the IP data plane. Hence, SP-1 is at risk of an Internet peer using IP routing tricks to circumvent BGP peering policies and, thereby, steal bandwidth in violation of established peering agreements. For more information on the BGP security techniques, refer to Chapter 5.

SPs are able to monitor peering policy violations through NetFlow and BGP policy accounting. However, these techniques do not filter traffic flows that violate policies. They only allow the SP to detect peering violations, not mitigate them. Data plane techniques are required to filter traffic flows that bypass BGP routing policies. For more information on NetFlow and BGP policy accounting, see Chapter 6.

As mentioned, ACLs may be used by SP-1 to prevent IP reachability between SP-2 and SP-3. Such an ACL would be applied, for example, on SP-1's external interfaces to SP-2 and SP-3 and would filter any traffic not destined to an SP-1 transit customer prefix. This seems relatively straightforward; however, in practice, this is not operationally deployable, for the following reasons:

- SP-1 has many transit customers, some of which use SP-1 assigned IP address blocks whereas others have their own address blocks allocated from an IP registry. Such customers may also be multihomed to multiple ISPs for redundancy purposes, which must be considered if they are also reachable via Internet peers. Transit customers may migrate from one ISP to another and, in the future, yet another.

- SP-1 customers may be downstream SPs themselves (for example, Tier 2). Hence, the prefix challenges just outlined are recursive among SP-1 and any transit customers that are also downstream SPs.

Because of the preceding reasons, the transit customer prefixes maintained by SPs are constantly changing. Conversely, ACLs are generally static. Therefore, to enforce peering policies using ACLs, an SP would be required to update and reapply the ACL policy whenever it gains or loses an IP prefix. Given the operational complexities and expense in maintaining constant changes to static ACL policies, SPs often do not enforce Internet peering policies within the data plane. Automated techniques similar to those used within BGP for filtering control plane advertisements are needed to filter IP data plane traffic that violates the BGP control plane policy.

A technique that may be used to enforce Internet peering policies is Cisco's QoS Policy Propagation on BGP (QPPB). QPPB provides prefix-based QoS such that traffic flows to and from specific IP prefixes may be prioritized above (or below) others or simply discarded. IP prefixes of interest are tagged via the control plane using common BGP route-map techniques, including the community attribute, AS Path, and ACLs. Traffic flows to and from the tagged BGP prefixes are then classified and filtered via the data forwarding plane using IOS MQC policing. For more information on policing, refer to the "Rate-Limiting" section earlier in the chapter. QPPB provides the glue between the BGP control plane and the data plane MQC capabilities (for example, policing) in support of IP prefix-based QoS. BGP, MQC, and QPPB are each configured independently; however, collectively they provide the QPPB solution.

In the context of Internet peering policy enforcement, QPPB is configured to apply distinct tags within the FIB (CEF) table to differentiate between peer IP prefixes and customer IP prefixes. Then, any traffic received from a peer and destined to a peer prefix can be discarded in accordance with Internet peering policies. Conversely, any traffic received from a peer and destined to a customer prefix is forwarded across the SP-1 backbone in accordance with Internet peering policies.

Standard BGP policy configurations may be used to tag peer prefixes differently from customer prefixes. The sample BGP configuration illustrated in Example 4-15 uses the BGP community attribute to distinguish between peer and customer prefixes, but you may also use the AS Path attribute and route-map ACLs.

Example 4-15 *QPPB Example BGP Configuration*

```
!
router bgp <SP1-ASN>
  table-map tag-prefix
  neighbor <ip-address> remote-as <SP1-ASN>
  neighbor 172.16.1.1 remote-as <SP2-ASN>
  neighbor 172.16.1.1 route-map peer-comm in
!
ip bgp-community new-format
ip community-list 1 permit <SP1-ASN>:1
ip community-list 2 permit <SP1-ASN>:2
!
access-list 1 permit 172.16.0.0 0.0.255.255
access-list 1 deny any
!
route-map peer-comm permit 10
  match ip address 1
  set community <SP1-ASN>:1
!
route-map tag-prefix permit 10
  match community 1
  set ip qos-group 1
route-map tag-prefix permit 20
  match community 2
  set ip qos-group 2
```

In this example, the BGP **tag-prefix** table map sets the QoS Group ID for each IP prefix within the FIB to 1 for peer prefixes and to 2 for customer prefixes. By default, IOS sets the QoS Group ID for each prefix within the FIB to 0. The QoS Group ID of a given prefix can be seen via the **show ip cef detail** IOS CLI command if the QoS Group ID is non-zero. As illustrated in Example 4-15, the BGP control plane classifies and tags prefixes within the router FIB. QPPB and MQC policing are then applied within the data forwarding plane to filter traffic flows sourced from Internet peers and destined to peer prefixes. Example 4-16 illustrates QPPB and MQC policing configurations.

Example 4-16 *QPPB and MQC Policing Configuration Illustrations*

```
class-map peer-prefix
  match qos-group 1
class-map customer-prefix
  match qos-group 2
!
policy-map peer-in
  class-map peer-prefix
    police <rate> conform-action drop exceed-action drop
!
interface pos1/1
  description SP-1 interface to SP-2
  ip address 10.1.1.1 255.255.255.252
  bgp-policy destination ip-qos-map
  service-policy input peer-in
  ip access-group <infrastructure-acl> in
```

In this example, interface POS1/1 connects to an Internet peer (SP-2). Destination-based QPPB is enabled on the interface along with MQC input policing. As a result, any traffic received from the Internet peer on interface POS1/1 and destined to a peer prefix is dropped via the MQC policer. Traffic received from the peer and destined to a customer prefix (in other words, QoS Group ID 2) is forwarded. Not only does this approach enforce peering policies within the data plane, thereby mitigating the risk of a peer using routing tricks to steal bandwidth, it also operates dynamically using BGP. In this way, any BGP prefix changes within the SP global IP routing table are automatically and rapidly distributed throughout the network. Peering routers may then use this information to filter traffic flows received from a peer and destined to another peer. No static or manually maintained ACL policies are required and, further, this works in conjunction with ingress ACL policies that provide infrastructure, transit, classification, and, optionally, antispoofing protection. Lastly, this QPPB technique not only filters transit traffic between remote peers connected via distinct SP-1 peering routers, but it also filters transit traffic between local Internet peers attached to the same SP-1 peering router.

IP Routing Techniques

The many techniques outlined in each of the previous sections are considered best common practices (BCP) to mitigate the risk of security attacks against the data plane of an IP network. You can apply ACLs, FPM, and rate limiting not only proactively as BCPs to help prevent attacks but also reactively as incident response tools to mitigate active security attacks.

Another group of valuable and recommended security mechanisms that you can use to mitigate the risk of attacks and to respond to incidents are IP routing techniques. IP routing techniques leverage the IP control plane to protect the data plane through packet filtering, because the lack of a route (or a route to Null0) results in packet discards. As with the data plane mechanisms described previously, these control plane–based mechanisms serve both as a proactive measure to help prevent attacks and as a reactive tool for mitigating active security attacks. Because no one technique or tool is applicable in all circumstances, having a security toolkit that includes IP routing techniques provides you greater flexibility to choose the most appropriate solutions for your specific network environment. The following sections describe how IP routing may be used as a BCP to mitigate the risk of attacks and as a tool for incident response.

IP Network Core Infrastructure Hiding

In this section we will examine the use of IS-IS advertise-passive only for hiding network core infrastructure.

IS-IS Advertise-Passive-Only

Intermediate System-to-Intermediate System (IS-IS) is a link-state protocol that is designed to operate in OSI Connectionless Network Service (CLNS) environments. OSI CLNS is a network layer service similar to IP, but it communicates over Connectionless Network Protocol (CLNP) with its CLNS peers. Integrated IS-IS was developed to support IP and CLNS, and may be used as an Interior Gateway Protocol (IGP) to support IP.

Because IS-IS uses CLNP for its underlying peer communications and carries IP prefixes as an overlay IP Routing Information Base (RIB), in certain cases it is possible to remove the so-called infrastructure links from the IS-IS IP RIB without impacting its primary role as an IGP. For example, iBGP peering is commonly established between loopback interfaces on edge and core routers. Hence, at a minimum, only these loopback interfaces need to be advertised in the IS-IS IP RIB for BGP sessions to be established.

IOS originally introduced a mechanism for IS-IS to exclude connected IP prefixes from LSP (link state protocol) advertisements to improve IS-IS protocol convergence times. This was later also identified as a useful router security tool; the connected prefixes are no longer carried within the IP routing table, so they are no longer reachable by (or susceptible to) direct attacks. This further reduces the risk of an attack against an IS-IS-enabled IP core network, because traffic destined to internal router interface addresses beyond the network edge routers have no associated IP route and thus are no longer reachable. (Infrastructure links on network edge routers remain reachable because they are represented as *connected* prefixes within the routing table.) Attacks against router loopback interfaces remain a threat; however, you can mitigate the risk by applying ingress interface ACLs at network edge routers, and Receive ACL (rACL) and CoPP policies on the local (target) router. For more information on rACL and CoPP, refer to Chapter 5.

Two methods are available for excluding infrastructure links from the IS-IS IP RIB. When only a small number of interfaces are involved, each interface may be explicitly configured for exclusion by issuing the **no isis advertise prefix** interface configuration mode command. When a large number of interfaces must be excluded from the IS-IS IP RIB, it is easier to advertise only the passive interfaces by configuring the **advertise-passive-only** command in IOS routing protocol configuration mode. To use this command, you must also configure the loopback interfaces as passive, which also prevents IS-IS from attempting to send unnecessary hello packets out through a loopback interface. Example 4-17 illustrates this concept.

Example 4-17 *IS-IS* **advertise-passive-only** *Configuration Illustration*

```
router isis Core
  advertise-passive-only
  passive-interface Loopback0
```

This mechanism is only supported for the IS-IS protocol within IOS today. IP networks that use an alternative IGP routing protocol may be similarly protected by using ingress interface ACLs, rACLs, and CoPP policies, as stated previously. The IS-IS **advertise-passive-only** technique simply adds another layer of protection, thus facilitating defense in depth and breadth, as outlined in Chapter 3. A drawback of this IS-IS technique, however, is that network management tasks become more difficult because this technique prevents the ping utility from verifying liveliness of these excluded links. As such, before deployment, you should take care to understand the implications of using this capability.

IP Network Edge External Link Protection

As described in the "Interface ACL Techniques" section earlier in the chapter, iACLs are widely deployed at the network edge to protect an organization's internal network infrastructure. Edge router external links, however, are typically not treated as internal infrastructure and, hence, are often carried within BGP aggregate routes that are widely distributed throughout the Internet routing architecture. This exposes these edge routers to potential DoS attacks from the wider Internet. Figure 4-10 illustrates the potential threat.

Figure 4-10 *PE-CE Link Reachability*

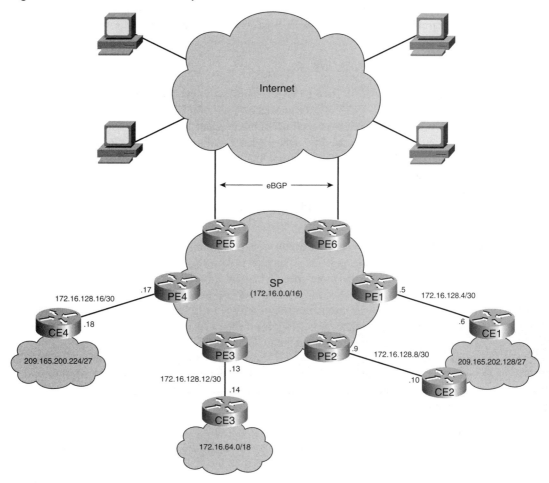

As shown in Figure 4-10, if these external interconnect links (including PE1-CE1, PE2-CE2, and so on) are carried within aggregate prefixes advertised to the wider Internet, they are potentially reachable and, thereby, vulnerable to attack from the wider Internet.

The same applies to the SP's peering interconnects, including PE5 and PE6. To mitigate the risk of attacks against the edge routers (both PEs and CEs) via these external (and public) links, any remote traffic destined to these external interface IP addresses needs to be filtered and discarded. Short of using RFC 3330 private addresses for these external links, you can filter and discard remote traffic by deploying any of several IP routing schemes or iACL techniques. These schemes block IP reachability to external interconnects including PE-CE links. In general, there is no underlying need for remote reachability to these links, but some customers may require reachability to their CE for specific applications, such as IPsec and GRE tunneling, VoIP gateway services, and so on. In those cases, filtering traffic to the CE may break such applications. For those specific PE-CE interconnects, you may need to filter remote traffic destined only to the PE address of the external link.

Protection Using More Specific IP Prefixes

As illustrated in Figure 4-10, the PE1-CE1 link is assigned 172.16.128.4/30, with a PE interface of 172.16.128.5 and a CE interface of 172.16.128.6. The 172.16.0.0/16 aggregate route is advertised to eBGP peers, including the wider Internet, providing to any Internet-connected device IP reachability to these PE-CE links. One approach to block reachability to these network edge (PE-CE) external links is to assign a static route to Null0 for the aggregate address block associated with external links on every core and edge router in the SP network (in other words, 172.16.128.0/18). In this case, the static route **ip route 172.16.128.0 255.255.192.0 Null0** would be configured. This prevents remote reachability across the SP network to the edge router external links.

When applying this, do not redistribute connected routes into BGP or IGP, and do not announce more specific aggregates, such as 172.16.128.0/19. Otherwise, IP reachability would remain, because the more-specific aggregate is preferred. Further, be sure to set BGP **next-hop-self** for iBGP sessions, because external peer BGP next hops (in other words, CEs) are also no longer reachable. The best route to 172.16.128.4/30 and all other PE-CE links on every router in the SP network is now the 172.16.128.0/18 static route to Null0. If a customer absolutely requires that their CE address be globally reachable via the Internet, then configure a static route to the CE /32 external address (for example, 172.16.128.6/32) pointing to the customer interface and redistribute that static route into iBGP on the associated PE. In this way, reachability is maintained for those customers who need it, but the majority of CE interfaces remain protected from direct attack.

The benefit of deploying this technique is that it makes it more difficult to remotely attack PE and, optionally, CE external interfaces (having public addresses). Any packets destined to such addresses are discarded, including ping, but IP traceroute is not impacted.

Providing IP reachability to CE devices while denying reachability to the associated PE external interfaces poses three challenges:

1 A potentially large number of /32 CE host routes may need to be installed within the SP global IP routing table. This may adversely impact IP prefix scalability within the SP routers.

2 PPP encapsulated PE-CE links also require the use of the **no peer neighbor-route**
IOS interface configuration command to ensure that the /32 connected prefix does not
appear in the router RIB, because it would be preferred over the /32 static route to the
CE. Without the **no peer neighbor-route** CLI, the /32 CE static route associated with
PPP interfaces would not be advertised within iBGP, preventing CE reachability, if
required for IPsec tunneling or other services.

3 This approach remains subject to local attacks that ingress and egress through the
same edge router, given that these PE public addresses are local CEF receive
adjacencies and the network edge cannot control what external traffic is sent its way
(as described in Chapter 3). Local attacks may be mitigated using interface ACLs, IP
rACLs, or CoPP. For more information on IP rACLs and CoPP, refer to Chapter 5.

Protection Using BGP Communities

An alternate technique to preventing IP reachability to edge router external links is to tag
the PE-CE prefixes (either the 172.16.128.0/18 aggregate or the individual /30s) with a
special iBGP community attribute that will be matched at remote edge routers. All remote
edge routers will then black hole any traffic to the tagged prefix(es) by setting the IP next
hop to a preconfigured static route that resolves to Null0, as is typically used for this
purpose. It is common practice to use a prefix from the TESTNET range (192.0.2.0/24) for
this purpose. In Example 4-18, the TESTNET prefix 192.0.2.1/32 is set with a next hop
of Null0.

Example 4-18 *PE-CE Link Protection via BGP Community Mechanisms*

```
router bgp 65535
  neighbor <ibgp peer> remote-as 65535
  neighbor <ibgp peer> route-map ibgp-peers in
!
ip community-list 1 permit 65535:66
!
route-map ibgp-peers permit 10
  match community 1
  set ip next-hop 192.0.2.1
  set local-preference 200
  set community no-export
  set origin igp
!
ip route 192.0.2.1 255.255.255.255 Null0
```

Similar to the previous solution of using more-specific IP prefixes, the benefit of deploying
this technique is that it makes it more difficult to remotely attack PE and, optionally, CE
external interfaces (having public addresses). Any packets destined to such addresses are
discarded, including ping, but IP traceroute is not impacted. The challenges with this
approach are the same as those outlined for the "Protection Using More Specific IP
Prefixes" approach above.

Protection Using ACLs with Discontiguous Network Masks

A third approach is to use iACLs to filter all remote traffic destined to the IP address block assigned to edge router external links. This is straightforward, provided that IP reachability to the CE is not required. If CE reachability is required, then discontiguous network masks within the ingress interface ACL policies are required to filter all remote packets destined to PE external addresses while permitting reachability to the associated CE external addresses.

NOTE	A discontiguous network mask within an ACL results when the wildcard bits set to *ignore* (1) are not contiguous within the address (source or destination) wildcard mask. For example, a source wildcard mask of 0.255.0.64 is considered a discontiguous network mask due to the separation of the 255 mask from the 64 mask by the intervening 0 mask.

An IP router will process packets destined to network addresses (in other words, 0 subnet), broadcast addresses (all 1s subnet), and unicast addresses assigned to router interfaces; hence, the ACL must consider all three of these CEF receive adjacencies. Consider the PE-CE addressing illustrated in Figure 4-10 where the prefix 172.16.128.4/30 has been assigned to the PE1-CE1 link. In this case, the prefixes would be allocated as follows:

- 172.16.128.4/32: Network address
- 172.16.128.5/32: PE external interface
- 172.16.128.6/32: CE external interface
- 172.16.128.7/32: Broadcast address

To filter traffic to the network, PE, and broadcast addresses while permitting traffic to the CE address, the interface ACL shown in Example 4-19 may be applied on all external interfaces of all PE routers.

Example 4-19 *PE-CE Link Protection via Discontiguous ACL Configurations*

```
interface pos1/1
 ip address 172.16.128.5 255.255.255.252
 ip access-group 150 in
!
access-list 150 deny ip any 172.16.128.5 0.0.63.254
access-list 150 deny ip any 172.16.128.0 0.0.63.252
access-list 150 permit ip any any
```

This approach requires a consistent IP addressing scheme across the SP edge router external links so that the PE-CE links may be aggregated within the ACL policy. For example, you could use odd IP addresses (.1) for PE external addresses and even IP addresses (.2) for CE external addresses. Otherwise, two distinct ACE entries may be required per PE-CE link, which increases the length of the ACL and is not operationally manageable.

Discontiguous ACL network mask support varies among IP router platforms. Both CRS-1 and the Cisco 12000 ISE (Engine 3 and Engine 5 line cards), for example, support the use of discontiguous ACLs in the hardware fast path. Conversely, other platforms may process these ACLs in the router slow path (CPU). Further, as outlined in the "Interface ACL Techniques" section earlier in the chapter, ACLs are difficult to manage, in particular, given all the exceptions required (for example, broadcast and multiaccess links).

The benefit of deploying any one of the preceding three edge router external link protection schemes is that it makes it more difficult to attack edge router external links. Any packets destined to such addresses are discarded, including ping, but IP traceroute is not impacted. The first two schemes (leveraging routing and the FIB) remain subject to local attacks that ingress and egress through the same edge router. Conversely, the third scheme (using interface ACLs with discontiguous network masks) mitigates both remote and local attacks, but requires a consistent PE-CE addressing scheme and interface ACL changes on each PE external link.

Remotely Triggered Black Hole Filtering

The most commonly deployed data plane incident response technique is the use of interface ACLs. The use of IP routing–based mechanisms to support data plane attack mitigation provides an alternate technique that potentially offers both speed and scalability advantages over ACL techniques. This is achieved by rerouting attacks to the Null0 interface, which results in those rerouted traffic flows being discarded. This is referred to as *black hole* filtering and is typically used in conjunction with BGP to trigger a network-wide response to an attack. When combined with BGP, it is referred to as remotely triggered black hole (RTBH) filtering.

Unlike ACL policies, which take time to be constructed, distributed, and installed across potentially hundreds to thousands of routers or interfaces, RTBH filtering policies are distributed throughout a network just as quickly as iBGP can update the network. This provides a tool that can be used for rapid response to security incidents. RTBH mechanisms must be predeployed before they can be used for incident response. The step necessary to accomplish this are as follows:

1 Configure all edge routers with a static route to Null0. It is common practice to use a prefix from the TESTNET range (192.0.2.0/24) for this purpose. Here, the TESTNET prefix 192.0.2.1/32 is set with a next hop of Null0 using the global command **ip route 192.0.2.1 255.255.255.255 Null0**.

2 Configure a trigger router as part of the iBGP mesh, whose role will be to support the real-time insertion and removal of prefixes that are to be discarded on a network-wide basis (attack mitigation). A dedicated trigger router or other BGP-speaking device (such as a Linux workstation running quagga or zebra, for example) is recommended. Note the trigger device only needs to advertise iBGP routes, not accept them. The trigger router is the device that will inject the iBGP announcement into the network. The baseline configuration of the trigger router is shown in Example 4-20.

Example 4-20   *Trigger Router Configuration Illustration*

```
router bgp 65535
  redistribute static route-map static-to-bgp
  neighbor <ibgp peer> remote-as 65535
!
route-map static-to-bgp permit 10
  match tag 66
  set ip next-hop 192.0.2.1
  set local-preference 200
  set community no-export
  set origin igp
!
route-map static-to-bgp deny 20
```

As you can see in Example 4-20, any static routes with a tag of 66 are matched and have their next hop set to 192.0.2.1. As previously configured, the same prefix, 192.0.2.1, was statically bound to Null0. Hence, once the two (2) predeployment steps are applied, the network is ready to respond to security incidents via RTBH filtering. To activate a black hole via the trigger router, simply configure a static route on the trigger router for the destination to be black holed, and make sure to mark the static route with the tag of 66 (as used within the route map of Example 4-20). For example, if the destination prefix 172.16.61.1/32 is being attacked and you want to black hole all traffic destined to this prefix, network-wide, install the static route **ip route 172.16.61.1 255.255.255.255 null0 tag 66** on the trigger router. Once you configure this static route on the trigger router, it will be automatically redistributed into iBGP and propagated to all edge routers. The edge routers then "glue" the more specific 172.16.61.1/32 prefix that was advertised by the trigger router to their preconfigured 192.0.2.1/32 static route, which resolves to Null0. Due to recursion, the attack target address now has a next hop of Null0. Traffic received at the network edge that is destined to the attack target (172.16.61.1) is now sent to Null0 (in other words, discarded). To view the number of packets discarded by the Null0 interface due to RTBH filtering, use the **show interface Null0** command as illustrated in Example 4-21.

Example 4-21   *Sample Null0 Interface Statistics*

```
Router> show int null0
Null0 is up, line protocol is up
  Hardware is Unknown
  MTU 1500 bytes, BW 10000000 Kbit, DLY 0 usec,
      reliability 0/255, txload 0/255, rxload 0/255
  Encapsulation ARPA, loopback not set
  Last input never, output never, output hang never
  Last clearing of "show interface" counters 00:03:31
  Input queue: 0/75/0/0 (size/max/drops/flushes); Total output drops: 0
  5 minute input rate 0 bits/sec, 0 packets/sec
  5 minute output rate 0 bits/sec, 0 packets/sec
     0 packets input, 0 bytes, 0 no buffer
     Received 0 broadcasts, 0 runts, 0 giants, 0 throttles
     0 input errors, 0 CRC, 0 frame, 0 overrun, 0 ignored, 0 abort
```

Example 4-21 *Sample Null0 Interface Statistics (Continued)*

```
       136414 packets output, 204621000 bytes, 0 underruns
       0 output errors, 0 collisions, 0 interface resets
       0 output buffer failures, 0 output buffers swapped out
  Router>
```

Null0 drop statistics are also available using the **show interface Null0 accounting** and **show interface Null0 stats** commands.

NOTE   This same technique can be used to provide source-based RTBH filtering by incorporating uRPF mechanisms into the solution. Source-based RTBH filtering is discussed later in this section.

Although destination-based RTBH filtering offers many benefits, including rapid deployment at BGP-update speed and network-wide filtering, it is not without its drawbacks. One drawback of RTBH is that it black holes all traffic to the target—attack and legitimate. Although this stops the attack, it also prevents IP connectivity to the target by legitimate applications. The second drawback is that this approach works at Layer 3 (IP address), and hence it is not as granular as ACLs, which can filter at the OSI Layer 4 port level. Nonetheless, this technique is useful under many circumstances, including the mitigation of attacks that may be causing collateral damage to the network.

This same technique that supports RTBH filtering may also be used to intercept and shunt traffic to a mitigation device (for example, traffic scrubber) and monitoring device (sinkhole). These schemes are often preferred because they aim to drop attack traffic and pass legitimate/authorized traffic onto the target. The only difference when implementing these schemes is that instead of forwarding the traffic to Null0 as with RTBH filtering, the next hop is set to the IP address corresponding to the sinkhole or scrubbing device. Expanding on Example 4-20, assume that a sinkhole device has been located at 192.0.2.2/32 within the core, and a scrubbing device has been located at 192.0.2.3/32. As illustrated in Example 4-22, additional route-map entries can be added on the trigger router to set the BGP next hop associated with each of these devices for prefixes matching specific tags, as shown.

Example 4-22 *Trigger Router Configuration Illustration*

```
  !
  router bgp 65535
    redistribute static route-map static-to-bgp
    neighbor <ibgp peer> remote-as 65535
  !
  route-map static-to-bgp permit 10
    match tag 66
    set ip next-hop 192.0.2.1
    set local-preference 200
```
continues

Example 4-22 *Trigger Router Configuration Illustration (Continued)*

```
   set community no-export
   set origin igp
 !
route-map static-to-bgp permit 20
  match tag 67
  set ip next-hop 192.0.2.2
  set local-preference 200
  set community no-export
  set origin igp
 !
route-map static-to-bgp permit 30
  match tag 68
  set ip next-hop 192.0.2.3
  set local-preference 200
  set community no-export
  set origin igp
 !
route-map static-to-bgp deny 40
```

As you can see in Example 4-22, any static routes with a tag of 67 will now have a BGP next hop set to 192.0.2.2 (the IP address of the sinkhole), and any static routes with a tag of 68 will now have a BGP next hop set to 192.0.2.3 (the IP address of the scrubbing device). These are activated exactly as in the RTBH case; simply configure a static route on the trigger router for the IP destination address that should be diverted to the sinkhole using tag 67 (or scrubber using tag 68). For example, if the destination prefix 172.16.61.1/32 is being attacked and you want to divert traffic to the sinkhole for further analysis, install the static route **ip route 172.16.61.1 255.255.255.255 null0 tag 67** on the trigger router. Note that the Null0 next hop applies only on the trigger router, which is not in the forwarding path of attack traffic anyway. When the trigger router advertises via iBGP the 172.16.61.1/32 prefix of the target, it rewrites the BGP next hop to 192.0.2.2, as shown in the route map illustrated in Example 4-22. All traffic to the victim is now diverted to the sinkhole. A similar approach applies when diverting traffic to the scrubber, but tag 68 and BGP next hop 192.0.2.3 are used instead.

Again, although this approach offers many benefits, including rapid network-wide deployment using BGP and network-wide diversion using Null0 black holes, sinkholes, or scrubbers, it also has its drawbacks. In this case, an issue arises if you want to return the traffic to the original destination IP address after the traffic has been processed by the sinkhole or scrubber. The challenge is that BGP has updated all routers to show the sinkhole or scrubbing device as the BGP next hop for the target destination prefix, which would result in a routing loop if traffic were simply forwarded back into the network. Hence, a tunnel must be used to reroute the traffic along the best path between the scrubbing device and the network valid exit point (to the original destination). Encapsulations using GRE, MPLS VPNs, or VLANs are typically used for this application. (Scrubbing is further discussed in the "Traffic Scrubbing" section later in this chapter.)

As you learned in the preceding discussion, by using various static route tags on the trigger device, you may invoke any number of different policies. In the preceding example:

- Tag 66 is used for RTBH filtering where the BGP next hop is set to 192.0.2.1, which in turn is mapped to Null0 for dropping traffic (in other words, black hole).

- Tag 67 is used for diverting traffic to a sinkhole where the BGP next hop is set to the sinkhole address.

- Tag 68 is used for diverting traffic to a scrubbing device where the BGP next hop is set to the scrubbing device address.

You may also use BGP communities instead of tags to extend the functionality and add fine-tuned control to the preceding traffic diversion techniques. For example, in a very large network, you may want to trigger RTBH on a regional basis instead of having it act globally throughout the entire network edge. This can be accomplished quite easily by using BGP communities. But to accommodate this, you must make a few changes to each of the edge routers and to the trigger router. These changes are as follows:

1 Convert the trigger router to send iBGP updates with specific, predefined communities. This is accomplished by adding something similar to the configuration shown in Example 4-23. In this example, trigger routes with a specific tag are assigned a corresponding community value. This value is propagated with the routing update within iBGP. In this example, trigger routes tagged with the value 123 are assigned a BGP community of 65535:123, and those tagged with a value of 124 are assigned a BGP community of 65535:124.

Example 4-23 *Trigger Router Configuration Example Using BGP Communities*

```
!
router bgp 65535
  redistribute static route-map static-to-bgp
  neighbor <ibgp peer> remote-as 65535
!
route-map static-to-bgp permit 10
  match tag 123
  set community 65535:123
  set local-preference 200
  set community no-export
  set origin igp
!
route-map static-to-bgp permit 20
  match tag 124
  set community 65535:124
  set local-preference 200
  set community no-export
  set origin igp
!
route-map static-to-bgp deny 30
```

2 Retain the configured static route to Null0 on the edge routers. Previously, the
   TESTNET prefix 192.0.2.1/32 was set with a next hop of Null0 using the global
   command **ip route 192.0.2.1 255.255.255.255 Null0**. In addition, configure iBGP
   to match on communities and assign the appropriate BGP next-hop behavior. In
   Example 4-24, it is assumed that the region this edge router is in will match only on
   the BGP community 65535:123 and divert this traffic to Null0. Other traffic will not
   be diverted.

Example 4-24 *Edge Router BGP Community-Based RTBH Configuration Illustration*

```
!
router bgp 65535
  neighbor <ibgp peer> remote-as 65535
  neighbor <ibgp peer> route-map ibgp-peers in
!
ip community-list 1 permit 65535:123
!
route-map ibgp-peers permit 10
  match community 1
  set ip next-hop 192.0.2.1
  set local-preference 200
  set community no-export
  set origin igp
!
route-map static-to-bgp permit 20
!
ip route 192.0.2.1 255.255.255.255 Null0
```

As shown in Example 4-24, the BGP community attribute is checked before accepting the
prefix from the trigger router. In this way, if the community matches, the BGP update is
installed within the RIB with the desired next-hop behavior (that is, 192.0.2.1). If the
community does not match, the BGP update is ignored and traffic is forwarded normally
along the IP routing best path. The use of communities allows you to customize policies on
different categories of routers; for example:

• Trigger community 1 can be for all routers in the network.

• Trigger community 2 can be for all Internet peering routers (no transit customer
  routers). In this way, transit customers have IP reachability to the target, whereas peers
  do not.

• Trigger community 3 can be for all transit customer routers, and can be used to push
  an inter-AS traceback to the edge of your network because only peers will have IP
  reachability to the target.

• Trigger communities assigned per ISP peer can be used to only black hole traffic
  received via one ISP peer's connection. This allows for a target to maintain partial
  service if the attack is coming predominantly from a single ISP network or peering
  point.

- Trigger communities assigned per geographic region can be used to black hole traffic only on routers deployed within a specific geographic region.

- Trigger communities assigned per desired service. For example, Null0 black hole, sinkhole, or scrubber, as previously described.

With some creativity, using BGP communities with the RTBH framework enables a wide range of possible applications.

The preceding RTBH techniques filter traffic based on destination IP addresses using standard routing mechanics. RTBH filtering may also be combined with uRPF (strict, loose, or VRF mode) to support source IP address–based RTBH filtering. That is, instead of dropping all traffic with the destination IP address of a specified target, you can drop all traffic with the source IP address of the attacker(s). Dropping traffic based on the source IP address, at the network edge, without ACLs, and installed at BGP-update speeds provides a very useful incident response capability. Using source IP address–based RTBH potentially allows you to mitigate an attack without taking the attack target offline.

Source-based RTBH is achieved using uRPF in combination with the RTBH architecture previously described. The mechanisms used include the following:

- The edge routers retain their configured static route to Null0. Previously, the TESTNET prefix 192.0.2.1/32 was set with a next hop of Null0 using the global command **ip route 192.0.2.1 255.255.255.255 Null0**.

- The trigger router continues to be used to support the real-time insertion and removal of prefixes that are to be discarded on a network-wide basis (attack mitigation). However, in this scenario, instead of setting trigger routes that represent the destination IP address for a target, you now install trigger routes that represent the source IP address(es) of the attacker(s).

- uRPF must be installed on the external interfaces of the edge routers. Any version of uRPF can be used; uRPFv1 (strict mode) and uRPFv2 (loose mode) support source-based RTBH with no additional configurations beyond those described in the earlier "Unicast RPF" section. If uRPFv3 (VRF mode) is used, the trigger router requires modifications in order to announce the trigger routes within the appropriate IPv4 VRF associated with uRPFv3.

Once you make the preceding configurations, when a source IP address is advertised by the trigger router, this IP prefix is then associated in each of the edge router FIBs with the Null0 interface. Hence, the uRPF address verification check for external packets received with source IP addresses matching the trigger route(s) will be resolved to Null0, which is an invalid interface for uRPF, resulting in these packets being dropped. Thus, any packets sourced from the attacker will be black holed. Note that spoofed sources are often used in attacks, as described in Chapter 2. Without proper validation and care, you may be tricked into black holing legitimate traffic sources. (This applies for any mitigation technique.)

In terms of scalability, BGP is capable of handling many hundreds of thousands of routes with ease. It is not inconceivable that the trigger router may need to install a large number of prefixes in reaction to a DoS attack, for example. This is no problem for RTBH. Conversely, this could challenge any ACL deployment technique.

Both destination IP address–based and source IP address–based RTBH techniques provide an effective incident response tool that:

- Rapidly distributes policy throughout the network at BGP-update speed.

- Requires no ACL changes.

- Supports filtering using both destination and source IP addresses.

- Drops matching traffic flows in the forwarding path, meaning there is no performance impact associated with destination-based RTBH deployment. There may be a performance impact for source-based RTBH because uRPF is required. uRPF performance impacts, if any, will vary among router platforms.

IP Transport and Application Layer Techniques

The many techniques described in the preceding sections operate at OSI Layers 2, 3, and 4 to protect against attacks within the data plane of an IP network. Additional techniques and mechanisms are available that operate even deeper within the packet at the application layer (OSI Layer 7) to provide additional security. It is not the intent of this book to cover every available security mechanism in detail. Entire books are dedicated to some of these individual techniques. The feature descriptions in this section are provided mainly as an introduction and point of reference.

TCP Intercept

IOS supports a TCP intercept feature that is intended to protect TCP protocol stacks from TCP SYN flood attacks that aim to exhaust system resources on a target device, as described in Chapter 2. The TCP intercept feature supports two operating modes:

- **Intercept mode:** The router intercepts TCP synchronization (SYN) packets sent between IP hosts that match an extended ACL. The ACL allows you to configure whether all TCP connection requests should be intercepted or only those sourced and destined to specific networks or devices as defined by the ACL policy. The router then acts as a TCP proxy and establishes its own connection with the source on behalf of the intended destination. If successful, the router then establishes a second TCP connection between itself and the destination. The two half connections are then knit together transparently within the IOS device, which maintains both until either one is terminated. This technique prevents TCP SYN connection requests from unreachable sources from ever reaching the destination. Note that aggressive TCP timeouts for half-open connections, as well as thresholds for all connection requests, further protect destination hosts from TCP SYN flood attacks while still allowing valid TCP connections. The number of supported TCP SYNs per second and the number of concurrent connections proxied vary depending on the particular router.

- **Watch mode:** The router passively monitors connection requests flowing through it. If a connection fails to become established in a configurable time interval, the router intervenes and terminates the connection attempt.

TCP intercept may be enabled using the IOS global configuration commands **ip tcp intercept list** and **ip tcp intercept mode** {**intercept** | **watch**}. The default TCP intercept mode is **intercept**. Note that the TCP intercept feature does not support the negotiation of TCP options (such as RFC 1323 on window scaling). Further, because the TCP intercept feature is handled entirely within the IOS process level of the router, it adds a tremendous burden to CPU load. TCP intercept should be enabled with caution and only after you are familiar with the impact it will have on the router performance. When TCP SYN-flood attacks are known to be a consistent problem, you should consider dedicated hardware for remediation in lieu of using the TCP intercept function.

Network Address Translation

IOS supports three major types of NAT services:

- Traditional IP NAT services, as specified in RFC 3022 (obsoletes RFC 1631)
- Network Address Port Translation (NAPT) services, as specified in RFC 3022
- Network Address Translation–Protocol Translation (NAT-PT) services, as specified in RFC 2766

In its simplest form, IP NAT operates on a router, firewall, or other network device that connects two (or more) networks together. Typically, one of these networks, referred to as the *inside* network, is addressed with either private (RFC 1918) or obsolete addresses that need to be converted into Internet-routable or globally unique addresses before packets are forwarded onto the other network, referred to as the *outside* network. NAT is a "stateful" process and works in conjunction with routing (see the IOS feature order of operations in Figure 3-1 of Chapter 3), so return packets are similarly translated back to their original addresses for delivery to the original source. NAT can be configured to work in the opposite direction as well. That is, packets arriving on the outside interface of a NAT device (such as a router) can be translated such that the destination IP address points to an inside, private destination address. This is a common deployment method within Internet data centers for web services, for example.

In IOS, this basic NAT functionality of converting one inside IP address to one outside IP address is referred to as a *simple translation*. As indicated previously, there are other, more-complex translation mechanisms that provide flexibility for other situations requiring NAT services. The most basic NAT mechanism maps one (Layer 3) IP address to another.

An *extended translation* maps one (Layer 3) IP address and (Layer 4) port pair to another. Both mechanisms, however, consume IP addresses on a one-for-one basis. Network Address Port Translation (NAPT), often called Port Address Translation (PAT), enhances NAT functionality by providing a mechanism that translates many inside addresses to a single outside address. PAT uses unique source port numbers on the translated addresses to distinguish between them. Because the port number is encoded in 16 bits, the total number could theoretically be as high as 65,536 per IP address. As IPv6 becomes more commonly deployed, an additional translation mechanism is needed as a migration tool. IOS provides functionality called Network Address Translation–Protocol Translation (NAT-PT) that converts inside network IPv6 addresses to outside network IPv4 addresses, allowing direct communication between hosts speaking these two different network protocols.

The intent of this section is not to show you how to configure NAT; there are many variations to NAT and many site-specific dependencies that make doing so infeasible. The intent is to make you aware of some of the performance, management, and security issues associated with deploying NAT.

NAT must perform several complex functions as part of the translation process, including translating the IP packet source and destination addresses and ports, and performing checksum adjustment computations. In addition, NAT is a stateful service and must maintain a translation table of all of the current sessions so that return traffic can be retranslated to the original header values. The initial connection setup process typically requires additional computation and memory to create the connection state, and often this adds latency to the first packet of a session. The initial packet requires processing within the IOS process level. Once the connection is established, NAT processes should be more transparent from a performance perspective.

In general, devices capable of performing NAT functions report two values: a connections-per-second setup rate, and a maximum-concurrent-sessions value. These parameters are important for understanding the overall performance of the system. IOS NAT has been optimized to perform NAT functions as efficiently as possible. However, NAT performance is still limited by the specifics of the individual platform capabilities. Note that when the memory and CPU utilization is very high due to the NAT process, collateral damage may potentially occur such that control and management plane functions are affected—potentially affecting network performance and leading to a DoS condition.

Firewalls, load balancers, and other dedicated hardware are usually capable of sustaining much higher rates of NAT translation and should be considered for high-performance environments. When application proxies are incorporated with NAT, such as for DNS translations, dynamic port assignments (for example, FTP), and so on, additional impacts to performance may be incurred. High-availability and failover scenarios also present challenges with NAT. Again, many firewalls, load balancers, and other dedicated hardware often provide stateful failover capabilities that maintain NAT translation tables on two devices to support highly available architectures.

NAT can present challenges for some management applications, especially when remote support is required by external network management applications. When remote management is required, it is common to use IPsec VPNs, both for data protection across external networks and to provide access into the inside NAT address space. (SPs that provide managed services may run into situations where customers have common [overlapping] private address space. In these situations, the SP typically installs a unique loopback address on each customer router for management purposes.) Alternatively, some management systems are capable of supporting virtualization to maintain customer segmentation within one unified management application.

NAT itself is not described as a security feature. However, it does obfuscate hosts within private address ranges behind NAT. Further, such hosts are only reachable during the period of time they make an outbound connection and an associated NAT translation exists. The more important concept to understand with NAT is how it interacts with other security mechanisms and impacts the overall network security posture. For example, when combined with certain IPsec encapsulation methods, NAT header modifications can break the imposed packet integrity checks and cause these packets to be discarded. That is, NAT makes it seem as if the packets have been tampered with (which they have, just not maliciously). Workarounds are available and are required when this issue arises. As another example, Internet worms can quickly overwhelm the translation tables and state checks within NAT devices when internal hosts become infected. When an internal host has been infected with a worm, it scans random destination addresses seeking additional vulnerable hosts for replication. Each of these individual requests starts a NAT translation and consumes state.

Tuning mechanisms are usually available to limit the total number of connections, purge half-open connections, and so on, but clearly it is undesirable to have this situation in the first place. This same situation occurs in reverse for Internet data center deployments where destination address translation is used (outside to inside) and a TCP SYN flood, for example, consumes all available translation slots, resulting in a DoS condition. In this case, mechanisms must be used to keep spoofed (or *bot*) traffic from consuming these resources. (See the "Traffic Scrubbing" section later in the chapter.)

As with any feature deployed in the network, you must be familiar with not only how NAT operates, but also how it behaves under all operational conditions, including attack conditions. Additional Cisco IOS NAT information can be found in the Cisco white paper "Cisco IOS Network Address Translation Overview," referenced in the "Further Reading" section.

IOS Firewall

IOS supports a fully functional, stateful firewall feature called IOS Firewall (IOS FW). IOS FW is usually deployed at the network edge, often placed in between internal or DMZ networks and an external network such as the Internet. Because IOS FW is incorporated as part of the router, it is quite easily deployed anywhere within the network where access control or segmentation is desired.

The most basic function of a firewall is to monitor and apply security policies (filters) to traffic. Like many firewalls, IOS FW examines Layer 3 and Layer 4 information, and application layer protocol information (such as FTP information) to learn about and maintain the state of TCP, UDP, and ICMP. The IOS FW uses state information to make intelligent decisions about whether packets should be permitted or denied, and then dynamically creates and deletes temporary openings in the firewall policy. Because IOS FW maintains connection state information on all connections, it is subject to the same performance, management, and security risks described in the previous section for NAT. In fact, all devices that maintain connection state face these same issues in one way or another.

Again, the intent of this section is not to show you how to configure IOS FW, but rather to make you aware of some of its associated performance, management, and security issues, described here:

- **Performance:** IOS FW performs traffic inspection for network, transport, and application layer information. It also forces protocol conformance for some protocols, and has limited vulnerability signature detection mechanisms and extensive DoS prevention mechanisms. However, many of these features are CPU intensive, and can adversely affect the performance of the router. When the memory and CPU utilization is very high due to the IOS FW processes, collateral damage can occur such that control plane and management plane functions are affected, potentially affecting network performance and leading to a DoS condition. Similar to NAT, the initial connection setup process in IOS FW typically requires additional computation and memory to create the connection state, and often this adds latency to the first packet of a session. The initial packet requires processing at the IOS process level. IOS FW parameters are also given in terms of connections-per-second setup rate, and a maximum-concurrent-sessions value. These parameters are important for understanding the overall performance of the system.

- **Management:** IOS FW may be managed through CLI or via the Cisco Security Device Manager (SDM) web GUI when deployed in a single location. When multiple IOS FW installations require management, it may be challenging to maintain consistent security policies across devices or maintain multiple policies without a dedicated security management system. The Cisco Security Manager (CSM) provides this functionality in an easy-to-use, central provisioning system that coordinates all aspects of device configurations and security policies for Cisco firewalls, Virtual Private Networks (VPN), and Intrusion Prevention Systems (IPS). Because IOS FW provides a security function, monitoring via SNMP or syslog is essential for situational awareness.

- **Security:** IOS FW is a security feature. It directly provides stateful traffic inspection and enforces security policy conformance. Given that it is stateful and in the path of data plane traffic, IOS FW deployments should be evaluated and sized appropriately for the intended environment. As with NAT, DoS conditions may severely impact any firewall implementation; IOS FW is no exception.

As with any feature deployed in the network, you must be familiar with not only how IOS FW operates, but also how it behaves under all operational conditions, including attack conditions. Additional Cisco IOS FW information can be found in "Cisco IOS Firewall Overview" (see the "Further Reading" section).

Firewall functionality may also be provided by dedicated hardware appliances and modules. Cisco products include the PIX Firewall appliance family, Adaptive Security Appliance (ASA) family, and the Firewall Service Module (FWSM) for the Catalyst 6500 family.

IOS Intrusion Prevention System

IOS provides mechanisms for incorporating IPS functionality directly within routers. IOS IPS is an inline, deep packet inspection (DPI) based traffic analyzer that helps mitigate a wide range of network attacks. You can either operate IOS IPS with a limited, default set of built-in signatures, or configure IOS IPS to dynamically load signature detection files (SDF) that incorporate the very latest signatures available to accurately identify, classify, and stop malicious or damaging traffic in real time. IOS IPS uses signature micro-engines (SME) to load the SDF and scan signatures. A feature called virtual fragment reassembly (VFR; not to be confused with virtual routing/forwarding instance, or VRF) is used to scan application layer signatures across fragments.

The intent of this section is to make you aware of some the performance, management, and security issues associated with IOS IPS, as described next:

- **Performance:** IOS IPS performs DPI-based traffic analysis. As with IOS FW, some IOS IPS features are CPU intensive, and can adversely affect the performance of the router. This is particularly true when these features require IOS process level support, and often, the initial packet requires processing in the slow path. When memory and CPU utilization is very high due to the IOS IPS processes, collateral damage can occur such that control plane and management plane functions are affected, potentially affecting network performance and leading to a DoS condition. These parameters are important for understanding the overall performance of the system.

- **Management:** IOS IPS may be managed through CLI or via the Cisco SDM web GUI when deployed in a single location. When multiple IOS IPS installations require management, it may be challenging to maintain security policies and SDFs across devices without a dedicated security management system. The CSM provides this functionality in an easy-to-use, central provisioning system that coordinates all aspects of device configurations and security policies for Cisco firewalls, VPNs, and IPS. Because IOS IPS provides a security function, monitoring of security events via syslog messages or Security Device Event Exchange (SDEE) alerts is essential for situational awareness.

- **Security:** IOS IPS is a security feature. It directly provides DPI-based traffic analysis. Given that it is stateful and in the path of data plane traffic, IOS IPS deployments should be evaluated and sized appropriately for the intended environment. As with IOS FW, DoS conditions may severely impact any IPS implementation; IOS IPS is no exception. Also note that the IOS IPS configuration on certain routers may not support the complete list of signatures due to memory constraints. Always be sure to provide sufficient memory for all security features.

As with any feature deployed in the network, you must be familiar with not only how IOS IPS operates, but also how it behaves under all operational conditions, including attack conditions. Additional Cisco IOS IPS information can be found in "Configuring Cisco IOS Intrusion Prevention System (IPS)" (referenced in the "Further Reading" section).

IPS functionality may also be provided by dedicated hardware appliances and modules. Cisco products include the IPS 4200 appliance family, and the Intrusion Detection Service Module (IDSM2) for the Catalyst 6500 family.

Traffic Scrubbing

As you learned earlier in the chapter, one of the fundamental techniques used by SPs and large enterprises for deploying network-wide traffic filtering is through BGP-triggered black hole filtering. One implementation of this technique involves directing traffic destined for a target toward a special-purpose traffic-scrubbing device, rather than toward Null0 (which represents a black hole). The benefit of such a solution is that instead of dropping all traffic destined to the victim, essentially accomplishing the objective of the DoS attack, this traffic can be *cleaned* such that only the bad traffic is discarded, allowing just the good traffic to be passed on to the target.

In this solution, the Cisco Traffic Anomaly Detector provides detection functionality by watching traffic destined for protected zones through Switched Port Analyzer (SPAN) traffic. That is, the detector is not inline with the traffic flows. Once an attack is detected, the detector can automatically trigger the companion Cisco Guard to provide scrubber-type DoS mitigation services. (The guard can also be configured to manually activate traffic scrubbing.) Once activated, the guard advertises the target prefix via BGP, much in the same way that the trigger router described earlier for RTBH advertises the target prefix, causing the traffic to flow to the guard rather than the target. The guard analyzes the diverted traffic for anomalies and, through a variety of mechanisms, drops attack traffic. The cleaned traffic from the guard is then redirected back to the target. Because the guard advertised within BGP a more-specific prefix for the target (in order to divert the flow to the guard), the cleaned traffic must be reinjected via some encapsulation method to prevent looping back to the guard. There are multiple injection methods available, depending on whether the core network topology is Layer 2 or Layer 3. Example methods include PBR, generic routing encapsulation (GRE), and MPLS VPN.

In addition to the Cisco Traffic Anomaly Detector and Cisco Guard appliances, this functionality may also be provided by similar modules for the Catalyst 6500 and Cisco 7600 families. Alternatively, NetFlow may be used in conjunction with third-party traffic analysis systems to activate traffic scrubbing using Cisco Guard. Details of the full traffic-scrubbing solution are beyond the scope of this book. However, additional details, including design guides and configuration examples, can be found at http://www.cisco.com/en/US/netsol/ns615/networking_solutions_sub_solution.html. NetFlow is further discussed in Chapter 6.

Deep Packet Inspection

The increasing expansion of broadband and mobile IP networks has provided greater opportunities for miscreants to conduct cyber attacks using unprotected and compromised IP devices. Malware such as worms, viruses, bots, and spam zombies threaten broadband and mobile subscribers and the IP network infrastructure by consuming available bandwidth capacity. The Cisco Service Control Engine (SCE) provides a solution that can proactively reduce the impact of malware and cyber attacks within broadband and mobile IP networks.

The Cisco SCE provides state-of-the-art detection and control capabilities. Using application layer stateful DPI, the Cisco SCE can accurately identify and classify application traffic by individual subscriber at multigigabit speeds. The Cisco SCE "stateful" DPI solution goes far beyond the simple counting of packets and can distinguish between many distinct small application sessions (for example, one thousand 1-KB messages) and a single large session (for example, 1-MB messages). Stateful DPI also enables the Cisco SCE to identify specific protocol signatures and, subsequently, monitor for malicious attack patterns and contain their effect.

If the Cisco SCE identifies suspicious traffic patterns, it can automatically apply traffic control policies that can block or rate limit the transmission and redirect it to a traffic scrubber, for example, as described in the preceding "Traffic Scrubbing" section. In this way, the Cisco SCE helps prevent the spread of malware or attack traffic by identifying the protocols and port numbers used and then blocking transit across the network. Further, the Cisco SCE also protects network resources by limiting the bandwidth capacity that may be consumed per subscriber and application flow.

The intent of this section is not to show you how to configure the Cisco SCE for DPI. The intent is simply to make you aware of the technology and its application in the context of IP data plane security. As with any feature deployed in the network, you must be familiar with not only how the Cisco SCE operates, but also how it behaves under all operational conditions, including attack conditions. Additional Cisco SCE information can be found at http://www.cisco.com/en/US/products/ps6135/index.html and http://www.cisco.com/en/US/products/ps6501/index.html.

Layer 2 Ethernet Security Techniques

Chapter 2 reviewed potential threats that may exist within a Layer 2 switched Ethernet network environment. This section describes security techniques to mitigate attacks within the data forwarding plane of Layer 2 Ethernet switches. Chapters 5 and 6 review techniques to mitigate attacks within the Layer 2 switched Ethernet control and management planes, respectively.

Port Security

Port security restricts a port's ingress traffic by limiting the MAC addresses that are allowed to send traffic into the port. The default number of secure MAC addresses for a port is one, but you may change this by using the **switchport port-security maximum** IOS CLI. Authorized MAC addresses are considered secure and may be assigned using any one of the following methods:

- **Static MAC addresses:** Secure MAC addresses may be explicitly and statically configured using the **switchport port-security mac-address** IOS interface configuration command. If fewer secure MAC addresses are configured than the port's maximum, the remaining MAC addresses may be learned dynamically. Statically configured secure MAC addresses do not age (expire) and they are not removed as a result of a link-down condition.

- **Dynamically learned MAC addresses:** The switch port may dynamically learn secure MAC addresses by using the source MAC address(es) of received ingress traffic. Dynamic learning of MAC addresses is the default configuration method when enabling **switchport port-security**. Secure MAC addresses that are not statically configured are learned dynamically up to the maximum allowable number (default of one). Dynamically learned secure MAC addresses are removed over time as they age out and as a result of a link-down condition. The aging time for dynamically learned secure MAC addresses may be configured using the **switchport port-security aging time** IOS interface configuration command. Aging may be disabled using the **no switchport port-security aging time** IOS interface configuration command.

- **Sticky MAC addresses:** Sticky MAC addresses provide many of the same benefits as static MAC addresses, but are learned dynamically. The difference between sticky and dynamically learned MAC addresses is that sticky MAC addresses are retained during a link-down condition, whereas (nonsticky) dynamically learned MAC addresses are removed. Further, if you enter a **write memory** or **copy running-config startup-config** command, then port security with sticky MAC addresses saves dynamically learned MAC addresses in the startup-config file and the port does not have to relearn addresses from ingress traffic flows after bootup or restart. To enable port security with sticky MAC addresses on a port, apply the **switchport port-security mac-address sticky** IOS interface configuration command.

Port security is supported on both access ports (nontrunks) and on nonnegotiating trunk ports. If port security is enabled and an unauthorized MAC address sends traffic into a secure port, then the switch port enters violation mode. Several violation modes are available and are configurable using the **switchport port-security violation** IOS interface configuration command. The violation mode determines the action to be taken when a security violation is detected. The available violation modes include:

- **Protect mode:** Drops packets with unknown source MAC addresses. When a sufficient number of secure MAC addresses are removed, thereby dropping the total number of secure MAC addresses below the maximum permitted value, a previously unknown source MAC address may be learned dynamically and become a secure MAC address. Secure MAC addresses are removed through aging, link-down conditions, or, in the case of static and sticky MAC addresses, configuration.

- **Restrict mode:** In a similar manner to protect mode, drops packets with unknown source MAC addresses until a sufficient number of secure MAC addresses are removed, thereby dropping the total number of secure MAC addresses below the maximum permitted value and allowing previously unknown MAC address to be added dynamically. The difference between restrict and protect modes is that restrict mode causes the SecurityViolation counter within the output of the **show port-security** IOS command to increment.

- **Shutdown mode:** Immediately drops the packet with the unknown source MAC address, puts the interface into the error-disabled state—which causes all packets, legitimate and attack, to be dropped—and sends an SNMP trap notification. To bring a secure port out of the error-disabled state, the **errdisable recovery cause shutdown** IOS global configuration command must be applied, or the port must be manually reenabled by entering the **shutdown** and **no shut down** interface configuration commands.

Port security restricts the authorized MAC addresses that are allowed to send traffic into the port and helps to mitigate the risk of CAM table overflow, MAC spoofing, and VLAN-hopping-based attacks.

MAC Address–Based Traffic Blocking

MAC address–based traffic blocking filters all traffic to or from a defined MAC address in a specified VLAN. This feature may be enabled using the **mac-address-table static** IOS global configuration command. Example 4-25 illustrates how to block all traffic to or from MAC address 0050.3e8d.6400 in VLAN 7.

Example 4-25   *Configuring a* **mac-address-table static** *Filter to Block a MAC Address*

```
Router# configure terminal
Router(config)# mac-address-table static 0050.3e8d.6400 vlan 7 drop
```

Disable Auto Trunking

A Layer 2 switched Ethernet trunk is a point-to-point link (or EtherChannel) between a switch and another networking device such as an IP router or an adjacent Ethernet switch. Trunks carry the traffic of multiple VLANs over a single physical link (or EtherChannel) and allow you to extend VLANs across an entire switched Ethernet network. Two trunking encapsulations are widely supported within Cisco Ethernet switches:

- **Inter-Switch Link (ISL):** Cisco-proprietary trunking encapsulation
- **802.1Q:** IEEE industry-standard trunking encapsulation

LAN ports may be configured to auto-negotiate the VLAN encapsulation type using the **switchport trunk encapsulation negotiate** IOS interface configuration command. The Dynamic Trunking Protocol (DTP) manages trunk autonegotiation on LAN ports. DTP is a point-to-point protocol and supports autonegotiation of both ISL and 802.1Q trunks. To autonegotiate trunking, the interconnected LAN ports must be in the same Virtual Trunking Protocol (VTP) domain. The **trunk** or **nonegotiate** keywords of the **switchport trunk encapsulation** IOS interface configuration command may be used to force LAN ports that are in different VTP domains to trunk. IOS Layer 2 Ethernet switch ports support several different modes of operation, including:

- **Access mode:** Puts the LAN port into permanent nontrunking mode and negotiates to convert the link into a nontrunk link. The LAN port becomes a nontrunk port even if the neighboring LAN port does not agree to the change. Access mode is enabled using the **switchport mode access** IOS interface configuration command. Note that access mode does not disable DTP on the LAN port.

- **Dynamic desirable mode:** Makes the LAN port actively attempt to convert the link to a trunk link using DTP. The LAN port becomes a trunk port if the neighboring LAN port is set to **trunk**, **desirable**, or **auto** mode. This is the default mode for all LAN ports. Dynamic desirable mode may also be reenabled using the **switchport mode dynamic desirable** IOS interface configuration command.

- **Dynamic auto mode:** Makes the LAN port willing to convert the link to a trunk link using DTP. The LAN port becomes a trunk port only if the neighboring LAN port is set to **trunk** or **desirable** mode. If the neighboring LAN port is set to **auto** mode, the LAN port becomes a nontrunk port. Dynamic auto mode is enabled using the **switchport mode dynamic auto** IOS interface configuration command.

- **Trunk mode:** Puts the LAN port into permanent trunking mode and negotiates to convert the link into a trunk link. The LAN port becomes a trunk port even if the neighboring port does not agree to the change. Trunk mode is enabled using the **switchport mode trunk** IOS interface configuration command, which will also disable DTP on the LAN port. Before entering the **switchport mode trunk** command, the VLAN encapsulation must be configured using the **switchport trunk encapsulation** IOS interface configuration command. Note trunk mode does not disable DTP on the LAN port.

- **No-negotiate mode:** Puts the LAN port into permanent trunking mode but prevents the port from generating DTP frames. No-negotiate mode disables DTP similarly to access mode. The neighboring port must be manually configured as a trunk port to establish a trunk link because DTP is disabled. No-negotiate mode is configured using the **switchport nonegotiate** IOS interface configuration command. Before entering the **switchport nonegotiate** command, the VLAN encapsulation must be configured and the port must be configured to trunk unconditionally using the **switchport trunk encapsulation** and **switchport mode trunk** IOS interface configuration commands, respectively.

Configuring LAN ports that do not serve as trunks in permanent nontrunking (access) mode using the **switchport mode access** IOS interface configuration command mitigates the threat of switch spoofing attacks because DTP is disabled.

VLAN ACLs

VLAN ACLs (VACL) provide access control for all packets that are either bridged within a VLAN or IP routed into or out of a VLAN. Unlike IOS IP ACLs that are configured only on IP router interfaces and are applied only to IP routed packets, VACLs may be applied to IP, IPX, and MAC-layer Ethernet packets, and may be applied to any defined VLAN. VACLs use IOS ACL CLI syntax; however, they ignore any IOS ACL fields that are not supported in hardware.

When a VACL is configured for a defined VLAN, all packets entering the VLAN are verified against this VACL. VACLs are supported in conjunction with interface IP ACLs and operate in the following manner:

- If a VACL is applied to a VLAN, and an input IP ACL is applied to a routed interface within the VLAN, then packets entering the VLAN are first verified against the VACL and, if permitted, are then verified against the input IP ACL.

- If a VACL is applied to a VLAN, and an output IP ACL is applied to a routed interface within the VLAN, then packets that egress the router interface are first verified against the output IP ACL and, if permitted, are then verified against the VACL.

If a VACL is configured for a specific packet type (for example, IP, IPX, and so on) and a received packet is not of that type, the default action of the VACL is to discard the packet. VACLs may be configured using the **vlan filter** and **vlan access-map** IOS global configuration commands. Note that IGMP packets are not checked against VACLs.

IP Source Guard

IP source guard is a technique available on Layer 2 Ethernet switches to prevent IP spoofing. It works in conjunction with DHCP snooping and allows only IP addresses that are obtained through DHCP snooping (refer to Chapter 5) to transmit traffic on a particular LAN port. Initially, all IP traffic on the port is blocked except for the DHCP packets that are captured via DHCP snooping. When a client receives a valid IP address from the DHCP server, a port access control list (PACL) is automatically installed on the LAN port that permits traffic sourced from the DHCP-assigned IP address. This process restricts the client IP traffic to those source IP addresses that are obtained from the DHCP server; any IP traffic with a source IP address other than one in the PACL's permit list is discarded. This filtering limits the ability of a device to spoof itself as another IP address.

A port's IP source address filter is changed when a new DHCP-snooping binding entry for the port is created or deleted. The port PACL is automatically modified and reapplied to the LAN port to reflect the IP source binding change. By default, if IP source guard is enabled without any DHCP-snooping bindings on the LAN port, a default PACL that denies all IP traffic is installed on the port. Disabling IP source guard removes any IP source filter PACL from the port.

IP source guard is not recommended on trunk ports because it is limited to ten IP addresses per LAN port. IP source guard cannot coexist with PACLs that you configure, because IP source guard installs its own PACL on enabled ports. IP source guard is also not supported on EtherChannel-enabled ports. High availability is also recommended when using IP source guard, Dynamic ARP Inspection (DAI), and DHCP snooping. Otherwise, if clients do not renew their IP addresses associated with these features, they may lose network connectivity after an RP switchover.

Before IP source guard may be enabled, DHCP snooping must be enabled on the VLAN to which the port belongs. To enable IP source guard, use the **set port dhcp-snooping source-guard enable** IOS configuration command. IP source guard provides a technique to mitigate the risk of IP source address spoofing on LAN ports of a Layer 2 Ethernet switch. For more information on DAI and DHCP snooping, refer to Chapter 5.

Private VLANs

As described in Chapter 2, private VLANs (PVLAN) provide Layer 2 isolation of hosts within the same VLAN and IP subnet. PVLANs work by limiting communication among switch ports within the same VLAN. There are three types of PVLAN ports: isolated, promiscuous, and community switch ports. Isolated switch ports within a VLAN may communicate only with promiscuous switch ports. Community switch ports may communicate only with promiscuous switch ports and other ports belonging to the same community. Promiscuous switch ports may communicate with any switch port and typically connect to the default gateway IP router.

PVLANs are often used to isolate traffic between customers within an SP server farm, for example, to circumvent VLAN scale and IP address management problems. The Cisco 7600 router, for example, supports up to 4096 defined VLANs. If an SP assigns one VLAN per customer, the number of customers that may be supported per router is limited to 4096. To enable IP routing to and from the customer VLANs, each VLAN is assigned a distinct subnet block of IP addresses. This may result in wasted IP addressing and may create IP address management problems.

PVLANs solve the VLAN scale and IP address management problems while providing isolation between customers. Note, however, as outlined in Chapter 2, that an attacker may use a default gateway router attached to a promiscuous port to bypass PVLAN restrictions and gain connectivity to another device on an isolated port within the same PVLAN. This, however, may be mitigated using IP ACLs on the default gateway router to filter traffic flows between IP hosts within the same PVLAN. To configure a PVLAN, use the **private-vlan** IOS VLAN configuration command.

Traffic Storm Control

Excessive LAN traffic may degrade network performance and increase the risk of broadcast storms and bridging loops. The traffic storm control feature prevents LAN ports from being disrupted by broadcast, multicast, and unicast traffic storms. Traffic storm control (also called traffic suppression) monitors incoming traffic levels on enabled LAN ports at 1-second intervals and, during each interval, compares the actual traffic level with the port's configured traffic storm control level. The traffic storm control level per LAN port is configured as a percentage of the total available bandwidth of the port. Three traffic control levels are available and configurable per LAN port: broadcast, multicast, and unicast thresholds.

Within a 1-second interval, if ingress traffic on a LAN port enabled for traffic storm control reaches the configured traffic storm control level, then traffic storm control drops any new traffic received on the LAN port until the traffic storm control 1-second interval ends. Higher thresholds allow more packets to pass through the LAN port. For more information on broadcast suppression using traffic storm control, refer to the Cisco.com document "Configuring Traffic Storm Control" (referenced in the "Further Reading" section). Traffic storm control is disabled within IOS by default. Note that the broadcast threshold applies only to broadcast traffic. However, the multicast and unicast thresholds apply to all traffic types, including multicast, unicast, and broadcast. Namely, when traffic storm control is active for either multicast or unicast and the rising threshold is hit, broadcast, unicast, and multicast frames are all filtered. Traffic storm control may be enabled using the **storm-control** IOS interface configuration command.

Unknown Unicast Flood Blocking

As described in Chapter 2, when the destination MAC address of a unicast Ethernet frame is not present within the CAM table, the frame is broadcast (flooded) out of every switch port within the associated VLAN. Broadcasting frames degrades network performance and increases the risk of broadcast storms and bridging loops. This default behavior may be prevented via the unknown unicast flood blocking (UUFB) feature available within IOS. The UUFB feature blocks unknown unicast traffic flooding and only permits egress traffic destined to known MAC addresses (in other words, installed in the CAM table) to exit on the UUFB-enabled port. The UUFB feature is supported on all ports that are configured with the **switchport** IOS interface configuration command, including PVLAN ports. UUFB is configured using the **switchport block unicast** IOS interface configuration command.

Summary

This chapter reviewed a wide array of techniques available to mitigate attacks within the IP data plane and within Layer 2 switched Ethernet networks. Many of the techniques are specifically intended for network security, including, for example, ACLs, uRPF, FPM, IP Options Selective Drop, and IP sanity checks. Conversely, many others, including the QoS, QPPB, ICMP, and IP routing techniques, are not intended (nor often considered) for network security but provide powerful tools that may be leveraged to mitigate the risk of security attacks. The optimal techniques that provide an effective security solution will vary by organization and depend on network topology, product mix, traffic behavior, operational complexity, and organizational mission. Defense in depth and breadth techniques (discussed in Chapter 3) can be helpful in understanding the interactions between various data plane security techniques and in optimizing the selection of appropriate measures. Chapters 5 through 7 review the techniques available within the IP control, management, and services planes, respectively, to mitigate the risk of attacks.

Review Questions

1 Which ACL types are commonly used for incident response during active security attacks?

2 What is a potential drawback of tuning the IOS BGP weight attribute so that strict uRPF operates correctly at the SP network edge for multihomed transit customers?

3 Describe two key differences between FPM and interface ACLs.

4 Which technique may be used to reserve a percentage of a router's interface bandwidth solely for control plane traffic?

   5 Name an IP option header type that results in IOS process level packet handling.

   6 Where is the logical place to disable the generation of ICMP Destination Unreachable reply messages (Type 3)?

   7 Name two distinct IOS features (other than CEF) that QPPB relies upon.

   8 What is the primary configuration difference between source-based RTBH filtering and destination-based RTBH filtering?

   9 Name three stateful data plane security techniques and three stateless techniques.

  10 Name the IOS Layer 2 Ethernet switch port mode that disables DTP.

Further Reading

Baker, F., and P. Savola. *Ingress Filtering for Multihomed Networks*. RFC 3704/BCP 84. IETF, March 2004. http://www.ietf.org/rfc/rfc3704.txt.

Evans, J., and C. Filsfils, "Deploying Diffserv at the Network Edge for Tight SLAs, Part I." *IEEE Internet Computing*, vol. 8, no. 1: 61–65 (2004).

Evans, J., and C. Filsfils. "Deploying Diffserv at the Network Edge for Tight SLAs, Part II." *IEEE Internet Computing*, vol. 8, no. 2: 61–69 (2004).

Ferguson, P., and D. Senie. *Network Ingress Filtering: Defeating Denial of Service Attacks which employ IP Source Address Spoofing*. RFC 2827/BCP 38. IETF, May 2000. http://www.ietf.org/rfc/rfc2827.txt.

Passmore, D. "Impact of P2P on Networks." *Business Communications Review*. vol. 35, no. 5: 14–15 (May 2005).

Parmakovic, D. "Service Provider Security." Cisco white paper. http://www.cisco.com/web/about/security/intelligence/sp_infrastruct_scty.html.

Savola, P. "Experiences from Using Unicast RPF." draft-savola-bcp84-urpf-experiences-02.txt. IETF, Nov. 15, 2006. http://tools.ietf.org/id/draft-savola-bcp84-urpf-experiences-02.txt.

"Access Control List Logging." Cisco white paper. http://www.cisco.com/web/about/security/intelligence/acl-logging.html.

"ACL IP Options Selective Drop." *Cisco IOS Software Releases 12.0S Feature Guide*. http://www.cisco.com/en/US/products/sw/iosswrel/ps1829/products_feature_guide09186a00801d4a94.html.

"ACL Support for Filtering IP Options." *Cisco IOS Software Releases 12.3T Feature Guide.* http://www.cisco.com/en/US/products/sw/iosswrel/ps5207/products_feature_guide09186a00801d4a7d.html.

"BGP and the Internet: Advanced Community Usage." Cisco Systems, 2000. http://www.questnet.net.au/questnet2001/ppt/pdf/BGP-AdvCommunities.pdf.

"BGP Support for IP Prefix Import from Global Table into a VRF Table." *Cisco IOS Software Releases 12.3T Feature Guide.* http://www.cisco.com/en/US/products/sw/iosswrel/ps5207/products_feature_guide09186a00803b8db9.html#wp1027265.

Cisco 7600 Series Cisco IOS Software Configuration Guide, 12.2SR. http://www.cisco.com/univercd/cc/td/doc/product/core/cis7600/software/122sr/swcg/index.htm.

"Cisco IOS Firewall Overview." *Cisco IOS Security Configuration Guide, Release 12.4.* http://cisco.com/en/US/products/ps6350/products_configuration_guide_chapter09186a0080455ae3.html.

"Cisco IOS Network Address Translation Overview." Cisco white paper. http://www.cisco.com/en/US/tech/tk648/tk361/technologies_white_paper09186a0080091cb9.shtml.

"Cisco IOS Quality of Service." Cisco white paper. http://www.cisco.com/en/US/products/ps6558/products_white_paper0900aecd802b68b1.shtml.

"Cisco IOS Software Support Resources." http://www.cisco.com/en/US/products/sw/iosswrel/tsd_products_support_category_home.html.

"Cisco Modular Quality of Service Command Line Interface." Cisco white paper. http://www.cisco.com/en/US/products/ps6558/products_white_paper09186a0080123415.shtml.

"Configuring Cisco IOS Intrusion Prevention System (IPS)." *Cisco IOS Security Configuration Guide, Release 12.4.* http://www.cisco.com/en/US/products/ps6350/products_configuration_guide_chapter09186a00804453cf.html.

"Configuring Traffic Storm Control." Cisco Documentation. http://www.cisco.com/univercd/cc/td/doc/product/core/cis7600/software/122sr/swcg/storm.htm.

"IS-IS Mechanisms to Exclude Connected IP Prefixes from LSP Advertisements." *Cisco IOS Software Releases 12.0S Feature Guide.* http://www.cisco.com/en/US/products/sw/iosswrel/ps1829/products_feature_guide09186a00800ad395.html.

"NANOG Security Curriculum." NANOG. http://www.nanog.org/ispsecurity.html.

"Network Based Application Recognition." Cisco Systems. http://www.cisco.com/en/US/products/ps6616/products_ios_protocol_group_home.html.

"Protecting Your Core: Infrastructure Protection Access Control Lists." (Doc. ID: 43920.) Cisco white paper. http://www.cisco.com/warp/public/707/iacl.html.

"Providing Service Security With Cisco Service Control Technology." *Cisco SCE 1000 Series Service Control Engine Brochure.* http://www.cisco.com/en/US/products/ps6150/prod_brochure0900aecd8024ff1a.html.

"Transit Access Control Lists: Filtering at Your Network Edge." (Doc. ID: 44541.) Cisco white paper. http://www.cisco.com/en/US/tech/tk648/tk361/technologies_white_paper09186a00801afc76.shtml.

"Using CAR During DoS Attacks." (Doc. ID: 12764.) Cisco Troubleshooting Tech Note. http://www.cisco.com/en/US/products/sw/iosswrel/ps1835/products_tech_note09186a00800fb50a.shtml.

"When Are ICMP Redirects Sent?" (Doc. ID: 13714.) Cisco Design Tech Note. http://www.cisco.com/en/US/partner/tech/tk365/technologies_tech_note09186a0080094702.shtml.

In this chapter, you learn about the following:

- Security techniques that may be used to protect the IP control plane

- Security techniques that may be used to protect the control plane of Layer 2 switched Ethernet networks

CHAPTER 5

IP Control Plane Security

This chapter describes techniques available to mitigate the risks of unauthorized traffic reaching the IP control plane. As control plane protocols enable IP host connectivity across a routed network, it is critical that:

- Control plane resources within an IP router are protected to mitigate the risk of DoS attacks because most control plane packets are handled at the IOS process level

- Control plane protocols are secured to mitigate the risk of protocol attacks, which may result in unauthorized traffic redirection to a black hole or, alternatively, to an insecure network where an attacker may eavesdrop on conversations and manipulate packet content

Several of the control plane techniques described here were previously referenced in Chapter 4, "Data Plane Security," given exception IP data plane traffic may require control plane processing. This includes data plane packets requiring ICMP handling, IP multicast state creation, or IP options header processing. Further, although data plane techniques such as infrastructure ACLs may help to protect internal control plane protocols such as OSPF, they offer limited protection for external control plane protocols that, by definition, peer with external devices. This chapter reviews the various IOS techniques available to protect BGP and to protect the router from ICMP attacks within the control plane. ICMP attacks that leverage the IP data plane were described in Chapter 4. Chapter 6, "Management Plane Security," and Chapter 7, "Services Plane Security," will review techniques to secure and mitigate attacks within the IP management and services planes, respectively.

As described previously, no single technology (or technique) makes an effective security solution. This applies not only to your wider IP network but also to individual IP traffic planes. Following the defense in depth and breadth principles outlined in Chapter 3, "IP Network Traffic Plane Security Concepts," you may consider deploying multiple complementary techniques, as described in this chapter, to mitigate the risk of control plane attacks.

Disabling Unused Control Plane Services

It is widely considered a network security best common practice (BCP) to disable any unused services and protocols on each device in the IP network. Unused services and protocols are generally not secured, and thus may be leveraged within an attack. The following services and protocols that are enabled by default within Cisco IOS represent a potential security risk. If you do not need these services, you should disable them. (Management plane services and protocols that should also be disabled if not used are described in Chapter 6.)

- **Gratuitous ARP:** To disable the transmission of gratuitous Address Resolution Protocol (ARP) messages on PPP/SLIP interfaces for an address in a local pool, use the **no ip gratuitous-arps** command in IOS global configuration mode.

- **IP source routing:** To disable source routing, enter the **no ip source-route** command in IOS global configuration mode. With IP source routing disabled, any IP packet containing a strict or loose source-route option (per RFC 791) will be discarded. Additional techniques available to mitigate the risk of IP options-based DoS attacks were reviewed in Chapter 4.

- **Maintenance Operation Protocol (MOP):** MOP is enabled on Ethernet interfaces and disabled on all other interface types by default within IOS. To disable MOP, use the **no mop enabled** command within IOS interface configuration mode.

- **Proxy ARP:** Proxy ARP is enabled for all interfaces by default within Cisco IOS. To disable it, use the **no ip proxy-arp** command in IOS interface configuration mode. Proxy ARP is generally only required for broadcast (or shared LAN) networks that connect IP routers with:

  — IP hosts that do not have a statically configured default gateway

  — IP hosts that do not use a dynamic routing protocol

  — IP hosts that do not use ICMP Router Discovery Messages (RFC 1256)

Most other control plane services and protocols are disabled by default within Cisco IOS. IOS management plane services that are enabled by default are described in Chapter 6. The IOS AutoSecure feature provides an automated mechanism to disable unnecessary IOS services. For more information on AutoSecure, refer to Chapter 6. Nevertheless, you should verify against your specific IOS devices and software releases that all unused services and protocols are disabled either by default or through the router configuration.

ICMP Techniques

ICMP, by its very definition per RFC 792, is a control plane protocol. However, it is generally used to report error conditions within IP data plane processing. As discussed in Chapter 2, "Threat Models for IP Networks," ICMP may be used as an attack vector for IP data plane DoS attacks. By triggering packet failures within the IP data plane, for example, using crafted IP packets with insufficient TTL values, attackers may adversely impact the IP control plane of affected routers. Because many of the attacks that target ICMP control plane functions are data plane attacks, the ICMP security techniques available to mitigate the risk of ICMP-related data plane attacks were described in Chapter 4. Refer to Chapter 4 for a detailed review of ICMP security techniques.

Nevertheless, there are specific techniques that you may use to mitigate the risk of control plane attacks that specifically use ICMP messages versus native IP data plane packet failures, per Chapter 4, including:

- **no ip information-reply:** Disables the router from generating ICMP Information Reply (Type 16) messages when it receives unsolicited ICMP Information Request (Type 15) messages. This command is applied by default within IOS interface configuration mode; hence, IOS routers will not respond to unsolicited ICMP Information Request messages. This command applies only to ICMP Information Request messages received. Example 5-1 illustrates how to explicitly disable the generation of ICMP Information Reply messages on an Ethernet interface, which again is the default IOS behavior.

Example 5-1   *IOS Interface Configuration for Disabling ICMP Information Replies*

```
interface Ethernet 0
  no ip information-reply
```

ICMP Information Request messages are not widely used. However, an attacker may use this IETF standard ICMP message type to conduct reconnaissance, as well as to spike the router CPU and potentially trigger a DoS condition. For these reasons, the default behavior of **no ip information-reply** should not be changed.

- **no ip mask-reply:** Disables the router from generating ICMP Address Mask Reply (Type 18) messages when it receives unsolicited ICMP Address Mask Request (Type 17) messages. This command is applied by default within IOS interface configuration mode; hence, IOS routers will not respond to unsolicited ICMP Address Mask Request messages. This command applies only to ICMP Address Mask Request messages received. Example 5-2 illustrates how to explicitly disable the generation of ICMP Address Mask Reply messages on an Ethernet interface, which again is the default IOS behavior.

Example 5-2   *Sample IOS Interface Configuration for Disabling ICMP Address Mask Replies*

```
interface Ethernet 0
  no ip mask-reply
```

ICMP Address Mask Request messages are not widely used. However, an attacker may use this IETF standard ICMP message type to conduct reconnaissance, as well as to spike the router CPU and potentially trigger a DoS condition. For these reasons, the default behavior of **no ip mask-reply** should not be changed.

- **Interface ACLs:** Infrastructure and transit ACLs, as described in Chapter 4, may be used to filter unnecessary ICMP messages destined to network infrastructure, including but not limited to ICMP Source Quench (Type 4), ICMP Echo (Type 8; in other words, ping), and ICMP Timestamp (Type 13) messages. If it is not necessary for external devices to send ICMP messages to your network infrastructure, you should filter them at your network edge. Only those ICMP messages that are specifically needed should be permitted—for example, ICMP Destination Unreachable (Type 3) and ICMP Echo Reply (Type 0) messages. Denying ICMP Echo Requests and permitting ICMP Echo Replies allows you to ping external hosts, such as a public Internet web server, but prevents external hosts from pinging your network infrastructure. If you wish to permit external pings to your DMZ that hosts public servers such as web and e-mail servers, be sure to make the ACL statement restrictive such that only pings are permitted to host addresses within the DMZ and not your wider network infrastructure. Further, you may use rate limiting to permit ICMP messages up to a configurable maximum rate. This allows specific ICMP messages to pass while limiting their potential impact as described in Chapter 4. In addition to interface ACLs and rate limiting, IP Receive ACLs (IP rACL) and Control Plane Policing (CoPP) may be used to filter and, optionally, rate limit ICMP messages from unauthorized sources. IP rACLs and CoPP are described in detail later in the chapter, in the sections "IP Receive ACLs" and "Control Plane Policing," respectively.

Selective Packet Discard

Selective Packet Discard (SPD) is an internal mechanism supported by many Cisco IOS platforms that manages ingress packets that are enqueued within the IOS process level input queues. SPD prioritizes control plane packets and other important traffic during periods of process level queue congestion. Prior to the advent of Cisco Express Forwarding (CEF), as described in Chapter 1, "Internet Protocol Operations Fundamentals," significant numbers of transit packets were forwarded by the IOS process level in order to populate the fast-switching cache. Consequently, SPD was required to prioritize the routing protocol packets over the transit packets that share the same process level queues. On modern platforms running CEF, only receive packets and some exception packets are handled at the IOS process level. Examples of these types of packets include but are not limited to the following:

- Example receive adjacency IP and non-IP packets:
    - IP control plane and routing protocol packets (for example, BGP, OSPF, and HSRP)
    - ICMP messages (for example, Echo Request/Reply and Information Request/Reply)

- — MPLS control protocol packets (for example, LDP and RSVP/MPLS-TE)
- — Management protocol packets (for example, Telnet, SSH, SNMP, TFTP, RADIUS, and TACACS+)
- — Multicast routing protocol packets (for example, PIM, DVMRP, and IGMP)
- — Layer 2 keepalives (for example, PPP, Frame Relay LMI, BFD, and ATM OAM)
- — ARP packets
- Example transit IP and non-IP exception packets:
  - — Multicast data plane packets (in other words, first packet of a multicast flow is punted to IOS process level for state creation, per Chapter 2)
  - — IP options packets (for example, router alert)
  - — MPLS packets with router alert label
  - — IP packets resulting in ICMP handling (for example, TTL expiry, IP Fragmentation Needed but Don't Fragment (bit) was Set)

After packets are punted and placed into the ingress queues, and before IOS starts processing those packets, the SPD mechanism takes place. SPD is an additional tool that ensures certain important packets are handled with higher priority, while in situations of high traffic load at the IOS process level, the less-important packets are discarded. For example, when an interface flap occurs, routing protocol traffic must be guaranteed a high priority and not discarded while the interface recovers. At a high level, the SPD mechanism can be illustrated as shown in Figure 5-1. Here, packets ingressing the router are first placed within ingress queues (left side of figure). From there, input queue checks are made against the per-hardware interface hold queues (middle of figure). Finally, they are enqueued into the IOS process queues (right side of figure). How these packets move from the ingress queue to the IOS process queue is managed by the SPD mechanisms.

SPD State Check

As stated in the preceding section, after packets are placed in the ingress queues, they are classified by SPD as *normal*, *high*, and *top* priority, as illustrated in the left side of Figure 5-1. It is during this classification process that the SPD state check is made. The SPD state check is the first of two checks during which time SPD is capable of discarding packets. To understand how SPD makes this state check, note in Figure 5-1 that the IOS process level reads packets from the process queue (on the right side of the figure), and that there are two queues from which it reads packets: the *general queue* and the *priority queue*. These queues will be covered in more detail shortly. At the moment, it is important to recognize that these queues will contain a certain number of packets at any given time. Further, SPD maintains a state machine that can be in one of three states, and whose state is predicated on the number of packets in the general queue. This is referred to as the SPD state check.

Figure 5-1 *IOS SPD Process*

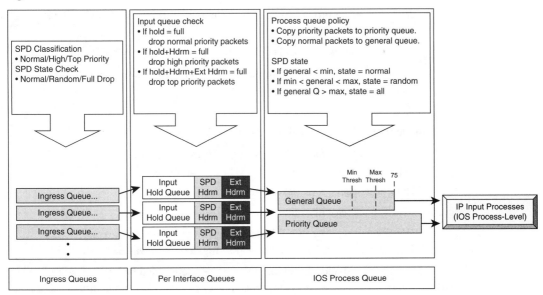

During the SPD classification process, packets with IP precedence 5 and below are classified as normal priority and are subject to the SPD state check and can be discarded. Packets with IP precedence 6 or 7 are classified as high priority and are not subject to the SPD state check. These high priority packets are never discarded by the SPD state check. Finally, non-IP packets are classified as top priority, and are also never subject to discard by the SPD state check. This concept of SPD classification queues is illustrated in Figure 5-2.

Figure 5-2 *IOS SPD Classification Process*

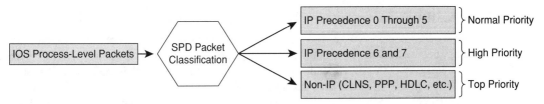

Whether packets classified as "normal" are discarded or not depends on the current depth of the general queue and the state of SPD. At any moment, the SPD state machine can be in one of three states:

- **NORMAL:** SPD is in this state when the number of normal priority packets in the general queue is less than the minimum threshold value (default 73) set for the general queue. In the NORMAL state, SPD will never drop any packets.

- **RANDOM DROP:** SPD is in this state when the number of normal priority packets in the general queue is greater than the minimum threshold but less than the maximum threshold (default 74) set for the general queue. In the RANDOM DROP state, SPD randomly drops well-formed packets. If SPD aggressive mode is configured (defined shortly), all malformed IP packets are discarded in this mode as well. Otherwise, all packets are treated as well-formed packets.

- **FULL DROP:** SPD is in this state when the number of normal priority packets in the general queue is greater than or equal to the maximum threshold for the general queue. In the FULL DROP state, all well-formed and malformed packets are discarded.

As just noted, SPD can be configured for normal (default) mode or aggressive mode. The only difference between the two is how the router accounts for malformed packets. SPD considers a malformed packet as one with an invalid checksum, incorrect version, incorrect header length, or incorrect packet length. When SPD is in normal mode (the default), all IP packets are treated as well formed. When SPD is in aggressive mode, which is configured using the **ip spd mode aggressive** command in IOS global configuration mode, malformed packets are recognized and discarded per the preceding rules. The SPD states and drop rules are illustrated in Figure 5-3.

Figure 5-3   *IOS SPD State Check IP General Queue Treatment*

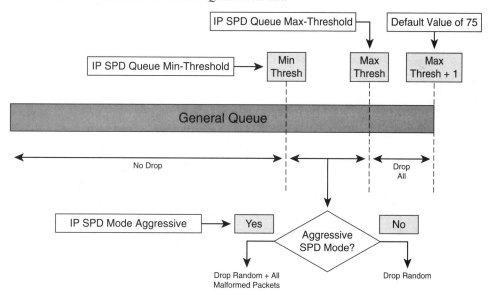

NOTE Aggressive mode is not required on the Cisco 12000 Series Router, because malformed IP packets are discarded directly by the ingress line card, and these packets are not punted to the IOS process level.

Further, on the Cisco 12000 Series, only packets punted to the central Route Processor (RP) are subject to the SPD functions outlined here. Packets handled exclusively by the distributed line card CPUs are not subjected to SPD handling.

The size of the general queue is set by default to 75 packets given the default minimum and maximum threshold values. The *general* queue minimum and maximum threshold default values are 73 and 74 packets, respectively. These values can be changed, however, using the **ip spd queue min-threshold** {*size*} and **ip spd queue max-threshold** {*size*} commands, respectively, in global configuration mode.

SPD Input Queue Check

Once IOS process level packets are classified and the SPD state check has completed, the packets are compared against the per-hardware interface hold queue (which are really just counters). It is at this point that SPD makes its second check and again has the capability of dropping packets. An input queue is maintained on a per-hardware interface basis, with its resources being shared among all subinterfaces. Maintaining SPD statistics on a per-hardware interface prevents any one interface from obtaining more that its fair share of IOS process level resources.

The concept of the per-hardware interface queue is illustrated in Figure 5-4. As shown, each per-hardware interface queue maintains counters in three regions: the *hold queue* region, the *SPD headroom* region, and the *SPD extended headroom* region. Packets classified as normal priority are copied into the IOS process generation queue only if there are free buffers available in the hold queue region; otherwise they are discarded. Packets classified as high priority are copied into the IOS process generation queue only if there are free counters available in either the hold queue region or in the SPD headroom region; otherwise they are discarded. Packets classified as top priority are copied into the IOS process priority queue if there are free counters available in any of hold queue region, SPD headroom region, or SPD extended headroom region; otherwise they are discarded. From that point, the IOS IP input processes dequeue packets in order of priority for protocol processing.

SPD Monitoring and Tuning

There are several important concepts that will aid in the understanding of SPD in operational environments. First, the input hold queue described in the preceding section is effectively a packet counter that IOS maintains per hardware (physical or channel) interface. The current and maximum depth of this queue may be viewed using the **show interface** command, as illustrated in Example 5-3.

Example 5-3 *Display of Current and Maximum Depth of Input Hold Queue*

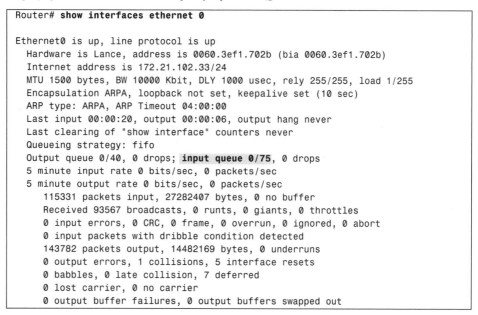

```
Router# show interfaces ethernet 0

Ethernet0 is up, line protocol is up
  Hardware is Lance, address is 0060.3ef1.702b (bia 0060.3ef1.702b)
  Internet address is 172.21.102.33/24
  MTU 1500 bytes, BW 10000 Kbit, DLY 1000 usec, rely 255/255, load 1/255
  Encapsulation ARPA, loopback not set, keepalive set (10 sec)
  ARP type: ARPA, ARP Timeout 04:00:00
  Last input 00:00:20, output 00:00:06, output hang never
  Last clearing of "show interface" counters never
  Queueing strategy: fifo
  Output queue 0/40, 0 drops; input queue 0/75, 0 drops
  5 minute input rate 0 bits/sec, 0 packets/sec
  5 minute output rate 0 bits/sec, 0 packets/sec
     115331 packets input, 27282407 bytes, 0 no buffer
     Received 93567 broadcasts, 0 runts, 0 giants, 0 throttles
     0 input errors, 0 CRC, 0 frame, 0 overrun, 0 ignored, 0 abort
     0 input packets with dribble condition detected
     143782 packets output, 14482169 bytes, 0 underruns
     0 output errors, 1 collisions, 5 interface resets
     0 babbles, 0 late collision, 7 deferred
     0 lost carrier, 0 no carrier
     0 output buffer failures, 0 output buffers swapped out
```

Figure 5-4 *IOS SPD Headroom and Extended Headroom*

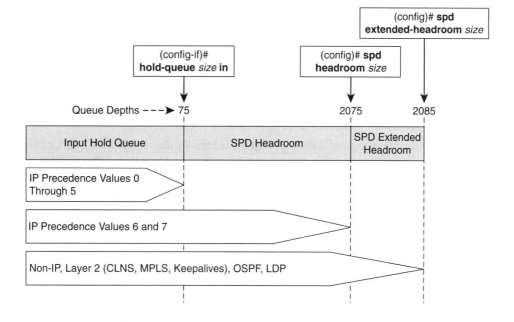

The input hold queue tracks the number of packets enqueued at the IOS process level for the associated physical (or channel) interface. As packets destined for the IOS process level arrive, the associated interface input hold queue counter is incremented by 1 for each packet enqueued. As these packets are dequeued and processed by IOS, the associated interface input hold queue counter is decremented by 1 for each packet dequeued. Without SPD enabled, when the current depth of an interface input hold queue equals its maximum configured limit, any new IOS process level packets received on that specific interface are silently discarded.

As previously stated, an input hold queue is available per physical or channel interface. It is not maintained per logical subinterface. Hence, all of the VLANs, DLCIs, and virtual circuits (VC) of an Ethernet, Frame Relay, and ATM interface, respectively, share the same input hold queue. Consequently, if one VLAN is flooded with IOS process level packets, for example, other VLANs on the same physical Ethernet interface may be starved of IOS control (and management) plane processing.

Operationally, SPD allows for prioritization of IOS process level packets while maintaining fairness among interfaces through the following mechanisms:

- **Hold queue:** The per-interface hold queue specifies the number of normal priority process level packets that may be enqueued to the interface hold queue region. To configure the size of the input hold queue for an interface, use the **hold-queue** {*length*} **in** command in IOS interface configuration mode. The IOS default size is 75 packets, except for asynchronous interfaces, which have a default size of 10 packets.

  — Up to 75 packets, irrespective of their priority, may be enqueued at one time, assuming available IOS process level system buffers. Once the interface input hold queue limit of 75 packets is reached for a given interface, normal priority process level packets received on the interface will be silently discarded.

- **SPD headroom:** SPD headroom specifies the number of high priority process level packets that may be enqueued beyond an interface's input hold queue limit. With the default interface input hold queue limit of 75 packets and the IOS 12.0(32)S default SPD headroom of 2000 packets:

  — An additional 2000 high priority and top priority process level packets may be enqueued into the SPD headroom region. Once the combined 2075 packet limit is reached for a given interface, high priority process level packets received on the interface will also be silently discarded.

  SPD headroom is configured using the **spd headroom** command in IOS global configuration mode and thus affects the size of the headroom region for all interface hold queues. The configured value for SPD headroom may be seen in the output of the **show spd** or **show ip spd** IOS commands, as illustrated in Example 5-4. The default value for SPD headroom varies across IOS releases because the percentage of IP traffic handled at the IOS process level varies across IOS releases and IOS router platforms.

Example 5-4 *Display of SPD Parameter Settings*

```
Router# show spd
Headroom: 2000, Extended Headroom: 10

Router# show ip spd
Current mode: normal
Queue min/max thresholds: 73/74, Headroom: 2000, Extended Headroom: 10
IP normal queue: 0, priority queue: 0.
SPD special drop mode: none
```

- **SPD extended headroom:** SPD extended headroom specifies the number of *top* priority process level packets that may be enqueued within the process level input queues above and beyond an interface's combined input hold queue and SPD headroom limits. Similar to the SPD headroom example just presented, given an interface input hold queue limit of 75 packets, an SPD headroom of 2000 packets, and the IOS 12.0(32)S SPD extended headroom default value of 10 packets:

  — An additional 10 *top* priority process level packets may be enqueued into the SPD extended headroom region. Once the combined 2085 packet limit is reached for a given interface, *top* priority process level priority packets received on the interface will also be silently discarded.

  SPD extended headroom is configured using the **spd extended** command in IOS global configuration mode and thus affects the size of the extended headroom region for all interface hold queues. The configured value for SPD extended headroom may also be seen in the output of the **show spd** or **show ip spd** IOS commands, as illustrated in Example 5-4. The default value for SPD extended headroom is typically 10 packets, but it may also vary across IOS releases, as previously explained for SPD headroom.

SPD is enabled by default within IOS and may be disabled using the **no spd enable** command in IOS global configuration mode. It applies only to ingress packets destined to the IOS process level and not to locally sourced router packets. SPD functions have proven effective during heavy IOS process level packet floods, because it gives priority service to important packets and ensures fairness among router interfaces of IOS process level router resources. The SPD headroom and extended headroom help to facilitate continuous operation of control plane protocols under such conditions. To mitigate the risk of attacks crafted as important packets (in other words, using IP precedence values 6 and 7), IP recoloring, as described in Chapters 4 and 7, may be applied as well as IP Receive ACL or Control Plane Policing techniques (or both) as described in the following sections. For additional information on SPD, refer to the references in the "Further Reading" section.

IP Receive ACLs

Chapter 2 described the different applications of IP interface ACLs, including infrastructure protection, antispoofing, classification, and transit packet filtering. IP interface ACLs are, as aptly named, applied directly to an IOS network interface, including a physical port, channel port (for example, T1 within a CT3), or logical port (for example, Ethernet VLAN, ATM VC, or Frame Relay DLCI). Consider, however, that when an IOS router interface has an input IP interface ACL applied, every packet that ingresses the interface is subject to the applied input ACL policy. (Similarly, every packet that egresses the interface is subject to any output IP interface ACL policy applied.) Consequently, IP interface ACLs apply not only to data plane traffic, but also to control plane, management plane, and services plane traffic. That is, even if the intended *use* of the ACL is to filter control plane traffic, when applied to an interface, any IP packet that passes through the interface is subject to the ACL policy applied in the corresponding direction (input versus output). There are two primary issues with the application of interface ACLs for the protection of control plane traffic:

- To protect the IP network infrastructure from security attacks, IP interface ACLs are generally applied on the external interfaces of all edge routers. In the event an attacker is able to bypass edge IP interface ACL policies, they may be able to attack IP core routers directly. IP interface ACLs may be applied on the internal interfaces of IP edge and core routers to mitigate this external threat and the potential risk of internal attacks. However, notwithstanding the potential performance impacts (if any), managing static IP interface ACL policies for both edge and core routers and for the many external and internal interfaces is operationally complex, as outlined in Chapter 4. Considering that some SP edge routers may have thousands of external interfaces, the operational challenges become all the more apparent.

- The actual construction of the ACL entries can be exceedingly challenging when interface ACLs are used to protect the control plane. For example, each router has a set of unique *receive* IP addresses associated with its own physical and logical interfaces, as described in Chapter 3. Thus, preventing attacks against receive addresses from spoofed sources purporting to be peer addresses requires the construction of unique ACLs for each interface on the platform. This is highly complex for large-scale routers and SP networks.

To simplify the operational security of IP routers, IOS Software Release 12.0S introduced IP Receive ACLs (rACL) as an interim step at solving a largely SP-related infrastructure protection issue. As such, IP rACLs were introduced in 12.0S only for the Cisco 7500, Cisco 12000 GSR, and, later, Cisco 10720 routers. (The long-term strategy that implements comparable but enhanced capabilities and that is included in most Cisco IOS releases and platforms is Control Plane Policing. CoPP is described in the next section.)

IP rACLs further improve the resistance of IOS devices from security attacks by filtering unauthorized traffic sent directly to the control plane of an IOS router using a single and interface-independent (in other words, global) ACL policy. That is, only ingress packets with an IP next hop of receive (otherwise known as a CEF receive adjacency) are subjected to the IP rACL policy, irrespective of the ingress interface. IP prefixes having a CEF receive adjacency include:

- /32 IP addresses automatically assigned to the local router IP interfaces after applying the **ip address** command within IOS interface configuration mode. After configuring 172.16.128.5/30 on a router interface, for example, 172.16.128.5/32 is automatically installed as a CEF receive adjacency. Note, this applies to physical, channel, logical, and loopback interfaces, as well as interfaces assigned to a VRF instance associated with an MPLS VPN. MPLS and IPsec VPNs are further described in Chapter 7.

- Broadcast addresses, including the all 1s IP address (255.255.255.255/32) and the all 1s IP subnets associated with the /32 IP addresses assigned to the local router interfaces (see the first bullet). For example, if a router interface is assigned IP address 172.16.128.5/30 (per the first bullet), the broadcast 172.16.128.7/32 address is treated as a CEF receive adjacency.

- Network addresses, including the all 0s IP subnets associated with the /32 IP addresses assigned to the local router interfaces (see the first bullet). As described in Chapter 4, if a router interface is assigned IP address 172.16.128.5/30 (per the first bullet), the subnet 172.16.128.4/32 address is treated as a CEF receive adjacency.

- Internet Assigned Numbers Authority (IANA) reserved IP multicast addresses in the range between 224.0.0.0 and 224.0.0.255, inclusive. This range of addresses is reserved for the use of routing protocols and other low-level topology discovery or maintenance protocols, such as gateway discovery and group membership reporting. Such multicast addresses are not IP routable and serve local network functions only. Hence, any packets destined to an address within this range are treated as CEF receive adjacencies.

Each of the above IP addresses are considered assigned to the router, and hence have an IP next hop of *receive*. CEF receive adjacencies may be viewed using the **show ip cef** IOS command, as illustrated in Example 5-5.

Example 5-5 *Sample Output from the **show ip cef** Command*

```
Router# show ip cef | include receive
0.0.0.0/32            receive
10.0.0.16/32          receive
10.0.1.4/32           receive
10.0.1.5/32           receive
10.0.1.7/32           receive
10.0.2.16/32          receive
10.0.2.17/32          receive
10.0.2.19/32          receive
10.82.69.0/32         receive
10.82.69.16/32        receive
10.82.69.255/32       receive
224.0.0.0/24          receive
255.255.255.255/32    receive
Router#
```

Given that IP rACL policies apply only to ingress IP packets destined to an IP prefix with a CEF receive adjacency—that is, to IP packets that are *punted* to the local IOS process level—they affect only the IP control and management planes (and possibly services plane traffic) associated with that specific router, and not data plane traffic that is *transiting* the router. Data plane traffic, whether CEF switched or IOS process level switched (slow path), is not affected by IP rACL policies. Ingress packets destined to an IP prefix having a *receive* IP next hop are always handled at the IOS process level and, hence, are often leveraged within router security attacks (whether purposefully or randomly as might occur during a worm outbreak).

IP rACL functions are implemented at the IOS process level in router CPU software (as opposed to hardware logic). On distributed router platforms (in other words, the Cisco 7500 and Cisco 12000 series routers), IP rACL functions are implemented on the distributed interface line card CPUs and unauthorized packets are filtered on the ingress distributed line card(s) without any central RP support. Figure 5-5 illustrates this concept of distributed support for IP rACLs. Thus, IP rACL filtered packets are prevented from adversely impacting the RP, protecting its ability to execute control and management plane services. Hence, under a DoS attack directed at a Cisco 7500 or 12000 series router, the distributed line card CPU utilization may increase because it absorbs the attack; however, the RP that serves as the master controller of the router will be unaffected. (Note that if the attack traffic is permitted by the IP rACL policy and is able to reach the RP, a DoS attack can obviously impact the RP.) Conversely, IP rACLs do not see transit traffic (DoS or otherwise). The Cisco 10720 router also supports IP rACLs, but only in the central RP CPU and not within the PXF hardware logic. IP rACL functions on the Cisco 7500 and 12000 series routers also operate on the RP to filter unauthorized IP traffic received on the out-of-band management interfaces. Security techniques relating to the management plane are described in Chapter 6.

IP Receive ACL Deployment Techniques

This section reviews best practices and implementation techniques necessary to deploy IP rACLs including the following:

- IP Receive ACL activation
- Configuration guidelines for IP Receive ACLs
- IOS feature support for IP Receive ACLs

Figure 5-5 *IP Receive ACL Operations on Distributed Routing Platforms*

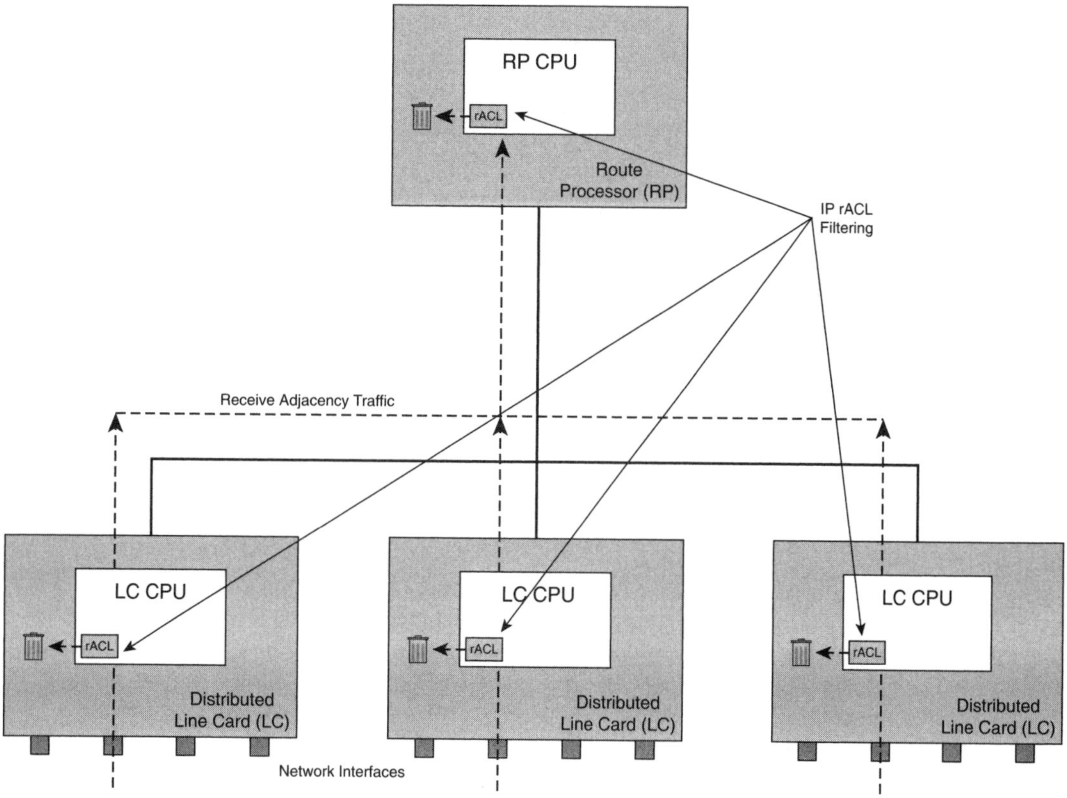

Activating an IP Receive ACL

To activate an IP rACL, use the **ip receive access-list** {*number*} command in IOS global configuration mode. The {*number*} parameter represents a standard or extended numbered IP ACL. Named IP ACLs are not supported. Further, because IP rACLs are implemented at the IOS process level in router CPU software, when the **ip receive access-list** command is entered on a Cisco 12000 or 7500 series router, the rACLs are *built* by the central RP and pushed out to each of the distributed line cards. Therefore, when changes are required, the entire rACL must first be removed using the **no ip receive access-list** command, and then reapplied after the required changes are made in order for them to become effective.

Example 5-6 shows a simple example of how to enable an IP rACL that permits only non-fragmented Telnet, OSPF, BGP, and ICMP Echo Reply (in other words, ping reply) packets. Any other packets destined to any one of the local IOS router's IP addresses described previously are silently discarded. (This example is provided simply to show how IP rACLs are deployed and should not be taken as representative of an operationally accurate deployment scenario. Additional information on deployment techniques follows.)

Example 5-6 *Sample IOS IP Receive ACL Configuration*

```
! - Create the access list entries---
access-list 100 deny ip any any fragments
access-list 100 permit tcp any any eq 23 precedence internet
access-list 100 permit ospf any any precedence internet
access-list 100 permit tcp any any eq bgp precedence internet
access-list 100 permit tcp any eq bgp any precedence internet
access-list 100 permit icmp any any echo-reply
access-list 100 deny ip any any
! - Apply the access list to the receive path
ip receive access-list 100
!
```

IP rACLs can be used to complement rather than replace IP interface ACLs. Deployed in combination, they support the defense in depth and breadth principles outlined in Chapter 3. A common IP ACL deployment model includes:

- IP interface ACLs applied on input to the external interfaces of all edge routers that are designed to protect the network infrastructure from attacks. That is, externally sourced packets with destination IP addresses belonging to internal infrastructure address space, for example, should be denied.

- IP rACLs applied on all capable edge and core routers to protect the RP on each individual router from attacks. This provides an additional layer of protection, for example, in the event that the IP interface ACLs (described in the first bullet) are bypassed. IP rACLs are also useful in protecting the RP in case of a reflection attack. (Reflection attacks against the IP infrastructure were described in Chapter 2.) In this way, IP rACLs also eliminate the need for IP interface ACLs on internal router interfaces.

IP Receive ACL Configuration Guidelines

IP rACLs are widely deployed within SP networks today. They are a proven technique for improving a router's resistance to attacks and, hence, are considered a network security BCP. Ideally, IP rACL policies should be made as restrictive as possible to prevent unauthorized sources and packet types from hitting the IOS process level of an IP router. During the initial IP rACL deployment phase, however, you must exercise caution to ensure that authorized traffic is not inadvertently filtered. Mistakenly filtering BGP or IGP protocol packets, for example, may cause a more detrimental impact than an attack itself. Therefore, when constructing IP rACL policies in a new deployment, it is recommended that IP rACL policies begin from a permissive state and gradually become more restrictive over time after gaining operational experience. Lab deployments and pilot deployments are also recommended to gain operational and router performance knowledge prior to full, network-wide IP rACL deployments.

The following guidelines have proven effective and may be used when deploying IP rACL policies.

Identify Protocols and Port Numbers Used

Identifying the protocols and port numbers used may be done by using a *classification* style IP rACL. As you learned in Chapter 4, classification ACLs consist of permit-only access control entries (ACE) and are useful for identifying types of traffic flowing on the network. In the case of IP rACLs, the classification ACL is applied to the receive path and, hence, identifies all IP traffic destined to the router itself. Thus, it simply serves as an informational logging mechanism to identify necessary IP protocols and TCP/UDP port numbers that must be considered before tightening the IP rACL policy per the "Filter Unnecessary Protocols and Port Numbers" section below. As a best practice, be sure to insert a **permit ip any any log** rule as the very last receive ACE so that any missed protocols not explicitly configured within the IP rACL policy are permitted and identified. Otherwise, CEF receive adjacency traffic may be inadvertently filtered by the implicit **deny ip any any** applied to the end of all IOS ACL policies.

Filter Unnecessary Protocols and Port Numbers

Filter unnecessary IP protocols and TCP/UDP port numbers. Using the information gathered in the preceding section, you may begin to construct your IP rACL policy. The IP rACL should be purposefully built to **permit** or **deny** IP traffic destined to CEF receive adjacency addresses. Begin constructing your IP rACL policy to allow only traffic associated with necessary IP protocols and TCP/UDP port numbers. Now that you have **deny** statements in the IP rACL, you can initially keep the **permit ip any any log** as the last ACL entry so that any traffic that does not match any explicit permit entries in the IP rACL policy will not be denied. As you gain experience with the IP rACL deployment and find that no legitimate packets end up hitting this **permit ip any any log** rule, you should strive to change the last line to a **deny ip any any log** rule so that all unauthorized packets are discarded and no legitimate traffic is discarded. Although there is an implicit **deny ip any any** at the end of the IP rACL policy, you should consider explicitly configuring a **deny ip any any** (log) at the end to ease configuration readability and to provide counters and, optionally, logging for denied packets. Note, a high volume of logged packets may overwhelm the distributed line card CPUs, hence use the **log** keyword option with caution. Other items you may consider include:

- **IP fragments:** As discussed in Chapter 2, IP reassembly is handled at the IOS process level with a limited number of reassembly packet buffers. This presents a potential DoS attack vector because IP fragment DoS attacks may exhaust reassembly buffers, starving legitimate IP fragments. Further, IP reassembly functions reduce available IOS process level CPU cycles for control and management plane protocols. Within properly architected networks, control plane traffic should never be fragmented, and it is a BCP to drop all IP fragments destined to the IOS process level. Therefore, the very first entries within the IP rACL policy should deny IP fragments. Typically, separate entries are applied for TCP, UDP, ICMP, and IP, as illustrated in the ACE configuration shown in Example 5-7. If only a single entry for IP fragments was included, you would achieve the same effect, but lose the information provided by the ACE counters that are maintained for each entry.

Example 5-7 *Sample IOS ACL Entries that Filter Noninitial IP Fragments*

```
! Add these lines to the IP rACL policy to drop all fragments
! These must be the first lines in the ACL!
!---Deny TCP, UDP, ICMP, and IP fragments---
access-list 100 deny tcp any any fragments
access-list 100 deny udp any any fragments
access-list 100 deny icmp any any fragments
access-list 100 deny ip any any fragments
!
```

Note that these IP fragment filters must be the very first set of configuration rules within the IP rACL policy. Otherwise, non-initial fragments may inadvertently match a permit ACE statement earlier within the IP rACL policy.

- **IP ToS:** IP control and management plane protocol standards often specify the use of a specific IP precedence value. The default IOS behavior with respect to the marking of router sourced traffic uses IP precedence value 6 for BGP, OSPF, RIP, ICMP, DVMRP, PIM, IGMP, HSRP, MPLS LDP, RSVP, SSH, and Telnet protocol packets. IP precedence value 0 is used for RADIUS, TACACS+, SNMP, and syslog protocol packets. IP rACL policies should consider these default IP precedence values when permitting such protocol packets. The IP rACL configuration shown in Example 5-6 permits Telnet, OSPF, and BGP protocol packets but only if the IP precedence value is 6 (Internetwork Control, per RFC 795). With IP QoS recoloring (for example, MQC **set ip dscp 0**) applied uniformly across the network edge, as described in Chapter 4, even if an attacker is able to bypass edge IP interface ACLs and hit infrastructure routers with, for example, Telnet, OSPF, and BGP protocol packets, if the IP precedence value of these external packets was recolored, they will be discarded by the IP rACL policy illustrated in Example 5-6. IP rACL policies that include IP precedence value filtering are very effective because attackers are not able to spoof IP precedence values when IP QoS recoloring is deployed across the network edge. The use of edge recoloring and IP precedence-aware IP rACL policies is another example of defense in depth and breadth security principles.

- **ICMP:** Although ICMP is integral to the IP protocol and traffic planes, as described in Chapter 2, not all ICMP message types are required within an IP network. Further, ICMP messages destined to an IP router are by default handled at the IOS process level and, hence, are often leveraged within an attack. Therefore, IP rACL policies should filter unnecessary ICMP message types (for example, Source Quench, Address Mask Request/Reply, and so on) to mitigate the risk of spoofed attacks.

Limit Permitted IP Source Addresses

Limit permitted IP source addresses to known source addresses and limit permitted IP router destination addresses. Using the guidelines previously described, you constructed your IP rACL policy to permit authorized protocols and port numbers from any IP source address. You can now start tightening this policy by specifying only the authorized IP source addresses from which authorized protocols and port numbers will be permitted. In addition, you can specify specific destination addresses as well. Each authorized protocol must be considered separately, however, as each may have a distinct set of authorized source and destination addresses. Consider the following protocols:

- **BGP:** Only valid eBGP peers and iBGP peers should be permitted within the IP rACL policy. Valid peers are statically defined using the **neighbor remote-as** command in IOS router configuration mode, so all source addresses should be easily identifiable. If you have taken care to summarize blocks of IP addresses for loopback interfaces from which iBGP is sourced, one strategy for IP rACL construction would be to use this address block in the ACL permit statements for iBGP, rather than use individual iBGP host addresses. This makes the IP rACL far easier to deploy by allowing for a single IP rACL policy for all routers. However, this adds some risk from spoofed attacks. That said, eBGP peers rarely fall within a consistent address block, making summarization for these connections improbable. Thus, some customization is likely to be required per router to achieve the most secure IP rACL policy. If a customized IP rACL policy can be deployed on each router, only the configured BGP peers should be permitted within the IP rACL policy, per Example 5-8.

Example 5-8   *IOS IP Receive ACL to Permit BGP from Static Peers Only*

```
! Add lines like these to the IP rACL policy to permit BGP protocol messages from
authorized peers only
!---iBGP Peers---
access-list 177 permit tcp host 10.0.10.1 gt 1024 host 10.0.10.11 eq bgp
access-list 177 permit tcp host 10.0.10.1 eq bgp host 10.0.10.11 gt 1024 established
access-list 177 permit tcp host 10.0.20.1 gt 1024 host 10.0.20.11 eq bgp
access-list 177 permit tcp host 10.0.20.1 eq bgp host 10.0.20.11 gt 1024 established
!---eBGP Peers---
access-list 177 permit tcp host 209.165.200.13 gt 1024 host 209.165.201.1 eq bgp
access-list 177 permit tcp host 209.165.200.13 eq bgp host 209.165.201.1 gt 1024
established
!
```

- **IGP protocols:** Unlike BGP, IGP peers are not statically configured within IOS router configuration mode. However, IGP peers generally fall within the same aggregate address range (in other words, classless inter-domain routing [CIDR] block) unlike eBGP peers. Because BGP peers typically include external sources, which are easier to spoof than internal sources, it makes sense to make the IP rACL policy for BGP as restrictive as possible using the /32 BGP peer addresses to reduce the risk of an external BGP attack. Conversely, because IGP peers are typically internal, fall within the same CIDR block, and are more difficult for external sources to spoof, an aggregate source address (for example, /24 as opposed to /32) may be specified as the permitted IGP peer source address range. This simplifies the IP rACL IGP policy rules significantly. This concept is illustrated in the IP rACL policy configuration shown in Example 5-9, which permits only OSPF packets sourced from the internal CIDR block 10.0.0.0/16.

Example 5-9   *IOS IP Receive ACL to Permit OSPF Messages from Internal 10.0.0.0/16 Sources Only*

```
! Add this line to the IP rACL policy to permit internal OSPF protocol messages
access-list 100 permit ospf 10.0.0.0 0.0.255.255 any precedence internet
!
```

You should also remember that uRPF or antispoofing ACL mechanisms can be deployed at the network edge, as described in Chapter 4, to prevent external sources from spoofing an address within an internal address range. Without antispoofing protection at the network edge, an attacker may be able to spoof an internal IP address within the permitted CIDR block specified by the IP rACL IGP policy rules. Hence, the combination of antispoofing protection at the edge and source-address-based IP rACL IGP policy rules narrows the scope for IGP attacks by preventing external ones. This is yet another example of defense in depth and breadth principles.

- **Management protocols:** Most organizations restrict by source IP address the management stations that have administrative access to infrastructure IP routers. (Management plane security is reviewed in detail in Chapter 6.) When IP rACLs are deployed, they must be constructed to permit specific management protocols, and you should also limit which IP hosts have management connectivity to IP routers. This includes limiting management protocol traffic such as Telnet, SSH, SNMP, ping, TACACS+, RADIUS, and NTP from only known network operations and security operations sources. As stated previously, IP rACLs apply to both the control and management planes and, optionally, the services plane. Therefore, IP rACL policies should also consider the known sources associated with each necessary management protocol. This concept is illustrated in the IP rACL policy configuration shown in Example 5-10, which permits only SSH, SNMP, DNS, TACACS+, NTP, FTP, ICMP, and traceroute. In this example, the 10.0.20.0/24 block is the aggregate address (CIDR) block associated with router management loopback interfaces, and 10.0.30.0/24 and 10.0.40.0/24 represent the network operations center (NOC) CIDR blocks.

Example 5-10 *Sample IOS IP Receive ACL Entries to Permit Management Traffic from Explicit Sources*

```
! Add lines such as these to the IP rACL policy to permit management protocols
!---SSH---(no telnet allowed!)
access-list 100 permit tcp 10.0.30.0 0.0.0.255 10.0.20.0 0.0.0.255 eq 22
access-list 100 permit tcp 10.0.30.0 eq 22 0.0.0.255 10.0.20.0 0.0.0.255 established
!--SNMP---
access-list 100 permit udp 10.0.30.0 0.0.0.255 10.0.20.0 0.0.0.255 eq snmp
!---DNS---
access-list 100 permit udp host 10.0.40.1 eq domain 10.0.20.0 0.0.0.255
!---TACACS+---
access-list 100 permit tcp host 10.0.40.2 10.0.20.0 0.0.0.255 established
!---NTP---
access-list 100 permit udp host 10.0.40.3 10.0.20.0 0.0.0.255 eq ntp
!---FTP---
access-list 100 permit tcp host 10.0.40.4 eq ftp 10.0.20.0 0.0.0.255
!---ICMP---
access-list 100 permit icmp any any echo-reply
access-list 100 permit icmp any any ttl-exceeded
access-list 100 permit icmp any any unreachable
access-list 100 permit icmp any any echo
!---TRACEROUTE---(this plus above icmp)
access-list 100 permit udp any gt 10000 any gt 10000
!
```

Limit Permitted IP Destination Addresses

A final phase of IP rACL configuration tightening is to limit permitted IP destination addresses. You may note that IP rACLs can be and often are written differently from typical interface ACLs due to their unique application point. That is, IP rACLs are applied on the *receive path* to the IOS process level. Because of their application point, IP rACLs only see IP packets with a destination of *receive*, and hence it is not mandatory that you explicitly define an IP destination address. The destination IP address can always be listed as **any** within the rACL. This difference from iACL construction can make IP rACLs simpler to deploy. However, specifying an explicit destination IP address, as is done in Examples 5-8 and 5-10 above, narrows the scope of spoofing attacks because the attacker must now know both the source and destination addresses associated with a permitted connection.

As outlined previously, a single IP router has many distinct IP addresses. Some are explicitly configured on an interface, as is the case with the 10.0.0.0/8 host addresses shown in Example 5-5. Others are implicitly assigned, such as the IANA-designated router multicast addresses (224.0.0.0 through 224.0.0.255), and the IP network and IP broadcast addresses associated with CIDR blocks (the .0 and .255 addresses for a /24 CIDR block, for example). Protocols based on TCP, such as BGP, Telnet, and SSH, as well as tunnel protocols such as GRE and IPsec, for example, use operator-configured IP addresses for protocol connections. It is quite common, for example, that router eBGP sessions use external interface IP addresses, whereas iBGP sessions use internal loopback IP addresses. Nevertheless, these protocols associate received protocol packets with (new or existing) connections using a 5-tuple representation including source address, destination address, source port, destination port, and IP protocol. Protocol packets having a 5-tuple that does not match a configured peer connection are discarded. TCP-based protocols also verify the integrity of the connection sequence numbers. These packet integrity checks, however, are performed at the IOS process level. Hence, a flood of invalid protocol packets that is discarded at the IOS process level may still adversely affect the router CPU.

This final phase of IP rACL configuration tightening is meant to limit the range of router destination addresses that will accept traffic for a permitted protocol. In this way, packets are filtered on the distributed line cards of the Cisco 7500 and 12000 series routers without any adverse impact on the router RP CPU. Router IP destination address integrity checks are not limited to static peer-defined TCP and tunnel protocols alone. They also apply to non-TCP protocols such as ICMP, OSPF, RIP, IGMP, PIM, and so on. One important difference with some (not all) of these protocols is the use of IANA-designated router multicast addresses (224.0.0.0 through 224.0.0.255). Any packets destined to an address within this range are automatically treated as CEF receive adjacencies. Individual protocols, however, use only specific addresses within this range. OSPF, for example, is designated the 224.0.0.5/32 and 224.0.0.6/32 addresses. Similarly, EIGRP and IGRP are designated the 224.0.0.10/32 address. Note that some protocols such as MPLS LDP have a UDP component for peer discovery as well as a TCP connection for reliable information exchange. Similar considerations must be applied for other protocols (for example, Multicast Source Discovery Protocol [MSDP]).

These guidelines provide an effective approach for deploying IP rACLs. You must also be sure to revisit IP rACL policies periodically to accommodate any network and configuration changes.

IP Receive ACL Feature Support

IP rACLs are widely deployed within IP networks today and have proven effective for filtering unauthorized traffic and packet types and for improving a router's resistance to attacks. Thus, IP rACLs are considered a network security BCP. They also complement other security techniques by adding an additional layer of protection in support of the defense in depth and breadth principles outlined in Chapter 3. Lastly, as stated at the beginning of this section, IP rACLs are supported only within IOS Software Release 12.0S and for selected routers. The long-term strategy for control plane protection that implements enhanced capabilities and that is included in most Cisco IOS releases and platforms is Control Plane Policing (CoPP), as described in the next section.

Control Plane Policing

The IP rACL policies described in the previous section provide filtering granularity that either permits or denies traffic flows destined to the local IOS router itself (in other words, CEF receive adjacencies). In some cases, this is too limited because you may wish to permit a particular traffic stream but limit the rate at which you accept packets. CoPP does exactly this by taking IP rACLs a step further and leveraging the IOS Modular Quality of Service CLI (MQC) to provide filtering and rate-limiting capabilities for control plane packets. This allows you to specify a maximum rate for ingress control and management plane traffic flows, as opposed to simply permitting without limits the same traffic flow. You may, for example, want to permit SNMP requests but only up to a specific maximum rate so as to not adversely impact the router.

In addition, CoPP is capable of protecting the IOS process level from a broader range of traffic. Whereas IP rACLs apply strictly to packets with CEF receive adjacencies (for example, control and management plane packets destined for the local router), CoPP is also capable of enforcing policies against all packet types that are handled by the IOS process level. For example, and as described in Chapter 2, certain IP data plane (transit) packets are punted to the IOS process level for handling (for example, IP router alert option). Because these are transit packets, they do not have receive adjacencies and thus are not seen by IP rACLs. However, they are handled by the IOS process level and can potentially impact router performance. Thus, CoPP provides broader support for policing data plane exception packets and, as such, is effective for mitigating the transit DoS attacks that were described in Chapter 2.

CoPP is also widely available within IOS, including Cisco IOS 12.0S, 12.2S, 12.2SX, 12.2SBC, 12.3T, and later releases. There are some obvious and some subtle CoPP feature differences between these supported IOS releases and between IOS router platforms. For example, the Cisco 12000 series is capable of deploying CoPP at both an aggregate level and a distributed level (per line card). Many other platforms are capable of deploying CoPP both for input and for output rate limiting. However, the goal of CoPP across all of these releases and platforms is consistent. That is, CoPP is intended to manage the traffic flow of packets capable of reaching the IOS process level so that control and management plane states are maintained in the face of an attack or heavy process level traffic loads on the router. Some of these differences are described further in the "Platform-specific CoPP Implementation Details" section below. These concepts of operation for CoPP are illustrated in Figure 5-6.

Figure 5-6 *Control Plane Policing Conceptual View*

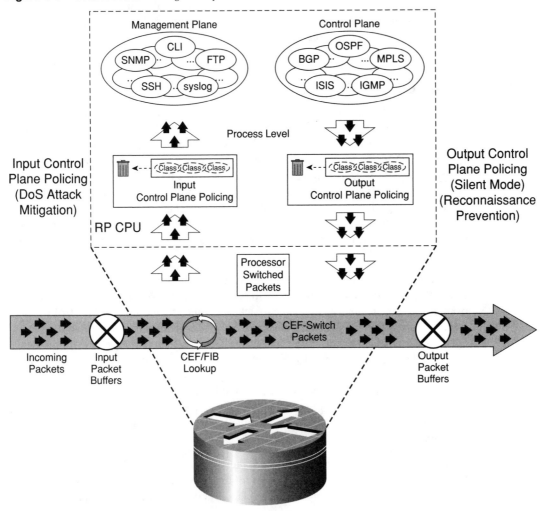

Before reviewing these variations, however, the basic techniques used to design and deploy CoPP policies must be discussed.

CoPP Configuration Guidelines

To protect an IOS router from an attack or heavy process level traffic loads, CoPP policies are applied to the *receive interface*, as described in Chapter 3, which is the forwarding path to the IOS process level from router network interfaces (both physical and channel ports). All traffic destined to the IOS process level is passed through this logical interface. In addition, locally sourced router traffic generated by the router egresses the IOS process level through this logical interface. CoPP input policies can be applied to traffic that ingresses this logical receive interface and, in certain routers, CoPP output policies can be applied to traffic that egresses this logical receive interface.

The general guidelines for deploying CoPP are similar to those for IP rACLs. Begin by creating fairly permissive policies, and gradually tighten them over time, after gaining operational experience. You should strive to make CoPP policies as restrictive as possible to prevent any unauthorized sources and packet types from hitting the IOS process level. In addition, use caution when creating CoPP policies to ensure that authorized traffic is not inadvertently filtered. Mistakenly filtering BGP or IGP protocol packets, for example, may cause a more detrimental impact than an attack itself. Lab deployments and pilot deployments are also recommended, to gain operational and router performance knowledge prior to full, network-wide CoPP deployments.

Defining CoPP Policies

CoPP leverages both IP ACLs and MQC to define its policies. Therefore, some of the steps for deployment are similar to those defined for IP rACLs. However, some additional steps are required, mainly to define traffic rates for authorized flows. Specific tasks to perform when deploying CoPP include the following:

Step 1 Identify appropriate traffic that is to be handled by CoPP for your network.

Step 2 Define packet classification ACLs.

Step 3 Define packet classification MQC class maps.

Step 4 Define the CoPP service policy.

Step 5 Apply the service policy to the control plane.

These steps are explained separately in the following sections.

Step 1: Identify Appropriate Traffic to Be Handled by CoPP for Your Network

This is analogous to the first of the IP rACL deployment guidelines detailed in the "IP Receive ACLs" section, but with some exceptions. Because CoPP sees *all* packet types that are handled by the IOS process level on the RP, you must identify not only the same *receive* adjacency traffic as before, but also the exception IP transit traffic and certain non-IP traffic that also hits the IOS process level. It is recommended that a classification ACL be used within a simple CoPP policy (as you will learn about in Steps 2 and 3 below) to identify IP traffic that is handled by the IOS process level on the RP. This will be useful for identifying both receive and punted transit IP traffic. As for non-IP traffic, the only protocol capable of being classified directly by CoPP today is ARP. As you will see in Step 4, all other non-IP packets (such as Layer 2 keepalives, and so on) are handled by the MQC-defined class-default traffic class.

NOTE   The process of identifying acceptable traffic to be handled by CoPP is a bit of a chicken-or-egg problem. How do you create a CoPP policy without identifying traffic hitting the IOS process level on the RP? And how do you identify traffic hitting the IOS process level without creating a CoPP policy? The answer is to create a very simple, single-class policy using a classification ACL (all permits), and then apply this classification CoPP policy to the logical receive interface for a period of time sufficient to collect the data required to build the formal CoPP policy.

Step 2: Define Packet Classification ACLs

Because the focus of CoPP is to provide rate limits (some of which could be *to* drop at any rate) to different traffic types, the prime focus of this step is to organize traffic that hits the IOS process level into groups of like priority. That is, some types of traffic, BGP and whatever IGP is being used, will always be allowed to reach the IOS process level with a rate limit, while others, such as ICMP, SNMP, and so on, will be allowed to reach the IOS process level but with a very restricted rate. Thus, the traffic types identified in Step 1 are separated into different traffic classes, and a suggested starting point includes the following:

- **Routing:** Control plane traffic that is crucial to the operation of the network, such as iBGP, eBGP, and whatever IGP is being used in the network.

- **Management:** Management plane traffic that is necessary for day-to-day operations, such as SSH, SNMP, NTP, FTP, DNS, Syslog, and so on, but that you may wish to constrain to some maximum rate limit.

- **Normal:** Other identifiable IP or non-IP (ARP) traffic that is expected, but that is not essential for network operations and that setting some rate limit for is appropriate.

- **Undesirable:** Traffic that can be identified as explicitly *bad* or *malicious* (for example, IP fragments or known worms, and so on) and that should be denied access to the IOS process level on the RP.

- **Remaining IP:** Because CoPP sees all traffic handled by the IOS process level, there will almost always be some exception transit IP traffic that cannot be identified ahead of time. This traffic must be permitted, but should definitely be rate limited to ensure that the RP CPU is not overrun.

Similar to MQC interface policies, CoPP policies use MQC traffic classes defined by the MQC **class-map** command in IOS global configuration mode. CoPP policies support the following MQC classification (**match**) criteria:

- Standard and extended IP ACLs using the **match access-group** keyword.

- IP ToS values including **match ip dscp** and **match ip precedence** keywords. Similar to the IP rACL deployment guidelines described previously, CoPP deployments should also consider IP precedence values within the policy configuration. The Cisco 10720 also supports **match mpls experimental** and **match qos-group**.

- ARP protocol packets using the **match protocol arp** command. Note, the **match protocol arp** command is not supported within the Cisco IOS 12.2SX release. The Cisco 10720 also supports the MQC **match protocol ipv6** command.

- Ingress router interface using **match input-interface**. This is supported only on the Cisco 10720 Internet router.

The most general approach within MQC for matching traffic types is to use classification ACLs. As you will recall in MQC, when ACLs are used to match traffic, a **permit** entry is equivalent to a **match**, and a **deny** entry is equivalent to a **match not**. For CoPP, you will most likely create classification ACLs that contain only permit statements. Therefore, you need to create a unique ACL for each traffic category (or class) defined. These ACLs should be as specific as possible, including protocol, source address, and destination address criteria, because this is how traffic types will be classified within the CoPP traffic classes. The definition of these ACLs is one of the most critical steps in the CoPP deployment process. MQC uses these ACLs to define the traffic classes, which in turn become the object of the policy actions (that is, policing). Appropriate granularity in the distribution of protocols within these ACLs also allows for better protection of the RP CPU.

Using the same traffic examples used for the IP rACL descriptions previously shown, Example 5-11 illustrates sample ACL policies that will be used for the routing, management, normal, undesirable and remaining IP traffic classes described previously.

Example 5-11 *Sample IOS CoPP Packet Classification ACLs*

```
! ROUTING ---------------- Defined as routing protocols this routing will process
!---iBGP Peers---
access-list 120 permit tcp host 10.0.10.1 gt 1024 host 10.0.10.11 eq bgp
access-list 120 permit tcp host 10.0.10.1 eq bgp host 10.0.10.11 gt 1024 established
access-list 120 permit tcp host 10.0.20.1 gt 1024 host 10.0.20.11 eq bgp
access-list 120 permit tcp host 10.0.20.1 eq bgp host 10.0.20.11 gt 1024 established
!---eBGP Peers---
```
continues

Example 5-11 *Sample IOS CoPP Packet Classification ACLs (Continued)*

```
access-list 120 permit tcp host 209.165.200.13 gt 1024 host 209.165.201.1 eq bgp
access-list 120 permit tcp host 209.165.200.13 eq bgp host 209.165.201.1 gt 1024
  established
!---OSPF protocol messages---
access-list 120 permit ospf 10.0.0.0 0.0.255.255 any precedence internet
!
! MANAGEMENT ------ Defined as traffic required to access and manage the router
!---SSH---(no telnet allowed!)
access-list 121 permit tcp 10.0.30.0 0.0.0.255 10.0.20.0 0.0.0.255 eq 22
access-list 121 permit tcp 10.0.30.0 0.0.0.255 eq 22 10.0.20.0 0.0.0.255 established
!---SNMP---
access-list 121 permit udp 10.0.30.0 0.0.0.255 10.0.20.0 0.0.0.255 eq snmp
!---DNS---
access-list 121 permit udp host 10.0.40.1 eq domain 10.0.20.0 0.0.0.255
!---TACACS+---
access-list 121 permit tcp host 10.0.40.2 10.0.20.0 0.0.0.255 established
!---NTP---
access-list 121 permit udp host 10.0.40.3 10.0.20.0 0.0.0.255 eq ntp
!---FTP---
access-list 121 permit tcp host 10.0.40.4 eq ftp 10.0.20.0 0.0.0.255
!---TRACEROUTE---(this plus below ICMP)
access-list 121 permit udp any gt 10000 any gt 10000
!
! NORMAL ------ Defined as other traffic destined to the router to track and limit
!---ICMP---
access-list 122 permit icmp any any echo
access-list 122 permit icmp any any echo-reply
access-list 122 permit icmp any any ttl-exceeded
access-list 122 permit icmp any any unreachable
access-list 122 permit icmp any any port-unreachable
access-list 122 permit icmp any any packet-too-big
!
! UNDESIRABLE ------------- Defined as traffic explicitly blocked (known malicious)
access-list 123 permit tcp any any fragments
access-list 123 permit udp any any fragments
access-list 123 permit icmp any any fragments
access-list 123 permit ip any any fragments
access-list 123 permit udp any any eq 1434
!
! REMAINING IP ------------- Defined as all previously unclassified packets
access-list 124 permit ip any any
!
```

As previously mentioned, these classification ACLs use only **permit** statements. Hence, all traffic that you want to explicitly group within a given class must be selected with a **permit** statement. The best example of this is the undesirable traffic class, as illustrated in Example 5-11. In this ACL (123), the use of the **permit** statement specifies that all IP noninitial fragments and SQL Slammer packets (in this case) are classified as undesirable. These packets will later be discarded in the policy statement definition configured for this class. As mentioned, packets that match a **deny** statement within an MQC **access-group** classification ACL are not classified within the associated MQC **class-map**. This also applies to the implicit deny at the end of the ACL policy as well. The policy actions that are applied to the traffic classes are specified within the CoPP policy configuration as described in Step 4 a bit later.

Step 3: Define Packet Classification MQC Class Maps

Now you must create class maps to complete the traffic-classification process using the previously defined ACLs from Step 2 to categorize IP packets into discrete classes. MQC class maps permit multiple match criteria, as well as nested class maps. The MQC **match-any** keyword requires that packets meet only one **match** criteria to be considered "in the class," whereas the MQC **match-all** keyword requires that packets meet all of the *match* criteria to be considered "in the class." If neither **match-any** nor **match-all** is specified, the default behavior is consistent with the **match-all** keyword. MQC **match-not** provides criterion that prevents a packet from being included in the class. In general, a **match-all** classification scheme with a simple, single-match criteria will satisfy initial deployments for CoPP. This is illustrated in Example 5-12 and leaves open the option for fine-tuning through multiple match criteria in the longer term.

Example 5-12 *Sample IOS MQC Class Map Format*

```
Router(config)# class-map match-all {class-map-name}
Router(config-cmap)# match access-group {acl-number}
```

In general, traffic destined to the undesirable class should follow a "match-any" classification scheme. Further, creating class maps with descriptive names also simplifies deployment and operational complexity.

Using the ACLs defined in Step 2, Example 5-13 constructs class maps for the specific traffic classes defined.

Example 5-13 *Sample IOS CoPP Traffic Classes Defined Using ACLs*

```
! Define a class for each type of traffic and associate the appropriate ACL
! Define a class-map to collect routing traffic…
class-map match-all CoPP-routing
  match access-group 120
! Define a class-map to collect management traffic…
class-map match-all CoPP-management
  match access-group 121
! Define a class-map to collect other normal traffic (icmp's etc.)
class-map match-all CoPP-normal
  match access-group 122
! Define a class-map to collect undesirable traffic (attacks, etc.)
class-map match-any CoPP-undesirable
  match access-group 123
! Define a class-map to collect all remaining IP traffic
class-map match-all CoPP-remaining-IP
  match access-group 124
!
```

Step 4: Define the CoPP Service Policy

Once the MQC class maps are defined in Step 3, they can be used to define policies to *enforce* each traffic class by referring to them within an MQC **policy-map**. The MQC policy map is used to associate specific policy actions with specific traffic classes. Two MQC commands are supported within CoPP policy maps, **police** and **drop**. Within IOS Software Release 12.0S, only the **police** command is available. However, **drop** may be used as an *action* within the **police** command for each of the **conform-action**, **exceed-action**, and **violate-action** arguments. This is similar to how traffic flows are permitted within CoPP policies except the **permit** action is used within the **police** command instead of **drop**. Example 5-14 illustrates a CoPP policy with four distinct traffic classes.

Example 5-14 *Sample IOS CoPP Drop, Rate-Limit, and Transmit Action Formats*

```
!
policy-map copp-in
  class class1
    drop
  class class2
    police 8000 conform-action drop exceed-action drop
  class class3
    police 10000 conform-action transmit exceed-action drop
  class class4
    police 20000 conform-action transmit exceed-action transmit
!
control-plane
    service-policy input copp-in
!
```

As illustrated in Example 5-14, all traffic associated with class1 and class2 is filtered (discarded). Traffic associated with class3 is rate limited to 10 kbps and traffic associated with class4 is allowed with no maximum rate limit specified. The 20-kbps rate specified for class4 is insignificant given the **exceed-action** is **transmit**. For more detailed information on MQC, refer to the white paper "Cisco Modular Quality of Service Command Line Interface" (listed in the "Further Reading" section). Refer to Chapters 4 and 7 for a discussion on QoS security techniques and the QoS services plane, respectively.

Typical deployments for CoPP use the general format shown in Example 5-15, where {*action*} is **transmit** or **drop**.

Example 5-15 *IOS MQC Policy Map Template*

```
Router(config)# policy-map {policy-map-name}
Router(config-pmap)# class {class-map-name}
Router(config-pmap-c)# police {rate} [burst-normal] [burst-max] conform-action
  {action} exceed-action {action}
```

For new CoPP deployments, it is best to start out with a basic, *forgiving* policy that does not police (rate limit) any traffic classes, with the exception of the CoPP-undesirable class, until you confirm that all protocols are properly classified among class maps and that no authorized traffic has been overlooked. An overly constraining policy can result in network issues, such as loss of management connectivity, or more impacting conditions, such as loss of routing protocols and link state. This is especially true for the catch-all CoPP-remaining-IP class and the always-present class-default class.

One deployment approach is to start out with **conform-action transmit exceed-action transmit** on all class maps except CoPP-undesirable, and tighten from there once operational experience is gained. Example 5-16 illustrates the CoPP policy configuration using the traffic classes defined previously. It is highly recommended that you start out with a pilot deployment on a few representative routers to gain experience and an understanding of traffic rates within each class map. Note that the **police** command rates used in Example 5-16 are for illustration purposes only. You must determine what the appropriate rates are for your network. Guidance on performing this task follows shortly.

Example 5-16 *Sample IOS CoPP Policy Configuration*

```
! Define a policy-map for CoPP…
policy-map CoPP
  class CoPP-undesirable
    police 8000 1500 1500 conform drop exceed drop
  class CoPP-routing
    police 125000 1500 1500 conform transmit exceed transmit
  class CoPP-management
    police 50000 1500 1500 conform transmit exceed transmit
  class CoPP-normal
    police 15000 1500 1500 conform transmit exceed transmit
  class CoPP-remaining-IP
    police 8000 1500 1500 conform transmit exceed transmit
  class class-default
    police 8000 1500 1500 conform transmit exceed transmit
!
```

Based on Example 5-16, there are several critical things you need to know about **policy-map CoPP** and its construction for use with CoPP:

- The class CoPP-undesirable is defined first. As with all MQC policy maps, class maps are processed in order and, hence, the order in which you arrange class maps within the policy map is critical to the operational effectiveness of CoPP. As soon as a match occurs, no further packet classification processing occurs with the current or any subsequent class maps. That is, a packet can be classified as belonging to only a single class map, and it is the first class map during which a match is determined. Therefore, because the desired policy is to deny fragments to the IOS process level on the RP, and fragments are included in the CoPP-undesirable class, this class must be defined first (with a drop policy) to prevent noninitial fragments from reaching the IOS process level. If the CoPP-undesirable class is not defined prior to other classes, fragmented packets may be matched by an earlier class map and handled by that class map's policy action. This applies to all undesirable traffic as well. Thus, the CoPP-undesirable traffic class should be specified first within the CoPP policy map configuration to prevent undesirable traffic from being mistakenly classified into another CoPP traffic class.

- The class CoPP-remaining-IP is defined second from last. Because class maps are processed in order, any IP traffic that is not explicitly matched by entries ahead of class CoPP-remaining-IP will be matched by this class. There are two main reasons why you want to define a catch all IP class immediately prior to class-default. First, exception IP transit traffic must be handled by the IOS process level but cannot be matched by explicit policies (for example, Router Alert option). Because some attack vectors attempt to exploit this, it is recommended that this catch all IP class be defined to appropriately rate limit this traffic class. Second, and equally as important, if this catch-all IP class is not defined, then all of these transit IP and exception IP traffic flows will fall into the class-default class. As you will see next, because other non-IP traffic also falls into class-default, it is not recommended that class-default be rate limited. Thus, without the catch-all IP class CoPP-remaining-IP, you would be unable to prevent transit IP and exception IP traffic from adversely impacting L2 protocol traffic, including keepalives.

- The class class-default is automatically placed last in the policy map. Any traffic that does not match any of the defined class maps previously described automatically falls into the class class-default. MQC class-default is a special class that is automatically defined and always included in MQC policies, whether it is specified by name or not. If it is not explicitly specified, it is still included but is not policed in any way. If it is included, as it is in Example 5-16, then an appropriate police action must be specified. In the current CoPP implementation (all IOS versions), the only Layer 2 protocol that can be matched by MQC within CoPP is ARP. (When ARP is not specifically classified, as it is not in Example 5-13 above, it will also fall into the class-default class.) All other non-IP and Layer 2 control plane packets will also fall into class-default. Non-IP and Layer 2 traffic includes Layer 2 keepalives, CLNS, as well as (at the time of this writing) MPLS labeled packets handled at the IOS process level, including those with the Router Alert Label or having an aggregate label that requires a second-level packet header lookup. Because of this, class-default should never be policed. As mentioned previously, this is why the class map immediately prior to class-default must be a catch-all for all remaining and unclassified IP traffic. This guarantees that class-default only contains non-IP and Layer 2 control plane traffic, and that it can safely be left unpoliced. You may also consider defining a distinct CoPP traffic class for ARP traffic, as illustrated in Example 5-17, to isolate ARP traffic from other types of Layer 2 traffic. A distinct CoPP class for ARP traffic would then limit the aggregate rate of ARP traffic received, thereby helping to mitigate the risk of ARP attacks.

Example 5-17 *Sample IOS CoPP Traffic Classes Defined for ARP Traffic*

```
! Define a class-map to collect ARP traffic…
class-map match-all CoPP-arp
  match protocol arp
```

- Finally, it is critical to note that, while CoPP policies are defined using MQC syntax, which is generally used for QoS services, this same usage within CoPP does not guarantee the specified bandwidth to the IOS process level for the relevant class. Rather, it is used to limit the bandwidth to the IOS process level that any one traffic class can consume. Also note that the configured maximum rate is the aggregate limit for all traffic associated with the specific class. Consider the case where the ACL used in a rate-limited class combines several protocols—for example, ACL 121 of Example 5-11 above used in the class CoPP-management. Each of those individual protocol's entries then is capable of consuming the entire amount of bandwidth dedicated to this class. Hence, under attack, it may not be possible to use one configured protocol if another one within the same class is consuming all of the allocated bandwidth. Using ACL 121 and the class CoPP-management as an example, suppose that SNMP was leveraged within a DoS attack and consumed the allocated bandwidth assigned to the CoPP-management class. In this case, you might find it difficult using SSH to gain remote access into the router. Thus, constructing class maps with ACLs that match a single protocol may be reasonable in certain cases (for example, SSH) to provide more-assured availability under attack. Note that if a class is not rate limited, as is the case with the class CoPP-routing of Example 5-16 above, then the class has no maximum limit and one protocol cannot starve another within the same class map. Traffic classes that are not policed are justifiable in certain cases (for example, routing). However, normal traffic that is expected but not essential for network operations should be policed to mitigate the risk of a heavy load of normal traffic from adversely affecting routing and management protocols.

Step 5: Apply the Service Policy to the Control Plane

The final step in deploying CoPP is to attach the policy map developed in Step 4 to the logical receive interface. The general commands for applying the CoPP policy in the input direction are illustrated in Example 5-18.

Example 5-18 *IOS CoPP Policy Attachment*

```
! Attached the CoPP policy to the control plane interface
control-plane
  service-policy input CoPP
!
```

This generalized form is available on all router platforms that support CoPP. The Cisco 12000 series includes an additional distributed mode of CoPP. This and other 12000-specific CoPP deployment guidelines are described later in this section.

Now that you have learned about CoPP policy construction methods, let's turn the attention toward CoPP policy tuning.

Tuning CoPP Policies

Policy construction is the key to operational success with CoPP. Policies will need to be adjusted over time, however. It is possible that adjustments such as adding class maps or adding or modifying ACLs may be required, especially as new routers and services are deployed. However, the primary effort that likely will be required is to make adjustments to the rate limits applied to policy map classes. Questions on how to best tune policy rate limits are the most frequently asked by network operators, and thus will be the main focus here.

When a CoPP policy is initially deployed, as previously mentioned, the initial policers should be **conform transmit exceed transmit** on all classes, except CoPP-undesirable. You can then use the results of the **show policy-map** command to understand the baseline measurements of the current traffic rates for each class within the policy map. After the production CoPP policy is deployed, you use these same techniques to validate rate-limit settings and fine-tune policies as necessary. The **show policy-map** command provides several keywords that help refine the output to information specific to the control plane. Some of the more important commands include the following:

- Verify and review the CoPP service policy map configuration and status:

  ```
  show policy-map control-plane [all] [input [class {class-name}] | output [class
  {class-name}]]
  ```

- Verify/review (all) policy map(s) configured on the router:

  ```
  show policy-map [policy-map-name]
  ```

- In addition to the **show policy-map** command, the **show class-map** command also provides invaluable information. Verify/review (all) class map(s) configured on the router:

  ```
  show class-map [class-map-name]
  ```

- Finally, reviewing the ACE counters on the access lists associated with class maps provides a wealth of information in terms of how effectively your policies are constructed to classify appropriate traffic. If you see a large number of hits against the ACL used in the catch-all IP class *CoPP-remaining-IP*, you should review the traffic types that are hitting this class and potentially modify other class map ACLs as appropriate to explicitly classify this traffic. Verify/review (all) access lists (associated with the class maps):

  ```
  show access-lists [ACL-number]
  ```

Example 5-19 shows a sample of the output generated by the **show policy-map control-plane input** command. As you can see, this output lists, per class map, the packet rates for matching traffic that both conforms or exceeds the policy, the names of the traffic classes and match criteria (ACLs in this case), and the policy action (police). These results should provide valuable guidance for policy tuning.

Example 5-19 *Sample* **show policy-map** *Output Detailing CoPP Class Statistics*

```
Router# show policy-map control-plane input
Control Plane

  Service-policy input: CoPP (225)

    Class-map: CoPP-undesirable (match-any) (4988273/4)
      0 packets, 0 bytes
      5 minute offered rate 0 bps, drop rate 0 bps
      Match: access-group 123 (4791698)
        0 packets, 0 bytes
        5 minute rate 0 bps
      police:
          cir 8000 bps, bc 1500 bytes
        conformed 0 packets, 0 bytes; actions:
          drop
        exceeded 0 packets, 0 bytes; actions:
          drop
        conformed 0 bps, exceed 0 bps

    Class-map: CoPP-routing (match-all) (7222977/1)
      0 packets, 0 bytes
      5 minute offered rate 0 bps, drop rate 0 bps
      Match: access-group 120 (11449986)
      police:
          cir 125000 bps, bc 1500 bytes
        conformed 0 packets, 0 bytes; actions:
          transmit
        exceeded 0 packets, 0 bytes; actions:
          transmit
        conformed 0 bps, exceed 0 bps

    Class-map: CoPP-management (match-all) (10957137/3)
      0 packets, 0 bytes
      5 minute offered rate 0 bps, drop rate 0 bps
      Match: access-group 121 (5208466)
      police:
          cir 50000 bps, bc 1500 bytes
        conformed 0 packets, 0 bytes; actions:
          transmit
        exceeded 0 packets, 0 bytes; actions:
          transmit
```

continues

Example 5-19 *Sample* **show policy-map** *Output Detailing CoPP Class Statistics (Continued)*

```
                   conformed 0 bps, exceed 0 bps

    Class-map: CoPP-normal (match-all) (12606385/2)
      0 packets, 0 bytes
      5 minute offered rate 0 bps, drop rate 0 bps
      Match: access-group 122 (8647266)
      police:
          cir 15000 bps, bc 1500 bytes
        conformed 0 packets, 0 bytes; actions:
          transmit
        exceeded 0 packets, 0 bytes; actions:
          transmit
        conformed 0 bps, exceed 0 bps

    Class-map: CoPP-remaining-IP (match-all) (1062113/5)
      40 packets, 8589 bytes
      5 minute offered rate 1000 bps, drop rate 0 bps
      Match: access-group 124 (10461554)
      police:
          cir 8000 bps, bc 1500 bytes
        conformed 40 packets, 8589 bytes; actions:
          transmit
        exceeded 0 packets, 0 bytes; actions:
          transmit
        conformed 1000 bps, exceed 0 bps

    Class-map: class-default (match-any) (9318433/0)
      18 packets, 46123 bytes
      5 minute offered rate 6000 bps, drop rate 0 bps
      Match: any  (4397474)
        18 packets, 46123 bytes
        5 minute rate 6000 bps
      police:
          cir 8000 bps, bc 1500 bytes
        conformed 8 packets, 1383 bytes; actions:
          transmit
        exceeded 10 packets, 44740 bytes; actions:
          transmit
        conformed 0 bps, exceed 6000 bps
Router#
```

Example 5-20 shows sample output generated by the **show access-lists** command. As you can see, this output lists the ACE classification rules associated with each ACL and nonzero hit counts per ACE rule. The output of Example 5-20 accounts for 1000 ping packets sent to the router and permitted by the CoPP policy.

Example 5-20 *Sample* **show access-lists** *Output Detailing ACL*

```
Router# show access-lists
Extended IP access list 120
    permit tcp host 10.0.10.1 gt 1024 host 10.0.10.11 eq bgp
    permit tcp host 10.0.10.1 eq bgp host 10.0.10.11 gt 1024 established
    permit tcp host 10.0.20.1 gt 1024 host 10.0.20.11 eq bgp
    permit tcp host 10.0.20.1 eq bgp host 10.0.20.11 gt 1024 established
    permit tcp host 209.165.200.13 gt 1024 host 209.165.201.1 eq bgp
    permit tcp host 209.165.200.13 eq bgp host 209.165.201.1 gt 1024 established
    permit ospf 10.0.0.0 0.0.255.255 any precedence internet
Extended IP access list 121
    permit tcp 10.0.30.0 0.0.0.255 10.0.20.0 0.0.0.255 eq 22
    permit tcp 10.0.30.0 0.0.0.255 eq 22 10.0.20.0 0.0.0.255 established
    permit udp 10.0.30.0 0.0.0.255 10.0.20.0 0.0.0.255 eq snmp
    permit udp host 10.0.40.1 eq domain 10.0.20.0 0.0.0.255
    permit tcp host 10.0.40.2 10.0.20.0 0.0.0.255 established
    permit udp host 10.0.40.3 10.0.20.0 0.0.0.255 eq ntp
    permit tcp host 10.0.40.4 eq ftp 10.0.20.0 0.0.0.255
    permit udp any gt 10000 any gt 10000
Extended IP access list 122
    permit icmp any any echo (1000 matches)
    permit icmp any any echo-reply
    permit icmp any any ttl-exceeded
    permit icmp any any unreachable
    permit icmp any any port-unreachable
    permit icmp any any packet-too-big
Extended IP access list 123
    permit tcp any any fragments
    permit udp any any fragments
    permit icmp any any fragments
    permit ip any any fragments
    permit udp any any eq 1434
Extended IP access list 124
    permit ip any any
Router#
!
```

SNMP queries may also be used to automate the process of gathering CoPP service policy transmit and drop rates. The Cisco QoS MIB CISCO-CLASS-BASED-QOS-MIB provides the primary mechanisms for MQC-based policy monitoring via SNMP. The implementation of this MIB is IOS release-dependent. Example 5-21 and Example 5-22 show simultaneous sample outputs generated by the **show policy map control-plane** IOS command and the **snmpwalk** SNMP command, respectively, and that indicate identical statistics for each class within the policy map.

Example 5-21 *Sample* **show policy-map control-plane** *Output Detailing CoPP Class Statistics*

```
Router# sh policy-map control-plane input | include packets
     0 packets, 0 bytes
        conformed 0 packets, 0 bytes; actions:
        exceeded 0 packets, 0 bytes; actions:
     0 packets, 0 bytes
        conformed 0 packets, 0 bytes; actions:
        exceeded 0 packets, 0 bytes; actions:
     1058 packets, 110704 bytes
        conformed 88 packets, 9824 bytes; actions:
        exceeded 970 packets, 100880 bytes; actions:
     1002 packets, 104196 bytes
        conformed 21 packets, 2172 bytes; actions:
        exceeded 981 packets, 102024 bytes; actions:
     6799 packets, 1398439 bytes
        conformed 6791 packets, 1394827 bytes; actions:
        exceeded 8 packets, 3612 bytes; actions:
     2923 packets, 7505870 bytes
        conformed 1285 packets, 177458 bytes; actions:
        exceeded 1638 packets, 7328412 bytes; actions:
Router#
```

Example 5-22 *Sample* **snmpwalk** *Output Detailing CoPP Class Statistics*

```
unix-station$ snmpwalk -v 2c -c cisco 10.82.69.121 .1.3.6.1.4.1.9.9.166.1.15.1.1.2
SNMPv2-SMI::enterprises.9.9.166.1.15.1.1.2.225.1062113 = Counter32: 6799
SNMPv2-SMI::enterprises.9.9.166.1.15.1.1.2.225.4988273 = Counter32: 0
SNMPv2-SMI::enterprises.9.9.166.1.15.1.1.2.225.7222977 = Counter32: 0
SNMPv2-SMI::enterprises.9.9.166.1.15.1.1.2.225.9318433 = Counter32: 2923
SNMPv2-SMI::enterprises.9.9.166.1.15.1.1.2.225.10957137 = Counter32: 1058
SNMPv2-SMI::enterprises.9.9.166.1.15.1.1.2.225.12606385 = Counter32: 1002
unix-station$
```

The bottom line is, you should review and tune your CoPP service policies based on the statistics learned through the use of IOS CLI **show** commands and/or management station **snmp** queries. You should review service policy transmit and drop rates to ensure that the appropriate traffic types and rates are receiving the appropriate policing policy. The IOS command **show policy-map control-plane** is invaluable for reviewing and tuning site-specific policies and troubleshooting CoPP. This displays dynamic information about the number of packets (and bytes) conforming or exceeding each policy definition. This command is useful for ensuring that appropriate traffic types and rates are reaching the IOS process level on the RP. You should also review the output of the IOS command **show access-list**, which displays hit counts on a per-ACE basis. The presence or absence of hits indicates flows or lack thereof for that packet type reaching the IOS process level. Large numbers of packets or an unusually rapid increase in rate of packets processed may be suspicious and should be investigated. The lack of packets may also indicate unusual behavior, or that a rule may need to be revisited.

When updating CoPP deployments, tighten existing policies based on confirmation of appropriate protocol distributions within each class map, and on confirmation of traffic rates within each class map under normal operating conditions. It is also highly recommended that you understand the behavior and performance of your CoPP policy when the router is under attack. This should be accomplished within a lab environment, and preferably before "the real thing" hits your operational network. When setting rate-limiting policies, take care to ensure that the required rates of traffic are well understood. A very low rate might discard necessary traffic, whereas a high rate might allow the IOS process level to be inundated with a flood of noncritical packets. Overall, the following general principles have proven effective in operational settings:

- Routing protocols should never be rate limited.

- Management traffic should be rate limited to prevent spoofed packets and to prevent rogue servers or processes from consuming excessive bandwidth to the IOS process level on the RP.

- User traffic that must be permitted (for example, ICMP and so forth) should be rate limited to prevent abuse (the main reason for CoPP, of course).

- An *undesirable* class should always be configured, should always come first, and should always have the policy actions of **conform-action drop exceed-action drop**.

- A catch-all IP class should always be configured, should always come second to last in ordering (just before *class-default*), and should always be carefully rate limited (based on operational experience).

- The *class-default* class should never be policed (**conform transmit exceed transmit**). Optionally, define a distinct ARP traffic class to limit the aggregate rate of ARP traffic received.

CoPP Handling of Malicious Traffic

As an advanced CoPP deployment technique, you may consider adding an additional class to your CoPP policy (in addition to an ARP traffic class). The CoPP policy map listed in Example 5-16 contains six classes in the following order: CoPP-undesirable, CoPP-routing, CoPP-management, CoPP-normal, CoPP-remaining-IP, and class-default. The CoPP-arp class illustrated in Example 5-17 represents a seventh class. If you follow the progression of authorized control and management plane traffic, legitimate but unclassifiable traffic (for example, exception IP transit traffic), and malicious (unauthorized) traffic flows through this CoPP policy map, recalling that classes are processed in order and the first match terminates the processing for each packet, you will see the following:

- Upon entering the policy map, authorized control and management plane traffic will pass through the CoPP-undesirable class, and then should be picked up by class CoPP-routing, CoPP-management, or CoPP-normal (assuming the traffic characterization process has been thoroughly completed). If this traffic is picked up by the class CoPP-remaining-IP, you must reconfigure your ACLs to move this traffic to the appropriate authorized traffic class.

- Upon entering the policy map, legitimate but unclassifiable traffic (for example, exceptions IP transit traffic) will pass through the classes CoPP-undesirable, CoPP-routing, CoPP-management, and CoPP-normal and then be picked up by the class CoPP-remaining-IP. This is the desired behavior.

- Upon entering the policy map, malicious IP traffic will have one of two things occur given the configuration shown in Example 5-16: If the malicious traffic matches the characteristics defined for the class CoPP-undesirable, it will match this class and be discarded. For example, SQL Slammer traffic destined to the RP would automatically be discarded in this case. However, other malicious traffic that does not hit the class CoPP-undesirable will continue on through the remaining classes until it hits CoPP-remaining-IP. In this case, malicious traffic and legitimate exceptions traffic are both matching this single class.

Obviously, you'd like to drop all malicious traffic and allow legitimate traffic at some specified rate. So how do you distinguish between legitimate and malicious traffic in this case? If you consider what *malicious* means from the perspective of the router and the RP, this can actually be reasonably well defined. Realistically, from the perspective of the router, it is not appropriate to define exception IP transit traffic as malicious because you just do not know whether it is or is not malicious. It could be, but you cannot be certain. In this case, it is completely appropriate, however, to rate limit how much of this traffic is able to hit the IOS process level on the RP—and that is in fact what the policy for the class CoPP-remaining-IP does. What you can define as malicious for certain is any traffic that has a CEF receive adjacency (receive) destination and that is not already classified by the classes CoPP-routing, CoPP-management, and CoPP-normal. For example, ACL 120 is used by class CoPP-routing to classify legitimate BGP traffic. However, if an attacker were to source malicious BGP traffic toward the same receive destination, that traffic would not match ACL 120 and would end up hitting the class CoPP-remaining-IP in this case. The fact that malicious traffic ends up in the class CoPP-remaining-IP along with legitimate exception IP transit traffic makes setting an appropriate rate for class CoPP-remaining-IP very difficult.

Therefore, as an advanced deployment technique, it is recommended that you create an additional class (call it *CoPP-bad-receive*, for example) that is designed to catch all traffic destined to the receive address space and that has not been previously identified as legitimate by any other classes. This new class must then be placed third from last within the policy map, just ahead of the class CoPP-remaining-IP, so that it can police this unauthorized traffic headed toward the receive address space (that is, the control and management plane). If you assume that ACLs 120, 121, and 122 cover all legitimate traffic destined to the receive address space, then a new ACL must be created to cover all other traffic for these same receive destinations. Example 5-23 shows this sample configuration, including the new classification ACL (125), **class-map** (CoPP-bad-receive), and **policy-map**

(CoPP-extra), as well as the required **class** ordering. (Note: it is assumed that the receive address space is fully contained within the 10.0.0.0/8 address block.)

Example 5-23 *IOS CoPP Configurations to Drop Malicious Traffic to the IOS Process Level on the RP*

```
! Define ACL - Anything not previously classified and destined to receive block
  should be matched (and discarded)
access-list 125 permit ip any 10.0.0.0 0.255.255.255
!
! Define a class-map to collect ACL 125 traffic...
class-map match-all CoPP-bad-receive
  match access-group 125
! Define the new policy-map for CoPP...
policy-map CoPP-extra
  class CoPP-undesirable
    police 8000 1500 1500 conform drop exceed drop
  class CoPP-routing
    police 125000 1500 1500 conform transmit exceed transmit
  class CoPP-management
    police 50000 1500 1500 conform transmit exceed transmit
  class CoPP-normal
    police 15000 1500 1500 conform transmit exceed transmit
  class CoPP-bad-receive
    police 8000 1500 1500 conform transmit exceed drop
  class CoPP-remaining-IP
    police 8000 1500 1500 conform transmit exceed drop
  class class-default
    police 8000 1500 1500 conform transmit exceed transmit
!
```

Because classes are processed top-down within a policy map, you should see that legitimate receive adjacency traffic will be properly classified in class *CoPP-routing, CoPP-management,* and *CoPP-normal.* Other packets with a receive destination are malicious and will be classified into the *CoPP-bad-receive* class. The policy in Example 5-23 rate limits this class to a very low level. This is done to leave some margin of error in case ACLs 120, 121, and 122 are not complete. However, over time, you should strive to change the policy for class *CoPP-bad-receive* to **conform-action drop exceed-action drop**.

Note also that this behavior can also be accomplished by modifying the already-existing class *CoPP-undesirable* rather than creating a new class and updating the policy map. Using this approach, however, requires the addition of pairs of ACL entries that first include a **deny** statement that mimics each legitimate (in other words, permitted) traffic specification in ACLs 120, 121, and 122, followed by a **permit** statement for the same protocols but using **any** in the source field and 10.0.0.0/8 (in this case) in the destination field. In this way, legitimate traffic will match the **deny** statements, causing no further processing for this class but allowing the legitimate traffic to still be classified against the remaining CoPP classes. Subsequently, this legitimate traffic would match the appropriate class as described earlier. However, malicious traffic will not match the **deny** statement but will instead hit the **permit** statement for the same protocol and be discarded.

These guidelines should provide you with the tools necessary to successfully deploy CoPP within your network. As stated at the beginning of the CoPP section, CoPP offers two different operating modes, aggregate and distributed. Aggregate mode CoPP generally operates within the central RP CPU of an IOS router. The Cisco 10720, 10000 (PRE-2 and PRE-3), 7600/6500 (PFC3), and Catalyst 4500 series, however, provide hardware-based (ASIC) support for aggregate mode CoPP. Hardware-based aggregate CoPP prevents filtered traffic from adversely affecting the central RP CPU because filtered packets are discarded in hardware and not at the IOS process level. Although software-based IOS router platforms (for example, ISR, 7200) support aggregate CoPP functions within the RP CPU only, aggregate software-based CoPP has still proven to be an effective added layer of protection because filtered packets are immediately discarded prior to any protocol processing at the IOS process level. The aggregate and distributed modes of CoPP are described further in the "Platform-specific CoPP Implementation Details" section that follows.

CoPP output policies are also supported within IOS Software Releases 12.2(25)S, 12.3(4)T, and later, excluding the Cisco 10720 and 7500 series. The CoPP output policy applies to egress packets that are locally sourced by the router—for example, ICMP replies. However, CoPP output policies do not reduce packet processing resources at the IOS process level because the router still generates the packet only to be silently discarded by the CoPP output policy. Hence, the benefit of a CoPP output policy is limited in terms of DoS protection. However, a CoPP output policy can provide a *stealth* capability to your router deployment by preventing router-generated responses from being emitted by the router. (In some forums, this is referred to as *emanations security*, or *EmSec* for short.)

Platform-Specific CoPP Implementation Details

There are some platform-specific implementation details that are important for operational CoPP deployments. These platform-specific implementation details are mainly due to hardware differences on the relevant platforms and are covered in detail next.

Cisco 12000 CoPP Implementation

The Cisco 12000 is a distributed routing platform and implements a special version of CoPP that takes advantage of this architecture. On the 12000, CoPP can be deployed in *aggregate mode* on the main RP (PRP), or it can be deployed in *distributed mode* on individual distributed line cards. This concept is illustrated in Figure 5-7.

Figure 5-7   *CoPP Operations on the Cisco 12000 Series Distributed Routing Platform*

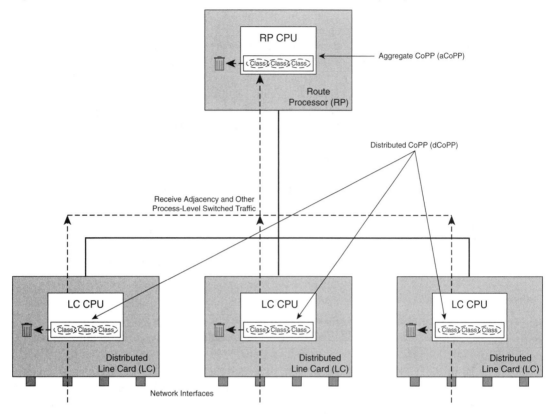

These two modes of CoPP, aggregate and distributed are described next.

Aggregate CoPP

Aggregate CoPP (aCoPP) applies a single and global CoPP input policy to the cumulative traffic destined for the IOS process level irrespective of the ingress router interface (or distributed line card slot). All packets that ingress the receive interface of the central PRP are subjected to the aCoPP input policy (if configured). aCoPP is configured using the **control-plane** command in IOS global configuration mode in exactly the same way as CoPP was described in the "CoPP Configuration Guildelines" section above. Because the 12000 is a distributed routing platform, only certain receive (and exception IP transit traffic) is required to be forward to the PRP for handling. Much of this load is handled directly by each ingress line card CPU. Hence, the construction of this aCoPP policy may differ from that used for distributed mode CoPP (discussed next).

Distributed CoPP

Distributed CoPP (dCoPP) is supported only on the Cisco 12000 series routers. When dCoPP is configured, a CoPP input policy may be assigned to each individual distributed line card slot within the chassis. Each distributed CoPP input policy is then applied to all traffic that ingresses the associated slot and is destined to the IOS process level of the central PRP specifically. That is, only packets punted to the central PRP are subject to dCoPP input policies. Punted traffic that is handled locally by the line card CPU is typically not subject to dCoPP policies. For example, the Cisco 12000 processes ICMP Echo Reply (Type 0) messages, ICMP Time Exceeded (Type 11) messages, ATM OAM packets, and BFD protocol packets directly on the distributed line card CPU, as opposed to on the central PRP. Therefore, these packets are not subject to dCoPP input policies, because they are not punted to the central PRP. The one exception is if these packets include IP header options, in which case they will be punted to the central PRP and consequently subject to the dCoPP input policy.

Distributed CoPP is configured using the **control-plane slot** {*slot-number*} command in IOS global configuration mode. Upon entering the **control plane slot** {*slot-number*} command, you enter IOS control plane configuration mode commands exactly as previously described. These general commands for applying input dCoPP are shown in Example 5-24.

Example 5-24 *IOS Distributed CoPP Policy Attachment*

```
Router(config)# control-plane slot {slot #}
Router(config-cp)# service-policy input {policy-name}
```

Distinct dCoPP input policies may be applied to each individual slot, or a common policy may be applied to each slot. In either case, the router applies policies and tracks all statistics on a per-slot basis. Each dCoPP input policy executes on the distributed line card CPU of the assigned slot. Unauthorized or rate-limited packets are then discarded on the ingress distributed line card(s) without involvement by the central PRP.

Distributed CoPP is generally applied to every slot on the 12000 chassis, including slots that do not contain line cards at the time of configuration. Applying the dCoPP policy to an empty slot will be accepted by the IOS CLI and kept within the router configuration. The router will automatically apply a configured dCoPP policy to a slot when a line card is later inserted, assuming dCoPP has previously been specified for that slot. If a line card is removed from a slot on which dCoPP is configured, the router will still retain the policy within the IOS router configuration. If the same or a different line card type is reinserted in the slot, the same dCoPP policy will be applied. Distributed mode also does not require that a dCoPP input policy be attached to each individual 12000 slot. You may decide, for example, to apply dCoPP input policies only on slots supporting external (untrusted) interfaces, versus slots supporting internal (trusted) core uplinks. In support of the defense in depth and breadth principles, however, distributed CoPP should be considered for each active slot, because it provides an added layer of protection for both external and internal router interfaces.

Similar to IP rACL processing, distributed CoPP prevents filtered packets from adversely impacting the Cisco 12000 central PRP, which executes most control and management plane services. Hence, under a directed or transit DoS attack aimed at the Cisco 12000 router, the distributed line card CPU utilization may increase; however, the central PRP, which serves as the master controller of the router, will not be adversely affected (unless, of course, the attack traffic is permitted by the distributed CoPP input policy to reach the central PRP).

As previously stated, aCoPP manages the cumulative amount of traffic destined for the IOS process level (central PRP). Distributed CoPP is applied on a per-slot basis, and hence manages the cumulative amount of traffic received by all interfaces on the associated line card within the slot. (That is, it is per-slot and not per-interface.)

NOTE	When considering the deployment of distributed mode CoPP, the question of whether a common policy or custom policies should be used for each slot often arises. The value in having custom policies per slot is that it gives you the opportunity to tailor permitted traffic types and rate limits that are appropriate for the interface types (speeds) and attached services. For example, external interfaces typically do not require IGP traffic to be supported. Thus, assuming that all interfaces for the line card in the slot support the same policy, a custom dCoPP policy that excludes (drops) IGP traffic would be beneficial. Then, for slots supporting backbone-facing uplinks, a different dCoPP policy that does support IGP traffic would be appropriate. In addition, different line cards support different performance rates, and again, different dCoPP policies may be appropriate. On the other hand, maintaining multiple dCoPP policies and ensuring that the correct policy type is applied to the correct slot adds significantly to the management burden. If line cards are moved between slots, or change functionality, having multiple dCoPP policies leaves open the possibility of adverse network impacts due to inappropriate traffic filtering. Whatever you decide, be conscious of the implications.

Both distributed and aggregate CoPP policies may be applied simultaneously on the Cisco 12000 series routers. Punted packets destined for the 12000 PRP would hit the dCoPP policy first, and then, assuming they are permitted, would be switched to the central PRP, where the aCoPP policy (if configured) would then be applied. The combination of dCoPP and aCoPP policies applied together is useful for simplifying per-slot traffic characteristics and rate limiters.

NOTE   When considering the deployment of distributed mode CoPP, the question of whether IP rACL and dCoPP/aCoPP can be deployed simultaneously on the same router often arises. The answer is yes. There may be value in deploying one, two, or all three techniques, depending on your network and traffic mix. Keep in mind that all three techniques are effective against somewhat different traffic sets. IP rACLs see only IP packets with receive destinations. They do not see exception IP transit packets. dCoPP sees some but not all IP packets with receive destinations, some but not all exception IP transit packets, and no Layer 2 traffic (*class-default* sees no traffic in dCoPP policies). aCoPP, on the other hand, sees the aggregate of all IP packets that reach the central PRP, including Layer 2 packets (these end up in *class-default*). Thus, the question of whether or not to deploy multiple mechanisms depends mostly on what needs to be protected. In addition, maintaining multiple techniques adds significantly to the management burden.

Cisco Catalyst 6500/Cisco 7600 CoPP Implementation

As previously stated, the Catalyst 6500 and Cisco 7600 series platforms (PFC3 and DFC3) provide ASIC-based (hardware) support for aggregate mode CoPP. Similar to the 12000 dCoPP described in the preceding section, ASIC-based aggregate CoPP prevents filtered traffic from adversely affecting the central MSFC (Multilayer Switch Feature Card) CPU because filtered packets are discarded in hardware before hitting the IOS process level. (In 12000 dCoPP, filtered packets are discarded on the ingress line card CPU before hitting the IOS process level on the PRP.) Aggregate CoPP is configured on the Catalyst 6500 and Cisco 7600 series platforms just as described in the previous section, but with the following differences:

- MLS QoS must be enabled using the **mls qos** command in global configuration mode prior to configuring CoPP. Otherwise, CoPP will work only in software (MSFC CPU) and will not provide any hardware (PFC3 and DFC3) filtering.

- CoPP uses hardware QoS TCAM resources. If you have a large QoS configuration, the system may run out of TCAM resources if CoPP is also enabled. In this event, CoPP may be performed in software (MSFC) only. With PFC3A, egress QoS and hardware-based CoPP cannot be configured at the same time. Use the **show tcam utilization** command to monitor TCAM resources.

- To display the hardware counters for bytes discarded and forwarded by the CoPP policy, use the **show mls qos ip** command. The **show access-list** and **show policy-map control-plane** commands, described earlier in the "Tuning CoPP Policies" section, are also available to monitor CoPP policies.

- Hardware CoPP is performed on a per-forwarding-engine (PFC3 or DFC) basis and software CoPP (MSFC) is performed on an aggregate basis. Hence, the global CoPP policy applied operates independently on each PFC3 and DFC within the system.

- MQC **police** is the only supported CoPP policy action.

- Only an input CoPP service policy is supported (not output CoPP).

- The only MQC **match** types supported include **match ip precedence**, **match ip dscp**, and **match access-group**. Note, only **match access-group** classification is supported in hardware (PFC and DFC). Classification ACEs defined with the **log** keyword are ignored by CoPP, and hence the **log** keyword is not recommended. Further, you may enter only one **match** command within a given CoPP-based MQC class map.

- Broadcast packets and CoPP classes that match multicast addresses are also not supported by CoPP in hardware (PFC and DFC) but are policed in software (MSFC). However, PFC3 supports built-in special-case hardware rate limiters (independent of CoPP), which can rate limit various types of traffic flows, including but not limited to broadcast and multicast packets.

The hardware-based rate limiters available on the PFC3 include:

- **Ingress and egress ACL bridged packets:** This rate limiter rate limits packets sent to the MSFC because of an ingress/egress ACL bridge result. You may configure this using the **mls rate-limit unicast acl** command in global configuration mode. This rate limiter is disabled by default and applies to unicast packets only.

- **uRPF check failures:** This rate limiter rate limits exception packets that failed the uRPF check but were permitted by the uRPF ACL. Such packets are sent to the MSFC. You may configure this using the **mls rate-limit unicast ip rpf-failure** command in global configuration mode. This rate limiter is enabled by default with a limit of 100 packets per second (PPS) and a burst size of ten packets.

- **TTL failure:** This rate limiter rate limits IPv4 packets sent to the MSFC due to IP TTL expiration. You may configure this using the **mls rate-limit all ttl-failure** command in global configuration mode. This rate limiter is disabled by default and applies to both unicast and multicast packets. It is an effective technique to mitigate the risk of IP TTL expiry–based attacks.

- **ICMP unreachable:** This rate limiter allows you to rate limit packets sent to the MSFC containing unreachable IP addresses. Such packets would normally result in an ICMP Destination Unreachable (Type 3) being generated by the MSFC. As outlined in Chapters 2 and 4, a flood of such packets represents a potential attack vector. Four distinct ICMP unreachable rate limiters are available to rate limit packets containing unreachable addresses, including ICMP unreachable no route, ICMP unreachable ACL drop, IP errors, and IP RPF failure. You may configure this using the **mls rate-limit unicast ip icmp unreachable** command in global configuration mode. These rate limiters are enabled by default with a limit of 100 pps and a burst size of ten packets, and only apply to unicast packets. This is an effective technique to mitigate the risk of ICMP Destination Unreachable–based attacks. Alternatively, you may configure the **no ip unreachable** command, as described in Chapter 4.

- **FIB (CEF) receive cases:** This rate limiter rate limits all packets that contain the MSFC IP address as the destination address (in other words, CEF receive adjacencies). Note, do not enable the FIB receive rate limiter if CoPP is enabled. The FIB receive rate limiter overrides any CoPP policy applied. You may configure this using the **mls rate-limit unicast cef receive** command in global configuration mode. This rate limiter is disabled by default and applies only to unicast traffic.

- **FIB glean:** This rate limiter does not limit ARP traffic, but provides the capability to rate limit traffic that requires ARP resolution and requires that it be sent to the MSFC. This situation occurs when traffic enters a port and contains the destination of a host on a subnet that is locally connected to the MSFC, but no ARP entry exists for that destination host. In this case, because the MAC address of the destination host will not be answered by any host on the directly connected subnet that is unknown, the "glean" adjacency is hit and the traffic is sent directly to the MSFC for ARP resolution. This rate limiter limits the possibility of an attacker overloading the CPU with such ARP requests. You may configure this using the **mls rate-limit unicast cef glean** command in global configuration mode. This rate limiter is disabled by default and applies only to unicast traffic.

- **Layer 3 security features:** Some Catalyst 6500 and Cisco 7600 security features are processed by first sending applicable packets to the MSFC. For these security features, you need to rate limit the number of these packets being sent to the MSFC to reduce any adverse MSFC CPU impact. The security features include authentication proxy (auth-proxy), IPsec, and inspection. Authentication proxy is used to authenticate inbound or outbound users, or both, and is described in further detail in Chapter 6. These users are normally blocked by an access list, but with auth-proxy, the users can bring up a browser to go through the firewall and authenticate on a TACACS+ or RADIUS server (based on the IP address). The server passes additional access list entries down to the router to allow the users through after authentication. These ACLs are stored and processed in software, and if there are many users utilizing auth-proxy, the MSFC may be overwhelmed. Rate limiting would be advantageous in this situation. IPsec and inspection are also done by the MSFC and may similarly require rate limiting. When the Layer 3 security feature rate limiter is enabled, all Layer 3 rate limiters for auth-proxy, IPsec, and inspection are enabled at the same rate. You may configure this using the **mls rate-limit unicast ip features** command in global configuration mode. This rate limiter is disabled by default and applies only to unicast traffic.

- **ICMP redirects:** This rate limiter rate limits traffic punted to the MSFC for ICMP Redirect (Type 5) message processing. As outlined in Chapters 2 and 4, a flood of such packets represents a potential attack vector. You may configure this using the **mls rate-limit unicast ip icmp redirect** command in global configuration mode. This rate limiter is disabled by default and applies only to unicast packets. This is an effective technique to mitigate the risk of ICMP Redirect–based attacks. Alternatively, you may configure the **no ip redirects** interface command, as described in Chapter 4.

- **VACL log:** This rate limiter rate limits packets that are sent to the MSFC for VLAN-ACL logging. A high volume of packets requiring logging may overwhelm the MSFC CPU. You may rate limit such packets using the **mls rate-limit unicast acl vacl-log** command in global configuration mode. This rate limiter is enabled by default with a limit of 2000 PPS and a burst size of ten packets, and applies to unicast packets only. Note, if you do not use VLAN logging, this rate limiter should be disabled.

- **MTU failure:** This rate limiter rate limits IPv4 packets sent to the MSFC due to MTU failures (in other words, packets requiring fragmentation but the Do Not Fragment bit is set within the IP header). As outlined in Chapter 2, a flood of such packets represents a potential attack vector. You may configure this using the **mls rate-limit all mtu** command in global configuration mode. This rate limiter is disabled by default and applies to both unicast and multicast packets. Best common practices relating to MTU handling and configuration are discussed in Chapter 7.

- **L2 multicast IGMP snooping:** This rate limiter limits the number of Layer 2 IGMP packets destined for the supervisor engine. If enabled, IGMP snooping listens to IGMP messages between the hosts and the supervisor engine. You may configure this using the **mls rate-limit multicast ipv4 igmp** command in global configuration mode. This rate limiter is disabled by default.

- **L2 PDU:** This rate limiter allows you to limit the number of Layer 2 PDU protocol packets (including BPDUs, DTP, PAgP, CDP, STP, and VTP packets) destined for the supervisor engine and not the MSFC CPU. You may configure this using the **mls rate-limit layer2 pdu** command in global configuration mode. This rate limiter is disabled by default.

- **L2 protocol tunneling:** This rate limiter limits the Layer 2 protocol tunneling packets, which include control PDUs, CDP, STP, and VTP packets destined for the supervisor engine. This may be configured using the **mls rate-limit layer2 l2pt** command in global configuration mode. This rate limiter is disabled by default.

- **IP errors:** This rate limiter rate limits packets with IP checksum and length errors. When a packet reaches the PFC3 with an IP checksum error or a length inconsistency error, it must be sent to the MSFC for further processing. You may configure this using the **mls rate-limit unicast ip errors** command in global configuration mode. This rate limiter is enabled by default with a limit of 100 pps and a burst size of ten packets.

- **Multicast IPv4:** This rate limiter rate limits IPv4 multicast packets. Within the IPv4 multicast rate limiter, there are three distinct rate limiters available to rate limit IPv4 multicast packets:
    - The FIB-miss rate limiter is enabled by default (100,000 pps, burst size of 100 packets) and allows you to rate limit the multicast traffic that does not match an entry in the mroute table.

- The multicast partially switched flow rate limiter is enabled by default (100,000 pps, burst size of 100 packets) and allows you to rate limit the flows destined to the MSFC3 for forwarding and replication. For a given multicast traffic flow, if at least one outgoing Layer 3 interface is multilayer switched, and at least one outgoing interface is not multilayer switched (no H-bit set for hardware switching), the particular flow is considered partially switched, or partial-SC (partial shortcut). The outgoing interfaces that have the H-bit flag are switched in hardware and the remaining traffic is switched in software through the MSFC3. For this reason, it may be desirable to rate limit the flow destined to the MSFC3 for forwarding and replication, which might otherwise increase CPU utilization.

- The multicast directly connected rate limiter is disabled by default and limits the multicast packets from directly connected sources.

  You may configure these using the **mls rate-limit multicast ipv4** command in global configuration mode. This rate limiter is enabled by default with a limit of 100 PPS and a burst size of ten packets.

- **Multicast IPv6:** This rate limiter rate limits IPv6 multicast packets. Within the IPv6 multicast rate limiter, there are five distinct rate limiters available to rate limit IPv6 multicast packets. The details of each of these IPv6 multicast rate limiters is beyond the scope of this book. Nevertheless, they are enabled by default and may be configured using the **mls rate-limit multicast ipv6** command in global configuration mode. For more information on these rate limiters, refer to the "Cisco 7600 Series: Configuring Denial of Service Protection" reference listed in the "Further Reading" section.

When you enable these hardware rate limiters, you should be aware that they override the CoPP policy for packets matching the rate-limiter criteria. Namely, the matching hardware rate-limiter policy takes precedence over a CoPP policy. Conversely, packets that do not match a hardware rate limiter are subject to the applied CoPP policy. The Catalyst 4500 series also supports hardware-based aCoPP and hardware rate limiters similar to the Catalyst 6500 and Cisco 7600 described here. There are differences between the hardware rate limiters; however, a review of the Catalyst 4500 series platform specifics is beyond the scope of this book. For further information on each of these platforms, refer to the references listed in the "Further Reading" section.

CoPP is a relatively new feature within Cisco IOS and, as such, is just beginning to become widely deployed within IP networks today. The relative complexity of deployment is somewhat higher than that of IP rACLs given the complexities of traffic classification and the added requirement to establish appropriate rate limits. Where CoPP has been deployed to date, it has proven itself as an effective technique for improving a router's resistance to attacks. When deployed in conjunction with infrastructure ACL policies, it provides an effective second layer of defense in support of the defense in depth and breadth principles described in Chapter 3. For additional platform-specific CoPP information on these IOS platforms, refer to the references in the "Further Reading" section. The IOS 12.4(4)T

Control Plane Protection feature, which is an extension of CoPP, allows for additional or separate aggregate CoPP policies to be configured and applied on different types of newly defined control plane subinterfaces, including host, transit, and CEF-exception subinterfaces. For more information on the Control Plane Protection feature, refer to the reference in the "Further Reading" section.

Neighbor Authentication

IP rACLs and CoPP are effective and proven techniques for increasing the resistance of an IOS router against security attacks. However, they both rely upon IP header information for packet classification, including, for example, IP source addresses. As outlined in Chapter 2, spoofed attacks are often used to bypass such security policies. Consider the restrictive IP rACL policy illustrated in Example 5-25, which only allows BGP and OSPF protocol packets sourced from 209.165.200.225/32 and 192.168.0.0/16, respectively.

Example 5-25 *Sample IOS IP Receive ACL Policy*

```
ip receive access-list 100
access-list 100 deny ip any any fragments
access-list 100 deny tcp any any eq 23 precedence internet
access-list 100 permit ospf 192.168.0.0 0.0.255.255 192.168.0.0 0.0.255.255
  precedence 6
access-list 100 permit tcp 209.165.200.225 209.165.200.226 eq bgp precedence 6
access-list 100 deny icmp any any echo
access-list 100 deny ip any any
```

Although this policy filters any BGP and OSPF protocol packets from any other IP source addresses, it would permit any spoofed packets that use 209.165.200.225/32 or 192.168.0.0/16 as the IP source addresses for BGP and OSPF, respectively. For "internal only" network protocols such as an IGP (for example, OSPF) or Telnet, this is simple to mitigate through antispoofing protection ACLs, uRPF, or infrastructure ACLs at the network edge. These techniques may be deployed to prevent an external source from sending internal protocol packets destined to the routers and to prevent external sources from spoofing internal infrastructure IP addresses. As a result, only a valid internal source is permitted to source OSPF or Telnet protocol packets. Conversely, for protocol packets exchanged with external peers (for example, BGP), source verification is much more difficult because you have limited ability to assure the integrity of a packet's source address beyond your network edge.

You must allow specific external protocol packets destined to your edge routers from valid external peers as required. For example, if you are running eBGP with an external peer, not only must your edge router's BGP configuration explicitly specify this external peer, but your edge infrastructure ACL policy as well as your IP rACL and/or CoPP security policies must also allow BGP protocol packets from this configured peer. This is a prerequisite of external protocols, and they will not operate otherwise. uRPF antispoofing mechanisms will drop at the network edge packets with spoofed source IP addresses that do not have a valid reverse path to the source address, but this does not prevent an attacker from spoofing any source addresses that do have valid reverse paths, such as, for example, sources within the prefix range of the ingress interface. Hence, a downstream attacker may easily spoof the address of an external peer (10.0.0.1 in this case), as shown in Figure 5-8.

Figure 5-8   *BGP Spoofing Attack*

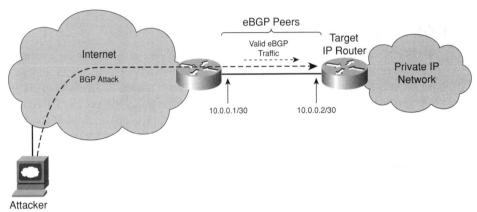

The threat depicted in Figure 5-8 illustrates the need for strict control over permitted external protocols. Internet SPs (ISP), for example, generally only use (and permit) eBGP with Internet peers (in other words, other ISPs), or with customers that are multihomed. Static IP routing is generally used with transit customers that are not multihomed, because only a single access line provides customer connectivity. This eliminates the need to permit BGP protocol packets on these single-homed access ports, thereby reducing the scope of a BGP security attack. ICMP is generally the only other external protocol that may be required between external peers. Techniques to reduce the scope of ICMP security attacks were described in the "ICMP Techniques" section above and in Chapter 4. Nevertheless, external protocols such as BGP are a fundamental requirement for connectivity between peer IP networks. Internet peering among ISPs (both settlement-free and settlement-based), for example, cannot function without eBGP. As such, neighbor authentication is critical for preventing routers from illegitimately joining a routing domain and for protecting routing protocols from malicious attacks and unintentional misconfigurations.

MD5 Authentication

A wide variety of control plane protocols—including, but not limited to, BGP (RFC 2385), OSPFv2 (RFC 2328), MPLS LDP (RFC 3036), RIPv2 (RFC 2082), IS-IS (RFC 3567), MSDP (RFC 3618), and Cisco's EIGRP, HSRP, Director Response Protocol (DRP) Server Agent, and Gateway Load Balancing Protocol (GLBP)—use the MD5 message digest algorithm (RFC 1321) to generate a 128-bit (16-byte) hash-based Message Authentication

Code (MAC) for protocol messages exchanged between peers. The use of a hash-based MAC allows a peer to verify that the message comes from a source who knows the secret key (authentication check), and that it has not been modified in transit (integrity check). The secret key is shared among valid peers to compute the cryptographic MAC inserted in transmitted messages, and to re-create the MAC for received messages. Receivers compare the MAC appended to messages received with what they recompute. If they do not match, the message is discarded. If they do match, the protocol message is accepted as authentic. These principles are illustrated in Figure 5-9.

Figure 5-9   *MD5 Neighbor Authentication*

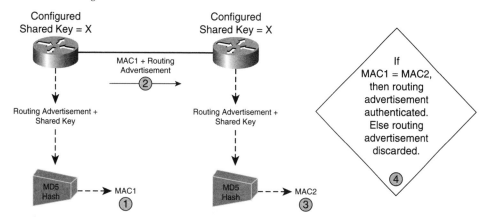

The procedure for computing and appending a MAC within protocol messages depends upon the specific control protocol and its underlying transport protocol. For example, the MAC for MD5-supported TCP-based protocols is computed and authenticated for each TCP segment exchanged between peers. In this case, as per RFC 2385, the MAC is transmitted as an option (kind 19) within the TCP header. Conversely, the MAC for non-TCP-based protocols is typically computed and authenticated for each individual protocol packet, as it is with OSPF for example. Nevertheless, the MD5 MAC is computed based on the data carried within the routing protocol update plus the shared secret. (Adding the shared secret to the routing update to compute the MAC prevents man-in-the-middle (MiTM) attacks that may attempt to modify these packets.) By using MD5 signatures, the receiving peer can detect even a single-bit change in a packet or TCP segment. For more information on protocol authentication using MD5, refer to the protocol-specific RFCs referenced at the beginning of this section above as well as RFC 1321. MD5 is also commonly used to hash router passwords and to verify the integrity of downloaded IOS software files. The use of MD5 within the IP management plane is further discussed in Chapter 6.

IOS also supports plaintext authentication for some routing protocols. Rather than computing an MD5 hash-based MAC for authentication, plaintext authentication methods simply append the shared key to the protocol messages as they are transmitted. Plaintext authentication is not considered a network security BCP because the shared secret itself is sent in the clear across the network. Conversely, MD5 authentication only transmits the hash-based MAC (or cryptographic signature) and never the shared key. Plaintext authentication is useful to protect against routing protocol misconfigurations, not security attacks. Therefore, plaintext authentication will not be covered further. MD5 helps to protect against both.

The required IOS configuration of MD5 authentication differs depending upon the specific protocol:

- **BGP:** BGP supports only MD5-based authentication and is configured on a neighbor or peer group basis using the **neighbor password** command in IOS router configuration mode or router address-family configuration mode. The neighbor router must have the same MD5 key value. Historically, changing a BGP MD5 key automatically caused BGP to reset the TCP protocol session (meaning the BGP session was also reset), which made it very difficult to dynamically manage MD5 keys in SP networks. As of 12.0(23)S, 12.2(15)T, 12.2(15)S, and later, BGP MD5 keys may be changed without causing a reset of the protocol session, provided the new keys are configured on both the local and remote sides before the BGP holddown timer expires. Otherwise, the session will be reset.

- **OSPF:** OSPF MD5 authentication can be configured on an interface, within an area, or both. OSPF MD5 authentication is configured on an interface using the **ip ospf message-digest-key md5** command within IOS interface configuration mode. OSPF MD5 authentication is configured within an area using the **area authentication message-digest** command within router configuration mode. OSPF MD5 authentication supports the configuration of multiple keys, which simplifies the migration of MD5 keys because neighbors do not need to be reconfigured within the OSPF holddown time to prevent adjacencies from being reset. Increased rotation of MD5 keys helps to mitigate the risk of keys being compromised.

- **LDP:** MPLS LDP authentication is configured using the **mpls ldp neighbor password** command in IOS global configuration mode. Changing the LDP MD5 keys will reset the protocol session. LDP support for changing MD5 keys without protocol session resets is not available at the time of this writing but is planned in the future.

- **RIPv2:** RIPv2 MD5 authentication is configured using the **ip rip authentication key-chain** and **ip rip authentication mode md5** IOS configuration commands within interface configuration mode. RIPv2 supports key chains, which simplifies the migration of MD5 keys. Key chains may be configured using the **key chain** command in IOS global configuration mode.

- **IS-IS:** IS-IS MD5 authentication is configured using the **authentication mode md5** command in router configuration mode, and the **authentication mode md5** command in interface configuration mode. IS-IS also supports key chains, similar to RIPv2.

- **RSVP:** RSVP authentication is configured using the **ip rsvp authentication type** [**md5** | **sha-1**] configuration command within IOS interface configuration mode. Note, only RSVP supports both MD5 and SHA-1 hashing algorithms. SHA-1 is newer and recognized as more secure.

- **EIGRP:** EIGRP MD5 authentication is configured using the **ip authentication mode eigrp md5** command in IOS interface configuration mode. EIGRP also supports key chains, similar to RIPv2 and IS-IS.

For information on MD5 configuration for other supported IOS protocols as well as **key chain** configurations, refer to the *IOS Configuration Guides*.

All MD5 hash processing is performed at the IOS process level. Hence, enabling MD5 authentication does increase resource utilization on the central RP CPU because it adds additional IOS process level packet processing overhead. The specific impact depends upon the authenticated protocol, session timers, router platform, routing table size, and protocol stability because the greater volume of authenticated protocol messages (transmit or received) requiring a hash-based MAC computation increases the impact. This increase in router CPU utilization is often used to argue that enabling MD5 authentication actually makes IP routers more susceptible to security attacks, because it takes less packets to flood the device. It is important to note, however, that this form of attack is a simple DoS attack and not a routing protocol attack. The primary driver for MD5 authentication is to prevent attackers from injecting false information into the control plane. It does not prevent packet flood attacks. Hence, although MD5 authentication may lower the PPS threshold for packet flood DoS attacks, such packet flood attacks are still feasible without MD5 authentication. Thus, MD5 does not introduce any new risk as argued but rather is intended to mitigate the risk of false routing information being injected into the control plane.

With that said, published results against MD5 show how to subvert its collision resistance. There have been no results that break the MD5 key that is used to compute a MAC. Going forward, in the worst-case scenario, if additional developments allowed an attacker to use this attack to somehow derive a new packet with a correct MAC, the attacker would still need to inject the packet into the conversation, and the receiving side would need to accept and process it. There are additional challenges here, including antispoofing techniques, TCP sequence numbers, and so on, that still make such an attack nontrivial. It is important to remember that the strength of the MAC is in the shared key. Even a hash function that may be considered weak by the standards of the cryptographic community can still provide significant protection. A poorly chosen, easy-to-guess shared key greatly diminishes the value of a MAC. Nevertheless, MD5 authentication adds yet another layer of defense that an attacker must overcome.

Generalized TTL Security Mechanism

In most cases, control plane messages are exchanged between adjacent routers that are directly connected. This is the default behavior for IGP adjacencies and MPLS LDP, and is the common deployment model for eBGP peering sessions. The Generalized TTL Security

Mechanism (GTSM) as defined in RFC 3682 takes advantage of these link-local protocol messages to provide antispoofing protection using the IP header TTL value. IOS provides GTSM support for eBGP (not iBGP) in releases 12.0(27)S, 12.2(25)S, 12.3(7)T, and later. This capability is also known as the IOS *BGP Support for TTL Security Check* feature. Further, this was originally known within the industry as the BGP TTL Security Hack (BTSH). The BTSH concept was then extended to allow support for other protocols, and is now known as GTSM.

For directly connected eBGP peers, IOS uses a default IP TTL value of 1 for locally sourced eBGP packets. Similarly, by default, an IOS eBGP peer only checks that received IP TTL values are equal to 1 or greater. Any IP TTL value greater or equal to 1 is considered valid per RFC 791. Because network and router security policies permit eBGP protocol packets from valid peers, only TCP port and sequence number verification and, if optionally enabled, MD5 authentication prevent a remote attacker from injecting spoofed eBGP protocol packets into the session, as previously illustrated in Figure 5-9. The weakness in this approach is that the receiving router does not know whether the packet traveled one hop or many.

Whether GTSM is enabled or not, TCP port and sequence number checking remains the same. Similarly, MD5 authentication is also independent of GTSM. However, with GTSM enabled on both sides of the eBGP session, the handling of IP TTL values for eBGP packets changes in the following manner:

- IOS transmits locally sourced eBGP packets with an IP TTL value of 255.
- IOS only accepts eBGP packets having an IP TTL value equal to or greater than 255, less the configured hop count for the associated eBGP peering session.

A hop count of 1 is generally configured for directly connected eBGP peers. Hence, eBGP accepts only packets having an IP TTL value of 254. Because remote attackers cannot spoof an IP TTL value of 254, they cannot inject spoofed packets into the session, as illustrated in Figure 5-10.

Thus, GTSM for eBGP reduces the scope of attacks against directly connected eBGP sessions. Namely, only attackers that are also directly connected—for example, through a shared LAN—may succeed against the IP TTL check provided by GTSM.

Figure 5-10 *BGP TTL Security Check (or GTSM)*

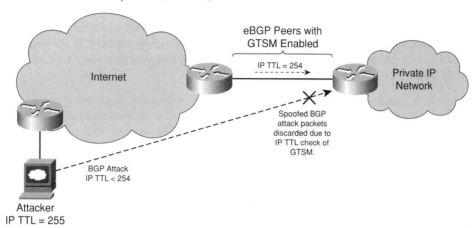

GTSM supplies greater security for directly connected eBGP peers than it does for multihop eBGP peers, because a higher hop count must be configured for multihop peers. Each additional hop between multihop eBGP peers increases the range (TTL diameter) of attack by that same amount, as illustrated in Figure 5-11.

Figure 5-11 *GTSM for eBGP Multihop*

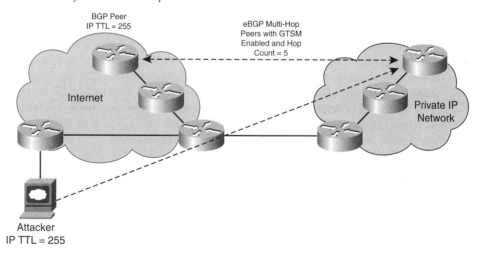

To attack a directly connected eBGP session, the attacker needs to be directly connected to spoof an IP TTL value of 254. Similarly, to attack a multihop eBGP session configured with a hop count of 10, for example, the attacker needs to be within only ten hops of either peer to spoof an IP TTL value of 245. Any farther away and the natural TTL decrement process would automatically reduce the IP TTL to a value less than 245, even if the attack packets started with an initial value of 255.

To maximize the effectiveness of this feature, the hop count should be tightly configured to match the number of hops between the two eBGP peers. However, you should also consider path variation when configuring this feature for multihop peers. To configure GTSM for eBGP, use the **neighbor ttl-security hops** {*hop-count*} command in IOS address-family or router configuration mode. This command applies to both directly connected and multihop eBGP sessions. However, when this command is configured for a multihop peering session, the **neighbor ebgp-multihop** router configuration command cannot be configured. These commands are mutually exclusive, and only one command is required to establish a multihop peering session. If you attempt to configure both commands for the same peering session, an error message will be displayed in the console.

When eBGP peering is configured from loopback-to-loopback (interfaces) between two directly connected peers, these sessions do not automatically come up. This is due to the connected-interface check that IOS does for default (TTL=1) eBGP sessions. That is, by default, the peer addresses for eBGP sessions with TTL=1 must be within the same subnet. Because loopback interfaces on two different routers will not be within the same subnet, the eBGP session is prevented from being established. The resolution to this issue was to use the **neighbor** {*peer address*} **ebgp-multihop 2** command in router configuration mode, which disabled this connected-interface check. (This led to the common confusion that loopback-to-loopback connections were two hops away, which is not the case.) Under certain conditions, this configuration opened a minor eBGP peering vulnerability. Therefore, a new command was added in IOS releases 12.0(22)S and 12.2(13)T that disables this connected-interface check and allows TTL=1 loopback-to-loopback eBGP sessions. This new command is **neighbor** {*peer address*} **disable-connected-check** and is configured in router configuration mode. When GTSM is used for loopback-to-loopback eBGP configurations, the connected-interface check still applies. Thus, to enable GTSM for loopback-to-loopback eBGP configurations, you may do either of the following:

- Configure **neighbor** {*peer address*} **ttl-security hops 2**
- Configure **neighbor** {*peer address*} **ttl-security hops 1** and **neighbor** {*peer address*} **disable-connected-check**

Note that the **neighbor update-source Loopback0** command is also required in either case.

The GTSM capability should also be configured on each side of the eBGP session to take full advantage of its protection capabilities. However, when this is not possible (for example, when GTSM is not supported in the version of IOS code used on one side), eBGP sessions may still be operated with only one side enabled for GTSM, provided that the other side (not enabled for GTSM) also has an adequate IP TTL value set via the **neighbor** {*peer address*} **ebgp-multihop** {*hop-count*} command in IOS router configuration mode.

At the time of this writing, software development of GTSM for OSPF is well under way but not yet available within IOS. OSPF support for GTSM will work similarly to eBGP, except, of course, OSPF is not TCP-based and it generally discovers its adjacencies dynamically instead of through static configuration. GTSM for OSPF may be enabled on individual OSPF interfaces using the **ip ospf ttl-security** command within IOS interface configuration mode. Alternatively, it may be enabled within IOS router configuration mode using the **ttl-security all-interfaces** command. Neither of these commands, however, applies to virtual or sham links. To enable GTSM for OSPF virtual links and sham links, use the **area virtual-link ttl-security** and **area sham-link ttl-security** commands, respectively, in IOS router configuration mode. The same {*hop-count*} value considerations that apply to eBGP multihop peering sessions also apply to OSPF virtual links and sham links.

GTSM is an effective way to increase the DoS resiliency of eBGP peering sessions. As you recall, BGP is processed at the IOS process level. Even when spoofed packets injected into the BGP control plane have incorrect TCP sequence numbers, if they are spoofing the correct TCP source and destination ports for an existing BGP session, these packets may cause excess CPU utilization due to the extent of processing invoked. Enabling MD5 authentication as described in the "MD5 Authentication" section above tends to exacerbate this condition because the MD5 check must be completed prior to the TCP sequence number check, and MD5 hash computations are resource-intensive. When GTSM is enabled, however, the low-impact TTL check is made very early in the packet-processing cycle, thus saving CPU resources for obviously spoofed packets. Although attackers may craft the initial IP TTL value for a packet, the fact is, this TTL field is decremented by 1 for each hop (or router interface) along the path to its final destination. Hence, IP TTL values outside the configured GTSM range cannot be spoofed. This makes GTSM an effective technique to mitigate remote attacks against a directly connected peering session. The strength of GTSM depends on an attacker not being inside a configured network diameter. If an attacker is within the configured hop-count diameter, GTSM cannot protect against packet floods or the injection of false routing information, although MD5 authentication can still protect against false routing information injection in this case. Other IOS protocols are expected to support GTSM in the future, including OSPF as described previously.

Protocol-Specific ACL Filters

Protocol-specific ACL filtering is another control plane security technique available for a limited number of control plane protocols. Whereas IP interface ACL policies are applied to specific router interfaces, and both IP rACL and CoPP policies are applied to the IOS receive interface, protocol-specific ACL policies are applied directly to a specific IOS control plane protocol. This generally allows you to control the valid protocol peers and the protocol information that peers exchange. One benefit in using this capability is that the ACL policy defined is specific to the associated protocol. Namely, IP rACL and CoPP ACL policies must consider all control, management, and services plane protocols and, in the case of CoPP, exception data plane packets punted to the IOS process level. Protocol-specific ACL filters, on the other hand, consider only the associated protocol, which helps with policy management. Some of the commonly deployed control protocol-specific ACL filter types include:

- **MPLS LDP:** LDP offers IOS commands to control label binding advertisements, including:

    — The **mpls ldp advertise-labels** command applied in IOS global configuration mode controls which local label bindings are advertised to which LDP neighbors. The specific local label bindings and specific LDP neighbors are defined using the distinct **for** ACL and **to** ACL arguments within the command syntax, respectively.

    — The **mpls ldp neighbor labels accept** command applied in IOS global configuration mode allows you to filter inbound label bindings from a particular LDP peer. The configurable ACL argument is used to filter label bindings advertised by the specified neighbor. If the prefix part of the label binding is permitted by the ACL, the router will accept the binding. If the prefix is denied, the router will not accept or store the binding. This functionality is particularly useful when two different organizations peer using LDP—for example, MPLS CsC and Inter-AS VPNs. For more information on this command, refer to Chapter 7.

- **PIM:** Using the **ip pim neighbor-filter** command within IOS interface configuration mode, you may restrict PIM protocol messages received on the associated interface such that only PIM messages from authorized neighbors are accepted. PIM messages received from sources not explicitly permitted within the configured neighbor filter ACL are discarded. Hosts, for example, should never be advertising PIM protocol messages.

- **IGMP:** Using the **ip igmp access-group** command within IOS interface configuration mode, you may restrict the multicast groups that hosts on the IP subnet serviced by the associated interface can join. This enables you to apply specific IGMP policies for an interface, including:

    — Deny all state for a multicast group G

    — Permit all state for a multicast group G

    — Deny all state for a multicast source S

- Permit all state for a multicast source S

- Filter a particular source S for a group G

- **MSDP:** MSDP offers IOS commands to control label binding advertisements, including:

  - The **ip msdp filter-sa-request** command applied in IOS global configuration mode may be configured within an ACL to control exactly which Source-Active (SA) request messages the router will honor. If an ACL is specified, only SA request messages from those groups explicitly permitted will be honored. All others will be ignored.

  - The **ip msdp sa-filter in** command applied in IOS global configuration mode is used to configure an incoming filter list for SA messages received from the specified MSDP peer. If the command is configured, but no ACL or route map is specified, all (S,G) pairs from the peer are filtered. If both the ACL and route-map keywords are used, only those (S,G) pairs explicitly permitted will be accepted.

  - The **ip msdp sa-filter out** command applied in IOS global configuration mode is used to configure an outbound filter list for SA messages advertised to the specified MSDP peer. If the command is configured, but no ACL or route map is specified, all (S,G) pairs are filtered from advertisement. If both the ACL and route-map keywords are used, only those (S,G) pairs explicitly permitted will be advertised.

Similar protocol-specific ACL filters may be available for other control plane protocols. This chapter simply introduces the concept, given the wide variety of configurable control plane protocols. You are tasked with determining if your specific control plane protocols support this capability. Chapter 6 reviews the commonly deployed management plane protocol-specific ACL filter types. For more detailed information on IP multicast security, refer to the Cisco Networkers Cannes 2007 Multicast Security (BRKIPM-2019) breakout session listed in the "Further Reading" section.

BGP Security Techniques

IOS support for GTSM was first introduced for eBGP, because eBGP is the primary external protocol and a common target for external attacks. IGP and other internal control protocols are much less susceptible to external attacks, given the nature of their operation, and assuming that infrastructure ACLs are used appropriately. Further, in support of defense in depth and breadth principles, IP rACLs, CoPP, and MD5 authentication provide an added layer of protection for internal protocols in the event that infrastructure ACLs are bypassed. Techniques to mitigate the risk of external ICMP attacks were described in the "ICMP Techniques" section above as well as in Chapter 4.

Infrastructure ACLs, IP rACLs, CoPP, and MD5 authentication, as well as the GTSM and IOS TCP sequence number generation improvements, also reduce the scope of external BGP attacks. Further, because eBGP operates over external links, it also makes sense to filter traffic destined to PE-CE and PE-PE links using any one of the available techniques outlined in Chapter 4. This prevents remote eBGP attacks that transit your network. However, despite all of these protection mechanisms, threats remain from a variety of sources:

- An attacker able to bypass the preceding BGP protection mechanisms

- A valid BGP peer that unintentionally triggers a DoS event or security event due to misconfiguration

- A valid BGP peer that intentionally launches an attack or that is compromised

To protect against these scenarios, you should consider deploying the BGP-specific protection mechanisms outlined in this section, which are available today within IOS. These mechanisms increase the level of robustness within BGP at its application layer and provide better controls for prefix and path information received (and advertised) to external peers.

BGP Prefix Filters

Prefix filters provide a means of filtering specific routes from routing advertisements learned from and sent to BGP peers. Prefix filters provide two main benefits:

- Filter false, hijacked, or unnecessary prefixes, including:

    — **Bogon prefixes:** These include DUSA (private and reserved addresses defined by RFC 1918 and RFC 3330) and address blocks that have not been allocated to a Regional Internet Registry (RIR) by the Internet Assigned Numbers Authority. Such IP prefixes should not be advertised within the public Internet. The IANA allocation of IPv4 address space to various registries is available at http://www.iana.org/assignments/ipv4-address-space. Regularly updated IP prefix configuration templates for bogon filters are available at http://www.cymru.com/Bogons/.

    — **Your own prefixes:** Your peer should not be advertising prefixes within your address block to you. Exceptions may include cases where you are multihomed or use the public Internet for connectivity between sites. In the latter case, your upstream ISP should advertise only the prefixes associated with your remote sites, and not local prefixes.

    — **A default route also known as the *gateway of last resort* or 0.0.0.0/0:** If you prefer to drop traffic destined to prefixes not explicitly carried within your routing table, then you should filter any default route advertisements received. Otherwise, you are at an increased risk of spoofing and transit attacks.

- Prevent deaggregation of CIDR address blocks. CIDR, as defined in RFC 1518 and RFC 1519, allows for classless route summarization, which reduces the amount of routing information maintained within routing tables. CIDR has helped to manage the growth of the global Internet routing table. The size of a routing table affects a router's scalability and stability, including convergence speed. Reducing or maintaining the number or prefixes to an acceptable level improves router performance. Conversely, significant and rapid expansion of the routing table size may adversely impact a router's performance and stability, because each router has a finite amount of memory in which to store the routing tables (and compute best paths), as described in Chapter 2. Consider the example illustrated in Figure 5-12.

Figure 5-12 *IP Prefix De-aggregation Example*

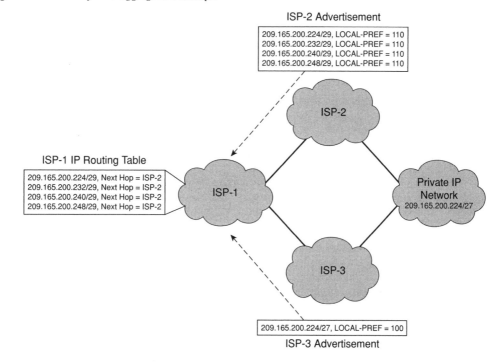

In Figure 5-12, ISP-1 receives many more-specific prefixes from ISP-2 than from ISP-3, which is advertising a single aggregate prefix for the same address block. Hence, rather than carrying 1 prefix, ISP-1 is forced to carry 4 prefixes. If all of ISP-1's peers advertised more-specific prefixes, as opposed to aggregate prefixes, the size of the ISP-1 routing table might exceed its routers' memory capacities and affect ISP-1's network stability. Therefore, to mitigate this risk, you should filter more-specific prefixes as appropriate for your network. IANA does not allocate address blocks longer than /24. Hence, at a minimum, it makes sense to filter all prefixes longer than /24. Some exceptions may exist, such as multihomed customers; however, you need to manage the number of prefixes maintained within your routing table so as to not affect network stability.

The preceding two scenarios may be advertised by the peer unintentionally via misconfiguration, for example, or intentionally with malice. Alternatively, the peering router may have been compromised, or perhaps your upstream provider has no filtering and one of its downstream customers is falsely advertising a hijacked prefix. Applying ingress prefix filters at the network edge (for all eBGP peers) helps to mitigate these risks. Policies need not be the same for each peer but may be customized per peer.

To create a prefix list or add a prefix-list entry, use the **ip prefix-list** command in IOS global configuration mode. To prevent distribution of BGP neighbor information as specified in a prefix list, use the **neighbor prefix-list** command in IOS address-family or router configuration mode. The configuration illustrated in Example 5-26 applies the prefix list named *foo* to incoming advertisements from neighbor 192.168.2.2.

Example 5-26   *Sample IOS BGP Prefix Filter Configuration*

```
router bgp 65001
address-family ipv4 unicast
 network 192.168.2.1
 neighbor 192.168.2.2 prefix-list foo in
 ! To accept a mask length of up to 24 bits in routes with the prefix 192/16:
 ip prefix-list foo permit 192.168.0.0/16 le 24
 ! To deny mask lengths greater than 25 bits in routes with the prefix 192/16:
 ip prefix-list foo deny 192.168.0.0/16 ge 25
 ! To deny mask lengths greater than 25 bits in all address space:
 ip prefix-list foo deny 0.0.0.0/0 ge 25
 ! To deny all routes with a prefix of 10/8:
 ip prefix-list foo deny 10.0.0.0/8 le 32
```

IP prefix filters are a widely deployed technique to filter improper prefix advertisements. They should be applied both on ingress and on egress so that you do not inadvertently advertise any bogus prefixes that slip through your ingress prefix filter policies.

IP Prefix Limits

In addition to prefix filtering, you may also limit the total number of prefixes that may be received from a specific peer. BGP prefix limits may be configured using the **neighbor maximum-prefix** command in IOS router configuration mode. This limits the total number of prefixes irrespective of their lengths and, thereby, prevents a peer from flooding your router with BGP advertised routes.

Peering sessions that exceed the maximum configured limit of prefixes will be torn down (by default). The session stays down until you bring the session back up by entering the **clear ip bgp** command. Entering the **clear ip bgp** command also clears stored prefixes. The optional **restart** keyword within the **neighbor maximum-prefix** command configures the router to automatically reestablish the peering session that has been disabled due to the maximum prefix limit being exceeded. An optional **restart-interval** is also configurable (in minutes), which specifies the time interval after which a peering session is reestablished after it was disabled. By using the **warning-only** optional keyword, you may also configure the router to generate a log message when the maximum prefix limit is exceeded, instead of terminating the peering session. Similarly, you may also configure a warning **threshold** specifying at what percentage of the maximum prefix limit the router starts to generate a warning message. The range is from 1 to 100; the default is 75.

Before applying such prefix limits, you should baseline your routing table and understand the prefixes advertised per peer. You must also consider potential network and topology changes and any associated impact they may have on the routing table and individual peering sessions. Further, the intention is to protect the router and not necessarily to micromanage the prefix limits of each peer.

AS Path Limits

Cisco IOS also supports a configuration command that allows you to filter BGP prefixes based on the total number of AS-PATH segments (or AS-PATH length). By default, there is no limit. To configure BGP to discard routes that have an AS-PATH length that exceeds a specified value, use the **bgp maxas-limit** command in IOS router configuration mode. With **bgp maxas-limit** enabled, if the AS-PATH length for a given prefix exceeds the configured limit, the offending prefix will be marked as invalid within the BGP table, which prevents it from being considered during best path selection and advertised to other BGP peers, and then logged.

The AS65000 BGP Routing Table Analysis Report (http://bgp.potaroo.net/as1221/bgp-active.html), at the time of this writing, reports a maximum AS-PATH length of 12 and a maximum prepended AS-PATH length of 30. These metrics provide useful guidelines for configuration of the **bgp maxas-limit** command, which should be tuned using the diameter of the Internet from the perspective of the configured router. This configuration command also applies to all BGP sessions associated with the configured address family and should be deployed specifically on edge routers with eBGP peers.

BGP Graceful Restart

An IOS router that is NSF-capable or NSF-aware for BGP can do the following:

- Detect an RP switchover on a peer
- Maintain the peering session
- Retain the routes associated with the session
- Continue forwarding for these routes while the peer recovers

Both peers need to be NSF-capable or NSF-aware, although they do not need to be operating in the same NSF mode (NSF-capable or NSF-aware).

Nonstop Forwarding (NSF)

An IP router is said to be NSF-aware if it is running NSF-compatible software. An IP router is said to be NSF-capable if it has been configured to support NSF. A router that is NSF-aware functions the same as an NSF-capable router, with one exception: an NSF-aware router is incapable of performing Stateful Switchover (SSO) operations whereby the active RP continuously synchronizes its FIB and adjacency tables with the standby RP such that state is maintained during RP failover events.

When an NSF router establishes a BGP session, it sends an OPEN message to the peer. Included in the message is a declaration that the NSF router has *graceful restart* capability. BGP graceful restart, as defined in RFC 4724, provides a mechanism by which BGP peers may avoid a routing flap following an RP switchover on the peer. SSO provides a mechanism by which the local BGP speaker may avoid a routing flap following a local RP switchover. If the BGP peer receives this graceful restart capability declaration, it becomes aware that the device sending it supports NSF. Both NSF peers need to exchange the graceful restart capability declaration in their OPEN messages at the time of session establishment. If both of the peers do not declare themselves graceful restart capable, the session will not provide NSF.

If the BGP session is established using graceful restart and one peer has an RP switchover, the other marks all the routes learned from the peer as stale; however, it continues to use these routes to make forwarding decisions for a (configurable) period of time. This functionality prevents any packet loss while the peer's newly active RP and forwarding tables converge. When the standby RP becomes active, it reestablishes the BGP session. In establishing the new session, it sends a new graceful restart message that identifies the peer as having restarted. At this point, the routing information is exchanged between the two BGP peers. Once this exchange is complete, the NSF peers use the routing information to update the RIB and the FIB with the new path and forwarding information, respectively. The NSF peers use the new routing information to remove stale routes from the BGP tables. Following that, the BGP protocol and CEF table are fully converged.

If a BGP peer does not support the graceful restart capability, it will ignore the graceful restart capability declaration in the OPEN message but will still establish a non-graceful restart capable BGP session with the NSF peer. This allows interoperability and backward compatibility between NSF and non-NSF peers.

BGP graceful restart provides an effective technique to reduce the impact of TCP RST attacks. If, for example, a BGP attack against an IP router results in the resetting of a BGP session, BGP graceful restart enables each peer to continue traffic forwarding for prefixes advertised by the lost peer while the session reestablishes itself. Hence, the data plane is not affected by a fault within BGP. Use the **bgp graceful-restart** command within IOS router configuration mode to enable the graceful restart capability and NSF behavior.

Layer 2 Ethernet Control Plane Security

Chapter 2 reviewed potential security threats that may exist within a Layer 2 switched Ethernet network environment. Security techniques available to mitigate attacks within the Layer 2 switched Ethernet data plane were described in Chapter 4. Techniques available to protect the control plane of Layer 2 switched Ethernet networks are described in this section. Chapter 6 reviews techniques available within the management plane.

In addition to the techniques described in this section, Cisco offers a Network Admission Control (NAC) solution that uses the network infrastructure, including but not limited to IEEE 802.1X port-based authentication, to enforce security policies on all devices seeking to access network computing resources. Details of the Cisco NAC technologies and solutions are beyond the scope of this book. However, additional details, including white papers and design guides, can be found on Cisco.com at http://www.cisco.com/en/US/netsol/ns617/networking_solutions_sub_solution_home.html.

VTP Authentication

VTP, as described in Chapter 2, is a Cisco-proprietary Layer 2 messaging protocol that enables network operators to centrally manage VLAN configurations within a switched Ethernet domain. Given that it is a Layer 2 protocol, VTP messages are not forwarded by IP routers. VTP messages are only exchanged between VTP servers and VTP clients within the same VTP domain, which generally includes neighboring L2 Ethernet switches. To mitigate the risk of spoofed VTP advertisements sourced from a local attacker, you may configure MD5 authentication using the **vtp passwd** command in VLAN configuration mode. The configured password is included in the calculation of the 16-byte MD5 checksum used within VTP messages. Specifically, the password is mapped to a hexadecimal secret key, which is then used in conjunction with VLAN information for calculating the MD5 checksum. All VTP-enabled Ethernet switches within the same VTP domain must be configured with the same shared password. Otherwise, VTP messages exchanged between server and client LAN switches will be discarded, similar to the manner in which messages are discarded for IP routers as depicted earlier in Figure 5-9. The default VTP configuration does not apply passwords.

VTP version 3 introduces the ability to hide configured passwords such that they do not appear in plaintext within the **show configuration** command similar to VTP versions 1 and 2 plaintext passwords. You may configure this by adding the **hidden** keyword to the **vtp passwd** command. When you use the **hidden** keyword, the hexadecimal secret key that is generated from the configured password is shown in the configuration instead of the plaintext password, as shown in Example 5-27.

Example 5-27   *Hiding VTP Version 3 Passwords*

```
Console> (enable) set vtp passwd foobar hidden
Generating the secret associated to the password.
The VTP password will not be shown in the configuration.
VTP3 domain server modified
Console> (enable) show config
 .
 .
 .
set vtp passwd 9fbdf74b43a2815037c1b33aa00445e2 secret
```

To configure the secret key directly, use the **secret** keyword of the **vtp passwd** command. The plaintext password and secret key are mutually exclusive. You cannot configure both simultaneously. If you configure a plaintext password, it replaces a current secret password, and similarly, if you paste a secret password into the configuration, the initial password is removed.

VTP version 3 also introduces the configuration of a primary server using the **set vtp primary** command configurable on a per-port basis. Only primary servers can make configuration changes within the VTP domain. If the VTP password is configured as hidden using the **hidden** password configuration keyword as described earlier in this section, you are prompted for the password when you try to configure the switch as a primary server. Only if your password matches the hidden password will the switch become a primary server allowing you to configure the domain. The use of a VTP password helps to mitigate the risk of spoofed VTP attacks, as outlined in Chapter 2.

DHCP Snooping

DHCP may be leveraged for a variety of attacks, as outlined in Chapter 2. To reduce the risk of such attacks, IOS supports a security feature called DHCP snooping. The DHCP snooping feature validates DHCP messages received on untrusted LAN interfaces. Invalid messages are discarded and the aggregate rate of DHCP messages (both invalid and valid) may be, optionally, rate limited. Rate limiting DHCP messages helps to mitigate the effects of DHCP-based DoS attacks that aim to exhaust DHCP server resources, including IP address pools. Such DHCP starvation attacks may also be mitigated using the *port security* technique described in Chapter 4.

To enable DHCP snooping, apply the **ip dhcp snooping** command in IOS global configuration mode. However, DHCP snooping is not active until you enable the feature on at least one VLAN. DHCP snooping is configurable on a per-VLAN basis and is also supported for private VLANs (PVLAN). By default, the feature is disabled on all VLANs. You can enable the feature on a single VLAN or a range of VLANs by using the **ip dhcp**

snooping vlan command in IOS global configuration mode. The following are DHCP messages considered invalid by the DHCP snooping feature when received on an untrusted interface associated with a DHCP snooping-enabled VLAN:

- Server-to-client DHCP message types, including DHCPOFFER, DHCPACK, and DHCPNAK, per RFC 2131.

- Relay agent-to-server DHCPLEASEQUERY message type, per IETF draft draft-ietf-dhc-leasequery.

- DHCP messages where the source MAC address of the Layer 2 Ethernet frame and the client hardware address within the DHCP message itself do not match. Note, this specific integrity check is performed only if the DHCP snooping MAC address verification option is enabled via the **ip dhcp snooping verify mac-address** command in IOS global configuration mode.

- DHCPRELEASE or DHCPDECLINE messages associated with an existing entry in the DHCP snooping binding table, where the interface information in the binding table does not match the ingress (untrusted) interface. The DHCP snooping binding table contains binding entries associated with untrusted ports. Each entry in the table includes the MAC address, the leased IP address, the lease time, the binding type, and the VLAN number and interface information associated with the untrusted host. To display the DHCP snooping binding table, use the **show ip dhcp snooping binding** command as illustrated in Example 5-28.

Example 5-28 *Display DHCP Snooping Binding Table*

```
Router# show ip dhcp snooping binding
MacAddress          IpAddress        Lease(sec)  Type          VLAN  Interface
-----------------   --------------   ----------  ------------  ----  -----------
--------
00:02:B3:3F:3B:99   10.1.1.1         6943        dhcp-snooping 10    FastEthernet6/10
```

- DHCP messages that include a relay agent IP address that is not 0.0.0.0, per RFC 2131.

- DHCP messages that include the relay agent information option (option 82). Option 82 enables a DHCP relay agent to include information about itself when forwarding client-originated DHCP packets to a DHCP server. The DHCP server can then use this information to implement IP address or other parameter-assignment policies. With IOS Software Release 12.2(18)SXF1 and later, you can change the default IOS behavior and enable the DHCP option 82 on untrusted port feature using the **ip dhcp snooping information option allow-untrusted** command in IOS global configuration mode. Normally, the switch drops packets with option 82 information when packets are received on an untrusted interface. This feature enables untrusted ports to forward DHCP packets that include option 82 information as may be required by IP aggregation routers that connect to IP edge routers serving as DHCP relay agents for attached IP hosts. When **ip dhcp snooping information option allow-untrusted** is enabled on the aggregation router shown in Figure 5-13, you can also still enable dynamic ARP on the aggregation switch while the switch receives packets with option 82 information on ingress untrusted interfaces to which hosts are connected, under the condition that the port on the edge switch that connects to the aggregation router is configured as a trusted interface. For more information on dynamic ARP inspection, refer to the next section.

Figure 5-13 *DHCP Relay Agent Using Option 82*

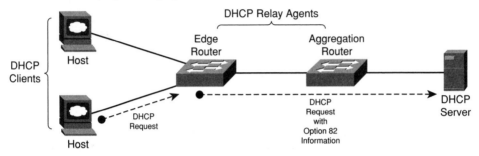

The default DHCP trust state of an IOS multilayer Ethernet switch LAN interface is untrusted. To configure the interface as trusted, use the **ip dhcp snooping trust** command within IOS interface configuration mode. You must explicitly configure LAN interfaces connected to valid DHCP servers as trusted. Ensure that DHCP servers are connected through trusted interfaces before enabling DHCP globally. Otherwise, DHCP itself will not function properly, given the DHCP snooping integrity checks outlined listed previously. DHCP host port LAN interfaces are generally configured as untrusted as are aggregation router interfaces that connect to edge routers since such aggregation router interfaces are in the forwarding path towards untrusted IP hosts. Conversely, edge router interfaces connecting to the aggregation router must be configured as trusted since such edge router interfaces are in the forwarding path towards the trusted DHCP server. Note that the edge router inserts the option 82 information, not the untrusted IP host. Hence, if the edge router is not considered a trusted device, do not apply the **ip dhcp snooping information option allowed-untrusted** command on the aggregation router. Otherwise, the edge router may spoof DHCP option 82 information as part of a security attack. Other security features, such as Dynamic ARP Inspection (DAI), discussed in the next section, also use the information stored in the DHCP snooping binding database.

To configure DHCP message rate limiting, use the **ip dhcp snooping limit rate** {*rate*} command within IOS interface configuration mode. This configured rate limit applies to both valid and invalid DHCP messages received on the interface. By default, DHCP snooping does not rate limit DHCP messages, so you must explicitly configure it if necessary. In the event the configured rate limit is exceeded, DHCP snooping places the associated port into the error-disabled state. The interface remains in the error-disabled state until either you manually enable error-disabled recovery using the **errdisable**

recovery dhcp-rate-limit global configuration command, or you enter the **shutdown** and **no shutdown** interface configuration commands.

When the DHCP snooping feature is enabled, all ARP messages received on untrusted interfaces within the applied VLAN(s) are intercepted and handled at the IOS process level on the RP where DHCP snooping integrity checks are applied. Hence, you must consider the CPU impacts of enabling DHCP snooping before deployment so as to not adversely affect the router or introduce a potential new attack vector. For more information on DHCP snooping, refer to the IOS platform-specific documents referenced in the "Further Reading" section.

Dynamic ARP Inspection

ARP may be also leveraged for a variety of attacks, as outlined in Chapter 2. To reduce the risk of ARP spoofing and ARP cache poisoning attacks, IOS supports a security feature called Dynamic ARP Inspection (DAI). The DAI feature behaves very similarly to the DHCP snooping feature whereby it validates all ARP messages received on untrusted interfaces. DAI, in fact, cannot function or be enabled without DHCP snooping being first configured, because DAI uses the DHCP snooping binding table to validate ARP messages. For untrusted IP host devices that do not use DHCP, you must configure a static entry within the DHCP snooping binding table or use ARP ACLs to permit or deny ARP messages. Otherwise, DAI will consider all ARP messages sourced from untrusted IP hosts with statically assigned IP addresses as invalid, thereby preventing network connectivity. Invalid messages are discarded and the aggregate rate of ARP messages (both invalid and valid) is rate limited. Unlike DHCP snooping, aggregate rate limiting of ARP messages received on an untrusted interface is enabled by default. Rate limiting ARP messages helps to mitigate the effects of ARP-based DoS attacks that aim to exhaust or poison ARP caches.

DAI is configurable on a per-VLAN basis and is also supported for PVLANs. By default, the feature is disabled on all VLANs. You can enable the feature on a single VLAN or a range of VLANs by using the **ip arp inspection vlan** command in IOS global configuration mode. The following ARP messages are considered invalid by the DAI feature when received on an untrusted interface associated with a DAI-enabled VLAN:

- ARP messages having an invalid IP-to-MAC address binding. DAI determines the validity of the IP-to-MAC address binding by using the local (and trusted) DHCP snooping binding database described in the preceding section. The **ip arp inspection vlan** command enables only this specific DAI integrity check. Additional DIA validation and integrity checks may be enabled using separate DIA-related commands as described in the rest of this list.

- ARP messages explicitly denied by a user-configured ARP ACL. DAI requires ARP ACLs for untrusted hosts with statically configured IP addresses, given that a valid IP-to-MAC address binding will not exist within the DHCP snooping binding table. ARP

ACLs may be configured using the **ip arp inspection filter** command in IOS global configuration mode. ARP ACL filtering is applied before the preceding DHCP snooping binding table check. Hence, if the ARP ACL denies an ARP message, it will be immediately discarded even if a valid binding exists in the DHCP snooping binding table. If the message is permitted by the ARP ACL, the DHCP snooping binding table is then used to verify the IP-to-MAC address binding per the preceding bullet.

- ARP messages (responses only) where the target MAC address within the ARP message itself is different from the destination MAC address specified within the Ethernet frame header. You may enable this specific integrity check using the **ip arp inspection validate dst-mac** command in IOS global configuration mode.

- ARP messages where the sender MAC address within the ARP message itself is different from the source MAC address specified within the Ethernet frame header. You may enable this specific integrity check using the **ip arp inspection validate src-mac** command in IOS global configuration mode. Note, this integrity check may be enabled in conjunction with the preceding destination MAC address integrity check using the **ip arp inspection validate dst-mac src-mac** command in IOS global configuration mode.

- ARP messages (both requests and responses) with invalid source IP addresses, including 0.0.0.0, 255.255.255.255, and all 224.0.0.0/4 IP multicast addresses, and ARP response messages (not requests) with invalid destination IP addresses, including 0.0.0.0, 255.255.255.255, and all IP multicast addresses (in other words, 224.0.0.0/4). You may enable these specific integrity checks using the **ip arp inspection validate ip** command in IOS global configuration mode. Note, this integrity check may be enabled in conjunction with either or both of the previous destination and source MAC address integrity checks using the **ip arp inspection validate {[dst-mac] [ip] [src-mac]}** command in IOS global configuration mode.

The default DAI trust state of a LAN interface on an IOS multilayer Ethernet switch is *untrusted*. On untrusted interfaces, the router forwards received ARP messages only if they pass the validation and integrity checks outlined in the preceding list. ARP packets received on trusted interfaces bypass any DAI validation and integrity checks. Therefore, use the DAI trust state configuration carefully. To configure the interface as trusted, use the **ip arp inspection trust** command within IOS interface configuration mode.

To configure DAI rate limiting, use the **ip arp inspection limit rate** {*pps*} command within IOS interface configuration mode. The IOS default rate limiting of ARP messages on untrusted interfaces is 15 ARP messages per second with a maximum burst interval of 1 second. In the event the configured (or default) rate limit is exceeded, DAI places the associated port into the error-disabled state. The interface remains in the error-disabled state until either you manually enable error-disabled recovery using the **errdisable recovery arp-inspection** global configuration command, or you enter the **shutdown** and **no shutdown** interface configuration commands.

DAI-filtered ARP messages are logged within IOS by default. DAI logging parameters are configurable as follows:

- Use the **ip arp inspection log-buffer entries** {*number*} command in IOS global configuration mode to configure the DAI logging buffer size. The default buffer size is 32.

- Use the **ip arp inspection log-buffer logs** {*number_of_messages*} **interval** {*length_in_seconds*} command in IOS global configuration mode to configure the logging-rate interval. The default logging-rate interface is 5 per second.

- Use the **ip arp inspection vlan** {*vlan_range*} **logging** {**acl-match** {**matchlog** | **none**} | **dhcp-bindings** {**all** | **none** | **permit**}} command in IOS global configuration mode to configure DAI log filtering to limit which denied ARP messages are logged.

When the DAI feature is enabled, all ARP messages received on untrusted interfaces within the applied VLAN(s) are intercepted and handled at the IOS process level on the RP where DAI integrity checks are applied. Hence, you must consider the CPU impacts of enabling DIA before deployment so as to not adversely affect the router or introduce a potential new attack vector. For more information on DAI, refer to the IOS platform-specific documents referenced in the "Further Reading" section. CoPP also supports ARP rate limiting using the MQC **match protocol arp** command. For more information on CoPP, refer to the "Control Plane Policing" section earlier in the chapter.

Sticky ARP

ARP (RFC 826), as described in Chapter 2, provides a mechanism to resolve an IP address to an L2 MAC address to provide IP connectivity between IP hosts within the same Layer 2 broadcast domain and between hosts on disparate IP networks. This latter case makes use of proxy ARP (RFC 1027), whereby the local IP default gateway routers advertise their own MAC addresses on behalf of the remote IP host associated with a subnetwork installed within their IP routing tables. IP routers including IP default gateways maintain IP/MAC address bindings (as well as interface and/or VLAN bindings) within their local ARP tables (or cache). Dynamically learned ARP table entries are maintained within the cache, provided the associated IP/MAC source address periodically transmits an IP-encapsulated Ethernet frame within a specified timeframe. The default ARP timeout value within IOS is 14400 seconds (or 4 hours). Excluding statically configured ARP cache entries, entries associated with inactive hosts are aged out of the ARP cache after their timeout value expires. ARP timeout values are configurable per interface using the **arp timeout** command within IOS interface configuration mode.

In addition to being refreshed, whereby the age is reset to 0, ARP table entries may also be updated or overridden within the cache. This includes modifying the IP/MAC address binding itself such that the IP address is associated with a new MAC address, or vice versa. Such ARP cache entry changes may be triggered by a variety of events, including but not limited to

- New ARP broadcasts, including gratuitous ARPs

- DHCP environments whereby a released IP address may be reassigned to a different IP host having its own unique MAC address

- IP and/or MAC spoofing (refer to Chapter 2)

To prevent dynamically learned ARP cache entries from being overridden or aged out, IOS Software Release 12.2SX introduced the sticky ARP feature. Sticky ARP entries do not age out and cannot be overridden. In the event that a different IP host uses an IP address already installed within the ARP cache, a logging message is generated, as illustrated in Example 5-29.

Example 5-29 *Sticky ARP Overwrite Attempt Log Message*

```
04:04:54: %IP-3-STCKYARPOVR: Attempt to overwrite Sticky ARP entry: 10.1.1.3, hw:
   0060.0804.09e0 by hw: 0060.9774.04a5
```

Further, the existing ARP cache is not modified in any way. Namely, a new entry is not created nor is the existing entry overridden. This helps to mitigate the risk of spoofing attacks within Layer 2 switched Ethernet networks. Sticky ARP is configured using the **ip sticky-arp** command in IOS global configuration mode. It is enabled by default within IOS 12.2SX and later and is supported on both native IP interfaces and PVLAN interfaces. The **ip sticky-arp** command is also configurable per interface. This allows you to overwrite the **ip sticky-arp** global configuration for specific interfaces. Note, the **no ip sticky-arp** command enables IP address reuse, such as may be required in DHCP environments. Given that sticky ARP entries cannot be overridden and do not age out, you must manually remove ARP entries if a MAC address changes. Also, unlike static entries, sticky ARP entries are not stored within the IOS configuration. Hence, when you reload the IOS device, sticky ARP entries must be dynamically relearned.

Spanning Tree Protocol

As outlined in Chapter 2, STP may also be leveraged for a variety of security attacks. To reduce the risk of STP attacks, IOS supports the following two security features:

- **BPDU Guard:** An Ethernet switch should receive Bridge PDUs (BPDU) only on interswitch interfaces. This applies to both point-to-point and shared LAN interswitch interfaces, as illustrated in Figure 5-14.

Figure 5-14 *Spanning Tree Protocol BPDUs*

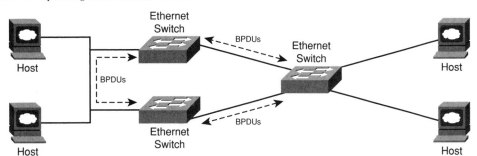

Reception of a BPDU on point-to-point or shared LAN access interfaces
providing connectivity *only* to IP hosts is an STP protocol violation. Only
a misconfiguration, software defect, or malicious attack would trigger this
error condition. Note, BPDUs will be exchanged between redundant
Ethernet switches providing IP host connectivity via a shared LAN, as
illustrated in Figure 5-14. When enabled on an access interface, the BPDU
Guard feature places the associated port into the error-disabled state if it
receives a BPDU, regardless of the interface's PortFast configuration. The
interface remains in the error-disabled state until either you manually
enable error-disabled recovery using the **errdisable recovery bpduguard**
global configuration command, or you enter the **shutdown** and **no
shutdown** interface configuration commands. This prevents such access
interfaces from participating in the STP protocol and, thereby, mitigates
the risk of a misconfiguration, software defect, or STP-based attack
sourced from an attached IP host or unauthorized device.

There are two options for enabling BPDU Guard:

— Apply the **spanning-tree portfast bpduguard default** command in IOS
   global configuration mode. This enables BPDU Guard on all interfaces in
   operational PortFast state.

— Apply the **spanning-tree bpduguard enable** command in IOS interface
   configuration mode. This allows you to configure BPDU Guard on
   individual interfaces and override the setting of the **spanning-tree portfast
   bpduguard default** global configuration command if configured.

- **Root Guard:** STP forwarding paths within a Layer 2 switched Ethernet network are
  calculated based on the elected root bridge. The Root Guard feature provides a way
  for you to enforce root bridge selection in the network. When enabled on an interface,
  the Root Guard feature places the associated port into the root-inconsistent (blocked)

state if it receives a superior BPDU from an attached device. This prevents Root Guard–enabled ports from becoming a root port. While in the root-inconsistent state, no traffic passes through the port. Only after the attached device stops sending superior BPDUs is the port unblocked again. Once unblocked, normal STP procedures will transition the port through the listening, learning, and forwarding states. Recovery is automatic; you do not need to enable error recovery or reenable the port. Root Guard is configured using the **spanning-tree guard root** command within IOS interface configuration mode. The deployment of Root Guard helps to prevent unauthorized devices from becoming the root bridge due to their spoofed BPDU advertisements.

Summary

This chapter reviewed a wide array of techniques available to mitigate attacks against the control plane within the IP networks. In addition, techniques available to mitigate attacks within the control plane of Layer 2 switched Ethernet networks were reviewed. The IP data, management, and services planes rely upon the IP control plane for correct operation. Therefore, attacks against the control plane may also adversely affect the data, management, and services planes. Protecting the control plane is critical. The optimal techniques that provide an effective security solution will vary by organization and depend on network topology, product mix, traffic behavior, operational complexity, and organizational mission. Defense in depth and breadth strategies discussed in Chapter 3 can be helpful in understanding the interactions between various IP traffic plane security techniques, and in optimizing the selection of control plane protection measures.

Review Questions

1 Name an ICMP message type (excluding ICMP replies) defined within RFC 792 that is processed by default within IOS and does not have a configuration command to disable processing.

2 SPD extended headroom applies to which specific control plane protocol packets?

3 True or False: IP rACLs apply to transit data plane packets punted to the IOS process level.

4 True or False: CoPP applies to transit data plane packets punted to the IOS process level.

5 Given that IOS BGP MD5 authentication does not support key chaining, how can you avoid resetting the BGP session when changing the MD5 key?

6 Explain the difference in the receive-side behavior of directly connected eBGP peers when GTSM is enabled (with a hop-count value of 1) versus when GTSM is not enabled.

7 Name techniques available within BGP to mitigate the risk of security attacks.

8 Name two techniques available to mitigate the risk of DHCP starvation attacks.

9 In a network environment that assigns IP host addresses dynamically, what other IOS security feature must be configured before enabling Dynamic ARP Inspection (DAI)?

10 Name two techniques available to reduce the risk of STP-based security attacks.

Further Reading

Antoine, V. et al. *Router Security Configuration Guide*, Version 1.1c. NSA, Dec. 15, 2005. http://www.nsa.gov/snac/routers/C4-040R-02.pdf.

Deleskie, J., T. Scholl, A. Popescu, and T. Underwood. "BGP Filtering—Myths Legends and Reality: Peer Filtering in the Modern Backbone." NANOG 35. Los Angeles. Oct. 24, 2005. http://www.nanog.org/mtg-0510/pdf/deleskie.pdf.

Eckert, T. "Multicast Security." (BRKIPM-2019.) Cisco Networkers 2007. Cannes, France.

Fuller, V., T. Li, J. Yu, and K. Varadhan. *Classless Inter-Domain Routing (CIDR): an Address Assignment and Aggregation Strategy.* RFC 1519. IETF, Sept. 1993. http://www.ietf.org/rfc/rfc1519.txt.

Gill, V., J. Heasley, and D. Meyer. "The BGP TTL Security Hack (BTSH)." draft-gill-btsh-01.txt. IETF, May 2003. http://tools.ietf.org/html/draft-gill-btsh-02.

Hoffman, P., and B. Schneier. *Attacks on Cryptographic Hashes in Internet Protocols.* RFC 4270. IETF, Nov. 2005. http://www.ietf.org/rfc/rfc4270.txt.

McDowell, R. "Implications of Securing Backbone Router Infrastructure." NANOG 31. San Francisco. May 4, 2004. http://www.nanog.org/mtg-0405/mcdowell.html.

McDowell, R. "Network Core Infrastructure Protection: Best Practices." Cisco Networkers 2006. Las Vegas. June 2006.

Mikle, O. "Practical Attacks on Digital Signatures Using MD5 Message Digest." Cryptology ePrint Archive, Report 2004/356. Dec. 2, 2004. http://eprint.iacr.org/2004/356.

Parmakovic, D. "Service Provider Security." Cisco white paper. http://www.cisco.com/web/about/security/intelligence/sp_infrastruct_scty.html.

Rivest, R. *The MD5 Message-Digest Algorithm.* RFC 1321. IETF, April 1992. http://www.ietf.org/rfc/rfc1321.txt.

Scholl, T. "BGP MD-5: The Good, Bad, Ugly?" NANOG 39. Toronto. Feb. 6, 2007. http://www.nanog.org/mtg-0702/presentations/Scholl.pdf.

Sherman, T. "Understanding, Preventing, and Defending Against Layer 2 Attacks." Cisco Networkers 2006. Las Vegas. June 2006.

Stevens, M., A. Lenstra, and B. de Weger. "Chosen-prefix Collisions for MD5 and Colliding X.509 Certificates for Different Identities." EuroCrypt 2007. March 22, 2007. http://www.win.tue.nl/hashclash/EC07v2.0.pdf.

Wang, X., D. Feng, X. Lai, and H. Yu. "Collisions for Hash Functions: MD4, MD5, HAVAL-128 and RIPEMD." Cryptology ePrint Archive, Report 2004/199. Aug. 17, 2004. http://eprint.iacr.org/2004/199.

Wang, X., Y. Yin, and H. Yu. "Collision Search Attacks on SHA1." CRYPTO 2005. August, 2005.

Welcher, P. "Secure Management of Routers." Chesapeake NetCraftsmen, March 5, 2001. http://www.netcraftsmen.net/welcher/papers/securemgmt.html. Wright, J., and J. Stewart. *Securing Cisco Routers: Step-by-Step*. SANS Institute, 2002. ISBN: 0-97242-733-3.

"Catalyst 3750 Switches." Cisco Documentation. http://www.cisco.com/univercd/cc/td/doc/product/lan/cat3750/index.htm.

"Catalyst 4500 Series: Configuring Control Plane Policing." Cisco Documentation. http://www.cisco.com/univercd/cc/td/doc/product/lan/cat4000/12_2_37s/config/cntl_pln.htm.

"Catalyst 4500 Series Switches." Cisco Documentation. http://www.cisco.com/univercd/cc/td/doc/product/lan/cat4000/index.htm.

"Catalyst 6500 Series Switches." Cisco Documentation. http://www.cisco.com/univercd/cc/td/doc/product/lan/cat6000/index.htm.

"Cisco 7600 Series: Configuring Denial of Service Protection." Cisco Documentation. http://www.cisco.com/univercd/cc/td/doc/product/core/cis7600/software/122sr/swcg/dos.htm.

Cisco 7600 Series Cisco IOS Software Configuration Guide, 12.2SR. Cisco Documentation. http://www.cisco.com/univercd/cc/td/doc/product/core/cis7600/software/122sr/swcg/index.htm.

"Cisco Modular Quality of Service Command Line Interface." Cisco white paper. http://www.cisco.com/en/US/products/ps6558/products_white_paper09186a0080123415.shtml.

"Configuring Advanced BGP Features." *Cisco IOS BGP Configuration Guide, Release 12.4T*. http://www.cisco.com/en/US/products/ps6441/products_configuration_guide_chapter09186a00805387d7.html.

"Control Plane Policing." *Cisco IOS Software Release 12.2(18)S Feature Guide*. http://www.cisco.com/en/US/products/sw/iosswrel/ps1838/products_feature_guide09186a008052446b.html.

"Control Plane Protection." *Cisco IOS Software Releases 12.4 T Feature Guide.* http://www.cisco.com/en/US/products/ps6441/ products_feature_guide09186a0080556710.html.

"Defining Strategies to Protect Against UDP Diagnostic Port Denial-of-Service Attacks." Cisco Tech Note. (Doc. ID: 13367.) http://cio.cisco.com/warp/public/ 707/3.html.

"Deploying Control Plane Policing." Cisco white paper. http://www.cisco.com/en/US/partner/products/ps6642/ products_white_paper0900aecd804fa16a.shtml.

"DHCPLEASEQUERY Message." Cisco Documentation. http://www.cisco.com/ univercd/cc/td/doc/product/rtrmgmt/ciscoasu/nr/nr50/cliref/clie.htm.

FIRST Best Practice Guide Library (BPGL). FIRST. http://www.first.org/resources/ guides/.

"GSR: Receive Access Control Lists." (Doc. ID: 43861.) Cisco white paper. http://www.cisco.com/en/US/tech/tk648/tk361/ technologies_white_paper09186a00801a0a5e.shtml.

"Internet Multicast Addresses." IANA. http://www.iana.org/assignments/multicast-addresses.

"Operational Security Capabilities for IP Network Infrastructure (opsec)." IETF. http://www.ietf.org/html.charters/opsec-charter.html.

"Protocol Numbers." IANA. http://www.iana.org/assignments/protocol-numbers.

"Spanning Tree PortFast BPDU Guard Enhancement." (Doc. ID: 10586.) Cisco Design Tech Note. http://www.cisco.com/en/US/tech/tk389/tk621/ technologies_tech_note09186a008009482f.shtml.

"Spanning Tree Protocol Root Guard Enhancement." (Doc. ID: 10588.) Cisco Design Tech Note. http://www.cisco.com/en/US/tech/tk389/tk621/ technologies_tech_note09186a00800ae96b.shtml.

"TCP and UDP Small Servers." (Doc. ID: 12815.) Cisco Tech Note. http://www.cisco.com/warp/public/66/23.html.

"The SANS Security Policy Project." SANS Institute. http://www.sans.org/resources/ policies/.

"Understanding Selective Packet Discard (SPD)." (Doc. ID: 29920.) Cisco Tech Note. http://www.cisco.com/warp/public/63/spd.html.

In this chapter, you learn about the following:

- Different types of management interfaces of IP routers
- Different access methods to IP routers
- Security techniques to secure the IP management plane
- Management of MPLS VPN customer edge routers using a secure Management VPN

CHAPTER 6

IP Management Plane Security

As described in Chapter 1, the management plane is used to provision, manage, and monitor IP networks, as well as individual network elements. This also includes the configuration of the many security techniques detailed throughout this book. Because the management plane enables network provisioning and telemetry, it is critical that:

- Management plane resources and protocols are secured to mitigate the threat of unauthorized access and malicious network reconnaissance, which inevitably leads to attacks within the IP data, control, and services planes

- Management plane resources within an IP router are protected to mitigate the risk of DoS attacks, because most management plane packets are handled at the Cisco IOS process level

- Management plane resources remain available during attacks such that attack sources can be identified and attacks themselves can be mitigated

The many threats against IP networks were described in Chapter 2, "Threat Models for IP Networks." This chapter describes techniques available to mitigate threats associated with the management plane. Data plane techniques such as infrastructure ACLs also help to protect the management plane, given that authorized management plane protocol traffic is generally limited to well-known, trusted, and internal sources. As described in Chapter 4, "Data Plane Security," infrastructure ACLs prevent unauthorized external traffic from gaining IP reachability to internal network infrastructure, including IP edge router addresses used for internal management plane protocols. This chapter also assumes that the network is physically secure. Network-based security measures become ineffective if physical security has been breached. The techniques described in this chapter also apply to multilayer Ethernet switches running IOS (subject to IOS release and platform-specific dependencies) and to routers configured for IPsec VPN services. Hence, a separate review for those topics, as was presented in earlier chapters, is not provided here. Conversely, specific management plane considerations for MPLS VPNs are described in this chapter. Chapter 7, "Services Plane Security," will review techniques to secure and mitigate attacks within the IP services plane.

No single technology (or technique) makes an effective security solution. This applies not only to IP networks but also to the individual IP traffic planes. Following the defense in depth and breadth principles outlined in Chapter 3, "IP Network Traffic Plane Security

Concepts," you may consider deploying multiple complementary techniques, including those described in this chapter and those described in earlier chapters, to mitigate the risk of management plane attacks.

Management Interfaces

As described in Chapter 1, "Internet Protocol Operations Fundamentals," one of the strengths of the IP protocol is that all packets are carried in a *common pipe* (also referred to as "in-band"). Legacy networks based on TDM, Frame Relay, ATM, and so forth typically relied on separate communications channels for data and control traffic. IP does not segment its traffic planes into separate channels. Thus, a router must look at every single packet entering an interface and decide what type of packet it is—data, control, management, or services plane—and apply the appropriate processes to each packet based on this determination. IP management plane packets are handled in-band with all other IP traffic. Although this is the native behavior of the IP protocol as defined within the IETF industry standards, many network operators build separate, out-of-band (OOB) management networks dedicated to carrying management plane traffic. The in-band and out-of-band management interface types are illustrated in Figure 6-1 and described further here:

Figure 6-1 *In-Band and Out-of-Band Management Architecture*

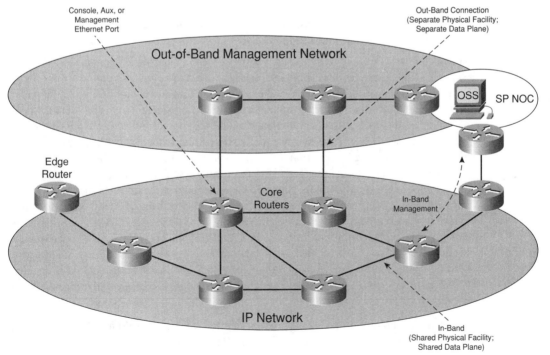

- **In-band management interface:** A physical (or logical) interface that carries both management and data plane traffic. An IP network that is managed in-band shares its physical facilities (that is, network links) and data plane (and the control plane and services plane) with management plane traffic. An in-band management interface is also referred to as a *shared* management interface. As described in Chapter 1, transit management plane traffic is processed in the CEF fast path by intermediate routers, just like data plane traffic. Management applications that operate in-band may use any of a router's interfaces or IP addresses for management connectivity. Loopback interfaces are commonly used as the in-band management interface (or IP address) because they are always *up*, unlike physical interfaces (provided the router itself is alive). Physical interfaces used for in-band management connectivity have no distinguishing characteristics. Any physical interface used for data plane forwarding may also be used for in-band management. To dedicate an in-band physical interface for OOB management, refer to the "Management Plane Protection" section later in the chapter.

- **Out-of-band management interface:** A physical interface that connects to a physically separate, isolated network dedicated exclusively to the operation and management of all network elements. An Out-of-band (OOB) network uses separate physical facilities (that is, network links, switches, and routers) and a separate control plane to carry management plane traffic to and from all network elements within the primary in-band network. Many SPs use separate, OOB management networks, which are commonly referred to as data communications networks (DCN). While such OOB networks have their own control planes, they are used exclusively for network management purposes. They never carry data plane traffic and isolation from data plane traffic within the in-band network is assured through the use of a separate control plane and separate physical network infrastructure. OOB management networks are deployed today for two primary reasons. The first is availability: an OOB network provides an alternate path to reach network elements if in-band management connectivity is lost. Note, you may design the OOB management network as the primary management path and use the in-band management path as backup. DCN designs vary widely. The second reason to deploy an OOB management network is for large-scale network management operations, including service provisioning, monitoring, billing, alarms, software upgrades, configuration backups, and so on. The following router interfaces are commonly used for OOB management:

    - **Console port:** The console port (CTY) is an asynchronous serial port that uses a DCE RJ-45 receptacle for connecting a data terminal (DTE). Any devices connected to this port must be capable of asynchronous transmission.

    - **Auxiliary port:** The auxiliary port (AUX) is also an asynchronous serial port but uses a DTE RJ-45 receptacle for connecting a modem or other DCE device (such as a CSU/DSU or another router) to the router. Any devices connected to this port must also be capable of asynchronous transmission. Unlike the console port, the asynchronous auxiliary port supports hardware flow control and modem control.

— **Management Ethernet port:** On certain routers, a separate Ethernet port
is made available strictly for OOB management connectivity. CEF is disabled
by default to prevent traffic forwarding between the OOB network and the
in-band network. Cisco strongly recommends against enabling CEF routing
functions on this port to prevent IP reachability between the in-band and OOB
networks. With CEF enabled, an in-band network failure may cause in-band
data plane traffic to be inadvertently rerouted across the OOB management
network. In this scenario, the OOB network no longer exclusively carries
management plane traffic, as intended.

Example 6-1 illustrates the four main types of management lines, as found by using the
show line command.

Example 6-1 *IOS* **show line** *Command Sample Output*

```
Router# show line
 Tty Typ     Tx/Rx     A Modem  Roty AccO AccI  Uses   Noise    Overruns
*   0 CTY               -   -      -    -    -     0      0        0/0
    1 TTY  38400/38400  - inout    -    -    -     0      0        0/0
    2 TTY  38400/38400  - inout    -    -    -     0      0        0/0
    3 TTY  38400/38400  - inout    -    -    -     0      0        0/0
    4 TTY  38400/38400  - inout    -    -    -     0      0        0/0
    5 TTY  38400/38400  - inout    -    -    -     0      0        0/0
    6 TTY  38400/38400  - inout    -    -    -     0      0        0/0
    7 TTY  38400/38400  - inout    -    -    -     0      0        0/0
    8 TTY  38400/38400  - inout    -    -    -     0      0        0/0
    9 AUX   9600/9600   - inout    -    -    -     0      0        0/0
   10 VTY   9600/9600   -   -      -    -    -     0      0        0/0
   11 VTY   9600/9600   -   -      -    -    -     0      0        0/0
   12 VTY   9600/9600   -   -      -    -    -     0      0        0/0
   13 VTY   9600/9600   -   -      -    -    -     0      0        0/0
   14 VTY   9600/9600   -   -      -    -    -     0      0        0/0
```

Console (CTY) and auxiliary (AUX) ports were described in the preceding list. VTY lines,
as aptly named, are virtual terminal lines with no associated physical interface. They are
used exclusively for remote terminal access, including inbound Telnet and Secure Shell
(SSH) connections. VTY lines appear as **line vty** within the IOS configuration. By default,
an IOS router has five VTY lines, numbered 0 through 4 (for example, **line vty 0 4**).
However, you can create additional VTY lines by using the **line vty** command in global
configuration mode. For more information on SSH, refer to the "Remote Terminal Access
Security" section later in the chapter.

TTY lines represent standard asynchronous lines, which are separate from the console and
auxiliary ports and the VTY lines. TTY lines are used for inbound or outbound modem and
terminal connections and appear as **line** {*line-number*} within the IOS configuration. The
specific line numbers are a function of the asynchronous interface hardware built into or
installed within the router. TTY lines are often used to connect to the console ports of other
devices or to connect to external modems for dial-in/out access.

By default, no password is defined for either the console or auxiliary parts. Hence, by connecting to a CTY or AUX line with the default IOS configuration, you are automatically placed into user EXEC mode. Conversely, VTY lines require a password (by default) to gain access to user EXEC mode. EXEC mode is the IOS software command interpreter. It interprets the commands you type and carries out the corresponding operations. By default, the IOS software command-line interface (CLI) has two levels of access to commands: user EXEC mode (privilege level 1) and privileged EXEC mode (privilege level 15). Level 1 provides the lowest EXEC mode user privileges and allows only *user-level* commands available at the **router>** prompt. Level 15 includes all *enable-level* commands at the **router#** enable prompt. You can use the **privilege** command in global configuration mode to configure additional privilege levels at which operators may log in, to allow or deny access to specific commands. The **privilege** command specifies the commands accessible at various levels. Up to 16 privilege levels can be configured, from level 0, which is the most restricted level, to level 15, which is the least restricted level. Which commands are available is based on your user privilege level. By default, there are only five commands associated with user privilege level 0: **disable**, **enable**, **exit**, **help**, and **logout**. You can display the commands available to you by typing a question mark (**?**) at the EXEC prompt. Screen output may vary depending upon your hardware and IOS software release. For more information on IOS CLI privilege levels, refer to the references listed in the "Further Reading" section.

Password Security

The use of password protection to control or restrict terminal access to the IOS CLI of your router is a fundamental element of router security. The following techniques enable you to control who is allowed access to the router and what IOS privilege levels they are granted once they gain access:

- **password (line configuration):** To specify a password on a line, use the **password** command in line configuration mode. A line is a console port (CTY), auxiliary port (AUX), virtual terminal (VTY), or asynchronous (TTY) line as described in the previous section.

  After specifying a password on a line using the **password** command, you must activate password checking at login using the **login** command in line configuration mode. Example 6-2 illustrates how to enable password security on each of the available lines. The **password** and **login** commands are widely available within IOS.

Example 6-2 *Enabling Password Security on Lines*

```
Router(config)# line con 0
Router(config-line)# password s3cr3t
Router(config-line)# login
Router(config-line)# line 1 8
Router(config-line)# password s3cr3t
Router(config-line)# login
Router(config-line)# line aux 0
```

continues

Example 6-2   *Enabling Password Security on Lines (Continued)*

```
Router(config-line)# password s3cr3t
Router(config-line)# login
Router(config-line)# line vty 0 4
Router(config-line)# password s3cr3t
Router(config-line)# login
```

Authentication, authorization, and accounting (AAA) and Role-based CLI Access are also available and are described in their corresponding sections later in this chapter.

- **username password:** The **password** command described above specifies a password for a specific line. Using the configuration in Example 6-2, any user that attempts to connect to a line must enter the configured line password to be granted user EXEC mode access. To establish local username-based password authentication, use the **username** command in global configuration mode. After specifying a username password, you must activate username-based password checking for the lines using the **login local** command in line configuration mode. The **username** command is widely available within IOS.

- **enable password:** To set a local router password to restrict access to the various EXEC mode privilege levels, use the **enable password** command in global configuration mode. By default within IOS, no enable password is defined, and entering the **enable** command in user EXEC mode automatically places you into privileged EXEC mode level 15, which is the least restricted level. The **enable password** command provides an optional [**level** {*level*}] argument that may be specified to define a unique enable password per EXEC mode privilege level. If the **level** argument is not specified within the **enable password** command, the privilege level of the configured enable password defaults to level 15. Only authorized users who need privileged EXEC mode access should know the enable password. As stated in the preceding section, you may use the **privilege** command in global configuration mode to specify commands accessible at various levels. To specify the default privilege level for a line, use the **privilege level** command in line configuration mode. The **enable password** command can also be specified with either one of two types of passwords. The first, Type 0, is a clear text password visible to any user who has access to privileged mode on the router or who can access the configuration. The second, Type 7, is a password with a weak, *exclusive-or* based encryption scheme. Type 7 passwords can be reversed from the encrypted form by using publicly available tools. Its benefit is mainly in preventing *shoulder surfers* from viewing clear text passwords. The **enable password** command is widely available within IOS.

- **enable secret:** To specify an additional layer of security over the **enable password** command, use the **enable secret** command in global configuration mode. The **enable secret** command provides better security by *storing* the configured **enable secret** password using a nonreversible cryptographic hash function, compared to the **enable password** command, which stores the configured password in clear text or in an easily reversible encrypted format (described in the **enable password** text above). Storing the password as a cryptographic hash helps to minimize the risk of password sniffing if the router configuration file is transferred across the network, such as to and from a TFTP server. It is also useful if an unauthorized user obtains a copy of your configuration file. Note, if neither the **enable password** command nor the **enable secret** command is configured, and if there is a line password configured for the console port, the console line password will serve as the enable password for all VTY lines, which includes Telnet, rlogin, and SSH connections. The **enable secret** command is widely available within IOS. Username passwords may also be stored in the router configuration file in cryptographic hash format, similar to the enable secret. The associated command is **username secret**.

- **security passwords min-length:** To ensure that all configured passwords are a specified minimum length, use the **security passwords min-length** command in global configuration mode. The IOS default is six characters. This command affects line passwords, username passwords, enable passwords, enable secrets, and username secrets. After this command is enabled, any newly configured passwords that are less than the specified minimum length will be rejected within EXEC mode. This command is available in IOS 12.3(1), 12.2(27)SBC, and later releases.

- **security authentication failure rate:** To configure the number of allowable unsuccessful login attempts, use the **security authentication failure rate** command in global configuration mode. The default number of allowable failed login attempts before a 15-second EXEC mode delay is ten. This command also activates the generation of system logging (syslog) messages if the number of allowable unsuccessful login attempts is exceeded. This command is available in IOS Software releases 12.3(1), 12.2(27)SBC, 12.3(7)T, and later releases. For more information on syslog, refer to the "Network Telemetry and Security" section later in the chapter.

- **service password-encryption:** To encrypt local router passwords, use the **service password-encryption** command in global configuration mode. This command applies to line passwords, username passwords, enable passwords, and authentication key passwords, including routing authentication passwords and key strings. By default, IOS does not encrypt passwords. Encrypting passwords in this way helps to minimize the risk of password sniffing if the router configuration file is transferred across the network such as to and/or from a TFTP server. It is also useful if an unauthorized user obtains a copy of your configuration file. This command is widely available within IOS. It should be noted that this command invokes the same Type 7 encryption algorithm described earlier in this list.

This section reviewed the basics of IOS password security. The techniques described provide local authentication whereby password storage and authentication is handled locally on the router. IOS also offers a variety of login enhancements, including delays between successive logins, login shutdown if an attack is suspected, and syslog generation for each successful or failed login attempt. For more information on these login enhancements and the password security commands described in this section, refer to the *IOS Configuration Guides* and *Command References* available on Cisco.com.

Further, using strong-password creation techniques can greatly reduce the risk of unauthorized access. These techniques include the use of mixed-case letters, numbers, and punctuation symbols. Avoid using dictionary words, names, phone numbers, and dates. Better passwords are greater than eight characters and include at least one of each of the following: lowercase letters, uppercase letters, digits, and special characters. For additional information on choosing a secure password, refer to the US-CERT Cyber Security Tip ST04-002, "Choosing and Protecting Passwords," available at http://www.us-cert.gov/cas/tips/ST04-002.html. For guidance on strong passwords, also refer to your organization's own security policy. As referenced earlier in this section, AAA and Role-based CLI Access are described in their respective sections later in the chapter.

SNMP Security

The Simple Network Management Protocol (SNMP) is an application layer protocol that facilitates the remote administration of network devices. SNMP operates between SNMP managers and SNMP agents. SNMP managers request management-related information of, and receive unsolicited management-related messages from, SNMP agents. Conversely, SNMP agents respond to SNMP manager requests and send unsolicited messages to SNMP managers. Some SNMP-enabled devices support the functions of both an SNMP manager and SNMP agent. Such devices are referred to as SNMP proxies. IOS routers generally operate as SNMP agents.

The SNMP request messages referenced in the preceding paragraph include solicited *get* and *set* messages with which the SNMP manager requests and modifies, respectively, the value(s) of object(s) managed by an SNMP agent. Similarly, the SNMP unsolicited messages include *trap* or *inform* messages with which the SNMP agent provides an unsolicited notification or alarm message to the SNMP manager relating to a managed object. The primary difference between the trap and inform messages is that the inform message is acknowledged by the SNMP manager. A collection of managed objects is organized into a Management Information Base (MIB). A wide variety of MIBs have been defined as IETF industry standards. In addition, all vendors, including Cisco, define private MIBs in addition to the generic IETF MIBs for managing vendor-specific network elements and functions. For more information on MIB support for a given IOS platform and/or release, refer to the MIB Locator available on Cisco.com at http://tools.cisco.com/ITDIT/MIBS/servlet/index.

All SNMP messages are transported over the User Datagram Protocol (UDP). Solicited operations are sent by the SNMP manager to the UDP destination port 161 on the SNMP agent. Unsolicited operations are sent by the SNMP agent to the UDP destination port 162 on the SNMP manager. The acknowledgement sent by the SNMP manager to an SNMP agent in reply to an inform operation is sent to a randomly chosen high UDP port that is determined when the SNMP agent process is started. As such, the SNMP agent process in IOS listens for SNMP operations on UDP ports 161, 162, and the random UDP port selected. The SNMP process is started within IOS either at the time the device boots or when SNMP is configured.

Many router configuration parameters are available through SNMP managed objects, including but not limited to enable passwords. Therefore, it is critical that if the SNMP process is enabled, it be secured. SNMP is disabled by default within IOS. Nevertheless, it is the primary and most widely deployed protocol for remote management of network devices. The following techniques are available to mitigate the risk of SNMP-based security attacks:

- **Community string:** An SNMP community string is included within each SNMP protocol message and functions much like a password. The SNMP agent authorizes SNMP messages received using the associated community string. Community strings may also be applied to unsolicited messages sent from an SNMP agent to the SNMP manager. Knowledge of an SNMP agent's community string provides access to all of its managed objects. To set the community string for the IOS SNMP agent and, thereby, restrict access, use the **snmp-server community** command in global configuration mode. Within this command you may define two different types of community strings: read-only (**ro**) and read-write (**rw**). Using the optional **ro** command argument, you can define a read-only community string, which provides read-only access to all of the device's managed objects. Management stations authorized for read-only access can retrieve only MIB objects. Using the optional **rw** command argument, you can define a read-write community string, which provides read-write access to all of the device's managed objects. Management stations authorized for read-write access can both retrieve and modify MIB objects. The strong-password creation techniques outlined earlier in the "Password Security" section should also be considered when you chose SNMP community strings. Note that no technique is available to encrypt or hash the assigned community strings within the router configuration file. Therefore, to reduce the risk of unauthorized access, you must restrict access and distribution of your router configuration files to protect your SNMP community strings and other router configuration information that can be leveraged for a security attack. Also note, SNMP community strings are transmitted in clear text across the IP network. More information on SNMP encryption is provided later in this list.

- **Community string ACLs:** The **snmp-server community** command described above also provides an optional {*access-list*} command argument. This allows for a numbered or named standard ACL to be specified in conjunction with the configuration of the community string(s) and is analogous to the protocol-specific ACL filters described in Chapter 5, "Control Plane Security." The community string ACL restricts the source IP addresses that are allowed access to the SNMP process. SNMP packets received from hosts not permitted within the ACL are silently discarded. Note, this ACL filter is applied at the IOS process level within the SNMP agent itself. Unauthorized SNMP management hosts should also be filtered within your infrastructure ACL, IP rACL, and/or CoPP policies, as described in Chapters 4 and 5. When deployed in combination, along with antispoofing protection, each of these data, control, and management plane security techniques supports the defense in depth and breadth principles outlined in Chapter 3.

- **snmp-server packetsize:** As outlined in Chapter 2, DoS attacks aim to exhaust router resources, including but not limited to CPU and packet memory. Further, attackers use malformed and crafted packets to discover new or exploit known software vulnerabilities. The classic ping of death (PoD) attack described in Chapter 2 is an example of an attack that used oversized packets to exploit a known software vulnerability at the time. To establish control over the largest SNMP packet size permitted when the SNMP server is receiving a request or generating a reply, use the **snmp-server packetsize** command in global configuration mode. The IOS default is 1500 bytes. This command is particularly useful if you do not filter IP fragments. As described in Chapter 5, it is a best common practice (BCP) to filter all IP fragments for management plane traffic.

- **SNMPv3:** There are three versions of the SNMP protocol defined within the IETF:

  — **SNMPv1:** SNMP version 1 is the original SNMP protocol specification, as defined in RFC 1157. The security of SNMPv1 is limited to the use of community strings for message authentication, as described earlier in this list.

  — **SNMPv2c:** SNMP version 2c provides a richer set of operation types and error codes, but its security remains limited to the use of community strings for message authentication. SNMPv2c is the most widely deployed version and is defined in RFC 1901, RFC 3416, RFC 3417, and RFC 3418.

  — **SNMPv3:** SNMP version 3 added advanced security mechanisms, including MD5 or SHA authentication of messages, DES encryption of messages, a View-based Access Control Model (VACM), SNMP contexts, and enforcement of message timeliness to defend against reply attacks. It is worth noting that many versions of IOS also support AES and 3DES encryption of SNMPv3 messages. Further, unlike SNMPv1 and SNMPv2c, which use cleartext community strings for message authentication, SNMPv3 uses a username and encrypted password. SNMPv3 user passwords are also not visible within the router configuration, unlike community strings. Similar to the community string ACLs outlined earlier in the "SNMP Security" section, SNMPv3 configuration commands also support the optional {*access-list*} command argument. This allows for a numbered or named standard ACL to be specified and, thereby, limit the IP addresses that are allowed access to the SNMP process. SNMP packets received from hosts not permitted within the ACL are discarded. Again, this ACL filter is applied at the IOS process level within the SNMP agent itself and should be used in conjunction with your infrastructure ACL, IP rACL, and/or CoPP policies as described earlier in this list. SNMPv3 is the current industry-standard SNMP version and is defined in RFC 3413, RFC 3414, RFC 3415, and RFC 3584.

IOS supports all three versions of SNMP (v1, v2c, and v3). The first **snmp-server** command that you enter enables all versions of SNMP. The **no snmp-server** command disables all versions of SNMP. To configure SNMPv3 parameters, use the **snmp-server engineID local**, **snmp-server group**, **snmp-server host**, **snmp-server user**, and **snmp-server view** commands in global configuration mode. For more information on SNMPv3, refer to the references listed in the "Further Reading" section.

Remote Terminal Access Security

SNMP provides remote management of network devices exclusively through the use of MIBs that define, organize, and name the managed objects available within a device, as described in the preceding section. For those objects that are not manageable through an SNMP MIB, you must use either the IOS EXEC mode or web-based console to view and/or modify them. Remote terminal access using the EXEC mode remains a widely used technique for configuring IOS devices and troubleshooting network events. Techniques to secure the console and auxiliary ports were described in the "Password Security" and "Disable Idle User Sessions" sections above. Such techniques also apply to remote console sessions via the VTY and TTY ports.

Telnet (originally specified in RFC 854) is the most widely used tool for remote console (VTY) access to IOS routers. Similarly, reverse Telnet is widely used to connect to a router with multiple terminal (TTY) lines that are in turn connected to consoles of other devices. Such routers with multiple terminal line connections are referred to as *terminal servers*. While you may configure the VTY and TTY lines for password authentication, Telnet (and reverse Telnet) sessions are not encrypted natively. Hence, usernames and passwords, and session data itself, are transmitted in clear text across the IP network between Telnet clients and servers. By using a man-in-the-middle (MiTM) attack as described in Chapter 2, for example, an attacker can eavesdrop on an unsecure remote console session and collect sensitive router configuration and network topology information. If an attacker intercepts a valid VTY (or TTY) username and password, the attacker can gain unauthorized access to the IP router itself. Because of this, Telnet is highly discouraged as a mechanism for remote console access.

In addition to the password security techniques outlined in the "Password Security" section, the following techniques are also available to mitigate the risk of unauthorized remote terminal access:

- **VTY access lists:** The **access-class** {*access-list*} **in** command allows for a numbered ACL to be applied to VTY lines and their associated incoming remote console connections. A VTY ACL restricts the source IP addresses that are allowed access to the VTY lines and is analogous to the protocol-specific ACL filters described in Chapter 5. Packets associated with incoming VTY connections that are received from hosts that are not permitted within the ACL are discarded. Similar to the SNMP community string ACL described earlier in the "SNMP Security" section, this ACL filter is also applied at the IOS process level within the VTY process itself. Unauthorized remote console management hosts should also be filtered within your infrastructure ACL, IP rACL, or CoPP policies, as described in Chapters 4 and 5. Deployed in combination, along with antispoofing protection, each of these data, control, and management plane security techniques supports the defense in depth and breadth principles outlined in Chapter 3. VTY ACL support is widely available within IOS.

- **Secure Shell:** SSH is a protocol that may be used to provide encrypted remote terminal access to a network device. As such, it offers greater security than Telnet and rlogin, which only provide session authentication in the clear. There are currently two versions of the SSH protocol, SSH Version 1 and SSH Version 2, both of which are supported by Cisco IOS. SSHv2 should be implemented when possible because it provides better host authentication as well as improvements to the transport layer. To determine whether the IOS image that your device is running supports SSH server functionality, the SSH protocol version, and whether it is enabled, use the **show ip ssh** command in global configuration mode. Note, the SSH server component of IOS identifies itself as version 1.5 if running only version 1 of the protocol, as version 2.0 if running only version 2 of the protocol, and as version 1.99 if running SSH version 2 with version 1 compatibility. To specify the version of SSH to be run on an IOS router, use the **ip ssh version** command in global configuration mode. To configure SSH control parameters on your router, use the **ip ssh** command in global configuration mode. Note, before you can configure SSH on your router, you must first define a hostname for the router using the **hostname** command, then define a domain name for the router using the **ip domain-name** command, and finally, generate the RSA key pairs required by SSH using the **crypto key generate rsa** command. After these steps have been completed, the SSH server will be enabled. To enable secure access to TTY (asynchronous) lines as opposed to using reverse Telnet, use the **ip ssh port** command in global configuration mode. The preceding IOS commands enable SSH functionality. They do not disable Telnet access, which is allowed by default within IOS for VTY lines. IOS does not accept incoming network connections to asynchronous ports (TTY lines) by default. This includes both Telnet and SSH. To define which *incoming* protocols are allowed to connect to a specific line of the router, use the **transport input** command in line configuration mode. Example 6-3 illustrates how you can enable only SSH on VTY and TTY lines.

Example 6-3 *Configuration Sample Enabling Only SSH on VTY and TTY Lines*

```
Router(config)# line vty 0 4
Router(config-line)# transport input ssh
Router(config-line)# line tty 1 8
Router(config-line)# transport input ssh
```

The IOS configuration shown in Example 6-3 also implicitly disables Telnet access on the VTY and TTY lines, because **telnet** is not specified as an argument within the **transport input** configuration command. To deny all forms of remote terminal access for a line, use the **transport preferred none** command in line configuration mode.

- **Secure HTTP (HTTPS):** IOS supports a secure HTTP server, which operates over the Secure Sockets Layer (SSL) 3.0 protocol. HTTP over SSL is abbreviated as HTTPS. The HTTPS server within IOS provides secure web-based administration of a device. Conversely, the IOS standard (and nonsecure) HTTP server, similar to Telnet, provides only authentication of HTTP connections, and not encryption. The secure HTTPS server is disabled by default within IOS. To enable the secure HTTPS server in support of web-based remote terminal access, use the **ip http secure-server** command in global configuration mode. Note, when enabling the secure HTTPS server, you should always disable the standard HTTP server to prevent unsecured connections to the same HTTP services. The standard HTTP server can be disabled using the **no ip http server** command in global configuration mode, which is discussed further in the next section, "Disabling Unused Management Plane Services." You may also enable selected HTTPS services within the IOS HTTPS server infrastructure, as opposed to enabling all HTTPS services, which is the default behavior. For more information on the IOS secure HTTPS server, including security certificates and applications, refer to the references listed in the "Further Reading" section.

Disabling Unused Management Plane Services

As described in Chapter 5, it is widely considered a network security BCP to disable any unused services and protocols on each individual device in the IP network. Unused services and protocols are generally not secured, and hence may be leveraged within an attack. This section describes those management plane services and protocols that are enabled by default within Cisco IOS and that represent a potential security risk. If you do not need these services, you should disable them. Control plane services and protocols that should also be disabled if not used were described in Chapter 5.

- **Bootstrap Protocol (BOOTP) services:** To disable BOOTP services, use the **no ip bootp server** command in IOS global configuration mode. Using the **no ip bootp server** command by itself will not stop the router from listening on UDP port 67 because this "well-known" port is also used by DHCP, which is described later in this list. This command is widely available within IOS.

- **Cisco Discovery Protocol (CDP):** CDP is a Cisco-proprietary data link layer protocol that facilitates autodiscovery of IOS (or Catalyst OS) neighbors and topologies. This can be very useful for network management applications and network troubleshooting. CDP is enabled by default on all Cisco IP routers, access servers, and switches except the Cisco 10000 ESR series. It is also supported on all LAN and WAN network interfaces that support Subnetwork Access Protocol (SNAP). ATM interfaces, for example, do not support SNAP and, consequently, CDP. As outlined in Chapter 2, CDP may be leveraged by an attacker for network reconnaissance purposes. Consequently, at a minimum CDP should be disabled on external interfaces. To disable CDP on an interface, use the **no cdp enable** IOS command within interface configuration mode. To disable CDP globally on a device, use the **no cdp run** IOS command in global configuration mode. To display information about the interfaces on which CDP is enabled, use the **show cdp interface** command in privileged EXEC mode. Example 6-4 illustrates how to disable CDP on an interface.

Example 6-4 *Configuration Sample Disabling CDP*

```
Router(config)# interface Ethernet0
Router(config-if)# no cdp enable
```

For more information on CDP, refer to the references listed in the "Further Reading" section. Also note that, because CDP is a Layer 2 protocol, it is not IP routable and therefore is not subject to remote attacks. Nevertheless, you do not want to provide external peers with knowledge of your network topology, IP router platforms, software releases, IP addressing plan, and so on, which can be leveraged for malicious reconnaissance purposes. CDP is widely available within IOS (and Catalyst OS).

- **Dynamic Host Configuration Protocol (DHCP) Server and Relay Agent:** To disable DHCP server and relay functions, use the **no service dhcp** command in IOS global configuration mode. Because DHCP is based on BOOTP, both of these services share the well-known UDP server port of 67 and client port of 68 (per RFC 951, RFC 1534, and RFC 2131). If both the BOOTP server and DHCP services are disabled using the **no ip bootp server** and **no service dhcp** IOS commands, ICMP Port Unreachable messages (Type 3, Code 3) will be sent in response to incoming requests on port 67, and the original incoming packet will be discarded. Disabling only one of the two BOOTP and DHCP services will not result in ICMP Port Unreachable messages. To disable BOOTP services (in IOS Software Releases 12.2(8)T and later) but leave DHCP services enabled, use the **ip dhcp bootp ignore** command in IOS global configuration mode. For more information on ICMP security, refer to Chapters 4 and 5. The **service dhcp** command is available in 12.0(1)T, 12.2(28)SB, and later IOS releases. The **ip dhcp bootp ignore** command is available in 12.2(8)T, 12.2(28)SB, and later IOS releases.

- **DNS-based host name-to-address translation:** By default, when an IOS command in user or privileged (enable) EXEC mode is entered into an IOS device and the command is not recognized, the device considers the invalid command as the host name of another device that the operator is attempting to connect to, for example, via Telnet or SSH. Therefore, the IOS device tries to resolve the unrecognized command into an IP address by performing an IP domain lookup via DNS. If no specific DNS server has been explicitly configured, the router will issue a local DNS broadcast for the unrecognized command to be translated into an IP address. As described in Chapter 2, a local attacker can exploit this and gain unauthorized access to the IOS device. Disabling IP DNS-based host name-to-address translation via the **no ip domain lookup** command in IOS global configuration mode mitigates this risk. Conversely, if DNS name resolution is required by the IOS device, configuring name servers using the **ip name-server** command in IOS global configuration mode is an alternate technique to mitigate this issue as are IP Receive ACLs, Control Plane Policing, VTY ACLs, and disabling default outbound Telnet behavior using the **transport preferred none** command in line configuration mode. Also note, the original syntax for disabling IP DNS-based host name-to-address translation was **no ip domain-lookup**. The syntax was changed to **no ip domain lookup** as of IOS Software Release 12.2 and later.

- **EXEC mode:** If you do not require EXEC mode on a line, disable it using the **no exec** command in line configuration mode. The **no exec** command disables the EXEC process for the associated line(s). Consequently, when an unauthorized user attempts to use Telnet, SSH, or rlogin to access a line with the EXEC process disabled, the user will get no response when attempting to connect. Note, by default, IOS enables EXEC mode on all lines as well as Telnet access. The **no exec** command affects only incoming connections and not outgoing connections—for example, using an asynchronous (TTY) line.

- **Finger service:** To disable the finger service (defined in RFC 742), use the **no ip finger** command in IOS global configuration mode. The finger service was enabled by default within IOS releases prior to 12.1(5) and 12.1(5)T. The **no ip finger** command replaced the IOS **service finger** command. For those earlier IOS versions that do not support the **no ip finger** command, the **no service finger** command should be used. If you are using IOS 12.1(5), 12.1(5)T or later, the finger service is disabled by default.

- **HTTP server:** For all Cisco IOS devices, the HTTP server is disabled by default (with the exception of Cisco 1003, Cisco 1004, and Cisco 1005 routers, on which the HTTP server is enabled by default). To display the status and configuration details of the HTTP server, use the **show ip http server** command in EXEC mode. If you choose to use HTTP for management, you should restrict access to well-known, trusted, and/or internal source hosts using the **ip http access-class** command. Note, this ACL filter is applied at the IOS process level within the HTTP process itself and is analogous to the protocol-specific ACL filters described in Chapter 5. Unauthorized HTTP clients should also be filtered within your infrastructure ACL, IP rACL, and/or CoPP policies, as described in Chapters 4 and 5. When deployed in combination with antispoofing protection, each of these data, control, and management plane security techniques supports the defense in depth and breadth principles outlined in Chapter 3. By default, the HTTP server listens on port 80, which is the industry-standard port for HTTP. To specify that the IOS HTTP server listen on a different port number, use the **ip http port** command in global configuration mode. Modifying the standard HTTP port number in this way increases security through obscuration only (for example, it may prevent automated scanners from discovering HTTP services on the default well-known port), but also requires authorized HTTP clients to be reconfigured with the new port number. If web-based administration is not required, be sure to disable the standard HTTP server using the **no ip http server** command in IOS global configuration mode if it has previously been enabled. IOS also supports HTTPS, as described in the earlier "Remote Terminal Access Security" section.

- **Maintenance Operation Protocol (MOP):** MOP is enabled on Ethernet interfaces and disabled on all other interface types by default within IOS. To disable MOP, use the **no mop enabled** IOS command within interface configuration mode. The **no mop enabled** command is widely available within IOS.

- **Network Time Protocol (NTP):** To disable the NTP server, use the **no ntp** command in IOS global configuration mode. NTP is enabled by default within Cisco IOS. The **ntp disable** IOS command may be used to disable NTP processing on specific interfaces such as external interfaces. NTP is very effective and widely deployed for correlating network events, including security incidents. NTP is discussed further in the "Network Telemetry & Security" section below and should be disabled only if it is not specifically used.

- **Packet assembler/disassembler (PAD):** All PAD commands associated with assembly and disassembly of data packets between an X.25 packet switching network and a group of terminal connections are enabled by default within IOS. To disable PAD services, use the **no service pad** IOS command in global configuration mode. The **no service pad** command is widely available within IOS.

- **Small TCP servers:** Within IOS Software Releases prior to 11.3, the TCP servers for Echo, Discard, Chargen, and Daytime services were enabled by default. To disable these services, use the **no service tcp-small-servers** command in IOS global configuration mode. When the minor TCP servers are disabled, access to the Echo, Discard, Chargen, and Daytime ports causes the IOS router to discard the initial incoming packet (TCP SYN request) and send a TCP RST packet to the source. Within IOS Software Releases 11.3 and later, these TCP servers are disabled by default.

- **Small UDP servers:** Within IOS Software Releases prior to 11.3, the UDP servers for Echo, Discard, and Chargen services were enabled by default. To disable these services, use the **no service udp-small-servers** command in IOS global configuration mode. When the minor UDP servers are disabled, access to the Echo, Discard, and Chargen ports causes the IOS router to discard the initial incoming packet and send an ICMP Port Unreachable message (Type 3, Code 3) to the source. Within IOS Software Releases 11.3 and later, these UDP servers are disabled by default.

Most other management plane services and protocols are disabled by default within Cisco IOS. Nevertheless, you should verify against your specific IOS Software Releases and platforms that all unnecessary services and protocols are disabled either by default or explicitly through the router configuration. You may also display detailed information about open IP sockets within your IOS device by using the **show ip sockets detail** command as well as display the status of TCP connections by using the **show tcp brief all** command, both from EXEC mode. IOS 12.4(11)T also introduced support for the **show udp** command to display IP socket information about UDP processes. To minimize the risk of a configuration error that could leave a router vulnerable, certain versions of IOS provide a *one touch* security lockdown configuration process known as AutoSecure, which is described further later in the chapter in the section "AutoSecure."

Disabling Idle User Sessions

Idle logged-in user sessions might be susceptible to unauthorized access and hijacking attacks. The following techniques are available to mitigate the risk associated with idle user sessions:

- **exec-timeout:** To disconnect incoming user sessions after a specific period of idle time, set the idle timeout interval that the EXEC command interpreter will wait by using the **exec-timeout** {*minutes*} [*seconds*] command in line configuration mode. Once the configured idle timeout interval is reached, IOS will terminate the session. This requires the user to log in again to gain access. By default, IOS disconnects idle user sessions after 10 minutes. The configuration illustrated in Example 6-5 sets a time interval of 5 minutes. This capability is widely available within IOS.

Example 6-5 *Configuring the EXEC Mode Idle Timeout Interval*

```
Router(config)# line console
Router(config-line)# exec-timeout 5 0
```

- **ip http timeout-policy idle:** To disconnect idle HTTP (or HTTPS) client connections after a specific period of idle time, set the idle timeout interval that the IOS HTTP server will wait by using the **ip http timeout-policy idle** command in global configuration mode. Once the configured idle timeout interval is reached, IOS will terminate the HTTP connection. This requires the web user to log in again to gain access. When using the **ip http timeout-policy idle** command, you must also specify the total lifetime of a connection since first established and irrespective of whether it is active or idle, using the **life** {*seconds*} argument.

By default, Cisco routers do not continually test whether the remote host associated with a previously connected TCP session is still active and reachable. If one side of the TCP session terminates abnormally, the host at the opposite end of the session may still believe the session is active. Orphaned TCP sessions consume router resources. Attackers have been known to take advantage of this weakness to attack TCP hosts, including IOS routers as described in Chapter 2. To mitigate the risk of orphaned TCP sessions, IOS routers can be configured to send periodic keepalive messages to verify whether the TCP peer is still available. If the TCP peer fails to respond to (that is, ACK) the keepalive message, the local router will disconnect the session and release the associated router resources. The following techniques are available to verify whether a remote host associated with a previously connected TCP session is still active and reachable:

- **service tcp-keepalives-in:** To generate keepalive packets on inactive incoming network connections (initiated by the remote host), use the **service tcp-keepalives-in** command in global configuration mode. This capability is widely available within IOS and is disabled by default.

- **service tcp-keepalives-out:** To generate keepalive packets on inactive outgoing network connections (initiated by a local user), use the **service tcp-keepalives-out** command in global configuration mode. This capability is widely available within IOS and is disabled by default.

System Banners

IOS enables you to define a variety of display banners that you may customize. A banner serves as a legal notice, such as "no trespassing" or a "warning" statement. A proper legal notice protects you such that it enables you to pursue legal actions against unauthorized users. Consult your legal staff for suitable language to use in your banner. The types of display banners available within IOS include but are not limited to the following:

- **EXEC banner:** To specify a message (or EXEC banner) to be displayed when an EXEC process is created, use the **banner exec** command in global configuration mode. If password checking is enabled, an EXEC process is created after password authentication. By default, no EXEC banner is defined or displayed when an EXEC process is created. The **banner exec** command is used simply to specify the EXEC banner message itself. To enable the display of the EXEC banner message specified by the **banner exec** command, use the **exec-banner** command in line configuration mode. Lines configured with the **exec-banner** command then display the message specified by the **banner exec** command when an EXEC session associated with the line is created. By default, **exec-banner** is enabled on all lines. However, because **banner exec** is disabled by default, no EXEC banner is displayed. Conversely, because **exec-banner** is enabled by default, specifying an EXEC banner using the **banner exec** command automatically results in EXEC banner messages being displayed when an EXEC process is created. This applies to all EXEC processes except for those associated with reverse Telnet sessions. Use the **banner incoming** command described later in the list to enable a display banner for reverse Telnet sessions. To disable the display of EXEC banner messages, you may use either the **no banner exec** or **no exec-banner** command.

- **MOTD (message-of-the-day) banner:** To specify a MOTD to be displayed immediately to all user sessions and when new users first connect to the router, use the **banner motd** command in global configuration mode. If password checking is enabled, the MOTD banner is displayed before the login prompt for new user sessions. By default, no MOTD banner is defined or displayed. The **banner motd** command is used simply to specify the MOTD banner message itself. To enable the display of the MOTD banner message specified by the **banner motd** command, use the **exec-banner** command in line configuration mode. Lines configured with the **exec-banner** command then display the message specified by the **banner motd** command immediately to all user sessions and when new users first connect to the router. By default, **exec-banner** is enabled on all lines. However, because **banner motd** is disabled, no MOTD banner is displayed by default. Conversely, because **exec-banner** is enabled by default, specifying an MOTD banner using the **banner motd** command automatically results in MOTD banner messages being displayed immediately to all user sessions and when new users first connect to the router. To disable the display of MOTD banner messages, you may use the **no banner motd**, **no motd-banner**, or **no exec-banner** command.

- **Incoming banner:** To specify an incoming banner to be displayed for incoming reverse Telnet sessions, use the **banner incoming** command in global configuration mode. If password checking is enabled, the incoming banner is displayed after password authentication of the reverse Telnet session. By default, no incoming banner is displayed for reverse Telnet sessions because **no banner incoming** is the IOS default configuration. Unlike the **banner exec** and **banner motd** commands described above, the **banner incoming** command alone determines whether an incoming banner is displayed for reverse Telnet sessions. If an incoming banner is defined using the **banner incoming** command, an incoming banner message is displayed for all reverse Telnet sessions. If an incoming banner is not defined (in other words, **no banner incoming**), an incoming banner is not displayed for reverse Telnet sessions. Consequently, to disable the display of incoming banner messages, use the **no banner incoming** command.

- **Login banner:** To specify a login banner to be displayed before username and password prompts, use the **banner login** command in global configuration mode. When a user connects to the router, the MOTD banner (if configured) appears first, followed by the login banner and prompts. After the user successfully logs in to the router, the EXEC banner or incoming banner is displayed, depending on the type of connection. (SSHv1 connections are the only exception to these rules, in which case the user is prompted for a username and password prior to any banner displays. SSHv2 works according to the normal banner processes described previously.) For a reverse Telnet login, the incoming banner is displayed. For all other connections, the router displays the EXEC banner. By default, no login banner is displayed because **no banner login** is the IOS default configuration. Similar to the **banner incoming** command described above, the **banner login** command alone determines whether a login banner is displayed. If a login banner is defined using the **banner login** command, a login banner message is displayed before username and password prompts. If a login banner is not defined (in other words, **no banner login**), a login banner is not displayed in any way. Consequently, to disable the display of login banner messages, use the **no banner login** command.

A banner may also be displayed when a Serial Line IP (SLIP) or PPP connection is made using the **banner slip-ppp** command. Example 6-6 illustrates the sequence of banner messages displayed based on the configuration shown in Example 6-7.

Example 6-6 *Sample Banner Output of Console Session*

```
Router con0 is now available


Press RETURN to get started.

Message of the Day banner displayed here.


Login banner displayed here.


User Access Verification

Password: {password}

EXEC banner displayed here.

Router>
```

Example 6-7 *Sample Console and Banner Configuration*

```
banner exec ^C

EXEC banner displayed here.

^C
banner login ^C

Login banner displayed here.

^C
banner motd ^C

Message of the Day banner displayed here

^C
!
line con 0
 password {password}
 login
```

Secure IOS File Systems

Certain versions of IOS support features to mitigate the risk of malicious attempts to erase the contents of persistent storage (NVRAM and flash) and features to prevent corrupted IOS images from being loaded. These features are known as *Cisco IOS Resilient Configuration* and *Cisco IOS Image Verification*, respectively. The IOS Resilient Configuration feature enables a router to securely archive copies of the running IOS image and configuration files. In this way, if the running files are tampered with or erased, you can restore them quickly using the secure copies and, as a result, minimize downtime. The IOS Image Verification feature allows you to automatically verify the integrity of IOS images. This was traditionally an optional user process. IOS Image Verification is now automated such that the integrity of any IOS image file downloaded is automatically verified. The following IOS commands are associated with these two features:

- **secure boot-config (IOS Resilient Configuration):** To take a snapshot of the router running configuration and securely archive it in persistent storage, use the **secure boot-config** command in global configuration mode. This command is supported only on routers configured with a PCMCIA Advanced Technology Attachment (ATA) disk. The archived configuration is hidden and cannot be viewed, copied, modified, or removed using EXEC mode commands (although it may be viewed in ROMMON mode). The archived configuration will even survive a disk format operation. Only the **show secure bootset** command can be used to display the archived filename. To restore the archived configuration, use the **secure boot-config restore** {*filename*} command in global configuration mode. The *filename* argument represents the restored copy of the archived configuration, which can then be loaded into the running or startup system configuration. If changes are made to the running configuration, you should disable and then reenter this command to archive a snapshot of the new configuration. This command can be disabled only through the console port of the router. Conversely, with the exception of the configuration upgrade scenario, enabling this command does not require console access.

- **secure boot-image (IOS Resilient Configuration):** To enable IOS image resilience, use the **secure boot-image** command in global configuration mode. When first enabled, the running IOS image (as displayed in the **show version** command output) is securely archived in persistent storage. This command is supported only on routers configured with a PCMCIA ATA disk. Images booted from a TFTP server cannot be secured using this command. The archived image is hidden and cannot be viewed, copied, modified, or removed from EXEC mode commands. The archived image will even survive a disk format operation. Only the **show secure bootset** command can be used to display the archived filename. The **no** form of this command releases the archived image so that it can be viewed or removed using EXEC mode commands. If **secure boot-image** is enabled at bootup by the startup system configuration and a different running IOS image is detected, a message similar to the one shown in Example 6-8 is generated.

Example 6-8 *IOS Resilient Configuration File Mismatch Message*

```
ios resilience :Archived image and configuration version 12.2 differs from running
version 12.3.
Run secure boot-config and image commands to upgrade archives to running version.
```

To upgrade the IOS image archive to the new running IOS image, reenter this command from EXEC mode. The former archived IOS image is then released and can be viewed or removed using EXEC mode commands.

- **file verify auto (IOS Image Verification):** To enable automatic image verification, use the **file verify auto** command in IOS global configuration mode. Image verification is disabled by default within IOS. With this command enabled, each IOS image that is copied or reloaded will be automatically verified. This includes computing a local MD5 hash of the image and comparing it to the MD5 hash embedded within the image. (Note that when this verification process is run, the Cisco.com MD5 hash is also displayed, which you can manually compare against the MD5 digest posted on Cisco.com.) If the MD5 hashes do not match, image verification fails and the image will not be loaded or copied. This helps to reduce the risk of images that are accidentally or maliciously corrupted from being loaded into a router. Image verification is supported only for IOS image files and is available in IOS Software Releases 12.2(18)S, 12.0(26)S, 12.3(4)T, and later releases. You may also use the **/verify** command and optional arguments within the **copy** and **reload** commands to perform image verification on individual IOS images.

- **ip scp server enable:** The IOS Secure Copy (SCP) feature provides a secure and authenticated method for copying router configuration and IOS image files to and from an IOS router. SCP relies on SSH, which, as described in the "Remote Terminal Access Security" section above, provides encrypted remote terminal access to a network device. Hence, prior to enabling SCP using the **ip scp server enable** command in global configuration mode, you must correctly configure SSH, including its RSA key pair, in addition to AAA authentication and authorization services. AAA, as described later in the chapter, is required by SCP to verify whether the user has proper EXEC privilege levels. Authorized users can then copy any file that exists in the IOS File System (IFS) by using the **copy** command.

For more information on IOS Resilient Configuration and IOS Image Verification, refer to the *Cisco IOS Configuration Guides* and *Command References* available on Cisco.com. For more information on AAA, refer to the "Authentication, Authorization, and Accounting" section later in this chapter.

Role-Based CLI Access

IOS EXEC mode provides for 16 different privilege levels to restrict user access to EXEC mode commands, as described earlier in the "Management Interfaces" section. The flexibility and level of detail available within the EXEC mode privilege levels, however, is somewhat limited given the following behavior:

- Commands available at lower privilege levels are executable at higher levels, because a privilege level inherits the privileges of all lower privilege levels. Therefore, a user authorized for privilege level 8, for example, is granted access not only to those commands allowed at privilege level 8 but also those commands allowed within privilege levels 0 through 7 (if also defined). A user authorized for privilege level 15 can execute all IOS commands.

- Assigning a command with multiple keywords to a specific privilege level also assigns the command associated with the first keyword to the specified privilege level. For example, if you assign the **show ip route** command to privilege level 8, for example, both the **show** command and the **show ip** command are automatically set to privilege level 8 unless you set them individually to a lower level or level 8. This is necessary because you cannot execute, for example, the **show ip route** command unless you have access to the **show** and **show ip** commands. Subcommands coming under **show ip route** are also automatically assigned to privilege level 8 within the preceding example.

- Most commands are automatically assigned level 15 privileges by default. If you want to create a user account that has access to most but not all commands, you must configure **privilege exec** statements for every command you want to make capable of being executed at a lower privilege level. Although this can be centralized through the use of TACACS+ (Terminal Access Controller Access-Control System Plus), it remains nonetheless somewhat tedious.

As an alternative, IOS introduced the Role-based CLI Access feature to provide more flexibility and command control than is possible with the EXEC mode privilege levels. Role-based CLI Access was introduced in IOS Software Release 12.3(7)T and allows you to define *CLI views*, which provide selective access and visibility to EXEC commands and configuration information. Similar to EXEC privilege levels, CLI views restrict user access to EXEC mode commands and limit visibility of router configuration information. Conversely, unlike EXEC privilege levels:

- CLI views are independent of one another. CLI views do not inherit the privileges (or authorized commands) associated with another CLI view. Thereby, CLI views limit the commands visible within the router configuration to only those that are specifically allowed within the view.

- Multiple keyword commands can be assigned to a CLI view without the view being automatically assigned the command associated with the first keyword. In this way, a user within a configured CLI view is allowed to use only those multiple keyword commands explicitly allowed within the CLI view. CLI views also support an optional wildcard keyword **all** that allows subcommands that begin with the same allowed keyword command to be allowed within the view.

- As of Cisco IOS Software Release 12.3(11)T, you can also specify an interface or a group of interfaces to a CLI view, thereby allowing command access on the basis of specified interfaces.

- CLI views also operate completely independently of EXEC mode privileges. That is, the list of commands allowed within a CLI view can span multiple privilege levels and, further, you can restrict the allowed commands regardless of the EXEC privilege level associated with a command.

Given the flexibility and detailed command control of CLI views, you may configure distinct and independent CLI views for different users and user groups, including but not limited to, for example, network management administrators, routing protocol administrators, services plane administrators (for example, IPSec VPNs), QoS policy administrators, and so on.

To configure a CLI view, use the **parser view** command in IOS configuration mode. Note, the **aaa new-model** global configuration command must be enabled prior to configuring a CLI view. You must also enter root view using the **enable view** command in order to configure a CLI view. The root view is password protected using the privilege level 15 enable password. The maximum number of CLI views that can be configured is 15, excluding the root view. To associate EXEC mode commands and a password to the CLI view, use the **commands** and **secret 5** commands, respectively, in view configuration mode. To bind a username to a CLI view, use the **username view** command in global configuration mode. Users assigned to a CLI view are placed into the CLI view after password authentication. From there they can only enter EXEC commands or view configuration information allowed within the assigned view. Alternatively, to gain access to a CLI view, you may also use the **enable view** command from EXEC mode. CLI views are enabled for password protection when first configured. Example 6-9 illustrates sample CLI view configurations for both a routing protocol administrator and a line administrator.

Example 6-9 *Sample CLI View Configuration*

```
Router# sh run | begin parser
parser view routing-admin
  secret 5 $1$s.U2$HCSJnzfUefaMLpQqjCWYt1
  commands configure include-exclusive router
  commands configure include all interface
  commands exec include configure terminal
  commands exec include configure
  commands exec include show running-config
  commands exec include show
 !
parser view line-admin
  secret 5 $1$.3Pu$rd7FFoI.Jr5TPxPOzto/T0
  commands configure include-exclusive line
  commands configure exclude interface
  commands exec include configure terminal
  commands exec include configure
  commands exec include show running-config
  commands exec include show
 !
 !
 end
```

Example 6-10 illustrates the commands available within the routing protocol administrator and line administrator CLI views. Notice that within the line administrator CLI view, you can only configure router lines. Conversely, within the routing protocol administrator CLI view, you can only configure router protocols and interfaces.

Example 6-10 *Sample CLI View-Specific Commands*

```
Router# enable view line-admin
Password: {password}
Router# ?
Exec commands:
  configure  Enter configuration mode
  enable     Turn on privileged commands
  exit       Exit from the EXEC
  show       Show running system information

Router# show ?
  disk0:          display information about disk0: file system
  disk1:          display information about disk1: file system
  running-config  Current operating configuration
  unix:           display information about unix: file system

Router# conf t
Enter configuration commands, one per line.  End with CNTL/Z.
Router(config)#
Router(config)# ?
Configure commands:
  do    To run exec commands in config mode
  exit  Exit from configure mode
  line  Configure a terminal line

Router(config)# exit
Router#
Router# enable view routing-admin
Password: {password}

Router# ?
Exec commands:
  configure  Enter configuration mode
  enable     Turn on privileged commands
  exit       Exit from the EXEC
  show       Show running system information

Router# show ?
  disk0:          display information about disk0: file system
  disk1:          display information about disk1: file system
  running-config  Current operating configuration
  unix:           display information about unix: file system

Router# config t
Enter configuration commands, one per line.  End with CNTL/Z.
Router(config)# ?
Configure commands:
```

continues

Example 6-10 *Sample CLI View-Specific Commands (Continued)*

```
  do        To run exec commands in config mode
  exit      Exit from configure mode
  interface Select an interface to configure
  router    Enable a routing process

Router(config)# exit
  Router#
```

For more information on Role-based CLI Access and the applicable commands described in this section, refer to the *IOS Configuration Guides* and *Command References* available on Cisco.com.

Management Plane Protection

Out-of-band management networks using dedicated management interfaces as described in the "Management Interfaces" section above are often used by SPs and large enterprises as an alternate path to network elements if in-band management connectivity is lost. Console, auxiliary, and management Ethernet ports are dedicated for OOB management. Given that the console and auxiliary ports are asynchronous serial interfaces, they offer limited bandwidth for OOB management access (for example, 9600 baud). Further, management Ethernet ports vary widely among router platforms in terms of transmission rate (for example, 10/100 Mbps versus Gigabit Ethernet) and port density (that is, one versus two management Ethernet ports).

IOS Software Release 12.4(6)T introduced the Management Plane Protection (MPP) feature, which allows any in-band (physical) interface to be dedicated for OOB management. This provides greater flexibility because you are no longer restricted to using the fixed console, auxiliary, and management Ethernet ports for OOB management. Not only can you dedicate in-band interfaces for OOB management, you can also restrict which management protocols are allowed (for example, SSH versus Telnet). With the MPP feature, the behavior of the console, auxiliary, and management Ethernet interfaces does not change. They remain dedicated for OOB management. Conversely, the behavior of in-band interfaces changes in the following manner:

- **MPP-enabled in-band interfaces:** An in-band interface configured as a dedicated management interface using the **management-interface allow** command in IOS control plane host configuration mode allows only authorized management plane protocol packets. Packets not authorized using the **management-interface allow** command are discarded, including all control, service, and data plane packets. The supported MPP protocols include FTP, HTTP, HTTPS, SSH, SCP, SNMP, Telnet, Blocks Extensible Exchange Protocol (BEEP), and TFTP. TACACS+ and RADIUS (Remote Authentication Dial-In User System) protocol packets, for example, are also filtered because they are not supported by the MPP feature. Because routing protocol packets are filtered, dynamic routing adjacencies will not be formed across such interfaces. This does not prevent, however, a misconfigured static route from transmitting data plane traffic out of an in-band interface dedicated for OOB management. Hence, you must use caution when configuring static routes associated with MPP-enabled interfaces.

- **Other in-band interfaces:** Other in-band interfaces not enabled for MPP automatically drop all ingress packets associated with any of the supported MPP protocols, including FTP, HTTP, HTTPS, SSH, SCP, SNMP, Telnet, BEEP, and TFTP. Hence, the remaining in-band interfaces not enabled for MPP are no longer accessible in-band, at least for those supported MPP protocols. TACACS+ and RADIUS protocol packets, for example, are not filtered on these interfaces because they are not supported by the MPP feature.

If you require OOB management access using an interface type other than the reserved console, auxiliary, or management Ethernet ports, you may use the MPP feature to dedicate an in-band interface for OOB management. The Example 6-11 configuration dedicates the POS2/1 interface shown in Figure 6-2 for OOB management. Notice that POS2/2 is no longer capable of in-band management.

Figure 6-2 *Management Plane Protection Illustration*

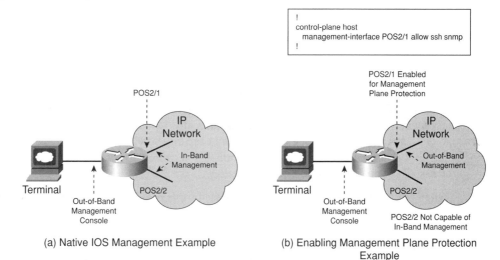

(a) Native IOS Management Example   (b) Enabling Management Plane Protection Example

Example 6-11 *Sample Management Plane Protection Configuration*

```
control-plane host
 management-interface POS2/1 allow snmp ssh
!
interface POS2/1
  ip address 192.168.1.1 255.255.255.0
  encapsulation ppp
!
interface POS2/2
ip address 192.168.2.1 255.255.255.0
  encapsulation ppp
!
```

As shown in Example 6-11, you may assign multiple in-band interfaces for OOB management. The MPP feature does not limit you to a single dedicated in-band interface. This capability, however, applies only to physical interfaces. Loopback and virtual interfaces not associated with physical interfaces cannot be enabled for MPP. To view the management interface configuration information, use the **show management-interface** command in EXEC mode. The MPP feature is also only supported on software-based centralized IOS router platforms using IOS 12.4(6)T or later. For more information on MPP, refer to the references listed in the "Further Reading" section.

Authentication, Authorization, and Accounting

The password security techniques described in the "Password Security" section earlier in the chapter are part of the built-in authentication features of IOS and control who is allowed to access the router. The EXEC mode privilege levels and Role-based CLI Access views are part of the built-in authorization features of IOS that define the EXEC mode commands and router configuration information available to an authorized user. As outlined previously, not all authorized users have the same privilege levels or require access to the same router configuration parameters. The remote terminal access techniques specify the methods (or protocols) by which authorized users can access the router. All of the the previously described password authentication and command authorization security checks are configured and executed on the local router. Although username, line, and enable password authentication, as well as EXEC privileges or CLI views, may be consistent across the IP network, each router must be configured independently when using local authentication and command authorization. Alternatively, IOS supports Authentication, Authorization, and Accounting (AAA) network security services, which provide a highly flexible and scaleable framework through which you can set up centralized access control across all of your IOS devices.

Figure 6-3 illustrates a typical AAA (pronounced *triple A*) network configuration that includes AAA-enabled IOS devices and redundant AAA security servers. The AAA servers represent RADIUS and/or TACACS+ security servers and serve to centralize access control for IP network access and/or remote terminal access to AAA clients such as IOS routers. AAA servers facilitate the configuration of three independent security functions in a consistent and modular manner, including:

- **Authentication:** The process of validating the claimed identity of a user
- **Authorization:** The act of granting access rights to a user or group of users
- **Accounting:** The methods of logging user connectivity and activity

Figure 6-3   *AAA Network Configuration Example*

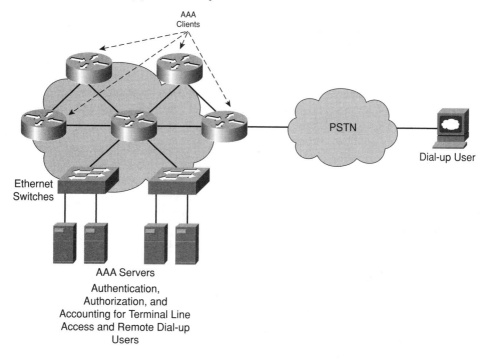

The use of centralized AAA servers and associated security policies facilitates uniform access control policy enforcement across the AAA-enabled network infrastructure, as opposed to configuring authentication and authorization policies on each individual IP router. The *Cisco Secure Access Control Server (ACS)* is an AAA server; its functionality and configuration is beyond the scope of this book. For more information on the Cisco Secure ACS product series, refer to the references listed in the "Further Reading" section. IOS routers and switches enabled for AAA are clients of the AAA servers.

The AAA protocol used between AAA clients and AAA servers can be RADIUS, TACACS+, or Kerberos. Kerberos only provides user authentication and hence is not discussed further here. TACACS+ is a Cisco-proprietary protocol and is not compatible with the deprecated protocols TACACS (RFC 1492) and extended TACACS, which, incidentally, are not compatible with AAA. TACACS+ provides reliable delivery (via TCP) of protocol packets transmitted between AAA clients and servers. The packet payload may be optionally encrypted using a byte-wise exclusive OR (XOR) function with a pseudo-random pad generated from a concatenated series of MD5 hashes. TACACS+ provides IOS EXEC mode command authorization per user as well as per group of users, and hence is better suited than RADIUS for centralized remote terminal access. This is the common deployment model for TACACS+. Although TACACS+ is a Cisco-proprietary protocol, it is widely supported within the industry today on both AAA servers and clients. It was also documented as an IETF Internet draft, as referenced in the "Further Reading" section.

RADIUS is an industry-standard protocol (RFC 2138) that uses UDP as an underlying transport protocol. As such, upper-layer services must handle RADIUS protocol timeouts and retransmissions. Further, RADIUS encrypts only passwords and not full protocol packets (as TACACS+ does) transmitted between AAA clients and servers. Further, RADIUS also combines authentication and authorization (TACACS+ separates all three functions), which prevents you from customizing the EXEC mode commands available per user. Nevertheless, RADIUS is less processing intensive and hence provides greater scalablity for devices supporting large numbers of connection requests, such as broadband aggregation routers and dial-up access servers. RADIUS also provides better accounting of dynamically established connections versus TACACS+, which is also a better match for broadband aggregation routers and dial-up access server deployments. This is the common deployment model for RADIUS.

Configuring AAA is relatively simple after you understand the basic process involved. To configure security on an IOS device using AAA, you must first enable AAA through the **aaa new-model** command in global configuration mode. If you decide to use a centralized AAA security server, you must configure the associated protocol parameters using either the **tacacs-server** or **radius-server** command, including, for example, the **tacacs-server host, tacacs-server timeout, tacacs-server key, radius-server host,** and **radius-server timeout** global configuration commands. Multiple TACACS+ or RADIUS servers can be specified for increased availability. When using centralized AAA security servers, IOS devices act as AAA clients. To configure AAA authentication, use the **aaa authentication** command in global configuration mode. To configure AAA authorization, use the **aaa authorization** command in global configuration mode. To configure AAA accounting, use the **aaa accounting** command in global configuration mode. Example 6-12 enables AAA services using TACACS+ for remote VTY access to the router.

Example 6-12 *AAA Sample Configuration*

```
aaa new-model
!
aaa authentication login VTY-A group tacacs+ local
aaa authentication enable default group tacacs+ enable
aaa authorization exec default group tacacs+ none
aaa accounting commands 1 default start-stop group tacacs+
aaa accounting commands 15 default start-stop group tacacs+
!
tacacs-server host 10.0.0.12
tacacs-server timeout 2
no tacacs-server directed-request
tacacs-server key 7 0017400516081F
!
line vty 0 4
 exec-timeout 5 0
 password 7 030752180500701E1D
 login authentication VTY-A
 transport input ssh
!
```

Note that there are a wide variety of AAA options and advanced features, a discussion of which is beyond the scope of this book. For a complete description of the commands applicable to AAA security services, refer to references listed in the "Further Reading" section.

AutoSecure

The management plane security techniques described in the preceding sections are most often configured individually. Beginning with IOS Software Releases 12.3(1), 12.2(18)S, and later, IOS offers a one-touch device lockdown capability known as *AutoSecure*. AutoSecure facilitates IP router security by simplifying the configuration process of security policies. Rather than apply each of the individual IOS security-related commands manually, AutoSecure uses a single command to both disable nonessential system services and protocols that can be exploited for network attacks and enable IP services and features that help protect against attacks. This feature is directed toward customers lacking a detailed understanding of IOS services and the associated security implications.

AutoSecure, in general, focuses on security of the management plane and, optionally, security of the data plane. Security of the data plane using AutoSecure is limited to the following:

- Enabling uRPF strict mode on external interfaces for antispoofing protection. For more information on uRPF and antispoofing protection, refer to Chapter 4.

- Enabling Cisco IOS Firewall (formerly known as Context-based Access Control, or CBAC) on external interfaces to prevent unauthorized external hosts from gaining access to your internal IP network. The IOS Firewall feature is outside the scope of this book. For more information, refer to the references listed in the "Further Reading" section.

Therefore, to fully secure the data plane, control plane, and services plane, you should consider deploying the techniques outlined in Chapters 4, 5, and 7, respectively.

AutoSecure helps secure the management plane by automatically:

- Disabling unnecessary and potentially insecure services. Alternatively, you may manually disable these services using the service-specific IOS commands described in the earlier "Disabling Unused Management Plane Services" section and those in the "Disabling Unused Control Plane Services" section of Chapter 5.

- Enabling certain services that help to increase the resistance of the router from attack.

- Securing remote management and terminal access to the router.

- Enabling appropriate security-related logging.

AutoSecure is invoked using the **auto secure** command in privileged EXEC configuration mode. The optional [**management** | **forwarding**] command arguments allow for the following:

- **management:** Only the management plane will be secured by AutoSecure.

- **forwarding:** Only the data plane will be secured by AutoSecure. As stated above, security of the data plane using AutoSecure is limited to uRPF strict mode and Cisco IOS Firewall.

By default, AutoSecure prompts you for any interactive questions—for example, an enable secret, local username, and password, whether SSH services should be enabled, and so on. You can also bypass interactive mode by using the optional **no-interact** command argument. AutoSecure then runs in noninteractive mode and configures the router using default AutoSecure settings. Noninteractive mode prevents you from customizing the AutoSecure-related configuration parameters. However, noninteractive mode is effective if you need to quickly secure a router. Note, when using noninteractive mode, no interactive-related configuration parameters such as usernames and passwords are configured. Default usernames and passwords, for example, are considered a security vulnerability and hence are not applied by AutoSecure.

AutoSecure can be enabled during initial system setup or during run time. If you modify any related configuration parameters after invoking AutoSecure, the AutoSecure configuration may not be fully effective. Be sure you have a thorough understanding of IOS services and the associated security implications before changing the AutoSecure configuration. IOS Software Release 12.3(8)T introduced rollback functionality for AutoSecure whereby you may revert back to the pre-AutoSecure router configuration state if the AutoSecure configuration process fails. Prior to IOS Software Release 12.3(8)T, you must save the running configuration before invoking AutoSecure. To display all of the configuration commands that have been added as part of the AutoSecure configuration, use the **show auto secure config** command from privileged EXEC mode. For more information on AutoSecure, including the supported IOS services, refer to the references listed in the "Further Reading" section.

Network Telemetry and Security

In addition to securing the network and network elements themselves, it is also critically important to be able to identify and classify security events. *Identification and classification* are two distinct phases defined within the six-phased approach for incident response that is widely recognized as the industry BCP. For more information on security incident handling and the six phases of incident response, refer to Appendix D, "Security Incident Handling."

Besides **show** commands from EXEC mode, there are a wide variety of tools and techniques available within IOS that facilitate identification and classification of network security events. Some of these tools are briefly described here:

- **BGP log neighbor changes:** The **bgp log-neighbor-changes** command enables syslog logging of BGP neighbor state changes (up or down events) and resets. This is very useful for troubleshooting network connectivity problems and measuring network stability, including security incident handling. Unexpected neighbor resets might indicate high error rates, high packet loss, or a security attack and thus should be investigated. The neighbor status change messages are not tracked if the **bgp log-neighbor-changes** command is not enabled, except for the reset reason, which is always available as output of the **show ip bgp neighbors** command.

- **BGP policy accounting:** BGP policy accounting provides an efficient method for measuring packet and byte volumes received from, or sent to, different BGP peers. As such it is typically deployed on network edges connecting to external BGP peers. From a security perspective, BGP policy accounting also facilitates traceback of attack entry points and sources. BGP policy accounting counters can be queried via SNMP or using the **show cef interface policy-statistics** command from EXEC mode. For more information on BGP policy accounting, including feature support and configuration guides, refer to the references listed in the "Further Reading" section.

- **Embedded Event Manager (EEM):** EEM is a framework within IOS that provides the components and methods to invoke custom, local actions trigged by user-defined events. EEM also provides mechanisms to enable the use of programmable scripting language based on Toolkit Command Language (TCL). EEM consists of Event Detectors, the Event Manager, and an Event Manager Policy Engine. The Policy Engine drives two types of policies that you can configure, Applet policies and Tcl policies. Thus, you can define policies to take specific actions when Cisco IOS recognizes certain events through the Event Detectors. The result is an extremely powerful and flexible set of tools to automate many network management tasks and direct the operation of Cisco IOS to increase availability, collect information, and notify external systems or personnel about critical events. For more information on EEM, refer to the references listed in the "Further Reading" section.

- **IP Source Tracker:** The IP Source Tracker feature allows you to trace back an attack to its network ingress point. In this way, you can block the attack at its entry point. Classification ACLs were commonly used in the past for this purpose. However, classification ACLs were very cumbersome because they needed to be applied hop by hop (and on every interface of each hop) along the upstream path from attack target to attack source. The classification ACLs were used to determine the ingress interface(s) at each hop. This information would then determine the next hop upstream router(s) toward the attack source(s). IP Source Tracker also works hop by hop but does not require classification ACLs to be applied on every interface of each hop along the upstream path. Instead, using IP Source Tracker, you specify the address of the attack target to be tracked using a single IOS command (**ip source-track**). The router then collects statistics of traffic flows destined to the tracked address. Similar to classification ACLs, this information enables you to determine the next-hop upstream router(s) and ultimately the attack ingress point(s). For more information on IP Source Tracker, refer to the reference listed in the "Further Reading" section. NetFlow also provides source traceback and is more widely deployed for this purpose. NetFlow is described a bit later in this list.

- **IP Traffic Export:** Similar to Switched Port Analyzer (SPAN) ports available with multilayer Ethernet switches such as the Catalyst product family, software-based IOS routers also allow for packet capture and export to traffic analysis systems. This is often useful for classifying an attack and determining the required mitigation action when TCP/IP header information is not sufficient. This also reduces the need to deploy traffic analysis systems inline and on the router itself—for example, enabling IOS Intrusion Prevention System (IPS) functions. Using IP Traffic Export, traffic can be selectively exported using classification ACLs and packet sampling, and exported directionally (ingress or egress traffic) on an interface. This feature is generally enabled in response to an attack to facilitate attack classification and mitigation, because its operation can be very data- and processor-intensive. You should measure any impact on router performance before deployment; otherwise, you risk collateral damage, which may have a greater impact than an attack itself. For more information on IP Traffic Export, refer to the references listed in the "Further Reading" section.

- **NetFlow:** NetFlow is a Cisco innovation that facilitates network and security monitoring, network planning, traffic analysis, and IP accounting. It is the primary technology for network anomaly detection technology and network accounting in the industry. It reports IP flow information similarly to a telephone bill, indicating who is talking to whom, over what interfaces, protocols, and ports, for how long, at what transmission rate, and so on. It is also widely available across IOS platforms, enabling each IOS device to act as a traffic analysis probe. Many hardware-based IOS platforms have dedicated hardware for NetFlow processing, minimizing the adverse impact, if any, on the router itself. The many benefits and broad software and hardware support have driven NetFlow's wide adoption. Although NetFlow was developed at Cisco, it is widely supported within the industry today by third-party routers, NetFlow collectors, and traffic analysis management systems. Support is also not limited to IP routers. Figure 6-4 illustrates a typical NetFlow network configuration that includes NetFlow-enabled IOS devices, NetFlow collectors, and traffic analysis systems.

Figure 6-4   *NetFlow Network Configuration Example*

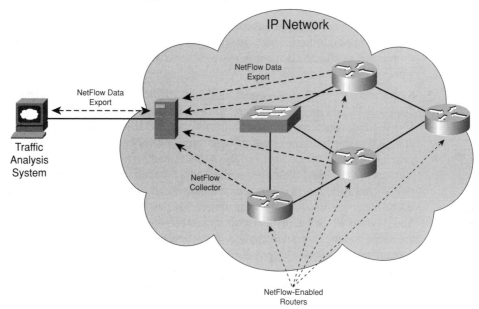

Network elements enabled for NetFlow will export (or push) IP flow information to their assigned NetFlow collectors as defined within the router configuration. The underlying protocol used to push flow records from NetFlow-enabled devices to NetFlow collectors is UDP. Flow records are exported when either the NetFlow cache is filled or flows expire. Flow information collected by the NetFlow collectors is then stored and, optionally, filtered and/or aggregated before being transferred to the traffic analysis system. There are a wide variety of NetFlow features, configuration options, and export formats. For more information on NetFlow, refer to the references listed in the "Further Reading" section.

- **NTP:** NTP is very effective and widely deployed for providing accurate timing that allows off-box systems to correlate network events, including security incidents. NTP provides a clock source and synchronized timekeeping between distributed time servers and network elements. Accurate timekeeping is critically important for correlating events (including security incidents) during network troubleshooting and for quantifying network performance (including packet delay and jitter). NTP is also widely available within IOS and supports MD5 authentication of NTP protocol packets.

- **SNMP:** As described in the "SNMP Security" section above, SNMP facilitates the remote administration of network devices. Using SNMP, you can collect and monitor a wide variety of device and network statistics, including but not limited to CPU load, memory utilization, link usage, control protocol activity, packet counters, and so on. Managed objects of the SNMP agent can be polled at regular intervals by the SNMP manager. Conversely, SNMP agents can also transmit unsolicited alarm messages such as trap or inform messages based on specific network events. SNMP is a rather simple way to effectively monitor network activity. SNMP is also widely available within IOS.

- **Syslog:** System logging messages, similar to SNMP traps (or informs), serve as unsolicited alarm messages and provide an audit trail of network activity. Unlike SNMP traps, which are formally defined within an MIB used between agent and manager, syslog messages are general purpose and very flexible. Syslog messages are generally provided for a wide variety of device and network events. In addition, IOS features such as EEM (described earlier in this list) allow you to define your own, customized syslog messages based on user-defined events that may be of particular interest to you, instead of relying on the general-purpose, predefined syslog messages. You can also set the facility and severity level for syslog messages, which determines the scope and logging detail applied. These levels can significantly increase or limit the number of messages logged. Syslog messages can be logged to a remote server by using the **logging host** command or to the local system buffer by using the **logging buffered** command. Logging syslog messages through a centralized syslog server allows messages to be stored and archived and facilitates the correlation of network-wide events. To include the date and time of the error or event within the syslog message, enable the **service timestamps log datetime msec localtime** command in global configuration mode. Use the **show logging** command to display the logging configuration and any buffered messages (if configured).

- **Remote Network Monitoring (RMON):** RMON is an IETF industry standard that defines a set of statistics and functions that can be exchanged between RMON-compliant console managers and network probes. As such, RMON provides sophisticated network performance reporting. IOS devices may be configured to operate as RMON probes at the IOS process level or using dedicated hardware for RMON processing with the Cisco Network Analysis Modules (NAM). The Cisco NAMs not only provide the ability to analyze packets and network performance, but also the ability to analyze this information from within the IOS device itself using a web browser. Although RMON is not as prevalent as SNMP and NetFlow, it remains an effective tool for gathering detailed analysis of network performance. For more information on RMON and the Cisco NAMs, refer to the references listed in the "Further Reading" section.

For more information on network telemetry and security, refer to the associated references listed in the "Further Reading" section.

Management VPN for MPLS VPNs

SPs that offer MPLS VPN services have in-band IP management connectivity to PE and core P routers defined within the MPLS VPN architecture through conventional IP routing using the global routing table, as illustrated in Figure 6-5.

Figure 6-5   *MPLS VPN Architecture*

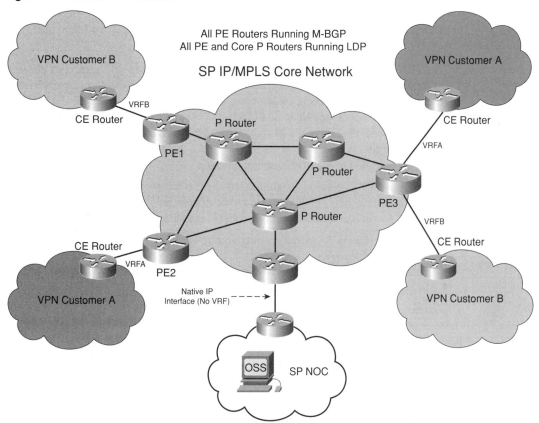

Given the IP addressing and routing separation provided by MPLS VPNs, the CE router is reachable only from within its assigned VPN. Once a CE is in an MPLS VPN, it is no longer accessible by means of conventional global IPv4 routing and, consequently, the SP loses in-band reachability to MPLS VPN-based CE routers. SPs can alternatively use OOB management access for management connectivity to CE routers; however, OOB management networks increase network complexity and costs, given a secondary WAN connection is required for OOB connectivity. Consequently, in-band management access is often preferred for large-scale managed CE router services. Note that if CE routers are not managed by the SP (otherwise referred to as *unmanaged*), then management connectivity is not necessary for the SP. Such unmanaged routers are managed by the VPN customers themselves, who will, by default, have in-band IP management connectivity given that they are provisioned within the VPN itself. Chapter 7 reviews in detail how to secure the MPLS VPN services plane. The remainder of this section reviews how an SP can use a dedicated *Management VPN* for the management of all managed CE routers participating within an MPLS VPN, irrespective of the assigned customer VPN.

The Management VPN (also referred to as the *gray VPN*) functions in the following manner:

- All VPN-based managed CE routers participate in their assigned (intranet) VPN and in the separate, SP-owned Management VPN. In one sense, this Management VPN can be thought of as a specialized version of an extranet that provides IP reachability to and from an SP-owned Management PE (MPE) and Management CE (MCE). The MPE represents the hub of the Management VPN and provides network connectivity between the SP network operations center (NOC) and the Management VPN. The SP NOC is connected to the MPE through the MCE.

- A customer VPN export map configured on the PEs allows only the routes to managed CE routers (for example, PE-CE links) to be distributed into the Management VPN; other VPN customer routes are not distributed into the Management VPN.

- Managed CE routers act as spokes only within the Management VPN regardless of which role the CE router has within its own customer VPN. Therefore, there is no IP reachability between CE routers within the Management VPN.

As a result, the Management VPN enables IP reachability in-band between the SP NOC and VPN-based CE routers for management and monitoring functions. The Management VPN is provisioned through the deployment of a parallel network link between the MPE and MCE, as illustrated in Figure 6-6.

The MPE assigns this secondary network link to the Management VPN (or VRF). The original network link between the MPE and MCE remains a native IP interface with no associated MPLS VPN (or VRF). The two network links between the MPE and MCE may be deployed as two distinct physical links or as two distinct logical interfaces (for example, VLANs, FR DLCIs, or ATM VCs) across a shared physical link. The only requirement is that they be two distinct IP subnets and that on the MPE side, one be assigned to the Management VPN and the other be routable via the global IP routing table (in other words, no VPN/VRF assignment). In this way, the SP NOC has in-band IP management connectivity both to PE and core (P) routers through the native IP interface and to the managed CE routers through the Management VPN interface. Note that the PE routers are reachable through either of the two MPE-MCE network links.

Figure 6-6   *Management VPN Architecture*

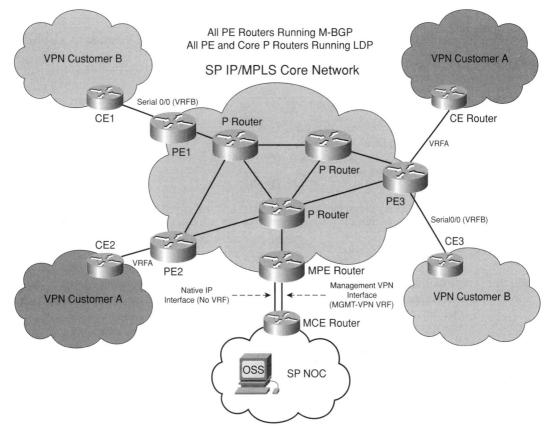

Example 6-13 illustrates how MPE, PE1, and PE3 from Figure 6-6 are configured to provide intranet VPN connectivity between Customer B managed CE routers and management connectivity to the SP NOC through the Management VPN. VPN managed routers CE1 and CE3 have IP connectivity to one another only through the intranet VPN (VRFB) and not through the Management VPN. At first glance, you might consider connectivity to the Management VPN extranet to be a security risk because it provides external connectivity to your VPN. However, this risk is minimized by the fact that external connectivity is provided only to the SP NOC that provides the MPLS VPN service. Further, because the SP owns the Management VPN, its trust level is the same as the underlying MPLS VPN service. Lack of connectivity between VPN sites of differing VPNs through the Management VPN is also assured given the hub-and-spoke topology of the Management VPN. Finally, only the PE-CE links are distributed into the Management VPN and, hence, only traffic sourced from these PE-CE link addresses is allowed access into the SP NOC.

Example 6-13 *Management VPN Sample Configurations*

```
! MPE router Management VPN related configuration
!
! The Management VPN uses route-target 65001:20 as a hub and 65001:30 as a spoke.
! Managed CPE routers are considered spokes.
ip vrf MGMT-VPN
 rd 65001:20
 route-target export 65001:20
 route-target import 65001:20
 route-target import 65001:30
!
interface Serial0/0
 description MPE-MCE link in MGMT-VPN VRF routing table
 ip vrf forwarding MGMT-VPN
 ip address 192.168.253.2 255.255.255.252
!
! The routing protocol for MPE-MCE Management VPN link is eBGP.
! M-iBGP is used for distribution of MPLS VPN prefixes between PEs and the MPE.
router bgp 65001
 bgp router-id 192.168.1.6
 neighbor 192.168.1.2 remote-as 65001
 neighbor 192.168.1.2 update-source Loopback0
 !
 address-family vpnv4
 neighbor 192.168.1.2 activate
 neighbor 192.168.1.2 send-community both
 exit-address-family
 !
 address-family ipv4 vrf MGMT-VPN
 neighbor 192.168.253.1 remote-as 65010
 neighbor 192.168.253.1 update-source Serial0/0
 neighbor 192.168.253.1 activate
 no synchronization
 exit-address-family
!
!
! PE1 router Management VPN related configuration
!
! The Customer B VPN uses route-target 65001:10 for any-to-any connectivity
! within the Customer B VPN. The Customer B VPN imports SP NOC prefix using
! route-target 65001:20. The mgmtvpn-filter export filter advertises only the
! PE-CE network prefix to the SP NOC.
ip vrf VRFB
 rd 65001:10
 export map mgmtvpn-filter
 route-target export 65001:10
 route-target import 65001:10
 route-target import 65001:20
!
interface Serial0/0
 description PE-CE link in Customer B VPN (VRFB) routing table
 ip vrf forwarding VRFB
 ip address 209.165.202.145 255.255.255.252
```

Example 6-13 *Management VPN Sample Configurations (Continued)*

```
!
! The routing protocol for PE-CE Customer B VPN link is eBGP.
! M-iBGP is used for distribution of MPLS VPN prefixes between PEs and the MPE.
router bgp 65001
 bgp router-id 192.168.1.3
 neighbor 192.168.1.2 remote-as 65001
 neighbor 192.168.1.2 update-source Loopback0
 !
 address-family vpnv4
 neighbor 192.168.1.2 activate
 neighbor 192.168.1.2 send-community both
 exit-address-family
 !
 address-family ipv4 vrf VRFB
 redistribute connected
 neighbor 209.165.202.146 remote-as 65004
 neighbor 209.165.202.146 update-source Serial0/0
 neighbor 209.165.202.146 activate
 no synchronization
 exit-address-family
 !
! Permit the PE-CE link
access-list 90 permit 209.165.202.144 0.0.0.3
 !
! Tag the PE-CE link as both a Customer B VPN prefix and a SP NOC spoke prefix
route-map mgmtvpn-filter permit 10
 match ip address 90
 set extcommunity rt  65001:10 65001:30
 !
! PE3 router Management VPN related configuration
 !
! The Customer B VPN uses route-target 65001:10 for any-to-any connectivity
! within the Customer B VPN. The Customer B VPN imports SP NOC prefix using
! route-target 65001:20. The mgmtvpn-filter export filter advertises only the
! PE-CE network prefix to the SP NOC.
ip vrf VRFB
 rd 65001:10
 export map mgmtvpn-filter
 route-target export 65001:10
 route-target import 65001:10
 route-target import 65001:20
 !
interface Serial0/0
 description PE-CE link in Customer B VPN (VRF) routing table
 ip vrf forwarding VRFB
 ip address 209.165.200.241 255.255.255.252
 !
! The routing protocol for PE-CE Customer B VPN link is eBGP.
! M-iBGP is used for distribution of MPLS VPN prefixes between PEs and the MPE.
router bgp 65001
 bgp router-id 192.168.1.1
```

continues

Example 6-13 *Management VPN Sample Configurations (Continued)*

```
 neighbor 192.168.1.2 remote-as 65001
 neighbor 192.168.1.2 update-source Loopback0
!
 address-family vpnv4
 neighbor 192.168.1.2 activate
 neighbor 192.168.1.2 send-community both
 exit-address-family
 !
 address-family ipv4 vrf VRFB
 redistribute connected
 neighbor 209.165.200.242 remote-as 65003
 neighbor 209.165.200.242 update-source Serial0/0
 neighbor 209.165.200.242 activate
 no synchronization
 exit-address-family
!
! Permit the PE-CE link
access-list 90 permit 209.165.200.240 0.0.0.3
 !
! Tag the PE-CE link as both a Customer B VPN prefix and a SP NOC spoke prefix
route-map mgmtvpn-filter permit 10
 match ip address 90
 set extcommunity rt  65001:10 65001:30
!
```

Only the PE routers (including the Management PE) are VRF-aware, as required, to maintain addressing and routing separation between different VPNs and from the global IP routing table. Although the SP can use the native IP interface between the MPE and MCE routers to manage the PE routers, it is not uncommon for SPs to manage MPLS VPN services separately from native IP services. This is illustrated in Figure 6-7, whereby NOC1 manages the PE and core (P) routers, with the exception of MPLS VPN services.

NOC1 management connectivity is in-band through the native IP interface. NOC2 is then exclusively responsible for management of MPLS VPN services on PE routers, and although management connectivity is also in-band, it is provided through the Management VPN, which enables IP reachability to all PE routers and managed CE routers.

Use of a VPN-specific management platform requires that management functions on PE routers be VRF-aware. This includes, for example, forwarding SNMP traps, syslog messages, and other management plane functions to management hosts within the Management VRF. Otherwise, management through the Management VPN would be limited and ineffective. IOS provides support for VRF-aware management plane functions, including but not limited to VRF-aware syslog, VRF-aware SNMP, VRF-aware AAA, VRF-aware VTY ACLs, VRF-aware DNS name resolution, VRF-aware NetFlow data export, and so on.

Figure 6-7   *MPLS VPN-Specific Management Platform*

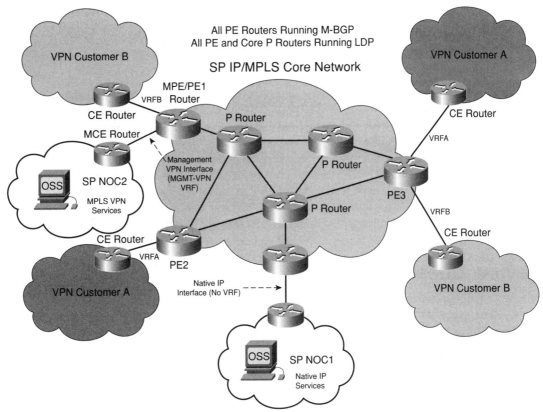

For more information on these capabilities and the Management VPN, refer to the *IOS Configuration Guides* and *Command References* available on Cisco.com. MPLS-enabled routers, including PE and core (P) routers, may also leverage MPLS OAM for detection of MPLS forwarding plane failures within the network. MPLS OAM makes use of MPLS echo requests (also referred to as *MPLS LSP pings*), which are assigned the destination UDP port of 3503 by IANA. Consequently, within your infrastructure ACL, IP rACL, and CoPP policies, you should filter packets from unauthorized sources that are destined to UDP port 3503. For more information on MPLS LSP ping, refer to RFC 4379 and to the references in the "Further Reading" section.

Summary

This chapter reviewed a wide array of techniques available to increase an IP router's resistance to security attacks within the IP management plane, including unauthorized access. If an attacker gains unauthorized access, they are able to launch a wide variety of attacks, as described in Chapter 2, that can affect all of the IP traffic planes and the wider IP network. Consequently, similar to the IP control plane, protecting the management plane is also critical given that it is used to configure and monitor all of the other IP traffic planes. Management plane security techniques were also reviewed in the context of MPLS VPNs. Network telemetry tools were also briefly reviewed because of the benefit they provide for detection and classification of security events.

This chapter also completes the review of the many security techniques available to protect the IP network traffic planes. The optimal techniques that provide an effective security solution will vary by organization and depend on network topology, product mix, traffic behavior, operational complexity, and organizational mission. The defense in depth and breadth strategies discussed in Chapter 3 can be helpful in understanding the interactions between various IP traffic plane security techniques and in optimizing the selection of IP network traffic plane protection measures. Part III of this book reviews how the interactions of different IP data, control, management, and services plane techniques when deployed in combination provide an effective security strategy for both enterprise and SP IP networks.

Review Questions

1 Describe the two primary reasons why out-of-band management networks are deployed.

2 How are management Ethernet interfaces different from in-band Ethernet interfaces?

3 Why should CEF not be enabled on a management Ethernet port dedicated for out-of-band management?

4 What should you do to mitigate the risk of reconnaissance attacks if CDP is required by your network management applications?

5 Which system banner does not apply to reverse Telnet sessions?

6 List the primary differences, from a security perspective, between SNMPv1, SNMPv2c, and SNMPv3.

7 What is the security advantage of SSH versus Telnet?

8 Identify the two primary management plane behavioral changes when enabling Management Plane Protection.

9 What are the primary benefits of network telemetry in the context of security?

10 How does the Management VPN prevent IP connectivity between managed CE routers associated with different MPLS VPNs?

Further Reading

Acheson, S. "Security for the Enterprise Network Engineer." (TECSEC-2002.) Cisco Networkers 2006. Las Vegas. June 2006.

Carrel, D., and L. Grant. "The TACACS+ Protocol." draft-grant-tacacs-00.txt. Cisco, Oct. 1996. http://www.cisco.com/warp/public/459/tac-rfc.1.76.txt.

Dobbins, R. "Detection and Classification of Network Traffic." (SEC-2104.) Networkers 2006. Las Vegas. June 2006.

Dobbins, R. "Listening to the Network: Network Telemetry and Security." (SEC-2102.) Networkers 2005. Las Vegas. June 2005.

Gudurvalmiki, S. "Understanding SNMP and MIBs." (NMS-2101.) Networkers 2006. Las Vegas. June 2006.

Stallings, W. "Security Comes to SNMP: The New SNMPv3 Proposed Internet Standards." *The Internet Protocol Journal*, vol. 1, no. 3 (Dec. 1998). http://www.cisco.com/web/about/ac123/ac147/archived_issues/ipj_1-3/snmpv3.html.

"Authentication, Authorization and Accounting (AAA): Part 1." Cisco Documentation. http://www.cisco.com/univercd/cc/td/doc/product/software/ios124/124cg/hsec_c/part05/index.htm.

"AutoSecure." *Cisco IOS Software Releases 12.2 SB Feature Guide.* http://www.cisco.com/en/US/products/ps6566/products_feature_guide09186a0080525232.html.

"BGP Policy Accounting." *Cisco IOS IP Routing Protocols Configuration Guide, Release 12.4.* http://www.cisco.com/en/US/products/ps6350/products_configuration_guide_chapter09186a008045561c.html#wp1036056.

"Cisco AAA Case Study Overview." *Cisco AAA Implementation Case Study.* http://www.cisco.com/en/US/products/hw/univgate/ps501/products_case_study_chapter09186a00800ee06a.html.

"Cisco AutoSecure White Paper." Cisco white paper. http://www.cisco.com/en/US/products/ps6642/products_white_paper09186a00801dbf61.shtml.

"Cisco IOS Firewall Overview." *Cisco IOS Security Configuration Guide, Release 12.4.* http://cisco.com/en/US/products/ps6350/products_configuration_guide_chapter09186a0080455ae3.html.

"Cisco IOS Login Enhancements (Login Block)." Cisco Documentation. http://www.cisco.com/univercd/cc/td/doc/product/software/ios124/124cg/hsec_c/part30/h_login.htm.

"Cisco IOS NetFlow." Cisco Documentation. http://www.cisco.com/en/US/products/ps6601/products_ios_protocol_group_home.html.

"Cisco Network Analysis Module Software." Cisco Documentation. http://www.cisco.com/en/US/products/sw/cscowork/ps5401/index.html.

"Cisco Secure Access Control Server 4.1 Overview." *User Guide for Cisco Secure Access Control Server 4.1.* http://www.cisco.com/en/US/docs/net_mgmt/ cisco_secure_access_control_server_for_windows/4.1/user/Overvw.html.

"Configuring RMON Support." *Cisco IOS Network Management Configuration Guide, Release 12.4T.* http://www.cisco.com/en/US/products/ps6441/ products_configuration_guide_chapter09186a008030c776.html.

"Configuring Security with Passwords, Privilege Levels, and Login Usernames for CLI Sessions on Networking Devices." Cisco Documentation. http://www.cisco.com/ univercd/cc/td/doc/product/software/ios124/124cg/hsec_c/part30/05ch/secpriv.htm.

"Embedded Event Manager Overview." *Cisco IOS Network Management Configuration Guide, Release 12.4T.* http://cisco.com/en/US/products/ps6441/ products_configuration_guide_chapter09186a00807c676c.html.

"HTTP Server – Enabling of Applications." *Cisco IOS Network Management Configuration Guide, Release 12.4T.* http://www.cisco.com/en/US/products/ps6441/ products_configuration_guide_chapter09186a0080455929.html.

"HTTPS – HTTP Server and Client with SSL 3.0." *Cisco IOS Software Releases 12.2T Feature Guide.* http://www.cisco.com/en/US/products/sw/iosswrel/ps1839/ products_feature_guide09186a008015a4c6.html.

"IOS Privilege Levels Cannot See Complete Running Configuration." (Doc. ID: 23383.) Cisco Tech Note. http://www.cisco.com/en/US/tech/tk59/ technologies_tech_note09186a00800949d5.shtml.

"IP Source Tracker." *Cisco IOS Software Releases 12.0S Feature Guide.* http://www.cisco.com/en/US/products/sw/iosswrel/ps1829/ products_feature_guide09186a00800e9d38.html.

"IP Traffic Export." *Cisco IOS Security Configuration Guide, Release 12.4.* http://www.cisco.com/en/US/products/ps6350/ products_configuration_guide_chapter09186a0080455b94.html.

"Management Plane Protection." *Cisco IOS Software Releases 12.4T Feature Guide.* http://www.cisco.com/en/US/products/ps6441/ products_feature_guide09186a0080617022.html.

"MPLS LSP Ping/Traceroute for LDP/TE, and LSP Ping for VCCV." *Cisco IOS Software Releases 12.4T Feature Guide.* http://www.cisco.com/en/US/products/ ps6441/products_feature_guide09186a0080618611.html.

"Remote Monitoring." Cisco Documentation. http://www.cisco.com/univercd/cc/td/ doc/cisintwk/ito_doc/rmon.htm.

"Secure Copy." *Cisco IOS Software Releases 12.2T Feature Guide.*
http://www.cisco.com/en/US/products/sw/iosswrel/ps1839/
products_feature_guide09186a0080087b18.html.

"Security Server Protocols: Part 2." Cisco Documentation. http://www.cisco.com/
univercd/cc/td/doc/product/software/ios124/124cg/hsec_c/part10/index.htm.

"SNMPv3." *Cisco IOS Software Releases 12.0T Feature Guide.*
http://www.cisco.com/en/US/products/sw/iosswrel/ps1830/
products_feature_guide09186a00800878fa.html.

"TCP and UDP Small Servers." Cisco Documentation.
http://www.cisco.com/warp/public/66/23.html.

"Telnet, Console and AUX Port Passwords on Cisco Routers Configuration Example."
(Doc. ID: 45843.) Cisco Configuration Example. http://www.cisco.com/en/US/
products/sw/iosswrel/ps1818/products_configuration_
example09186a0080204528.shtml.

In this chapter, you learn about the following:

- How services plane traffic differs from data, control, and management plane traffic in terms of packet processing and forwarding

- How services plane traffic can be protected by direct packet classification and policy enforcement mechanisms

- How additional services plane security techniques that use indirect mechanisms can be used to protect signaling and other protocol-specific service support components

CHAPTER 7

IP Services Plane Security

Chapter 1, "Internet Protocol Operations Fundamentals," reviewed the IP traffic planes and provided an introductory explanation of how these traffic planes were processed by various hardware and software architectures. As you learned, the services plane and data plane are both defined as carrying user traffic—that is, traffic that is sourced by and destined to end stations, servers, and other nonrouting infrastructure devices. What distinguishes services plane traffic from data plane traffic is the way in which routers and other network devices must handle these packets.

For example, data plane traffic typically receives very basic processing that mainly involves best-effort, destination-based forwarding. Services plane traffic, on the other hand, typically requires additional, specialized processing above and beyond basic forwarding. In addition, it often also requires end-to-end handling across the network. Examples of services plane traffic include VPN tunneling (MPLS, IPsec, SSL, GRE, and so on), private-to-public translation (IPv6-to-IPv4, NAT, firewall, and IDS/IPS), QoS, voice and video services, and many others.

Services Plane Overview

The services plane refers to user traffic that requires specialized packet handling by network elements above and beyond the standard forwarding logic that is typically applied. That is, services plane traffic includes customer traffic that would normally be part of the data plane and that would normally appear as *transit* traffic to the routers without specialized handling in the normal forwarding path. However, because specialized services are applied, routers and other forwarding devices must treat these packets in a more complex manner. In some cases, packets must be punted to the slow path for CPU handling. In other cases, dedicated hardware may be required to handle services plane traffic. For example, IPsec and SSL VPNs require high-speed encryption and decryption services, which are often performed in dedicated hardware optimized for this purpose. This is just one example of how services plane traffic differs from data plane traffic. Others are covered in this chapter.

Many aspects of the services plane are heavily dependent upon unique factors such as hardware and software performance, service functions applied, and network architecture and topology. This limits the ability to provide a full range of specific security recommendations. As such, this chapter is organized in a manner that is somewhat different from Chapters 4, 5, and 6, in which you learned about specific mechanisms dedicated exclusively to the protection of their respective IP traffic plane. What you will find for the services plane is that although there are some specific mechanisms designed to protect a specific service, it is not exclusively the case that just these specific protection mechanisms are used. Instead, protection mechanisms used in securing the data plane and control plane must also be configured to provide protection for the services plane functions.

To illustrate how services plane traffic is handled in this regard, this chapter takes a detailed look at several example services plane applications and the special requirements that must be employed to secure these services. From these examples, you will see that several overarching and consistent themes are evident that lead to a set of general processes that you can use to assess and secure other services that you may find in your unique environment. In preview, these overarching themes for services plane traffic include the following:

- The IP services plane often requires specialized packet handling to implement the defined service. For example, the application of QoS markings and policing may require processing support that cannot be provided by hardware within the CEF fast path and results in forwarding performance impacts. (This is very platform dependent.) Whenever performance impacts occur, this should be an indication that protections must be deployed.

- The IP services plane often requires the use of service-specific control plane mechanisms to support the underlying service. For example, IPsec uses the IKE protocol suite for control plane support. Whenever control planes are created and maintained, this should be an indication that protections must be deployed.

- The IP services plane often involves the creation and management of *state* to establish and maintain the defined service. For example, firewalls create and manage state for TCP sessions passing through them. The creation and management of state always enables attack vectors that would not otherwise exist. Whenever state creation and management is required, this should be an indication that protections must be deployed.

IP services are deployed to provide specialized treatment of user packets in some way. When a service is deployed, it requires capital and operational expenses to roll out the service. Because of this, the service is built and deployed to support a defined capacity within well-defined service-level agreements (SLA). As this is the case, there are several key reasons why the IP services plane must be protected and several goals for selecting appropriate protection mechanisms. These include the following:

- Because each deployed service has finite resources to draw upon, you must ensure the integrity of the services plane such that only legitimate traffic is allowed to take advantage of a specific service type. Services plane traffic generates higher revenues than non-services traffic (as in the case of SPs) or costs more money to deploy (as in the case of enterprises). If unauthorized traffic can use these finite resources, either maliciously or unintentionally, then these resources may not be available for the intended legitimate traffic. This leads to lost revenues or the need to spend additional capital to increase capacity unnecessarily. Thus, the protection requirements here are to permit only authorized traffic to use the service and deny unauthorized traffic from using the service.

- Because services plane traffic often consumes more general-purpose shared resources (memory, CPU interrupt cycles, and so on) that are required to support all traffic planes, you must ensure both that normal data plane traffic does not consume resources to the point where the deployed services plane lacks sufficient resources to function properly, and that when multiple services are deployed, one service type does not impact any other service type. Sufficient network resources must be available during all operating conditions—normal loads, flash-crowd conditions, failover conditions, and so on—so that higher-priority services can receive proper handling, as required. In some cases, this may even be done at the expense of lower-priority traffic. Thus, the requirements here are to protect the network and router resources to support services, but also to prevent services or non-services traffic from jeopardizing the entire network infrastructure.

NOTE	It is important to distinguish between a *secure service* and *securing a service*. The former is something provided by MPLS or IPsec, for example, where aspects of separation, confidentiality (encryption), authentication, and data integrity are applied to specific traffic that belongs to the service. Different to this is securing a service, which is described in this chapter. This includes the things done and steps taken to prevent unauthorized traffic from using a service (theft), and to prevent the service from being rendered unavailable (DoS) to legitimate traffic. IPsec and MPLS are both examples of secure services. However, both of these secure services must themselves be secured for the reasons mentioned in the preceding list.

Finally, it is worth noting that this chapter is not intended to be a primer on the deployment of various services. In most cases, services deployment strategies and options involve complexities that in and of themselves are often the subject of entire books. Instead, this chapter provides, through examples, an illustration of how services operate within the network environment and a method by which to secure them. To accomplish this, three services are used as illustrations: QoS, MPLS VPNs, and IPsec VPNs. Important techniques are identified here, and pointers to additional references are provided for completeness.

As outlined in Chapter 3, "IP Network Traffic Plane Security Concepts," no single technology (or technique) makes an effective security solution. In addition, not every technology is appropriate in every case, as some may only increase complexity and may actually detract from overall network security. Developing a defense in depth and breadth strategy provides an effective approach for deploying complementary techniques to mitigate the risk of security attacks when appropriate security layers are considered. The optimal techniques will vary by organization and depend on network topology, product mix, traffic behavior, operational complexity, and service requirements. The examples in this chapter illustrate the points outlined in this section and give you the background necessary to evaluate these same or any other services plane applications deployed in your network.

Quality of Service

The term quality of service (QoS) covers a wide range of mechanisms that are applied at the network edge and sometimes within the core to provide *differentiated* and *predictable* packet experiences through the network for a variety of reasons. QoS is often described as providing priority processing and access through a congested IP core network. For most modern networks, the core is typically *not* where congestion occurs, but rather congestion events more commonly happen at the edge. Typical service provider (SP) core networks today are built on OC192 backbones (10 Gbps), and many are scaling to OC768 (40 Gbps) core designs. The edge is typically the more interesting place when considering QoS services.

Although QoS can be applied as a service in and of itself, it is not often deployed in this manner. QoS is most frequently combined with other service offerings such as VPNs (MPLS and IPsec) to prioritize the usage of limited resources (for example, network bandwidth or encryption capacity) and to minimize delay and jitter for voice, video, and other delay-sensitive traffic. For example, a corporation may prioritize voice traffic over other traffic types across its MPLS VPN to prevent lower-priority traffic from disrupting delay sensitive VoIP traffic. In this case, SPs must deploy appropriate QoS mechanisms *within* the MPLS VPN network to give priority and provide bandwidth guarantees to voice traffic. In Chapter 4, "Data Plane Security," and Chapter 5, "Control Plane Security," you already learned about several other practical applications for QoS as data plane and control plane enforcement techniques.

To deploy QoS, you must be capable of identifying the traffic type(s) that you want prioritized, and be willing to sacrifice some traffic at the expense of the higher-priority traffic under congestion conditions. Currently, the scope of this QoS control is limited to a single administrative domain. An enterprise, for example, can control what happens within its network, but it cannot control, by itself, what happens to its traffic as it traverses external networks. In the case of an MPLS VPN, the SP network for all intents becomes an extension of the enterprise network. But since it is administratively part of the SPs domain, SLAs are often negotiated between enterprises and SP to formally define the level of service that will be delivered.

Two distinct IP QoS models are defined here: *Integrated Services* and *Differentiated Services*. These two models augment the traditional IP best-effort service model. Integrated Services (IntServ), defined in RFC 1633, is a dynamic resource reservation model based upon RSVP (RFC 2205) signaling. Differentiated Services (DiffServ), defined in RFC 2475, removes the per-flow reservations associated with RSVP and instead uses a simplified (*passive*) signaling mechanism of classifying individual packets based on a well-defined packet classifier (for example, IP precedence). Only the DiffServ QoS model (using IP precedence) is discussed here.

NOTE   RSVP is essentially the control plane for the IntServ QoS model. RSVP-based signaling uses the ROUTER-ALERT IPv4 header option to signal end-to-end QoS requirements along a path. A detailed discussion of the RSVP-based QoS model is not discussed here and is considered outside the scope of this book. However, issues and protection mechanisms related to packets with IPv4 header options have been discussed at length in previous chapters. In addition, routing protocol and other control plane protections previously described also apply to RSVP. Without protections, attacks on the RSVP signaling system could result in QoS routing malfunctions, interference of resource reservation, or even failure of QoS provisioning.

Regardless of the model implementation, without suitable protections, QoS is vulnerable to both theft of service and denial of service, which inhibits the delivery of both high- and low-priority services as well as network availability as described in Chapter 4.

This chapter is not intended to be a primer on QoS methods, deployments, and mechanisms, but rather is intended to briefly introduce the methods used to protect a QoS service. To accomplish this, a brief overview is provided that describes the important mechanisms used by the DiffServ QoS model to implement its many functions. In this way, it will become evident that design and implementation considerations must be made when deploying QoS services. Additional details on QoS implementations may be found in the Cisco Press book *QoS for IP/MPLS Networks* (see the "Further Reading" section), which covers QoS methods and deployment topics in thorough detail.

QoS Mechanisms

Cisco IOS uses an idealized QoS configuration model to provide consistent behavior across platforms. Even though the underlying hardware and software may differ, the end result is intended to be identical, regardless of which device is configured. Understanding exactly how QoS is implemented and how QoS policies are translated within the router will help you understand how to protect this service.

In Cisco IOS, QoS is implemented through the Modular Quality of Service CLI (MQC) command set. You first learned about MQC in Chapters 4 and 5, because it also is the basis for implementing several data and control plane security techniques. MQC itself is discussed in more detail later in this section to help you understand how to secure a QoS implementation. Prior to reviewing MQC, however, some of the basic principles of QoS must be described.

There are four main functional components required for a QoS implementation: classification, marking, policing, and queuing. Referring to Figure 7-1, which you were first introduced to in Chapter 3, you can see that the first three of these four QoS mechanisms apply to ingress and egress processing, but queuing applies only to the egress path. (Note that the Cisco 12000 family is one exception in that it implements ingress queuing in addition to egress queuing.) Functionally, each component performs its job based on seeing an individual packet, comparing it to a policy, and taking some action. Packet statistics (*counters*) are maintained, primarily so that *rate* values can be calculated, and this represents the only *state* involved in the QoS process. Recognizing where state is required and maintained always provides clues as to where protection is required for any service. The concept of state is most often associated with devices like stateful firewalls, which maintain significantly more state, such as per-flow inter-packet relationships for TCP sessions. In the case of QoS, packet counters are the only state maintained. But as you will see, because QoS uses these counters to compute *rates* that it uses as the basis for its actions, protecting the manipulation of these counters is one of the most important goals in protecting the QoS service.

Figure 7-1 *Cisco IOS Feature Order of Operations*

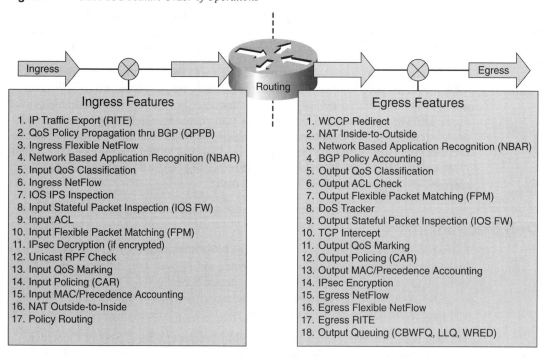

Ingress | Routing | Egress

Ingress Features

1. IP Traffic Export (RITE)
2. QoS Policy Propagation thru BGP (QPPB)
3. Ingress Flexible NetFlow
4. Network Based Application Recognition (NBAR)
5. Input QoS Classification
6. Ingress NetFlow
7. IOS IPS Inspection
8. Input Stateful Packet Inspection (IOS FW)
9. Input ACL
10. Input Flexible Packet Matching (FPM)
11. IPsec Decryption (if encrypted)
12. Unicast RPF Check
13. Input QoS Marking
14. Input Policing (CAR)
15. Input MAC/Precedence Accounting
16. NAT Outside-to-Inside
17. Policy Routing

Egress Features

1. WCCP Redirect
2. NAT Inside-to-Outside
3. Network Based Application Recognition (NBAR)
4. BGP Policy Accounting
5. Output QoS Classification
6. Output ACL Check
7. Output Flexible Packet Matching (FPM)
8. DoS Tracker
9. Output Stateful Packet Inspection (IOS FW)
10. TCP Intercept
11. Output QoS Marking
12. Output Policing (CAR)
13. Output MAC/Precedence Accounting
14. IPsec Encryption
15. Egress NetFlow
16. Egress Flexible NetFlow
17. Egress RITE
18. Output Queuing (CBWFQ, LLQ, WRED)

Within QoS, even though each of the four components provides its own functionality, there exists an order to their operation and some interdependency from one component to the next. Not every component is required to be deployed, but if they are not all deployed, certain trusts and assumptions must be made about the traffic. These trust relationships and interdependencies are the main focus for securing QoS services. Let's review each of the four components.

Classification

Classification is the first step in the QoS process and involves identifying packets and comparing each against the configured DiffServ QoS policies to find matches. There is an implied assumption, of course, that some engineering effort has occurred to define policies. The process of classification affects every other step in the QoS process and thus is critical for ensuring correct QoS performance. Classification can be based on any number of items within each packet, as described in Chapter 4, such as source and destination IP address, protocol type and port, IP header precedence/DSCP setting, ingress interface, or even payload contents. The desired outcome of the packet classification process is to end up associating *every* packet with a particular class of service based on configured explicit or implicit policies that define the packet match criteria.

It is important to note that the classification process only accounts for packets. Within Cisco IOS, counters associated with a defined class of service are incremented as packets that match the traffic class are seen. Cisco IOS also maintains an *internal* header associated with every packet that is forwarded by the router to keep track of applied features and helps accelerate the processing speed. This internal header is also adjusted to reflect the outcome of the classification process. (As noted in Figure 7-1, the classification process occurs at Step 5, whereas the application of the desired service does not occur until Step 14.)

From a services plane security perspective, you should recognize that *all* packets must be classified as belonging to *some* group. That is, no packet should be left unclassified. To facilitate this task, there is a simple mechanism within IOS MQC that allows everything that has not been classified to end up in a catch-all *default* class that has its own associated policy (that is, **class-default**).

Note that when QoS is combined with other services such as MPLS or IPsec VPNs, IOS provides a classification mechanism that allows traffic to be either *pre-* or *post*-classified with respect to encapsulation within or de-encapsulation from the tunnel. This enables several different versions of QoS transparency, as described in Chapter 4. These are defined within the RFC 3270 *MPLS Diffserv Tunneling* specification.

Marking

Once classification has identified particular packets, the optional second step of marking can be taken for each packet. Although the classification process sets certain IOS *internal* flags and increments counters, the marking process (ingress Step 13 or egress Step 11 in Figure 7-1) actually modifies each packet IP header itself in the specified manner. This optional process may be critical for the implementation of an end-to-end QoS policy, network wide. For example, the marking process can set the precedence or DSCP field within the IP header to a particular value. Packets might enter the router with one marking but exit with a different marking based upon the classification and marking. This process is often referred to as packet *recoloring*, as described in Chapter 4. Other marking options are possible, including manipulations of various Layer 2 and MPLS header fields.

From a services plane security perspective, marking can be critical for enforcing policies elsewhere in the network. Whereas the classification process sets the packet's internal header (whose scope is effective only within the router), marking modifies the real packet header, which allows for actions to be taken downstream. As an example, an SP may mark (recolor) all packets ingressing its network from untrusted domains in one particular way, and mark its own internal (trusted) traffic in a different way. This gives the SP an additional mechanism to use when securing its control and management plane traffic. To prevent leakage, however, 100 percent coverage must be guaranteed, as described in Chapter 4.

NOTE	One interesting side note in this example is that because classification and marking of untrusted traffic is done based on ingress interface, there is no concern for spoofed internal IP addresses. Packets arriving via an external interface cannot possibly have originated from inside the network. Positively marking the packet reinforces its origin to other devices within the network and, hence, helps to mitigate spoofing attacks.

Policing

Traffic policing is the third step in the QoS process, and is configured to restrict the rate of traffic as dictated against a particular policy. Policing (ingress Step 14 or egress Step 12 in Figure 7-1) is an optional process and is dependent on classification, but it is unrelated to marking unless the policer policy is explicitly configured to do so, as described below. Policing provides the functional mechanisms to enforce the rate thresholds per class, and drop (or re-mark) traffic when it exceeds the thresholds. It is most useful when applied at the network edge to enforce some agreed traffic rate from or to a network user. As you learned in Chapter 4, policing can also augment interface ACLs by rate limiting traffic up to a configured maximum rate. From a services plane security perspective, policing is applied to traffic matching some classification policy. This is why it is critical to classify *all* packets accurately. For further information, refer to Chapter 4.

Queuing

Queuing is an optional egress-only function (Step 18 in Figure 7-1) that provides bandwidth management during periods of egress link congestion. Note, some IP router platforms such as the Cisco 12000 series also support ingress queuing. In some cases, the Cisco 12000 uses this ingress queuing, as triggered by a backpressure mechanism signaled through the backplane, to manage egress link congestion. In other cases, the

Cisco 12000 uses input queuing to manage internal switch fabric or router backplane congestion. Whether ingress or egress queuing is configured, when congestion is not occurring, queuing is not a factor. Queuing can be implemented either to support congestion avoidance, as in the case where Weighted Random Early Detection (WRED) is deployed, or to support congestion management, as in the case where Low-Latency Queuing (LLQ), Class-Based Weighted Fair Queuing (CBWFQ), or Modified Deficit Round Robin (MDRR) is deployed.

MQC

As mentioned earlier in this section, Cisco IOS implements QoS via the MQC mechanisms. MQC uses three types of constructs to implement QoS:

- **class-map:** MQC uses the **class-map** construct as the method within which classification descriptors are defined for a traffic class. Class maps implement the classification function described in the previous list. The **class-map** construct includes one or more **match** statements to define the traffic descriptor rules for the class. These **match** commands allow a wide range of criteria for packet classification, including many Layer 2, 3, 4, and, in some cases, certain Layer 7 attributes. Typically, multiple **class-map** statements are defined, each representing a distinct traffic class and each containing one or more **match** statements describing the match criteria for the associated traffic class. When multiple **match** statements are included, these can be considered as logical AND or logical OR operations using the **match-all** or **match-any** keywords, respectively. Class map names are case sensitive. Note that Cisco IOS predefines one class map, **class-default** (lowercase), as a catch-all class, which simplifies the task of classifying all packets that do not match other class maps defined within a policy map.

- **policy-map:** MQC uses the **policy-map** construct to tie together one or more class maps into an overall QoS policy. The **policy-map** defines the specific QoS actions to be applied for each traffic class. Hence, within the **policy-map** construct, previously defined class maps are referenced, and then corresponding **MQC** actions are specified per **class-map**. QoS actions may include but are not limited to marking using MQC **set**, policing using MQC **police**, and queuing using MQC **bandwidth** commands. Policy maps are processed top-down, and a packet may match one and only one traffic class. Once a packet is classified into a defined traffic class, all subsequent classes are ignored. Only the MQC actions associated with the matched traffic class are applied. Packets that do not satisfy any match criteria for any referenced classes become part of the implicit **class-default** class. As with **class-map** names, **policy-map** names are also case sensitive.

- **service-policy:** MQC uses the **service-policy** construct to associate a **policy-map** with an interface and to specify the direction of applicability. The **input** or **output** keyword is used to specify the direction in which the defined actions are taken.

Service policies can be attached to physical interfaces and *logical* interfaces, such as VLANs and tunnels, and to control plane (receive) interfaces (see the description of CoPP in Chapter 5).

The separation of the classification definitions, policing definitions, and service policy deployment provides flexibility during the creation phase and simplifies the overall QoS configuration process because it allows you to specify a traffic class independently of QoS policy actions. Class maps are created to identify specific traffic types and may be used in one or more policy maps. Each policy map may be applied to one or more interfaces concurrently. Policy statistics and counters are maintained on a per-interface basis.

When creating a QoS policy using MQC, the typical construction chronology is as follows:

1 Create classification ACLs (if needed) for use in the **class-map** statements as traffic descriptors.

2 Create traffic classes using **class-map** and **match** statements, referencing the previously created ACLs as needed.

3 Create **policy-map** statements to combine the previously defined **class-map** statements with appropriate QoS actions.

4 Apply each **policy-map** statement to the appropriate interface(s) using the **service-policy** statement.

The following examples will help illustrate the use of MQC for QoS.

Packet Recoloring Example

As previously mentioned, recoloring is the term used to describe the process of changing the precedence setting in the IP header of packets as they ingress your network. The IP header Precedence field (see Appendix B, Figure B-1) is used to indicate the level of importance for the packet. The defined values and their meanings are listed in Table 7-1.

Table 7-1 *IP Header Precedence Field Settings*

Precedence Field Bit Setting	Defined Meaning
000 (0)	Routine
001 (1)	Priority
010 (2)	Immediate
011 (3)	Flash
100 (4)	Flash Override
101 (5)	Critical

Table 7-1   *IP Header Precedence Field Settings (Continued)*

Precedence Field Bit Setting	Defined Meaning
110 (6)	Internetwork Control
111 (7)	Network Control

As an example, most routing protocols set their own traffic with a precedence value of 6—Internetwork Control. Cisco IOS uses this precedence value for some internal functions as well, such as Selective Packet Discard (SPD), to prioritize these packets within the IOS process-level queues that feed the route processor, as described in Chapter 5. Many QoS deployments take advantage of precedence marking as well. Some Internet sites have been known to purposely set their traffic with IP header Precedence values of 5, 6, or 7 in hopes that their content is provided higher-priority service. Attackers have also been known to set the precedence value in attack packets in hopes of giving their attack higher priority. The general guidance then is to reset (recolor) the IP header Precedence field to a value of 0 for all packets that ingress an external interface, or to whatever value is appropriate for your network and service. Example 7-1 uses MQC match access-group constructs. MQC accomplishes this by defining an ACL that describes the IP header Precedence values (Step 1), configuring a **class-map** to match on this ACL (Step 2), configuring a **policy-map** to recolor packets matching this **class-map** (Step 3), and then applying this policy to the desired interface on the ingress (input) direction using a **service-policy** (Step 4).

Example 7-1   *MQC-Based Recoloring Implementation*

```
! Step 1 - Create ACLs to match IP header Precedence (color)
access-list 160 permit ip any any precedence priority
access-list 160 permit ip any any precedence immediate
access-list 160 permit ip any any precedence flash
access-list 160 permit ip any any precedence flash-override
access-list 160 permit ip any any precedence critical
access-list 160 permit ip any any precedence internet
access-list 160 permit ip any any precedence network
!
! Step 2 - Create a class-map to match ACLs in Step 1
class-map match-color
  match access-group 160
!
! Step 3 - Create a policy-map to apply policy (drop/drop)
policy-map re-color
  class match-color
    set ip precedence routine
!
! Step 4 - Apply service-policy to interface
interface pos1/1
  encapsulation ppp
  ip address 209.165.200.225 255.255.255.224
  service-policy input re-color
!
```

Notice in Example 7-1 that **access-list 160** only matches on IP header Precedence values of 1 through 7, but no explicit test is done for packets with a precedence value of 0. Because tests look for 1 through 7, which represents all other possible values, it is not necessary to test explicitly for 0 to ensure that all packets are being classified. Zero is the default value, and most packets should be set to this value. Of course, it is possible to define another ACL entry to match on 0 (routine), but strictly speaking it is not required. One reason to do so would be to provide statistics via ACL counters, as described next.

Tracking how packets are initially marked can be accomplished most easily by using the **show access-list** command to display the counters for ACL lines matching different precedence levels of incoming packets. Example 7-2 illustrates this concept.

Example 7-2 *Monitoring Recoloring Access List Counters*

```
router-a# show access-list 160

Extended IP access list 160
  permit ip any any precedence priority (5637629 matches)
  permit ip any any precedence immediate (3916144 matches)
  permit ip any any precedence flash (1967437 matches)
  permit ip any any precedence flash-override (4034766 matches)
  permit ip any any precedence critical (2306059 matches)
  permit ip any any precedence internet (8024235 matches)
  permit ip any any precedence network (919538 matches)
```

Monitoring these values over time may give you some indication of impending attacks or even misconfigurations within the network. The use of EEM or custom scripts, as described in Chapter 6, "Management Plane Security," can be used to provide this type of information.

Traffic Management Example

The following example illustrates the use of QoS and MQC in a traffic management role. In Example 7-3, traffic egressing the PE heading toward the CE is prioritized by IP precedence. This of course assumes that IP precedence values are properly set and can be trusted to reflect the nature of the traffic. In this case, several **class-map** statements are configured to match on IP precedence directly (no ACL is required), and a **policy-map** is used to allocate bandwidth via LLQ. LLQ allocates the assigned bandwidth to the priority queue, if configured, using the **priority percent** keyword. The remaining bandwidth is then allocated to each of the other configured traffic classes belonging to the policy map by using the **bandwidth percent** keyword. In this case, traffic matching precedence 5 is associated with the priority queue and given 35 percent of the bandwidth, perhaps to accommodate real-time voice traffic. Traffic matching precedence 4 and precedence 3 are given 25 percent and 15 percent of the bandwidth, respectively.

Example 7-3 *QoS-Based Traffic Management Implementation*

```
! Step 1 - Create class-map statements to classify traffic based on IP precedence
class-map match-any precedence3
  match ip precedence 3
class-map match-any precedence4
  match ip precedence 4
class-map match-any precedence5
  match ip precedence 5
!
! Step 2 - Create policy-map to allocate bandwidth by class from Step 1
policy-map TrafficMgmt
  class precedence5
    priority percent 35
  class precedence4
    bandwidth percent 25
  class precedence3
    bandwidth percent 15
!
! Step 3 - Apply service-policy to interface
interface Serial1/0/0/2:0
 description Circuit-123, Customer ABC-10
 bandwidth 1536
 ip vrf forwarding ABC
 ip address 10.0.1.13 255.255.255.252
 no ip directed-broadcast
 no ip proxy-arp
 no fair-queue
 no cdp enable
 service-policy output TrafficMgmt
!
```

NOTE   In Example 7-3, explicit **class-map** configurations are only used to match IP precedence 3, 4, and 5 because these classes have explicit bandwidth assignments. The remainder of the traffic (IP precedence values 0, 1, 2, 6, and 7) is handled within the **class-default** traffic class, which is implicitly defined and controlled. Additional details on this behavior are covered in the Cisco Press book *QoS for IP/MPLS Networks* (listed in the "Further Reading" section).

The **show policy-map** command is the primary tool for verifying the operation and configuration of QoS policies within MQC. The output of this command displays counters and rates for the configured actions on each **class-map** within the **policy-map**, as well as the always-defined **class-default** policy. The **clear counters** command resets all interface counters, including MQC counters, which is useful when comparative measurements are required for troubleshooting or traffic analysis. Example 7-4 illustrates the output of the

show policy-map command for the policy defined in Example 7-3. There are no **debug** commands, however, because the MQC mechanisms are applied in the CEF fast path and the performance impact of debugging would be too great.

Example 7-4 *Sample Output from the* **show policy-map** *Command*

```
router-a# show policy-map interface Serial 0/0
Serial0/0

  Service-policy output: TrafficMgmt

    Class-map: precedence5 (match-any)
      0 packets, 0 bytes
      5 minute offered rate 0 bps, drop rate 0 bps
      Match: ip precedence 5
        0 packets, 0 bytes
        5 minute rate 0 bps
      Queueing
        Strict Priority
        Output Queue: Conversation 264
        Bandwidth 35 (%)
        Bandwidth 540 (kbps) Burst 13500 (Bytes)
        (pkts matched/bytes matched) 0/0
        (total drops/bytes drops) 0/0

    Class-map: precedence4 (match-any)
      0 packets, 0 bytes
      5 minute offered rate 0 bps, drop rate 0 bps
      Match: ip precedence 4
        0 packets, 0 bytes
        5 minute rate 0 bps
      Queueing
        Output Queue: Conversation 265
        Bandwidth 25 (%)
        Bandwidth 386 (kbps) Max Threshold 64 (packets)
        (pkts matched/bytes matched) 0/0
        (depth/total drops/no-buffer drops) 0/0/0

    Class-map: precedence3 (match-any)
      0 packets, 0 bytes
      5 minute offered rate 0 bps, drop rate 0 bps
      Match: ip precedence 3
        0 packets, 0 bytes
        5 minute rate 0 bps
      Queueing
        Output Queue: Conversation 266
        Bandwidth 15 (%)
        Bandwidth 231 (kbps) Max Threshold 64 (packets)
        (pkts matched/bytes matched) 0/0
        (depth/total drops/no-buffer drops) 0/0/0
```

Example 7-4 *Sample Output from the* **show policy-map** *Command (Continued)*

```
       Class-map: class-default (match-any)
         3 packets, 72 bytes
         5 minute offered rate 0 bps, drop rate 0 bps
         Match: any
router-a#
```

Now that the basic mechanisms of MQC and QoS have been described, it is possible to discuss the main aspects of QoS services plane security.

Securing QoS Services

To deploy QoS and, implicitly, to secure the QoS service, you must take several considerations into account:

- You must expend the *engineering effort* to adequately define the traffic classes that make up your differentiated services architecture. Ensure that all packets entering or exiting the system can be classified, and that appropriate QoS policies can be applied to each class of traffic. No traffic should be unclassified and uncontrolled. This requires a complete understanding of the network topology, and the traffic flows within this topology.

- You must be able to accurately identify all points in the network where traffic *classification* can be accomplished. All traffic crossing defined points in the network (for example, the ingress link, egress link, and tunnel interface) must be *classified* and in many cases *marked* so that QoS mechanisms can be applied to the traffic either at that point or elsewhere within the network. QoS mechanisms (rates and percentages) assume that all traffic is accounted for. Thus, all traffic should be properly classified and marked because exceptions can disrupt these QoS mechanisms. This high-value service should be protected from theft or abuse by purposeful (malicious) mismarking. Therefore, you must deploy positive classification and marking schemes across all traffic types and boundaries to account for all traffic. From an IP traffic plane security perspective, *where* the QoS components are deployed is important. In theory, any network element can provide QoS services, assuming the platform is capable of implementing the appropriate mechanisms and performing the required actions. However, as highlighted in prior chapters, there are specific points in the network where implementing certain services makes more sense. In the case of DiffServ QoS, this is primarily (but not exclusively) at the edge of the network, and often in both the ingress and egress directions. External interfaces offer the most logical implementation point for ingress classification and marking. As described in Chapter 3, using the network edge as a reference point allows certain assumptions to be made about ingress packets that cannot be made elsewhere in the network. Recoloring at the edge enables you to perform other QoS and security functions deeper within the network by signaling QoS classification information that indicates the origin of the packets.

- You must be able to apply policies (actions) on all traffic to accomplish the desired goals of the QoS service without impacting overall network operations. If this is a new service, you must ensure that the hardware is capable of adequately supporting the deployment of the service without undue stress. Older platforms may be incapable of deploying certain QoS features at line rate, or may experience a significant increase in CPU utilization, for example. When this is the case, this alone opens a potential vulnerability by exposing other traffic planes, most notably the control plane, to stress potential instability. The deployment of QoS services cannot jeopardize the operations of the network. This can be assured through the use of appropriately scaled hardware and by allowing only applicable traffic to use the higher-priority QoS services. For the Cisco 12000, for example, legacy Engine 0–based line cards not only have limited MQC and QoS support (minimal match support, no marking support, and limited congestion management support), but they also suffer a significant performance degradation of approximately 50 percent when QoS is enabled. Modern Cisco 12000 line cards, such as those based on Engine 3 and Engine 5 (ISE) technologies, are designed as edge services cards and therefore support ingress and egress QoS and MQC (and other services) at line rate. Most CPU-based IOS devices, on the other hand, experience some performance degradation when QoS is enabled, although all MQC functions should be supported. For example, Cisco ISR routers may experience a 10 percent increase in CPU utilization with QoS functions enabled. Designers must also budget for QoS performance impacts and alternate solutions if routers are already stressed (high CPU). When deploying QoS, you should always consult the hardware release notes for your specific platforms to ensure that you understand the implications that enabling these features may have on system performance. In addition, it is always useful to perform laboratory tests under conditions simulating your production environment (including attack conditions) if feasible.

- You should apply defense in depth and breadth principles such as transit ACLs and uRPF to prevent unauthorized traffic from impacting the QoS service. DoS attacks are always more difficult to deal with when they target features that require special processing or that add extra processor burdens.

The preceding list represents recommendations based on generalized QoS and MQC deployments. Obviously, it is not possible to cover every scenario and situation in this chapter. Many other recommendations that are specific to topology and QoS service deployment should be considered based on your particular environment. It is the intention of these discussions and guidelines that you be able to recognize within your specific deployment scheme where potential vulnerabilities exist and how QoS must be protected. For more information on available QoS techniques to mitigate attacks within the IP data plane, see to Chapter 4.

MPLS VPN Services

Multiprotocol Label Switching (MPLS) Virtual Private Networks (VPN) provide traffic isolation and differentiation to create virtual networks across a shared IP network infrastructure. MPLS-based Layer 3 VPNs combine Multiprotocol BGP (M-BGP) using extended community attributes and VPN address families, LDP (RFC 3036) or RSVP-TE (RFC 3209) for label distribution, and router support for Virtual Routing and Forwarding (VRF) instances to create these virtual IP networks. These operate based on the Internet Engineering Task Force (IETF) RFC 4364 specification (which obsoletes RFC 2547bis).

An extensive discussion of the threats to MPLS VPNs was covered in Chapter 2, "Threat Models for IP Networks." The purpose of this section is to review techniques available to protect MPLS VPN services from the threats described in Chapter 2. This section is not intended to provide detailed MPLS VPN design and implementation guidelines. A short overview of some of the components used in creating MPLS VPNs and some of the more common deployment aspects are covered in review, however. Some level of understanding of MPLS VPN arechitectures and their operational concepts is assumed. For additional information on deploying and securing MPLS VPNs, refer to the Cisco Press book entitled *MPLS VPN Security* (listed in the "Further Reading" section), which provides details on their architecture, deployment models, and security.

MPLS VPN Overview

As described in previous chapters, MPLS VPNs provide a site-to-site IP VPN service and are rapidly replacing legacy Frame Relay and ATM networks. SPs offer MPLS VPN services across a shared IP infrastructure. The SP IP network not only is shared among MPLS VPN customers but it may also be shared by SP customers of other services, including, for example, Internet transit, IPv6 VPNs (otherwise known as 6VPE), and Layer 2 VPNs (or pseudowires). Although the SP IP network is shared, addressing and routing separation, as well as privacy, are assured between customer VPNs, and between VPNs and the SP global IP routing table. This is inherently achieved through the use of the following mechanisms, as defined by RFC 4364 and as were described in Chapter 2:

- VPN-IPv4 addressing, to ensure unique addressing and routing separation between VPNs
- VRFs, to associate VPNs to physical (or logical) interfaces on provider edge (PE) routers
- Multiprotocol BGP (M-BGP), to exchange VPN routing information between PE routers

RFC 4364 also categorizes the different roles of IP routers within the MPLS VPN architecture, including customer edge (CE), provider edge (PE), provider core (P), and autonomous system boundary routers (ASBR), also described in Chapter 2 and illustrated in Figure 2-15. Unlike an Internet service, an MPLS VPN service is considered trusted; hence, often few or no security measures are applied. The following sections review techniques available to protect each of these different MPLS VPN router types (or categories) from the threats outlined in Chapter 2.

Customer Edge Security

Given the IP addressing and routing separation provided by MPLS VPNs, the CE router is reachable only from within its assigned VPN. Therefore, by default, the CE router is only susceptible to attacks sourced from inside the VPN. Only if the VPN has Internet or extranet connectivity configured (excluding the secure Management VPN per Chapter 6) is it susceptible to external attacks, as was described in Chapter 2. Keep in mind that the CE router is an IP router and is not enabled for any MPLS functionality (with the exception of the Carrier Supporting Carrier [CsC] model, which is described in the "Inter-Provider Edge Security" section later in the chapter). Hence, to mitigate the risk of attacks against the CE router, the data, control, and management plane security techniques described in Chapters 4 through 6 may be applied, including:

- Data plane security
  - Interface ACLs
  - Unicast RPF
  - Flexible Packet Matching (FPM)
  - QoS
  - IP Options handling techniques
  - ICMP data plane techniques
  - Disabling IP directed broadcasts
  - IP transport and application layer techniques
- Control plane security
  - Disabling unnecessary services
  - ICMP control plane techniques
  - Selective Packet Discard
  - IP Receive ACLs (rACLs)
  - Control Plane Policing (CoPP)
  - Neighbor authentication (MD-5)
  - Protocol specific ACL filters
  - BGP security techniques (GTSM, prefix filtering, etc.)
- Management plane security
  - SNMP techniques
  - Disabling unused management plane services
  - Disabling idle user sessions
  - System banners

 — Secure IOS file systems

 — AutoSecure

 — SSH

 — AAA/TACACS+/RADIUS

 — Syslog

 — NTP

 — NetFlow

 — Management VPN (specifically designed for managed MPLS VPN CE routers)

The preceding techniques would be deployed in the same manner as was described in Chapters 4 through 6; hence, they will not be repeated here.

NOTE Note, however, the CE router is deployed within a private IP (MPLS) VPN versus being reachable from the wider Internet. Therefore, you may consider deploying only those security techniques that mitigate the risk of significant threats. Spoofing attacks, for example, may not be considered a significant threat within MPLS VPNs. The optimal techniques that provide an effective security solution will vary by organization and depend on network topology, product mix, traffic behavior, operational complexity and organizational mission.

Provider Edge Security

As described in Chapter 2, PE routers associate physical (or logical) interfaces to customer VPNs using VRFs. VRFs are statically assigned to interfaces and cannot be modified without PE router reconfiguration. Using a static VRF configuration provides complete separation between VPNs, and between VPNs and the SP global IP routing table. VPN customer packets cannot travel outside of the assigned VPN unless the SP VPN policies specifically allow for it. Conversely, external packets cannot be injected inside the VPN unless specifically allowed by policy. That is, only a misconfiguration or software vulnerability would allow illegal unauthorized packets to leak into or out of a customer VPN.

Although the PE provides routing and addressing separation between VPNs, it is also IP reachable within each configured VPN. This makes it susceptible to internal IP attacks sourced from within a VPN. Internal attacks sourced from within a private VPN may be considered low risk. However, given that a PE router aggregates many customers and VPNs, an attack against the PE from within one VPN may adversely affect other VPN customers because the PE router shares its resources, including CPU, memory, and (uplink) interface bandwidth, among the different customer VPNs. Hence, although an MPLS VPN assures routing and addressing separation between VPNs and between VPNs and the global IP routing table, collateral damage remains a valid threat.

The PE router appears as a native IP router to VPN customers (excluding CsC customers, as described in the "Inter-Provider Edge Security" section later in the chapter). A single VPN customer site generally has IP reachability to all of the PEs configured for the associated customer VPN. Hence, to mitigate the risk of VPN customer attacks against PE routers, many of the data, control, and management plane security techniques described in Chapters 4 through 6 may be applied. Note, all of these techniques are generally supported for MPLS VPNs and VRF interfaces; however, specific platform restrictions may apply. Further, these techniques would be generally deployed in the same manner as was described in Chapters 4 through 6 and so their application will not be repeated here. However, some additional considerations for MPLS VPN PE routers are described in the following list, including resource management per VPN to limit the risk of collateral damage.

Infrastructure ACL

VPN customers and CE routers require minimal, if any, protocol access to the PE routers. Most MPLS VPN deployments only require dynamic routing (for example, eBGP or EIGRP) between the PE and the directly connected CE. Infrastructure ACLs are specifically designed to prevent IP packets from reaching destination addresses that make up the SP core network, including the PE external interface addresses themselves. Thus, iACLs may be applied on the PE router, inbound on each CE-facing interface to filter all traffic destined to the PE except routing protocol traffic from the directly connected CE router. This type of policy may be applied on the PE, on each CE-facing interface. Note that if the iACLs filter traffic from the directly connected CE router only and not from CE routers associated with other sites within the VPN, additional protection steps may be required. To protect PEs from remote attacks sourced from other sites within the VPN, you could simply not carry the IP prefixes associated with the PE-CE links within the VRF routing table. Or, if CE reachability is required in support of VoIP gateway, firewall, or IPsec services, for example, you may use any one of the three techniques outlined in the "Edge Router External Link Protection" section of Chapter 4. If static routing is used on the PE-CE link, the infrastructure ACL should simply deny all traffic destined to the PE external interfaces. IP rACLs and/or CoPP should also be applied as a second layer of defense in the event that the infrastructure ACL and external link protection policies are bypassed. IP rACLs and CoPP in the context of MPLS VPNs are discussed next.

IP Receive ACL

As described in Chapter 5, IP rACL policies apply to all CEF receive adjacency traffic. However, IP rACLs are not VRF-aware, and thus polices applied on PE routers are unable to distinguish between receive adjacency traffic that is associated with each customer VRF or the global table when filtering solely based upon IP source addresses. Given that the PE supports a distinct VRF table for each customer VPN, and that each customer VPN, as well as the PE itself, may use overlapping IP addressing, this leaves open the possibility for ambiguities within IP rACL policies and potentially allows unauthorized traffic to incorrectly be permitted by the IP rACL. For example, if the IP rACL policy permits all BGP traffic from the 209.165.200.224/27 subnet, then traffic sourced from any 209.165.200.224/27 address within *any* VPN configured on the PE, or any traffic sourced from an 209.165.200.224/27 address within the global table will be permitted by the IP rACL. This situation can be resolved by also configuring infrastructure ACLs as needed, to fully rationalize each traffic source. It should be noted that IP rACL filtering based upon IP destination address information is not exposed to the same issues because any permitted destination address must be that of a CEF receive adjacency.

Control Plane Policing

CoPP policies that use IP source address information will suffer from the same issues just described for IP rACLs. That is, CoPP is not VRF-aware at this time, and thus does not consider the ingress VRF. This is conceivably less of an issue for CoPP than for IP rACLs in that CoPP typically is provisioned to rate limit traffic types to infrastructure destination IP addresses.

VRF Prefix Limits

Although BGP neighbor prefix limits may be applied as described in Chapter 4 per BGP peer, you may also configure a maximum prefix limit for each VRF table defined within the PE routers. This allows you to limit the maximum number of routes in a VRF table to prevent a PE router from importing too many routes. The VPN prefix limit is protocol independent as well as independent of the number of CE peers or sites within a VPN. To enable this feature, use the **maximum routes** <*limit*> {*warn-threshold* | **warn-only**} command in IOS VRF configuration mode. This allows you to monitor and limit PE routing table resources used per VPN/VRF. You can use the **maximum routes** command to monitor and limit the number of routes in a VRF on a PE router. By default, IOS does not limit the maximum number of prefixes per VRF table. You may specify a limit by using the **maximum routes** command. Routes are rejected when a maximum number as set by the *limit* argument is reached. A percentage of this maximum number of permitted routes can also be defined by specifying the *warn-threshold* argument. When configured, IOS generates a Syslog warning message every time a route is added to a VRF when the VRF route count is above the warning threshold. IOS also generates a route rejection Syslog notification when the maximum threshold limit is reached and every time a route is rejected after the limit is reached. To generate a warning message only instead of a imposing a hard VRF prefix limit, use the **warn-only** keyword within the **maximum routes** command.

IP Fragmentation and Reassembly

As described in Chapter 2, MPLS VPN PE routers impose an 8-byte MPLS shim for all unicast traffic received from connected CE routers and destined to remote VPN sites across the MPLS core. The addition of the 8-byte MPLS shim may result in IP fragmentation of customer VPN traffic. If IP fragmentation occurs, a flood of VPN traffic may adversely affect the ingress PE router because this traffic must be handled in the slow path. For unicast VPN traffic, any PE fragmented IP packets will be reassembled by the destination address specified within the customer VPN packets. Hence, only the ingress PE router is affected. Conversely, for multicast VPN (MVPN) traffic (which is encapsulated within a 24-byte GRE point-to-multipoint tunnel header and not an MPLS header, per IETF draft-rosen-vpn-mcast-08.txt), the egress PE may be required to reassemble the fragmented MVPN (GRE) packets because the GRE tunnel endpoint (or destination address) is the egress PE itself.

As outlined in Chapter 2, IP routers have a limited number of IP fragment reassembly buffers. Further, fragment reassembly is handled at the IOS process level. If PE routers are required to fragment VPN traffic and/or reassemble fragmented MVPN traffic, they are potentially susceptible to DoS attacks crafted with large packets. Given the different tunnel header encapsulations used for unicast and MVPN traffic (in other words, 8 versus 24 bytes), avoiding unicast fragmentation does not necessarily mitigate the risk associated with MVPN fragmentation and reassembly. Multicast fragmentation must be considered if MVPN services are offered. Additionally, it is also possible for large packets to be used for an ICMP attack. In this scenario, the attacker simply sets the Don't Fragment (DF) bit of the oversized packets. If the PE router cannot fragment the packet due to the DF bit being set, it sends an ICMP Packet Too Big message back to the source. An excessive volume of these crafted packets can trigger a DoS condition on the router.

The only technique available to mitigate the risks associated with IP fragmentation and reassembly is to engineer the network to simply avoid it. This may be achieved only by ensuring that the MPLS core network from ingress PE to egress PE supports an MTU greater than that of all IP access and aggregation networks (in other words, PE-CE links) and must be large enough to accommodate the additional MPLS and/or GRE encapsulations imposed. In this way, any VPN packets received at the edge are guaranteed not to be fragmented when transiting the core. Further, the MTU setting should be universal across the network edge. Otherwise, fragmentation may occur depending upon the entry or exit points at the network edge.

When fragmentation cannot be eliminated through network design, every effort must be made to mitigate the impacts of any fragmentation and reassembly that may still occur. There are a number of strategies for resolving fragmentation within the context of MPLS VPNs, and the best approach depends on your particular environment and on how much work you are willing to do to prevent fragmentation. There is no panacea, however, and some engineering effort must be expended to determine the best approach.

To avoid fragmentation (and possibly reassembly) on the PEs, the MPLS core network must support an MTU greater than that of the PE-CE links. The best-case scenario, then, is to set the egress interface MTU value of every CE router to a suitable value that guarantees there will be no fragmentation within the MPLS core. For example, assume that the interface MTU is 1500 bytes everywhere within the MPLS core network. The CE egress interface MTU must be reduced, then, by an amount equal to or greater than the maximum combination of tunnel headers imposed across the MPLS core. This includes either the 8-byte label stack imposed for unicast VPN traffic or the 24-byte GRE header imposed for MVPN traffic. If other encapsulations are also used within MPLS core, their overhead must be accommodated as well. For example, MPLS TE tunnels between MPLS core P routers can also influence the maximum packet size to avoid fragmentation. In the preceding example, because all interfaces have an MTU of 1500 bytes, all unicast traffic greater than 1492 bytes would be fragmented by the ingress PE. Similarly, all MVPN traffic greater than 1476 bytes would be fragmented at the ingress PE and then require reassembly at the egress PE.

The main approaches to modifying the interface MTU of the CE links include the following:

- **Modify the Interface Layer 2 MTU:** By making modifications to the CE egress interface Layer 2 MTU, fragmentation may be avoided on the PE. The interface command **mtu** *<value>* is used to set the maximum transmission unit (MTU)—that is the maximum packet size for outbound packets at Layer 2. Thus, any Layer 3 protocols will be subjected to this value (for example, IP). The IOS default MTU setting depends on the interface medium. Table 7-2 lists IOS default MTU values according to media type.

Table 7-2   *Cisco IOS Default MTU Values*

Media Type	Default MTU (Bytes)
Ethernet	1500
Gigabit Ethernet	1500
DS1/E1 Serial and below	1500
DS3/E3 Serial	4470
ATM	4470
POS	4470
HSSI	4470

- **Modify the Interface Layer 3 (IP) MTU:** To modify the CE egress interface Layer 3 MTU value, use the **ip mtu** *<value>* interface configuration command. Note that the Layer 3 interface MTU is protocol-specific. Namely, this Layer 3 interface MTU command applies only to IP packets, whereas the Layer 2 interface MTU command applies to any upper-layer protocols that are transmitted on the interface. With the proper interface or IP MTU setting on the CE, the CE will then perform the IP fragmentation when necessary, and not the ingress PE.

When the CE router is not managed by the SP, the SP cannot rely on each of its customers to set the MTU accordingly on the CE router. Hence, instead of reducing the MTU on the CE router, ideally the SP should increase the MTU within the core of their network to accommodate the maximum PE-CE MTU size plus sufficient overhead for any possible MPLS label stack. Given wide deployment of POS interfaces within MPLS VPN core networks as well as Gigabit Ethernet interfaces enabled for jumbo frames, MTUs of 4470 bytes or 9000 bytes, respectively, are commonly supported. This allows SPs to eliminate the likelihood of fragmentation and reassembly within their MPLS core, assuming the MTU of the PE-CE link is 1500 bytes.

| NOTE | Changing default MTU settings may cause the router to recarve system packet buffers to accommodate the new MTU applied. This may disrupt packet-forwarding operations during the period of time it takes to complete the buffer recarve operations. |

Provider Core Security

Excluding the PE router, the SP infrastructure is inherently hidden from MPLS VPN customers, given VPN routing separation. Consequently, it is not possible for a VPN customer to launch direct attacks against core (P) routers due to the absence of IP reachability. Further, MPLS core (P) routers do not carry VPN customer prefixes, hence, the IP rACL, CoPP and VRF prefix limits issues outlined for PE routers do not apply to core (P) routers. Nevertheless, core (P) routers remain susceptible to transit attacks, as described in Chapter 2. Hence, to mitigate the risk of attacks from VPN customers against the core (P) routers, the following techniques may be applied.

Disable IP TTL to MPLS TTL Propagation at the Network Edge

By default, when IP packets are MPLS encapsulated, the IP TTL is copied down into the TTL fields of the imposed MPLS labels. Not only does this allow VPN customer packets to expire within the MPLS core network, but it also provides VPN customers with visibility of the core network using IP traceroute. Both of these conditions represent potential security risks. RFC 3032 and IETF draft-ietf-mpls-icmp-07 specify the interaction between MPLS and ICMP, and allow for ICMP messages generated by the core (P) routers to be sent to a source host within a customer VPN as required, including ICMP Time Exceeded (Type 11) messages. To mitigate the risk of VPN customer packets expiring on core (P) routers, the **no mpls ip propagate-ttl forwarded** command must be applied on all PE and ASBR routers within IOS global configuration mode. This command disables the propagation of the IP TTL into the MPLS label stack. Instead, the MPLS TTL values are set to 255 (the maximum available value per RFC 3032), preventing VPN customer packets from expiring within the MPLS core network (unless of course a routing loop exists, in which case TTL expiration is desired). Note that disabling IP TTL to MPLS TTL propagation in this way does not break VPN customer IP traceroute. It simply prevents the core (P) routers from being reported when the VPN customer performs IP traceroute. The VPN customer will see only the CE routers and ingress PE router, and not the core (P) routers. In this way, the MPLS core network remains hidden and appears as a single hop. The egress PE router is optionally reported depending upon the MPLS tunneling model applied per RFC 3443. As stated, the **no mpls ip propagate-ttl forwarded** command must be applied on all edge routers (PEs and ASBRs), because this is where the MPLS encapsulation of VPN customer packets takes place. Further, disabling IP TTL to MPLS TTL propagation does not affect the SP's ability to use IP traceroute across the internal infrastructure either. For more information on TTL processing in MPLS networks, refer to RFC 3443.

IP Fragmentation

Similar to the description in the previous section for PE routers without proper MTU support across the MPLS core, P routers are also susceptible to fragmentation and/or ICMP attacks resulting from large packets. Excessive fragmentation may trigger a DoS condition in core (P) routers. This can be mitigated with a proper Layer 2 or Layer 3 interface MTU setting at the network edge, as described for PE security techniques in the Provider Edge Security section above, or by ensuring that the MTU within the core of the network is sufficiently large to accommodate the maximum PE-CE MTU size plus sufficient overhead for any possible MPLS label stack.

Router Alert Label

As described in Chapters 2 and 4, VPN customer traffic both with and without IP header options is always MPLS-encapsulated at the ingress PE and forwarded downstream across the MPLS core. There are exceptions, however. VPN packets with IP Source Route options will be MPLS label switched only if the IP addresses specified in the Source Route option are valid addresses within the associated VRF. If not, these packets will be discarded. Once MPLS-encapsulated, however, core (P) routers forward packets based upon the MPLS label stack and do not consider the IP header options of VPN customer packets (because it is beneath the labels and not seen by core (P) routers). RFC 3032 defines an MPLS Router Alert Label, which is analogous to the IP header Router Alert option. When applied, MPLS packets tagged with the Router Alert Label will be punted to the IOS process-level for packet handling. At the time of this writing, there is no industry or IETF standard for IP header option processing in MPLS networks to specify when the MPLS Router Alert Label should (or should not) be imposed. Consequently, each MPLS VPN PE router platform may potentially behave differently in this regard. MPLS PE router platforms that impose the Router Alert Label (at the top of the label stack) may make downstream core (P) routers susceptible to security attacks, given that such packets will be handled at the IOS process level. A sustained attack that sends crafted IP packets having the IP header Router Alert option, for example, to an MPLS VPN PE that imposes the MPLS Router Alert label may trigger a DoS condition within the MPLS core. At the time of this writing, Cisco IOS MPLS VPN PE routers do not impose the MPLS Router Alert label for VPN customer packets. But, again, because there is no industry standard, non-IOS MPLS VPN PE routers may behave differently. If your MPLS VPN PE router imposes the Router Alert label for VPN packets which have an IP header Router Alert option, you should consider filtering these packets at the PE to mitigate the risk they present to the core. Techniques to filter IP options packets on IOS routers are described in Chapter 4.

Network SLAs

Similar to IP TTL handling described at the beginning of this list, when IP packets are MPLS encapsulated, the IP precedence value, by default, is copied down into the EXP fields of the imposed MPLS labels. Hence, without proper QoS policies at the PE, VPN customers may craft their low-priority traffic as high-priority in an attempt to either steal high-priority MPLS core bandwidth from other high-priority services or to launch attacks against high-priority traffic classes, including control plane protocols. Both of these scenarios assume that a DiffServ QoS architecture is implemented within the MPLS core. To mitigate this risk, packet recoloring and policing should be applied uniformly across the network edge, as described in the "Securing QoS Services" section above, and earlier in Chapter 4.

The preceding techniques outline specific steps you may take to protect core P routers in the context of MPLS VPN–based attacks. Only a PE router misconfiguration or software vulnerability would provide IP reachability between a VPN customer and the MPLS core (P) routers. Further, if the SP network also provides other services such as Internet transit, the core P routers may be susceptible to other threats, as described in Chapter 2. Hence, you should also consider deploying the applicable data, control, and management plane security techniques described in Chapters 4 through 6 to mitigate the risks associated with these other threats. Note that IOS also supports MD5 authentication for MPLS LDP, which is the most widely deployed label distribution protocol for MPLS VPN services. Chapter 9, "Service Provider Network Case Study," illustrates the combination of techniques and defense in depth and breadth principles that SPs should consider to protect their infrastructure and services, including MPLS VPNs.

Inter-Provider Edge Security

As described in Chapter 2, there are two primary components of the inter-provider MPLS VPN architecture: Carrier Supporting Carrier (CsC) and Inter-AS VPNs. CsC is a hierarchical VPN model that enables downstream service providers (DSP), or customer carriers, to interconnect geographically diverse IP or MPLS networks over an MPLS VPN backbone. This eliminates the need for customer carriers to build and maintain their own private IP or MPLS backbone.

Inter-AS is a peer-to-peer model that enables customer VPNs to be extended through multiple SP or multi-domain networks. Using Inter-AS VPN techniques, SPs peer with one another and offer end-to-end VPN connectivity over extended geographical locations for those VPN customers who may be out of reach for a single SP. Both CsC and Inter-AS VPNs maintain segmentation between distinct customer VPNs.

Carrier Supporting Carrier Security

From a security perspective, the CsC-PE router is subject to the same threats as the native MPLS VPN PE router. Similarly, the CsC-CE router is subject to the same threats as the native MPLS VPN CE router. Further, because the customer carrier is itself an SP, the CsC-CE is also a core (P) router from the perspective of DSP customers. The potential threats against the CsC-CE as a customer carrier core router depend upon whether the DSP offers Internet transit or MPLS VPN services, or both. Each of these types of threats were detailed in Chapter 2.

The primary difference from a security perspective between native MPLS VPNs and the CsC model is that data plane packets exchanged between the CsC-CE and CsC-PE routers are MPLS encapsulated. This makes some IP data plane security techniques such as IP ACLs ineffective (as described in the list below). Again, however, this only applies to MPLS labeled data plane packets not native IP packets. Despite the use of MPLS labeled data plane packets, the CsC-CE router is reachable only from within the associated customer carrier VPN and is not susceptible to external attacks through the CsC provider. This is strictly enforced at the CsC-PE through an automatic MPLS label spoofing avoidance mechanism that prevents the CsC-CE from using spoofed MPLS labels to transmit unauthorized packets into another customer VPN. MPLS packets with spoofed labels are automatically discarded upon ingress of the CsC-PE. This is possible because, within IOS, the labels distributed from the CsC-PE to the CsC-CE using either LDP or RFC 3107 (BGP plus labels) are VRF-aware. Hence, CsC provides addressing and routing separation between VPNs equivalent to native MPLS VPNs. Therefore, the security techniques outlined above in the "Customer Edge Security," "Provider Edge Security," and "Provider Core Security" sections also apply to CsC services. Additionally, the following security considerations also apply to CsC services:

- **Interface IP ACLs:** Interface ACLs are IP-based and hence do not apply to MPLS labeled packets. Although IP ACLs may be ineffective against MPLS labeled data plane packets, unlabeled control plane traffic between the CsC-CE and CsC-PE may be filtered using infrastructure IP ACLs.

- **CoPP:** Similar to IP ACLs outlined directly above, labeled data plane exception traffic such as MPLS packets with the Router Alert Label are always classified into the **class-default** traffic class of a CoPP policy. This is because (at the time of this writing) MPLS packets are considered Layer 2 and will not match any IP ACL MQC match criteria configured within the CoPP policy.

- **IP TTL propagation:** The **no mpls ip propagate-ttl forwarded** command (outlined earlier in the "Provider Core Security" section) which was used to protect the MPLS core (P) routers from TTL expiry attacks, does not apply to CsC-PE routers (or PE interfaces enabled for CsC). This command only applies to ingress IP packets being encapsulated into MPLS. It does not apply to ingress MPLS packets being MPLS label switched because no IP TTL to MPLS TTL propagation operation is performed. Given that the CsC-PE (or PE interface enabled for CsC) receives MPLS labeled packets from the CsC-CE, this command does not apply to CsC services. Hence, in the CsC model, unless this command is applied upstream in the CsC customer's network, it is possible for CsC customer packets to TTL-expire within the MPLS core of the SP providing the CsC service (in other words, between the ingress and egress CsC-PEs).

- **Label distribution:** Label distribution between the CsC-CE and CsC-PE may be done using either MPLS LDP or BGP (RFC 3107). Using only BGP, the control plane between the CsC-CE and CsC-PE routers operates similarly to native MPLS VPNs and the different BGP security techniques reviewed in Chapter 5 may be applied. Conversely, MPLS LDP supports MD5 authentication as well as inbound and outbound filtering of label advertisements. Each of these MPLS LDP security techniques were also described in Chapter 5.

Inter-AS VPN Security

Inter-AS VPNs are intended to expand the reach of customer VPNs through multiple SP networks. This is meant to overcome issues where the primary SP footprint may not match the required footprint of the VPN customer, most notably in multinational deployments. RFC 4364 Section 10 outlines three techniques to achieve this, which are widely known within the industry as options (a), (b), and (c). Each has trade-offs in terms of scalability, security, and service awareness. Chapter 2 presented the security threats associated with each option under the condition that the interconnect between each distinct MPLS VPN network is under the control of different SPs (that is, is untrusted). The security of each Inter-AS VPN option is briefly described here:

- **Option (a):** Within option (a), the ASBR router of each SP network effectively operates as a PE router. Further, each ASBR sees its peer ASBR as a CE router. Hence, all of the security techniques previously outlined for native MPLS VPN PE routers apply equally to ASBR routers configured for Inter-AS VPN option (a). As such, this is the only Inter-AS VPN interconnect model that provides for resource management on a per-VPN basis. That is, option (a) maintains separate data plane and control plane instances per VPN (for example, VRF prefix limits, eBGP peering, IP interface per VRF, and so on), unlike options (b) and (c). For this reason, option (a) is the only IOS Inter-AS VPN interconnect model known at the time of this writing to be deployed in production between two (2) distinct SPs. This technique is illustrated in Figure 2-17.

- **Option (b):** Within option (b), the ASBR routers use a single Multiprotocol eBGP session to exchange all Inter-AS VPN customer prefixes over a single native IP (non-VRF) interface between SPs. Although this improves ASBR scaling since only a single interconnect and eBGP session required, it prevents ASBR resource management and security policies on a per-VPN basis. That is, all of the per-VPN techniques such as VRF prefix limits, eBGP peering, IP interface per VRF, and so forth, cannot be applied because option (b) carries all Inter-AS VPNs using a shared interconnect and eBGP peering session for each SP peer. In fact, an option (b) ASBR does not need to be configured with any VRF instances. Because there is no VPN isolation, option (b) Inter-AS VPNs share a common fate whereby one Inter-AS VPN may adversely impact connectivity of another, given the shared data and control plane within the ASBR. Also, because no VRF interface configurations are applied on the ASBR, MPLS label spoofing avoidance checks similar to CsC cannot be enforced on the interconnect, which may allow unauthorized access to a customer VPN. Further, the data plane security techniques described in Chapter 4 do not apply to MPLS label switched packets. Hence, Inter-AS VPN option (b) is susceptible to a variety of security risks that cannot be properly mitigated. Because of these weaknesses, option (b) is not known at the time of this writing to be deployed in production between two 2) distinct SPs for Inter-AS VPN connectivity using IOS. Conversely, for multi-domain (or multi-AS) SP networks, option (b) may be considered since the different domains are managed by the same single SP. (This technique is illustrated in Figure 2-18.)

- **Option (c):** Within option (c), the ASBR routers exchange only PE /32 loopback addresses and associated label information using either MPLS LDP or BGP + Labels (RFC 3107). VPN customer prefixes are then exchanged between route reflectors (RRs) within each SP network (AS) using multihop Multiprotocol-eBGP. (This technique is illustrated in Figure 2-19.) Because this option requires external IP reachability between each SPs (internal) M-BGP route reflector (RR), not only are the RRs exposed to attack, but the MPLS core network of each SP is also now exposed. Similar to option (b), there is no way to verify the integrity of the MPLS label stack, making VPN label spoofing possible. Hence, Inter-AS VPN option (c) also suffers from a variety of security risks, and at the time of this writing, is not known to be deployed in production using IOS because this model is deemed insecure for Inter-AS VPN connectivity between different SPs. Conversely, for multi-domain (or multi-AS) SP networks, option (c) may be considered since the different domains are managed by the same single SP.

The preceding guidelines are based on generalized MPLS VPN deployments. Obviously, it is not possible to cover every MPLS VPN deployment scenario in this chapter. Many other topology and service -specific considerations may apply. This section provided you with general guidelines for enhancing the security of MPLS VPN services. Additional MPLS VPN security topics and details are provided in the Cisco Press book entitled *MPLS VPN Security*, which is listed in the "Further Reading" section.

Although MPLS VPNs provide addressing and routing separation between customer VPNs similar to FR and ATM VPNs, they do not provide cryptographic privacy. The next section reviews IP services plane deployments involving IPsec VPNs.

IPsec VPN Services

The IP Security (IPsec) protocol suite encompasses a set of RFC standards, including RFC 2401 and related standards RFC 2402 through 2412 and 2451, which provide mechanisms for securing Layer 3 IP communications. Although IPsec standards apply to both IPv4 and IPv6 environments, only IPv4 is discussed here. IPsec can be deployed by itself, generally for corporate network extensions over public networks, although it is frequently combined with other services such as GRE or MPLS VPNs as a means of adding security layers to these other services. For example, many companies are now implementing IPsec within their MPLS VPN networks as a means of providing confidentiality (data privacy) along with the segmentation provided by MPLS VPNs. IPsec VPNs, by themselves, provide limited support for things such as dynamic routing, multicast, and so on, which other services such as GRE and MPLS VPNs provide. Hence, the combination of these services often provides the most operationally sound deployment environment.

An extensive discussion of the major threats to IPsec VPNs was already covered in Chapter 2. The purpose of this section is to take these areas where IPsec VPN services are most vulnerable to attack and to describe how to protect these services. This section is not intended to provide detailed IPsec VPN design and implementation guidelines. A short overview of some of the components used in creating IPsec VPNs and some of the more common deployment aspects are covered in review, however. Some level of understanding of IPsec VPNs and their operational concepts, architecture, design, and deployment options is assumed. For additional information on deploying and securing IPsec VPNs, refer to the Cisco Press book *IPSec VPN Design* (listed in the "Further Reading" section), which provides details on their architecture, deployment models, and security.

IPsec VPN Overview

As introduced in Chapter 2, IPsec VPNs are used to provide confidentiality, authentication, and integrity to IP traffic. To provide these features, IPsec VPNs use a two-part system, not unlike other VPN technologies, where a control channel component is first established to manage the IPsec VPN attributes, and then a separate data channel provides the secure mechanisms for transmitting the actual data stream. In IPsec VPNs, the control channel is provided by the Internet Key Exchange (IKE) protocol, and the data protection is provided by one or both of two IPsec protocols know as the Encapsulating Security Payload (ESP) protocol and the Authentication Header (AH) protocol. Each of these components is described briefly next.

IKE

IKE functions as the control channel for IPsec VPNs. In this role, IKE actually performs two separate functions. The first, known as IKE Phase 1, provides VPN endpoint authentication and establishes the method by which IKE will protect itself (encryption and hashing algorithms). To do this, IKE establishes a single, bidirectional security association (SA) for itself, and then brings up the control channel using this SA. It is through this control channel that IKE manages subsequent connections on behalf of IPsec. The second function, known as IKE Phase 2, is the actual IPsec session management function in which IKE negotiates how IPsec connections should be protected, and builds the set of SAs, one for each direction of the IPsec connection. SAs for IPsec are unidirectional and specific to ESP or AH, so there will be at least two SAs per IPsec connection and possibly four if both ESP and AH are invoked. IKE Phase 2 then manages these IPsec connections (negotiates setup, teardown, key refresh, and so on).

Figure 7-2 illustrates these concepts, showing the single IKE control channel (bidirectional) and two IPsec (unidirectional) data channels (one in each direction). Note that IKE Phase 2 is also where the ESP and AH protocols negotiate such parameters as encryption, hashing algorithms, keys, and values for timers and keepalives.

Figure 7-2   *IPsec Control Channel (IKE SA) and Data Channel (IPsec SAs)*

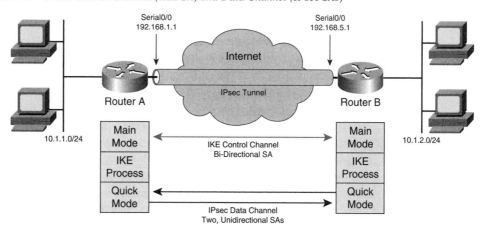

Diffie Hellman (DH) is a cryptographic key exchange protocol that allows two parties that have no prior knowledge of each other to jointly establish a shared secret key over an insecure communications channel. DH is the basic mechanism of the Oakley key exchange protocol that is used in the IKE process for deriving the shared secret keys between two

IPsec parties that are subsequently used for the data encryption process. IKE uses the DH mechanisms both during Phase 1 in the establishment of its own bi-direction (control channel) SA, as well as during Phase 2 in the establishment of both unidirectional (data plane) IPsec SAs.

IKE control channel sessions can be established using one of two modes: *main mode* or *aggressive mode*. Main mode is normally used for site-to-site VPN connections, whereas aggressive mode is normally used for remote-access VPN client session establishment. The primary difference between the two modes is in the number of messages they use to exchange endpoint attributes. Main mode uses more messages, and certain endpoint information exchange is delayed until they can be exchanged securely. Aggressive mode attempts to complete IKE session establishment within a minimum number of packets, albeit via a less secure packet exchange. This being the case, main mode consumes more processing and resources before knowing whether a session request is legitimate or not (in other words, before completing or deleting the IKE session), and thus is more susceptible to resource exhaustion attacks. This issue, which occurs in the original version of IKE (IKEv1), is corrected in IKEv2. Also, it is worth noting that IKE uses UDP as transport, defaulting to port 500, but typically using UDP port 4500 when NAT transparency mode is used.

After IKE has established its control plane, IPsec can be brought up for the actual data exchange portion of the VPN. User data can be encrypted, authenticated, or both, using the IPsec protocols ESP or AH (individually or both) to process and encapsulate user data. Each of these two IPsec protocols has its own IP protocol number, 50 and 51 respectively. These protocols are briefly described in the next section.

IPsec

As just stated, IPsec provides two protocols to define how the data will be processed within the VPN—the Encapsulating Security Protocol (ESP), and the Authentication Header (AH) protocol. These two protocols are described as follows:

- **Encapsulating Security Payload (ESP):** ESP is identified by IP protocol number 50 and is the protocol that handles encryption of IP data at Layer 3 to provide data confidentiality. It uses symmetric-key cryptographic algorithms, including NULL, Data Encryption Standard (DES), Triple DES (3DES), and Advanced Encryption Standard (AES), to encrypt the payload of each IP packet. When IPsec builds packets using the ESP protocol, an ESP header is either inserted between the original IP packet header and payload (for example, Layer 4 header + data) in *transport mode* or prefixed to the original IP header and full payload along with a new IP header in *tunnel mode*. These two modes of operation for ESP are described in more detail shortly. ESP by itself also provides some authentication and integrity capabilities, albeit with slightly less scope of coverage over each IP packet than what AH provides. As such, ESP can be used to provide encryption only, encryption plus authentication, or authentication only. (ESP can be used to provide similar services to AH using NULL encryption. The difference from ESP with authentication only is that AH also authenticates parts of the outer IP header—for instance, source and destination addresses—making certain that the packet really came from whom the IP header claims it is from.)

- **Authentication Header (AH):** AH is identified by the IP protocol number 51, and provides authentication and integrity services used to verify that a packet has not been altered or tampered with during transmission. The Authentication Header is either inserted between the original IP packet header and payload (for example, TCP header + data) in *transport mode* or prefixed to the original IP header and full payload along with a new IP header in *tunnel mode*. These two modes of operation for AH are described in more detail shortly. AH can be used in combination with ESP if privacy and full authenticity and integrity are required, or it can be used by itself to guarantee only the authenticity and integrity (not privacy) of each IP packet. When used in conjunction with digital certificates, the use of AH also provides non-repudiation functions for received packets. AH authenticates all parts of the IP packet, including the data, and all parts of the IP header.

Through the use of these protocols, the set of security services offered by IPsec includes access control, connectionless integrity, data origin authentication, protection against replay, confidentiality (encryption), and limited traffic flow confidentiality (tunnel mode only).

As noted, the tunnels shown in Figure 7-2 are represented by SAs stored on each device. SAs are an important part of the IPsec process because they define the trust relationships negotiated between any two IPsec endpoints. Through SAs, end devices agree on the security policies that will be used and identify the SA by an IP address, a security protocol identifier, and a unique security parameter index (SPI) value.

IPsec may be operated in one of two modes:

- **Transport mode:** IPsec transport mode retains the original IP header of the transported datagram. It can be used to secure a connection from a VPN client directly to the security gateway, for example, for IPsec protected remote configuration. Transport mode is generally used to support direct host-to-host communications. Transport mode for ESP or AH encapsulates the upper-layer payload, above the IP layer. These are typical Layer 4 and higher payloads such as TCP, UDP, and so on. This leaves the original Layer 3 IP header intact, allowing it to be used for other network services, such as the application of QoS. AH transport mode would be used for applications that need to maintain the original IP header and just need authentication and data integrity services. ESP transport mode would be used for applications that need to maintain the original IP header but also want to encrypt the remainder of the packet payload. Examples of the ESP and AH IPsec header additions for transport mode are shown in Figure 7-3(a) and Figure 7-4(a), respectively.

- **Tunnel mode:** IPsec tunnel mode completely encapsulates and protects the contents of an entire IP packet, including the original IP header. Tunnel mode indicates that the traffic will be tunneled to a remote gateway, which will decrypt/authenticate the data, extract it from its tunnel, and pass it on to its final destination. When using tunnel mode, an eavesdropper would see all traffic as sourced from and destined to the IPsec VPN tunnel endpoints, and not the true source and destination endpoints of the established data session. IPsec tunnel mode adds a new, 20-byte outer IP header to each packet, in addition to a minimum of 36 bytes for ESP or 24 bytes for AH as required for other packet header and trailer parameters applied by each protocol. When IPsec tunnel mode is combined with GRE, an additional 24 bytes is added by the GRE shim and GRE tunnel IP header. Examples of the ESP and AH IPsec header additions for tunnel mode are shown in Figure 7-3(b) and Figure 7-4(b), respectively.

Figure 7-3 *Application of IPsec ESP to IP Datagrams in Tunnel Mode and Transport Mode*

(a) IP Datagram – ESP Transport Mode

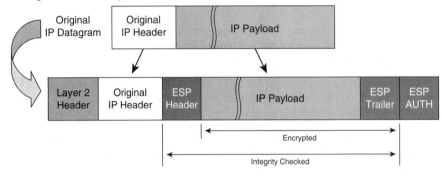

(b) IP Datagram – ESP Tunnel Mode

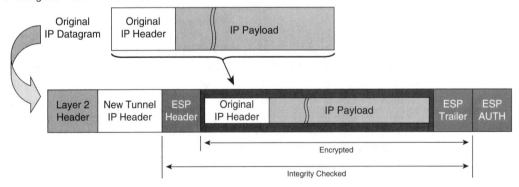

Figure 7-4   *Application of IPsec AH to IP Datagrams in Tunnel Mode and Transport Mode*

(a) IP Datagram – AH Transport Mode

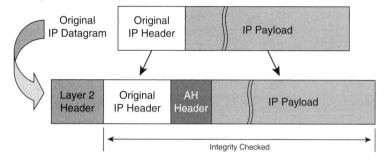

(b) IP Datagram – AH Tunnel Mode

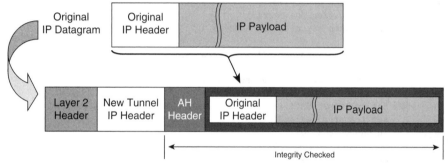

IPsec is designed per IETF standards for IP unicast-based traffic only. As such, when there are requirements to apply IPsec to multicast applications, non-IP traffic, or routing protocols that use multicast or broadcast addressing, then the additional use of a generic route encapsulation (GRE) tunneling is necessary. GRE provides the means for encapsulating many traffic types within unicast IP packets, hence meeting the requirement for IPsec encapsulation. With IPsec and GRE working together, support is available for multicast applications; routing protocols such as Open Shortest Path First (OSPF), Routing Information Protocol (RIP), and Enhanced Interior Gateway Routing Protocol (EIGRP); or even the transport of non-IP traffic such as IPX or AppleTalk within an IPsec environment.

A simple example configuration of an IPsec VPN using ESP encapsulation in tunnel mode is illustrated in Figure 7-5, with the corresponding configuration being given in Example 7-5. Figure 7-6 and corresponding configuration Example 7-6 show the same topology again for the comparable IPsec plus GRE architecture as a direct comparison.

Figure 7-5 *IPsec VPN Deployment Using ESP Tunnel Mode*

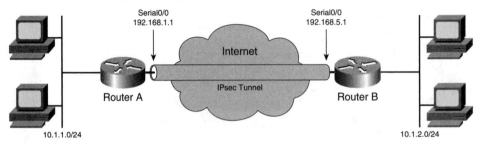

Example 7-5 *IPsec VPN Configuration Using ESP Tunnel Mode*

```
Router-A Configuration
!
crypto isakmp policy 10
  authentication pre-share
crypto isakmp key cisco123 address 192.168.5.1
!
crypto ipsec transform-set VPN-trans esp-3des esp-md5-hmac
!
crypto map vpnmap local-address Serial0//0
crypto map vpnmap 10 ipsec-isakmp
  set peer 192.168.5.1
  set transform-set VPN-trans
  match address 101
!
interface Ethernet1
  ip address 10.1.1.1 255.255.255.0
interface Serial1/0
  ip address 192.168.1.1 255.255.255.252
  crypto map vpnmap
!
access-list 101 permit ip 10.1.1.0 0.0.0.255 10.1.2.0 0.0.0.255
!
ip route 0.0.0.0 0.0.0.0 192.168.1.2

Router-B Configuration
!
crypto isakmp policy 10
  authentication pre-share
crypto isakmp key cisco123 address 192.168.1.1
!
crypto ipsectransform-set VPN-trans esp-3des esp-md5-hmac
!
crypto map vpnmap local-address Serial0//0
crypto map vpnmap 10 ipsec-isakmp
  set peer 192.168.1.1
  set transform-set VPN-trans
```

Example 7-5 *IPsec VPN Configuration Using ESP Tunnel Mode (Continued)*

```
   match address 101
!
interface Ethernet1
  ip address 10.1.2.1 255.255.255.0
interface Serial1/0
  ip address 192.168.5.1 255.255.255.252
  crypto map vpnmap
!
access-list 101 permit ip 10.1.2.0 0.0.0.255 10.1.1.0 0.0.0.255
!
ip route 0.0.0.0 0.0.0.0 192.168.5.2
```

The example illustrated in Figure 7-5 and the corresponding configurations in Example 7-5 draw on many default conditions and represent a very basic IPsec VPN setup in Cisco IOS. For brevity, only the relevant configuration components are shown. This example is useful nonetheless for illustrating the details of IPsec VPNs.

The components of relevance include the **crypto isakmp** configuration, which provisions the IKE Phase 1 process, and the **crypto ipsec transform-set** configuration, which provisions the IKE Phase 2 process. The **crypto map** elements tie the Phase 1 and Phase 2 components together, and the use of an **access-list** (101 in Example 7-5) specifies which traffic should be subjected to the IPsec VPN process.

It should be noted that the Phase 1 and Phase 2 attributes match in both router configurations, and that the access list entries in ACL 101 are reciprocals (mirror images) of each other. These are requirements for Cisco IPsec VPN configurations. Note also the use of the default route (**ip route**) as well. In this case, all traffic is forwarded toward the same next hop. However, only the traffic matching the crypto ACL will be encrypted and sent across the IPsec VPN tunnel. The remaining traffic (that which does not match the crypto ACL) is forwarded unaltered. In one sense, you may think of this as being similar to a static routing decision, because the router encrypts and encapsulates packets matching this ACL and forwards them not based on the original destination IP address, but instead based on the IPsec header destination IP address (in other words, the **set peer** address). For Cisco IOS, it is important to note that each entry in the crypto ACL causes the creation of a unique pair of SAs because these ACL entries represent IPsec policy enforcement specifications. SA creation and maintenance consumes resources on the router, and thus a finite number can be allocated.

Similar to the way in which managing static routes becomes overwhelming as your network size increase (and thus the benefit of the use of dynamic routing protocols), IPsec VPNs often enlist the aid of the GRE tunneling mechanisms to enable the use of dynamic routing protocols for similar efficiencies. Managing crypto ACL entries can become overwhelming and resource-consuming as IPsec VPN networks increase in size. One way to minimize the creation of SAs and at the same time obtain the benefits of dynamic routing is to use GRE tunneling within IPsec VPNs. IPsec (by IETF standards) is only capable of carrying unicast IP packets. Because GRE is itself a unicast IP packet, it is possible to apply the IPsec VPN policy to GRE-encapsulated traffic. This not only greatly simplifies the crypto ACL construction, as illustrated in Example 7-6, but also allows for the use of a dynamic routing protocol (across the GRE tunnel). The example illustrated in Figure 7-6 and the corresponding configurations in Example 7-6 show a very simplified IPsec plus GRE VPN deployment.

Figure 7-6 *IPsec + GRE VPN Deployment Using ESP Tunnel Mode*

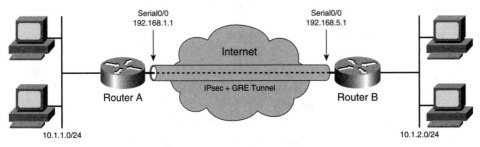

Example 7-6 *IPsec + GRE VPN Configuration Using ESP Tunnel Mode*

```
Router-A Configuration

crypto isakmp policy 10
  authentication pre-share
crypto isakmp key cisco123 address 192.168.5.1
!
crypto ipsec transform-set VPN-trans esp-3des esp-md5-hmac
!
crypto map vpnmap local-address Serial0//0
crypto map vpnmap 10 ipsec-isakmp
  set peer 192.168.5.1
  set transform-set VPN-trans
  match address 102
!
interface Ethernet1
  ip address 10.1.1.1 255.255.255.0
interface Serial1/0
  ip address 192.168.1.1 255.255.255.252
interface Tunnel0
  ip address 10.10.255.1 255.255.255.252
  ip mtu 1400
  tunnel source Serial0/0
  tunnel destination 192.168.5.1
  crypto map vpnmap
!
router eigrp 100
 network 10.0.0.0 0.0.0.255
 no auto-summary
!
ip route 0.0.0.0 0.0.0.0 192.168.1.2
```

Example 7-6 *IPsec + GRE VPN Configuration Using ESP Tunnel Mode (Continued)*

```
!
access-list 102 permit gre host 192.168.1.1 host 192.168.5.1


Router-B Configuration

crypto isakmp policy 10
  authentication pre-share
crypto isakmp key cisco123 address 192.168.1.1
!
crypto ipsectransform-set VPN-trans esp-3des esp-md5-hmac
!
crypto map vpnmap local-address Serial0//0
crypto map vpnmap 10 ipsec-isakmp
  set peer 192.168.1.1
  set transform-set VPN-trans
  match address 102
!
interface Ethernet1
  ip address 10.1.2.1 255.255.255.0
interface Serial1/0
  ip address 192.168.5.1 255.255.255.252
interface Tunnel0
  ip address 10.10.255.2 255.255.255.252
  ip mtu 1400
  tunnel source Serial0/0
  tunnel destination 192.168.1.1
  crypto map vpnmap
!
router eigrp 100
 network 10.0.0.0 0.0.0.255
 no auto-summary
!
ip route 0.0.0.0 0.0.0.0 192.168.5.2
!
access-list 102 permit gre host 192.168.5.1 host 192.168.1.1
```

Because the topologies in Figure 7-5 and Figure 7-6 include only two endpoints, the efficiency gains in using GRE are perhaps not obvious from the configurations in Example 7-5 and Example 7-6. It should be apparent, however, that as more networks are added behind the IPsec gateways (Routers A and B), additional entries in the crypto ACL would be required in Example 7-5 (and as a result, more SAs would be built). The crypto ACL in Example 7-6, on the other hand, would remain unchanged because it only refers to the GRE tunnel endpoints in the crypto ACLs, and dynamic routing takes care of the rest.

The preceding examples are very basic and are intended solely to illustrate the service components required for IPsec VPNs for the purpose of providing a point of reference for the security recommendations described next. There are many excellent references that deal specifically with IPsec VPN architectures and their optimizations. Some of these are referenced in the *Further Reading* section at the end of this chapter.

Securing IPsec VPN Services

It may sound odd that a security protocol such as IPsec requires protection itself. However, when considering that implementing IPsec requires significant additional packet processing resources above and beyond normal data plane forwarding, not to mention the establishment and maintenance of a separate control plane, it is easy to see why the IPsec process itself must be protected. Additional CPU processing (mainly for IKE functions), memory consumption (for SA storage), and specialized hardware (for encryption) are used to implement IPsec VPNs. The two main reasons for protecting IPsec include the following:

- **IPsec is a complex service:** IPsec involves extra packet handling, the maintenance of state, and additional interconnected complexities with routing, NAT, and other processing functions. Thus, IPsec can itself become a potential DoS target. Whether malicious or unintentional through misconfigurations and inadvertent resource consumption, it is possible to impact the IPsec service itself, or even the platform(s) upon which the service is hosted.

- **IPsec is a specialized service:** IPsec is a specialized service that requires additional resources beyond normal forwarding. Although newer hardware options are available to increase the capacity and performance of IPsec VPNs, these still remain premium services. Because this hardware represents a finite resource, only selected packets should be capable of using the service. In addition, the encryption process itself can add delay in forwarding, so QoS mechanisms may also need to be applied to prioritize flows within the IPsec VPN.

The main ideas here are essentially the same as with the other services previously described. The services plane applies additional packet handling requirements, implying that they can become DoS targets. In addition, services represent scarce resources (as compared with standard data plane forwarding), implying that the service should be reserved for selected packets. Thus, the following considerations should be made when deploying IPsec VPNs.

IKE Security

As described above in the IPsec VPN Overview section, the IKE establishes and maintains the control plane for IPsec VPNs. IKE uses UDP as transport, defaulting to port 500. IKE packets are *receive* packets and are normally processed by the router CPU itself. Because the IKE process must be publicly reachable, it is exposed to direct attack. In addition, the first version of IKE (IKEv1), the most generally deployed version today, requires that some fairly significant amount of processing be accomplished within the IKE Phase 1 negotiation process before it can determine whether the IKE request is legitimate or not. (IKEv2 provides some corrective measures to help alleviate this issue.) Thus, you should take steps to protect the IKE process. The following approaches can be taken, and may be layered with other mechanisms for additional protection:

- **Interface ACLs:** Interface ACLs may be used to limit the sources permitted to reach the IKE process if specific source IP addresses are known. This mainly applies for site-to-site VPNs with fixed IP addresses, because remote-access VPNs generally are sourced from unknown addresses. In the case where this is acceptable, the access list entries should permit selected traffic to reach UDP port 500. (Infrastructure ACL construction and deployment for control plane protection is covered in Chapter 5.)

- **CoPP:** Because IKE packets are *receive* packets that are processed by the router CPU, they are seen by CoPP mechanisms. CoPP can be used to rate limit IKE connection requests to the router. This has proven effective in cases where the source of the IKE requests is not previously known. Keep in mind that both legitimate and malicious requests will be rate limited. (Specific details on CoPP construction and deployment for control plane processes are covered in Chapter 5.)

- **Call Admission Control:** In later versions of Cisco IOS, a feature named Call Admission Control (CAC) was introduced to protect processes such as IKE session establishment. CAC may be configured and applied to IKE in one of two ways:

  - To limit the number of IKE SAs that a router can establish, you may configure an absolute IKE SA limit by entering the **crypto call admission limit ike sa** command in IOS global configuration mode. In this case, the router drops new IKE SA requests when the configured value has been reached.

  - To limit the system resources that the router may dedicate to IKE, expressed as a percentage of maximum global system resources available, you may configure the **call admission limit** command, also in IOS global configuration mode. In this case, the router drops new IKE SA requests when the specified percentage of system resources being used exceeds the configured value.

  More information on CAC may be found in the Cisco.com "Call Admission Control for IKE" reference in the "Further Reading" section.

Fragmentation

Fragmentation occurs when the IP packet size exceeds the egress link MTU. In modern networks, this is normally not an issue for standard IP forwarding, but, just as in the case of MPLS section above, when services plane protocols such as IPsec encapsulate packets, the added overhead results in oversized IP packets that may require fragmentation before transmission. IP packet fragmentation is never desirable. As previously described in

Chapter 2, fragmentation requires slow path processing and results in performance impacts. This performance impact manifests itself in several ways, some of which are generic to fragmentation in general, and some of which are specific to IPsec in particular. The following discusses both types of issues and then describes options for avoiding or managing fragmentation:

- **General fragmentation issues:** Generally, fragmentation requires the support of slow path processing on routers. Because of this, there is a performance impact simply due to slow path forwarding when fragmentation is required. In addition, fragmentation involves splitting one packet into two, and if the original packet is only slightly oversized, these two new packets will include one large packet and one small packet. Because there are now twice as many packets to forward, and when looking at the maximum forwarding rate of the platform on a PPS basis, you have now consumed twice the resources (headers, trailers, inter-packet delays, routing decisions, and so on) for the same amount of data. In addition, all intermediate routers must forward these additional packets as well. Finally, the receiver must reassemble the fragments, and if any fragments are lost along the way, the entire packet must be retransmitted.

- **IPsec specific fragmentation issues:** More specifically for IPsec, fragmentation can have an even more significant impact on router performance. One thing that should be obvious from Figures 7-3 and 7-4 is that the original packet size increases by up to 84 bytes, depending on IPsec options and mode. By default, packets are fragmented after encryption. When that happens, it causes reassembly to be required by the IPsec VPN peer router prior to decryption. Routers are not designed for fragmentation reassembly, and reassembly is even more processor intensive than fragmentation. For IPsec VPNs, two interrupts are required: one to get packets to the reassembly process, and one to get packets to the decryption process. (Reassembly is not normally required to be performed by the router for normal data plane traffic because the destination address is the end host, not the router itself.) When fragmentation and reassembly must be done in support of IPsec, this can reduce the forwarding performance by as much as 70 percent. As described in Chapter 2, IP routers have a limited number of reassembly buffers, which may also limit the rate of packet retransmissions. Finally, as mentioned above in the previous bullet point, fragmentation often results in the generation of two packets—one large and one small. This intermingling of large and small packets can result in very uneven delays in encryption processing and serialization and may have significant impacts on latency and jitter-sensitive applications deployed across the IPsec VPN.

Of course, the best scenario is to avoid fragmentation altogether. When applications are sending small data packets, fragmentation is never an issue. However, when large packets are involved, fragmentation consequences must be considered. There are a number of strategies for resolving fragmentation within the context of IPsec VPNs, and the best approach depends on your particular environment and on how much work you are willing to do to prevent fragmentation. There is no panacea, however, and some engineering effort must be expended to determine the best approach. The main approaches for preventing or managing fragmentation follow. The main idea for all of these techniques is to avoid both fragmentation and reassembly if possible. When this is not possible, minimize its impact on network performance by using these techniques.

Host MSS Modification

Hosts participating in IPsec VPNs can be hard coded to transmit IP packets that will not exceed a specified size. This technique completely eliminates fragmentation for all packet types. Many IPsec remote-access clients, including the Cisco client for example, provide options for setting this value on the host. (Typically, a value of 1400 bytes is used.) For hosts behind IPsec gateways, manual configuration of this value can be accomplished as well. More information on setting this value on common operating systems may be found in the Cisco Tech Note "Adjusting IP MTU, TCP MSS, and PMTUD on Windows and Sun Systems," referenced in the "Further Reading" section. You should also review your host operating system guide for specific details on setting this value. Note, however, that you cannot trust a compromised host to send properly sized packets that will not require fragmentation and reassembly.

Path MTU Discovery (PMTUD)

PMTUD (RFC 1191) was designed to dynamically determine the lowest MTU between two endpoints. There are several inherent requirements for PMTUD to work successfully, and when it works correctly, it can eliminate fragmentation for certain packet types. First, from the originating end host perspective, PMTUD only works for TCP sessions. Second, PMTUD requires that originating packets be transmitted by the host with the IP header DF bit set to 1 (enabled). This causes these packets to be dropped along the path by any forwarding device that is unable to forward the packet when fragmentation is required. In such a case, when the packet is dropped, an ICMP Type 3, Code 4 message (Fragmentation Needed and DF Was Set) is sent from the device that cannot forward the packet due to fragmentation requirements, to the originating IP address. This ICMP Type 3 Code 4 message also contains the required MTU setting necessary for successful transmission. (See Appendix B for more details on this ICMP message type.) In this way, the end host can dynamically learn the correct MTU and reduce packet size automatically to accommodate IPsec overhead.

IPsec participates in PMTUD conversations by default (per RFC 2401) and no extra configuration is required. When GRE is used in conjunction with IPsec, PMTUD must be enabled for the GRE tunnel as well by using the **tunnel path-mtu-discovery** command within the interface configuration mode. Any firewalls or ACLs along the return path that block ICMP packets will cause PMTUD to fail. PMTUD includes timers that age out the dynamically learned MTU value (the default is 10 minutes). This causes the PMTUD process to be repeated periodically. Finally, from the end host perspective, TCP is the only protocol that participates in PMTUD. Hence, if other protocols are used—say, for example, you are "testing" your links with large ICMP Echo Request packets and setting the DF bit—they will fail to be transmitted. (Other options must be pursued for non-TCP applications.)

Interface TCP MSS Modification

The TCP protocol Maximum Segment Size (MSS) (or Maximum Send Segment as it is sometimes referred to) option is sent by hosts within the TCP SYN packet during the TCP connection establishment phase. Each TCP end host then obey the MSS value conveyed by the other end. When IP traffic involves the TCP protocol, Cisco IOS CLI provides a mechanism (per interface) to intercept TCP SYN packets and insert a specific MSS value. The relevant interface command is **ip tcp adjust-mss** *<size>*, where *size* represents the maximum TCP segment size (in bytes) and must account for the header lengths (in bytes) for IP (20), TCP (20), GRE (24), and IPsec (up to 60) header components, meaning the value for *<size>* could be as small as 1376 bytes. This command should be configured on ingress interfaces toward the private side (originating hosts), or on the GRE tunnel interface. Obviously, this configuration option applies only to TCP traffic, but it can eliminate fragmentation issues when TCP protocols are involved.

Interface MTU Modification

As previously discussed in the MPLS VPN section above, the interface MTU may be set at either Layer 2 or Layer 3 to leave room in advance for IPsec overhead. To modify the Layer 2 interface MTU, use the **mtu** *<value>* interface configuration command. To modify the Layer 3 interface MTU value, use the **ip mtu** *<value>* interface configuration command. The Layer 3 form of this command may be used for GRE tunnels as well. The difference between the Layer 2 interface MTU and the Layer 3 interface MTU is that the Layer 3 interface MTU is protocol-specific. Namely, the **ip mtu** command only applies to IP packets, whereas the Layer 2 **mtu** command applies to any upper-layer protocols transmitted on the interface (for example, MPLS, L2TPv3, ARP, CDP, and so on). Using either of these techniques will have one of two effects on fragmentation:

- If PMTUD is enabled and host packets are TCP and originated with DF = 1, reducing the interface MTU will cause PMTUD to occur once (upon packet ingress to the router), which is not only much earlier in the processing, but also before the IPsec encryption occurs. This ensures that the receiving router will not be required to perform reassembly prior to decryption. If GRE is used, this configuration may save two PMTUD iterations (once prior to GRE encapsulation and a second after IPsec encryption.

- When PMTUD is not an option (DF = 0 or non-TCP protocol), modifying the interface MTU will at least cause fragmentation to occur prior to IPsec encryption (or GRE encapsulation), thereby saving precious resources on the tunnel receive end because reassembly is no longer required prior to IPsec decryption.

NOTE	Changing default MTU settings may cause the router recarving system packet buffers to accommodate the new MTU applied. This may disrupt packet-forwarding operations during the period of time it takes to complete the buffer recarve operations.

Look Ahead Fragmentation

When fragmentation absolutely cannot be avoided for whatever reason (for example, non-TCP, ICMP filtered, and so on), as a last resort the best option is to ensure that the DF bit is cleared so that all packets can at least be transmitted through the network (albeit with fragmentation being required). This can be accomplished within Cisco IOS using the **crypto ipsec df-bit clear** command, and then applying the **crypto ipsec fragmentation before-encryption** command (in either interface or global configuration mode). This feature, also known as *look-ahead fragmentation*, requires IPsec tunnel mode for support. Note that this Cisco IOS allows you to change the default (RFC specified) behavior of IPsec which is to fragment *after* encryption. This "looking ahead" feature causes IPsec to check the outbound interface MTU on a per-packet basis prior to encryption to predetermine if fragmentation will be required. If the packet will require fragmentation after IPsec encapsulation, IOS will fragment the packet prior to the encryption process. This saves precious resources on the tunnel receive end in that only decryption (as standard) is required and fragments can be forwarded downstream to the final destination for reassembly. This method does not prevent fragmentation, but does avoid reassembly at the tunnel receive end.

IPsec VPN Access Control

When you deploy an IPsec tunnel to encrypt data between private sites, it does not speak to the type of traffic being carried within the tunnel. For example, if an infected host on one side of the VPN attempts to infect hosts on the other side of the VPN, instead of having good traffic traversing your encrypted tunnel, you now have bad traffic traversing the tunnel. At a minimum, these precious IPsec VPN resources are being consumed by malicious traffic, which reduces their availability to legitimate traffic. This is not the only scenario where traffic flows must be considered. Thus, several IPsec VPN deployment techniques must be considered.

Crypto ACLs

Crypto ACLs (for example, ACL 101 in Example 7-5) define the IPsec SA proxy identities, and hence what traffic is to be encrypted (protected) by IPsec. You must use care when defining crypto ACLs, and consider them in conjunction with your routing tables. Just as over-summarizing routes can cause traffic black-holing, over-summarizing (or mis-summarizing) crypto ACL policies can cause unexpected behaviors, especially when default routes are used.

For example, consider the topology in Figure 7-5 and the configuration in Example 7-5. Note that default routes are used on both sides, and that crypto ACLs are specifically defined to include only the specific /24 owned by each router. If a packet is sourced from 10.1.1.1 behind Router-A and is destined to 10.1.2.1, it will be routed according to the default route, and then match the crypto ACL. Hence, it will be encrypted and sent across the IPsec tunnel as expected. But what if the destination was something other than 10.1.2.0/24? Say the destination is 10.10.2.1 or something that is not explicitly allocated by either endpoint. In this case, this packet would be routed by the default route, but fail the crypto ACL check. That is, it will be forwarded to the next hop (192.168.1.2 in this case) unaltered by IPsec. This may be what you intend, but if it is not, you must make accommodations to achieve the proper response. (It is not uncommon for SPs to receive many IP packets with private addresses due to errors like these.) It may be that a NAT policy should be implemented (also know as split tunneling), or it may be appropriate to drop such packets.

Considering Example 7-5 again, suppose the crypto ACL on each side was changed to **access-list 101 permit ip 10.0.0.0 0.255.255.255 10.0.0.0 0.255.255.255**. How would the packet forwarding behavior change? In this case, a packet sourced from 10.1.1.1 behind Router-A destined to 10.1.2.1 will be routed according to the default route, and then match the crypto ACL. Hence, it will be encrypted and sent across the IPsec tunnel and decrypted by Router-B as expected. But what about a packet sourced from 10.1.1.1 behind Router-A that is destined to some address that Router-B does not own, such as 10.10.2.1? In this case, the packet will be routed according to the default route, and then match the crypto ACL and be IPsec tunneled to Router-B, which will then decrypt the packet, perform a route lookup for the original destination (10.10.2.1 in this case), and route the packet via the default route *back* across the tunnel. This will continue until the packet TTL expires. Due to an imbalance between the routing table and the crypto ACL, a routing loop has been created. Packets from an infected host scanning for other vulnerable machines could generate this kind of traffic and would certainly consume all of the available encryption capacity. Host or server misconfigurations could also result in these kinds of packet loops and present the appearance of a DoS attack.

The main idea here is to ensure that your crypto ACLs are appropriately configured to account for the prefixes they can reach. Just as with routing, be careful not to over-summarize within crypto ACLs for addresses you do not own or have access to. Many administrators use GRE and dynamic routing protocols for this exact reason (as illustrated in Figure 7-6 and Example 7-6) because this type of configuration separates the crypto ACL policies from the routing policies and simplifies the overall IPsec configuration.

As illustrated in the case, when a default route is used, unintended behaviors can result. This is especially critical under attack scenarios. For example, worms often scan the entire network block associated with the host they infect. In the preceding scenario, this would mean the worm would scan the entire 10/8 network. Due to the default route, packets destined for prefixes in the 10/8 block and that are not covered by the crypto ACL will be forwarded toward the next hop. If NAT is employed, these bogus packets will consume all of the NAT resources. In this case, it is best practice to install a static route for 10/8 that points to Null0 (that is, **ip route 10.0.0.0 255.0.0.0 Null0**). This covers all networks that are not accounted for by *more specific* routes acquired through either static routes or dynamic routing protocols. These more specific routes will forward traffic to legitimate destinations, and the Null0 route will drop packets destined to bogus prefixes within your network block. The default route can still be used to provide access to the Internet for appropriate prefixes. This does not prevent bogus traffic from traversing the IPsec tunnel. However, it does protect the NAT process that would be used for split tunneling (to the Internet). End host security mechanisms should still be deployed, which are out of the scope of this book.

Interface ACLs

Interface ACLs may be used to apply stateless filtering on ingress interfaces toward the private side (originating hosts) to limit access to the IPsec process to only those packets and protocols that require IPsec encryption. This not only eliminates unnecessary packets from consuming precious encryption resources, but can make the task of defining crypto ACLs less complex. Remember that each crypto ACL entry results in the generation of two SA pairs. The SA database represents *state* in the router, which is a finite resource, and limiting the number of SAs that need to be created is prudent. In addition, during failover, IPsec will attempt to rebuild all failed SAs. Minimizing the number of SAs also improves high-availability performance.

CoPP

As noted earlier in the IKE section, IKE is a process on the router CPU and, hence, can be controlled by the CoPP mechanism. GRE also hits the router CPU and is also subject to CoPP mechanisms. Therefore, any policies applied to the control plane using CoPP must include specific entries for IKE and GRE when employed. (Specific details on CoPP construction and deployment are covered in Chapter 5.)

QoS

There are potentially two issues that may require the use of QoS with IPsec VPNs:

- **Specialized hardware:** IPsec services are often provided using specialized hardware or platforms. Typically, the performance of this hardware (in terms of PPS or bandwidth) is some fraction of the total bandwidth of the overall network itself. Thus,

IPsec represents a finite resource that may be oversubscribed. Therefore, QoS is often deployed in conjunction with IPsec VPNs to prioritize traffic within the tunnel. Typically this is accomplished by configuring the QoS service policies on all IPsec VPN endpoints (gateways). By default, QoS functions occur within Cisco IOS after IPsec encryption on egress interfaces. (See the Cisco IOS feature order of operations illustration in Figure 7-1.) Because the entire original packet is encrypted when using IPsec VPNs, viewing the original IP header DSCP values or TOS bits would normally not be possible.

Cisco IOS provides the QoS pre-classify feature to allow both IPsec VPNs and QoS to occur on the same system. This feature preserves the DSCP/TOS bit setting of the original packet by copying this information to the IP header of the final IPsec VPN packet. This allows for normal QoS functions to operate on the outer IP header associated with the IPsec VPN tunnel. This feature is enabled via the **qos pre-classify** interface configuration command, which may be applied to physical interfaces and to tunnel interfaces.

• **Encryption hardware and LLQ:** Encryption hardware processes packets on a first-in, first-out (FIFO) basis, and when large packets precede small packets, delay and jitter for the small packets can vary significantly. This can happen, for example, when voice traffic and large data transfers are intermixed in IPsec VPNs without prioritization. Cisco IOS provides low latency queuing (LLQ) to IPsec encryption engines to help reduce packet latency. Instead of treating the input to the encryption processor as a single queue that gives equal status to all packets and results in FIFO processing, this LLQ capability designates two queues: a best-effort queue for data packets, and a priority queue for delay-sensitive packets. The encryption hardware processes packets in a manner that favors the priority queue and guarantees a minimum processing bandwidth. Additional information on LLQ and IPsec VPNs may be found in "Low Latency Queuing (LLQ) for IPSec Encryption Engines," referenced in the "Further Reading" section.

Other IPsec Security-Related Features

There are many other security-related features applicable to highly available architectures, including resilient/redundant failover scenarios that also play a role in securing IPsec VPNs. These are outside the scope of this book. For more information, see the Cisco Press book *IPSec VPN Design* (see the "Further Reading" section), which covers many of these topics in detail.

Other Services

The preceding three IP services plane examples were selected for two primary reasons. First, they are widely deployed and, hence, you may already have familiarity with one if not all of them. In that case, hopefully the preceding discussions provided you an opportunity to review your own security deployments in support of these services (or encouraged you to do so). Second, they are useful for illustrating the thought process used to identify underlying weaknesses and attack vectors that exist within various services. Often times these challenges are obvious or direct, as is the case for IKE call admission for example, while other times they are not, as is the case for IPsec fragmentation impacts. Hopefully, the three examples above illustrate the common themes that must be well assessed when developing security methodologies for other services plane applications.

As indicated at the outset of this chapter, the services plane includes the application of processes that require additional packet handling above and beyond normal IP data plane forwarding processes. Within the context of this book, all services plane functions use at least the data plane. As in the case of MPLS and IPsec VPNs, these services also directly use the control plane. For QoS services, the control plane may also be used directly, as in the case of RSVP signaling. Although there is no way to completely generalize where or how all services are deployed, you will most likely find that these links and interdependencies between data plane and control plane components may provide attack vector opportunities within most services plane deployments.

Many other services are deployed within IP networks in addition to those covered by the three examples above. It is simply not possible to cover all possible services in detail within a single chapter, nor even a single book. However, a quick review and brief description of some of the more common services is appropriate and follows next.

SSL VPN Services

Secure Sockets Layer (SSL) VPNs are typically used to provide secure, clientless remote-access connectivity to corporate networks and assets. In contrast to IPsec, which was designed to provide secure services for IP packets (the network layer, Layer 3), SSL (and its successor, Transport Layer Security [TLS]) was designed to provide secure services for the transport layer (Layer 4). Officially, SSL can be used to add security to any protocol that uses reliable connections. However, SSL is predominantly associated with securing TCP-based applications, and within TCP, it is most commonly associated with securing web applications through the Secure Hypertext Transport Protocol (HTTPS, TCP port 443).

In contrast to IPsec, which requires the deployment and maintenance of a separate control plane through IKE for proper operations, SSL does not depend on a separate control plane to establish encrypted sessions between endpoints. Instead, all security negotiations are performed in-band between the server and client. Therefore, no separate control channel must be protected as is the case of IKE for IPsec. Similarly to IPsec, however, SSL can have a significant impact on the CPU levels of an SSL gateway when large numbers of session terminations occur due to the relatively high processing demands incurred by public-key cryptography. This implies that efforts must be taken to prevent precious CPU resources from being consumed, just as in the case of IPsec. In this regard, endpoint security cannot be ignored. One often-discussed disadvantage of SSL VPNs is that their universal access via web browsers allows connectivity from virtually anywhere, including untrusted locations and hosts (Internet cafes, kiosks, hotels, and so on), which poses significant risks for the corporate network.

For additional information on Cisco deployments of SSL VPNs, refer to the Cisco Press book *Comparing, Designing, and Deploying VPNs*, which provides details on architecture and deployments, or the Cisco.com article "SSL VPN Security," both of which are listed in the "Further Reading" section.

VoIP Services

Voice over IP (VoIP) services carry voice signals over an IP network, and are one of the most compelling emerging technologies. VoIP services typically use standards-based protocols, including H.323, Session Initiation Protocol (SIP), or Media Gateway Control Protocol (MGCP). Officially called "Recommendation H.323," H.323 refers to an umbrella recommendation from the International Telecommunication Union (ITU) for packet-based multimedia communications systems, including VoIP and IP-based videoconferencing (see the reference for H.323 in the "Further Reading" section). SIP is an application layer control protocol, defined in RFC 3261, and similarly, MGCP is defined by RFC 3435 (see the reference for these RFCs in the "Further Reading" section). All of these protocols use some combination of both TCP and UDP for transport, define fixed port numbers for a separate control channel used for call setup and management, and use dynamic port ranges for media streams. Real-time Transport Protocol (RTP) is used for audio streams. The main differences between these protocols primarily involve their call control architectures and call control signaling.

In many respects, VoIP services have similar design characteristics to IPsec VPN services, and thus many of the same security questions and solutions apply. For example, because VoIP services establish their own separate control channel to support call setup and call control, these control channels are subject to very similar security requirements as those created by IPsec VPNs.

VoIP services are also delay and jitter dependent, and are quite intolerant of packet loss. As such, QoS services are almost always deployed in conjunction with VoIP services, especially for business-class deployments. The deployment of security mechanisms and low-latency QoS techniques are often orthogonal, however, and security can negate the effectiveness of QoS in some cases. For example, RTP ports used for audio streams are usually dynamically assigned during call setup within the control channel. This complicates firewall deployments as they are now required to either permit a wide range of UDP ports access to the network, or have features to inspect the control channel to determine which ports to allow for each call. (Cisco firewalls perform this dynamic port tracking with a feature called *fixups*.)

Less-capable devices may add unacceptable latency in this inspection process, impacting the VoIP service quality. In addition, when encryption is used, QoS services may not be able to recognize and prioritize VoIP traffic from any other traffic. A session border controller (SBC) may also be used along with firewalls to exert control over the signaling involved in setting up and tearing down calls and the media streams.

Attacks directly against VoIP services are not necessarily required to break or disable the service entirely. Simply degrading the performance of the network may be sufficient to render the VoIP service unusable. VoIP relies upon a number of ancillary services as part of the configuration process and to deliver its services. These include but are not limited to DNS, DHCP, HTTP, HTTPS, SNMP, SSH, RSVP, and TFTP services. Securing the underlying infrastructure, as described in previous chapters, is requisite for securing VoIP services. DoS attacks against the network infrastructure (Layer 3 and Layer 2 attacks), against VoIP clients and servers, and against other essential but ancillary services (DNS, DHCP, TFTP, and so on) can all impact VoIP services.

Because VoIP protocols are still evolving, the features required to secure VoIP networks and services are still under development as well. For additional information on VoIP security based on Cisco SIP-enabled products, refer to the Cisco white paper "Security in SIP-Based Networks" and NIST Special Publication 800-58, *Security Considerations for Voice Over IP Systems*, both of which are listed in the "Further Reading" section.

Video Services

Video services are another one of the compelling emerging technologies, and are part of the new "triple play" of data, voice, and video offered by service providers. Video services share many common attributes with voice services and therefore share many of the same security concerns and solutions.

Like voice services, video services also require real-time delivery of data streams and are also dependent on delay and jitter (the variability in delay from one packet to the next). Video requires a constant bit stream to maintain the quality of the image. However, the single most important factor in the delivery of acceptable video services is the protection of the video stream from frame drops. When too many frames are lost, the video quality is impaired. Thus, network congestion must be avoided and so QoS is often applied as part of video services. Thus, the concerns previously described for VoIP and QoS apply here as well. Video services also establish their own separate control channel to support session setup and session control, and these control channels are subject to very similar security requirements as those described in the preceding section for voice services. DoS attacks against the control channel. Thus, attacks against video services, like attacks against voice services, may simply attempt to degrade the performance of the network, rendering the video service unusable.

Similar to voice services, video services may also be impacted by the deployment of security services. For example, the same dynamic port assignment issues described for voice services also apply for video services, and hence firewall deployments must be handled in a similar manner.

One potentially critical problem for video delivery that is not found in voice services is related to packet size. Whereas voice applications tend to require fairly small packets to transport audio streams, video applications (such as video conferencing, for example) can use large packet sizes. Video streams with typical MPEG-2 or MPEG-4 (Moving Pictures Experts Group) encoding and transported over RTP or other transport protocols can generate packets as large as the network MTU. From a security perspective, when video services are combined with VPN services such as MPLS or IPsec, there is the potential for IP fragmentation to be required due to the extra overhead involved in the VPN encapsulation process, as described in detail above in both the MPLS VPN and IPsec VPN sections. One of the main issues with fragmentation in the case of video is that each slightly oversized video packet is fragmented into one large and one small packet. This results in significant jitter through encryption engines and forwarding processes and causes significant impacts on the quality of video services. For dedicated video conferencing equipment, for example, the solution is simply to configure smaller maximum packet sizes to prevent fragmentation in the first place.

Video streams also may be carried in IP unicast or multicast packets, depending on the type of service (on-demand versus live broadcast, for example). In Chapters 2, you learned about several important issues related to securing IP multicast. Multicast can require a significant amount of packet punts within the control plane for state creation. Control signaling via Protocol Independent Multicast (PIM) or Internet Multicast Group Protocol (IGMP) must be protected, and control plane policing can be deployed for this purpose, as well as best practice techniques such as PIM neighbor filters and IGMP access groups. Similar techniques can be deployed for other multicast protocols as applicable.

Like voice services, video services also rely upon the same ancillary network support services as other applications, such as DNS, DHCP, HTTP, HTTPS, SNMP, SSH, RSVP, and TFTP services. Securing the underlying infrastructure, as described in previous chapters, is requisite for securing video services. DoS attacks against the network infrastructure (Layer 3 and Layer 2 attacks) and against other essential but ancillary services (DNS, DHCP, TFTP, and so on) can all impact video services.

Additional information on video services and security can be found in the Cisco Press book *Voice and Video Conferencing Fundamentals*, listed in the "Further Reading" section.

Summary

This chapter described security issues related to the IP services plane. The services plane refers to user traffic that requires specialized packet handling by network elements above and beyond the standard IP data plane forwarding process. Three IP services plane examples were described in detail; QoS, MPLS VPNs, and IPsec VPNs. The intention of describing these IP services plane examples was to illustrate the thought process used to identify underlying weaknesses and security threats that exist within these services. Hopefully, these examples illustrate the common themes that must be well understood when developing security methods for other services plane applications.

Within the context of this book, all services plane traffic uses at least the IP data plane and control plane of the network, but may also optionally establish a separate control plane session to support the underlying service. It is most often the case that interactions and interdependencies between data plane and control plane components are the most vulnerable areas in any services plane deployment. Also, many services depend on tight, or at least predictable, SLAs for operational deployments. In these cases, QoS impacts must be considered. In addition, it was shown that when VPN services are combined with other services, fragmentation can become problematic due to encapsulation overhead. In these cases, accommodations must be made to eliminate fragmentation. Finally, most services are highly dependent upon a number of ancillary services such as DNS, DHCP, HTTP, HTTPS, SNMP, SSH, RSVP, TFTP, and other baseline services, which all require protection. DoS attacks against the network infrastructure (Layer 3 and Layer 2 attacks) and against other ancillary but essential services (DNS, DHCP, TFTP, and so on) can impact nearly every IP service.

Review Questions

1 The services plane is distinguished from other IP traffic planes by what main attribute?

2 When deploying the DiffServ QoS model, what network edge technique should you deploy to prevent unauthorized use of high-priority traffic classes, and how is it implemented?

3 Name the three categories of MPLS VPN router types (excluding ASBRs) and identify the one that does not require MPLS functionality.

4 What, if any, are the challenges with IP rACL and CoPP policies applied on the PE router that use source address filtering?

   5 How many bytes of transport overhead does an MPLS VPN ingress PE impose?

   6 What is the IOS command to disable IP TTL to MPLS TTL propagation?

   7 Which of the Inter-AS VPN architectural options is considered the most secure?

   8 IPsec VPNs use IKE as a control plane. Briefly describe the functions provided by IKE, and indicate what protocol it uses for transport.

   9 IPsec supports what two protocols, and what services do these two protocols provide?

   10 IPsec VPNs may require fragmentation of IP packets. When fragmentation is of concern, name three options for preventing or minimizing fragmentation impacts.

Further Reading

Alvarez, S. *QoS for IP/MPLS Networks*. Cisco Press, 2006. ISBN: 1-58705-233-4.

Andreasen, F., and B. Foster. *Media Gateway Control Protocol (MGCP) Version 1.0*. RFC 3435. IETF, Jan. 2003. http://www.ietf.org/rfc/rfc3435.txt.

Behringer, M. H., and M. J. Morrow. *MPLS VPN Security*. Cisco Press, 2005. ISBN: 1-58705-183-4.

Bollapragada, V., M. Khalid, and S. Wainner. *IPSec VPN Design*. Cisco Press, March 2005. ISBN: 1-58705-111-7.

Evans, J. W., and C. Filsfils. *Deploying IP and MPLS QoS for Multiservice Networks: Theory & Practice*. Morgan Kaufmann, 2007. ISBN: 0-123-70549-5

Firestone, S., T. Ramalingam, and S. Fry. *Voice and Video Conferencing Fundamentals*. Cisco Press, 2007. ISBN: 1-58705-268-7.

Kuhn, D. R., T. J. Walsh, and S. Fries. *Security Considerations for Voice Over IP Systems*. NIST Special Publication 800-58. National Institute for Standards and Technology, January 2005. http://csrc.nist.gov/publications/nistpubs/800-58/SP800-58-final.pdf.

Lewis, M. *Comparing, Designing, and Deploying VPNs*. Cisco Press, 2006. ISBN: 1-58705-179-6.

Rosenberg, J. et al. *SIP: Session Initiation Protocol*. RFC 3261. IETF, June 2002. http://www.ietf.org/rfc/rfc3261.txt.

Song, S. "SSL VPN Security." Cisco Documentation. http://www.cisco.com/web/about/security/intelligence/05_08_SSL-VPN-Security.html.

"Adjusting IP MTU, TCP MSS, and PMTUD on Windows and Sun Systems." (Doc. ID: 13709.) Cisco Tech Note. http://www.cisco.com/warp/public/105/38.shtml.

"Call Admission Control for IKE." *Cisco IOS Software Releases 12.3T Feature Guide*. http://www.cisco.com/en/US/products/sw/iosswrel/ps5207/products_feature_guide09186a0080229125.html.

"H.323: Packet-based Multimedia Communications Systems." ITU Recommendation, June 2006. http://www.itu.int/rec/T-REC-H.323/en.

"Low Latency Queuing (LLQ) for IPSec Encryption Engines." *Cisco IOS Software Releases 12.2T Feature Guide*. http://www.cisco.com/en/US/products/sw/iosswrel/ps1839/products_feature_guide09186a008013489a.html.

"Pre-Fragmentation for IPSec VPNs." *Cisco IOS Security Configuration Guide, Release 12.4*. http://www.cisco.com/en/US/products/ps6350/products_configuration_guide_chapter09186a0080455b91.html.

"Resolve IP Fragmentation, MTU, MSS, and PMTUD Issues with GRE and IPSEC." (Doc. ID: 25885.) Cisco white paper. http://www.cisco.com/en/US/tech/tk827/tk369/technologies_white_paper09186a00800d6979.shtml.

"Security in SIP-Based Networks." Cisco white paper. http://www.cisco.com/warp/public/cc/techno/tyvdve/sip/prodlit/sipsc_wp.htm.

"Why Can't I Browse the Internet when Using a GRE Tunnel?" (Doc. ID: 13725.) Cisco Tech Note. http://www.cisco.com/warp/public/105/56.html.

Case Studies

In this chapter, you will learn about the following:

- How to apply IP traffic plane security techniques to a typical Internet-based, IPsec VPN enterprise network design

- How to apply IP traffic plane security techniques to a typical MPLS VPN enterprise network design

- How the combination of IP traffic plane techniques provides an effective defense in depth and breadth security architecture

CHAPTER 8

Enterprise Network Case Studies

The purpose of this chapter is to demonstrate the use of the concepts and techniques described in Chapters 4 through 7 by applying them to conceptual enterprise networks as case studies. The intent is to clarify your understanding of how all of these security techniques are brought together to form an effective defense in depth and breadth security strategy that secures the enterprise network and each of its IP traffic planes.

Two case studies are presented, one being a site-to-site Internet-based IPsec VPN, and the other being a site-to-site MPLS VPN. Defense in depth and breadth principles are applied to protect IP traffic planes within each architecture. The common topology for both of these case studies is illustrated in the high-level, conceptual diagram shown in Figure 8-1. As shown in Figure 8-1, a service provider (SP) IP/MPLS core network provides access for both case studies. Customer A has three sites, two that connect directly to the SP (Corporate HQ and Remote 1) and one that obtains Internet access through some other provider (Remote 2). These three Customer A sites will be used to illustrate a very common IPsec VPN and Internet access topology. Customer B also has three sites, but in this case all of them connect directly to the SP IP/MPLS network. These three Customer B sites will be used to illustrate a very common MPLS VPN case.

The case studies in this chapter focus on the enterprise (customer) side of the network. That is, in each case study, the focus is on the customer edge routers and their respective security requirements. In Chapter 9, "Service Provider Network Case Studies," the focus will be turned on the SP side of the network for these same case studies. Thus, Chapters 8 and 9 are companions to each other and share a common topology whereby external interfaces interconnect the enterprise and SP networks in both case studies.

The following information is presented for both case studies in this chapter:

- The network topology, including IP addressing plans, and the requirements for network data plane, control plane, management plane, and services plane traffic, as appropriate
- The derived router configurations, along with detailed comments describing the relationship between specific entries and each entry's respective contribution to IP traffic plane security

Figure 8-1 *Conceptual View of Enterprise and Service Provider Networks for Chapters 8 and 9 Case Studies*

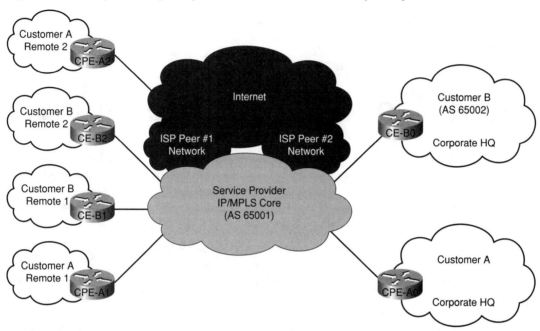

Obviously, no single enterprise network design case study can cover all aspects of IP traffic plane security, and these case studies will not be able to cover every possible topology, variation, nuance, or condition. What should be evident from these case studies, however, is the defense in depth and breadth methodology used to identify and protect each IP traffic plane component within the enterprise network designs presented. With this understanding, you will be able to apply similar methods and procedures to your particular network topology, product mix, and organizational mission, with the goal of developing appropriate IP traffic plane security policies.

Case Study 1: IPsec VPN and Internet Access

Case Study 1 focuses on a typical enterprise scenario where IPsec is used within an Internet access environment to connect headquarters and remote sites into a private IP VPN. A description of the case study network topology, functional requirements for the network, and translated security requirements follows.

Network Topology and Requirements

The network topology and assigned IP addressing schemes used within this case study are illustrated in Figure 8-2. Customer A has three sites with Internet access. Two sites, Corporate HQ (on the right side of the figure) and Remote 1 (on the lower-left side of the figure), obtain their Internet connectivity by direct connections to the same SP IP/MPLS network. The third site, Remote 2 (on the upper-left side of the figure), obtains its Internet access through a different provider.

The functional requirements assumed in this case study are as follows:

- **IPsec VPN hub-and-spoke topology:** To provide the necessary functionality of privacy between headquarters and remote sites, Customer A deploys GRE + IPsec to create its VPN topology. GRE is used in conjunction with IPsec so that Customer A can also run OSPF within the VPN to provide dynamic routing-based reachability information for internal networks. In this way, each IPsec VPN tunnel appears as a single-hop forwarding path between remote sites and the HQ site. Remote CPE routers appear as if they are one IP hop away from the HQ CPE router. Because GRE is used, IPsec is run in transport mode.

- **User (internal) access to Internet:** Customer A uses NAT to provide Internet reachability from the private address space within its enterprise networks. In this case study, assume that all 10/8 addresses are private and that NAT is used for external traffic destined to the Internet. Outbound traffic is limited to web-based resources (HTTP port 80 and HTTPS port 443).

- **Static IP default routing between SP and customer sites:** Customer A uses OSPF as its Interior Gateway Protocol (IGP), including between remote sites. All external sites, including the Internet, are found via a static default route directed toward each PE interface IP address.

- **Internet (external) access to Customer A web services:** Customer A requires that web services within its DMZ network located at the HQ site shall be reachable from the Internet. In this case study, assume that the 172.16.0.0/24 DMZ network is Internet routable, and that a single web server (or proxy) located at 172.16.0.16/32 must be reachable from the Internet.

- **Management:** Customer A manages its own routers in this case study. Management plane traffic is only permitted on internal interfaces and from internal (private) addresses. For operational reasons, certain ICMP packets for example, Echo Reply, Time Exceeded (for traceroute), and a few other selected types, must be permitted from the Internet. Management applications assumed in this case study include SSH, HTTPS, Syslog, SNMP, NTP, SCP, TACACS+, and DNS.

Figure 8-2 *Conceptual Enterprise Network Architecture for Internet-Based IPsec VPN Case Study 1*

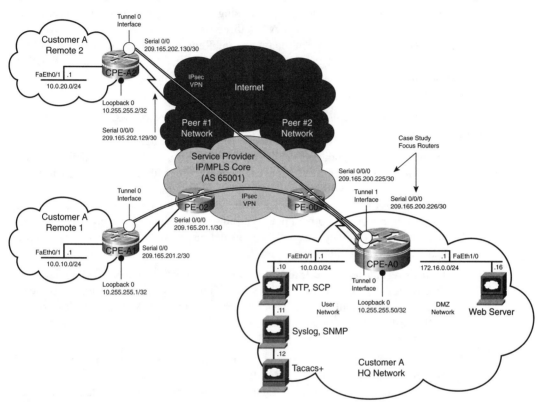

Figure 8-3 highlights the types and relationships of the interfaces found on the customer edge (CE) routers in this case study. These interface types were first introduced in Chapter 3, "IP Network Traffic Plane Security Concepts." The following interfaces are included in this case study:

- **Internal:** Internal interfaces connect network assets wholly within the administrative domain of Customer A. All three Customer A routers include at least one internal interface. In this case study, FastEthernet0/1 for CPE-A1 and FastEthernet0/1 for CPE-A2 are internal for the remote sites. The headquarters router, CPE-A0, includes two internal interfaces represented by FastEthernet0/1 for the user network and FastEthernet1/0 for the DMZ network. (Of course, the trust levels are very different for these two internal interfaces.) The assigned IP addresses for this case study are shown in Figure 8-2 for each internal interface. In all cases, /24 subnet masking is assigned. The prefixes associated with these internal interfaces are routed within the IGP (OSPF in this case study) to form the Customer A private network.

- **External:** External interfaces connect networks belonging to two different administrative domains. All three Customer A routers include one external interface, Serial0/0 in all cases, that connects each CE router to its upstream Internet provider. CPE-A0 and CPE-A1 connect to the SP IP/MPLS network that is the focus of the Chapter 9 SP case study. CPE-A2 connects to a different provider. (This is solely to show that for IPsec VPNs, CPEs only require Internet access and not connectivity to one specific SP.) The assigned IP addresses for this case study are shown in Figure 8-2 for each of these serial connections. In all cases, /30 address masking is assigned. The prefixes associated with these external interfaces are not routed within the IGP in this case study because they are provided by the upstream SP and serve as transit links only with no attached IP hosts.

- **Loopback:** All three Customer A CPE routers implement a single loopback interface that is primarily used for management plane traffic. In this case study, Loopback0 is used. The assigned IP addresses for this case study are shown in Figure 8-2 for each loopback interface. In all cases, /32 address masking is assigned. These loopback interfaces are routed within the IGP and are reachable via the Customer A VPN for management plane purposes.

- **Tunnel:** All three Customer A routers implement a tunnel interface that is used to deliver services plane traffic. That is, the tunnel interface provides GRE encapsulation for Customer A traffic that is to be encrypted with the IPsec VPN. In this case study, CPE-A1 and CPE-A2 each require a single tunnel interface, Tunnel0, to connect to the HQ router. The HQ router, CPE-A0, requires two tunnel interfaces, Tunnel0 and Tunnel1, in this case study, one for each remote site. Several options exist for tunnel interface addressing. In this case study, each tunnel interface takes on the IP address of the loopback interface on the same router.

- **Receive:** All routers include by default a receive interface that "logically" represents the slow path to the IOS process level. This applies to any ingress packets that must be punted from the CEF fast path to the router's CPU for local processing.

Figure 8-3 highlights in particular the router of focus for this case study, CPE-A0, and illustrates the relationship among its interfaces. This router is also the focus for the sample IOS configuration in the "Router Configuration" section that follows.

Router Configuration

Security configurations may be derived based upon the preceding topology and functional requirements. Router CPE-A0 is used as the focal point for the remaining discussions. The other Customer A CPE routers shown in the topology in Figure 8-2 have similar but locally specific configurations.

Figure 8-3 *IP Traffic Plane Relationships to Router Interfaces for Internet-Based IPsec VPN Case Study 1*

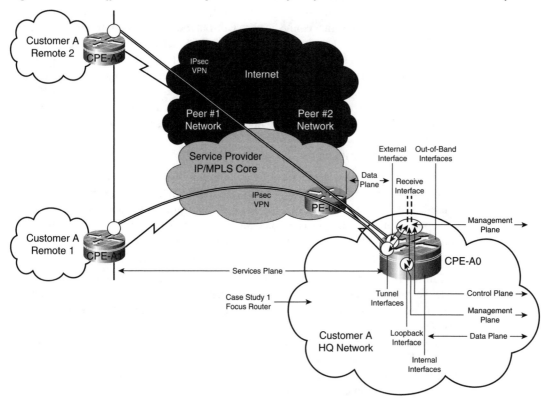

Example 8-1 provides the derived Cisco IOS configuration that implements the preceding requirements and defense in depth and breadth security principles. This configuration assumes that CPE-A0 is a Cisco ISR class router (1800, 2800, or 3800 series), and that it is running Cisco IOS version 12.4 software with IPsec AES/3DES feature support and advanced IP services support. Line numbers precede each configuration command shown in Example 8-1 and serve as reference points for the remainder of the discussion that directly follows, which is organized by IP traffic plane.

Example 8-1 *Case Study 1 Enterprise Customer Premises Edge Router Configuration*

```
1 : !
2 : version 12.4
3 : service nagle
4 : no service pad
5 : service tcp-keepalives-in
6 : service tcp-keepalives-out
7 : service timestamps debug datetime msec localtime show-timezone
8 : service timestamps log datetime msec localtime show-timezone
```

Example 8-1   *Case Study 1 Enterprise Customer Premises Edge Router Configuration (Continued)*

```
 9 : service password-encryption
10 : no service dhcp
11 : !
12 : hostname CPE-A0
13 : !
14 : boot-start-marker
15 : boot system flash c3845-advipservicesk9-mz.124-10.bin
16 : boot-end-marker
17 : !
18 : logging buffered 4096 debugging
19 : no logging console
20 : logging monitor errors
21 : enable secret 5 $1$Vmt.$SYiN8ZjKPe7DuTvNHm/vS.
22 : !
23 : aaa new-model
24 : !
25 : aaa authentication banner ^C
26 : **** AUTHORIZED ACCESS ONLY *****
27 : **** This system is the property of Customer A
28 : **** Disconnect IMMEDIATELY if you are not an authorized user!
29 : **** ********************* *****^C
30 : aaa authentication password-prompt Customer_A-Password:
31 : aaa authentication username-prompt Customer_A-Username:
32 : !
33 : aaa authentication login CustA group tacacs+ local
34 : aaa authentication enable default group tacacs+ enable
35 : aaa authorization exec default group tacacs+ none
36 : aaa accounting commands 1 default start-stop group tacacs+
37 : aaa accounting commands 10 default start-stop group tacacs+
38 : aaa accounting commands 15 default start-stop group tacacs+
39 : !
40 : aaa session-id common
41 : !
42 : memory-size iomem 15
43 : ip subnet-zero
44 : no ip source-route
45 : no ip gratuitous-arps
46 : ip icmp rate-limit unreachable 100
47 : ip spd mode aggressive
48 : ip options drop
49 : ip tcp window-size 32768
50 : ip tcp synwait-time 5
51 : ip tcp path-mtu-discovery
52 :!
53 :!
54 : ip cef
55 : ip domain name customer-a.com
56 : no ip domain lookup
```

continues

Example 8-1 *Case Study 1 Enterprise Customer Premises Edge Router Configuration (Continued)*

```
 57 : !
 58 : !
 59 : no ip bootp server
 60 : ip ssh time-out 20
 61 : ip ssh source-interface Loopback0
 62 : ip ssh version 2
 63 : ip scp server enable
 64 : !
 65 : !
 66 : memory free low-watermark processor 100000
 67 : memory free low-watermark IO 1000000
 68 : username gregg privilege 15 secret 5 $1$c/vj$kAzIb.llu.OBhGH1hRVS2/
 69 : username dave privilege 10 secret 5 $1$gCTJ$wjUiXxisNBZfxQeJr67a91
 70 : !
 71 : !
 72 : class-map match-all CoPP-management
 73 :   match access-group 121
 74 : class-map match-all CoPP-normal
 75 :   match access-group 122
 76 : class-map match-all CoPP-remaining-IP
 77 :   match access-group 124
 78 : class-map match-all CoPP-routing
 79 :   match access-group 120
 80 : class-map match-any CoPP-undesirable
 81 :   match access-group 123
 82 : !
 83 : !
 84 : policy-map CoPP
 85 : class CoPP-undesirable
 86 :    police 8000 1500 1500 conform-action drop  exceed-action drop
 87 : class CoPP-routing
 88 :    police 125000 1500 1500 conform-action transmit  exceed-action transmit
 89 : class CoPP-management
 90 :    police 50000 1500 1500 conform-action transmit  exceed-action drop
 91 : class CoPP-normal
 92 :    police 15000 1500 1500 conform-action transmit  exceed-action drop
 93 : class CoPP-remaining-IP
 94 :    police 8000 1500 1500 conform-action transmit  exceed-action drop
 95 : class class-default
 96 :    police 8000 1500 1500 conform-action transmit  exceed-action transmit
 97 : !
 98 : !
 99 : crypto isakmp policy 10
100 :   encr 3des
101 :   authentication pre-share
102 : crypto isakmp key s3cr3t address 209.165.201.2
103 : crypto isakmp key s3cr3t address 209.165.202.130
104 : !
105 : crypto ipsec transform-set CRYPTO esp-3des esp-sha-hmac
106 :   mode transport
107 : !
108 : crypto call admission limit ike sa 2
```

Example 8-1 *Case Study 1 Enterprise Customer Premises Edge Router Configuration (Continued)*

```
109 : !
110 : crypto map GREIPSEC local-address Serial0/0
111 : crypto map GREIPSEC 10 ipsec-isakmp
112 :  set peer 209.165.201.2
113 :  set transform-set CRYPTO
114 :  match address GRE1
115 : crypto map GREIPSEC 20 ipsec-isakmp
116 :  set peer 209.165.202.130
117 :  set transform-set CRYPTO
118 :  match address GRE2
119 : !
120 : !
121 : interface Tunnel0
122 :  description - To Customer A Remote 1
123 :  ip unnumbered Loopback0
124 :  ip verify unicast source reachable-via rx
125 :  ip mtu 1400
126 :  tunnel source Serial0/0
127 :  tunnel destination 209.165.201.2
128 : !
129 : interface Tunnel1
130 :  description - To Customer A Remote 2
131 :  ip unnumbered Loopback0
132 :  ip verify unicast source reachable-via rx
133 :  ip mtu 1400
134 :  tunnel source Serial0/0
135 :  tunnel destination 209.165.202.130
136 : !
137 : interface Null0
138 :  no ip unreachables
139 : !
140 : interface Loopback0
141 :  description - Loopback for Management access
142 :  ip address 10.255.255.50 255.255.255.255
143 :  no ip unreachables
144 : !
145 : interface Serial0/0
146 :  description - To SP PE-00
147 :  ip address 209.165.200.226 255.255.255.252
148 :  ip access-group iACL-external in
149 :  ip verify unicast source reachable-via rx allow-default
150 :  no ip redirects
151 :  no ip unreachables
152 :  no ip proxy-arp
153 :  ip nat outside
154 :  ip virtual-reassembly
155 :  no fair-queue
156 :  crypto map GREIPSEC
157 : !
158 : interface FastEthernet0/0
159 :  no ip address
```

continues

Example 8-1 *Case Study 1 Enterprise Customer Premises Edge Router Configuration (Continued)*

```
160 :   shutdown
161 : !
162 : interface FastEthernet0/1
163 :  description - Customer A HQ Internal
164 :  ip address 10.0.0.1 255.255.255.0
165 :  ip access-group iACL-internal out
166 :  ip verify unicast source reachable-via rx
167 :  no ip redirects
168 :  no ip unreachables
169 :  no ip proxy-arp
170 :  ip nat inside
171 :  ip virtual-reassembly
172 :  ip route-cache flow
173 :  ip ospf message-digest-key 1 md5 7 044858051D7258
174 :  no mop enabled
175 : !
176 : interface FastEthernet1/0
177 :  description - Customer A HQ DMZ
178 :  ip address 172.16.0.1 255.255.255.0
179 :  ip access-group iACL-DMZ in
180 :  ip verify unicast source reachable-via rx
181 :  no ip redirects
182 :  no ip unreachables
183 :  no ip proxy-arp
184 :  ip ospf message-digest-key 1 md5 7 0017400516081F
185 :  no mop enabled
186 : !
187 : interface FastEthernet1/1
188 :  no ip address
189 :  shutdown
190 : !
191 : router ospf 10
192 :  log-adjacency-changes
193 :  area 0 authentication message-digest
194 :  passive-interface FastEthernet0/1
195 :  passive-interface FastEthernet1/0
196 :  passive-interface Loopback0
197 :  network 10.0.0.0 0.0.0.255 area 0
198 :  network 10.255.255.50 0.0.0.0 area 0
199 :  network 172.16.0.0 0.0.0.255 area 0
200 : !
201 : no ip http server
202 : ip http access-class 10
203 : ip http authentication local
204 : ip http secure-server
205 : ip classless
206 : ip route 0.0.0.0 0.0.0.0 209.165.200.225
207 : ip route 10.0.0.0 255.0.0.0 Null0
208 : ip route 14.0.0.0 255.0.0.0 Null0
209 : ip route 24.0.0.0 255.0.0.0 Null0
210 : ip route 39.0.0.0 255.0.0.0 Null0
211 : ip route 127.0.0.0 255.0.0.0 Null0
```

Example 8-1 *Case Study 1 Enterprise Customer Premises Edge Router Configuration (Continued)*

```
212 : ip route 128.0.0.0 255.255.0.0 Null0
213 : ip route 169.254.0.0 255.255.0.0 Null0
214 : ip route 172.16.0.0 255.240.0.0 Null0
215 : ip route 192.0.2.0 255.255.255.0 Null0
216 : ip route 192.168.0.0 255.255.0.0 Null0
217 : !
218 : ip nat inside source list NATADD interface Serial0/0 overload
219 : !
220 : ip access-list extended GRE1
221 :  permit gre host 209.165.200.226 host 209.165.201.2
222 : ip access-list extended GRE2
223 :  permit gre host 209.165.200.226 host 209.165.202.130
224 : ip access-list extended NATADD
225 :  deny   ip 10.0.0.0 0.0.0.255 10.0.0.0 0.255.255.255
226 :  permit ip 10.0.0.0 0.0.0.255 any
227 : ip access-list extended iACL-DMZ
228 :  permit tcp host 172.16.0.16 eq www any established
229 : ip access-list extended iACL-external
230 :  permit udp host 209.165.201.2 host 209.165.200.226 eq isakmp
231 :  permit udp host 209.165.202.130 host 209.165.200.226 eq isakmp
232 :  permit esp host 209.165.201.2 host 209.165.200.226
233 :  permit esp host 209.165.202.130 host 209.165.200.226
234 :  deny ip 0.0.0.0 0.255.255.255 any
235 :  deny ip 10.0.0.0 0.255.255.255 any
236 :  deny ip 14.0.0.0 0.255.255.255 any
237 :  deny ip 24.0.0.0 0.255.255.255 any
238 :  deny ip 39.0.0.0 0.255.255.255 any
239 :  deny ip 127.0.0.0  0.255.255.255 any
240 :  deny ip 128.0.0.0 0.0.255.255 any
241 :  deny ip 169.254.0.0 0.0.255.255 any
242 :  deny ip 172.16.0.0  0.31.255.255 any
243 :  deny ip 192.0.2.0   0.0.0.255 any
244 :  deny ip 192.168.0.0 0.0.255.255 any
245 :  deny ip any 224.0.0.0 0.0.0.255
246 :  deny ip 224.0.0.0 0.0.0.255 any
247 :  permit tcp any host 172.16.0.16 eq www
248 :  permit tcp any host 209.165.200.226 established
249 :  permit icmp any 209.165.200.226 echo-reply
250 :  permit icmp any 209.165.200.226 ttl-exceeded
251 :  permit icmp any 209.165.200.226 port-unreachable
252 :  permit icmp any 209.165.200.226 protocol-unreachable
253 :  permit icmp any 209.165.200.226 packet-too-big
254 : ip access-list extended iACL-internal
255 :  permit tcp host 172.16.0.16 eq www 10.0.0.0 0.0.0.255 established
256 :  deny   ip 172.16.0.0 0.0.0.255 any
257 :  permit tcp any 10.0.0.0 0.0.0.255 established
258 :  permit tcp host 10.0.0.1 host 10.0.0.10 eq 22
259 :  permit udp host 10.255.255.50 eq snmp host 10.0.0.11
260 :  permit udp host 10.255.255.50 eq snmptrap host 10.0.0.11
261 :  permit udp host 10.255.255.50 host 10.0.0.11 eq syslog
```

continues

Example 8-1 *Case Study 1 Enterprise Customer Premises Edge Router Configuration (Continued)*

```
262 :  permit udp host 10.255.255.50 host 10.0.0.10 eq ntp
263 :  permit icmp any 10.0.0.0 0.0.0.255 echo-reply
264 :  permit icmp any 10.0.0.0 0.0.0.255 packet-too-big
265 :  permit icmp any 10.0.0.0 0.0.0.255 time-exceeded
266 :  permit icmp any 10.0.0.0 0.0.0.255 port-unreachable
267 :  permit icmp any 10.0.0.0 0.0.0.255 protocol-unreachable
268 : logging trap notifications
269 : logging source-interface Loopback0
270 : logging 10.0.0.11
271 : access-list 10 permit 10.0.0.0 0.255.255.255
272 : access-list 120 remark -- Routing Protocol ACL for CoPP
273 : access-list 120 remark -- -- permit ospf
274 : access-list 120 permit ospf 10.0.0.0 0.255.255.255 any precedence internet
275 : access-list 121 remark -- Management Protocol ACL for CoPP
276 : access-list 121 remark -- -- permit ssh (and also scp)
277 : access-list 121 permit tcp 10.0.0.0 0.255.255.255 10.0.0.0 0.255.255.255 eq 22
278 : access-list 121 remark -- -- permit snmp
279 : access-list 121 permit udp 10.0.0.0 0.255.255.255 10.0.0.0 0.255.255.255
       eq snmp
280 : access-list 121 remark -- -- permit tacacs+
281 : access-list 121 permit tcp 10.0.0.0 0.255.255.255 eq tacacs 10.0.0.0
       0.255.255.255 established
282 : access-list 121 remark -- -- permit DNS
283 : access-list 121 permit udp 10.0.0.0 0.255.255.255 eq domain 10.0.0.0
       0.255.255.255
284 : access-list 121 remark -- -- permit ntp
285 : access-list 121 permit udp 10.0.0.0 0.255.255.255 10.0.0.0 0.255.255.255
       eq ntp
286 : access-list 121 remark -- -- permit https
287 : access-list 121 permit tcp 10.0.0.0 0.255.255.255 10.0.0.0 0.255.255.255
       eq 443
288 : access-list 121 remark -- -- permit traceroute
289 : access-list 121 permit udp any gt 10000 any gt 10000
290 : access-list 121 remark -- -- permit IKE (udp 500)
291 : access-list 121 permit udp any any eq isakmp
292 : access-list 122 remark -- Normal Traffic ACL for CoPP
293 : access-list 122 remark -- -- permit ICMP types
294 : access-list 122 permit icmp any any echo
295 : access-list 122 permit icmp any any echo-reply
296 : access-list 122 permit icmp any any ttl-exceeded
297 : access-list 122 permit icmp any any unreachable
298 : access-list 122 permit icmp any any port-unreachable
299 : access-list 122 permit icmp any any packet-too-big
300 : access-list 123 remark -- Undesirable Traffic ACL for CoPP
301 : access-list 123 remark -- -- Block Fragments
302 : access-list 123 permit tcp any any fragments
303 : access-list 123 permit udp any any fragments
304 : access-list 123 permit icmp any any fragments
305 : access-list 123 permit ip any any fragments
306 : access-list 123 remark -- -- Block Slammer
307 : access-list 123 permit udp any any eq 1434
308 : access-list 124 remark -- Catch-All IP ACL for CoPP
309 : access-list 124 remark -- -- permit all IP
```

Example 8-1 *Case Study 1 Enterprise Customer Premises Edge Router Configuration (Continued)*

```
310 : access-list 124 permit ip any any
311 : snmp-server community s3cr3t RO 10
312 : snmp-server packetsize 1400
313 : snmp-server enable traps tty
314 : snmp-server trap-source Loopback0
315 : snmp-server host 10.0.0.11 version 2c s3cr3t
316 : no cdp run
317 : !
318 : tacacs-server host 10.0.0.12
319 : tacacs-server timeout 2
320 : no tacacs-server directed-request
321 : tacacs-server key 7 0017400516081F
322 : !
323 : control-plane
324 :   service-policy input CoPP
325 : !
326 : !
327 : banner motd ^C
328 : **** AUTHORIZED ACCESS ONLY *****
329 : **** This system is the property of Customer A
330 : **** Disconnect IMMEDIATELY if you are not an authorized user!
331 : **** ********************** *****^C
332 : privilege exec level 10 show ip ospf
333 : privilege exec level 10 show ip route
334 : privilege exec level 10 show ip interface
345 : privilege exec level 10 show ip
336 : privilege exec level 10 show logging
337 : !
338 : line con 0
339 :  exec-timeout 60 0
340 :  login authentication CustA
341 : line aux 0
342 :  transport input none
343 :  transport output none
344 : line vty 0 4
345 :  access-class 10 in
346 :  exec-timeout 60 0
347 :  login authentication CustA
348 :  transport input ssh
349 : !
350 : scheduler allocate 6000 1000
351 : process cpu threshold type total rising 80 interval 5 falling 20 interval 5
352 : ntp authentication-key 1 md5 0505121F6C471D10 7
353 : ntp authenticate
354 : ntp trust-key 1
355 : ntp source Loopback0
356 : ntp access-group serve-only 10
357 : ntp server 10.0.0.10 key 1
358 : !
359 : end
```

Data Plane

In this case study, and from the perspective of router CPE-A0, data plane traffic includes the following:

- **Internal to internal traffic:** Data plane traffic in this category includes traffic that is sourced from and destined to devices wholly within the administrative domain of the enterprise. In the case of CPE-A0, this includes all packets routed between local LANs (that is, only those packets routed between FastEthernet0/1 and FastEthernet1/0). Packets traversing the IPsec VPN are converted from the data plane to the services plane as described in the "Services Plane" section later in the chapter. Even though this traffic remains within a single administrative domain, this traffic is considered to be in the services plane due to the extra processing and specialized handling performed by the router.

- **Internal to external traffic:** Data plane traffic in this category includes traffic that is sourced internally but destined to external networks (Internet traffic, for example) outside the administrative domain of this enterprise. In the case of CPE-A0, this type of internal to external traffic is sourced from internal users on the 10.0.0.0/24 private network and destined to networks outside of the 10.0.0.0/24 private network. User traffic sourced from the private 10.0.0.0/24 network is converted from the data plane to the services plane through the NAT process (as discussed below in the "Services Plane" section later in this chapter). For the purposes of this case study, there should not be any traffic sourced from the 172.16.0.0/24 DMZ network except for the replies from the web server located at 172.16.0.16/32. This traffic remains in the data plane.

- **External to internal traffic:** Data plane traffic in this category includes traffic that is externally sourced and destined to internal resources. In the case of CPE-A0, the web server at 172.16.0.16/32 on the DMZ network is the only authorized internal host granted reachability from external networks. (IPsec traffic from remote sites is included in the "Services Plane" section.)

Data Plane Security

From the perspective of router CPE-A0, the security mechanisms used for data plane traffic segmentation and control include the following:

- **Interface ACL:** An interface ACL is applied to the Serial0/0 interface in the ingress (in) direction to limit the traffic permitted to enter CPE-A0. Example 8-1 configuration lines 229 through 253 implement this functionality via the named extended ACL iACL-external, which is then applied to the Serial0/0 interface in the inbound direction on line 148. Note that this ACL accounts for all ingress traffic, so entries are included for data, management, and services plane traffic. (No IP layer control plane traffic traverses this interface.) An interface ACL is also applied to FastEthernet0/1 in the egress (out) direction to limit the traffic permitted to reach the user LAN. Configuration lines 254 through 267 implement this functionality via the named extended ACL iACL-internal, which is applied to the FastEthernet0/1 interface in the outbound direction on line 165. Note that this ACL only permits return HTTP traffic from the DMZ LAN, and return TCP traffic, management plane traffic, and certain ICMP traffic from the Internet. Finally, an interface ACL is applied to the FastEthernet1/0 interface in the ingress direction to limit the permitted traffic *sent from* the DMZ LAN. Configuration lines 227 through 228 implement this functionality via the named extended ACL iACL-DMZ, which is applied to the FastEthernet1/0 interface in the inbound direction on line 179. This ACL only permits established HTTP traffic from the DMZ LAN to be transmitted. Although these ACLs have some duplication of coverage, together they provide defense in depth and breadth protection and increase the overall security posture of router CEP-A0.

Note   The use of the *stateful* IOS Firewall feature is also feasible and can provide additional security when compared to *stateless* ACLs. IOS Firewall is capable of tracking outbound requests and dynamically tracking these requests to permit return traffic in a stateful manner. Refer to the "Further Reading" section for more details.

- **Antispoofing ACL:** Assuming RFC 3330 special-use IPv4 addresses should not be routed within the Internet, all IP packets with RFC 3330 addresses as sources must be dropped because they are obviously spoofed packets. Thus, these prefixes are included in the iACL-external interface ACL applied to Serial0/0 in the ingress direction. (Note that the CPE-A0 DMZ prefix 172.16.0.0/32 is assumed to be routable for the purposes of this case study but is otherwise part of the RFC 3330 reserved address space. Regardless, packets should not enter Serial0/0 with source addresses of internal infrastructure prefixes.) Antispoofing functionality is implemented as part of the named extended ACL iACL-external via lines 234 through 246.

- **uRPF:** Unicast RPF strict mode is deployed on all interfaces. For the Serial0/0 interface, the **allow-default** keyword must be used for this implementation, as shown on line 149, given that a default route is used for forwarding to external prefixes reachable via the Internet. For the internal interfaces, FastEthernet0/1 and FastEthernet1/0, uRPF strict mode can be applied without the **allow-default** keyword, as shown on lines 166 and 180. In addition, uRPF strict mode is applied to the Tunnel0 and Tunnel1 interfaces, as shown on lines 124 and 132. Note that the static routes to Null0 improve the effectiveness of uRPF (as described in the upcoming "Control Plane" section). uRPF provides antispoofing protection in conjunction with the interface ACL described above in support of defense in depth and breadth principles.

- **IP options:** The ability for the router to process IP packets with option headers is disabled with the global **ip options drop** configuration (line 48). The default IOS behavior of processing IP packets with the Source Route option header is also disabled with the **no ip source-route** configuration (line 44). While overlap exists between these two commands for IP packets with source route header options, but this supports in depth and breadth principles.

- **IP directed broadcasts:** The dropping of IP directed broadcast packets is the default behavior in this IOS image, so the best common practice (BCP) for earlier IOS images to include the **no ip directed-broadcast** command is not required.

- **ICMP techniques:** On a per-interface basis, several ICMP BCPs are also enabled. Disabling IP redirects is configured using the **no ip redirects** interface command (lines 150, 167, and 181), and disabling the generation of ICMP Destination Unreachable messages is configured using the **no ip unreachables** interface command (lines 151, 168, and 182). The global rate limiting of ICMP Destination Unreachable messages is also enabled via line 46. The generation of ICMP Address Mask Reply messages and ICMP Information Reply messages is disabled by default in this IOS image, so the BCP for earlier IOS images to include the **no ip information-reply** and **no ip mask-reply** interface commands is not required.

Control Plane

In this case study, and from the perspective of router CPE-A0, control plane traffic includes the following:

- **IGP traffic:** IP layer control plane traffic in this category includes OSPF, which is used as the IGP in the case study. OSPF is configured for all private prefixes. In the case of CPE-A0, this includes the 10.0.0.0/24 and 172.16.0.0/24 networks, and the 10.255.255.50/32 prefix for Loopback0. In this case study, OSPF adjacencies will only be formed between CPE routers across the IPsec-protected GRE tunnels. Thus, OSPF control plane traffic does not need to be sent out internal interfaces. OSPF traffic from other sites will appear as services plane traffic to the external (Serial) and tunnel interfaces.

- **Layer 2 keepalives:** Layer 2 keepalives will exist on the Serial interfaces of CPE-A0. Layer 2 keepalives are not defined within the IEEE Ethernet specifications, nor are they applicable to virtual interfaces such as Loopback0.

Control Plane Security

From the perspective of CPE-A0, the security mechanisms that will be used for control plane traffic segmentation and control include the following:

- **Control Plane Policing (CoPP):** CoPP is one of the primary mechanisms for protecting the route processor CPU. When configured, all punted packets reach the route processor CPU through the CoPP mechanism, including all control plane and management plane packets, most services plane packets, and exceptions IP data plane packets. In the case of CPE-A0, CoPP is implemented via MQC mechanisms. In total, the CoPP configuration includes the ACLs 120, 121, 122, 123, and 124 shown on lines 272 through 310, the class-map statements shown on lines 72 through 81, and the policy-map statements shown on lines 84 through 96. CoPP is enabled by applying the service policy to the control plane, as shown on lines 323 through 324. Note that the **class-default** portion of the CoPP **policy-map** (lines 95 and 96) should be left unpoliced here because it only sees Layer 2 keepalive traffic, due to the existence of the catch-all CoPP-remaining-IP traffic class (lines 93 and 94) directly preceding it in the policy map.

- **Default route:** A default route to the Internet is configured on line 206. Because a default route matches *any* destination prefix, other security measures are implemented to prevent the router from forwarding spoofed traffic (for example, in the case where malware infects a user network device). These include the ACLs and uRPF configurations that prevent spoofed traffic from reaching the Internet (described earlier in the "Data Plane" section), the static routes to Null0 (described in this section), and portions of the NAT configuration that help protect NAT and IPsec encryption resources (described in the "Services Plane" section later in the chapter).

- **OSPF MD5 authentication:** OSPF is enabled on lines 191 through 199. The **passive-interface** commands on lines 194 through 196 prevent OSPF from sending its control plane traffic out these interfaces. (The network prefixes associated with these interfaces will still be carried within and advertised by OSPF.) The MD5 hash-based authentication feature is turned on for OSPF with the **area 0 authentication message-digest** configuration (line 193) to prevent OSPF message spoofing. The interfaces FastEthernet0/1 and FastEthernet1/0 apply the MD5 key for OSPF router authentication, as shown on lines 173 and 184, respectively. Note that even though the prefix associated with Loopback0 is carried in OSPF, this interface does not require the MD5 key to be applied because it is a virtual interface.

- **Selective Packet Discard (SPD):** SPD is turned on by default, and the hold-queue, headroom, and extended headroom default settings are adequate. However, SPD aggressive mode is not enabled by default and should be turned on. SPD aggressive mode is enabled via the *hidden* global EXEC command **ip spd mode aggressive** (line 47). (This command will then appear in the configuration.)

- **Static routes to Null0:** A static route to Null0 is installed for the 10.0.0.0/8 prefix. Only certain prefixes within the 10.0.0.0/8 IP address block are actually used by Customer A sites. However, because a default route points toward the Internet, any traffic generated toward unknown destinations will flow toward the Internet and consume NAT resources. This static route to Null0 prevents packets destined to unknown addresses within the 10.0.0.0/8 block from reaching the Internet by way of the NAT process (which helps protect NAT resources). Similar rationale applies for the other prefixes assigned static routes to Null0. These static routes also aid uRPF strict mode, especially with the **allow-default** keyword, in distinguishing spoofed source addresses. (Legitimate sources will match the uRPF check based on the more-specific 10.0.x.0/24 prefixes installed via OSPF. Spoofed packets outside these more-specific prefixes will fail the uRPF check due to the Null0 match.) Static routes to Null0 are applied via lines 207 through 216. The Null0 interface is configured on line 137, and the generation of ICMP Destination Unreachable messages is disabled on the Null0 interface on line 138.

- **Disable unused services:** BCP router security configurations related to the control plane include disabling the proxy ARP feature on a per-interface basis via the **no ip proxy-arp** command (lines 152, 169, and 183) and, for the FastEthernet interfaces, disabling the MOP protocol via the **no mop enabled** command (lines 174 and 185).

Management Plane

In this case study, and from the perspective of router CPE-A0, management plane traffic includes the following:

- **Provisioning traffic:** Management plane traffic in this category includes SSH, HTTPS, and SCP traffic. This traffic must be sourced internally per the case study requirements. Telnet, FTP, and TFTP are not permitted because they are inherently insecure protocols. In the case of CPE-A0, ingress management traffic of this type will be destined to the 10.255.255.50/32 address of Loopback0. Management traffic of this type will be destined to the 10.0.0.0/24 prefix range (all provisioning occurs from within the HQ site).

- **Monitoring traffic:** Management plane traffic in this category includes SNMP and Syslog, and this traffic exists only within the internal network. In the case of CPE-A0, ingress SNMP traffic will be destined to the 10.255.255.50/32 address of Loopback0. For this case study, Customer A is assumed to have collocated the SNMP and Syslog services on the server at 10.0.0.11.

- **Other traffic:** Several other protocols are configured within the management plane, including NTP and TACACS+ traffic. In the case of CPE-A0, management traffic of this type will all be within the 10.0.0.0/24 prefix range. For this case study, the TACACS+ server is at 10.0.0.12 and the NTP device is at 10.0.0.10. In addition, several types of ICMP packets (management plane traffic) must be permitted for operational needs (Echo Reply, Time Exceeded, and certain IP Unreachable messages). CDP is globally disabled.

- **OOB traffic:** The console interface is configured for OOB management plane access.

Management Plane Security

From the perspective of CPE-A0, the security mechanisms that will be used for management plane traffic segmentation and control include the following:

- **Loopback0 interface:** The interface Loopback0 is configured on lines 140 through 143 to support management plane traffic.

- **AAA:** AAA is fully configured for authentication, authorization, and accounting. This begins with the **aaa new-model** configuration (line 23). An authentication banner is configured (lines 25 through 29), and customized authentication username and password prompts are configured (lines 30 and 31). Login authentication is configured to use TACACS+ and then local information with the list name CustA (line 33). Enable-mode authentication is configured to use TACACS+ and then the enable secret (line 34). (The TACACS+ server implementation is not shown.) Command authorization is configured to use TACACS+ and then none (line 35). Command accounting is configured to use TACACS+ (lines 36 through 38). Finally, two local usernames are configured with different privilege levels (lines 68 and 69). Several commands have been added at privilege level 10 for users granted this level of enable access, as shown on lines 332 through 336.

- **SSH services:** Configuring SSH requires that a domain name be specified (for RSA encryption key generation), as shown on line 55. (The RSA encryption key is generated outside the configuration during router setup.) SSH protocol parameters are configured on lines 60 through 62.

- **In-band VTY access:** In-band VTY management plane access is configured on lines 344 through 348. VTY access is restricted to sources matching ACL 10 via line 345, and in-band VTY access is restricted to using the SSH protocol only, on line 348.

- **HTTPS and SCP services:** HTTPS access is enabled via lines 202 through 204. Line 202 restricts HTTPS access to sources matching ACL 10. ACL 10 is defined on line 271. HTTP is disabled on line 201. Secure Copy (SCP) server functionality is enabled on line 63.

- **SNMP and Syslog:** SNMP configuration parameters are implemented via lines 311 through 315. SNMP access is restricted to read-only by the community string *s3cr3t* and is limited to sources matching ACL 10 via line 311. (SNMP is restricted to only monitoring in this case study. Write access is not permitted.) Syslog configurations are included on lines 268 through 270. In addition, to generate Syslog messages when OSPF adjacency changes occur, logging of these changes is enabled on line 192.

- **TACACS+, NTP, and DNS:** The TACACS+ server parameters are configured via lines 318 through 321. The DNS name resolution by the router is disabled on line 56. NTP is configured via lines 352 and 357. Ingress NTP messages are restricted to sources permitted by ACL 10 (line 356). Further, MD5 authentication is enabled for NTP message exchanges with the configured NTP server (lines 352 through 354 and line 357).

- **Out-of-band console access:** OOB (console port) access is configured on lines 338 through 340. Console login authentication is referred to the AAA list CustA on line 340. AUX port transport is disabled (effectively shutting down the port) on lines 341 through 343.

- **Disable unused services:** Several global service settings are disabled, including PAD service (line 4), DHCP services (line 10), and (globally) CDP (line 316). Note that CDP could be disabled on a per-interface basis if its use was desired within the Customer A network. In this case, it would be disabled only on external interfaces.

The processing of gratuitous ARP messages is disabled on line 45, and the BOOTP service is disabled on line 59. Note that disabling IP finger services is the default in this IOS image, so the **no ip finger** or **no service finger** commands are not required.

- **Other BCPs:** Other BCP router security configurations related to the management plane are implemented. The router host name is configured on line 12. Global service settings are modified, including enabling timestamps for all debug and logging messages (lines 7 and 8) and enabling password encryption services (line 9). The router boot image is specified on line 15 (lines 14 and 16 are auto-generated). Buffered logging is enabled at debug level and the buffer size is set (line 18). The display of logging messages to the console is disabled (line 19), and logging to the monitor at the error level is enabled (line 20). The enable secret is set on line 21. Several global settings for router self-generated TCP sessions are adjusted, including enabling Nagle services (line 3), enabling TCP keepalives (lines 5 and 6), increasing the TCP window size (line 49), reducing the TCP SYN wait time (line 50), and enabling Path MTU Discovery (line 51). In order to generate Syslog messages when free memory resources are low, low-watermark levels are set for processor and I/O memory on lines 66 and 67. A message of the day (MOTD) login banner is configured on lines 327 through 331. To guarantee CPU time for processes, **scheduler allocate** is configured on line 350. Finally, in order to generate Syslog messages when CPU resources are low, processor CPU threshold levels are set on line 351.

Services Plane

In this case study, and from the perspective of router CPE-A0, services plane traffic includes the following:

- **GRE + IPsec VPN traffic:** Services plane traffic in this category includes all traffic traversing the GRE + IPsec VPN tunnels between headquarters and remote sites. All packets (data plane, control plane, and management plane) that are exchanged between headquarters and remote sites are routed through the established GRE tunnels. All GRE packets have source and destination addresses corresponding to each Serial0/0 interface. The GRE tunnel interfaces themselves are unnumbered, but reference the Loopback0 interface. All GRE packets are then encrypted using the IPsec ESP protocol. All IPsec packets also have source and destination addresses corresponding to each Serial0/0 interface. IKE provides the control channel for IPsec and also has source and destination addresses corresponding to each Serial0/0 interface.

- **NAT traffic:** Services plane traffic in this category includes all traffic that is sourced internally but destined to external networks (for instance, Internet traffic) outside the administrative domain of this enterprise. In the case of CPE-A0, user traffic from the private 10.0.0.0/24 network is converted from the data plane to the services plane using NAT resources. (Return traffic to the NAT process is also permitted.)

Services Plane Security

From the perspective of CPE-A0, the security mechanisms that will be used for services plane traffic segmentation and control include the following:

- **GRE:** GRE is configured to provide unicast IPv4 encapsulation of all packets considered to be within the Customer A private network. From the perspective of CPE-A0, two tunnels are configured, one to Remote 1 and a second to Remote 2. The GRE tunnel interfaces are configured on lines 121 through 127 and lines 129 through 135. The tunnel IP MTU is set to 1400 bytes on lines 125 and 133 to cause GRE to prefragment IP packets that exceed 1400 bytes in length to account for GRE and IPsec encapsulation overhead. GRE would normally prefragment for packets exceeding 1476 bytes by default. (This prevents packets from potentially being fragmented by the router after IPsec encapsulation, which would result in significant performance degradation due to the need for reassembly prior to decryption on the receiving side. That is, if fragmentation is required, it is done prior to IPsec encryption.)

- **IPsec:** IPsec is configured to encrypt the GRE tunneled traffic between headquarters and remote sites. The IKE (IPsec Phase 1) configuration is listed on lines 99 through 101. This policy enables 3DES encryption (line 100) for IKE, and defines that the authentication mechanism should use a preshared key (line 101). The preshared key used for each IKE peer is configured on lines 102 and 103. Finally, IKE call admission protection is enabled on line 108, which limits the number of simultaneous IKE sessions to two in this case. The IPsec Phase 2 protection scheme is defined on lines 105 and 106. Note that the transport mode is enabled (line 106) because GRE tunneling is being used. The IPsec tunnel is configured to use the IP address of interface Serial0/0 (line 110), and the crypto map is configured for the two IPsec tunnels on lines 112 through 118. Note that encryption is applied to all packets matching the named extended ACLs GRE1 and GRE2 as configured on lines 114 and 118. These named extended ACLs are defined on lines 220 through 223. Because IPsec is securing GRE tunnels, the ACL classification used to match traffic requiring IPsec support is trivial. Finally, the crypto map is applied to the Serial0/0 interface on line 156.

- **NAT:** Outbound traffic from the internal private address space (in other words, the 10.0.0.0/8 network) and destined for the Internet uses NAT services. The NAT policy is defined on line 218, which indicates that *inside* packets with source IP addresses matching ACL NATADD shall be use the NAT service, and the Serial0/0 IP address shall be used as a port address translation (PAT) pool. The ACL NATADD is defined on lines 224 through 226. As shown, the first entry (line 225) denies packets that are sourced from the private network behind CPE-A0 and destined to any other Customer A VPN site. These packets will use the GRE + IPsec tunnel and thus do not require NAT services. The second entry (line 226) permits packets to use NAT services when destined to the Internet. (Note that the static routes to Null0, defined on lines 207 through 216, are extremely useful for protecting the NAT services. Packets sent toward bogus destinations (for example, in the case where an internal host is infected by a worm and is scanning random networks in search of vulnerable hosts) would be dropped rather than following the default route to the Internet and consuming valuable NAT resources. Finally, line 170 assigns the FastEthernet0/1 interface as NAT inside, and line 153 assigns the Serial0/0 interface as NAT outside to provide the appropriate inside and outside context to NAT services. (The DMZ interface does not require NAT services because this address space is assumed to be Internet routable in this case study.)

Case Study 2: MPLS VPN

Case Study 2 focuses on a typical enterprise scenario where an MPLS VPN service is used to connect customer headquarters and remote sites within a private IP VPN across the SP's shared IP network infrastructure. A description of the case study network topology, functional requirements for the network, and translated security requirements follows.

Network Topology and Requirements

The network topology and assigned IP addressing schemes used within this case study are illustrated in Figure 8-4. Customer B has three sites connected using a managed MPLS VPN topology, and all three sites obtain their VPN connectivity by direct connections to the same SP IP/MPLS network. Hence, the RFC 4364 section 10 Inter-AS VPN architectural options (a), (b), and (c) do not apply to this case study. MPLS VPN configurations and security techniques for PE and core P routers are reviewed in the companion SP case study within Chapter 9.

The functional requirements assumed in this case study are as follows:

- **MPLS VPN:** Customer B obtains any-to-any IP VPN connectivity from its SP for access between all private sites. The IP VPN is built within the SP network using RFC 4364 MPLS VPNs, and thus Customer B has few requirements on its side of the network. In this case study, being a rather small network, each CE router is assumed to have only a single internal interface for user access at each site. Because each internal interface must be reachable by all other remote sites, these connected interfaces are redistributed into eBGP, and the SP in turn carries these customer-specific prefixes within Multiprotocol BGP (M-BGP) to provide reachability between sites within a single customer IP VPN. By using M-BGP, the SP is assured of addressing and routing separation between different customer IP VPNs. In this case study, the SP is assumed to be AS 65001, and Customer B is assumed to be AS 65002.

- **Access:** All users of the Customer B MPLS VPN are considered internal, and have access to all Customer B locations and network prefixes. There is no access from the Customer B MPLS VPN to the Internet. Conversely, external access to the Customer B MPLS VPN is not required other than the SP Management VPN, described next, because the customer CE routers are managed.

- **Management:** In this case study, it is assumed that all Customer B CE routers are managed by the SP. For operational reasons, then, the SP must have in-band access to each CE device. This is achieved using the Management VPN technique, which was described in Chapter 6, "Management Plane Security."

Figure 8-4 *Conceptual Enterprise Network Architecture for MPLS VPN Connectivity Case Study 2*

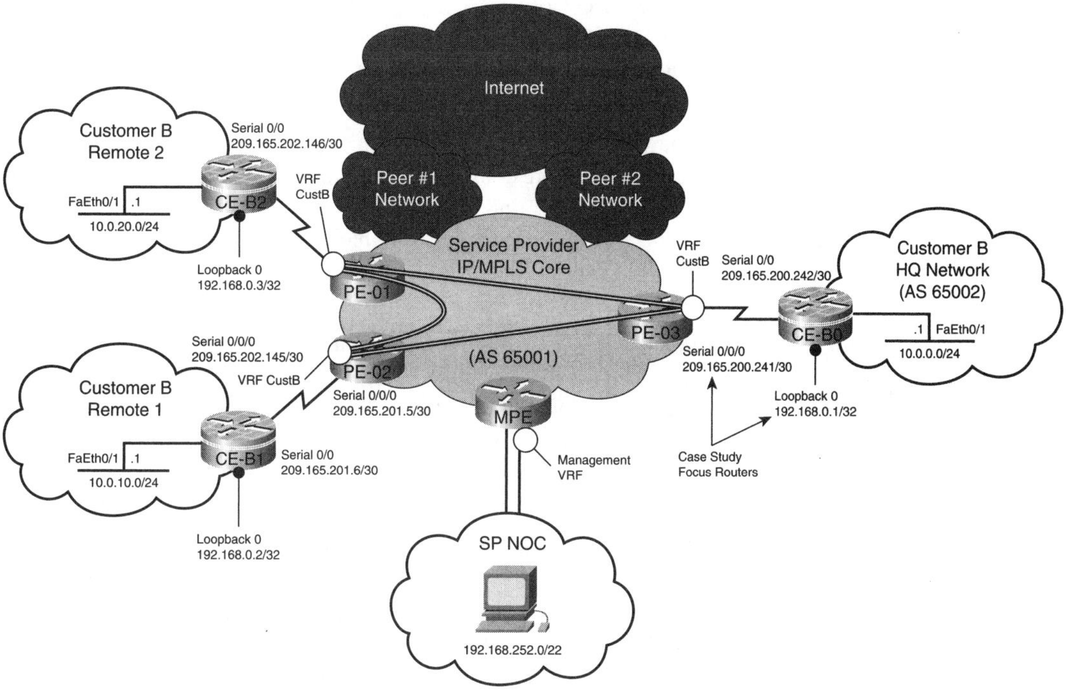

Figure 8-5 highlights the types and relationships of the interfaces found on the customer edge (CE) router in this case study. These interface types were first introduced in Chapter 3. The following interfaces are included in this case study:

- **Internal:** Internal interfaces connect network assets wholly within one administrative domain. In this case study, Customer B CE routers only have internal interfaces. That is, even the CE-PE link is considered internal because the PE side of the link is installed in a VRF that binds the link to the private IP VPN of Customer B. Thus, all three Customer B routers include one internal CE-PE interface (in other words, the Serial0/0 interface of all CE routers) that connects each CE router to the SP IP/MPLS network. The assigned IP addresses for this case study are shown in Figure 8-4 for each of these serial connections. In all cases, /30 subnet masking is assigned, and the CE-PE address space is provided by the SP. Even though these interfaces are internal for Customer B, in the context of this case study, the SP restricts access to these prefixes (via ACLs) to prevent Customer B generated packets from reaching the PE and CE interfaces within the VRF (described in the upcoming "Data Plane" section). All three Customer B routers also include a single FastEthernet internal interface. In this case study, FastEthernet0/1 is the common internal interface for all three CE routers. The assigned IP addresses for this case study are also shown in Figure 8-4 for each FastEthernet internal interface. In all cases, /24 subnet masking is assigned. The prefixes associated with these connected interfaces are redistributed into eBGP, and the SP in turn carries these customer-specific prefixes within MBGP to provide reachability between sites within a single customer IP VPN and to provide addressing and routing separation between different customer IP VPNs.

- **External:** External interfaces connect networks belonging to two different administrative domains. Although the PE-CE links connect the customer and SP networks (and use eBGP), they are considered internal because the PE side of the link is installed in a VRF that binds the link to the private IP VPN of the customer. Thereby, reachability to CE and PE routers is only available from within the IP VPN or via the Management VPN. Therefore, in this case study, all CE router interfaces are considered internal.

- **Loopback:** All three Customer B routers implement a single loopback interface, Loopback0, which is used for SP management plane traffic (SP management access to the CE routers using the Management VPN). The assigned IP addresses for this case study are shown in Figure 8-4. In all cases, /32 subnet masking is assigned. Because the SP is assumed to be managing all CE routers, these loopback interface addresses are assigned by the SP, and they are reachable within the Management VPN.

- **Receive:** All routers include by default a receive interface that "logically" represents the slow path to the IOS process-level. This applies to any ingress packets that must be punted from the CEF fast path to the router's CPU for local processing.

Figure 8-5 highlights in particular the router of focus for this case study, CE-B0, and illustrates the relationship among its interfaces. This router is also the focus for the sample IOS configuration in the "Router Configuration" section that follows.

Router Configuration

Security configurations may be derived based upon the topology shown in Figure 8-4 and the previously described functional requirements. Router CE-B0 is used as the focal point for the remaining discussions. The other Customer B CE routers shown in the topology in Figure 8-4 have similar but locally specific configurations.

Example 8-2 provides the derived Cisco IOS configuration that implements the preceding requirements and defense in depth and breadth security principles. This configuration assumes that CPE-B0 is a Cisco ISR class router (1800, 2800, or 3800 series), and that is running Cisco IOS version 12.4 software.

Figure 8-5   *IP Traffic Plane Relationships to Router Interfaces for MPLS VPN Case Study 2*

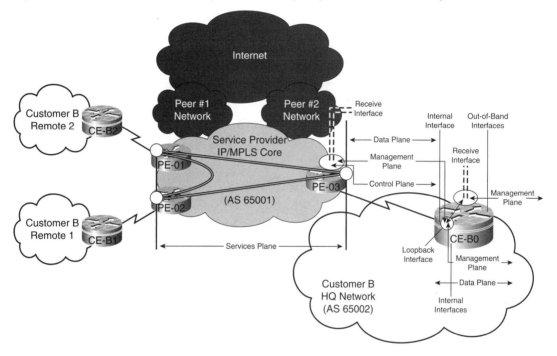

NOTE   Even though limited requirements are defined for the CE routers in this case study and thus only a basic IOS image is required, implementing more complex security features may be useful in some MPLS VPN network environments. For example, IOS Firewall and IOS IPS features may be useful for enforcing security policies within the MPLS VPN. In addition, IPsec encryption may be required on top of the MPLS VPN to provide confidentiality and integrity mechanisms. In these cases, an IOS image similar to the one used in Case Study 1 is appropriate.

As in Case Study 1, line numbers precede each configuration command shown in Example 8-2 and serve as reference points for the remainder of the discussion that directly follows, which is organized by IP traffic plane.

Example 8-2 *Case Study 2 Enterprise Customer Edge Router Configuration*

```
 1 : !
 2 : version 12.4
 3 : service nagle
 4 : no service pad
 5 : service tcp-keepalives-in
```
continues
```
 6 : service tcp-keepalives-out
 7 : service timestamps debug datetime msec localtime show-timezone
 8 : service timestamps log datetime msec localtime show-timezone
 9 : service password-encryption
…10 : no service dhcp
11 : !
12 : hostname CE-B0
13 : !
14 : boot-start-marker
15 : boot system flash c3845-advipservicesk9-mz.124-10.bin
16 : boot-end-marker
17 : !
18 : logging buffered 4096 debugging
19 : no logging console
20 : logging monitor errors
21 : enable secret 5 $1$Vmt.$SYiN8ZjKPe7DuTvNHm/vS.
22 : !
23 : aaa new-model
24 : !
25 : aaa authentication login SPnoc group tacacs+ local
26 : aaa authentication enable default group tacacs+ enable
27 : aaa authorization exec default group tacacs+ none
28 : aaa accounting commands 1 default start-stop group tacacs+
29 : aaa accounting commands 15 default start-stop group tacacs+
30 : !
31 : memory-size iomem 15
32 : ip subnet-zero
33 : no ip source-route
34 : no ip gratuitous-arps
35 : ip icmp rate-limit unreachable 100
36 : ip spd mode aggressive
37 : ip options drop
38 : ip tcp window-size 32768
39 : ip tcp synwait-time 5
40 : ip tcp path-mtu-discovery
41 : !
42 : !
43 : ip cef
44 : ip ip domain name spnet.com
45 : no ip domain-lookup
46 : !
```

Example 8-2 *Case Study 2 Enterprise Customer Edge Router Configuration (Continued)*

```
47 : !
48 : no ip bootp server
49 : ip ssh time-out 20
50 : ip ssh source-interface Loopback0
51 : ip ssh version 2
52 : ip scp server enable
53 : !
54 : !
55 : memory free low-watermark processor 100000
56 : memory free low-watermark IO 1000000
57 : username sp-noc privilege 15 secret 5 $1$c/vj$kAzIb.llu.0BhGH1hRVS2/
58 : !
59 : !
60 : class-map match-all CoPP-management
61 :  match access-group 121
62 : class-map match-all CoPP-normal
63 :  match access-group 122
64 : class-map match-all CoPP-remaining-IP
65 :  match access-group 124
66 : class-map match-all CoPP-routing
67 :  match access-group 120
68 : class-map match-any CoPP-undesirable
69 :  match access-group 123
70 : !
71 : !
72 : policy-map CoPP
73 :  class CoPP-undesirable
74 :    police 8000 1500 1500 conform-action drop   exceed-action drop
75 :  class CoPP-routing
76 : police 125000 1500 1500 conform-action transmit  exceed-action transmit
77 :  class CoPP-management
78 :    police 50000 1500 1500 conform-action transmit  exceed-action drop
79 :  class CoPP-normal
80 :    police 15000 1500 1500 conform-action transmit  exceed-action drop
81 :  class CoPP-remaining-IP
82 :    police 8000 1500 1500 conform-action transmit  exceed-action drop
83 :  class class-default
84 :    police 8000 1500 1500 conform-action transmit  exceed-action transmit
85 : !
86 : !
87 : interface Null0
88 :  no ip unreachables
89 : !
90 : interface Loopback0
91 :  description – Loopback for SP Management access
92 :  ip address 192.168.0.1 255.255.255.255
93 :  no ip unreachables
94 : !
95 : interface Serial0/0
96 :  description – To SP PE-03
97 :  ip address 209.165.200.242 255.255.255.252
98 :  ip access-group iACL-extin in
```

Example 8-2 *Case Study 2 Enterprise Customer Edge Router Configuration (Continued)*

```
 99 :  ip access-group iACL-extout out
100 :  ip verify unicast source reachable-via rx
101 :  no ip redirects
102 :  no ip unreachables
103 :  no ip proxy-arp
104 :  no fair-queue
105 : !
106 : interface FastEthernet0/0
107 :  no ip address
108 :  shutdown

109 : !
110 : interface FastEthernet0/1
111 :  description - Customer B HQ Internal
112 :  ip address 10.0.0.1 255.255.255.0
113 :  ip access-group iACL-internal in
114 :  ip verify unicast source reachable-via rx
115 :  no ip redirects
116 :  no ip unreachables
117 :  no ip proxy-arp
118 :  no mop enabled
119 : !
120 : interface FastEthernet1/0
121 :  no ip address
122 :  shutdown
123 : !
124 : interface FastEthernet1/1
125 :  no ip address
126 :  shutdown
127 : !
128 : !
129 : router bgp 65002
130 :  no synchronization
131 :  bgp log-neighbor-changes
132 :  redistribute connected route-map CustB
133 :  neighbor 209.165.200.241 remote-as 65001
134 :  neighbor 209.165.200.241 ttl-security hops 1
135 :  neighbor 209.165.200.241 update-source Serial0/0
136 :  neighbor 209.165.200.241 send-community extended
137 :  no auto-summary
138 :!
139 :!
140 : no ip http server
141 : ip http access-class 10
142 : ip http authentication local
143 : ip http secure-server
144 : ip classless
145 : !
146 : !
147 : !
148 : ip bgp-community new-format
```

continues

Example 8-2 *Case Study 2 Enterprise Customer Edge Router Configuration (Continued)*

```
149 : ip prefix-list Connected seq 5 permit 10.0.0.0/24
150 : !
151 : ip access-list extended iACL-extin
152 :   deny ip 10.0.0.0 0.255.255.255 host 209.165.200.242
153 :   deny ip 10.0.0.0 0.255.255.255 host 192.168.0.1
154 :   permit tcp host 209.165.200.241 host 209.165.200.242 eq bgp
155 :   permit tcp host 209.165.200.241 eq bgp host 209.165.200.242
156 :   deny tcp any any eq bgp
157 :   deny tcp any eq bgp any
158 :   permit icmp 192.168.252.0 0.0.3.255 host 192.168.0.1 echo
159 :   permit icmp 192.168.252.0 0.0.3.255 host 192.168.0.1 echo-reply
160 :   permit icmp 192.168.252.0 0.0.3.255 host 209.165.200.242 echo
161 :   permit icmp 192.168.252.0 0.0.3.255 host 209.165.200.242 echo-reply
162 :   permit icmp 10.0.0.0 0.255.255.255 10.0.0.0 0.0.0.255 echo-reply
163 :   permit icmp 10.0.0.0 0.255.255.255 10.0.0.0 0.0.0.255 packet-too-big
164 :   permit icmp 10.0.0.0 0.255.255.255 10.0.0.0 0.0.0.255 time-exceeded
165 :   permit icmp 10.0.0.0 0.255.255.255 10.0.0.0 0.0.0.255 port-unreachable
166 :   permit icmp 10.0.0.0 0.255.255.255 10.0.0.0 0.0.0.255 protocol-unreachable
167 :   deny icmp any any
168 :   permit udp 192.168.252.0 0.0.3.255 host 192.168.0.1 eq snmp
169 :   permit udp 192.168.252.0 0.0.3.255 host 192.168.0.1 eq ntp
170 :   deny udp any any eq snmp
171 :   permit ip any any
172 : ip access-list extended iACL-extout
173 :   deny ip 10.0.0.0 0.0.0.255 209.165.200.240 0.0.0.3
174 :   deny ip 10.0.0.0 0.0.0.255 209.165.201.4 0.0.0.3
175 :   deny ip 10.0.0.0 0.0.0.255 209.165.202.144 0 0.0.0.3
176 :   deny ip 10.0.0.0 0.0.0.255 192.168.0.0 0.0.0.255
177 :   deny ip 10.0.0.0 0.0.0.255 192.168.252.0 0.0.3.255
178 :   permit ip host 192.168.0.1 192.168.252.0 0.0.3.255
179 :   permit ip host 192.168.0.1 host 209.165.200.241
180 :   permit tcp host 209.165.200.242 host 209.165.200.241 eq bgp
181 :   permit tcp host 209.165.200.242 eq bgp host 209.165.200.241
182 :   deny tcp any any eq bgp
183 :   deny tcp any eq bgp any
184 :   permit tcp host 192.168.0.1 192.168.252.0 0.0.3.255 eq 22
185 :   permit icmp host 192.168.0.1 192.168.252.0 0.0.3.255 eq echo
186 :   permit icmp host 192.168.0.1 192.168.252.0 0.0.3.255 eq echo-reply
187 :   permit icmp host 209.165.200.242 192.168.252.0 0.0.3.255 eq echo
188 :   permit icmp host 209.165.200.242 192.168.252.0 0.0.3.255 eq echo-reply
189 :   permit icmp 10.0.0.0 0.0.0.255 10.0.0.0 0.255.255.255 echo-reply
190 :   permit icmp 10.0.0.0 0.0.0.255 10.0.0.0 0.255.255.255 packet-too-big
191 :   permit icmp 10.0.0.0 0.0.0.255 10.0.0.0 0.255.255.255 time-exceeded
192 :   permit icmp 10.0.0.0 0.0.0.255 10.0.0.0 0.255.255.255 port-unreachable
193 : permit icmp 10.0.0.0 0.0.0.255 10.0.0.0 0.255.255.255 protocol-unreachable
194 :   deny icmp any any
195 :   permit ip any any
196 : ip access-list extended iACL-internal
197 :   permit ip 10.0.0.0 0.0.0.255 10.0.0.0 0.255.255.255
198 :   deny ip any any
199 : logging trap notifications
200 : logging source-interface Loopback0
201 : logging 192.168. 255.11
```

Example 8-2 *Case Study 2 Enterprise Customer Edge Router Configuration (Continued)*

```
202 : access-list 10 permit 192.168.252.0 0.0.3.255
203 : access-list 120 remark -- Routing Protocol ACL for CoPP
204 : access-list 120 remark -- -- permit bgp
205 : access-list 120 permit tcp host 209.165.200.241 eq bgp host 209.165.200.242
206 : access-list 120 permit tcp host 209.165.200.241 host 209.165.200.242 eq bgp
207 : access-list 121 remark -- Management Protocol ACL for CoPP
208 : access-list 121 remark -- -- permit ssh (and also scp)
209 : access-list 121 permit tcp 192.168.252.0 0.0.3.255 host 192.168.0.1 eq 22
210 : access-list 121 remark -- -- permit snmp
211 : access-list 121 permit udp 192.168.252.0 0.0.3.255 host 192.168.0.1 eq eq
      snmp
```

continues

```
212 : access-list 121 remark -- -- permit tacacs+
213 : access-list 121 permit tcp 192.168.252.0 0.0.3.255 eq tacacs host
      192.168.0.1established
214 : access-list 121 remark -- -- permit ntp
215 : access-list 121 permit udp 192.168.0.0 0.0.0.255 host 192.168.0.1 eq ntp
216 : access-list 121 remark -- -- permit https
217 : access-list 121 permit tcp 192.168.252.0 0.0.3.255 host 192.168.0.1 eq 443
218 : access-list 121 remark -- -- permit traceroute
219 : access-list 121 permit udp any gt 10000 any gt 10000
220 : access-list 122 remark -- Normal Traffic ACL for CoPP
221 : access-list 122 remark -- -- permit ICMP types
222 : access-list 122 permit icmp any any echo
223 : access-list 122 permit icmp any any echo-reply
224 : access-list 122 permit icmp any any ttl-exceeded
225 : access-list 122 permit icmp any any unreachable
226 : access-list 122 permit icmp any any port-unreachable
227 : access-list 122 permit icmp any any packet-too-big
228 : access-list 123 remark -- Undesirable Traffic ACL for CoPP
229 : access-list 123 remark -- -- Block Fragments
230 : access-list 123 permit tcp any any fragments
231 : access-list 123 permit udp any any fragments
232 : access-list 123 permit icmp any any fragments
233 : access-list 123 permit ip any any fragments
234 : access-list 123 remark -- -- Block Slammer
235 : access-list 123 permit udp any any eq 1434
236 : access-list 124 remark -- Catch-All IP ACL for CoPP
237 : access-list 124 remark -- -- permit all IP
238 : access-list 124 permit ip any any
239 :!
240 : route-map CustB permit 10
241 :   match ip address prefix-list Connected
242 :!
243 : snmp-server community s3cr3t RO 10
244 : snmp-server packetsize 1400
245 : snmp-server enable traps tty
246 : snmp-server trap-source Loopback0
247 : snmp-server host 192.168. 255.11 version 2c s3cr3t
248 : no cdp run
249 : !
250 : tacacs-server host 192.168. 255.12
```

Example 8-2 *Case Study 2 Enterprise Customer Edge Router Configuration (Continued)*

```
251 : tacacs-server timeout 2
252 : no tacacs-server directed-request
253 : tacacs-server key 7 0017400516081F
254 : !
255 : control-plane
256 :  service-policy input CoPP
257 : !
258 : banner motd ^C
259 : **** AUTHORIZED ACCESS ONLY *****
260 : **** This system is the property of Customer B
261 : **** Disconnect IMMEDIATELY if you are not an authorized user!
262 : **** ********************** *****^C
263 : !
264 : line con 0
265 :  exec-timeout 60 0
266 :  login authentication SPnoc
267 : line aux 0
268 :  transport input none
269 :  transport output none
270 : line vty 0 4
271 :  access-class 10 in
272 :  exec-timeout 60 0
273 :  login authentication SPnoc
274 :  transport input ssh
275 : !
276 : scheduler allocate 6000 1000
277 : process cpu threshold type total rising 80 interval 5 falling 20 interval 5
278 : ntp authentication-key 1 md5 0505121F6C471D10 7
279 : ntp authenticate
280 : ntp trust-key 1
281 : ntp source Loopback0
282 : ntp access-group serve-only 10
283 : ntp server 192.168. 255.10 key 1
284 : !
285 : end
```

Data Plane

In this case study, and from the perspective of router CE-B0, data plane traffic includes the following:

- **Internal to internal traffic:** Data plane traffic in this category includes traffic that is sourced by and destined to devices wholly within the administrative domain of the enterprise. In the case of CE-B0, this includes all packets routed between each LAN located at sites within the Customer B MPLS VPN. For CE-B0, this interface is represented by FastEthernet0/1. From the perspective of CE-B0, all user traffic is data plane traffic because the MPLS VPN *services plane* is only defined within the SP side of the network. The CE router has no MPLS VPN awareness.

Data Plane Security

From the perspective of CE-B0, the security mechanisms used for data plane traffic segmentation and control include the following:

- **Interface ACLs:** Interface ACLs are applied to interface Serial0/0 in both the ingress (in) and egress (out) directions to limit the traffic permitted to enter and exit CE-B0. Example 8-2 configuration lines 151 through 171 implement the ingress functionality via the named extended ACL iACL-extin, which is applied to Serial0/0 in the inbound direction on line 98. Note that this ACL accounts for all ingress traffic, so entries are included for data, management, and control plane traffic. This ACL denies user traffic destined to the Serial0/0 and Loopback0 interfaces because these are controlled exclusively by the SP for control plane and management plane purposes. Further, only the SP NOC address block (192.168.252.0/22) is permitted to reach the Loopback0 destination. The named extended ACL iACL-extout, shown on lines 172 through 195, is applied to Serial0/0 in the outbound direction on line 99 to limit the traffic permitted to enter SP network. This ACL denies user traffic destined to the PE interface address and to the SP NOC address block. Only traffic from the Loopback0 address is permitted to reach the PE interface or SP NOC address block. All other user traffic is permitted to transit the MPLS VPN. Finally, an interface ACL is applied to the FastEthernet0/1 interface in the ingress direction to limit the traffic permitted to reach CE-B0. Configuration lines 196 through 198 implement this functionality via the named extended ACL iACL-internal, which is applied to the FastEthernet0/1 interface in the inbound direction on line 113. This ACL only permits user traffic from the internal LAN that is destined for any address within the Customer B MPLS VPN address range (assumed 10.0.0.0/8). Although these ACLs have some duplication of coverage, together they provide defense in depth and breadth protection and increase the overall security posture of router CE-B0.

Note The use of the *stateful* IOS Firewall feature is also feasible and can provide additional security when compared to *stateless* ACLs. IOS Firewall is capable of tracking outbound requests and dynamically tracking these requests to permit return traffic in a stateful manner. Refer to the "Further Reading" section for more details.

- **uRPF:** Unicast RPF strict mode is deployed on all interfaces to prevent packets with obviously spoofed IP source addresses from entering the network. For the interface Serial0/0, this implementation is shown on line 100. For interface FastEthernet0/1, uRPF strict mode is applied as shown on line 114.

- **IP options drop:** The ability for the router to process IP packets with option headers is disabled with the global **ip options drop** configuration (line 37). The default IOS behavior of processing IP packets with the Source Route option header is also disabled with the **no ip source-route** configuration (line 33). Again, overlap exists between these two commands for IP header source route options, but this supports in depth and breadth principles.

- **IP directed broadcasts:** The dropping of IP directed broadcast packets is the default behavior in this IOS image, so the BCP for earlier IOS images to include the **no ip directed-broadcast** command is not required.

- **ICMP techniques:** On a per-interface basis, several ICMP BCPs are also enabled. Disabling IP redirects is configured using the **no ip redirects** interface command (lines 101 and 115), and disabling the generation of ICMP Destination Unreachable messages is configured using the **no ip unreachables** interface command (lines 93, 102, and 116). Globally, rate limiting of ICMP Destination Unreachable messages is enabled via line 35. The generation of ICMP Address Mask Reply messages and ICMP Information Reply messages is disabled by default in this IOS image, so the BCP for earlier IOS images to include the **no ip information-reply** and **no ip mask-reply** interface commands is not required.

Control Plane

In this case study, and from the perspective of router CE-B0, control plane traffic includes the following:

- **External BGP (eBGP):** Control plane traffic in this category includes eBGP traffic between the interface addresses on CE-B0 and the PE link. In this case study, the prefix associated with the FastEthernet0/1 interface is redistributed into BGP, and then the SP carries this prefix within MBGP to create the Customer B MPLS IP VPN.

- **Layer 2 keepalives:** Layer 2 keepalives will exist on the Serial interfaces of CPE-B0. Layer 2 keepalives are not defined within the IEEE Ethernet specifications, nor are they applicable to virtual interfaces such as Loopback0.

Control Plane Security

From the perspective of CE-B0, the security mechanisms that will be used for control plane traffic segmentation and control include the following:

- **Control Plane Policing (CoPP):** CoPP is one of the primary mechanisms for protecting the route processor CPU. When configured, all punted packets reach the route processor CPU through the CoPP mechanism, including in this case all control plane and management plane packets, and some exceptions IP data plane packets. In the case of CE-B0, CoPP is implemented via MQC mechanisms. In total, the CoPP configuration includes the ACLs 120, 121, 122, 123, and 124 shown on lines 203 through 238, the class-map statements shown on lines 60 through 69, and the policy-map statements shown on lines 72 through 84. CoPP is enabled by applying the service policy to the control plane, as shown on lines 255 and 256. Note that the **class-default** portion of the CoPP **policy-map** (lines 83 and 84) should be left unpoliced here because it only sees Layer 2 keepalive traffic, because of the existence of the catch-all CoPP-remaining-IP traffic class (lines 81 and 82) directly preceding it in the policy map.

- **BGP and BGP TTL security:** BGP is configured on lines 129 through 137. Interface Serial0/0 is specified as the source of the CE-B0 BGP traffic on line 135. Connected interfaces are redistributed into BGP on line 132 using the route-map CustB as a filter. Route-map CustB is configured on lines 240 and 241. This route map refers to the **ip prefix-list** Connected (line 241), which is defined on line 149. Because BGP extended communities will be exchanged, **bgp-communities new-format** is enabled on line 148. The BGP implementation of the Generalized TTL Security Mechanism (GTSM) is enabled on line 134.

- **Selective Packet Discard (SPD):** SPD is turned on by default, and the hold-queue, headroom, and extended headroom default settings are adequate. However, SPD aggressive mode is not enabled by default and should be turned on. SPD aggressive mode is enabled via the *hidden* global configuration command **ip spd mode aggressive** (line 36).

- **Null0 interface:** The Null0 interface is configured on lines 87 and 88. The generation of ICMP Destination Unreachable messages for this interface is disabled on line 88.

- **Disable unused services:** BCP router security configurations related to the control plane include disabling the proxy ARP feature on a per-interface basis via the **no ip proxy-arp** command (lines 103 and 117). For the FastEthernet interface, the MOP protocol is also disabled via the **no mop enabled** command (line 118).

Management Plane

In this case study, all CE routers are assumed to be managed by the SP. Thus, the SP assigns a globally unique IP address to a loopback interface that is used for management plane purposes. These loopback interface IP addresses are reachable within the SP Management VPN defined within the SP infrastructure. (See Case Study 2 in Chapter 9 for details on this Management VPN configuration.) From the perspective of router CE-B0, management plane traffic includes the following:

- **Provisioning traffic:** Management plane traffic in this category includes SSH, HTTPS, and SCP traffic. This traffic must be sourced from within the SP Management VPN and must be destined to the 192.168.0.1/32 address of Loopback0. VTY traffic is restricted to SSH only (Telnet is not permitted). Egress management traffic of this type will be destined to the 192.168.252.0/22 prefix range associated with the SP NOC management block.

- **Monitoring traffic:** Management plane traffic in this category includes SNMP and Syslog. In the case of CE-B0, ingress SNMP traffic will be destined to the 192.168.0.1/32 address of Loopback0. Egress management traffic of this type will be destined to the 192.168.252.0/22 prefix range associated with the SP NOC management block.

- **Other traffic:** Several other protocols are used within the management plane and include NTP and TACACS+ traffic. In the case of CE-B0, management traffic of this type will be destined to the 192.168.0.1/32 address of Loopback0. Egress management traffic of this type will be destined to the 192.168.252.0/22 prefix range associated with the SP NOC management block. In addition, several types of ICMP packets (management plane traffic) must be permitted by the iACL (as described under ICMP Techniques section of the "Data Plane" section above) as well for operational needs (Echo Reply, Time Exceeded, and certain IP Unreachable messages). CDP is globally disabled.

- **OOB traffic:** The console interface is configured for OOB management plane access.

Management Plane Security

From the perspective of CE-B0, the security mechanisms that will be used for management plane traffic segmentation and control include the following:

- **Loopback0 interface:** The interface Loopback0 is configured on lines 90 through 93. CoPP policies described in the "Control Plane" section above only allow management plane traffic destined to this IP address of the CPE-B0 router.

- **AAA:** AAA is fully configured for authentication, authorization, and accounting. This begins with the **aaa new-model** configuration (line 23). Login authentication is configured to use TACACS+ and then local information with the list name SPnoc (line 25). Enable-mode authentication is configured to use TACACS+ and then the enable secret (line 26). (The TACACS+ implementation is not shown.) Command authorization is configured to use TACACS+ and then none (line 27). Command accounting is configured to use TACACS+ (lines 28 and 29). Finally, a local username is configured on line 57.

- **SSH services:** Configuring SSH requires that a domain name be specified (for RSA encryption key generation). This is done via line 44. (The RSA encryption key is generated outside the configuration during router setup.) SSH protocol parameters are configured on lines 49 through 51.

- **In-band VTY access:** In-band VTY management plane access is configured on lines 270 through 274. VTY access is restricted to sources matching ACL 10 via line 271, and in-band VTY access is restricted to using the SSH protocol only, on line 274.

- **HTTPS and SCP services:** HTTPS access is enabled via lines 141 through 143. Line 141 restricts HTTPS access to sources matching ACL 10. ACL 10 is defined on line 202. The HTTP server is disabled on line 140. SCP server functionality is enabled on line 52.

- **SNMP and Syslog:** SNMP configuration parameters are implemented via lines 243 through 247. SNMP access is restricted to read-only by the community string *s3cr3t* and is limited to sources matching ACL 10 via line 243. (SNMP is restricted to only monitoring in this case study. Write access is not permitted.) Syslog configurations are included on lines 199 through 201. In addition, in order to generate Syslog messages when BGP changes occur, logging of these changes is enabled on line 131.

- **TACACS+, NTP, and DNS:** The TACACS+ server parameters are configured via lines 250 through 253. DNS name resolution is disabled for queries generated by the router on line 45. NTP is configured via lines 278 and 283. Ingress NTP messages are restricted to sources permitted by ACL 10 (line 282). Further, MD5 authentication is enabled for NTP message exchanges with the configured NTP server (lines 278 through 280 and line 283).

- **Out-of-band console access:** OOB (console port) access is configured on lines 264 through 266. Console and VTY login authentication refer to the AAA list SPnoc on lines 266 and 273, respectively. AUX port transport is disabled (effectively shutting down the port) on lines 267 through 269.

- **Disable unused services:** Several global service settings are disabled, including PAD service (line 4), DHCP services (line 10), and (globally) CDP (line 248). The processing of gratuitous ARP messages is disabled on line 34, and the BOOTP service is disabled on line 48. Note that disabling IP finger services is the default in this IOS image, so the **no ip finger** or **no service finger** commands are not required.

- **Other BCPs:** Other BCP router security configurations related to the management plane are implemented. The router host name is configured on line 12. Global service settings are modified, including enabling timestamps for all debug and logging messages (lines 7 and 8) and enabling password encryption services (line 9). The router boot image is specified on line 15 (lines 14 and 16 are auto-generated). Buffered logging is enabled at debug level and the buffer size is set (line 18). The display of logging messages to the console is disabled (line 19), and logging to the monitor at the error level is enabled (line 20). The enable secret is set on line 21. Several global settings for router self-generated TCP sessions are adjusted, including enabling Nagle services (line 3), enabling TCP keepalives (lines 5 and 6), increasing the TCP window size (line 38), reducing the TCP SYN wait time (line 39), and enabling Path MTU Discovery (line 40). In order to generate Syslog messages when free memory resources are low, low-watermark levels are set for processor and I/O memory on lines 55 and 56. A message of the day (MOTD) login banner is configured on lines 258 through 262. To guarantee CPU time for processes, **scheduler allocate** is configured on line 276. Finally, in order to generate Syslog messages when CPU resources are low, processor CPU threshold levels are set on line 277.

Services Plane

There are no services plane requirements from the perspective of router CE-B0 in this case study. All services plane requirements occur on the SP side of the network and are instantiated on the PE routers. Chapter 9 provides these details.

Summary

This chapter demonstrated the use of various concepts and techniques described in Chapters 4 through 7 by applying them to conceptual enterprise networks as case studies. Two case studies were presented, one being an Internet-based site-to-site IPsec VPN, and the other being a site-to-site MPLS VPN. Defense in depth and breadth principles were applied to protect IP traffic as it travels across the Internet or a shared IP infrastructure. Full configurations were provided for both case studies, and annotations were included for all security components to provide the appropriate context for each mechanism.

These case studies focused on the enterprise (customer) side of the network. In Chapter 9, the focus will be turned on the SP side of the network for these same cases.

Further Reading

Cisco IOS Firewall Design Guide. Cisco Documentation. http://www.cisco.com/en/ US/products/sw/secursw/ps1018/products_implementation_design_ guide09186a00800fd670.html.

"Cisco IOS Firewall Performance Guidelines for Cisco Integrated Services Routers." http://www.cisco.com/en/US/partner/products/ps5855/products_white_ paper0900aecd8061536b.shtml.

In this chapter, you will learn about the following:

- How to apply IP traffic plane security techniques within an Internet transit SP network design

- How to apply IP traffic plane security techniques within an MPLS VPN SP network design

- How the combination of IP traffic plane techniques provides an effective defense in depth and breadth security architecture

CHAPTER 9

Service Provider Network Case Studies

The purpose of this chapter is to demonstrate the use of the security concepts and techniques described in Chapters 4 through 7 by applying them to a conceptual service provider (SP) network as case studies. The intent is to clarify your understanding of how all of these individual security techniques are brought together to form an effective defense in depth and breadth strategy that secures the SP network and each of its IP traffic planes. The same IPsec VPN and MPLS VPN case studies presented in Chapter 8 "Enterprise Network Case Studies," are reviewed in this chapter, but now from the perspective of the SP. This chapter complements Chapter 8, which reviewed these two case studies from the perspective of enterprise networks.

Two different SP edge router configurations are studied in this chapter, including a dedicated Internet edge router and a dedicated MPLS VPN edge router. Although Internet and MPLS VPN services can be integrated onto a shared edge router with routing and address separation assured, for the purposes of this chapter, we review the security techniques applicable to Internet and MPLS VPN services separately using distinct edge router configurations. The common topology for both of these case studies is illustrated in the high-level, conceptual diagram shown in Figure 9-1. As shown in Figure 9-1, an SP IP/MPLS core network provides transport for both case studies. Customer A has three sites, two that connect directly to the SP network that is the focus of the case studies (Corporate HQ and Remote 1) and one that obtains Internet access through some other provider (Remote 2). These three Customer A sites will be used to illustrate a very common Internet access topology. Customer B also has three sites, all of which connect directly to the same SP IP/MPLS network (AS 65001). These three Customer B sites will be used to illustrate a very common MPLS VPN topology.

As previously stated, the case studies in this chapter focus on the SP side of the network. That is, in each case, the focus is on the SP edge routers and their respective security requirements. In Chapter 8, the focus is on the enterprise side of the network (CPE routers) for these same case studies. Thus, Chapters 8 and 9 complement one another by sharing a common network topology whereby physical network links interconnect the enterprise and SP networks in both case studies.

Figure 9-1 *Conceptual View of Enterprise and Service Provider Networks for Chapters 8 and 9 Case Studies*

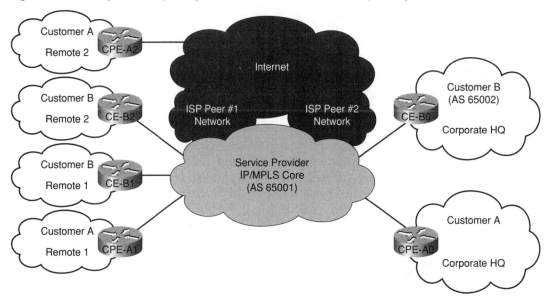

The following information is presented for each of the two SP case studies in this chapter:

- The network topology, including IP addressing, and the functional requirements for each of the case study routers of focus, as appropriate

- The derived router configurations, along with detailed comments describing the relationship between specific configuration command entries and the respective contribution of each entry to IP traffic plane security

No single example case study can cover all of the many aspects of IP traffic plane security from the perspective of an SP. SP networks vary widely due to product mix, topology, services, protocols, traffic behavior, and organizational mission. Nevertheless, what should be evident from these case studies is the defense in depth and breadth methodology used to identify and protect each IP traffic plane component within the SP network presented. With this understanding, you will be able to apply similar methods and procedures to mitigate the risk of security attacks against your specific network.

Case Study 1: IPsec VPN and Internet Access

Case Study 1 focuses on a typical scenario where an SP provides Internet access to different enterprise sites. An IPsec VPN is used to connect the headquarters and remote sites of the enterprise into a private IP VPN. In this scenario, the SP simply provides Internet access to the enterprise. IPsec VPN services are provided by the CPE routers, which are managed by the enterprise itself. Hence, the SP has no awareness of IPsec VPN services used within the enterprise and, therefore, handles all traffic received from or destined to the enterprise as native IP data plane traffic. Conversely, the enterprise handles all IPsec VPN traffic within the IP services plane as described in Chapter 8. A description of the SP network topology, functional requirements, and translated security requirements follows.

Network Topology and Requirements

The SP network topology and assigned IP addressing schemes used within this case study are illustrated in Figure 9-2. Customer A has three sites with Internet access. Two sites, Corporate HQ (on the right side of the figure) and Remote 1 (on the lower-left side of the figure), obtain their Internet connectivity by direct connections to the same SP IP/MPLS network (AS 65001). The third site, Remote 2 (on the upper-left side of the figure), obtains its Internet access through a different provider.

Figure 9-2   *Conceptual SP Network Architecture for Internet-Based IPsec VPN Case Study 1*

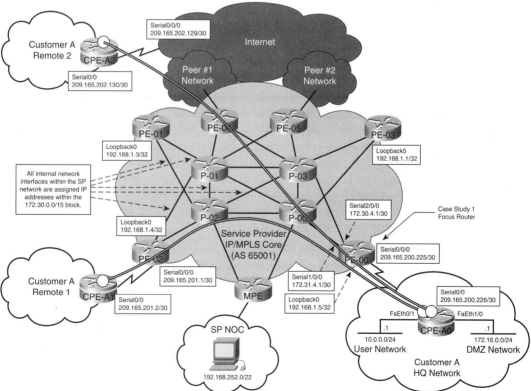

The functional requirements assumed in this case study are as follows:

- **Customer access to Internet:** The SP network simply provides Internet transit services to the enterprise and, therefore, has no awareness of IPsec VPN services, which are fully contained within the enterprise network. Nevertheless, given that the IPsec VPN service tunnels terminate on the Customer A CPE routers, the SP network must provide remote IP reachability to the CPE routers from the wider Internet. Remote IP reachability to the CPE routers is provided exclusively through the data plane within the SP network.

- **Internet access to Customer A web services:** In addition to remote IP reachability to the Customer A CPE routers, Customer A requires that its public web server (172.16.0.16/32), located within the DMZ network of the HQ site, be accessible from the wider Internet. In this case study, assume that the SP installs a static route for the DMZ network address of 172.16.0.0/24 with a next hop pointing toward the Customer A router CPE-A0, and that this prefix is also advertised via eBGP to the SP's Internet peers and, therefore, carried within the global Internet routing table.

Note	In reality, this address range is private and would never be advertised or routable within the wider Internet. This is used solely as an example for the purposes of this case study.

- **Static IP default routing between SP and customer sites:** Static IP default routing is used between the SP and Customer A CPE routers. Although the customer uses OSPF as its Internal Gateway Protocol (IGP), including between remote sites per Chapter 8, this is transparent to the SP because it runs above the IPsec VPN services layer. All remote traffic received from or destined to a Customer A site is handled by the SP as native IP data plane traffic per above. Note, because static routing is used, not all of the BGP security techniques outlined in Chapter 4, "Data Plane Security," are reviewed here—specifically, those applicable to eBGP sessions, including prefix filters, prefix limits, and BGP graceful restart.

- **Global Internet routing:** Through a combination of Internet peering and Internet transit agreements with upstream SPs, the SP in this case study (AS 65001) carries the full Internet routing table within its global IP routing table. This enables the SP to offer Internet transit services itself to downstream customers. BGP is used to exchange prefix information with Internet peers and multi-homed customer sites. IP reachability between edge networks within the SP network is provided through OSPF, which serves as the IGP.

- **Unmanaged CPE router:** The SP manages its own routers in this case study via in-band methods, including the Internet edge routers and shared core (P) routers. The SP has no specific requirements for CPE router access because those routers are unmanaged (in other words, managed by the enterprise, not the SP). In this case study, it is assumed that the SP has a dedicated NOC that performs provisioning, management, and monitoring functions, and that the NOC is contained within the 192.168.252.0/22 address block. Therefore, all management plane traffic associated with the SP edge and core routers must be either sourced from or destined to a host within the 192.168.252.0/22 address block. Management applications assumed in this case study include SSH, Syslog, SNMP, NTP, TFTP, and TACACS+ only.

Figure 9-3 highlights the types and relationships of the interfaces associated with the SP Internet edge router in this case study.

Figure 9-3   *IP Traffic Plane Relationships to Router Interfaces for Internet-Based IPsec VPN Case Study 1*

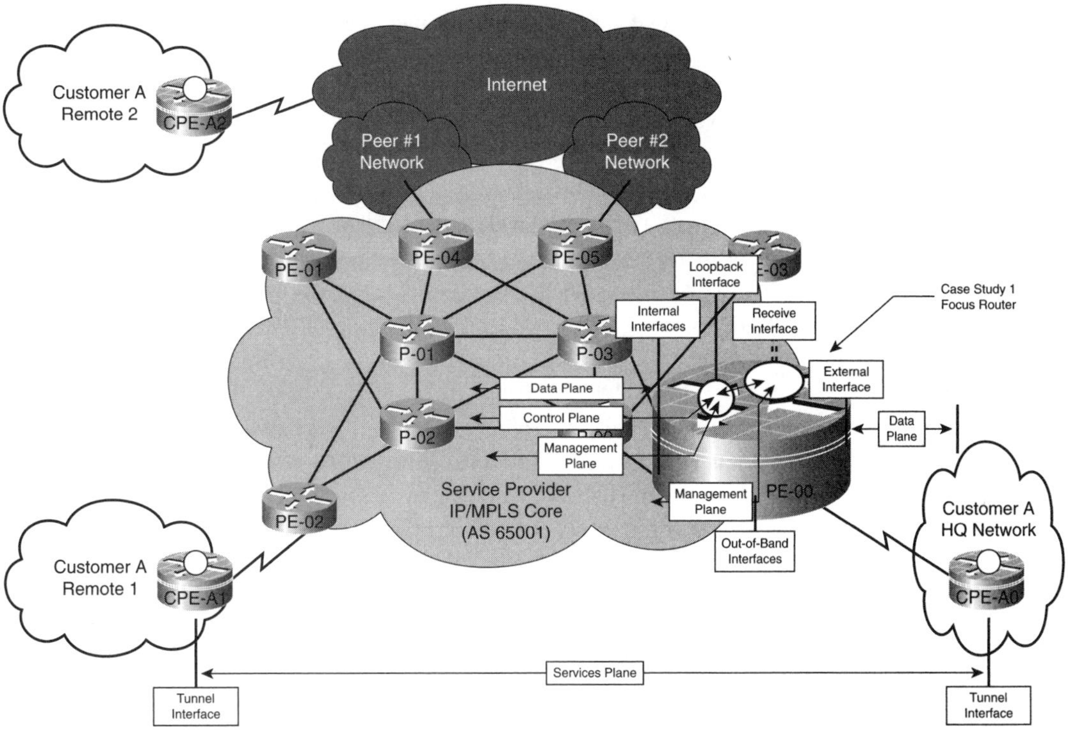

You were first introduced to these interface types in Chapter 3, "IP Network Traffic Plane Security Concepts." The following interfaces are included in this case study:

- **External:** External interfaces connect networks belonging to two different administrative domains. Hence, by definition, an edge router includes at least one external interface. In this case study, two Customer A customer edge (CE) routers, CPE-A0 and CPE-A1, connect directly to the SP network (AS 65001) via PE-00 and PE-02, respectively. CPE-A2 connects to a different SP but has IP reachability to the other Customer A sites via the Internet. For both connections of CPE-A0 and CPE-A1, the associated edge router (PE) interfaces are assumed to be Serial0/0/0. The IP addresses assigned to these PE-CE links are shown in Figure 9-2. For all external PE-CE links, /30 subnet masking is assigned.

- **Internal:** Internal interfaces connect network infrastructure wholly within one administrative domain. All SP edge and core routers shown in Figure 9-2 include at least two internal interfaces. Interfaces Serial1/0/0 and Serial2/0/0 of PE-00 are considered internal to the SP network. All internal interfaces within this case study are assigned from the 172.30.0.0/15 address block. The IP subnets associated with these internal interfaces are carried within the SP IGP (OSPF in this case study).

- **Loopback:** All SP edge and core routers shown in Figure 9-2 implement a single loopback interface that is used for control and management plane traffic. All loopback interfaces within this case study are assigned from the 192.168.1.0/24 address block, as shown in Figure 9-2. The /32 IP subnets associated with these internal interfaces are also carried within the SP IGP (OSPF in this case study).

- **Receive:** All routers include by default a receive interface that "logically" represents the slow path to the IOS process level on the RP. The receive path applies to any ingress packets that must be punted from the CEF fast path to be processed locally by the router's CPU whether transit or receive adjacency packets. Because the receive path represents an exception packet processing path between the CEF fast path and IOS process level, it is not assigned or associated with a specific IP subnet. However, as you will see, control plane security features are applied to these logical interfaces.

Figure 9-3 highlights in particular the router of focus for this case study, PE-00, and illustrates the relationship among its interfaces. This router is also the focus for the sample IOS configuration that follows.

Router Configuration

Security configurations may be derived based upon the preceding topology and functional requirements. Router PE-00 is used as the focal point for the remaining discussions; however, the other Internet edge routers shown within the topology of Figure 9-2 have similar but locally specific configurations.

Example 9-1 provides the derived Cisco IOS configuration that satisfies the preceding requirements and defense in depth and breadth security principles. This configuration assumes that PE-00 is a Cisco 12000 series router (12416), and that it is running IOS Software Release 12.0(32)S with the SSH feature set. Line numbers precede each configuration command shown in Example 9-1 and serve as reference points for the remainder of the discussion that directly follows, which is organized by IP traffic plane.

Example 9-1 *Case Study 1 SP Internet Edge Router PE-00 Configuration*

```
 1 : version 12.0
 2 : service nagle
 3 : no service pad
 4 : service tcp-keepalives-in
 5 : service tcp-keepalives-out
 6 : service timestamps debug datetime msec localtime show-timezone
 7 : service timestamps log datetime msec localtime show-timezone
 8 : service password-encryption
 9 : no service dhcp
10 : !
11 : hostname PE-00
12 : !
13 : boot-start-marker
14 : boot system disk0:gsr-k3p-mz.120-32.S3.bin
15 : boot-end-marker
16 : !
17 : logging buffered 4096 debugging
18 : no logging console
19 : logging monitor errors
20 : !
21 : aaa new-model
22 : aaa authentication login default tacacs+ local
23 : aaa authentication enable default tacacs+ enable
24 : aaa authorization exec default tacacs+ none
25 : aaa accounting commands 1 default start-stop tacacs+
26 : aaa accounting commands 15 default start-stop tacacs+
27 : enable secret 5 $1$rdYk$45iBa5oBI.QGmjoFDS9j00
28 : !
29 : username noc-admin secret 5 $1$z.rf$jFH3rwXPQdsXP8FxUeCV5.
30 : memory free low-watermark processor 100000
31 : ip subnet-zero
32 : no ip source-route
33 : no ip gratuitous-arps
34 : ip icmp rate-limit unreachable 100
35 : ip options drop
36 : ip cef
37 : no ip finger
38 : ip tcp window-size 32768
39 : ip tcp synwait-time 5
40 : ip tcp path-mtu-discovery
41 : no ip bootp server
42 : ip ssh time-out 20
43 : ip ssh source-interface Loopback0
44 : ip ssh version 1
45 : no ip domain-lookup
46 : ip domain-name sp-as65001.com
47 : !
48 : ip receive access-list 101
```

continues

Example 9-1 *Case Study 1 SP Internet Edge Router PE-00 Configuration (Continued)*

```
49  : !
50  : class-map match-all gold
51  :  match ip precedence 4  5
52  : class-map match-all bronze
53  :  match ip precedence 0  1
54  : class-map match-all control
55  :  match ip precedence 6  7
56  : class-map match-all silver
57  :  match ip precedence 2  3
58  : class-map match-all CoPP-management
59  :  match access-group 121
60  : class-map match-all CoPP-normal
61  :  match access-group 122
62  : class-map match-all CoPP-remaining-IP
63  :  match access-group 124
64  : class-map match-all CoPP-undesirable
65  :  match access-group 123
66  : class-map match-all CoPP-routing
67  :  match access-group 120
68  : !
69  : !
70  : policy-map edge-recolor
71  :  class class-default
72  :   set precedence 0
73  : policy-map CoPP
74  :  class CoPP-undesirable
75  :   police 8000    conform-action drop     exceed-action drop
76  :  class CoPP-routing
77  :   police 8000    conform-action transmit    exceed-action transmit
78  :  class CoPP-management
79  :   police 50000   conform-action transmit    exceed-action drop
80  :  class CoPP-normal
81  :   police 15000   conform-action transmit    exceed-action drop
82  :  class CoPP-remaining-IP
83  :   police 8000    conform-action transmit    exceed-action drop
84  :  class class-default
85  :   police 8000    conform-action transmit    exceed-action transmit
86  : policy-map diffserv-qos
87  :  class control
88  :   bandwidth percent 20
89  :  class gold
90  :   bandwidth percent 40
91  :  class silver
92  :   bandwidth percent 30
93  :  class bronze
94  :   bandwidth percent 10
95  : !
96  : !
97  : !
98  : !
99  : interface Loopback0
```

Example 9-1   *Case Study 1 SP Internet Edge Router PE-00 Configuration (Continued)*

```
100 :  ip address 192.168.1.5 255.255.255.255
101 :  no ip unreachables
102 :  no ip directed-broadcast
103 : !
104 : interface Null0
105 :  no ip unreachables
106 : !
107 : interface Serial0/0/0
108 :  description - Link to Customer A CPE-A0 router
109 :  ip address 209.165.200.225 255.255.255.252
110 :  ip access-group 100 in
111 :  ip verify unicast source reachable-via rx
112 :  no ip redirects
113 :  no ip unreachables
114 :  no ip directed-broadcast
115 :  encapsulation ppp
116 :  ntp disable
117 :  no peer neighbor-route
118 :  no cdp enable
119 :  service-policy input edge-recolor
120 : !
121 : interface Serial1/0/0
122 :  description - Link to P-00 router
123 :  mtu 4072
124 :  ip address 172.31.4.1 255.255.255.252
125 :  no ip directed-broadcast
126 :  encapsulation ppp
127 :  ip ospf message-digest-key 1 md5 7 095F4B0A0B0003
128 :  service-policy output diffserv-qos
129 : !
130 : interface Serial2/0/0
131 :  description - Link to P-03 router
132 :  mtu 4072
133 :  ip address 172.30.4.1 255.255.255.252
134 :  no ip directed-broadcast
135 :  encapsulation ppp
136 :  ip ospf message-digest-key 1 md5 7 095F4B0A0B0003
137 :  service-policy output diffserv-qos
138 : !
139 : router ospf 1
140 :  router-id 192.168.1.5
141 :  log-adjacency-changes
142 :  area 0.0.0.0 authentication message-digest
143 :  passive-interface Loopback0
144 :  network 172.31.0.0 0.0.255.255 area 0.0.0.0
145 :  network 172.30.0.0 0.0.255.255 area 0.0.0.0
146 :  network 192.168.1.0 0.0.0.255 area 0.0.0.0
147 : !
148 : router bgp 65001
149 :  bgp router-id 192.168.1.5
```

continues

Example 9-1 *Case Study 1 SP Internet Edge Router PE-00 Configuration (Continued)*

```
150 :  bgp maxas-limit 100
151 :  bgp log-neighbor-changes
152 :  neighbor 192.168.1.2 remote-as 65001
153 :  neighbor 192.168.1.2 password 7 02050D480809
154 :  neighbor 192.168.1.2 update-source Loopback0
155 :  !
156 :  address-family ipv4
157 :   redistribute static
158 :   neighbor 192.168.1.2 activate
159 :   neighbor 192.168.1.2 next-hop-self
160 :   no auto-summary
161 :   no synchronization
162 :   network 172.16.0.0 mask 255.255.255.0
163 :   exit-address-family
164 :  !
165 : ip classless
166 : ip route 172.16.0.0 255.255.255.0 Serial0/0
167 : ip route 192.0.2.1 255.255.255.255 Null0
168 : ip route 209.165.200.0 255.255.252.0 Null0
169 : ip route 209.165.200.226 255.255.255.255 Serial0/0
170 : no ip http server
171 : !
172 : !
173 : logging trap notifications
174 : logging source-interface Loopback0
175 : logging 192.168.255.50
176 : access-list 10 permit 192.168.252.0 0.0.3.255
177 : access-list 100 deny   ip any 172.30.0.0 0.1.255.255
178 : access-list 100 deny   ip any 192.168.1.0 0.0.0.255
179 : access-list 100 deny   ip any 192.168.252.0 0.0.3.255
180 : access-list 100 deny ip 0.0.0.0 0.255.255.255 any
181 : access-list 100 deny ip 10.0.0.0 0.255.255.255 any
182 : access-list 100 deny ip 127.0.0.0 0.255.255.255 any
183 : access-list 100 deny ip 169.254.0.0 0.255.255.255 any
184 : access-list 100 deny ip 172.16.0.0 0.0.15.255 any
185 : access-list 100 deny ip 192.0.2.0 0.0.0.255 any
186 : access-list 100 deny ip 192.168.0.0 0.0.255.255 any
187 : access-list 100 deny ip 198.18.0.0 0.1.255.255 any
188 : access-list 100 deny ip 224.0.0.0 63.255.255.255 any
189 : access-list 100 permit ip any any
190 : access-list 101 permit ospf 192.168.1.0 0.0.0.255 any precedence internet
191 : access-list 101 permit tcp host 192.168.1.2 host 192.168.1.5 eq 179
         precedence internet
192 : access-list 101 permit tcp host 192.168.1.2 eq 179 host 192.168.1.5
         precedence internet
193 : access-list 101 permit tcp 192.168.252.0 0.0.3.255 host 192.168.1.5 eq 22
194 : access-list 101 permit tcp 192.168.252.0 0.0.3.255 eq 22 host 192.168.1.5
195 : access-list 101 permit udp 192.168.252.0 0.0.3.255 host 192.168.1.5 eq 123
```

Example 9-1 *Case Study 1 SP Internet Edge Router PE-00 Configuration (Continued)*

```
196  : access-list 101 permit tcp 192.168.252.0 0.0.3.255 eq tacacs host
         192.168.1.5 established
197  : access-list 101 permit udp 192.168.252.0 0.0.3.255 host 192.168.1.5 eq 69
198  : access-list 101 permit udp 192.168.252.0 0.0.3.255 host 192.168.1.5 eq 161
199  : access-list 101 permit icmp any any echo
200  : access-list 101 permit icmp any any echo-reply
201  : access-list 101 permit icmp any any ttl-exceeded
202  : access-list 101 permit icmp any any unreachable
203  : access-list 101 permit icmp any any port-unreachable
204  : access-list 101 permit icmp any any packet-too-big
205  : access-list 101 deny   ip any any
206  : access-list 120 permit ospf 192.168.1.0 0.0.0.255 any precedence internet
207  : access-list 120 permit tcp host 192.168.1.2 host 192.168.1.5 eq 179
         precedence internet
208  : access-list 120 permit tcp host 192.168.1.2 eq 179 host 192.168.1.5
         precedence internet
209  : access-list 121 permit tcp 192.168.252.0 0.0.3.255 host 192.168.1.5 eq 22
210  : access-list 121 permit udp 192.168.252.0 0.0.3.255 host 192.168.1.5 eq 123
211  : access-list 121 permit tcp 192.168.252.0 0.0.3.255 eq tacacs host
         192.168.1.5 established
212  : access-list 121 permit udp 192.168.252.0 0.0.3.255 host 192.168.1.5 eq 69
213  : access-list 121 permit udp 192.168.252.0 0.0.3.255 host 192.168.1.5 eq 161
214  : access-list 121 permit ip 192.168.252.0 0.0.3.255 any
215  : access-list 122 permit icmp 172.30.0.0 0.1.255.255 any echo
216  : access-list 122 permit icmp 192.168.1.0 0.0.0.255 any echo
217  : access-list 122 permit icmp 209.165.200.0 0.0.3.255 any echo
218  : access-list 122 permit icmp 172.30.0.0 0.1.255.255 any echo-reply
219  : access-list 122 permit icmp 192.168.1.0 0.0.0.255 any echo-reply
220  : access-list 122 permit icmp 209.165.200.0 0.0.3.255 any echo-reply
221  : access-list 122 permit icmp 172.30.0.0 0.1.255.255 any packet-too-big
222  : access-list 122 permit icmp 192.168.1.0 0.0.0.255 any packet-too-big
223  : access-list 122 permit icmp 209.165.200.0 0.0.3.255 any packet-too-big
224  : access-list 122 permit icmp 172.30.0.0 0.1.255.255 any ttl-exceeded
225  : access-list 122 permit icmp 192.168.1.0 0.0.0.255 any ttl-exceeded
226  : access-list 122 permit icmp 209.165.200.0 0.0.3.255 any ttl-exceeded
227  : access-list 123 permit icmp any any fragments
228  : access-list 123 permit udp any any fragments
229  : access-list 123 permit tcp any any fragments
230  : access-list 124 permit ip any any
231  : !
232  : !
233  : tacacs-server host 192.168.255.30
234  : tacacs-server timeout 2
235  : no tacacs-server directed-request
236  : tacacs-server key 7 s3cr3t
237  : snmp-server community s3cr3t RO 10
238  : snmp-server trap-source Loopback0
239  : snmp-server enable traps tty
240  : snmp-server host 192.168.255.1 version 2c s3cr3t
```

continues

Example 9-1 *Case Study 1 SP Internet Edge Router PE-00 Configuration (Continued)*

```
241 : !
242 : control-plane slot 0
243 :  service-policy input CoPP
244 : control-plane slot 1
245 :  service-policy input CoPP
246 : control-plane slot 2
247 :  service-policy input CoPP
248 : control-plane slot 3
249 :  service-policy input CoPP
250 : control-plane slot 4
251 :  service-policy input CoPP
252 : control-plane slot 5
253 :  service-policy input CoPP
254 : control-plane slot 6
255 :  service-policy input CoPP
256 : control-plane slot 9
257 :  service-policy input CoPP
258 : control-plane slot 10
259 :  service-policy input CoPP
260 : control-plane slot 11
261 :  service-policy input CoPP
262 : control-plane slot 12
263 :  service-policy input CoPP
264 : control-plane slot 13
265 :  service-policy input CoPP
266 : control-plane slot 14
267 :  service-policy input CoPP
268 : control-plane slot 15
269 :  service-policy input CoPP
270 : !
271 : banner motd ^C
272 : **** AUTHORIZED ACCESS ONLY *****
273 : **** This system is the property of SP AS65001.
274 : **** Disconnect IMMEDIATELY if you are not an authorized user!
275 : **** ********************** *****
276 : ^C
277 : !
278 : line con 0
279 :  exec-timeout 5 0
280 :  login authentication default
281 : line aux 0
282 :  no exec
283 : line vty 0 4
284 :  access-class 10 in
285 :  access-class 10 out
286 :  exec-timeout 5 0
287 :  transport input ssh
288 : !
289 : process cpu threshold type total rising 80 interval 5 falling 20 interval 5
```

Example 9-1 *Case Study 1 SP Internet Edge Router PE-00 Configuration (Continued)*

```
290  : ntp authentication-key 1 md5 0017400516081F 7
291  : ntp authenticate
292  : ntp trusted-key 1
293  : ntp source Loopback0
294  : ntp access-group serve-only 10
295  : ntp server 192.168.255.40 key 1
296  : no cns aaa enable
297  : !
298  : end
```

Data Plane

In this case study, and from the perspective of router PE-00, data plane traffic includes the following:

- **Internal to internal traffic:** Data plane traffic in this category includes traffic that is sourced by and destined to devices wholly within the administrative domain of the SP (AS 65001). In the case of PE-00, this includes all packets routed between the redundant uplinks (that is, only those packets routed between Serial1/0/0 and Serial2/0/0). Many SP network designs are architected such that *internal to internal* data plane traffic is routed exclusively through core routers and not through edge routers except during multiple core failure conditions. In this way, the PE-00 uplink interface capacity is used exclusively for traffic routed between internal and external interfaces and, of course, control and management plane protocols. Hence, in this case study and from the perspective of PE-00, no data plane traffic is included in this category.

- **Internal to external traffic:** Data plane traffic in this category includes traffic that is sourced within the SP internal infrastructure but destined to external networks outside the SP's administrative domain. Support for such internal to external traffic forwarding is required by some external applications such as IP traceroute and Path MTU Discovery (PMTUD). For the purposes of this case study and from the perspective of PE-00, this type of internal to external data plane traffic is limited to certain ICMP types—for example, Fragmentation Needed but Do Not Fragment Bit Set (Message Type 3, Code 4) and Time Exceeded (Message Type 11)—and comes from internal interfaces within the SP internal infrastructure prefix range 172.30.0.0/15.

- **External to internal traffic:** Data plane traffic in this category includes traffic that is sourced externally and destined for internal SP infrastructure, such as in the case of SPs with hosted content. However, in this case study and from the perspective of PE-00, no legitimate data plane traffic is included in this category. Therefore, such traffic is filtered at the network edge to mitigate the risk of an attack against the internal SP infrastructure.

- **External to external traffic:** Data plane traffic in this category includes traffic that is sourced externally and destined to an external network. Such traffic requires transit from the SP and possibly the wider Internet for remote connectivity. For SPs, this often represents the vast majority of the data plane traffic seen within the network. In this case study and from the perspective of PE-00, this includes any traffic that ingresses an external interface, such as Serial0/0/0, and that is destined to a prefix only reachable through another external interface. The egress external interface can exist on either PE-00 or a different edge router within the SP network (AS 65001). Either way, external to external traffic simply transits the SP network.

Data Plane Security

From the perspective of PE-00, the techniques used for data plane security include the following:

- **Interface ACL:** A combined infrastructure and antispoofing ACL is applied to the Serial0/0/0 interface to filter any ingress traffic destined to SP internal infrastructure, including the SP NOC, and any special-use and reserved IP addresses (per RFC 3330). This policy is defined through the extended ACL 100 (lines 177 through 189), which is attached to the Serial0/0/0 interface in the input direction on line 110. Note that this input ACL applies to all ingress traffic. Because PE-00 exchanges only data plane packets with CPE-A0, no permit ACL entries are included for control, management, and services plane traffic. The only traffic that is filtered is traffic destined to internal SP infrastructure addresses and spoofed traffic that is using special-use and reserved IP addresses. All other traffic is allowed. Although it is possible for the SP to also configure an egress ACL on Serial0/0/0 as well, rarely would it do so for unmanaged Internet access customers. In this case, Customer A has taken the responsibilities for managing its Internet access (CPE) router itself, as was described in Chapter 8. The interface ACL policy mitigates the risk of both direct attacks against the SP internal infrastructure and spoofing attacks using special-use and reserved IP addresses.

- **uRPF:** Unicast RPF strict mode is deployed on the PE-00 external interface to Customer A for antispoofing protection. The use of uRPF strict mode will filter (drop) any ingress traffic sourced from outside the Customer A HQ network public address blocks, including 172.16.0.0/24 and 209.165.200.226/32. Only ingress traffic having an IP source address within these two address blocks is permitted by uRPF strict mode. Configuration line 111 enables uRPF for antispoofing protection on the Serial0/0/0 interface. The uRPF policy mitigates the risk of spoofing attacks.

- **QoS:** QoS is deployed within the SP network in support of differentiated services and to isolate important control plane traffic from the other IP traffic planes. The associated policy map (lines 86 through 94) and class maps (lines 50 through 57) are defined using MQC. The policy is then attached to the PE-00 uplink interfaces, including Serial1/0/0 and Serial2/0/0 per lines 128 and 137. If the PE-00 uplinks become congested, QoS will reserve 20 percent of uplink bandwidth for control plane traffic. To ensure that low-priority external traffic does not inadvertently or maliciously enter the high-priority traffic classes (in other words, *gold*, *silver*, *control*), a QoS recoloring policy is applied to Internet access ports, including the PE-00 serial interface (Serial0/0/0) to CPE-A0 (line 119). The associated policy (lines 70 through 72) simply recolors all traffic with IP precedence 0. This prevents any transit Internet traffic from being classified into the SP's high-priority traffic classes. Hence, the queuing and recoloring policies mitigate the risk of resource (bandwidth) exhaustion attacks against high-priority traffic classes including control plane protocols.

- **IP options:** IP packets with option headers are filtered by the **ip options drop** global configuration command (line 35). The IOS default behavior of IP source routing is also disabled with the **no ip source-route** global configuration command (line 32). Disabling IP options in this way mitigates the risk of IP options–based attacks.

- **ICMP techniques:** On a per-interface basis, several ICMP best common practices (BCP) are also applied. ICMP Destination Unreachable and Redirect message generation is disabled using the **no ip unreachables** (line 113) and **no ip redirects** (line 112) interface configuration commands, respectively. Global rate limiting of ICMP Destination Unreachable message generation is also enabled via line 34. ICMP Information Request and Address Mask Request processing is disabled by default within IOS; hence, the **no ip information-reply** and **no ip mask-reply** interface commands are applied by default. Disabling ICMP processing in this way mitigates the risk of transit IP data plane attacks and ICMP-based control plane attacks.

- **IP directed broadcasts:** The dropping of IP directed broadcast packets is the default behavior in IOS 12.0(32)S and, hence, the **no ip directed-broadcast** interface command is applied by default (line 114). Earlier versions of IOS forwarded IP directed broadcast packets by default. You should confirm the default behavior for your IOS release in order to properly mitigate the risk of directed broadcast based attacks.

- **Edge router external link protection:** Whereas IP reachability from the wider Internet to the CPE-A0 Serial0/0 interface is required for IPsec VPN services as outlined previously, it is not required to the PE-00 Serial0/0/0 interface. To mitigate the risk of remote attacks against PE routers that leverage IP reachable external interface addresses, an aggregate static route to Null0 is configured on every edge and core router within the SP network (line 168). As a result, remote external traffic destined to an external PE-CE (Internet access) interface is now discarded as described in detail in Chapter 4. Because this configuration has the additional impact of making local eBGP next hops no longer reachable, BGP **next-hop-self** (line 159) must be set for iBGP sessions. Further, to maintain IP reachability to CPE-A0 in support of IPsec VPN and NAT services, a static route for the host prefix 209.165.200.226/32 is also configured (line 169) and redistributed into iBGP (line 157). The **no peer neighbor-route** command (line 117) is also configured on the Serial0/0 interface to ensure that the 209.165.200.226/32 connected prefix does not appear in the router RIB, which would prevent the 209.165.200.226/32 static route from being redistributed into iBGP. Redistributing 209.165.200.226/32 into iBGP enables remote IP reachability to CPE-A0 in support of IPsec VPN services. Note that the generation of ICMP Destination Unreachable messages is also disabled on the Null0 interface via line 105. This is important, because without this configuration, ICMP Destination Unreachable messages would be generated by the Null0 interface, possibly causing high CPU utilization. (Note that the Null0 interfaces will not appear in the router configuration unless default interface configuration parameters are modified, such as **no ip unreachables**.) The PE-CE link protection policy using an aggregate static route to Null0 mitigates the risk of remote attacks against PE external interfaces.

- **Remotely triggered black hole (RTBH) filtering:** As detailed in Chapter 4, RTBH mechanisms must be predeployed before they can be used for security incident response. The configuration necessary on PE-00 is simply a static route to the Null0 interface (line 167). This prepares the router for destination-based RTBH filtering, which would be invoked by a remote trigger router. Because uRPF is also enabled on PE-00, as described previously in this list, source-based RTBH filtering can also be invoked by a remote trigger router.

Control Plane

In this case study, and from the perspective of router PE-00, control plane traffic includes the following:

- **IGP traffic:** The SP uses OSPF as its IGP, which is enabled on all internal and loopback interfaces throughout the SP infrastructure. Because static IP default routing is used by the Customer A CPE routers, neither OSPF nor BGP is enabled on the PE-00 external interface to CPE-A0. Although Customer A uses OSPF as its IGP between remote sites, it runs within the IPsec VPN services layer, and hence appears as native data plane traffic to the PE-00. Further, these two instances of OSPF are completely unique because they support completely unrelated administrative domains. Therefore, no OSPF adjacencies are formed between PE-00 and CPE-A0. In the case of PE-00, OSPF is enabled on the uplinks, which represent the 172.30.4.1/30 and 72.31.4.1/30 networks, and on the 192.168.1.5/32 prefix associated with Loopback0.

- **BGP:** Although eBGP is not used between PE-00 and CPE-A0, iBGP is enabled on all edge and core routers within the SP network in support of interdomain (Internet) routing.

- **Layer 2 keepalives:** L2 keepalives will be used on all of the Serial interfaces of PE-00. L2 keepalives are not used for Ethernet nor are they applicable to virtual interfaces such as Loopback0.

Control Plane Security

From the perspective of PE-00, the techniques used for control plane security include the following:

- **Selective Packet Discard (SPD):** SPD is turned on by default, and on 12000 series routers, aggressive mode is the only mode available. Hence, no additional configuration is required. The hold-queue, headroom, and extended headroom default settings are adequate as well.

- **IP Receive ACLs:** An IP rACL is applied to filter unauthorized traffic destined to the IOS process level on PE-00. Configuration lines 190 through 205 define the IP rACL policy using the extended ACL 101, which is then applied to the receive interface in the inbound direction on line 48. All traffic flows are denied by the IP rACL except for the following:

  — OSPF traffic sourced from 192.168.1.0/24 and with IP precedence 6 (line 190).

  — BGP traffic sourced from an internal BGP route reflector (192.168.1.2/24) and with IP precedence 6 (lines 191 and 192).

  — Management traffic sourced from the SP NOC 192.168.252.0/22 (lines 193 through 198).

  — Several types of ICMP packets (management plane traffic) must be permitted by the rACL for operational needs (Echo Reply, Time Exceeded, and certain IP destination unreachables). These ACE rules are configured on lines 199 through 204.

  Per Chapter 5, "Control Plane Security," all CEF receive adjacency traffic has to be accounted for within the IP rACL policy, including both control and management plane traffic. IP rACLs mitigate the risk of unauthorized (attack) traffic from reaching the IOS process level.

- **Control Plane Policing (CoPP):** CoPP is enabled to protect IOS process level functions, including control and management plane services. Only distributed CoPP is enabled by applying MQC service policies to the control plane, as shown on lines 242 through 269. The associated MQC policies that permit, deny, or rate limit control and management plane traffic flows are defined via lines 73 through 85. The MQC class maps and extended ACLs used for CoPP packet classification are configured via lines 58 through 67, and 206 through 230, respectively. Because the catch-all

CoPP-remaining-IP traffic class (line 82) directly precedes it, the class-default portion of the CoPP policy map (lines 84 and 85) accounts for all Layer 2 keepalive traffic only. Note, the routing and class-default traffic classes are unpoliced. The management, normal (ICMP), and remaining IP traffic classes are rate limited. Traffic classified into the undesirable class is dropped. Per Chapter 5, all IOS process level traffic has to be accounted for within the CoPP policy, including control and management plane traffic as well as exception data plane traffic. CoPP mitigates the risk of unauthorized traffic and exception IP transit traffic from reaching the IOS process level.

- **OSPF MD5 authentication:** OSPF is enabled on lines 139 through 146. Further, within the OSPF routing process itself, **passive-interface** is configured for the Loopback0 interface, as shown on line 143. MD5 authentication for configured OSPF areas is also enabled (line 142). MD5 authentication passwords are configured on each of the internal physical interfaces, including Serial1/0/0 (line 127) and Serial2/0/0 (line 136). Note that even though the prefix associated with Loopback0 is enabled for OSPF, this interface does not require the MD5 key to be applied because it is a virtual interface and no adjacency is formed. MD5 authentication helps to mitigate the risk of attacks against OSPF.

- **BGP MD5 authentication:** BGP is enabled on lines 148 through 163. BGP MD5 authentication (line 153) is enabled between PE-00 and the BGP route reflector (192.168.1.2/32) within the SP network. MD5 authentication helps to mitigate the risk of attacks against BGP.

Management Plane

In this case study, and from the perspective of router PE-00, in-band management plane traffic includes the following:

- **Provisioning traffic:** Management plane traffic in this category includes SSH and TFTP traffic and must be sourced internally from the SP NOC (192.168.252.0/22). Telnet and HTTP are not permitted. In the case of PE-00, ingress management traffic of this type will be destined to the 192.168.1.5/32 address of Loopback0. Egress management traffic of this type will be destined to the 192.168.252.0/22 prefix of the SP NOC.

- **Monitoring traffic:** Management plane traffic in this category includes SNMP, NetFlow, and Syslog, and this traffic is only authorized to and from the internal network. In the case of PE-00, ingress SNMP traffic will be destined to the 192.168.1.5/32 address of Loopback0. Egress management traffic of this type will be destined to the 192.168.252.0/22 prefix of the SP NOC. Local NetFlow collectors are not included in this case study, which would generally require export to an internal address outside of the SP NOC 192.168.252.0/22 address block.

- **Other traffic:** Several other protocols are configured within the management plane, including NTP, DNS, and TACACS+. In the case of PE-00, management traffic of this type will all be within the SP NOC 192.168.252.0/22 address block. In addition, several types of ICMP packets must be permitted by the IP rACL and CoPP policies (see the preceding "Control Plane" section) for operational needs, including ICMP Echo Request, Echo Reply, Time Exceeded, and specific IP Unreachable types. CDP is disabled on external interfaces but enabled on internal interfaces.

- **Out-of-band traffic:** The console interface is used for OOB management access.

Management Plane Security

From the perspective of PE-00, the techniques used for management plane security include the following:

- **Out-of-band management:** Password authentication is enabled for terminal access using the console port (line 280). Password authentication mitigates the risk of unauthorized access.

- **SNMP:** SNMP parameters are configured via lines 237 through 240, which includes sending SNMP traps in v2c format to the SP NOC (line 240). Only read-only SNMP access is allowed (line 237) given that no read-write community string is configured. Further, SNMP read access is restricted to sources permitted within the SNMP configured standard ACL 10 (line 176). SNMP packets greater than 1500 bytes are also discarded, given the IOS default behavior for **snmp-server packetsize**. These SNMP security techniques mitigate the risk of unauthorized access and network reconnaissance.

- **Disable unused services:**
    - **BOOTP:** BOOTP services are disabled on line 41.
    - **CDP:** CDP is disabled on external interfaces only (line 118).
    - **DHCP:** DHCP server functions are disabled on line 9.
    - **DNS-based host name-to-address translation:** DNS-based name resolution by the router is disabled on line 45.
    - **EXEC mode:** Because the auxiliary port is not used for in-band or out-of-band management, EXEC mode is disabled (line 282) on the auxiliary port.
    - **Finger service:** The finger service is disabled on line 37.
    - **HTTP server:** The (unsecure) HTTP server is disabled on line 170.
    - **Minor servers:** Both the minor TCP and UDP servers are disabled by default within IOS.

— **NTP:** NTP is disabled on external interfaces only (line 116). The NTP configuration associated with internal interfaces is described later in this list.

— **PAD:** The PAD service is disabled on line 3.

These management plane security techniques mitigate the risk of unauthorized access and network reconnaissance.

- **AAA:** AAA is fully enabled for authentication, authorization, and accounting. This begins with the **aaa new-model** configuration command (line 21). TACACS+ serves as the primary authentication mechanism (lines 22 and 23) for both user-level and privilege-level (enable) EXEC mode access. If PE-00 loses IP connectivity to the TACACS+ server for whatever reason, local username/password authentication will be used for user-level EXEC mode access (line 22) and enable password authentication will be used for privilege-level (enable) EXEC mode access (line 23). A local *noc-admin* username and password is configured (lines 29) in support of local username/password authentication. The enable secret is configured (line 27) in support of enable password authentication. Command authorization is configured to use TACACS+ and then none (in other words, no authorization) if IP connectivity to the TACACS+ server is lost (line 24). Command accounting is also configured to use TACACS+ (lines 25 and 26). The TACACS+ server-related parameters are configured via lines 233 through 236. The configuration of the TACACS+ server itself is outside the scope of this book. The preceding AAA policies mitigate the risk of unauthorized access and provide user accounting.

- **SSH services:** Configuring SSH requires that an IP domain name be specified (for RSA key generation). This is done via line 46. The RSA encryption key is generated outside the configuration during router setup. SSH protocol parameters are configured on lines 42 through 44, and VTY lines are restricted to SSH transport (line 287). Remote terminal access is further restricted to sources matching ACL 10, per lines 284 and 285. SSH provides secure remote terminal access to IP routers. As such, it mitigates the risk of session eavesdropping, which may compromise router configurations, passwords, and so on and be leveraged for an attack.

- **Disable idle user sessions:** Idle EXEC sessions are disabled after 5 minutes (lines 279 and 286). Further, TCP keepalives are enabled via lines 5 and 6 and serve to terminate connections where the remote host disappears (provide no positive acknowledgement [ACK]). Disabling idle user sessions in this way reduces the risk of unauthorized access.

- **NTP:** NTP is enabled to facilitate correlation of network events (line 290 through 295). Ingress NTP protocol messages are restricted to sources permitted within the NTP configured standard ACL 10 (line 294). Further, MD5 authentication is enabled for NTP protocol message exchanged with the configured NTP server (lines 290 through 292 and line 295). MD5 authentication helps to mitigate the risk of attacks against NTP, which is valuable for network event correlation, including security incident response.

- **Syslog:** Syslog parameters are configured on lines 173 through 175, which includes directing Syslog messages to the SP NOC (line 175). Timestamps are also appended to each Syslog (and debug) message per lines 7 and 8. In addition, Syslog is configured to report OSPF adjacency changes (line 141) and BGP neighbor state changes (line 151). In order to generate Syslog messages when free memory resources are low, low-watermark levels are set for processor memory on line 30. Further, in order to generate Syslog messages when CPU resources are low, processor CPU threshold levels are set on line 289. Syslog provides valuable network telemetry and is useful for security incident response.

- **Other BCPs:** Other BCP router security configurations related to the management plane are implemented. The router host name is configured on line 11. Global service settings are modified, including enabling timestamps for all debug and logging messages (lines 6 and 7) and enabling password encryption services (line 8). The router boot image is specified on line 14 (lines 13 and 15 are auto-generated). Buffered logging is enabled at debug level and the buffer size is set (line 17). The display of logging messages to the console is disabled (line 18). The enable secret is set on line 27. Several global settings for router self-generated TCP sessions are adjusted, including enabling Nagle services (line 2), enabling TCP keepalives per "Disable idle user sessions" above (lines 4 and 5), increasing the TCP window size (line 38), reducing the TCP SYN wait time (line 39), and enabling PMTUD (line 40). In order to generate Syslog messages when free memory resources are low, a low-watermark level is set for processor memory on line 30. A message of the day (MOTD) login banner is configured on lines 271 through 276. Finally, in order to generate Syslog messages when CPU resources are low, processor CPU threshold levels are set on line 289.

Services Plane

In this case study, there are no services plane requirements from the perspective of router PE-00. All services plane requirements occur on the customer side of the network in the form of GRE + IPsec VPNs, and are instantiated on the CPE routers as was demonstrated in Chapter 8.

Case Study 2: MPLS VPN

Case Study 2 focuses on a typical scenario where an MPLS VPN service is used to connect customer headquarters and remote sites within a private IP VPN across the SP's shared IP network infrastructure. A description of the case study network topology, functional requirements, and translated security requirements follows.

Network Topology and Requirements

The SP network topology and assigned IP addressing schemes used within this case study are illustrated in Figure 9-4. Customer B has three sites connected using a managed MPLS VPN service, and all three sites obtain their any-to-any VPN connectivity by direct connections to the same SP network. Hence, the Inter-AS VPN architectural options (a), (b), and (c) per RFC 4364 section 10 (see Chapter 2, "Threat Models for IP Networks," and Chapter 7, "Services Plane Security") do not apply to this case study. The configurations and security techniques for the managed CE routers are reviewed in the companion enterprise case study in Chapter 8.

Figure 9-4 *Conceptual Enterprise Network Architecture for MPLS VPN Case Study 2*

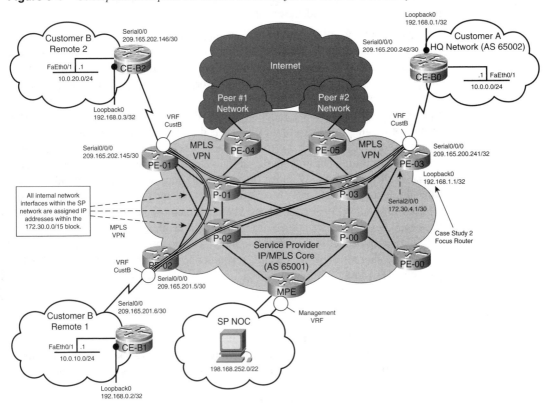

The functional requirements assumed in this case study are as follows:

- **MPLS VPN:** The SP (AS 65001) provides any-to-any IP VPN connectivity between all of the geographically disperse Customer B offices. The IP VPN is built within the SP network using RFC 4364 MPLS VPNs. BGP routing is used between the Customer B CE routers and the associated SP MPLS VPN PE routers to exchange Customer B prefix information. The SP in turn carries these customer-specific prefixes within Multiprotocol BGP (MBGP) to provide reachability between customer sites within a single customer IP VPN and to provide addressing and routing separation between different customer IP VPNs.

- **Intranet Access:** Access to Customer B's MPLS VPN and associated network prefixes is restricted to Customer B offices only. There is no Internet access from the Customer B VPN, or vice versa. External IP reachability is only provided between the CE router loopback addresses and the SP NOC for management purposes given that the Customer B CE routers are managed (as described directly below).

- **Managed CE router:** All Customer B CE routers are managed by the SP. For operational reasons, then, the SP must have in-band access to each managed CE router. The SP also manages the MPLS VPN PE and core (P) routers. The PE and P routers are managed both in-band and out-of-band using the console ports. Management applications assumed in this case study include SSH, Syslog, SNMP, NTP, TFTP, and TACACS+.

Figure 9-5 highlights the types and relationships of the interfaces associated with the MPLS VPN PE router in this case study.

You were first introduced to these interface types in Chapter 3. The following interfaces are included in this case study:

- **Internal:** Internal interfaces connect network assets wholly within one administrative domain. All SP routers shown in Figure 9-4 include at least two internal interfaces. In this case study, interfaces Serial1/0/0 and Serial2/0/0 of PE-03 are considered internal to the SP network. For all internal interfaces, /30 subnet masking is used for the purposes of this case study. The prefixes associated with these internal interfaces are routable within the IGP (OSPF in this case study). External reachability to these internal prefixes is not allowed per the MPLS VPN architecture, as outlined in Chapter 7.

- **External:** External interfaces connect networks belonging to two different administrative domains. All SP MPLS VPN edge (PE) routers include at least one external interface. Hence, by definition, an edge router normally includes at least one external interface. In the MPLS VPN case, the PE-CE link is contained within a VRF. Although the VRF routing table is customer specific, it is associated with customer routing and not the SP IGP. Hence, from the SP perspective, the PE-CE link is considered external. Conversely, from the enterprise perspective, because the link is contained within the IP VPN, it may be treated as internal, per Chapter 8.

- **Loopback:** All SP edge and core routers shown in Figure 9-4 implement a single loopback interface that is used for control and management plane traffic. All loopback interfaces within this case study are assigned from the 192.168.1.0/24 address block, as shown in Figure 9-4. The /32 IP subnets associated with these internal interfaces are also carried within the SP IGP (OSPF in this case study).

- **Receive:** All routers include by default a receive interface that "logically" represents the slow path to the IOS process level. The receive path applies to any ingress packets that must be punted from the CEF fast path to be processed locally by the router's CPU whether transit or receive adjacency packets. Because the receive path represents an exception packet processing path between the CEF fast path and IOS process level, it is not assigned or associated with a specific IP subnet.

Figure 9-5   *IP Traffic Plane Relationships to Router Interfaces for MPLS VPN Case Study 2*

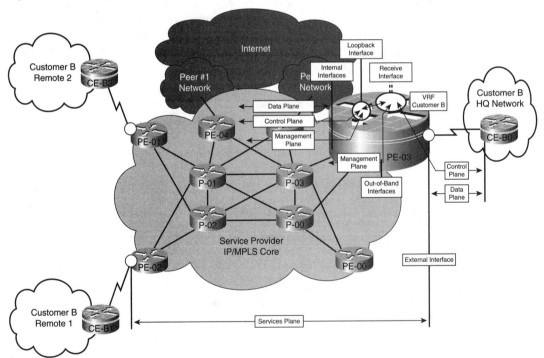

Figure 9-5 highlights in particular the router of focus for this case study, PE-03, and illustrates the relationship among its interfaces. This router is also the focus for the sample IOS configuration that follows.

Router Configuration

Security configurations may be derived based upon the topology and functional requirements presented in the preceding section. Router PE-03 is used as the focal point for the remaining discussions; however, the other MPLS VPN PE routers shown in the topology in Figure 9-4 have similar but locally specific configurations. Note that PE-02 represents a shared edge router supporting both Internet and MPLS services.

Example 9-2 provides the derived IOS configuration that satisfies the preceding requirements and the defense in depth and breadth security principles. This configuration assumes that PE-03 is a Cisco 12000 series router (12416), and that it is running Cisco IOS Software Release 12.0(32)S with the SSH feature set. Similar to Example 9-1, line numbers precede each configuration command shown in Example 9-2 and serve as reference points for the remainder of the discussion that directly follows, which is organized by IP traffic plane.

Example 9-2 *Case Study 2 SP MPLS VPN Provider Edge Router Configuration*

```
 1 : version 12.0
 2 : service nagle
 3 : no service pad
 4 : service tcp-keepalives-in
 5 : service tcp-keepalives-out
 6 : service timestamps debug datetime msec localtime show-timezone
 7 : service timestamps log datetime msec localtime show-timezone
 8 : service password-encryption
 9 : no service dhcp
10 : !
11 : hostname PE-03
12 : !
13 : boot-start-marker
14 : boot system disk0:gsr-k3p-mz.120-32.S3.bin
15 : boot-end-marker
16 : !
17 : logging buffered 4096 debugging
18 : no logging console
19 : logging monitor errors
20 : aaa new-model
21 : aaa authentication login default tacacs+ local
22 : aaa authentication enable default tacacs+ enable
23 : aaa authorization exec default tacacs+ none
24 : aaa accounting commands 1 default start-stop tacacs+
25 : aaa accounting commands 15 default start-stop tacacs+
26 : enable secret 5 $1$rdYk$45iBa5oBI.QGmjoFDS9j00
27 : !
28 : username noc-admin secret 5 $1$z.rf$jFH3rwXPQdsXP8FxUeCV5.
29 : memory free low-watermark processor 100000
30 : ip subnet-zero
31 : no ip source-route
32 : no ip gratuitous-arps
```

continues

Example 9-2 *Case Study 2 SP MPLS VPN Provider Edge Router Configuration (Continued)*

```
33 : ip icmp rate-limit unreachable 100
34 : ip options drop
35 : ip cef
36 : no ip finger
37 : ip tcp window-size 32768
38 : ip tcp synwait-time 5
39 : ip tcp path-mtu-discovery
40 : no ip bootp server
41 : ip ssh time-out 20
42 : ip ssh source-interface Loopback0
43 : ip ssh version 1
44 : no ip domain-lookup
45 : ip domain-name sp-as65001.com
46 : !
47 : ip vrf CustB-VPN
48 :   rd 65001:10
49 :   export map mgmtvpn-filter
50 :   route import 65001:10
51 :   route export 65001:10
52 :   route import 65001:20
53 :   maximum routes 1000 90
54 : !
55 : mpls label protocol ldp
56 : mpls ldp neighbor 192.168.1.2 password 7 04480E051D2458
57 : no mpls ip propagate-ttl forwarded
58 : tag-switching advertise-tags for 91
59 : !
60 : ip receive access-list 101
61 : !
62 : class-map match-any gold
63 :   match ip precedence 4  5
64 :   match mpls experimental 4 5
65 : class-map match-any bronze
66 :   match ip precedence 0  1
67 :   match mpls experimental 0 1
68 : class-map match-any silver
69 :   match ip precedence 2  3
70 :   match mpls experimental 2 3
71 : class-map match-any control
72 :   match ip precedence 6  7
73 :   match mpls experimental 6 7
74 : class-map match-all CoPP-management
75 :   match access-group 121
76 : class-map match-all CoPP-normal
77 :   match access-group 122
78 : class-map match-all CoPP-remaining-IP
79 :   match access-group 124
80 : class-map match-all CoPP-undesirable
81 :   match access-group 123
82 : class-map match-all CoPP-routing
83 :   match access-group 120
```

Example 9-2   *Case Study 2 SP MPLS VPN Provider Edge Router Configuration (Continued)*

```
 84 : !
 85 : policy-map edge-recolor
 86 :  class class-default
 87 :   set mpls experimental imposition 0
 88 : policy-map CoPP
 89 :  class CoPP-undesirable
 90 :   police 8000 conform-action drop exceed-action drop
 91 :  class CoPP-routing
 92 :   police 8000 conform-action transmit exceed-action transmit
 93 :  class CoPP-management
 94 :   police 50000 conform-action transmit exceed-action drop
 95 :  class CoPP-normal
 96 :   police 15000 conform-action transmit exceed-action drop
 97 :  class CoPP-remaining-IP
 98 :   police 8000 conform-action transmit exceed-action drop
 99 :  class class-default
100 :   police 8000 conform-action transmit exceed-action transmit
101 : policy-map diffserv-qos
102 :  class control
103 :   bandwidth percent 20
104 :  class gold
105 :   bandwidth percent 40
106 :  class silver
107 :   bandwidth percent 30
108 :  class bronze
109 :   bandwidth percent 10
110 : !
111 : !
112 : !
113 : !
114 : interface Loopback0
115 :  ip address 192.168.1.1 255.255.255.255
116 :  no ip unreachables
117 :  no ip directed-broadcast
118 : !
119 : interface Null0
120 :  no ip unreachables
121 : !
122 : interface Serial0/0/0
123 :  description - Link to Customer B CE-B0 router
124 :  ip vrf forwarding CustB-VPN
125 :  ip address 209.165.200.241 255.255.255.252
126 :  ip access-group 100 in
127 :  no ip redirects
128 :  no ip unreachables
129 :  no ip directed-broadcast
130 :  encapsulation ppp
131 :  ntp disable
132 :  no cdp enable
133 :  service-policy input edge-recolor
```

continues

Example 9-2 *Case Study 2 SP MPLS VPN Provider Edge Router Configuration (Continued)*

```
134 : !
135 : interface Serial1/0/0
136 :  description - Link to P-03 router
137 :  mtu 4072
138 :  ip address 172.31.5.1 255.255.255.252
139 :  no ip directed-broadcast
140 :  encapsulation ppp
141 :  mpls label protocol ldp
142 :  tag-switching ip
143 :  ip ospf message-digest-key 1 md5 7 095F4B0A0B0003
144 :  service-policy output diffserv-qos
145 : !
146 : interface Serial2/0/0
147 :  description - Link to P-00 router
148 :  mtu 4072
149 :  ip address 172.30.5.1 255.255.255.252
150 :  no ip directed-broadcast
151 :  encapsulation ppp
152 :  mpls label protocol ldp
153 :  tag-switching ip
154 :  ip ospf message-digest-key 1 md5 7 095F4B0A0B0003
155 :  service-policy output diffserv-qos
156 : !
157 : router ospf 1
158 :  router-id 192.168.1.1
159 :  log-adjacency-changes
160 :  area 0.0.0.0 authentication message-digest
161 :  passive-interface Loopback0
162 :  network 172.31.0.0 0.0.255.255 area 0.0.0.0
163 :  network 172.30.0.0 0.0.255.255 area 0.0.0.0
164 :  network 192.168.1.0 0.0.0.255 area 0.0.0.0
165 : !
166 : router bgp 65001
167 :  bgp router-id 192.168.1.1
168 :  bgp maxas-limit 100
169 :  bgp log-neighbor-changes
170 :  neighbor 192.168.1.2 remote-as 65001
171 :  neighbor 192.168.1.2 password 7 02050D480809
172 :  neighbor 192.168.1.2 update-source Loopback0
173 :  neighbor 209.165.200.242 remote-as 65002
174 :  neighbor 209.165.200.242 update-source Serial0/0
175 : !
176 :  address-family ipv4
177 :   no neighbor 192.168.1.2 activate
178 :   no neighbor 209.165.200.242 activate
179 :   no auto-summary
180 :   no synchronization
181 :   exit-address-family
182 : !
183 :  address-family vpnv4
184 :   neighbor 192.168.1.2 activate
```

Example 9-2 *Case Study 2 SP MPLS VPN Provider Edge Router Configuration (Continued)*

```
185 :   neighbor 192.168.1.2 send-community both
186 :   no auto-summary
187 :   no synchronization
188 :   exit-address-family
189 : !
190 :  address-family ipv4 vrf CustB-VPN
191 :   redistribute connected
192 :   neighbor 209.165.200.242 remote-as 65002
193 :   neighbor 209.165.200.242 update-source Serial0/0
194 :   neighbor 209.165.200.242 activate
195 :   neighbor 209.165.200.242 maximum-prefix 250 restart 2
196 :   neighbor 209.165.200.242 ttl-security hops 1
197 :   no auto-summary
198 :   no synchronization
199 :   exit-address-family
200 : !
201 : ip classless
202 : !
203 : no ip http server
204 : !
205 : logging trap notifications
206 : logging source-interface Loopback0
207 : logging 192.168.255.50
208 : access-list 10 permit 192.168.252.0 0.0.3.255
209 : access-list 90 permit 209.165.200.240 0.0.0.3
210 : access-list 91 permit 192.168.1.0 0.0.0.255
211 : access-list 100 permit ip 209.165.200.242 0.0.0.0 192.168.252.0 0.0.3.255
212 : access-list 100 permit ip 209.165.200.242 0.0.0.0 209.165.200.241 0.0.0.0
213 : access-list 100 deny ip any 192.168.252.0 0.0.3.255
214 : access-list 100 deny ip any 209.165.200.241 0.0.0.0
215 : access-list 100 permit ip any any
216 : access-list 101 permit ospf 192.168.1.0 0.0.0.255 any precedence internet
217 : access-list 101 permit tcp host 192.168.1.2 host 192.168.1.5 eq 179
        precedence internet
218 : access-list 101 permit tcp host 192.168.1.2 eq 179 host 192.168.1.5
        precedence internet
219 : access-list 101 permit tcp host 209.165.200.242 host 209.165.200.241 eq 179
        precedence internet
220 : access-list 101 permit tcp host 209.165.200.242 eq 179 host 209.165.200.241
        precedence internet
221 : access-list 101 permit tcp 192.168.252.0 0.0.3.255 host 192.168.1.5 eq 22
222 : access-list 101 permit udp 192.168.252.0 0.0.3.255 host 192.168.1.5 eq 123
223 : access-list 101 permit tcp 192.168.252.0 0.0.3.255 eq tacacs host
        192.168.1.5 established
224 : access-list 101 permit udp 192.168.252.0 0.0.3.255 host 192.168.1.5 eq 69
225 : access-list 101 permit udp 192.168.252.0 0.0.3.255 host 192.168.1.5 eq 161
226 : access-list 101 permit ip 192.168.252.0 0.0.3.255 any
227 : access-list 101 permit udp 192.168.1.0 0.0.0.255 any eq 646 precedence
        internet
228 : access-list 101 permit udp 192.168.1.0 0.0.0.255 eq 646 any precedence
        internet
```

continues

Example 9-2 *Case Study 2 SP MPLS VPN Provider Edge Router Configuration (Continued)*

```
229 : access-list 101 permit tcp 192.168.1.0 0.0.0.255 any eq 646 precedence
        internet
230 : access-list 101 permit tcp 192.168.1.0 0.0.0.255 eq 646 any precedence
        internet
231 : access-list 101 permit icmp any any echo
232 : access-list 101 permit icmp any any echo-reply
233 : access-list 101 permit icmp any any ttl-exceeded
234 : access-list 101 permit icmp any any unreachable
235 : access-list 101 permit icmp any any port-unreachable
236 : access-list 101 permit icmp any any packet-too-big
237 : access-list 101 deny   ip any any
238 : access-list 120 permit ospf 192.168.1.0 0.0.0.255 any precedence internet
239 : access-list 120 permit tcp host 192.168.1.2 host 192.168.1.1 eq 179
        precedence internet
240 : access-list 120 permit tcp host 192.168.1.2 eq 179 host 192.168.1.5
        precedence internet
241 : access-list 120 permit tcp host 209.165.200.242 host 209.165.200.241 eq 179
        precedence internet
242 : access-list 120 permit tcp host 209.165.200.242 eq 179 host 209.165.200.241
        precedence internet
243 : access-list 120 permit udp 192.168.1.0 0.0.0.255 any eq 646 precedence
        internet
244 : access-list 120 permit udp 192.168.1.0 0.0.0.255 eq 646 any precedence
        internet
245 : access-list 120 permit tcp 192.168.1.0 0.0.0.255 any eq 646 precedence
        internet
246 : access-list 120 permit tcp 192.168.1.0 0.0.0.255 eq 646 any precedence
        internet
247 : access-list 121 permit tcp 192.168.252.0 0.0.3.255 host 192.168.1.5 eq 22
248 : access-list 121 permit udp 192.168.252.0 0.0.3.255 host 192.168.1.5 eq 123
249 : access-list 121 permit tcp 192.168.252.0 0.0.3.255 eq tacacs host
        192.168.1.5 established
250 : access-list 121 permit udp 192.168.252.0 0.0.3.255 host 192.168.1.5 eq 69
251 : access-list 121 permit udp 192.168.252.0 0.0.3.255 host 192.168.1.5 eq 161
252 : access-list 121 permit ip 192.168.252.0 0.0.3.255 any
253 : access-list 122 permit icmp 172.30.0.0 0.1.255.255 any echo
254 : access-list 122 permit icmp 192.168.1.0 0.0.0.255 any echo
255 : access-list 122 permit icmp 209.165.200.0 0.0.3.255 any echo
256 : access-list 122 permit icmp 172.30.0.0 0.1.255.255 any echo-reply
257 : access-list 122 permit icmp 192.168.1.0 0.0.0.255 any echo-reply
258 : access-list 122 permit icmp 209.165.200.0 0.0.3.255 any echo-reply
259 : access-list 122 permit icmp 172.30.0.0 0.1.255.255 any packet-too-big
260 : access-list 122 permit icmp 192.168.1.0 0.0.0.255 any packet-too-big
261 : access-list 122 permit icmp 209.165.200.0 0.0.3.255 any packet-too-big
262 : access-list 122 permit icmp 172.30.0.0 0.1.255.255 any ttl-exceeded
263 : access-list 122 permit icmp 192.168.1.0 0.0.0.255 any ttl-exceeded
264 : access-list 122 permit icmp 209.165.200.0 0.0.3.255 any ttl-exceeded
265 : access-list 123 permit icmp any any fragments
266 : access-list 123 permit udp any any fragments
267 : access-list 123 permit tcp any any fragments
268 : access-list 124 permit ip any any
269 : !
270 : tacacs-server host 192.168.255.30
```

Example 9-2 *Case Study 2 SP MPLS VPN Provider Edge Router Configuration (Continued)*

```
271 : tacacs-server timeout 2
272 : no tacacs-server directed-request
273 : tacacs-server key 7 s3cr3t
274 : snmp-server community s3cr3t RO 10
275 : snmp-server trap-source Loopback0
276 : snmp-server enable traps tty
277 : snmp-server host 192.168.255.1 vrf CustB-VPN s3cr3t
278 : snmp-server host 192.168.255.1 version 2c s3cr3t
279 : !
280 : route-map mgmtvpn-filter permit 10
281 :   match ip address 90
282 :   set ext-community rt 65001:10 65001:30
283 : !
284 : tag-switching tdp router-id Loopback0
285 : control-plane slot 0
286 :   service-policy input CoPP
287 : control-plane slot 1
288 :   service-policy input CoPP
289 : control-plane slot 2
290 :   service-policy input CoPP
291 : control-plane slot 3
292 :   service-policy input CoPP
293 : control-plane slot 4
294 :   service-policy input CoPP
295 : control-plane slot 5
296 :   service-policy input CoPP
297 : control-plane slot 6
298 :   service-policy input CoPP
299 : control-plane slot 9
300 :   service-policy input CoPP
301 : control-plane slot 10
302 :   service-policy input CoPP
303 : control-plane slot 11
304 :   service-policy input CoPP
305 : control-plane slot 12
306 :   service-policy input CoPP
307 : control-plane slot 13
308 :   service-policy input CoPP
309 : control-plane slot 14
310 :   service-policy input CoPP
311 : control-plane slot 15
312 :   service-policy input CoPP
313 : !
314 : banner motd ^C
315 : **** AUTHORIZED ACCESS ONLY *****
316 : **** This system is the property of SP AS65001.
317 : **** Disconnect IMMEDIATELY if you are not an authorized user!
318 : **** ********************** *****
319 : ^C
320 : !
```

continues

Example 9-2 *Case Study 2 SP MPLS VPN Provider Edge Router Configuration (Continued)*

```
321 : line con 0
322 :  exec-timeout 5 0
323 :  login authentication default
324 : line aux 0
325 :  no exec
326 : line vty 0 4
327 :  access-class 10 in vrf-also
328 :  access-class 10 out
329 :  exec-timeout 5 0
330 :  transport input ssh
331 : !
332 : process cpu threshold type total rising 80 interval 5 falling 20 interval 5
333 : ntp authentication-key 1 md5 0017400516081F 7
334 : ntp authenticate
335 : ntp trusted-key 1
336 : ntp source Loopback0
337 : ntp access-group serve-only 10
338 : ntp server 192.168.255.40 key 1
339 : ntp server vrf CustB-VPN 192.168.255.40 key 1
340 : no cns aaa enable
341 : !
342 : end
```

Data Plane

In this case study, and from the perspective of router PE-03, no data plane traffic is included in this category. Rather VPN customer transit traffic is handled within the IP services plane.

Data Plane Security

External traffic is not associated with the IP data plane in any way given that this is an MPLS VPN service. External traffic is associated with the control, management, and services planes only, as described in the respective sections that follow. Therefore, in this case study, there are no data plane security requirements from the perspective of router PE-00.

Control Plane

In this case study, and from the perspective of router PE-03, control plane traffic includes the following:

- **BGP:** Control plane traffic in this category includes eBGP traffic between the PE-03 Serial0/0/0 address and the Serial0/0 address on CE-B0. BGP routing is used to dynamically exchange VPN prefix information between Customer B offices and the SP network. This category also includes MBGP traffic, which operates between the PE-03 and its internal MBGP (M-iBGP) peers. M-iBGP routing is used to dynamically exchange VPN prefix information between SP MPLS VPN PE routers within the SP network. Deployed in combination, eBGP and M-iBGP provide reachability between customer sites within a single customer IP VPN as well as addressing and routing separation between different customer IP VPNs.

- **IGP traffic:** Control plane traffic in this category includes OSPF, which is used as the IGP within the SP network. OSPF is configured for all internal and loopback interfaces within the SP infrastructure and provides IP reachability between BGP next hops and, optionally, to the SP NOC. In the case of PE-03, OSPF is enabled on the uplinks, including the 172.31.5.1/24 and 172.30.5.1/24 networks, and on the 192.168.1.1/32 prefix for Loopback0.

- **Label Distribution Protocol:** Control plane traffic in this category includes LDP (RFC 3036), which is used as the label distribution protocol by the SP in this case study. LDP is configured for all internal interfaces within the SP infrastructure and distributes MPLS labels for all of the MPLS VPN PE /32 loopback prefixes carried within the IGP (OSPF in this case). Distributing labels only for /32 loopback addresses of PE routers results in MPLS label switched paths (LSP) being established between ingress and egress PE routers only. In this way, only services plane traffic is label switched across the SP network, and not internal SP data, control, and management plane traffic. Nevertheless, LDP serves as a control plane protocol for the establishment of MPLS LSPs across the SP network between ingress and egress MPLS VPN PE routers.

- **Layer 2 keepalives:** L2 keepalives will be used on all of the Serial interfaces of PE-03. L2 keepalives are not used for Ethernet nor are they applicable to virtual interfaces such as Loopback0.

Control Plane Security

From the perspective of PE-03, the security mechanisms that will be used for control plane traffic segmentation and control include the following:

- **Selective Packet Discard (SPD):** SPD is turned on by default, and on 12000 series routers, aggressive mode is the only mode available. Hence, no additional configuration is required. The hold-queue, headroom and extended headroom default settings are adequate as well.

- **IP Receive ACLs:** An IP rACL is applied to filter unauthorized traffic destined to the IOS process level on PE-03. Configuration lines 216 through 237 define the IP rACL policy using the extended ACL 101, which is then applied to the receive interface in the inbound direction on line 60. All traffic flows are denied by the IP rACL except for the following:

    — OSPF traffic sourced from 192.168.1.0/24 and with IP precedence 6 (line 216).

    — BGP traffic sourced from an internal BGP route reflector (192.168.1.2/24) and with IP precedence 6 (lines 217 and 218).

— BGP traffic sourced from CE-B0 external Serial0/0 interface
  (209.165.200.242/32) and with IP precedence 6 (lines 219 and 220).

— Management traffic sourced from the SP NOC 192.168.252.0/22 (lines 221
  through 226).

— LDP traffic sourced from 192.168.1.0/24 and with IP precedence 6 (line 227
  through 230).

— Several types of ICMP packets (management plane traffic) must be permitted
  by the rACL for operational needs (Echo Reply, Time Exceeded, and certain
  IP Destination Unreachables). These ACE rules are configured on lines 231
  through 236.

Per Chapter 5, all CEF receive adjacency traffic has to be accounted for
within the IP rACL policy, including both control and management plane
traffic. IP rACLs mitigate the risk of unauthorized (attack) traffic from
reaching the IOS process level.

- **Control Plane Policing (CoPP):** CoPP is enabled to protect IOS process level
  functions, including control and management plane services. Only distributed CoPP
  is enabled by applying MQC service policies to the control plane, as shown on lines
  285 through 312. The associated MQC policies that permit, deny, or rate limit control
  and management plane traffic flows are defined via lines 88 through 100. The MQC
  class maps and extended ACLs used for CoPP packet classification are configured
  via lines 74 through 83, and 238 through 268, respectively. Because the catch-all
  CoPP-remaining-IP traffic class (line 97) directly precedes it, the class-default
  portion of the CoPP policy map (lines 99 and 100) accounts for all Layer 2 keepalive
  traffic only. Note, the routing and class-default traffic classes are unpoliced. The
  management, normal (ICMP), and remaining IP traffic classes are rate limited.
  Traffic classified into the undesirable class is dropped. Per Chapter 5, all IOS process
  level traffic has to be accounted for within the CoPP policy, including control and
  management plane traffic as well as exception data plane traffic. CoPP mitigates the
  risk of unauthorized traffic and exception IP transit traffic from reaching the IOS
  process level.

- **OSPF MD5 authentication:** OSPF is enabled on lines 157 through 164. Further,
  within the OSPF routing process itself, **passive-interface** is configured for the
  Loopback0 interface, as shown on line 161. MD5 authentication for configured OSPF
  areas is also enabled (line 160). MD5 authentication passwords are configured on
  each of the internal physical interfaces, including Serial1/0/0 (line 143) and Serial2/
  0/0 (line 154). Note that even though the prefix associated with Loopback0 is enabled
  for OSPF, this interface does not require the MD5 key to be applied because it is a
  virtual interface and no adjacency is formed. MD5 authentication helps to mitigate the
  risk of attacks against OSPF.

- **BGP MD5 authentication:** BGP MD5 authentication is applied to the internal M-iBGP session (line 171). MD5 authentication helps to mitigate the risk of attacks against BGP.

- **BGP TTL Security Check:** GTSM is only supported for eBGP sessions and is also configured on a per-neighbor basis. Because PE03 and CE-B0 are directly connected eBGP peers, a GTSM hop count of 1 is configured (line 196). The BGP TTL Security Check helps to mitigate the risk of attacks against eBGP.

- **BGP prefix limits:** Neighbor maximum prefix limits are configured on line 195. This prevents CPE-B0 from flooding PE-03 with a large number of VPN prefixes and, thereby, consuming the full Customer B VPN routing table, which is limited to 1000 prefixes (line 53).

- **VPN prefix maximum:** To control the maximum number of routes within the Customer B VPN routing table and the aggregate VPN routes maintained by PE-03, a maximum limit is imposed per customer VPN (line 53).

- **LDP MD5 authentication:** MD5 authentication is enabled for LDP (line 56). MD5 authentication helps to mitigate the risk of attacks against LDP.

Management Plane

In this case study, all CE routers are assumed to be managed in-band by the SP. Thus, the SP assigns a globally unique IP address to each CE Loopback0 interface for management plane purposes. These loopback interface addresses are reachable within the Management VPN defined within the SP infrastructure. Management plane traffic from the perspective of CE-B0 was reviewed in Chapter 8. From the perspective of router PE-03, management plane traffic includes the following:

- **Provisioning traffic:** Management plane traffic in this category includes SSH and TFTP traffic and must be sourced internally from the SP NOC (192.168.252.0/22). Telnet and HTTP are not permitted. In the case of PE-03, ingress management traffic of this type will be destined to the 192.168.1.1/32 address of Loopback0. Egress management traffic of this type will be destined to the 192.168.252.0/22 prefix of the SP NOC.

- **Monitoring traffic:** Management plane traffic in this category includes SNMP, NetFlow, and Syslog, and this traffic is only authorized to and from the internal network. In the case of PE-03, ingress SNMP traffic will be destined to the 192.168.1.1/32 address of Loopback0. Egress management traffic of this type will be destined to the 192.168.252.0/22 prefix of the SP NOC. Local NetFlow collectors are not included in this case study, which would generally require export to an internal address outside of the SP NOC 192.168.252.0/22 address block.

- **Other traffic:** Several other protocols are configured within the management plane, including NTP, DNS, and TACACS+ traffic. In the case of PE-03, management traffic of this type will all be within the SP NOC 192.168.252.0/22 address block. In addition, several types of ICMP packets must be permitted by the IP rACL and CoPP policies (see the preceding "Control Plane" section) for operational needs, including ICMP Echo Request, Echo Reply, Time Exceeded, and specific IP Unreachable types. CDP is disabled on external interfaces but enabled on internal interfaces.

- **Out-of-band traffic:** The console interface is used for out-of-band management access.

Management Plane Security

From the perspective of PE-03, the techniques used for management plane security include the following:

- **OOB management:** Password authentication is enabled for terminal access using the console port (line 323). Password authentication mitigates the risk of unauthorized access.

- **SNMP:** SNMP parameters are configured via lines 274 through 278, which includes sending SNMP traps in v2c format to the SP NOC (line 278). Only read-only SNMP access is allowed (line 274) given that no read-write community string is configured. Further, SNMP read access is restricted to sources permitted within the SNMP configured standard ACL 10 (line 274). SNMP packets greater than 1500 bytes are also discarded, given the default IOS behavior for **snmp-server packetsize.** These SNMP security techniques mitigate the risk of unauthorized access and network reconnaissance.

- **Disable unused services:**
    - **BOOTP:** BOOTP services are disabled on line 40.
    - **CDP:** CDP is disabled on external interfaces only (line 132).
    - **DHCP:** DHCP server functions are disabled on line 9.
    - **DNS-based host name-to-address translation:** DNS-based name resolution by the router is disabled on line 44.
    - **EXEC mode:** Because the auxiliary port is not used for in-band or out-of-band management, EXEC mode is disabled (line 325) on the auxiliary port.
    - **Finger service:** The finger service is disabled on line 36.
    - **HTTP server:** The (unsecure) HTTP server is disabled on line 203.
    - **Minor servers:** Both the minor TCP and UDP servers are disabled by default.

— **NTP:** NTP is disabled on external interfaces only (line 131). The NTP configuration associated with internal interfaces is described later in this list.

— **PAD:** The PAD service is disabled on line 3.

These management plane security techniques mitigate the risk of unauthorized access and network reconnaissance.

- **AAA:** AAA is fully enabled for authentication, authorization, and accounting. This begins with the **aaa new-model** configuration command (line 20). TACACS+ serves as the primary authentication mechanism (lines 21 and 22) for both user-level and privilege-level (enable) EXEC mode access. If PE-03 loses IP connectivity to the TACACS+ server for whatever reason, local username/password authentication will be used for user-level EXEC mode access (line 21) and enable password authentication will be used for privilege-level (enable) EXEC mode access (line 22). The local username *noc-admin* and password is configured (line 28) in support of local username/password authentication. The enable secret is configured (line 26) in support of enable password authentication. Command authorization is configured to use TACACS+ and then none (that is, no authorization) if IP connectivity to the TACACS+ server is lost (line 23). Command accounting is also configured to use TACACS+ (lines 24 through 25). The TACACS+ server-related parameters are configured via lines 270 through 273. The configuration of the TACACS+ server itself is outside the scope of this book. The preceding AAA policies mitigate the risk of unauthorized access and provide user accounting.

- **SSH services:** Configuring SSH requires that an IP domain name be specified (for RSA key generation). This is done via line 45. The RSA encryption key is generated outside the configuration during router setup. SSH protocol parameters are configured on lines 41 through 43, and VTY lines are restricted to SSH transport (line 330). Remote terminal access is further restricted to sources matching ACL 10, per lines 327 and 328. SSH provides secure remote terminal access to IP routers. As such, it mitigates the risk of session eavesdropping, which may compromise router configurations, passwords, and so on and be leveraged for an attack.

- **Disable idle user sessions:** Idle EXEC sessions are disabled after 5 minutes (lines 322 and 329). Further, TCP keepalives are enabled via lines 4 and 5 and serve to terminate connections where the remote host disappears (provides no positive acknowledgement [ACK]). Disabling idle user sessions in this way reduces the risk of unauthorized access.

- **NTP:** NTP is enabled to facilitate correlation of network events (lines 333 through 339). Ingress NTP protocol messages are restricted to sources permitted within the NTP configured standard ACL 10 (line 337). Further, MD5 authentication is enabled for NTP protocol messages exchanged with the configured NTP server (lines 333 through 335 and line 338). MD5 authentication helps to mitigate the risk of attacks against NTP, which is valuable for network event correlation, including security incident response.

- **Syslog:** Syslog parameters are configured on lines 205 through 207, which includes directing Syslog messages to the SP NOC (line 207). Timestamps are also appended to each Syslog (and debug) message per lines 6 and 7. In addition, Syslog is configured to report OSPF adjacency changes (line 159) and BGP neighbor state changes (line 169). In order to generate Syslog messages when free memory resources are low, low-watermark levels are set for processor memory on line 29. Further, in order to generate Syslog messages when CPU resources are low, processor CPU threshold levels are set on line 332. Syslog provides valuable network telemetry and is useful for security incident response.

- **Management VPN:** The Management VPN is primarily used for management of managed CE routers. Nevertheless, it provides an alternate in-band management path to PE routers in addition to the existing in-band access via the IGP (OSPF) and OOB access via the console port. A route map is configured (lines 280 through 282) such that only the MPLS VPN PE-CE links are distributed (line 49) into the Management VPN. Management plane functions—including but not limited to SNMP traps (line 277), NTP (line 339), and VTY access (line 327)—may also be configured to operate within the Management VPN. Further, PE-03 is configured as a spoke within the Management VPN (line 52), which prevents IP reachability between any two PEs (and CEs) within the Management VPN.

- **Other BCPs:** Other BCP router security configurations related to the management plane are implemented. The router host name is configured on line 11. Global service settings are modified, including enabling timestamps for all debug and logging messages (lines 6 and 7) and enabling password encryption services (line 8). The router boot image is specified on line 14 (lines 13 and 15 are auto-generated). Buffered logging is enabled at debug level and the buffer size is set (line 17). The display of logging messages to the console is disabled (line 18). The enable secret is set on line 26. Several global settings for router self-generated TCP sessions are adjusted, including enabling Nagle services (line 2), enabling TCP keepalives per "Disable idle user sessions" above (lines 4 and 5), increasing the TCP window size (line 37), reducing the TCP SYN wait time (line 5), and enabling PMTUD (line 39). In order to generate Syslog messages when free memory resources are low, a low-watermark level is set for processor memory on line 29. A message of the day (MOTD) login banner is configured on lines 314 through 319. Finally, in order to generate Syslog messages when CPU resources are low, processor CPU threshold levels are set on line 332.

Services Plane

In this case study, and from the perspective of router PE-03, services plane traffic includes only MPLS VPN customer traffic, which includes all remote IP traffic transmitted between Customer B offices. All IP data plane packets that are exchanged between Customer B offices are MPLS encapsulated at the associated ingress PE router. The traffic is then MPLS label switched across the SP network through the IP services plane. The egress PE uses the imposed MPLS label to determine the next-hop CE router, and then de-encapsulates the IP packet from the MPLS label stack and forwards the IP packet downstream to the next-hop CE router.

Services Plane Security

From the perspective of PE-03, the techniques used for services plane security include the following:

- **Virtual routing/forwarding (VRF) instance:** Customer B is placed into an MPLS VPN by attaching the associated VRF to the Serial0/0/0 interface (line 124). The MPLS VPN architecture (RFC 4364) ensures addressing and routing separation, as described in Chapters 2 and 7.

- **Interface ACL:** An infrastructure ACL is applied to the Serial0/0/0 interface (line 126) to filter any unauthorized traffic destined to SP internal infrastructure, including PE loopbacks, PE external interfaces, and the SP NOC. Note, because this is an MPLS VPN service, external reachability to the SP core network is natively denied because the external interface is assigned to a VRF (line 124). The ACL policy is defined through the extended ACL 100 (lines 211 through 215), which is attached to the Serial0/0/0 interface in the input direction on line 126. This ACL mitigates the risk of attacks that are sourced from within a customer VPN and that target PEs within the customer VPN. This is necessary to protect other customers attached to the same PE. Namely, a successful attack against the PE can cause collateral damage that affects other connected customers.

- **QoS:** QoS is deployed within the SP network in support of differentiated services and to isolate important control plane traffic from the other IP traffic planes. The associated policies (lines 101 through 109) and class maps (lines 62 through 73) are defined using MQC. The policy is then attached to the PE-03 uplink interfaces, including Serial1/0/0 and Serial2/0/0 per lines 144 and 155. If the PE-03 uplinks become congested, QoS will reserve 20 percent of uplink capacity for control plane traffic. To ensure that low-priority external traffic does not inadvertently or maliciously enter the high-priority traffic classes (in other words, *gold*, *silver*, *control*), a QoS recoloring policy is applied to MPLS VPN access ports, including the PE-03 serial interface to CE-B0 (line 133). The associated policy (lines 85 through 87) simply marks all traffic with MPLS experimental bits 0. This prevents any transit MPLS VPN traffic from being classified into the SP's high-priority traffic classes. Note, IP differentiated services are widely available for MPLS VPN networks. Such QoS policies applied to the MPLS VPN PE-CE link are outside the scope of this book. Note, however, that with MPLS VPN services, encapsulated IP packets need not be modified in any way while transiting the SP network. Notice that in Case Study 1 in this chapter, the edge recoloring policy sets the IP precedence to 0 for all ingress packets. Conversely, in this case study, the edge recoloring policy sets the MPLS experimental bits to 0 (line 87) for all ingress packets. Given that MPLS VPN services tunnel IP traffic across the SP network through the use of an MPLS label stack, QoS transparency is available whereby the SP does not re-mark Customer B's IP precedence markings in any way. The queuing and recoloring policies outlined directly above mitigate the risk of resource (bandwidth) exhaustion attacks against high-priority traffic classes including control plane protocols.

- **IP options:** IP packets with option headers are filtered by the **ip options drop** global configuration command (line 34). The IOS default behavior of IP source routing is also disabled with the **no ip source-route** global configuration command (line 31). Disabling IP options in this way mitigates the risk of IP options–based attacks.

- **ICMP techniques:** On a per-interface basis, several ICMP BCPs are also applied. ICMP Destination Unreachable and Redirect message generation is also disabled using the **no ip unreachables** (line 128) and **no ip redirects** (line 127) interface configuration commands, respectively. Global rate limiting of ICMP Destination Unreachable message generation is also enabled via line 33. ICMP Information Request and Address Mask Request processing is disabled by default within IOS; hence, the **no ip information-reply** and **no ip mask-reply** interface commands are applied by default. Disabling ICMP processing in this way mitigates the risk of transit IP data plane attacks and ICMP-based control plane attacks.

- **IP directed broadcasts:** The dropping of IP directed broadcast packets is the default behavior in IOS 12.0(32)S and, hence, the **no ip directed-broadcast** interface command is applied by default (line 129). Earlier versions of IOS forwarded IP directed broadcast packets by default. You should confirm the default behavior for your IOS release in order to properly mitigate the risk of directed broadcast based attacks.

- **Disable TTL propagation:** IP to MPLS TTL propagation is disabled (line 57), which mitigates the risk of TTL expiry attacks against core (P) routers within the SP network.

- **Interface MTU:** The SP core network is configured with an MTU (lines 137 and 148) greater than that of the PE-CE links, which have a default interface MTU of 1500. This mitigates the risk of IP fragmentation of MPLS VPN services plane traffic, given the MPLS shim header (see Appendix B, "IP Protocol Headers") imposed by ingress MPLS VPN PE routers in support of MPLS VPN services.

Summary

This chapter demonstrated the use of the concepts and techniques described in Chapters 4 through 7 by applying them to conceptual SP network case studies. Two edge router case studies were presented: a typical enterprise IPsec VPN and Internet access case, and an MPLS VPN case. Full configurations were provided for both case studies, and included annotations for all security components to provide the appropriate context for each mechanism.

These case studies focused on the SP side of the network. In Chapter 8, the focus is on the enterprise side of the network for these same cases.

Further Reading

Behringer, M., and M. Morrow. *MPLS VPN Security.* Cisco Press, 2005. ISBN 1-58705-183-4.

Greene, B. R., and P. Smith. *ISP Essentials.* Cisco Press, 2002. ISBN: 1-58705-041-2.

PART IV

Appendixes

Answers to Chapter Review Questions

Chapter 1

1 • IP is connectionless.

   • IP provides end-to-end and any-to-any connectivity.

   • IP performs everything in-band whereas legacy protocols tend to have separate control channel and data channel mechanisms.

2 Building and operating IP network infrastructures for converged services that meet carrier-class requirements must consider multiple, diverse services that have distinct bandwidth, jitter, and latency requirements. In addition, the interactions between these services must be considered as they may affect one another, along with the scale and security requirements.

3 • **Transit IP packets:** Any IP packet that has a destination IP address that is not one considered to be owned by the forwarding device (e.g. router) itself.

   • **Receive IP packets:** Any IP packet that has a destination IP address that is owned by the forwarding device (e.g. router) itself (for example, interface IP, loopback, and so on).

   • **Exception IP packets:** Any transit IP packet that requires specialized handling for forwarding (for example, contains options in the IP header) and thus must be punted and handled in the slow path.

   • **Non-IP packets:** Any non-IP packet such as a Layer 2 keep alive or CLNS/IS-IS packet.

4 • **Process switching:** Utilizes only the router CPU to directly process and forward packets.

   • **Fast switching:** Forwards packets in the CPU interrupt process by taking advantage of cache entries created during process switching of the first packet of each new flow.

   • **CEF switching:** Forwards packets using a pre-computed and very well-optimized version of the routing table.

5 True. Data plane traffic uses only standard forwarding processes and should never have destination IP addresses that belong to the router itself.

6 True. Control plane packets are generated by network protocols, signaling and link state protocols, and other control protocols used to build network services.

7 The management plane supports all required provisioning, maintenance, and monitoring functions for the network.

8 Services plane traffic requires specialized network-based processing to be applied when forwarding packets.

9 • **Centralized CPU-based router:** Relies on a single CPU to perform forwarding, control plane operations, network management, and services delivery.

• **Centralized ASIC-based router:** Similar to a centralized CPU-based router but also includes a forwarding ASIC to offload forwarding duties from the CPU to improve overall device performance, mainly for data plane traffic.

• **Distributed CPU-based router:** Supports discrete line cards, each capable of performing the CPU-based processing and forwarding functions normally done by a single, centralized CPU.

• **Distributed ASIC-based router:** Supports discrete line cards, but each line card has its own forwarding ASIC to offload forwarding duties from any CPU and operates independently from all other line cards.

Chapter 2

1 • **Layer 1—physical layer:** Defines the conversion between digital data and electrical signals transmitted over a physical cable (or other communications channel).

• **Layer 2—data link layer:** Provides reliable transit of data across a physical link. The data link layer is concerned with physical addressing, network topology, line discipline, error notification, ordered delivery of frames, and flow control. The IEEE divided this layer into two sublayers: the MAC sublayer and the LLC sublayer (sometimes simply called link layer).

• **Layer 3—network layer:** Provides connectivity and path selection between two end systems. The network layer is the layer at which routing occurs.

• **Layer 4—transport layer:** Is responsible for reliable network communication between end nodes. The transport layer provides mechanisms for the establishment, maintenance, and termination of virtual circuits, transport fault detection and recovery, and information flow control.

• **Layer 5—session layer:** Establishes, manages, and terminates sessions between applications and manages the data exchange between presentation layer entities.

• **Layer 6—presentation layer:** Ensures that information sent by the application layer of one system will be readable by the application layer of another system. The presentation layer also is concerned with the data structures used by programs and therefore negotiates data transfer syntax for the application layer.

- **Layer 7—application layer:** Provides services to application processes (such as e-mail, file transfer, and terminal emulation) that are outside the OSI reference model. The application layer identifies and establishes the availability of intended communication partners (and the resources required to connect with them), synchronizes cooperating applications, and establishes an agreement on the procedures for error recovery and the control of data integrity.

Note   For more information on the OSI reference model, refer to *Internetworking Terms and Acronyms* on Cisco.com: http://www.cisco.com/en/US/tech/tk1330/tsd_technology_ support_ technical_reference_chapter09186a00807598b4.html#wp998586.

---

2 CAM table overflow and MAC spoofing attacks. Such attacks must be locally sourced because they rely on MAC address spoofing within data link layer headers, which are link local only and not routed across an IP network.

3 Traceroute. Traceroute operates by sending a UDP packet to the target destination with a Time to Live (TTL) of 1. The first-hop router then sends back an ICMP Time Exceeded (Message Type 11) message indicating that the packet could not be forwarded. The packet is then re-sent with the TTL value of 2 (incremented by 1), with the packet expiring at the second hop this time. This process continues until the target destination is reached. The target destination returns an ICMP Port Unreachable message in response to the UDP packet (which attempts to connect to an unopened port). By recording the source address of each ICMP Time Exceeded message, plus looking for the final ICMP Port Unreachable message, traceroute provides a trace of the path the packet took to reach the destination.

For more information, refer to RFC 2151.

4 Ping sweep. Ping sweep is a network-scanning technique used to find live (reachable) IP hosts within a specified IP address block. Because ping sweep is automated to send many ICMP Echo Requests (Message Type 8) as opposed to a single ping packet, it simplifies the discovery of potential attack targets.

5 A malformed packet is one that violates the TCP/IP protocol specifications—for example, using invalid header field lengths or values. Software implementations without adequate protocol integrity checks may be susceptible to malformed packet attacks. A crafted packet adheres to the TCP/IP protocol specification but is specifically constructed in a manner to exploit a weakness within a software implementation or protocol state machine.

6 - **Direct attack:** An attack launched directly at the target, whereby the IP destination address equals the target. Such an attack requires IP reachability to the target.

- **Transit attack:** An attack that does not specify the target router as the IP destination address, but rather uses crafted packets to trigger a DoS condition on an intermediate IP router in the forwarding path toward a specific destination. IP reachability is not required to the intermediate IP router. Only a valid downstream network address is required.

- **Reflection attack:** An attack that spoofs the IP address of the target. In this way, a flood of protocol request messages to innocent IP hosts (or broadcast addresses) become *reflectors*. These reflectors simply respond to the spoofed request messages, flooding the unsuspecting target.

7 Collateral damage.

8 A virtual routing and forwarding instance (VRF).

9 IPsec.

10
- Hide identity and hinder traceback.
- Launch reflection attacks.
- Bypass ACLs or authentication policies.

Chapter 3

1 The *depth* component refers to multiple defense layers defined and applied against a single attack vector. For example, when protecting SNMP, two layers supporting the same attack vector could be interface ACLs to block all but configured management station peers from connecting to UDP port 161, and then adding SNMP application-layer ACLs to also block all but the same traffic.

2 *Breadth* refers to multiple defense layers defined and applied against different attack vectors for the same service. For example, when protecting BGP, one layer could use interface ACLs to block all but configured peers from connecting to TCP port 179, which mitigates spoofing attacks, and a second layer of BGP neighbor authentication with MD5 hashing could be used to mitigate fraudulent route updates.

3 False.

4 True.

5 A, B, D, and E.

6 True.

7 The enterprise edge security policy is typically described as "deny everything unless explicitly permitted," whereas the SP edge security policy is typically described as "permit everything unless explicitly denied."

8 False. TTL expiry reflection attacks are one example where transit traffic can impact internal interfaces.

9 True.

Chapter 4

1 Transit and classification ACLs.

2 Customer RFC 1998 routing policy may be inadvertently changed.

3 FPM provides the ability to match (and filter) on arbitrary bits within the packet as opposed to using predefined fields. Further, FPM can also match (and filter) on packet header and payload information.

4 Queuing.

5 Router Alert option.

6 At the network edge.

7 BGP and MQC (QoS).

8 Unicast RPF on the edge router(s) and the static route on the trigger router specify the attacker (source address) not the target (destination address).

9 • **Stateful:** Firewall, IDS/IPS, traffic scrubbing.

   • **Stateless:** ACL, FPM, uRPF.

10 No-negotiate mode.

Chapter 5

1   ICMP Echo (Type 8) and Timestamp (Type 13) messages. For the complete list of ICMP message types, refer to http://www.iana.org/assignments/icmp-parameters. IOS does not process ICMP Source Quench (Type 4) messages and therefore is not vulnerable to attacks that are based on crafting this type of message.

2   SPD extended headroom is reserved for Layer 2 keepalives, CLNS, OSPF, and MPLS LDP protocol packets only.

3   False. IP rACLs apply only to ingress packets having a CEF receive adjacency.

4   True. Ingress packets punted to the IOS process level—regardless of whether they are data, control, management, or services plane protocol packets—are subject to CoPP policies. On the Cisco 12000 series, only packets punted to the central PRP are subject to CoPP policies. This includes all IOS process level packets except ICMP Echo (Type 8), ICMP Time Exceeded (Type 11), and BFD protocol packets, which are handled on the distributed line card CPUs unless they include IP option headers.

5   Reconfigure the new MD5 keys on both sides of the BGP peering session before the holddown timer expires.

6   When GTSM is enabled (with a hop-count value of 1), the receive-side peer only accepts eBGP packets having an IP TTL value of 254 or greater. When GTSM is not enabled, the receive-side peer accepts eBGP packets having an IP TTL value of 1 or greater.

7   • MD5 authentication.

   • GTSM.

   • IP prefix lists.

   • IP prefix limits.

   • AS path limits.

   • Graceful restart.

   • Disabled connected check for loopback-to-loopback directly connected eBGP peers.

8   DHCP snooping and port security.

9   DHCP snooping.

10   • BPDU Guard.

    • Root Guard.

Chapter 6

1 • **Availability:** An out-of-band network provides an alternate path to each network element if in-band management connectivity is lost. Alternatively, you may design the OOB management network as the primary management path and use the in-band management path as backup. DCN designs vary widely.

   • **Day-to-day network operations:** These include service provisioning, monitoring, billing, alarms, software upgrades, configuration backups, and so on.

2 CEF is disabled by default on management Ethernet interfaces, making the IOS router appear as an IP host to the (out-of-band) IP network connected to the management Ethernet interface.

3 Cisco strongly recommends against enabling CEF routing functions on this port to prevent IP reachability between the in-band and out-of-band networks. Otherwise, if an in-band network failure occurs, in-band data plane traffic may be inadvertently rerouted across the OOB management network. In this scenario, the OOB network no longer exclusively carries management plane traffic as intended.

4 Disable CDP on external interfaces only by using the **no cdp enable** command within IOS interface configuration mode.

5 MOTD, login, and incoming banners all apply to reverse Telnet sessions. The EXEC banner does not.

6 The same security techniques apply to both SNMPv1 and SNMPv2c, including community strings and community string ACLs. Neither provides means for encryption. SNMPv3 provides *strong security* by supporting sender identification, message modification checks, and message content encryption.

7 SSH provides encrypted remote terminal access, whereas native Telnet transmits protocol packets in clear text.

8 • The configured in-band interface(s) is dedicated for out-of-band management and, as a result, discards any ingress control, services, or data plane traffic received.

   • All other in-band interfaces discard any ingress management plane protocol traffic received. This includes FTP, HTTP, HTTPS, SSH, SCP, SNMP, Telnet, BEEP, and TFTP protocol packets.

9 Identification, classification, and source traceback of security events.

10 Through its hub-and-spoke topology configuration, which allows connectivity only between managed CE routers and the SP NOC.

Chapter 7

1 The services plane refers to user traffic that requires specialized packet handling by network elements above and beyond the standard forwarding processing typically applied to data plane traffic.

2 Recoloring of ingress IP packets should be applied at the edge of the network. Recoloring is the process of changing the DiffServ marking within the IP header of each packet as it ingresses the network edge. For Cisco IOS routers, this would be accomplished by using MQC and interface service policies.

3 CE, PE, and P routers. The CE router does not require MPLS functionality and operates as a native IP router except in the case of the CsC model.

4 Such policies do not consider the associated VRF; hence, given MPLS VPN support for overlapping IP addressing, unauthorized traffic may incorrectly permitted through a source address-based IP rACL and CoPP policy.

5 An MPLS VPN ingress PE imposes 8 bytes for unicast traffic and 24 bytes for multicast traffic, assuming no other MPLS services such as TE/FRR tunnels are applied.

6 The command is **no mpls ip propagate-ttl forwarded** and is applied in IOS global configuration mode.

7 RFC 4363 Section 10, option (a) is considered most secure given that it provides for resource management per VPN, similar to a PE router, which helps to mitigate the risk of label spoofing and collateral damage.

8 IKE performs two separate functions. The first, IKE Phase 1, provides VPN endpoint authentication, and establishes a bidirectional SA (control channel) by which IKE protects itself (encryption and hashing algorithms). It is through this control channel that IKE Phase 2 manages subsequent connections on behalf of IPsec. IKE Phase 2 negotiates how IPsec connections should be protected, and builds a set of SAs, one for each direction of the IPsec connection. IKE Phase 2 then manages these IPsec connections (negotiates setup, teardown, key refresh, and so on). The IKE protocol uses UDP as transport, defaulting to port 500.

9 IPsec supports the Encapsulating Security Payload (ESP) and Authentication Header (AH) protocols. ESP handles encryption of IP data at Layer 3 to provide data confidentiality. ESP also provides some authentication and integrity capabilities. AH provides authentication and integrity services used to verify that a packet has not been altered or tampered with during transmission.

10 Fragmentation may be prevented either by modifying each hosts MSS configuration to limit the size of any packets sent by clients, or by configuring IP Path MTU Discovery on each router to allow IPsec to dynamically modify permitted packet sizes. Fragmentation effects may be minimized by configuring the clearing of the DF bit within the original IP packet header and at the same time enabling the Cisco unique IPsec look-ahead fragmentation feature.

IP Protocol Headers

Many network attacks are accomplished by manipulating or spoofing the packet header fields within TCP/IP protocols. With few exceptions, these protocol header fields can be manipulated or spoofed by an attacker to achieve one of two broad goals: circumvent security policies (to steal or modify data), or cause a denial of service (DoS) condition somewhere within the network. The fact that protocol header value manipulation and spoofing can be used to accomplish these goals is made possible because of the following reasons:

- **Protocol weaknesses:** Many protocol definitions are insufficiently specific or lack inherent security mechanisms, leaving them exposed to manipulation and spoofing. For example, ICMP is designed to provide unauthenticated messages from unknown sources as a feedback mechanism. As an illustration, ICMP Type 3, Code 4 messages are used by Path MTU Discovery mechanisms for other, more-secure protocols such as IPsec. Other protocols, such as TCP, are more complex and have many interactions within the state machine, making it very difficult to consider how these interactions and state machine transition affect security. And other protocols are defined so simply, such as UDP, that there is virtually no way to completely secure them. DoS attacks, malicious data insertion, and loss of confidentiality often exploit protocol weakness.

- **Operating system/network stack weaknesses:** Insecure coding techniques used in operating system implementations for TCP/IP network stacks lead to inappropriate processing of packets. The main objective in this case is to cause a DoS condition or, more dangerously, to cause a buffer-overflow condition, which may provide the ability to install and run arbitrary code. This is often the result of inadequate integrity or sanity checks against received packet headers.

- **Network configuration exploitation:** Networks may be designed with QoS rules, filtering/ACL rules, firewalls, IDS/IPS, and other mechanisms installed. By spoofing certain protocol header values, an attacker may be able to circumvent these rules. For example, some networks have been known to apply QoS rules to give priority treatment to packets marked in a certain way (via the IP header ToS field). A user could then mark packets to take advantage of this service. Although this is not really an attack in the traditional sense, it nonetheless could be considered *stealing* if the user is gaining a service advantage illegally. Further, illegitimate traffic that is improperly classified may adversely affect legitimate traffic within the same class. This may be exploited to trigger a DoS condition.

NOTE Protocol header anomalies are very often a sign of an attack. However, this does not rule out several other possibilities. First, some protocols are not as rigidly defined as would be expected. Occasionally, interpretation nuances result in differences in software implementation, especially in terms of default values. At a minimum, this can lead to vendor interoperability issues. In the extreme, network outages can result. Early IPsec protocol implementations often come to mind as an example of this kind of problem. The second problem is the periodic software *glitch* that can occur during network operating system upgrades. Occasionally, software errors cause protocol header violations. Neither of these cases has a malicious underpinning, yet each may cause a network outage that potentially has all the appearances of an attack from the user's perspective.

Nearly every field in most protocol headers can be modified, manipulated, misinterpreted, and/or spoofed. Some network devices look for protocol violations and manipulations as part of their operation. Intrusion detection and prevention systems (IDS/IPS) and many firewalls, anomaly detection (AD) systems, and a new class of deep packet inspection (DPI) devices often provide this function. Many Cisco routers perform certain "IP sanity checks" on each packet as it is being forwarded as well (with illegal packets being silently dropped). Misconfigured, manipulated, and/or spoofed packets will always be seen in networks, whether due to malicious packet crafting, misconfigurations, or poor software coding. The bottom line is, protocol header values are spoofed for many reasons, and having the knowledge of each protocol header and its expected values gives you an advantage in recognizing when this occurs, and how best to mitigate negative effects.

This appendix provides detailed information about the most important TCP/IP protocol headers:

- The IP version 4 protocol header (Layer 3)
- The TCP protocol header (Layer 4)

- The UDP protocol header (Layer 4)
- The ICMP protocol header (Layer 3)

NOTE   IP version 6 is not discussed here. However, the IPv6 header is subject to many of the same, plus new forms of, modifications, manipulations, misinterpretations, and spoofing attacks as the IPv4 header.

In addition, the following Layer 2 headers are also described:

- Ethernet/802.1Q header (Layer 2)
- MPLS header (Layer 2)

Each protocol header is discussed individually in its own section. Each section provides a short description of the protocol, along with an illustration of that protocol header. A table then follows that provides details about each field contained within the header, including the size and offset of the field, and a description of the field. Finally, a short discussion of the security implications of the field is provided.

IP Version 4 Header

The minimum IP version 4 (IPv4) packet header consists of 12 fields requiring 20 bytes to specify the data necessary to route a packet. The IP header is capable of allowing an additional 13th field for specifying *optional* content to enable specialized services during routing. With certain exceptions, IPv4 options are not normally used. The IPv4 header is shown below in Figure B-1.

Figure B-1 *IP Version 4 Header*

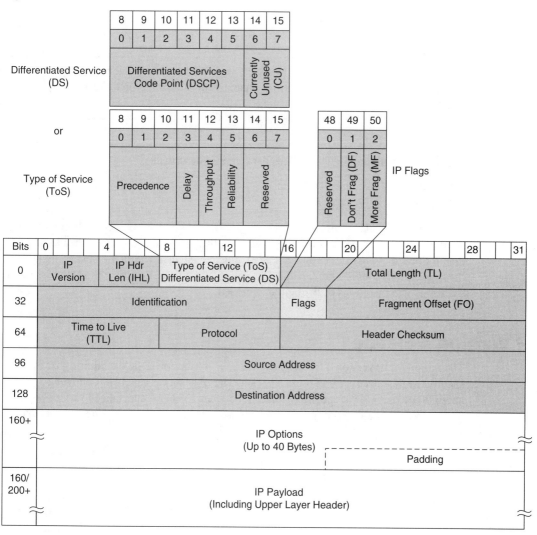

IPv4 header fields are listed and described in Table B-1. Table B-1 also includes a brief description of some known modifications or spoofs to relevant header fields that have been seen in common attacks.

Table B-1   *IP Version 4 Header Fields and Their Security Implications*

Bit Offset	Header Field	Header Value and Description
0–3 (4 bits)	IP Version	Indicates the version of IP used by the packet. A value of 4 (binary 0100) indicates IPv4.
	Security Implications: All TCP/IP network stacks check this field to determine which IP version to hand the packet off to for processing. A value of 4 basically tells the stack how to parse the remainder of the header (how many fields, and the number of bits per field). It is plausible that a poorly written network stack may improperly process packets with an unexpected version number (any value other than 4 or 6), possibly leading to a DoS condition or buffer overflow condition. Software that simply checks for a specific value (for example, ip->version == 4) but does not provide suitable error handling for exception conditions may be susceptible to attack.	
4–7 (4 bits)	IP Header Length (IHL)	Indicates the length in 32-bit words of the IPv4 packet header. Standard IPv4 packets with a header length of 20 bytes have an IHL value of 5 (binary 0101), indicating five, 4-byte (32-bit) words, or 5 x 4 = 20. When IP options are included, the IHL can indicate a maximum of 60 bytes (a value of 15, or binary 1111).
	Security Implications: All TCP/IP network stacks should check this header field to determine how far into the packet the IP header extends (in other words, whether IP options are included or not). Packets that include IP options generally require additional processing by routers (potentially causing increases in processor load) and may require additional memory to be buffered to accommodate the longer header. It is plausible that a poorly written network stack could improperly process packets with an unexpected IHL value. Software that simply checks for a specific value (for example, ip->ihl == 5) but does not provide suitable error handling may be susceptible to attack. For example, packets that specify a value greater than 5 in the IHL but then do not include IP options could cause a DoS condition or buffer overflow condition. At least one vulnerability was reported for packets where ip->ihl == 0 caused an infinite-loop and system core dump (DoS condition).[1]	

continues

Table B-1 *IP Version 4 Header Fields and Their Security Implications (Continued)*

Bit Offset	Header Field	Header Value and Description
8–15 (8 bits)	RFC 791 Type of Service (ToS) RFC 2474 Differentiated Services (DS)	Specifies how an upper-layer protocol would like packets to be queued and processed by network elements as they are forwarded through the network. The original (RFC 791) designation of this 8-bit-long field used the 3 most significant bits as precedence bits. For normal traffic, this value is set to 0, but it may be assigned a different value to indicate another level of importance to network elements along the IP forwarding path. The 5 least significant bits set type of service flags and were originally used to indicate packet drop priority in the event an intermediate router became congested. The newer DS field (RFC 2474) obsoletes the ToS designation, although backward compatibility has been maintained. Six bits of the DS field are used as a codepoint (DSCP) to select the per-hop behavior (PHB) a packet experiences at each node. A 2-bit currently unused (CU) field is reserved. PHBs and mechanisms to classify them on a per-packet basis can be deployed in network nodes. The forwarding path may require that some fancy QoS mechanisms be applied on the network traffic designated for *special* treatment to satisfy requirements associated with the delivery of the special treatment.
	Security Implications: ToS/DSCP bits are permitted to be set by user applications and IP routers. For example, many voice and video applications include menus for configuring DSCP settings. Comparable settings must be made within the network infrastructure for DSCP bits to be honored. In addition, this is only important during network congestion conditions. Thus, there are not any direct attacks per se that are caused by spoofing DSCP bits. However, if the network is configured to allow some packets to receive different (for instance, better) service, then an attacker may be able to steal this service by modifying the DSCP value for that service. Given sufficient traffic injection, this could result in DoS conditions for legitimate users of that service. In addition, some IP control plane mechanisms take advantage of IP precedence settings to alert routers to the need for high-priority processing. OSPF, for example, uses an IP precedence setting of 6 for this purpose. The attack Stacheldraht v1.666 (aka Trinoo and Tribe Flood Network [TFN]) launched an IP header attack using IP precedence 7, in theory to obtain special processing.[2]		

Table B-1   *IP Version 4 Header Fields and Their Security Implications (Continued)*

Bit Offset	Header Field	Header Value and Description
16–31 (16 bits)	Total Length (TL)	Specifies the length, in bytes, of the entire IP packet, including the data and IP header. The maximum possible size of an IP packet is 65,535 bytes.
	Security Implications: The expected value represents the total length of the datagram. The minimum value is 20 (0x0014) and the maximum value is 65,535 (0xFFFF). Direct attack may use a value that does not represent the true packet length. A poorly written network stack may improperly process these packets, resulting in a DoS condition. Indirectly, this field has been exploited by many attacks. The classic attack, jolt2.c, sends identical, illegally fragmented ICMP or UDP packets with a Fragment Offset (described later in this table) of 65,520 octets and a Total Length value of 68 octets.[3] The resulting datagram has a length of 65,588 octets, which exceeds the maximum allowable datagram size of 65,535 octets ($2^{16} - 1$). *Ping of death* is another famous attack that uses a similar technique.[4] Several operating systems have been reported as having problems with zero-length fragments.[5] Although technically not spoofed, this field may be exploited in conjunction with the Fragment Offset field to produce a malformed (illegal) packet. A poorly written network stack may improperly process these packets, resulting in a DoS condition.	
32–47 (16 bits)	Identification	This 16-bit field contains an integer that identifies the current datagram. It is only used when packet fragmentation occurs (that is, when a datagram is carried in multiple, fragmented packets). This field is used by the destination host to identify packets that belong to the same datagram, and then in conjunction with the Flags and Fragment Offset fields to reassemble the fragmented datagrams belonging to the same packet (same identification value). (Note that packets are reassembled by the destination host, not in transit.)
	Security Implications: This header field is important only when packet fragmentation occurs. The value is set by the user application and, thus, there are few direct attacks that are caused by spoofing the Identification value. One attack has been proposed that uses the IP Identification field as a *covert channel* to transmit information without detection by anyone other than the entities operating the covert channel.[6] The Identification field may potentially be useful as part of an attack identification system. Many times, attackers hard-code the Identification field value to simplify the source code. Receiving repeated datagrams from a single source IP address with identical Identification values suggests a hard-coded attack packet.	

continues

Table B-1   *IP Version 4 Header Fields and Their Security Implications (Continued)*

Bit Offset	Header Field	Header Value and Description
48–50 (3 bits)	Flags	Consists of a 3-bit field, the 2 low-order (least-significant) bits of which control fragmentation. The high-order (first) bit is not used and must be set to 0. The middle (second) "Don't Fragment" (DF) bit specifies whether the packet is permitted to be fragmented (0 = fragmentation permitted, 1 = fragmentation not permitted). The low-order (third) "More Fragments" (MF) bit specifies whether the packet is the last fragment in a series of fragmented packets (set to 1 for all fragments except the last one, telling the end station which fragment is the last).
	Security Implications: When used in conjunction with the Total Length field (see above) and Fragment Offset field (see below), attacks are often created that produce mismatched, overlapping, or gapped fragmentation patterns, causing malformed (illegal) packets. Examples include the references cited in table footnotes 3, 4, and 5. A poorly written network stack may improperly process these packets, resulting in a DoS condition. Another attack has been suggested that uses purposefully misordered IP packets that have been artificially fragmented across the Layer 4 header (such that the TCP parameters are not completely available within a single packet) to evade access control in filtering devices.[7]	
51–63 (13 bits)	Fragment Offset (FO)	Provides the position (offset), in bytes, of this fragment's data relative to the start of the data in the initial datagram. This enables the destination IP process to properly reconstruct the original datagram.
	Security Implications: When used in conjunction with the Total Length field (see above) and Flag field (see above), attacks are often created that produce mismatched, overlapping, or gapped fragmentation patterns, causing malformed (illegal) packets. Examples include the references cited in table footnotes 3, 4, and 5. A poorly written network stack may improperly process these packets, resulting in a DoS condition. This field would also be used with the attack suggested previously for the Flags field that uses purposefully misordered IP packets that are artificially fragmented across the Layer 4 header to evade access control in filtering devices.[7]	

Table B-1   *IP Version 4 Header Fields and Their Security Implications (Continued)*

Bit Offset	Header Field	Header Value and Description
64–71 (8 bits)	Time to Live (TTL)	Specifies the maximum number of links (hops) that the packet may be routed over. This counter is decremented by each IP router processing the packet while forwarding it toward its destination. When the TTL value reaches 0, the datagram is discarded. This prevents packets from looping endlessly, as would otherwise occur during accidental routing loops, for example. This 8-bit value can range anywhere from 255 to 0.
	Security Implications: The stated (legitimate) use of the TTL field is to limit the life of a packet in the event of a routing loop. The TTL value is set by the sending application, but each IP network device that forwards the packet decrements the TTL value until it reaches 0. When this occurs, the ICMP error message Time to Live Exceeded in Transit (Type 11, Code 0) is generated by the device dropping the packet and sent back to the (apparent) source IP address of the offending packet. The legitimate application traceroute takes advantage of this ICMP feedback mechanism to map the hop-by-hop path a packet would take through the network from source to destination by artificially manipulating the TTL field within the IP packet header. Although legitimate uses for traceroute exist, such as a variety of network management and troubleshooting tasks, it is also useful in the reconnaissance phase leading up to an attack. The information returned by traceroute may be useful for mapping the target network, including layout, host distribution, diameter (hop distance), and so on, and for determining whether filtering devices may be encountered along the path (often indicated by a "* * *" response). Crafting TTL values may also be used to cause the purposeful expiration of a large quantity of packets in the middle of a network. In this case, the destination IP address of the packet is not the intended target, but merely useful in providing the information necessary for the packet to take the desired path through the network. The TTL value is crafted such that it decrements to 0 upon reaching the appropriate device (intended target). Certain network devices may require more computational energy to respond to TTL expiry packets, thus potentially resulting in a DoS condition. Also, an attack of this nature may be able to circumvent filtering devices that may be encountered along the way if the destination IP address is reachable through them (even though the packet is never intended to fully reach the destination).		

continues

Table B-1   *IP Version 4 Header Fields and Their Security Implications (Continued)*

Bit Offset	Header Field	Header Value and Description
	Finally, TTL expiry attacks may be combined with spoofed source IP addresses to form a reflection attack. In a reflection attack, the source IP address of the attack packets is spoofed to be that of the intended target (not to hide the source of the attack). In this case, when the packet expires, the ICMP Time Exceeded message is flooded back toward the spoofed source, the intended target, with the intended result being a DoS condition.	
	Methods for defending against numerous classes of attacks are also being developed that take advantage of the TTL field and its behavior. Interestingly, even though the TTL can be set initially within an attack packet, this value is changed (decremented) at each step in its journey by each IP networking device within the forwarding path. Hence, the TTL value can never be larger than the initial value, and it can never be larger than 255 (the maximum starting value). Mechanisms are now available for BGP[8] and for general use[9] (mainly for control plane and management plane services) that limit the diameter in which an attack can occur. Of course, access list mechanisms that can filter on TTL field values are also useful for enforcing similar policies.	
72–79 (8-bits)	Protocol	Indicates the upper-layer protocol that should receive the incoming packets after IP processing is complete. Normally, this indicates the type of transport packet being used. For example, a value of one (1) indicates IP is carrying an ICMP packet; six (6) indicates a TCP packet, and 17 indicates that a UDP packet is being carried by IP. This 8-bit value can range anywhere from 255 to 0.
	Security Implications: Officially recognized protocols and their assigned numbers are maintained by the Internet Assigned Numbers Authority (IANA). The latest officially recognized and reserved protocol numbers are listed at IANA.[10] Values between 0 and 137 have already been assigned, and values between 138 and 252 have not been assigned. The values of 253 and 254 are designated for experimentation and testing, and the value of 255 is reserved. Notable (common) protocol values are 1 (ICMP), 2 (IGMP), 4 (IP-IP), 6 (TCP), 17 (UDP), 47 (GRE), 88 (EIGRP), 89 (OSPF), and 115 (L2TP). It's plausible that a poorly written network stack could improperly process packets with an unexpected protocol value. Software that simply checks for the standard (well known) values (e.g. ip->protocol == 6) but does not provide suitable error handling may be susceptible to attack.	

Table B-1   *IP Version 4 Header Fields and Their Security Implications (Continued)*

Bit Offset	Header Field	Header Value and Description
80–95 (16-bits)	Header Checksum	A 16-bit 1's-compliment hash inserted by the sender and updated by each router that modifies the packet while forwarding it toward its destination (which essentially means every router since, at a minimum, the TTL value is modified at each hop). This value is used to detect errors that may be introduced into the packet as it traverses the network. Packets with an invalid checksum are required to be discarded by any receiving node in the network as well as any intermediate routers along the forwarding path.
	Security Implications: The IP header checksum is first computed by the sending network stack, and then recomputed/compared upon receipt–and recomputed/stored upon forwarding by each network device along the path. Packets with invalid checksums are discarded (usually silently–that is, without causing the generation of an ICMP error message). No useful attacks seem plausible that manipulate or spoof this header field.	
96–127 (32-bits)	Source Address	Specifies the unique IP address of the sending node (the originator of the IP packet).
	Security Implications: The source IP address field is likely, the most-often spoofed field in the IP header. Source IP addresses are spoofed for one of three reasons: (1) for hiding the true source of the attack, (2) for providing the feedback target IP address in a reflection-based attack or, (3) for bypassing filtering policies based on source IP address. In the case of attack source-hiding, spoofed addresses are often generated in the so-called *bogon* and *Martian* address ranges. On the public Internet, a *bogon* address is one that claims to be from reserved, but not yet allocated or delegated IP address space (by the Internet Assigned Numbers Authority (IANA) or a delegated Regional Internet Registry (RIR).[11] A Martian address is one that claims to be from a prefix not in the routing table, or from private or reserved address block as defined by RFC 1918 and RFC 3330.[12] In the case of reflection attacks, the source IP address is spoofed so that the response to the attack packet (often an ICMP error message) is directed against the *true* victim–the spoofed source IP address. This may be used to circumvent network defenses, or to simply take advantage of a protocol operational function. In the case of bypassing filtering policies, a source IP address is spoofed to masquerade as a trusted host, thereby exploiting a trust-relationship and bypassing filtering policies and gaining unauthorized access.	

continues

Table B-1 *IP Version 4 Header Fields and Their Security Implications (Continued)*

Bit Offset	Header Field	Header Value and Description
128–159 (32-bits)	Destination Address	Specifies the unique IP address of the receiving node (the final destination of the packet).
	Security Implications: The destination IP address can represent one of three potential values.	
	1 – In the case of a *direct attack*, the destination is actually that of the true target of the attack packet. This may or may not be used in combination with spoofed source IP addresses (depending on whether or not attack-hiding is applied).	
	2 – In the case of a *transit attack*, the destination is actually that of a downstream device that causes the packet to follow a path leading it *through* the intended target. This is also used in combination with TTL field manipulations, as described above, to accomplish the TTL expiry attack or TTL expiry reflection attack.	
	3 – In the case of a *reflection attack*, the destination is actually that of a device that is used as a packet reflector or amplifier. In this case, the destination is not the intended target. This attack is combined with a spoofed IP source address (as described above) such that a response packet (often an ICMP error message) is directed against the *true* target–the spoofed source IP address.	
	Destination IP addresses may also be scanned during the reconnaissance phase in preparation for future attacks. Numerous programs exist that perform these *horizontal* scans (across a range of IP addresses, usually against a single well-known port) to locate live hosts and map a network (for example, Nmap).	
160+ (variable)	IP Options + Padding (optional)	Allows IP to support various options, such as timestamp, record route, and strict source route. IP options are not normally used. Various option types are assigned by IANA.[13] Padding is used as a filler to guarantee that the data that follows starts on a 32-bit boundary.
	Security Implications: Option values must range between 0 and 31, with the values between 25 and 31 being currently undefined.[13] It is plausible that a poorly written network stack could improperly process packets with an unexpected option value, resulting in a DoS or buffer overflow condition.	
	IPv4 options are mostly a legacy concept and are deprecated by advances in IP protocols. There are several cases where specific options remain useful. The Router Alert option (20) is used by the Resource Reservation Protocol for automatic QoS resource allocation in IP networks, for example. Security options (5) are used in some military network applications to enforce policy.	

Table B-1   *IP Version 4 Header Fields and Their Security Implications (Continued)*

Bit Offset	Header Field	Header Value and Description
		Some of the IP options, such as Loose Source Router (3) and Strict Source Router (9), can be used in network attacks to potentially circumvent deployed network filtering devices. Legitimate network traffic rarely uses either of these options. Invoking IP options often causes slow path processing by routing devices due to the variable length of the IP header (see Chapters 1 and 2). This can potentially lead to network congestion, or possibly even a DoS condition.

1. "CVE-1999-1024" (Zero-Length Header Vulnerability). Common Vulnerabilities and Exposures (CVE) List. The MITRE Corp.
    http://cve.mitre.org/cgi-bin/cvename.cgi?name=CVE-1999-1024.

2. Cheng, G. "Analysis on DDOS Tool Stacheldraht v1.666." SANS Institute.
    http://www.sans.org/resources/malwarefaq/stacheldraht.php.

3. "CVE-2000-0305" (IP Fragment Reassembly Vulnerability). CVE List. The MITRE Corp.
    http://cve.mitre.org/cgi-bin/cvename.cgi?name=CVE-2000-0305.

4. "Ping of Death." Wikipedia.
    http://en.wikipedia.org/wiki/Ping_of_death.

5. "CVE-1999-0431" (IP Zero-Length Fragmentation Attack) CVE List. The MITRE Corp.
    http://cve.mitre.org/cgi-bin/cvename.cgi?name=CVE-1999-0431.

6. Rowland, C. "Covert Channels in the TCP/IP Protocol Suite." *First Monday*, volume 2, issue 5 (1997).
    http://www.firstmonday.org/issues/issue2_5/rowland/.

7. Ptacek, T., and T. Newsham. "Insertion, Evasion, and Denial of Service: Eluding Network Intrusion Detection." Secure Networks, Jan. 1988. Accessed at Snort.org.
    http://www.snort.org/docs/idspaper/.

8. Gill, V., J. Heasley, and D. Meyer. "BGP TTL Security Hack (BTSH)." Internet draft <draft-gill-btsh-01.txt>. NANOG 27. Phoenix. Oct. 2002.
    http://www.nanog.org/mtg-0302/ppt/meyer.pdf.

9. Gill, V., J. Heasley, and D. Meyer. *The Generalized TTL Security Mechanism (GTSM)*. RFC 3682. IETF, Feb. 2004.
    http://www.ietf.org/rfc/rfc3682.txt.

10. "Protocol Numbers." IANA.
    http://www.iana.org/assignments/protocol-numbers.

11. "Internet Protocol v4 Address Space." IANA.
    http://www.iana.org/assignments/ipv4-address-space.

12. "Special-Use IPv4 Addresses." RFC 3330. IETF, Sept. 2002.
    http://www.ietf.org/rfc/rfc3330.txt.

13. "IP Option Numbers." IANA.
    http://www.iana.org/assignments/ip-parameters.

TCP Header

The minimum Transmission Control Protocol (TCP) header consists of ten fields requiring 20 bytes to specify the data necessary to establish and maintain this connection-oriented session. The TCP header is capable of allowing an additional 11th field for specifying *optional* content to enable specialized services for the session. The TCP header is shown in Figure B-2.

Figure B-2 *TCP Header*

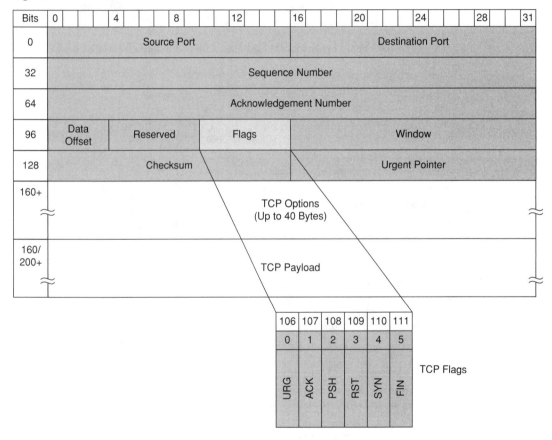

The TCP header fields shown in Figure B-2 are listed and described in Table B-2. Table B-2 also provides a brief description of some known modifications or spoofs to relevant header fields that have been seen in common attacks.

NOTE	TCP is a complex, connection-oriented Layer 4 protocol that is designed to provide the reliable delivery of its segments using the connectionless, best-effort networking (Layer 3) IP protocol. TCP uses many *moving parts* to support reliable data delivery. This section does not attempt to cover or address each and every one of these components. Additional TCP resources may be found in *TCP/IP Illustrated, Volume 1*, listed in the "Further Reading" section at the end of the appendix.

Table B-2 *TCP Header Fields and Their Security Implications*

Bit-Offset	Header Field	Header Value and Description
0–15 (16 bits)	Source Port	The source port number. TCP source and destination ports are used in pairs to support bidirectional communication. The range of possible values is 0–65,535, which is split into multiple groups. In the client/server model, the initial TCP client connection request usually sets the source port value to an *ephemeral* port number, typically within the 1024–4999 range (although, OS-dependent settings can be configured to extend this range to the full 65,535 value). Ports in the 1–1023 range are the so-called *well-known* or *privileged* ports and are reserved for system services. These are typically used as the destination port for the initial TCP client connection request. Hence, TCP connection replies from servers have source port values in the 1–1023 range.
		Security Implications: All TCP attacks against existing sessions assume that the destination IP address and source and destination TCP ports are known. The destination port is easy; it is generally published. The destination IP addresses is known (it is the target). The source IP address may be spoofed (depending on attack type) or may also have to be known. The most difficult port value to find is the source port (because it is ephemeral). A TCP reset (RST) attack can be accomplished by sending packets to each port above 1024 (and within every possible TCP window). Although this requires the generation of quite a few packets, it is relatively simple (albeit noisy) to accomplish.
		Port 0 is reserved for special use (see RFC 1700).[1] This port is intended for client use to indicate to the underlying OS network stack that it should reassign this value to something in the ephemeral range. No traffic should flow over the Internet using this port. Each OS may use a different approach for handling source port 0 packets, leading to the potential for OS fingerprinting.[2] OS fingerprinting is often used by attackers during the reconnaissance phase prior to an attack. In addition, it is plausible that a poorly written network stack may improperly process packets with a source port number of 0, possibly leading to a DoS condition or buffer overflow condition. Software that does not provide suitable error handling for exception conditions may be susceptible to attack.

continues

Table B-2   *TCP Header Fields and Their Security Implications (Continued)*

Bit-Offset	Header Field	Header Value and Description
16–31 (16 bits)	Destination Port	The destination port number. TCP source and destination ports are used in pairs to support bidirectional communication. The range of possible values is 0–65,535, which is split into multiple groups. In the client/server model, the initial TCP client connection request usually sets the destination port value to a port in the 1–1023 range (the so-called *well-known* or *privileged* port range), which is reserved for system services. Several well-known destination ports include: 20 (FTP-data), 21 (FTP-control), 22 (SSH), 23 (Telnet), 25 (SMTP), 80 (HTTP), 110 (POP), 179 (BGP), and 443 (SSL).
	Security Implications: For attacks against existing TCP sessions, see the Security Implications for the Source Port field earlier in the table. TCP destination ports are often scanned during the reconnaissance phase in preparation for future attacks. Numerous programs, such as Nmap,[3] hping2, Nessus, and others perform these *vertical* scans (across a range of ports, against a single IP address) to locate live services (and their versions) to expose potential points of vulnerability for future attacks. One other notable attack that manipulates TCP port numbers is the LAND attack (IP source address = IP destination address, TCP source port = TCP destination port, and TCP SYN flag set). This causes some systems to consume all available CPU resources, resulting in a DoS condition.[4]	
32–63 (32 bits)	Sequence Number	The sequence number has a dual role. If the SYN flag is present, then this is the initial sequence number (ISN), and the first byte of data that will be sent when a new connection is established is the sequence number plus 1. Otherwise, if the SYN flag is not present, then the first byte of data in that particular segment is the sequence number.
	Security Implications: TCP is a connection-oriented protocol that maintains its understanding of session state through a combination of flags (see the Flags field that follows) and sequence and acknowledgement numbers. Sequence and acknowledgment numbers allow the TCP stack at both ends to ensure that all packets transmitted have been received. Not all packets travel through the same route and in the same order, and some packets may be lost in transit. Based on the sequence number, TCP can request the retransmission of missing packets. Only the missing packet will be retransmitted. The sender may also retransmit packets that have not been acknowledged. Note that the TCP sender maintains a copy of each packet it has sent in its *retransmission buffer* for just this purpose, until each packet has been *acknowledged* by the receiver. This requires that a memory buffer of up to the *window size* (see the Window field that follows) be committed for each established connection. Data segments will only be sent within this window size, which is negotiated at connection setup time.	

Table B-2   *TCP Header Fields and Their Security Implications (Continued)*

Bit-Offset	Header Field	Header Value and Description
		The initial sequence number (ISN) should be chosen at random for each new TCP connection. Originally, this was not the case and attacks were developed based on TCP sequence number guessing. (Each operating system had a characteristic signature for its ISN, leading this to also be used for OS fingerprinting.) A TCP sequence prediction attack is an attempt to hijack an existing TCP session by injecting packets that pretend to come from one host involved in the TCP session. This can be used in blind spoofing attacks for the purposes of denial of service (such as a reset attack), and nonblind spoofing attacks for the purposes of malicious data/theft insertion (such as an MiTM attack).[5]
64–95 (32 bits)	Acknowledgement Number	If the ACK flag is set, then the value of this field is the sequence number the sender expects next (SYN+1). For the initial connection request (SYN flag set, no ACK flag), the acknowledgement number should be 0.
	Security Implications: For attacks against existing TCP sessions, see the preceding Security Implications for the Sequence Number field.	
96–99 (4 bits)	Data Offset	This 4-bit field specifies the size of the TCP header in 32-bit words, and indicates the offset from the start of the TCP packet to the start of the data.
	Security Implications: The minimum header size is 0x5, meaning five 32-bit words (or 5×4 bytes = 20 bytes). When TCP options are included, the Data Offset field can indicate a maximum of 0xF, or up to fifteen 32-bit words (or 15×4 bytes = 60 bytes). Thus, up to 40 bytes are available for TCP options (see the TCP Options field that follows). When options are included and this value improperly points to the start of data, for example by indicating a length of 0 (or some other improper offset), the network stack will not know where the data portion begins. This may result in a DoS condition.[6] It is plausible that a poorly written network stack may improperly process these packets, possibly leading to a DoS condition or buffer overflow condition.	
100–105 (6 bits)	Reserved	This 6-bit field is reserved for future use and should be set to 0.
	Security Implications: The 6-bit Reserved field should always be 0. It is plausible that a poorly written network stack may improperly process a non-zero Reserved bit field, possibly leading to a DoS condition or buffer overflow condition.	

continues

Table B-2 *TCP Header Fields and Their Security Implications (Continued)*

Bit-Offset	Header Field	Header Value and Description
106–111 (6 bits)	Flags (Control bits)	This field contains six bit flags: **URG:** Urgent pointer field is set **ACK:** Acknowledgement field is set **PSH:** Push function **RST:** Reset the connection **SYN:** Synchronize sequence numbers (initial connection request) **FIN:** No more data from sender (close connection)
	Security Implications: Only ten valid combinations of these six TCP flags should be seen in a TCP packet header, including: SYN, SYN-ACK, ACK, FIN-ACK, RST, RST-ACK, FIN-PSH-ACK, PSH-ACK, URG-ACK, and URG-PSH-ACK.	
	• **Valid flag combinations:** The trio of SYN, SYN-ACK, and ACK are the most well-known and are used during the three-way handshake that establishes a TCP connection. The equally well-known FIN-ACK and ACK flags are used during the graceful teardown of an existing TCP connection. A RST-ACK can be used to immediately terminate an existing connection. An RST can appear by itself; it is generated in response to an unsolicited ACK to an open or closed port. The FIN-ACK (and possibly, the FIN-ACK-PSH) is used during the connection teardown process. All packets sent during the session after the three-way handshake and before the teardown sequence must have the ACK bit set. Optionally, the PSH and URG flags may also be set (PSH-ACK, URG-ACK, or PSH-URG-ACK).	
	• **Invalid flag combinations:** TCP packets having no flags set are referred to as *null packets* and are always illegal. Packets of this type are used by some scanning programs in so-called *null scan* or *stealth scan* modes to identify open ports on hosts (an open port will not reply to a null scan, whereas a closed port will reply with an RST). All valid TCP packets must have at least one flag set. TCP packets having just the FIN flag set are also illegal. Packets of this type are used by some scanning programs in the so-called *fin scan* mode, which produces the same results as a null scan. The fact that no reply is generated from open ports gives these scans their *stealth* attributes. The SYN-FIN combination is probably the most well-known illegal scanning packet; these flags should never appear together (one starts a connection and the other one terminates it, and there is no legitimate point to having these appear together). Packets of this type may elicit a response from a host that is	

Table B-2   *TCP Header Fields and Their Security Implications (Continued)*

Bit-Offset	Header Field	Header Value and Description
		protected by a personal firewall, for example.[7] One other well-known scan is the so-called *xmas-tree* scan. The scanning tool Nmap uses the flags FIN-URG-PSH in its xmas scan mode (–sX option). Other tools use the full set of TCP flags (URG-ACK-PSH-RST-SYN-FIN), hence the name *xmas-tree* (or *all flags lit up*) for these scans. *Xmas Tree* scanning (also referred to as *nastygram*, *kamikaze*, and *lamp-test*) is most often used to bypass simple firewalls and in OS fingerprinting techniques. Any packet that uses the URG or PSH flags may always carry data. *WinNuke* is an older attack against a Windows system that caused a *Blue Screen of Death* (BSOD). The exploit consisted of setting the URG flag but not following it with data, and then sending an RST to tear down the connection. The combination SYN-PSH is invalid because a SYN would never be used in a packet carrying data. Other variations exist as well; all are illegal.
112–127 (16 bits)	Window	This value is exchanged by each side of the TCP connection to tell the opposite side how much data it is capable of buffering, and hence how much data the opposite side can send before pausing and waiting for acknowledgement from the receiver of the data. Because TCP is a full-duplex protocol, there are two window sizes: one in each direction.
		Security Implications: This is perhaps the most important field in legitimate TCP connections in that it is a key factor for efficient data transmission. The window value is also used as a form of flow control. The maximum value is 65,535 bytes. Typically, the window value fluctuates as data is received and processed. Under normal conditions, if the receiver's input buffer is full, it will advertise a window size of 0, indicating that the other side should stop sending data until it is told to do so (with an increased window size).
		All TCP attacks against existing connections require knowledge of source and destination IP addresses, source and destination ports, and the sequence and acknowledgement numbers. Given that the sequence and acknowledgement numbers are incremented based on the amount of data transmitted, knowing the window size can be advantageous to an attacker. Because the receiving TCP implementation will accept any sequence number that falls within a certain range of the expected sequence numbers—as dictated by the window—this makes TCP vulnerable to reset attacks.[8] This vulnerability has been exacerbated due to higher-bandwidth links and increased window sizes (to meet the so-called *bandwidth-delay product*).

continues

Table B-2   *TCP Header Fields and Their Security Implications (Continued)*

Bit-Offset	Header Field	Header Value and Description
128–143 (16 bits)	Checksum	This field is calculated as the 16-bit one's complement of the one's complement sum of all 16-bit words in the TCP segment header and TCP segment data. If the segment contains an odd number of octets (that is, it does not end on a 16-bit boundary), then it is padded with 0s for checksum calculation purposes. While computing the checksum, the Checksum field itself is replaced with 0s. A 12-byte pseudo-header is also used in the checksum calculation, and contains the IP header Source Address, Destination Address, and Protocol fields, as well as a calculated TCP segment length (header and data) in bytes.
	Security Implications: Attacks using invalid checksums (purposely) are limited, because all TCP segments with invalid checksums are dropped. Checksum errors occur in fragmentation-based attacks that split the packet across the TCP header. Another interesting attack that has been hypothesized to actually take advantage of this behavior is a *covert channel* attack (surreptitiously passing confidential data without discovery). In this case, the sender creates TCP segments carrying the data to be divulged, but all packets are built with invalid TCP checksums. The destination address is selected to ensure that these packets travel through the network and pass a monitoring point employed by the attacker(s), where each packet is *sniffed*. When these packets reach their destination, they are simply discarded due to the invalid checksum.[9] As a result, packet interception at the monitoring point goes undetected.		
144–159 (16 bits)	Urgent Pointer	When the URG flag is set, this value, when added to the sequence number in the packet, is a pointer to the last urgent data byte.
	Security Implications: The URG flag and urgent pointer have been known to be used to cause a DoS condition. These TCP packets with URG set are referred to as *out-of-band* packets. When the urgent pointer points to the end of the frame but no normal data follows, a DoS condition may occur.[10] A TCP packet with a non-zero Urgent Pointer field value but without the URG flag set must also be considered invalid.		
160+ (32 bits)	TCP Options	Additional header fields (called options) may follow the urgent pointer and be identified by an option *kind* field. Currently defined *kind* values are maintained by IANA.[11]

Table B-2   *TCP Header Fields and Their Security Implications (Continued)*

Bit-Offset	Header Field	Header Value and Description
		Security Implications: To date, 30 different *kind* values are specified.[11] The *kind* value indicates the type of TCP option being invoked, and depending on the *kind* value, the length of the option varies. The total length of the option field must be a multiple of a 32-bit word, and the Data Offset field must be adjusted appropriately. The *kind* options End of List (0) and No-Operation (1) are exactly one octet (which is just their *kind* field) and are used to pad out other options to the 32-bit word boundary. All other options have a one-octet *kind* field, followed by a one-octet *length* field, followed by (*length*–2) octets of option data. Some well-known options include: No-Operation (1), Maximum Segment Size (2), Window Scale (WSOPT) (3), Selective Acknowledgement Permitted (SACKOK) (4), and Timestamp (8). Option kinds MSS, SACKOK, and WSOPT are only permitted during connection establishment (with the SYN flag). It is not valid to include these options otherwise. Not all options are required to be (or are) supported by all network stacks. Poorly written network stacks may improperly process unsupported or improperly specified options, possibly leading to a DoS condition or buffer overflow condition.
		The MD5 Signature Option (19) is used by BGP to provide some protection against spoofed TCP segments (hijacking and blind insertion) attacking BGP sessions on Internet core and customer premises equipment (CPE) routers.[12]
		As indicated above, there are two types of TCP options: a single-octet option (option-kind) and a two-octet option (option-kind+option-length+option-data). When TCP options are used, the Data Offset field indicates the total length of the TCP header, including the length of the options. If the TCP header length does not match the cumulative total of the lengths listed with each option, it is likely that the packet will be improperly processed, possibly leading to a DoS condition.

1. Reynolds, J., and J. Postel. *Assigned Numbers*. RFC 1700. IETF, Oct. 1994. http://www.ietf.org/rfc/rfc1700.txt.

2. Jones, S. "Port 0 OS Fingerprinting." Network Penetration, 2003. http://www.networkpenetration.com/port0.html.

3. Nmap. Developed by Gordon Lyon. Available at Insecure.org. http://insecure.org/nmap/.

4. "Microsoft Windows Malformed TCP DoS (LAND)." Open Source Vulnerability Database, March 5, 2005. http://osvdb.org/displayvuln.php?osvdb_id=14578.

5. "What Is a TCP Sequence Prediction Attack?" Tech-FAQ. http://www.tech-faq.com/tcp-sequence-prediction.shtml.

6. "CVE-2004-0375" (Symantec Multiple Firewall TCP Options Denial of Service). CVE List. The MITRE Corp.
    http://cve.mitre.org/cgi-bin/cvename.cgi?name=2004-0375.

7.   "Symantec Norton Personal Firewall 2002 SYN/FIN Scan Issue." Symantec Security Response Advisory. Symantec, May 16, 2002. http://www.symantec.com/avcenter/security/Content/2002.05.16.html.

8.   "Vulnerability Issues in TCP." National Cyber Alert System Technical Cyber Security Alert TA04-111A., Last revised: September 9, 2005. http://www.us-cert.gov/cas/techalerts/TA04-111A.html.

9.   Paxson, V. "Subterfuge Attacks." Section in "Bro: A System for Detecting Network Intruders in Real-Time." *Proceedings of the 7th USENIX Security Symposium.* San Antonio, Texas, Jan. 1998. http://www.sagecertification.org/publications/library/proceedings/sec98/full_papers/paxson/paxson_html/node17.html.

10. "Multiple Vendor 'Out Of Band' Data Denial Of Service Vulnerability." SecurityFocus. http://www.securityfocus.com/bid/2010/discuss.

11. "TCP Option Numbers." IANA. http://www.iana.org/assignments/tcp-parameters.

12. Heffernan, A. *Protection of BGP Sessions via the TCP MD5 Signature Option.* RFC 2385. IETF, Aug. 1998. http://www.ietf. org/rfc/rfc2385.txt.

UDP Header

The User Datagram Protocol (UDP) is used for unreliable, minimal overhead transport services that give applications direct access to the datagram service of the IP layer. UDP provides no guarantees for delivery and no protection from duplication. Its simplicity in implementation is its strength when considering transport overhead, but its weakness when considering security implications.

The UDP header consists of only four fields, of which two are optional, and requires 8 bytes to specify the necessary values. The UDP header is shown in Figure B-3.

NOTE   Because UDP is stateless, unauthenticated, and often used in unidirectional data flows, it is highly susceptible to spoofing attacks against nearly every port and every service. This section does not attempt to cover or address each and every type of UDP attack known to exist.

Figure B-3   *UDP Header*

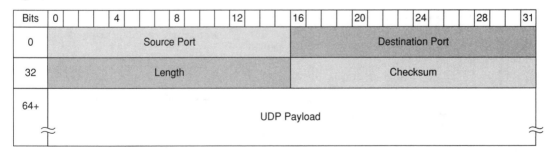

The UDP header fields shown in Figure B-3 are listed and described in Table B-3. Table B-3 also provides a brief description of some known modifications or spoofs to relevant header fields that have been seen in common attacks.

Table B-3   *UDP Header Fields and Their Security Implications*

Bit-Offset	Header Field	Header Value and Description
0–15 (16 bits)	Source Port	This optional field identifies the sending port when meaningful and should be assumed to be the port to reply to if needed. If not used, then it should be 0.
		Security Implications: UDP spoofing attacks have been possible since day one. One well-known DoS attack that spoofed the UDP source port is the so-called *UDP Echo/Chargen attack* (or *UDP Bomb*, or *UDP Packet Storm*). This attack spoofs a UDP packet with a *source port* of echo (7) and a destination port of chargen (19), causing it to send a datagram back to port 7, which causes this loop to continue endlessly.[1] This was effective against a single host (spoofing the same source and destination IP address), or between two hosts. The source port is often spoofed in reflection-based attacks or where feedback mechanisms can be abused to flood the target (purported source) and cause a DoS condition. The *UDP Snork Attack* used a similar technique, but targeted UDP source/destination port 135.[2]
16–31 (16 bits)	Destination Port	This mandatory field identifies the destination port number. The range of possible values is 0–65,535. (Unlike TCP, many port numbers above 1023 are registered as services.) Several well-known destination ports include: 53 (DNS), 67 (BOOTPS), 68 (BOOTPC), 69 (TFTP), 123 (NTP), 137 (WINS), 138 (NETBIOS), 139 (NETBIOS), 161 (SNMP), 162 (SNMPTRAP), 500 (IKE), 514 (SYSLOG), 1701 (L2TP), 1812 (RADIUS AUTH), and 1813 (RADIUS ACCT). An up-to-date list of ports can be found in Wikipedia.[3]
		Security Implications: Attacks directed at specific UDP destination ports are used for several reasons. Reconnaissance attacks may be useful in identifying live services in preparation for future attacks. Security scanners such as Nmap[4] have built-in UDP probing capabilities that conduct vertical UDP scans looking for open ports. Because UDP is stateless, scanning involves a *negative-response* technique. UDP probes reaching closed ports elicit ICMP Port Unreachable error messages, while probes to open (or filtered) ports receive either no response or a positive data response.

continues

Table B-3   *UDP Header Fields and Their Security Implications (Continued)*

Bit-Offset	Header Field	Header Value and Description
		DoS attacks against open UDP ports mainly attempt to simply overwhelm the victim with traffic (brute force). These attacks can be direct or reflected. One well-known DoS attack directs crafted UDP packets against the Internet Key Exchange (IKE) service (port 500), causing IKE to expend tremendous resources on basically, illegitimate new service requests, and making valid requests slow or impossible.[5]
		Because UDP is unauthenticated and stateless, it is highly susceptible to spoofed data insertion attacks. As a result, many UDP-based application protocols implement their own authentication schemes to protect against such attacks. For example, NTP implements its own MD5-based authentication mechanism for this purpose. Another example is SNMP, which implements the community-string concept. If SNMP were unprotected, an attacker may be able to either query SNMP (to gain unauthorized information) or insert bogus data (to change routing parameters, for example).
32–47 (16 bits)	Length	This mandatory field specifies the length, in bytes, of the entire datagram (header plus data). The minimum length is 8 bytes, because that is the length of the header, and the theoretical maximum is 65,535 (meaning 65,535–8 = 65,527 bytes for the data carried by a single UDP datagram).
	Security Implications: Even though the minimum length is 8 bytes, an empty datagram to certain services may cause a DoS condition. The Internet Printing Protocol (IPP) is one such service that was noted to be affected by this form of attack.[6]	
48–63 (16 bits)	Checksum	The optional 16-bit Checksum field is used for error checking the UDP header and data. The Checksum field is calculated as the 16-bit one's complement of the one's complement sum of a pseudo-header of information from the IP header, the UDP header, and the data, padded with 0 octets at the end (if necessary) to make a multiple of 16-bit boundary. The 12-byte pseudo-header contains the IP header Source Address, Destination Address, Protocol (17), and calculated UDP datagram length (header and data) in bytes. If a checksum is not used, it should be sent as 0 (all 0s), because 0 indicates an unused checksum.
	Security Implications: If a UDP datagram is received with a checksum that is non-zero and invalid, UDP silently discards the datagram. Hence, there is little point in purposely miscalculating or spoofing this value.	

1.   "CVE-1999-0103: UDP Bomb or UDP Packet Storm." (Status: Entry.) CVE List. The MITRE Corp.
      http://cve.mitre.org/cgi-bin/cvename.cgi?name=1999-0103.

2.   "CVE-1999-0969: Snork Denial of Service Attack, Windows NT RPC Service." (Status: Entry.) CVE List.
      The MITRE Corp.
      http://cve.mitre.org/cgi-bin/cvename.cgi?name=CVE-1999-0969.

3.   "List of TCP and UDP Port Numbers." Wikipedia.
      http://en.wikipedia.org/wiki/List_of_TCP_and_UDP_port_numbers.

4.   Nmap. Developed by Gordon Lyon. Available at Insecure.org.
      http://insecure.org/nmap/.

5.   "Multiple Vulnerability Issues in Implementation of ISAKMP Protocol." Vulnerability Note VU#226364,
      Nov. 15, 2005.
      http://www.kb.cert.org/vuls/id/226364.

6.   "CVE-2004-0558: Internet Printing Protocol (IPP) Empty UDP Datagram DoS Vulnerability." (Status:
      Candidate.) CVE List. The MITRE Corp.
      http://cve.mitre.org/cgi-bin/cvename.cgi?name=2004-0558.

ICMP Header

The Internet Control Message Protocol (ICMP) is used for error reporting and debugging of the IP protocol. ICMP uses IP at the network layer and hence it is unreliable (by the same definition that IP is considered unreliable). In general, there are two types of ICMP messages:

- **Query messages:** ICMP query messages are generated by users or client programs and are used to probe the network and gather status information at any moment. Query messages are primarily intended for use as troubleshooting and diagnostic tools. For example, the ICMP Echo Request/Echo Reply function sends a packet with a specific payload to a destination host, where it is expected to be copied and returned to the sending host. The user application ping is the most familiar management tool that provides access to the ICMP Echo Request/Echo Reply function.

- **Error messages:** ICMP error messages are automatically generated by network elements or hosts when certain error conditions within the network are encountered. ICMP may, for example, announce that a host or a network is unreachable by issuing the ICMP Destination Unreachable message, or that a routing loop has occurred by issuing the ICMP Time Exceeded message.

In the previous protocol header examples, a single header could be used to fully describe each protocol. This is not the case with ICMP. Although a basic ICMP header format can be described, the full format and content of any individual ICMP query or error message varies with the type of ICMP message.

The basic ICMP header illustrated in Figure B-4 shows the major fields that are included in all ICMP messages. The primary fields are the 8-bit Type field, the adjacent 8-bit Code field, followed by the 16-bit ICMP Header Checksum. After that, a variable-format data field appears. The format and contents of this field depend on the ICMP message type. Valid ICMP message types, as defined by their type and code field values, are listed in Table B-4.

Figure B-4 *Basic ICMP Header*

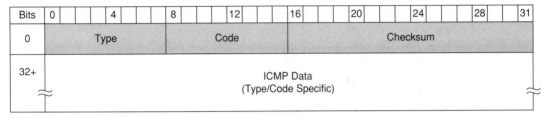

Table B-4 *ICMP Message Types and Codes*[1]

Type	Codes	Description	Use
0	0	Echo Reply	Query-Reply
1		Unassigned	—
2		Unassigned	—
3	Destination Unreachable		
	0	Network Unreachable	Error
	1	Host Unreachable	Error
	2	Protocol Unreachable	Error
	3	Port Unreachable	Error
	4	Fragmentation Needed and Don't Fragment was Set	Error
	5	Source Route Failed	Error
	6	Destination Network Unknown	Error
	7	Destination Host Unknown	Error
	8	Source Host Isolated	Error
	9	Communication with Destination Network is Administratively Prohibited	Error
	10	Communication with Destination Host is Administratively Prohibited	Error
	11	Destination Network Unreachable for ToS	Error

Table B-4   *ICMP Message Types and Codes[1](Continued)*

Type	Codes	Description	Use
	12	Destination Host Unreachable for ToS	Error
	13	Communication Administratively Prohibited	Error
	14	Host Precedence Violation	Error
	15	Precedence Cutoff in Effect	Error
4	0	Source Quench	Error
5	Redirect		
	0	Redirect Datagram for the Network (or Subnet)	Error
	1	Redirect Datagram for the Host	Error
	2	Redirect Datagram for the Type of Service and Network	Error
	3	Redirect Datagram for the Type of Service and Host	Error
6	0	Alternate Address for Host	—
7		Unassigned	—
8	0	Echo	Query
9	Router Advertisement		
	0	Normal Router Advertisement	Query
	16	Does not route common traffic	Query
10	0	Router Solicitation	Query
11	Time Exceeded		
	0	Time to Live exceeded in Transit	Error
	1	Fragment Reassembly Time Exceeded	Error
12	Parameter Problem		
	0	Pointer indicates the error	Error
	1	Missing a Required Option	Error
	2	Bad Length	Error
13	0	Timestamp	Query
14	0	Timestamp Reply	Query-Reply

continues

Table B-4   *ICMP Message Types and Codes*[1]*(Continued)*

Type	Codes	Description	Use
15	0	Information Request	Query
16	0	Information Reply	Query-Reply
17	0	Address Mask Request	Query
18	0	Address Mask Reply	Query-Reply
19		Reserved (for Security)	—
20–29		Reserved (for Robustness Experiment)	—
30		Traceroute	Query
31		Datagram Conversion Error	Error
32		Mobile Host Redirect	—
33		IPv6 Where-Are-You	—
34		IPv6 I-Am-Here	—
35		Mobile Registration Request	Query
36		Mobile Registration Reply	Query-Reply
37		Domain Name Request	Query
38		Domain Name Reply	Query-Reply
39		SKIP (Simple Key-Management for Internet Protocol)	—
40	Photuris		
	0	Bad SPI	Error
	1	Authentication Failed	Error
	2	Decompression Failed	Error
	3	Decryption Failed	Error
	4	Need Authentication	Error
	5	Need Authorization	Error

1.   "ICMP Type Numbers." IANA.
      http://www.iana.org/assignments/icmp-parameters.

Although ICMP is a legitimate protocol and is required for the proper operations of IP networks, it has historically been one of the most exploited and *exploitable* protocols. The most commonly exploited ICMP message types are reviewed in the following four subsections.

ICMP Echo Request/Echo Reply Query Message Headers

The ICMP Echo Request/Echo Reply query messages (Type 8, Code 0 and Type 0, Code 0, respectively) function as a pair, with the Echo Request sending a packet with a specific payload to a destination host, where the payload is expected to be copied and returned to the sending host as an Echo Reply. The user application ping is the most familiar network management and diagnostic tool that provides access to the ICMP Echo Request/Echo Reply message function. Ping transmits a series of packets to a destination host, and then waits for their return. Based on how many are returned and the time it takes, ping computes average round-trip times and loss percentages. Hence, ping is the most widely used tool for verifying network connectivity, and IP reachability to destination hosts (or attack targets!).

NOTE   More-advanced network diagnostics can be performed with ping by modifying various IP header and ICMP header parameters. For example, setting the IP header Don't Fragment (DF) bit and increasing the ICMP payload size can be used to identify locations along the packet path where fragmentation is required (due to smaller link MTUs). Ping typically allows for other parameters to be set as well, such as TTL, QoS markings, record-route IP options, and timestamp options.

The ICMP Echo Request/Echo Reply header consists of five fields, plus a Data field, as shown in Figure B-5. The ICMP Echo Request/Echo Reply header fields shown in Figure B-5 are listed and described in Table B-5, along with a brief description of the security implications relevant to each header field.

Figure B-5   *ICMP Header—Echo Request/Echo Reply Query Message*

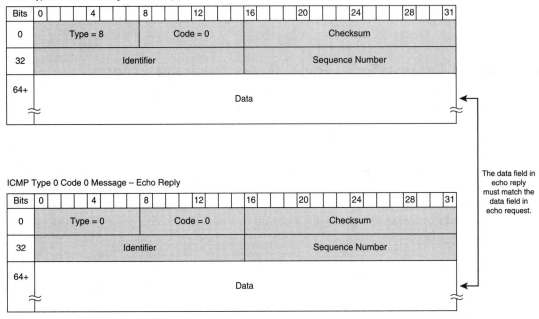

Table B-5   *ICMP Echo Request/Echo Reply Header Fields and Their Security Implications*

Bit Offset	Header Field	Header Value and Description
0–7 (8 bits)	Type	This field indicates the ICMP message type being carried by the ICMP payload. ICMP Echo Request messages have a type value of 8. ICMP Echo Reply messages have a type value of 0. (See Table B-4 for a full list of message types.)
		Security Implications: When correctly specified, there really are not any security issues with this field. You either want an ICMP Echo Request or you do not. One potential issue that might arise could be when the value of this field indicates an unknown ICMP type. It is plausible that a poorly written network stack could have issues under such conditions. ICMP error messages are never supposed to be generated and sent in response to other ICMP error messages (to avoid infinite loops). Sending a spoofed ICMP Echo Reply to a host that never generated an ICMP Echo Request should result in that host silently dropping the message. It is plausible that a poorly written network stack could cause the receiving host to have issues under such conditions.

Table B-5   *ICMP Echo Request/Echo Reply Header Fields and Their Security Implications (Continued)*

Bit Offset	Header Field	Header Value and Description
8–15 (8 bits)	Code	This field indicates, when appropriate for the ICMP message type, the particular *code* (or submessage type) to further specify the message being carried by the ICMP payload. Neither ICMP Echo Request nor Echo Reply messages have codes; thus this field is set to 0. (See Table B-4 for a full list of message codes per message type.)
	Security Implications: When correctly specified, there really are not any security issues with this field. You either want an ICMP Echo Request or you do not. One potential issue that might arise could be when the value of this field indicates a code value of other than 0 (which would be inappropriate for an ICMP Type 8 message). It is plausible that a poorly written network stack could have issues under such conditions.	
16–31 (16 bits)	Checksum	This field contains a 16-bit one's complement of the one's complement sum of the ICMP message, starting with the ICMP Type field.
	Security Implications: When correctly specified, there really are not any security issues with this field. You either want an ICMP Echo Request or you do not. If this field is computed incorrectly, the packet is supposed to be silently dropped on ingress. It is plausible that a poorly written network stack might improperly process such packets with unknown consequences.	
32–47 (16 bits)	Identifier	This field allows for the insertion of a unique, 16-bit identifier so that ICMP Echo Request messages can be matched to corresponding ICMP Echo Reply messages. This field may be set to 0. The ping application commonly sets the value of this field to some random value and then increments the sequence number (see the Sequence Number field which follows) when multiple packets to a common destination are sent by a single ping session.
	Security Implications: The value selected for this field may be OS-specific, possibly allowing for OS fingerprinting.	

continues

Table B-5   *ICMP Echo Request/Echo Reply Header Fields and Their Security Implications (Continued)*

Bit Offset	Header Field	Header Value and Description
48–63 (16 bits)	Sequence Number	This field allows for the insertion of a unique, 16-bit sequence number so that ICMP Echo Request messages can be matched to ICMP Echo Reply messages. This field may be set to 0. The ping application commonly sets the value of the Identifier field (see above) to some random value and then increments this field (for example, 0x0000, 0x0001, 0x0002, and so on) when multiple packets to a common destination are sent from a single ping session.
		Security Implications: The value selected for this field may be OS-specific, possibly allowing for OS fingerprinting.
64+ (variable)	Data	This field provides a space for the insertion of a (normally arbitrary) data block.
		Security Implications: The default values (size and content) specified in the Data field may be OS-specific, possibly allowing for OS fingerprinting. For example, "*nix" variants seem to insert 56 bytes of data, giving a total packet length of 84 bytes (20 bytes IP header, 8 bytes ICMP header, and 56 bytes of data). Windows OS variants seem to insert only 32 bytes of data, giving a total packet length of 60 bytes (20 bytes IP header, 8 bytes ICMP header, and 32 bytes of data). The content of the Data field in the ICMP Echo Request message may be compared with the companion Echo Reply message. If the content matches, in theory, the process has been successfully completed. Whether or not all implementations actually compare companion data blocks is unclear. The maximum data size is dictated by the maximum for all IP packets, that being 65,536 bytes in total. Obviously, this would result in fragmented packets.

Overall Security for ICMP Echo Request/Echo Reply Query Messages

Reconnaissance attacks: Ping is often the first application used for network discovery. Although not destructive, this is often described as the first phase in preparation for broader attacks. By manipulating, and/or observing various ping parameters, OS fingerprinting can be accomplished, potentially allowing further attack vectors to be identified. Tools such as hping2,[1] SING,[2] and Nemesis[3] are often used to accomplish this task. One of the very best references covering the gamut of ICMP reconnaissance attacks is "ICMP Usage in Scanning, Version 3.0."[4]

DoS attacks: ICMP Echo Request/Echo Reply packets have been successfully used in several ways to accomplish DoS attacks. The famous ICMP smurf attack sends forged ICMP Echo Request packets to the network broadcast address (destination IP), using a source IP address of the

Table B-5   *ICMP Echo Request/Echo Reply Header Fields and Their Security Implications (Continued)*

Bit Offset	Header Field	Header Value and Description
		intended target.[5] All of the systems on the network respond with ICMP Echo Reply messages back to the purported originator—in this case, the spoofed IP address of the target—thus consuming the target's resources and creating a DoS condition. In this case, the network broadcast address is used as an amplifier for the attack. The equally famous ping of death attack sends an ICMP Echo Request packet (fragmented) that exceeds the maximum 65,536 bytes of data allowed by the IP specification.[6] The target cannot reassemble the packets, often resulting in a system crash (or hang or reboot).
		Other security issues: ICMP Echo Request/Echo Reply packets have been used for many other purposes than for what they were originally intended. Because the Data field can carry any specified content, ICMP Echo Request/Echo Reply packets may be used as a covert channel (tunnel) for carrying traffic surreptitiously, perhaps when firewalls are used to close other ports (or perhaps because ICMP Type 8, Type 0 packets are so common that they may not be scrutinized closely).[7,8]

1.   hping2. Developed by Salvatore Sanfilippo. Available at SourceForge.net. http://sourceforge.net/projects/hping2.

2.   SING. Developed by Alfredo Andres Omella. Available at SourceForge.net. http://sourceforge.net/projects/sing.

3.   Nemesis. Developed by Jeff Nathan. Available at SourceForge.net. http://nemesis.sourceforge.net/.

4.   Arkin, O. "ICMP Usage in Scanning, Version 3.0." Sys-Security Group, June 2001. http://www.sys-security.com/archive/papers/ICMP_Scanning_v3.0.pdf.

5.   "CERT Advisory CA-1998-01 Smurf IP Denial-of-Service Attacks." CERT, original date issued Jan. 5, 1998. http://www.cert.org/advisories/CA-1998-01.html.

6.   "CERT Advisory CA-1996-26 Denial-of-Service Attack via Ping." CERT, original date issued Dec. 18, 1996. http://www.cert.org/advisories/CA-1996-26.html.

7.   "Project Loki." http://www.phrack.org/archives/49/P49-06.

8.   ICMPTX. Developed by Thomer Gil. http://thomer.com/icmptx/.

ICMP Time to Live Exceeded in Transit Error Message Header

The ICMP Time to Live Exceeded in Transit error message (Type 11, Code 0) is generated by network elements that drop IP packets when they have a Time to Live (TTL) field value that decrements to 0 while in the forwarding process. Under normal circumstances, IP packets should be able to reach their destination within the allotted TTL scope. The TTL field is included within the IP header and is a means of preventing packets from "circling the network forever" (and clogging the Internet!) as would otherwise occur under a routing-loop condition, for example. When a packet is dropped during forwarding due to a TTL expiry condition, the ICMP Time to Live Exceeded in Transit error message is generated and sent back to the source IP address of the offending packet. In this case, a portion of the offending IP packet is also copied into the ICMP Time to Live Exceeded in Transit message payload as a feedback mechanism to the origination host.

The user application traceroute is the most familiar network management and diagnostic tool that purposefully takes advantage of this feedback mechanism. Traceroute maps the hop-by-hop path a packet would take through the network from source to destination by artificially manipulating the TTL field within an IP packet header to cause a TTL expiry at each node along the path. It then watches for the ICMP Time to Live Exceeded in Transit announcements in reply to map the entire path (in one direction).

The ICMP Time to Live Exceeded in Transit header consists of three fields, plus a data field, as shown in Figure B-6. The ICMP Time to Live Exceeded in Transit header fields shown in Figure B-6 are described in Table B-6, along with a brief description of the security implications relevant to each header field.

Figure B-6 *ICMP Header—Time to Live Exceeded in Transit Error Message*

ICMP Type 11 Code 0 Message – Time Exceeded in Transit

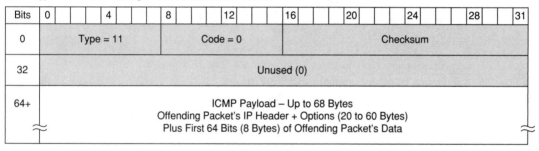

Table B-6 *ICMP Time to Live Exceeded in Transit Error Message Header Fields and Their Security Implications*

Bit Offset	Header Field	Header Value and Description
0–7 (8 bits)	Type	This field indicates the ICMP message type being carried by the ICMP payload. The ICMP Time to Live Exceeded in Transit error message has a type value of 11. (See Table B-4 for a full list of message types.)

Table B-6   *ICMP Time to Live Exceeded in Transit Error Message Header Fields and Their Security Implications (Continued)*

Bit Offset	Header Field	Header Value and Description
		Security Implications: When correctly specified, there really are not any security issues with this field. You either want an ICMP Time to Live Exceeded in Transit message or you do not. One potential issue that might arise could be when the value of this field indicates an unknown ICMP type. It is plausible that a poorly written network stack could have issues under such conditions.
8–15 (8 bits)	Code	This field indicates, when appropriate for the ICMP message type, the particular *code* (or submessage type) to further specify the message being carried by the ICMP payload. The ICMP Time Exceeded (Type 11) error message actually permits two codes: Code 0, for Time to Live Exceeded in Transit, and Code 1, for Fragment Reassembly Time Exceeded. (See Table B-4 for full list of message codes per message type.)
		Security Implications: When correctly specified, there really are not any security issues with this field. You either want an ICMP Time to Live Exceeded in Transit message or you do not. One potential issue that might arise could be when the value of this field indicates a code value of other than 0 or 1 (which would be inappropriate for an ICMP Type 11 message). It is plausible that a poorly written network stack could have issues under such conditions.
16–31 (16 bits)	Checksum	This field contains a 16-bit one's complement of the one's complement sum of the ICMP message, starting with the ICMP Type field.
		Security Implications: When correctly specified, there really are not any security issues with this field. You either want an ICMP Time to Live Exceeded in Transit message or you do not. If this field is computed incorrectly, the packet is supposed to be silently dropped on ingress. It is plausible that a poorly written network stack might improperly process such packets with unknown consequences.
32–63 (32 bits)	Unused	This field is unused by ICMP Time Exceeded error messages and is required to be set to 0.
		Security Implications: This field is required to be set to 0. Any value inserted in this field should be ignored by the receiver regardless. It is plausible that a poorly written network stack might improperly process packets that do not have a value of 0, resulting in unknown consequences.

continues

Table B-6 *ICMP Time to Live Exceeded in Transit Error Message Header Fields and Their Security Implications (Continued)*

Bit Offset	Header Field	Header Value and Description
64+ (variable)	Data	This field includes a copy of the IP header (20 bytes plus IP options if they exist) and the first 64 bits of the offending packet's data. This field is intended for use by the receiver to match the ICMP error message to the appropriate process that created the original, offending packet. For higher-level protocols that use port numbers (for example, TCP and UDP), the first 64 bits will also include the source and destination ports of the offending packet. The minimum length of this field is 28 bytes (20 bytes for the offending packet IP header, plus 8 bytes [64 bits] of additional data from the offending packet).

Security Implications: In theory, the contents of this Data field are meant to help the originating source determine which application (by protocol and port) had a packet experience a TTL expiry while in flight. With the exception of traceroute, it does not appear that any other applications actually consume and use the information contained in ICMP Time to Live Exceeded in Transit (Type 11, Code 0) messages. If it is assumed that this field is consumed at the application level as a feedback mechanism, it should be incredibly simple to build spoofed ICMP Time to Live Exceeded in Transit messages, including spoofing the correct elements within the Data field.

Overall Security for ICMP Time to Live Exceeded in Transit Error Messages

Reconnaissance attacks: Although legitimate uses for traceroute exist, it is also useful in the reconnaissance phase leading up to an attack. The information returned by traceroute may be useful for mapping the target network layout, host distribution, diameter (hop distance), and so on, and for determining whether filtering devices (or private address space) are encountered along the path (as indicated by a "*   *   *" response).

DoS attacks: As described in Chapters 1 and 2, many routers must *punt* TTL expiry packets to the CPU for error handling (primarily because of the requirement to insert a portion of the offending packet IP header and data within the payload of the ICMP Time to Live Exceeded in Transit [Type 11, Code 0] error message it must generate). When a flood of TTL expiry packets must be handled by the router, it is possible that the CPU may be overwhelmed in generating error messages for these packets, leaving little or no processing resources for performing other control plane and/or management plane activities and potentially resulting in a DoS condition. Chapter 2, "Threat Models for IP Networks," describes a transit attack of this type where the destination IP address of the attack packet is not the intended target, but rather is simply designed to take the packet along the desired path through the network. The TTL value is crafted such that it decrements to 0 upon reaching the appropriate device in the middle of the network (the intended target). Attacks of this nature are frequently able to circumvent filtering devices because the destination address is not the true target. (Strategies for preventing these attacks are discussed in Part II, Chapters 4 through 7.)

Table B-6   *ICMP Time to Live Exceeded in Transit Error Message Header Fields and Their Security Implications (Continued)*

Bit Offset	Header Field	Header Value and Description
Other security issues: The issues described here are not directly the result of spoofed or malicious ICMP Time to Live Exceeded in Transit messages, but rather are primarily due to the fact that when IP packets with expiring TTL values are dropped, ICMP Time to Live Exceeded in Transit error messages must be generated. One interesting side effect of this (and for other ICMP error messages as well) is that when attack packets use spoofed IP source addresses that are not routable (such as RFC 1918 addresses), these ICMP error messages (including ICMP Time to Live Exceeded in Transit error messages) are sent back to the purported origination point—the spoofed source. Service providers (SPs) often deploy *sink holes* within the core of their networks to gather up all of these wayward ICMP error messages—often referred to as *backscatter* for the purposes of monitoring DoS and other malicious network activity.[1,2]		

1. Moore, D., G. Voelker, and S. Savage. "Inferring Internet Denial-of-Service Activity." *Proceedings of the 10th USENIX Security Symposium.* Washington D.C., Aug. 2001.
    http://www.caida.org/outreach/papers/2001/BackScatter/usenixsecurity01.pdf.

2. "Service Provider Infrastructure Security Techniques." Cisco.com.
    http://www.cisco.com/web/about/security/intelligence/sp_infrastruct_scty.html.

ICMP Destination Unreachable, Fragmentation Needed and Don't Fragment was Set Error Message Header

The ICMP Destination Unreachable, Fragmentation Needed and Don't Fragment was Set (Type 3, Code 4) error message is generated by network elements that drop IP packets during the forwarding process when the router determines the following:

- The packet size exceeds the MTU of the forwarding interface.

- The packet DF bit is *set* (DF = 1) in the IP header, indicating that forwarding routers are not allowed to fragment the packet.

When IP packets with the DF bit set traverse the Internet (or any IP network) from source to destination, an ICMP Destination Unreachable, Fragmentation Needed and Don't Fragment was Set error message can be generated anywhere along the path by any forwarding router when the preceding error condition occurs.

NOTE   Fragmentation should be avoided where possible. Most enterprises are using Ethernet-based links with an MTU of 1500 bytes, and most SPs are running IP core network links with an MTU of 4470 bytes or greater. IP packets should have little trouble traversing such networks, even if the DF bit is set. Fragmentation issues mainly result when tunnel encapsulations, such as IPsec, GRE, MPLS, or L2TPv3, are applied. In these cases, additional encapsulation protocol headers are added to the original packet, potentially resulting in oversized packets (as compared to the 1500-byte MTU). Methods to address these issues are described in Chapter 7, "IP Services Plane Security."

ICMP Destination Unreachable, Fragmentation Needed and Don't Fragment was Set (Type 3, Code 4) error messages are used to support Path MTU Discovery (RFC 1191). The application or protocol that sent the offending packet is responsible for listening for ICMP Type 3, Code 4 error messages and adjusting future packet sizes accordingly.

The ICMP Type 3, Code 4 header consists of five fields, plus a Data field, as shown in Figure B-7. The ICMP Type 3, Code 4 header fields shown in Figure B-7 are listed and described in Table B-7, along with a brief description of the security implications relevant to each header field.

Figure B-7 *ICMP Header—Destination Unreachable, Fragmentation Needed and Don't Fragment was Set Error Message*

ICMP Type 3 Code 4 Message – Destination Unreachable, Fragmentation Needed but DF Bit Set

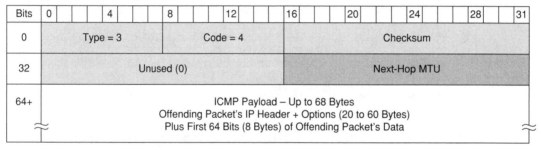

Table B-7 *ICMP Destination Unreachable, Fragmentation Needed and Don't Fragment was Set Header Fields and Their Security Implications*

Bit Offset	Header Field	Header Value and Description
0–7 (8 bits)	Type	This field indicates the ICMP message type being carried by the ICMP payload. ICMP Destination Unreachable, Fragmentation Needed and Don't Fragment was Set messages have a type value of 3. (See Table B-4 for a full list of message types.)
	Security Implications: When correctly specified, there really are not any security issues with this field. If this packet is spoofed, this field must be correctly formed to specify an ICMP Destination Unreachable message. One potential issue that might arise could be when the value of this field indicates an unknown ICMP type. It is plausible that a poorly written network stack could have issues under such conditions.	

Table B-7   *ICMP Destination Unreachable, Fragmentation Needed and Don't Fragment was Set
Header Fields and Their Security Implications (Continued)*

Bit Offset	Header Field	Header Value and Description
8–15 (8 bits)	Code	This field indicates, when appropriate for the ICMP message type, the particular *code* (or submessage type) to further specify the message being carried by the ICMP payload. The ICMP Destination Unreachable (Type 3) error message actually specifies 16 different types of submessages via 16 different codes (values of 0 through 15). The particular Destination Unreachable message described here is Code 4–Fragmentation Needed and Don't Fragment was Set. (See Table B-4 for a full list of sub-message codes per message type.)
	Security Implications: When correctly specified, there really are not any security issues with this field. If this packet is spoofed, this field must be correctly formed to specify an ICMP Destination Unreachable message. One potential issue that might arise could be when the value of this field indicates a code value of other than 0 through 15 (which would be inappropriate for an ICMP Type 3 message). It is plausible that a poorly written network stack could have issues under such conditions.	
16–31 (16 bits)	Checksum	This field contains a 16-bit one's complement of the one's complement sum of the ICMP message, starting with the ICMP Type field.
	Security Implications: When correctly specified, there really are not any security issues with this field. If this packet is spoofed, this field must be correctly formed to specify an ICMP Destination Unreachable message. If this field is computed incorrectly, the packet is supposed to be silently dropped on ingress. It is plausible that a poorly written network stack might improperly process such packets with unknown consequences.	
32–47 (16 bits)	Unused	This field is unused by ICMP Destination Unreachable, Fragmentation Needed and Don't Fragment was Set error messages and is required to be set to 0.
	Security Implications: When correctly specified, there really are not any security issues with this field. If this packet is spoofed, this field must be correctly formed to specify an ICMP Destination Unreachable message. This field is required to be set to 0. If this field is not set to 0, as required, it is plausible that a poorly written network stack might improperly process such packets with unknown consequences.	

continues

Table B-7   *ICMP Destination Unreachable, Fragmentation Needed and Don't Fragment was Set Header Fields and Their Security Implications (Continued)*

Bit Offset	Header Field	Header Value and Description
48–63 (16 bits)	Next-Hop MTU	This field provides the size, in bytes, of the MTU of the next-hop link that caused the packet to be discarded (and that if adhered to, would permit the packet to be forwarded without fragmentation). The size indicated is the maximum length of the IP header plus data that can be accommodated by the next-hop link that caused the error. This size value does not include the length of any lower-layer headers. This field was not specified within the original ICMP protocol specification (RFC 792), but was added later in support of PMTUD per RFC 1191.
	Security Implications: When taken in conjunction with the Data field, this is the most interesting field in this error message. In the legitimate case, this value is the next-hop MTU value of the interface that caused the drop. The source of the offending packet is supposed to read this value and adjust all future packet transmission accordingly, when running PMTUD. In the case where this value is spoofed, an attacker might specify an absurdly small next-hop MTU value that does not kill the connection, but rather substantially impedes it by forcing the source to send many small packets. Interestingly, TCP should maintain separate path MTU states for each connection it opens. Hence, an attacker could essentially cause a DoS condition on one connection, but all others will be unaffected, making troubleshooting particularly onerous. In theory, this field should never contain a value less than 68 bytes, because every router must be able to forward a 68-byte datagram without fragmentation. It is plausible that a poorly written network stack might improperly process packets with inappropriate values, resulting in a DoS condition, or other unknown condition.		
64+ (variable)	ICMP Payload	This field includes a copy of the IP header (20 bytes plus IP options if they exist) and the first 64 bits of the offending packet's data. This field is intended for use by the receiver to match the ICMP error message to the appropriate process that created the original, offending packet. For higher-level protocols that use port numbers (for example, TCP and UDP), the first 64 bits also includes the source and destination ports of the offending packet. The minimum length of this field is 28 bytes (20 bytes for the offending packet IP header, plus 8 bytes [64 bits] of payload data from the offending packet).

Table B-7   *ICMP Destination Unreachable, Fragmentation Needed and Don't Fragment was Set Header Fields and Their Security Implications (Continued)*

Bit Offset	Header Field	Header Value and Description
		Security Implications: When taken in conjunction with the Next-Hop MTU field, this is the most interesting field in this error message. In the legitimate case, this field includes a copy of the IP header (20 bytes plus IP options if they exist) and the first 64 bits of the offending packet's data. Because ICMP error messages are unauthenticated, they are highly susceptible to spoofing. In order to correctly spoof an ICMP Type 3, Code 4 message, the data included in this field would need to correctly match the parameters of the session/connection that this packet is attempting to disrupt. How challenging this is depends entirely on the protocol of the session/connection being spoofed. For example, in the case of a GRE tunnel, only the source and destination IP addresses of the tunnel endpoints need to be spoofed. In the case of a TCP session, however, in addition to the IP source and destination addresses of both sides to the connection, the spoofed packet must correctly identify the TCP source and destination ports, and the sequence and acknowledgement numbers that fit within the current connection window. The bottom line is, the spoofed data included in this field must only include what is required by the target protocol, and must only be as accurate as necessary to pass any checks conducted by the target network stack. Obviously for TCP, for example, the source and destination IP addresses and TCP ports must be accurate, as these identify the individual connections, but the accuracy of the sequence number depends on the receiving OS stack. It is plausible that a poorly written network stack might ignore this field altogether (in PMTUD), making it more susceptible to spoofing attacks.

Overall Security for ICMP Destination Unreachable, Fragmentation Needed and Don't Fragment was Set Error Messages

DoS attacks: When protocols use PMTUD (RFC 1191), they may be susceptible to DoS attacks via ICMP Destination Unreachable, Fragmentation Needed and Don't Fragment was Set (Type 3, Code 4) error messages. There are several reasons for this:

- These error messages are unauthenticated and can be generated by any router within the forwarding path of a packet, or spoofed by any device with IP reachability to either endpoint. If a protocol participates in PMTUD, then it is going to consume any received ICMP Type 3, Code 4 messages and adjust its send size accordingly. Because routers in the core of some networks have infrastructure link addresses in private address ranges (for example, RFC 1918), it is completely plausible to receive a legitimate ICMP Type 3, Code 4 error message with a source IP address from a private IP address. This makes it extremely difficult to construct a strong security policy to protect against spoofed ICMP Type 3, Code 4 attacks. This also makes it incredibly easy to spoof the IP header of this packet, because literally any IP address may be used as a source, and only the destination IP address is relevant (it must be the target of the attack).

continues

Table B-7 *ICMP Destination Unreachable, Fragmentation Needed and Don't Fragment was Set Header Fields and Their Security Implications (Continued)*

Bit Offset	Header Field	Header Value and Description
		• ICMP error messages are, by themselves, stateless. In the case of ICMP error messages, any concept of *state* would need to be maintained by the protocol to which the ICMP message was indicating an error. For example, TCP could look at the sequence number indicated within the Data field of an ICMP error message to determine if the message was valid and still within state (window) of the current TCP session. (ICMP query messages, on the other hand, tend to maintain state within the application that uses them; for example, ping and traceroute each match up requests and replies at the application layer). • ICMP error messages can circumvent the security mechanisms enabled for other protocols. For example, TCP is capable of using MD5 Signature Option (TCP Option Type 19). BGP uses this capability to provide some protection against spoofed TCP segments. However, because TCP listens for ICMP Type 3, Code 4 error messages, it is relatively simple to impact the TCP session—even with the additional MD5 security mechanism—because of the *coupling* between the two protocols. (Discussions related to defense in depth and breadth are appropriate at this point!)

Also, instead of traditional DoS attacks, which attempt to overwhelm a link (or CPU) with a large volume of packets, using ICMP Type 3, Code 4 packets may require only a *single packet* to be effective, making it less susceptible to discovery. In addition, using a technique of *squeezing* the session down in size (send a small MTU value instead of 0) may make a service operate very slowly, but not disappear! Leaving the service "up" but "really slow" creates a troubleshooting nightmare.

Other security issue: One additional security issue may occur as a result of Type 3, Code 4 error messages. In looking at the Next-Hop MTU field, it is seen that this field provides the size, in bytes, of the maximum length of the IP header plus data that can be accommodated by the next-hop link. Thus, the receiving protocol must do some math (subtraction) to determine exactly how much data it can carry so that the final packet size ends up meeting the PMTUD requirements. For example, a normal TCP connection (no IP or TCP options) has a 20-byte IP header and a 20-byte TCP header. Thus, the maximum data segment size that TCP computes must be 40 bytes less than the Next-Hop MTU value it receives from the ICMP Type 3, Code 4 error message. What happens when a spoofed ICMP Type 3, Code 4 error message sends a Next-Hop MTU of 40 bytes? Does TCP compute a maximum segment size of 0 bytes? Or what if the Next-Hop MTU is 38 bytes? Does TCP compute a maximum segment size of –2 bytes? It should be noted that *whenever* math is done within source code, it is always possible that errors can occur (especially when boundary checks are not performed), potentially leading to software vulnerabilities.

The security implications of ICMP Destination Unreachable, Fragmentation Needed and Don't Fragment was Set error messages have literally been known since day one. RFC 1191 describes the exact issues.[1] Privately, exploits using this knowledge had been developed. However, the first *public* description of specific attacks against TCP appears in 2004 by F. Gont[2] and the related advisories.[3]

Similar attacks against other protocols that participate in PMTUD are possible, including GRE, IPsec, and L2TP.[4]

1. Mogul, J., and S. Deering. *Path MTU Discovery*. RFC 1191. IETF, Nov. 1990.
    http://www.ietf.org/rfc/rfc1191.txt.

2. Gont, F. "ICMP Attacks Against TCP."
    http://www.gont.com.ar/drafts/icmp-attacks-against-tcp.html.

3. "Vulnerability Issues in ICMP Packets with TCP Payloads." NISCC Vulnerability Advisory 532967/
    NISCC/ICMP.
    http://www.cpni.gov.uk/docs/re-20050412-00303.pdf?lang=en.

4. "Crafted ICMP Messages Can Cause Denial of Service." (Doc. ID: 64520.) Cisco Security Advisory.
    http://www.cisco.com/en/US/products/products_security_advisory09186a0080436587.shtml.

Other ICMP Destination Unreachable Error Message Headers

Under normal circumstances, IP packets should be able to reach their destination without incident. For a variety of reasons, this may not be the case, however. The ICMP Destination Unreachable (Type 3) error message header provides 16 different submessage categories (codes) to describe the various error conditions. The focus here is on four particularly useful Destination Unreachable error messages:

- **ICMP Destination Unreachable, Network Unreachable (Type 3, Code 0):** When a router cannot forward a packet because it has no routes at all (including no default route) to the destination specified in the packet, then the router *may* generate this ICMP message back to the host.

- **ICMP Destination Unreachable, Host Unreachable (Type 3, Code 1):** When a router cannot forward a packet to a host on a network that is directly connected to the router (in other words, the router is the last-hop router) and the router has ascertained that there is no path to the destination host, then the router *must* generate this ICMP message. In this scenario, the destination network exists, but the destination host within the network does not. If, for example, the last-hop router cannot resolve the MAC address for the destination address via ARP, it considers the host unreachable.

- **ICMP Destination Unreachable, Port Unreachable (Type 3, Code 3):** When a packet is received by the destination host and the indicated destination transport protocol (for example, UDP) is unable to associate the packet to a local port number, then the host *should* generate this ICMP message. In this scenario, the destination host may not be configured for servicing the specified protocol port number (for example, HTTP).

- **ICMP Destination Unreachable, Communication Administratively Prohibited (Type 3, Code 13):** When a router cannot forward a packet because a security policy (for example, an access list) has been applied that denies the packet from being forwarded, the router *should* generate this ICMP message.

The ICMP Destination Unreachable header consists of three fields, plus a Data field, as shown in Figure B-8. The ICMP Destination Unreachable header fields shown in Figure B-8 are listed and described in Table B-8, along with a brief description of the security implications relevant to each header field.

Figure B-8   *ICMP Header—Destination Unreachable Error Messages*

ICMP Type 3 Code 0 Message – Destination Unreachable, Network Unreachable
ICMP Type 3 Code 1 Message – Destination Unreachable, Host Unreachable
ICMP Type 3 Code 3 Message – Destination Unreachable, Port Unreachable
ICMP Type 3 Code 13 Message – Destination Unreachable, Communication Administratively Prohibited

Bits	0			4			8			12			16			20			24			28		31
0	Type = 3						Code = 0, 1, 3, or 13							Checksum									
32	Unused (0)																						
64+	ICMP Payload – Up to 68 Bytes Offending Packet's IP Header + Options (20 to 60 Bytes) Plus First 64 Bits (8 Bytes) of Offending Packet's Data																						

Table B-8   *ICMP Destination Unreachable Error Message Header Fields and Their Security Implications*

Bit Offset	Header Field	Header Value and Description
0–7 (8 bits)	Type	This field indicates the ICMP message type being carried by the ICMP payload. The ICMP Destination Unreachable error message has a type value of 3. (See Table B-4 for a full list of message types.)
		Security Implications: When correctly specified, there really are not any security issues with this field. If this packet is spoofed, this field must be correctly formed to specify an ICMP Destination Unreachable message. One potential issue that might arise could be when the value of this field indicates an unknown ICMP type. It is plausible that a poorly written network stack could have issues under such conditions.
8–15 (8 bits)	Code	This field indicates, when appropriate for the ICMP message type, the particular *code* (or submessage type) to further specify the message being carried by the ICMP payload. The ICMP Destination Unreachable (Type 3) error message actually specifies 16 different types of submessages via 16 different codes (values of 0 through 15). The particular Destination Unreachable messages described here are: Code 0–Network Unreachable, Code 1–Host Unreachable, Code 3–Port Unreachable, and Code 13–Communication Administratively Prohibited. (See Table B-4 for a full list of submessage codes per message type.)

Table B-8   *ICMP Destination Unreachable Error Message Header Fields and Their*
Security Implications (Continued)

Bit Offset	Header Field	Header Value and Description
		Security Implications: When correctly specified, there really are not any security issues with this field. If this packet is spoofed, this field must be correctly formed to specify an ICMP Destination Unreachable message. One potential issue that might arise could be when the value of this field indicates a code value of other than 0 through 15 (which would be inappropriate for an ICMP Type 3 message). It is plausible that a poorly written network stack could have issues under such conditions.
16–31 (16 bits)	Checksum	This field contains a 16-bit one's complement of the one's complement sum of the ICMP message, starting with the ICMP Type field.
		Security Implications: When correctly specified, there really are not any security issues with this field. If this packet is spoofed, this field must be correctly formed to specify an ICMP Destination Unreachable message. If this field is computed incorrectly, the packet is supposed to be silently dropped on ingress. It is plausible that a poorly written network could have issues under such conditions.
32–63 (32 bits)	Unused	This field is unused by ICMP Time Exceeded error messages and is required to be set to 0.
		Security Implications: When correctly specified, there really are not any security issues with this field. If this packet is spoofed, this field must be correctly formed to specify an ICMP Destination Unreachable message. This field is required to be set to 0. If this field is not set to 0, as required, it is plausible that a poorly written network stack could have issues under such conditions.
64+ (variable)	ICMP Payload	This field includes a copy of the IP header (20 bytes plus IP options if they exist) and the first 64 bits of the offending packet's data. This field is intended for use by the receiver to match the ICMP error message to the appropriate process that created the original, offending packet. For higher-level protocols that use port numbers (for example, TCP and UDP), the first 64 bits also includes the source and destination ports of the offending packet. The minimum length of this field is 28 bytes (20 bytes for the offending packet IP header, plus 8 bytes [64 bits] of additional data from the offending packet).

continues

Table B-8 *ICMP Destination Unreachable Error Message Header Fields and Their Security Implications (Continued)*

Bit Offset	Header Field	Header Value and Description
		Security Implications: In the legitimate case, this field includes a copy of the IP header (20 bytes plus IP options if they exist) and the first 64 bits of the offending packet's data. Because ICMP error messages are unauthenticated, they are highly susceptible to spoofing. Ironically, even though routers and hosts must/should send these particular ICMP error messages, there are not many (if any) mechanisms on the receiver side to listen for or act upon them. Hence, ICMP Destination Unreachable error messages (with the exception of the previous Type 3, Code 4 case) are typically not spoofed with the one-packet, one-kill mentality. They are often spoofed for DoS attacks, however. ICMP error messages are also very useful for reconnaissance attacks. Numerous network mappers, security scanners, and vulnerability assessment tools rely on these particular ICMP message replies to extract information about topologies and the state of services and patches on network elements.[1]

Overall Security for ICMP Destination Unreachable Error Messages

Reconnaissance attacks: Numerous network assessment tools take advantage of various ICMP Destination Unreachable messages to accomplish their goals.

Traceroute is an excellent example of one of the first applications that was built to take advantage of the behavior and interrelationship between UDP and ICMP. UDP does not have an error-signaling mechanism of its own (in the way TCP does with its flags and sequence numbers), and so applications using UDP for transport can monitor for any ICMP error messages that may be related to their packets. Traceroute (the original, *nix version) sends UDP packets toward the destination, incrementing the TTL value and UDP destination port value by 1 each time. These packets are constructed using very high UDP destination port numbers, typically above 33,434. The intermediate routers drop the TTL expiring packets and respond with ICMP Time to Live Exceeded in Transit (Type 11, Code 0) error messages. Traceroute matches the UDP destination port number contained in the Data field of the ICMP TTL Exceeded messages to reliably match the ICMP error messages with the individual UDP probes. The very last probe that is sent has sufficient TTL to finally reach the destination IP address, and in this case, the host responds with an ICMP Destination Unreachable, Port Unreachable (Type 3, Code 3) error message. It is in this way that traceroute knows it has reached the final destination.[2] (Windows uses ICMP Echo Request messages in its tool called *tracert* instead of UDP probes as used in the traditional *nix tool called *traceroute*.)

Nmap is an excellent example of a network exploration/security auditing tool that can use UDP scans to identify active UDP-based services on target platforms.[3] Nmap sends UDP probes toward the destination (target) when the–sU option is selected. If the host responds with an ICMP Destination Unreachable, Port Unreachable (Type 3, Code 3) error message, it is certain that the port is closed. However, if the host does not respond, the UDP port is assumed to be open or filtered. (Obviously, if data is returned the port is open.)

Table B-8   *ICMP Destination Unreachable Error Message Header Fields and Their Security Implications (Continued)*

Bit Offset	Header Field	Header Value and Description
		One of the very best references covering the gamut of ICMP reconnaissance attacks is "ICMP Usage in Scanning, Version 3.0."[4]
		On the defensive side, IDS and other network monitoring tools often look at various ICMP statistics as an indication of OS fingerprinting and UDP-based port scans.[5] High numbers of ICMP Destination Unreachable, Port Unreachable (Type 3, Code 3) error messages may also be an indication of a worm that spreads through UDP, such as *MS SQL*, *Slammer*, or *Sapphire*, or a DoS attack that uses UDP packets, such as *trin00/TFN*.[6]

ICMP Destination Unreachable Header References:

1.   "Top 100 Network Security Tools."
     <http://sectools.org/>

2.   "Original Van Jacobson/Unix/LBL Traceroute."
     <http://kb.pert.geant2.net/PERTKB/VanJacobsonTraceroute>

3.   "Nmap Network Mapper."
     <http://insecure.org/nmap/>

4.   "ICMP Usage in Scanning, Version 3.0" Ofir Arkin. June 2001.
     <http://www.sys-security.com/archive/papers/ICMP_Scanning_v3.0.pdf>

5.   "Looking for Trouble: ICMP and IP Statistics to Watch."
     <http://www.securitypronews.com/2003/1028.html>

6.   "Denial of Service Attack using the trin00 and Tribe Flood Network programs."
     <http://xforce.iss.net/xforce/alerts/id/advise40>

Ethernet/802.1Q Header

As outlined in Chapter 2, a wide variety of network attacks are accomplished by manipulating and spoofing the header fields within Layer 2 Ethernet frames. While there are several different variants, the two most common are the IEEE 802.3 Ethernet Frame, and the IEEE 802.1Q VLAN Frame. This section reviews these different Ethernet frame formats, their header fields, and associated security implications.

IEEE 802.3 Ethernet Frame Header Format

Ethernet operates at Layer 2 of the OSI protocol stack. The IEEE 802.3 standard defines a basic data frame format that is required for all Ethernet implementations, plus several additional optional formats that are used to extend the protocol's basic capability.

The basic IEEE 802.3 Ethernet frame format contains seven fields, as shown in Figure B-9. The IEEE 802.3 Ethernet frame header fields shown in Figure B-9 are described in Table B-9, along with a brief description of some known modifications or spoofs to relevant header fields that have been seen used in common Ethernet attacks.

Figure B-9 *IEEE 802.3 Ethernet Frame Header*

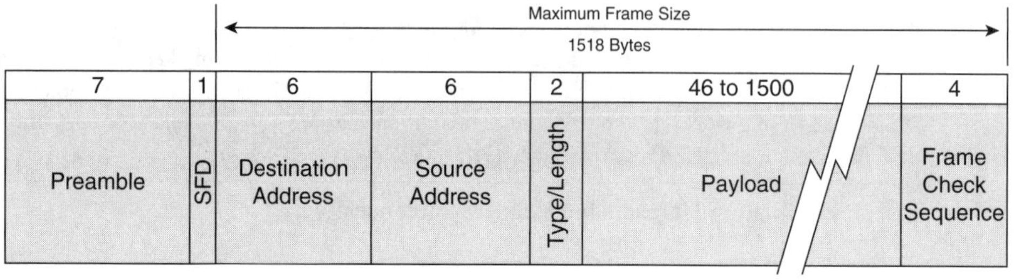

Table B-9 *IEEE 802.3 Ethernet Frame Header Fields and Their Security Implications*

Field Length	Header Field	Header Value and Description
7 bytes	Preamble (PRE)	This field provides an alternating pattern of 1s and 0s (binary 10101010), indicating to receiving stations that a frame follows, and used to synchronize receiving stations with the incoming bit stream on the wire. The specific pattern varies depending upon the specific Ethernet encoding used, which is outside the scope of this book.
		Security Implications: No security implications exist because this field is used solely for physical and data link layer bit and Ethernet frame synchronization. Of course, in switchless Ethernet topologies, a faulty or malicious host may continuously transmit bits on the wire, causing collisions and preventing other hosts from transmitting. This does not apply to the switched Ethernet topologies, which are most commonly deployed today.
1 byte	Start of Frame Delimiter (SFD)	This field provides an alternating pattern of 1s and 0s, ending with two consecutive 1 bits (binary 10101011), indicating that the next bit is the leftmost bit in the leftmost byte of the frame's destination address.
		Security Implications: Similar to the preamble above, no security implications exist because this field is used solely for physical and data link layer bit and Ethernet frame synchronization.

Table B-9   *IEEE 802.3 Ethernet Frame Header Fields and Their Security Implications (Continued)*

Field Length	Header Field	Header Value and Description
6 bytes	Destination Address (DA)	This field identifies the Media Access Control (MAC) address of the station(s) that should receive the Ethernet frame. The leftmost bit in the DA field indicates whether the address is an individual address (indicated by a 0) or a group address (indicated by a 1). The second bit from the left indicates whether the DA is globally administered (indicated by a 0) or locally administered (indicated by a 1). The remaining 46 bits are a uniquely assigned value that identifies a single station (unicast), a defined group of stations (multicast), or all stations on the network (broadcast).
		Security Implications: In the legitimate case, the IP protocol dynamically resolves IP address to MAC address bindings, and vice versa, using ARP and RARP (Reverse ARP). In the malicious case, an attacker may craft the destination address within an Ethernet frame in an attempt to launch ARP spoofing, switch spoofing, double 802.1Q encapsulation, private VLAN, and Spanning Tree Protocol (STP) attacks, as outlined in Chapter 2.
6 bytes	Source Address (SA)	This field identifies the MAC address of the sending station. The SA must always be an individual (unicast) address, and the leftmost bit in the SA field is always 0.
		Security Implications: In the legitimate case, the sending host inserts its MAC address in this field. In the malicious case, an attacker may craft the MAC source address within an Ethernet frame in an attempt to launch CAM table overflow and ARP spoofing attacks, as outlined in Chapter 2. Note that ARP spoofing affects both source and destination Ethernet addresses. The attacker first advertises itself as an IP host using a spoofed gratuitous ARP, at which point hosts may begin transmitting packets destined to the spoofed IP host to the attacker's Ethernet address. For more information on ARP spoofing attacks, refer to Chapter 2.
2 bytes	Type/Length	This field indicates either the number of data bytes contained in the Data field of the frame (length) or the frame type ID if the frame is assembled using an optional format (Ethernet II frame). Specifically, if the Type/Length field value is less than or equal to 1500 bytes (0x05DC), the frame is considered an IEEE 802.3 frame.

continues

Table B-9 *IEEE 802.3 Ethernet Frame Header Fields and Their Security Implications (Continued)*

Field Length	Header Field	Header Value and Description
		If the Type/Length field value is greater than 1536 bytes (0x0600), it is considered an Ethernet II frame. A value of 0x0800, for example, represents an Ethernet II encapsulated TCP/IP packet. Similarly, a value of 1500 (0x05DC) represents an IEEE 802.3 frame with a total frame length of 1518 bytes, including Destination Address, Source Address, Type/Length, and FCS header fields. The IEEE 802.2 LLC/SNAP header located within the Data field is outside the scope of this book.
		Security Implications: DoS attacks may use a value that does not represent the true frame length or Ethernet II subprotocol identifier. A poorly written network stack may improperly process these packets, resulting in a DoS or buffer overflow condition. Note, many Ethernet vendors have also added support for jumbo Ethernet frames to increase overall networked application throughput and to accommodate VLAN and MPLS header information.[1] Jumbo frames are frames that are bigger than the standard IEEE 802.3 Ethernet frame size of 1518 bytes. Because jumbo frames are not part of the IEEE standard, the definition of jumbo frame size is vendor-dependent.
46 to 1500 bytes	Data/Payload	This field carries the payload of the Ethernet frame. The Data field can be anywhere from 46 to 1500 bytes in size.
		Security Implications: In the legitimate case, if the frame does not have 46 bytes' worth of information to convey, the station pads the end of this field with 1s. Short frames (runts) are typically an indication of collisions (on old switchless topologies). In the malicious case, runts could be injected on the network artificially.
4 bytes	Frame Check Sequence (FCS)	This field contains a 32-bit cyclic redundancy check (CRC) value. The FCS is generated over the DA, SA, Type/Length, and Data fields, and excludes the Preamble and SFD.
		Security Implications: The FCS is created by the source MAC and is recalculated by receiving MACs to check for damaged frames. Frames with invalid checksums are discarded silently, and hence no useful attacks seem plausible that manipulate or spoof this header field.

1. "Jumbo/Giant Frame Support on Catalyst Switches Configuration Example." (Doc. ID: 24048.) Cisco Documentation.
http://www.cisco.com/warp/public/473/148.html.

IEEE 802.1Q VLAN Header Format

The IEEE 802.1Q VLAN header extends the IEEE 802.3 Ethernet protocol's basic capability (see the Cisco Tech Note "Inter-Switch Link and IEEE 802.1Q Frame Format," referenced in the "Further Reading" section). The IEEE 802.1Q VLAN header format consists of the original IEEE 802.3 Ethernet frame header, plus two additional 2-byte fields inserted as shown in Figure B-10. (A reference for IEEE 802.1Q is included in the "Further Reading" section.) The IEEE 802.1Q VLAN header fields shown in Figure B-10 are listed and described in Table B-10, along with a brief description of some known modifications or spoofs to relevant header fields that have been seen used in common VLAN attacks.

Figure B-10   *IEEE 802.1Q VLAN Frame Header*

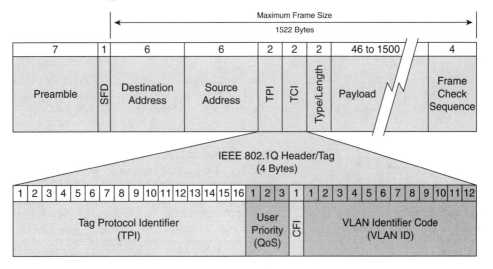

Table B-10   *IEEE 802.1Q VLAN Frame Header Fields and Their Security Implications*

Field Length	Header Field	Header Value and Description
7 bytes	Preamble (PRE)	This field provides an alternating pattern of 1s and 0s (binary 10101010), indicating to receiving stations that a frame follows, and used to synchronize receiving stations with the incoming bit stream on the wire. The specific pattern varies depending upon the specific Ethernet encoding used, which is outside the scope of this book.

continues

Table B-10 *IEEE 802.1Q VLAN Frame Header Fields and Their Security Implications (Continued)*

Field Length	Header Field	Header Value and Description
		Security Implications: No security implications exist because this field is used solely for physical and data link layer bit and Ethernet frame synchronization. Of course, in switchless Ethernet topologies, a faulty or malicious host may continuously transmit bits on the wire, causing collisions and preventing other hosts from transmitting. This does not apply to the switched Ethernet topologies, which are most commonly deployed today.
1 byte	Start of Frame Delimiter (SFD)	This field provides an alternating pattern of 1s and 0s, ending with two consecutive 1 bits (binary 10101011), indicating that the next bit is the leftmost bit in the leftmost byte of the frame's destination address.
		Security Implications: Similar to the Preamble above, no security implications exist because this field is used solely for physical and data link layer bit and Ethernet frame synchronization.
6 bytes	Destination Address (DA)	This field identifies the MAC address of the station(s) that should receive the Ethernet frame. The leftmost bit in the DA field indicates whether the address is an individual address (indicated by a 0) or a group address (indicated by a 1). The second bit from the left indicates whether the DA is globally administered (indicated by a 0) or locally administered (indicated by a 1). The remaining 46 bits are a uniquely assigned value that identifies a single station (unicast), a defined group of stations (multicast), or all stations on the network (broadcast).
		Security Implications: In the legitimate case, the IP protocol dynamically resolves IP address to MAC address bindings, and vice versa, using ARP and RARP. In the malicious case, an attacker may craft the destination address within an Ethernet frame in an attempt to launch ARP spoofing, switch spoofing, double 802.1Q encapsulation, private VLAN, and STP attacks, as outlined in Chapter 2.
6 bytes	Source Address (SA)	This field identifies the MAC address of the sending station. The SA must always be an individual (unicast) address, and the leftmost bit in the SA field is always 0.

Table B-10   *IEEE 802.1Q VLAN Frame Header Fields and Their Security Implications (Continued)*

Field Length	Header Field	Header Value and Description
		Security Implications: In the legitimate case, the sending host inserts its MAC address in this field. In the malicious case, an attacker may craft the MAC source address within an Ethernet frame in an attempt to launch CAM table overflow and ARP spoofing attacks, as outlined in Chapter 2. Note that ARP spoofing affects both source and destination Ethernet addresses. The attacker first advertises itself as an IP host using a point hosts may begin transmitting packets destined to the spoofed IP host to the attacker's Ethernet address. For more information on ARP spoofing attacks, refer to Chapter 2.
2 bytes	Tag Protocol Identifier (TPI)	The TPI field indicates that the Ethernet frame is an IEEE 802.1Q VLAN tagged frame. IEEE 802.1Q VLAN tagged frames have a TPI value of 0x8100.
		Security Implications: It is possible that if this field indicates a value that does not represent the 802.1Q VLAN tag, a poorly written network stack may improperly process such packets, resulting in a DoS or buffer overflow condition.
2 bytes	Tag Control Information (TCI)	The TCI field consists of three subfields: • **User Priority (3 bits):** Defines user priority, giving eight (2^3) priority levels for the frame as specified by the IEEE 802.1P standard. • **Canonical Format Identifier (1 bit):** Provides compatibility between Ethernet and Token Ring networks. If the value of this field is 1, the MAC address is in noncanonical format. If the value is 0, the MAC address is in canonical format. A value of 0 is used within Ethernet-only networks. • **VLAN ID Code (12 bits):** Identifies the VLAN to which the frame belongs. This field allows for up to 4096 possible VIDs (2^{12}). A value of 0 is used to identify priority frames and value 4095 (FFF) is reserved, so the maximum possible VLAN configurations are 4094.
		Security Implications: An attacker may craft the VLAN ID within an 802.1Q VLAN tagged Ethernet frame in an attempt to launch switch spoofing and double 802.1Q encapsulation attacks, as outlined in Chapter 2.

continues

Table B-10 *IEEE 802.1Q VLAN Frame Header Fields and Their Security Implications (Continued)*

Field Length	Header Field	Header Value and Description
2 bytes	Type/Length	This field indicates either the number of data bytes that are contained in the Data field of the frame (length) or the frame type ID if the frame is assembled using an optional format (Ethernet II frame). Specifically, if the Type/Length field value is less than or equal to 1500 bytes (0x05DC), the frame is considered an IEEE 802.3 frame. If the Type/Length field value is greater than 1536 bytes (0x0600), it is considered an Ethernet II frame. A value of 0x0800, for example, represents an Ethernet II encapsulated TCP/IP packet. Similarly, a value of 1500 (0x05DC) represents an IEEE 802.3 frame with a total frame length of 1518 bytes, including Destination Address, Source Address, Type/Length, and FCS header fields. The IEEE 802.2 LLC/SNAP header located within the Data field is outside the scope of this book.
	Security Implications: DoS attacks may use a value that does not represent the true frame length or Ethernet II subprotocol identifier. A poorly written network stack may improperly process these packets, resulting in a DoS or buffer overflow condition. Note, many Ethernet vendors have also added support for jumbo Ethernet frames to increase overall networked application throughput and to accommodate VLAN and MPLS header information.[1] Jumbo frames are frames that are bigger than the standard IEEE 802.3 Ethernet frame size of 1518 bytes. Because jumbo frames are not part of the IEEE standard, the definition of jumbo frame size is vendor-dependent.	
46 to 1500 bytes	Data/Payload	This field carries the payload of the Ethernet frame. The data field can be anywhere from 46 to 1500 bytes in size.
	Security Implications: In the legitimate case, if the frame does not have 46 bytes' worth of information to convey, the station pads the end of this field with 1s. Short frames (runts) are typically an indication of collisions (on old switchless topologies). In the malicious case, runts could be injected on the network artificially.	
4 bytes	Frame Check Sequence (FCS)	This field contains a 32-bit cyclic redundancy check (CRC) value. The FCS is generated over the DA, SA, Type/Length, and Data fields, and excludes the Preamble and SFD.
	Security Implications: The FCS is created by the source MAC and is recalculated by receiving MACs to check for damaged frames. Frames with invalid checksums are discarded silently, and hence no useful attacks seem plausible that manipulate or spoof this header field.	

1.   "Jumbo/Giant Frame Support on Catalyst Switches Configuration Example." (Doc. ID: 24048.) Cisco Documentation.
      http://www.cisco.com/warp/public/473/148.html.

MPLS Protocol Header

MPLS is deployed for a variety of applications, including Layer 3 IP VPNs, Layer 2 VPNs, traffic engineering, and fast network convergence (reroute). Most current MPLS deployments are intradomain, where MPLS labeled packets are not exchanged between external or untrusted peers. With the growth of interdomain MPLS VPNs and Carrier Supporting Carrier (CsC) services, MPLS labeled packets are increasingly being exchanged at interprovider boundaries. This section reviews the MPLS label header formats, the label fields, and associated security implications.

RFC 3032 and RFC 4182 define the MPLS label stack encoding (see the "Further Reading" section for links to these RFCs). For IP-based MPLS services, the MPLS header appears after the Layer 2 headers (for example, Ethernet) but before the IP packet, as shown in Figure B-11. The MPLS header is represented by a label stack that consists of a sequence of label stack entries. Each label stack entry is 4 bytes in length. The depth of the label stack often varies between MPLS networks and is dependent upon the MPLS services deployed (for example, MPLS VPNs, MPLS TE/FRR, and AToM). The MPLS label format contains four fields, as illustrated in Figure B-12. Each of these fields is listed and described in Table B-11, along with a brief description of applicable security considerations.

Figure B-11 *MPLS Encapsulation Example of an IP Packet Transported over an Ethernet Interface*

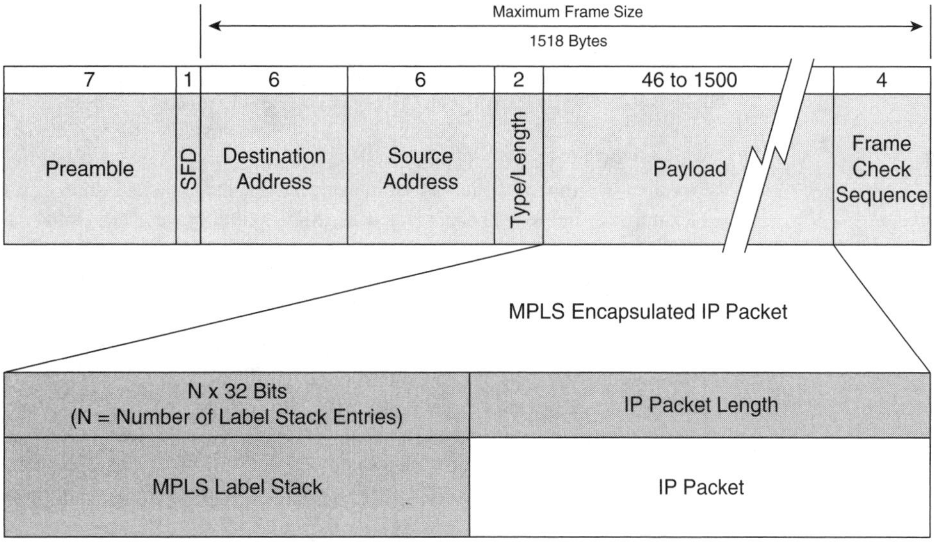

Figure B-12 *MPLS Label Stack Encoding*

Bits	0			4			8			12			16			20			24			28		31
0	Label															EXP		S		TTL				

Table B-11 *MPLS Label Fields and Security Considerations*

Bit Offset	Header Field	Header Value and Description
0–19 (20 bits)	Label	This field carries the actual value of the MPLS label, which may be assigned by a variety of MPLS label distribution protocols, including but not limited to LDP, BGP, and M-BGP.[1,2,3]
		Security Implications: Label distribution protocols allocate labels per IP prefix or Forwarding Equivalence Class (FEC). An FEC is used by MPLS routers to determine how packets are mapped to MPLS label switched paths (LSP). Received MPLS packets should also always be discarded on interfaces where no MPLS application is enabled. It is plausible that a poorly written network stack may improperly process MPLS packets on an interface not enabled for MPLS. Such a condition would facilitate MPLS label spoofing, enabling attacks against downstream devices.
		MPLS provides for the discarding of any labeled packet having an invalid label. This is analogous to dropping IPv4 packets having no corresponding route (or next hop) in the local IP routing table. A label is considered valid if the label was advertised by the MPLS router itself in accordance with label distribution protocols. Conversely, labels are not verified against an MPLS source (for example, using RPF checking), and the MPLS label space is not global (network wide). Labels are local to, and assigned by, each individual transit MPLS router in support of the label-switching paradigm. An MPLS router considers a label invalid if it was not assigned by itself from its own label pool.
		Labels are allocated from a global system pool within an MPLS router and not per interface (the exception being cell mode MPLS, which is not widely deployed). A global label pool within the MPLS router makes label spoofing less difficult because the label of received MPLS packets is not verified against the ingress router interface or MPLS source. Hence, as long as the ingress router interface is enabled for MPLS and the label received is valid within the local MPLS router's global label pool, the MPLS packet is forwarded downstream based on the received label's associated LSP. Given that interface IP ACLs do not apply to MPLS label encapsulated packets, label spoofing may allow unauthorized access and reachability to downstream network devices and to secure VPNs. For this reason, MPLS is not widely deployed using Inter-AS VPN options (b) and (c) between untrusted peers, as outlined in Chapter 2. If Inter-AS

Table B-11   *MPLS Label Fields and Security Considerations (Continued)*

Bit Offset	Header Field	Header Value and Description
		VPN is configured using options (b) and (c), then all valid labels (spoofed or not) will be accepted. Hence, there must be a trust relationship between peers doing Inter-AS VPN options (b) and (c). Conversely, the CsC configuration maintains label bindings per VRF (or VPN). This enables label spoofing avoidance mechanisms that verify that the MPLS labels of packets received are, in fact, associated with the assigned VRF. If not, the MPLS labeled packets are discarded. Hence, within a CsC configuration, the inherent label spoofing avoidance mechanisms ensure that routing and address separation between VPNs is maintained.
20–22 (3 bits)	Experimental Use (EXP)	This field is reserved for experimental use. However, it is widely used for QoS classification and drop precedence of MPLS packets. The value within this field may range from 0 through 7.
	Security Implications: When IP packets are encapsulated within MPLS, Cisco IOS will copy the (3-bit) IP precedence value into the MPLS EXP of each imposed label entry by default. Attackers may attempt to exploit this default behavior by marking malicious IP traffic with high priority—for example, IP precedence values 5–7. In this way, such malicious traffic may receive high-priority treatment (EXP 5–7) within the MPLS network. Further, using this technique, attacks may be launched against high-priority traffic classes, which may trigger a DoS condition or adversely impact network SLAs. To change this default behavior, an interface QoS policy must be applied using Cisco MQC.	
23 (1 bit)	Bottom of Stack (S)	This field (or bit) indicates whether the associated label entry is the bottom of the label stack. A value of 1 represents the last label stack entry. Conversely, all other label stack entries have a value within this field of 0. Per RFC 3032, the top of the label stack appears earliest in the packet, and the bottom appears latest. The encapsulated IP packet immediately follows the bottom label stack entry, which has the S bit set to 1.
	Security Implications: No useful attacks seem plausible that manipulate or spoof this header field. It is plausible that a poorly written network stack may improperly process MPLS packets with an unexpected *S* bit. For example, setting a value of 0 when the label entry is the bottom label of the label stack or a value of 1 when the label entry is not the bottom of the label stack should cause the router to silently discard such packets. A poorly written network stack may incur a buffer overflow or DoS condition, making it susceptible to such an attack.	

continues

Table B-11   *MPLS Label Fields and Security Considerations (Continued)*

Bit Offset	Header Field	Header Value and Description
24–31 (8 bits)	Time to Live (TTL)	This field carries the MPLS packet's TTL value. Similar to the IP TTL, the MPLS TTL specifies the maximum number of links (hops) that the MPLS packet may be forwarded over. This counter is decremented by each MPLS router processing the packet while forwarding it toward its destination. When the TTL value reaches 0, the MPLS packet is discarded. This prevents MPLS packets from looping endlessly, as would otherwise occur during accidental forwarding loops, for example. This 8-bit value can range anywhere from 255 to 0. The processing of this field is further described in RFC 3443.[4]
	Security Implications: When IP packets are encapsulated within MPLS, Cisco IOS will copy the (8-bit) IP TTL value into the MPLS TTL of each imposed label entry by default. This makes MPLS routers visible via IP traceroute, and enables IP packets to TTL expire within the MPLS network. Attackers may attempt to exploit this default behavior for reconnaissance purposes or to launch transit DoS attacks or ICMP reflection attacks,[5] as outlined in Chapter 2. To change the default behavior and mitigate the risk of such attacks, IP to MPLS TTL propagation may be disabled using the IOS **no mpls ip propagate-ttl forwarded** CLI command, as described in Chapter 7.		

1. Andersson, L., P. Doolan, N. Feldman, A. Fredette, and B. Thomas. *LDP Specification*. RFC 3036. IETF, Jan. 2001.
    http://www.ietf.org/rfc/rfc3036.txt.

2. Rekhter, Y., and E. Rosen. *Carrying Label Information in BGP-4*. RFC 3107. IETF, May 2001.
    http://www.ietf.org/rfc/rfc3107.txt.

3. Rosen, E., and Y. Rekhter. *BGP/MPLS IP Virtual Private Networks (VPNs)*. RFC 4364. IETF, Feb. 2006.
    http://www.ietf.org/rfc/rfc4364.txt.

4. Agarwal, P., and B. Akyol. *Time To Live Processing in MPLS Networks*. RFC 3443. IETF, Jan. 2003.
    http://www.ietf.org/rfc/rfc3443.txt.

5. Bonica, R., D. Gan, D. Tappan, and C. Pignataro. *ICMP Extensions for Multiprotocol Label Switching*. RFC 4950. IETF, Aug. 2007.
    http://www.rfc-editor.org/rfc/rfc4950.txt.

Further Reading

Rosen, E., D. Tappan, G. Fedorkow, Y. Rekhter, D. Farinacci, T. Li, and A. Conta. *MPLS Label Stack Encoding*. RFC 3032. IETF, Jan. 2001. http://www.ietf.org/rfc/rfc3032.txt.

Rosen, E. *Removing a Restriction on the Use of MPLS Explicit NULL*. RFC 4182. IETF, Sept. 2005. http://www.ietf.org/rfc/rfc4182.txt.

Stevens, W. R. *TCP/IP Illustrated, Volume 1*. Addison-Wesley Professional, 1993. ISBN: 0-20163-346-9.

"Ethernet Technologies." *Internetworking Technology Handbook*. Cisco Documentation. http://www.cisco.com/univercd/cc/td/doc/cisintwk/ito_doc/ethernet.htm.

IEEE 802.3 LAN/MAN CSMA/CD Access Method. IEEE 802.3-2005/COR 1-2006. IEEE, 2005. http://standards.ieee.org/getieee802/802.3.html.

IEEE 802.1Q-2003, Virtual Bridged Local Area Networks. IEEE, 2003. http://standards.ieee.org/getieee802/download/802.1Q-2005.pdf.

"Inter-Switch Link and IEEE 802.1Q Frame Format." (Doc. ID: 17056.) Cisco Tech Note. http://www.cisco.com/en/US/tech/tk389/tk689/technologies_tech_note09186a0080094665.shtml.

Cisco IOS to IOS XR Security Transition

Cisco IOS has been the mainstay for all Cisco routers for more than 20 years. This monolithic operating system, which disassociates the software architecture from hardware, has proven resilient to massive upgrades in both hardware and software technologies over the years. The term monolithic means that Cisco IOS runs as a single image and all processes share the same memory space, and that it uses a non-preemptive scheduler. In support of carrier-class IP networks, including continuous system operation and unprecedented service flexibility, the Cisco IOS XR operating system was pioneered for the Cisco CRS-1 and 12000 series platforms. Cisco IOS XR uses a real-time microkernel operating system (QNX) at its core, and incorporates modularity and memory protection between processes, lightweight threads, preemptive scheduling, and the ability to independently restart failed processes to maximize network availability.

Cisco IOS XR represents a new direction and thus provides an opportunity to diverge from legacy requirements and protocols of Cisco IOS. Although some attempt was made to maintain a certain level of familiarity between the command sets, there are many differences between these two distinct software systems. This can make converting from one system to the other challenging. The purpose of this appendix is to provide a brief cross-reference between the security-related commands and operations that you may be familiar with in Cisco IOS and their counterparts in Cisco IOS XR. In many cases, similar commands and functions exist, but there are some instances where comparable configurations are not required. Note that because Cisco IOS XR is applicable only to Cisco CRS-1 and 12000 series routers, it only makes sense to compare it with Cisco IOS version 12.0S, which is the service provider IOS version used today on Cisco 12000 series routers. For the purposes of this appendix, the Cisco IOS version assumed is 12.0(32)S, and the Cisco IOS XR version assumed is IOS XR 3.5. Both are the latest available at the time of this writing. Note that IOS XR also offers a wide variety of security enhancements, including but not limited to authenticated software installation, image validation, and code signing. These capabilities are outside the scope of this book. For further information on these topics, refer to the IOS XR configuration guides referenced in the "Further Reading" section.

The four IP traffic planes presented throughout this book are used to facilitate this cross-referencing task. As such, the following command categories are reviewed:

- Data plane security commands: Table C-1
- Control plane security commands: Table C-2
- Management plane security commands: Table C-3
- Services plane security commands: Table C-4

Each table includes the Cisco IOS command, its Cisco IOS XR counterpart, if any, and a short example of how each command is used.

Data Plane Security Commands

Data plane-specific commands refer to those commands that configure direct security features, such as interface access lists, Unicast RPF, and other features. Table C-1 lists Cisco IOS commands and their Cisco IOS XR counterparts, if any, along with a short example of how each command is used.

Table C-1 *Data Plane Security Commands*

IOS 12.0S	IOS XR
Interface Access Control Lists	
Standard IPv4 Access List	—

Standard access list: Filter on IPv4 destination IP addresses.
 	
`(config)# access-list 101 permit 192.168.0.0 0.0.0.255 eq 80`
`(config)# interface POS0/4`
`(config-if)# ip access-group 1 in`
	Only named IPv4 access lists exist in IOS XR. Refer to Named IPv4 Access List below.

Extended IPv4 Access List	—

Extended access list: Filters on IPv4 source/ destination IP addresses, Layer 4 protocol, ports, and other parameters.
 	
`(config)# access-list 101 permit tcp any 192.168.0.0 0.0.0.255 eq 80`
`(config)# interface POS0/4`
`(config-if)# ip access-group 101 in`
	Only named IPv4 access lists exist in IOS XR. Refer to Named IPv4 Access List below.

Table C-1   *Data Plane Security Commands (Continued)*

IOS 12.0S	IOS XR
Named IPv4 Access List	Named IPv4 Access List

Named access list: Defined as standard or extended (as above) using a name instead of a number.
 	
`(config)# ip access-list extended GoodTraffic`
`(config-ext-nacl)# permit tcp any host 192.168.0.10 eq 80`
 	
Caveats: Named ACLs cannot be used for distributed functions such as Receive ACLs or Control Plane Policing until 12.0(33)S.
	IOS XR named access lists include support for standard and extended ACL types. Numbers may be used for names, as they are simply stored as strings.
	
	`(config)# ipv4 access-list cisco`
	`(config-ipv4-acl)# 10 deny 192.168.34.0 0.0.0.255`
	`(config-ipv4-acl)# 20 permit 172.16.34.0 0.0.0.255`
	`(config)# interface POS0/4/0/0`
	`(config-if)# ipv4 access-group cisco in`
	
	IOS XR ACLs have sequence numbers, can be reordered in place, and can be dynamically modified in place.
	
	Additional commands are available for IOS XR ACLs.
	
	Global commands:
	
	ipv4 access-list log-update rate {*rate*}
	ipv4 access-list log-update threshold {*update-number*}
	ipv4 access-list maximum ace threshold {*ace-number*}
	ipv4 access-list maximum acl threshold {*acl-number*}
	
	Exec command:
	
	resequence access-list ipv4 {*name*} {*base*} {*increment*}

Unicast Reverse Path Forwarding (uRPF)	
uRPFv1 (Strict Mode)	uRPFv1 (Strict Mode)

Strict mode (v1): Apply uRPF "strict" check to IP source addresses.
 	
ip verify unicast source reachable-via rx {*acl*} [**allow-default**] [**allow-self-ping**]
 	
`(config)# interface POS0/4`
`(config-if)# ip verify unicast source reachable-via rx 111 allow-self-ping`
	Strict mode (v1): Apply uRPF "strict" check to IP source addresses.
	
	ipv4 verify unicast source reachable-via rx [**allow-default**] [**allow-self-ping**]
	
	`(config)# interface POS0/0/0/0`
	`(config-if)# ipv4 verify unicast source reachable-via rx allow-self-ping`

continues

Table C-1 *Data Plane Security Commands (Continued)*

IOS 12.0S	IOS XR
Caveat: uRPF ACL bypass is supported only on Engine 0 (CPU-based) line cards. It is not available on hardware-based line cards such as the Engine 3 and Engine 5 ASIC-based line cards.	Caveat: uRPF ACL bypass is not available in IOS XR.
uRPFv2 (Loose Mode)	uRPFv2 (Loose Mode)
Loose mode (v2): Apply uRPF "loose" check to IP source addresses. **ip verify unicast source reachable-via any** {*acl*} [**allow-default**][**allow-self-ping**] (config)# **interface POS0/4** (config-if)# **ip verify unicast source reachable-via any**	Loose mode (v2): Apply uRPF "loose" check to IP source addresses. **ipv4 verify unicast source reachable-via any** [**allow-default**] [**allow-self-ping**] (config)# **interface POS0/0/0/0** (config-if)# **ipv4 verify unicast source reachable-via any**
uRPFv3 (VRF Mode)	—
VRF mode (v3): Compare IP source addresses to IP VRF table (vs. global routing table). Note, this is an IPv4 VRF, not an MPLS VPN–based VRF. **ip verify unicast vrf** {*vrf-name*} [**permit** | **deny**] (config)# **interface POS0/4** (config-if)# **ip verify unicast vrf DropSrc deny** Caveat: uRPFv3 is supported only on Engine 0 (CPU-based) line cards. It is not available on hardware-based line cards such as Engine 3 and Engine 5 ASIC-based line cards.	uRPFv3 is not available in IOS XR at the time of this writing.
IP Options	
IP Options [ignore | drop]	—
ip options ignore: When this mode is configured, IP option headers within transit IPv4 packets are ignored. Such packets are forwarded downstream but the IOS router does not consider the IP option header during packet processing. This prevents IP options such as Router Alert from adversely affecting the 12000 RP. Receive-path IPv4 packets with option headers are processed normally (not ignored).	No directly comparable command exists in IOS XR. IOS XR employs hardware rate limiters supported by the Local Packet Transport Services (LPTS) functionality to mitigate the impact of IPv4 packets with IP option headers. LPTS is described in more detail in several of the references provided in the "Further Reading" section.

Table C-1   *Data Plane Security Commands (Continued)*

IOS 12.0S	IOS XR
(config)# **ip options ignore** **ip options drop**: When this mode is configured, both transit and receive-path IPv4 packets with options are punted to the LC CPU and dropped immediately. (config)# **ip options drop**	
IP Source-Route Processing	
IP Source-Route Command	IP Source-Route Command
no ip source-route: Disable the ability to process source-route header options (both strict and loose) within IP datagrams. By default, IOS 12.0S processes all IP datagrams that contain the source-route header option. These packets are punted, and then processed by the 12000 distributed line card CPU. (config)# **no ip source-route**	**no ipv4 source-route**: Disable the ability to process source-routing header options (both strict and loose) within IPv4 datagrams. By default, IOS XR discards (does not process) all IPv4 datagrams that contain the source-route header option. Thus, this command is not required, unless the default behavior has been changed. (config)# **no ipv4 source-route**
IP Directed Broadcast	
IP Directed Broadcast Command	IP Directed Broadcast Command
no ip directed-broadcast: Drop directed broadcasts destined for the subnet to which that interface is attached. (Dropped by default). config-if)# **no ip directed-broadcast**	**no ipv4 directed-broadcast**: Drop directed broadcasts destined for the subnet to which that interface is attached. (Dropped by default). config-if)# **no ipv4 directed-broadcast**
Edge Recoloring	
Edge Recoloring	Edge Recoloring
Edge recoloring: Change the precedence or DSCP field of the IPv4 packet header as it enters the network.	Edge recoloring: Change the precedence or DSCP field of the IPv4 packet header as it enters the network.

continues

Table C-1   *Data Plane Security Commands (Continued)*

IOS 12.0S	IOS XR

`(config)# access-list 160 permit ip any`
`any precedence priority`
`(config)# access-list 160 permit ip any`
`any precedence immediate`
`(config)# access-list 160 permit ip any`
`any precedence flash`
`(config)# access-list 160 permit ip any`
`any precedence flash-override`
`(config)# access-list 160 permit ip any`
`any precedence critical`
`(config)# access-list 160 permit ip any`
`any precedence internet`
`(config)# access-list 160 permit ip any`
`any precedence network`
 	
`(config)# class-map Colors`
`(config-cmap)# match access-group 160`
 	
`(config)# policy-map ReColor`
`(config-pmap)# class Colors`
`(config-pmap)# set ip precedence routine`
 	
`(config)# interface POS0/4`
`(config-if)# service-policy input`
`ReColor`
 	
Note: The use of ACLs and the **class-map** Colors in the preceding example, rather than **class-default**, is solely to provide additional instrumentation through the use of the **show access-list** command in order to track the number of packets with various IP precedence values ingressing the network. This may be useful as an indication of a pending or ongoing attack.
	`(config)# ipv4 access-list Precedence`
	`(config-ipv4-acl)# 10 permit ipv4 any`
	`any precedence priority`
	`(config-ipv4-acl)# 20 permit ipv4 any`
	`any precedence immediate`
	`(config-ipv4-acl)# 30 permit ipv4 any`
	`any precedence flash`
	`(config-ipv4-acl)# 40 permit ipv4 any`
	`any precedence flash-override`
	`(config-ipv4-acl)# 50 permit ipv4 any`
	`any precedence critical`
	`(config-ipv4-acl)# 60 permit ipv4 any`
	`any precedence internet`
	`(config-ipv4-acl)# 70 permit ipv4 any`
	`any precedence network`
	
	`(config)# class-map Colors`
	`(config-cmap)# match access-group`
	`Precedence`
	
	`(config)# policy-map ReColor`
	`(config-pmap)# class Colors`
	`(config-pmap)# set ip precedence routine`
	
	`(config)# interface POS0/4/0/0`
	`(config-if)# service-policy input`
	`ReColor`
	
	IOS XR also uses MQC to configure QoS policies, including queuing and policing.

Control Plane Security Commands

Control plane–specific commands refer to those commands that configure, directly or indirectly, security features within control plane functions such as routing protocols, route filtering mechanisms, and other control plane mechanisms. Table C-2 lists Cisco IOS commands and their Cisco IOS XR counterparts, if any, along with a short example of how each command is used.

Table C-2 *Control Plane Security Commands*

IOS 12.0S	IOS XR
Receive Path Access Control List (rACL)	
Receive Path Access List (rACL)	—

rACL: Filter CEF receive adjacency packets on the LC CPU and PRP.
 	
ip receive access-list {*number*}
 	
`(config)# access-list 111 deny ip any any fragments`
`(config)# access-list 111 permit host 192.168.1.1 any eq 22`
`(config)# access-list 111 permit host 192.168.1.1 any established`
`(config)# access-list 111 permit icmp any any echo-reply`
`…<etc.>…`
`(config)# ip receive access-list 111`
	No directly comparable configuration command exists in IOS XR. rACLs are not available in IOS XR, because it uses Local Packet Transport Services (LPTS) to automatically manage and rate-limit (police) all receive-adjacency traffic that will be handled by any CPU on the platform.
	
	LPTS and related policers are not user-configurable at the time of this writing.

Control Plane Policing (CoPP)	
Distributed Mode CoPP (dCoPP)	Dynamic Control Plane Protection (DCoPP)

dCoPP: Filter punted packets on the Cisco 12000 GSR distributed line card CPU.
 	
`(config)# access-list 101 permit ip any any`
 	
`(config)# class-map match-any All_IP`
`(config-cmap)# match access-group 101`
 	
`(config)# policy-map CoPP`
`(config-pmap)# class All_IP`
`(config-pmap-c)# police 10000 1500 1500 conform transmit exceed drop`
 	
`(config)# control-plane slot 5`
`(config-cp-slot)# service-policy input CoPP`
 	
Caveats: Only packets punted to the 12000 PRP are subject to the dCoPP policy, even though the dCoPP policy is applied to a line card slot. This function is intended to protect the PRP from resource-based attacks. Further, the dCoPP policy applies only to packets ingressing the configured slot.
	The IOS XR function DCoPP provides a function similar to IOS dCoPP. IOS XR DCoPP is an *automatic* feature and requires no user configuration.
	
	IOS XR DCoPP relies on LPTS and related policers to automatically manage and rate-limit (police) all receive-adjacency traffic and exceptions packets that will be handled by any CPU (line card or router processor) on the platform. LPTS and related policers work on a per-line card basis, not at an aggregate system level, and are not user-configurable at the time of this writing.
	
	DCoPP is not configurable in IOS XR at the time of this writing. DCoPP is described in more detail in several of the references provided in the "Further Reading" section.

continues

Table C-2 *Control Plane Security Commands (Continued)*

IOS 12.0S	IOS XR
Aggregate Mode CoPP (aCoPP)	—

aCoPP: Filters on the PRP.
 	
`(config)# access-list 101 permit ip any any`
 	
`(config)# class-map match-any All_IP`
`(config-cmap)# match access-group 101`
 	
`(config)# policy-map CoPP`
`(config-pmap)# class All_IP`
`(config-pmap-c)# police 10000 1500 1500 conform transmit exceed drop`
 	
`(config)# control-plane`
`(config-cp)# service-policy input CoPP`
 	
Caveats: Only packets punted to the 12000 PRP are subject to aCoPP policies.
	No directly comparable command exists in IOS XR. The IOS XR function DCoPP provides a function similar to IOS dCoPP, but the IOS XR DCoPP policers work on a per-line card basis, not at an aggregate system level, and are not user-configurable at the time of this writing.

Selective Packet Discard (SPD)	
Selective Packet Discard (SPD)	—

SPD: Manage the IOS process level input queues on the Route Processor (RP).
 	
Global configuration commands:
 	
`(config)# ip spd enable`
`(config)# ip spd queue max-threshold 100`
`(config)# ip spd queue min-threshold 90`
`(config)# ip headroom 2000`
`(config)# ip extended-headroom 20`
`(config)# ip spd mode aggressive`
 	
Interface configuration commands:
 	
`(config)# interface POS0/4`
`(config-if)# hold-queue <xxx> in`
	No directly comparable commands exist in IOS XR. The IOS XR feature LPTS supersedes the IOS feature SPD. Hence, SPD is not required in IOS XR.
	
	LPTS is an automatic service and requires no configuration on the part of the user.

BGP Security-Related Commands	
BGP Global Commands	—
ip bgp-community new-format: Converts BGP communities. `(config)# ip bgp-community new-format`	No comparable command exists in IOS XR, nor is one required. Community lists, which support old-style numbering, are deprecated. Refer instead to the IOS XR **community-set** command.

Table C-2   *Control Plane Security Commands (Continued)*

IOS 12.0S	IOS XR
Router BGP Commands	Router Policy Language (RPL) as path length Command
bgp maxas-limit {*number*}: Configure a maximum limit for the number of AS-PATH segments that are permitted within inbound routes. If a route is received with an AS-PATH segment that exceeds the configured limit, the BGP routing process discards the route. `(config)# `**`router bgp 65001`** `(config-router)# `**`address-family ipv4`** `(config-router-af)# `**`bgp maxas-limit 30`**	BGP AS path filtering is done using the IOS XR Route Policy Language (RPL). Within RPL, the as-path length *{eq | is | ge | le} {number | parameter}* command to configure a maximum limit for the number of AS-PATH segments that are permitted within inbound routes. `(config)# `**`route-policy FOO`** `(config-rpl)# `**`if as-path length ge 30 then`** `(config-rpl-if)# `**`drop`**` (config-rpl-if)# `**`endif`** `(config-rpl)#` `(config)# `**`router bgp 65001`** `(config-bgp)# `**`neighbor 192.168.1.1`** `(config-bgp-nbr)# `**`address-family ipv4 unicast (config-bgp-nbr-af)# route-policy FOO in`**
BGP Neighbor Commands	BGP Neighbor Commands
neighbor {*ip-address*} **password** {*string*}: Configure MD5 authentication for a BGP peer. `(config)# `**`router bgp 65001`** `(config-router)# `**`neighbor 192.168.1.1 password s3cr3t`**	**neighbor** {*ip-address*} **password clear** {*string*}: Configure MD5 authentication for a BGP peer `(config)# `**`router bgp 65001`** `(config-bgp)# `**`neighbor 192.168.1.1`** `(config-bgp-nbr)# `**`password clear s3cr3t`**
No comparable command exists in IOS 12.0S at this time.	**neighbor** {*ip-address*} **keychain** <*key-chain-name*>: Configures key-chain-based authentication for a BGP peer. `(config)# `**`router bgp 65001`** `(config-bgp)# `**`neighbor 192.168.1.1`** `(config-bgp-nbr)# `**`keychain 18`**
neighbor {*ip-address*} **ttl-security hops** {*hops*}: Configure the TTL security check for a BGP peer to prevent spoofed attacks. `(config)# `**`router bgp 65001`** `(config-router)# `**`neighbor 192.168.1.1 ttl-security hops 1`**	**neighbor** {*ip-address*} **ttl-security** {*hops*}: Configure the TTL security check for a BGP to prevent spoofed attacks. `(config)# `**`router bgp 65001`** `(config-bgp)# `**`neighbor-group 192.168.1.1`** `(config-bgp-nbr)# `**`ttl-security`**

continues

Table C-2 *Control Plane Security Commands (Continued)*

IOS 12.0S	IOS XR

neighbor {*ip-address*} **maximum-prefix** {*max*}: Configure the number of prefixes that can be received from a BGP peer.
 	
`(config)# router bgp 65001`
`(config-router)# neighbor 192.168.1.1`
`maximum-prefix 500`
	maximum-prefix {*max*} [*threshold*] [**warning-only**]: Configure the number of prefixes that can be received from a BGP peer.
	
	`(config)# router bgp 65001`
	`(config-bgp)# neighbor 192.168.1.1`
	`(config-bgp-nbr)# address-family ipv4`
	`unicast`
	`(config-bgp-nbr-af))# maximum-prefix 500`

neighbor {*ip-address*} **disable-connected-check**: Disable the directly connected check for eBGP thus enabling multihop peer session to be established between directly connected neighbors when eBGP peering is established from loopback to loopback.
 	
`(config)# router bgp 65001`
`(config-router)# neighbor 192.168.1.1`
`disable-connected-check`
	No comparable command exists in IOS XR.

neighbor {*ip-address*} **distribute-list** {*list*} [**in** | **out**]: Configures a distribute list to filter BGP neighbor information in or out.
 	
`(config)# router bgp 65001`
`(config-router)# neighbor 192.168.1.1`
`distribute-list 101 in`
 	
IOS prefix lists are recommended versus IOS distribute lists.
	No directly comparable command exists in IOS XR. BGP ingress/egress prefix filtering is done using the IOS XR Route Policy Language (RPL). RPL uses logical if-then-else constructs and parameter passing to achieve unprecedented flexibility and modularity of routing policy. RPL greatly simplifies complex routing policy configurations.

neighbor {*ip-address*} **prefix-list** {*list*}: Used to prevent distribution of BGP neighbor advertised prefix information as specified in a prefix list. Can be used in address-family or router configuration mode.
 	
`(config)# router bgp 65001`
`(config-router)# neighbor 192.168.1.1`
`prefix-list AsiaPeer out`
	No directly comparable command exists in IOS XR. BGP ingress/egress prefix filtering is done using the IOS XR RPL. RPL uses logical if-then-else constructs and parameter passing to achieve unprecedented flexibility and modularity of routing policy. RPL greatly simplifies complex routing policy configurations.

neighbor {*ip-address*} **route-map** {*name*} [**in** | **out**]: Apply a route map to incoming or outgoing route updates for a BGP peer.	**neighbor** {*ip-address*} **route-policy** {*name*}: Apply a route policy to incoming or outgoing route updates for a BGP peer.

Table C-2   *Control Plane Security Commands (Continued)*

IOS 12.0S	IOS XR
(config)# **route-map FOO permit 10** (config-route-map)# **match community 5** (config)# **router bgp 65001** (config-router)# **address-family ipv4** (config-router-af)# **neighbor** **192.168.1.1 route-map FOO in**	(config)# **route-policy FOO** (config-rpl)# **pass** (config-rpl)# **end-policy** (config)# **router bgp 65001** (config-bgp)# **neighbor 192.168.1.1** (config-bgp-nbr)# **address-family ipv4** **unicast** (config-bgp-nbr-af)# **route-policy FOO in**
bgp graceful-restart: Enable the Border Gateway Protocol (BGP) graceful restart capability. (config)# **router bgp 65001** (config-router)# **bgp graceful-restart**	**bgp graceful-restart**: Enable the BGP graceful restart capability. (config)# **router bgp 65001** (config-bgp)# **bgp graceful-restart**
IP Prefix List Commands	
IP Prefix List	Prefix Set
ip prefix-list: Define an IP prefix list. (config)# **ip prefix-list rootservers** **description DNS root servers** (config)# **ip prefix-list rootservers** **seq 5 permit 198.41.0.0/24** (config)# **ip prefix-list rootservers** **seq 10 permit 128.9.0.0/16** (config)# **ip prefix-list rootservers** **seq 15 permit 192.33.4.0/24** (config)# **ip prefix-list rootservers** **seq 20 permit 128.8.0.0/16** (config)# **ip prefix-list rootservers** **seq 25 permit 192.203.230.0/24** (config)# **ip prefix-list rootservers** **seq 30 permit 192.5.4.0/23** (config)# **ip prefix-list rootservers** **seq 35 permit 192.112.36.0/24** (config)# **ip prefix-list rootservers** **seq 40 permit 128.63.0.0/16** (config)# **ip prefix-list rootservers** **seq 45 permit 192.36.148.0/24** (config)# **ip prefix-list rootservers** **seq 50 permit 193.0.14.0/24** (config)# **ip prefix-list rootservers** **seq 55 permit 198.32.64.0/24** (config)# **ip prefix-list rootservers** **seq 60 permit 202.12.27.0/24**	**prefix-set**: Configure IPv4 prefix match specifications, each of which has four parts: an address, a mask length, a minimum matching length, and a maximum matching length. (config)# **prefix-set rootservers** (config-pfx)# **#DNS root servers** (config-pfx)# **128.9.0.0/16,** (config-pfx)# **192.33.4.0/24,** (config-pfx)# **128.8.0.0/16,** (config-pfx)# **192.203.230.0/24,** (config-pfx)# **192.5.4.0/23,** (config-pfx)# **192.112.36.0/24,** (config-pfx)# **128.63.0.0/16,** (config-pfx)# **192.36.148.0/24,** (config-pfx)# **193.0.14.0/24,** (config-pfx)# **198.32.64.0/24,** (config-pfx)# **202.12.27.0/24** (config-pfx)# **end-set**

continues

Table C-2 *Control Plane Security Commands (Continued)*

IOS 12.0S	IOS XR
IP Community List Commands	
IP Community List	Community Set

ip community-list: Define an IP community list:
 	
{**1-99**}: Standard community list
{**100-500**}: Expanded community list
standard {*name*}: Standard named community list
expanded {*name*}: Expanded named community list
 	
`(config)# ip community-list 10 permit 65001:110`
 	
Or
 	
`(config)# ip community-list 123 deny ^6500[0-4]:.*`
`(config)# ip community-list 123 deny ^650[1578][0-4]:.*`
	community-set: Configure community values for matching against the BGP community attribute. Integer community values must be split in half and expressed as two unsigned decimal integers in the range from 0 to 65535, separated by a colon. Single 32-bit community values are not allowed.
	
	`(config)# community-set emea`
	`(config-comm)# #EMEA peers`
	`(config-comm)# 65001:110`
	`(config-comm)# end-set`

ip extcommunity-list: Define an IP community list:
 	
{**0–99**}: Standard community list
{**100–500**}: Expanded community list
 	
`(config)# ip extcommunity-list 500 deny _123_`
`(config)# ip extcommunity-list 500 deny ^123.*`
	extcommunity-set: Configure extended community values for matching against BGP community attributes. An extended community-set is analogous to a community-set except that it contains extended community values instead of regular community values. It also supports named forms and inline forms. There are three types of extended community sets: **cost**, Site-of-Origin (**soo**), and Route Target (**rt**).
	
	`(config)# extcommunity-set rt RT_set`
	`(config-ext)##Route Targets`
	`(config-ext)# 65001:666`
	`(config-ext)# end-set`

AS-Path Access List Commands	
IP AS-Path Access List	AS-Path Set

ip as-path access-list: Configure an autonomous system path filter using regular expressions, to be applied to inbound and outbound BGP paths.
 	
`(config)# ip as-path access-list 500 deny _65535_`
`(config)# ip as-path access-list 500 deny ^65535$`
	as-path-set: Configure a set of autonomous system operations for matching an AS path attribute. The only matching operation is a regular expression (regex) match.
	
	`(config)# as-path-set aset1`
	`(config-as)##AS Path Set`
	`(config-as)# ios-regex '_65535_',`
	`(config-as)# ios-regex '^65535$'`
	`(config-as)# end-set`

Table C-2   *Control Plane Security Commands (Continued)*

IOS 12.0S	IOS XR
Route Map Commands	
Route Map Commands	Route Policy Commands

route-map {*name*}: Configure a route map to instruct the router to inspect, filter, and/or modify routes and their attributes on peer ingress or egress, or redistribution from one routing protocol to another.
 	
`(config)# route-map DDoS-Select permit 5`
`(config-route-map)# description - route traffic to Null0`
`(config-route-map)# match community 1`
`(config-route-map)# set ip next-hop 192.0.2.1`
`(config-route-map)# set local-preference 200`
`(config-route-map)# set community no-advertise additive`
	route-policy {*name*} [parameter1, etc.]: Configure a route policy to instruct the router to inspect, filter, and/or modify routes and their attributes on peer ingress or egress, or redistribution from one routing protocol to another. The **route-policy** command is available within the IOS XR RPL, which uses logical if-then-else constructs and parameter passing to achieve unprecedented flexibility and modularity of routing policy. RPL greatly simplifies complex routing policy configurations.

`(config)# router bgp 65001`
`(config-router)# neighbor 10.20.2.2 route-map DDoS-Select in`
	`(config)# route-policy DDoS`
	`(config-rpl)# route traffic to Null0`
	`(config-rpl)# if community matches-any ddos-comm then`
	`(config-rpl-if)# set next-hop 192.0.2.1`
	`(config-rpl-if)# set local-preference 200`
	`(config-rpl-if)# set community no-advertise`
	`(config-rpl-if)# endif`
	`(config-rpl)# end-policy`
	
	`(config)# router static`
	`(config-static)# address-family ipv4 unicast`
	`(config-static-afi)# 192.0.2.1/32 Null 0`
	`(config-static-afi)# exit`
	`(config-static)# exit`
	
	`(config)# router bgp 65001`
	`(config-bgp)# neighbor 10.0.0.1`
	`(config-bgp-nbr)# address-family ipv4 unicast`
	`(config-bgp-nbr-af))# route-policy DDoS in`

Class Map Commands	
Class Map Commands	Class Map Commands

class-map {*name*}: Configure a class map to be used for matching packets to a specified class.
 	
`(config)# class-map match-all data`
`(config-cmap)# match ip precedence 1 2 3 4 5`
	class-map {*name*}: Configure a class map to be used for matching packets to a specified class.

continues

Table C-2 *Control Plane Security Commands (Continued)*

IOS 12.0S	IOS XR

```(config-cmap)# exit```
```(config)# class-map match-all control```
```(config-cmap)# match ip precedence```
```6 7```
	```(config)# class-map match-any Data```
	```(config-cmap)# match precedence 1 2 3 4 5```
	```(config-cmap)# exit```
	```(config)# class-map match-any Control```
	```(config-cmap)# match precedence 6 7```
	```(config-cmap)# commit```

Policy Map Commands	
Policy Map Commands	Policy Map Commands

policy-map {*name*}: Create a policy map.
 	
```(config)# policy-map CoPP_Policy```
```(config-pmap)# class class-default```
```(config-pmap-c)# police 10000 1500```
```1550 conform transmit exceed transmit```
	policy-map {*name*}: Create a policy map.
	
	```(config)# policy-map Rate-Limit```
	```(config-pmap)# class class-default```
	```(config-pmap-c)# police 10000 conform```
	```transmit```
	```(config-pmap-c)# exit```
	```(config-pmap)# commit```

Static Route to Null0 Commands	
Null0 Static Route	Null0 Static Route

ip route *{prefix} {netmask}* **Null0**: Define a static route pointing to the Null0 logical interface for packet discard.
 	
```(config)# ip route 192.168.2.1```
```255.255.255.255 Null0```
	router static: Define an IP static route to the Null0 logical interface. Static routes are defined within the routing protocol **static** configuration mode.
	
	```(config)# router static```
	```(config-static)# address-family ipv4```
	```unicast```
	```(config-static-afi)# 192.168.2.1/32 Null0```
	```(config-static-afi)# exit```
	```(config-static)# exit```
	```(config)# commit```

IS-IS Security-Related Commands	
Router IS-IS Commands	Router IS-IS Commands

passive-interface {*interface*}: Disable advertisement of routing updates out an interface and do not form adjacencies out the interface. Note, the connected prefix of the interface is still advertised within the IS-IS domain.
 	
```(config)# router is-is Core```
```(config-router)# passive-interface```
```loopback0```
	Similar functionality is accomplished with the IOS XR **passive** command.

Table C-2   *Control Plane Security Commands (Continued)*

IOS 12.0S	IOS XR

advertise passive-only: Configure IS-IS to advertise only prefixes associated with interfaces marked as passive (via the **passive-interface** command), and not prefixes associated with connected interfaces.
 	
`(config)# router is-is Core`
`(config-router)# advertise`
`passive-only`
	Similar functionality is accomplished with the IOS XR **suppressed** command described which immediately follows.

IS-IS Interface Commands	IS-IS Interface Commands

[no] is-is advertise prefix: Disable IS-IS from advertising the connected prefix, but still form adjacencies over the interface.
 	
`(config)# interface POS0/4`
`(config-if)# ip router is-is`
`(config-if)# no is-is advertise prefix`
	suppressed: Disable IS-IS from advertising the connected prefix, but still form adjacencies over the interface.
	
	`(config)# router is-is isp`
	`(config-is-is)# interface POS0/0/0/0`
	`(config-is-is-if)# suppressed`

No directly comparable interface configuration command exists in IOS 12.0S. The IOS routing configuration command **passive-interface** {*interface*} provides similar functionality.	**passive**: Disable the forming of adjacencies over the interface, but still advertise connected prefixes within the IS-IS domain.
	
	`(config)# router is-is isp`
	`(config-is-is)# interface loopback0`
	`(config-is-is-if)# passive`

IS-IS Authentication Commands	IS-IS Authentication Commands

**authentication mode [md5	text][level-1	level-2]**: Specify the authentication mode used in IS-IS as either MD5 or text.
		
		`(config)# router is-is Core`
		`(config-router)# authentication mode`
		`md5 level-1`
			No directly comparable command exists in IOS XR. See the IS-IS related **lsp-password hmac-md5** and **hello-password hmac-md5** IOS XR commands directly below.

authentication key-chain {*name*} **[level-1	level-2]**: Specify the key chain to use when authentication (clear text or MD5) is applied to IS-IS.
	
	`(config)# router is-is Core`
	`(config-router)# authentication key-chain S3cr3ts level-1`
		lsp-password hmac-md5 {*password*}: Configure the authentication password and MD5 hashing method for the IS-IS domain.
		
		`(config)# router is-is Core`
		`(config-is-is)# lsp-password hmac-md5`
		`s3cr3t level 1`

continues

Table C-2   *Control Plane Security Commands (Continued)*

IOS 12.0S	IOS XR

No directly comparable command exists in IOS 12.0S.	**hello-password hmac-md5** {*password*}: Configure the authentication password and MD5 hashing method for the IS-IS interface.
	
	`(config)# router is-is Core`
	`(config-is-is)# interface POS0/0/0/0`
	`(config-is-is-if)# hello-password`
	`hmac-md5 p4ssw0rd level 1`

OSPF Security-Related Commands	
OSPF Authentication Commands	OSPF Authentication Commands

area {*area*} **authentication message-digest**: Enable OSPF MD5 authentication within an area.
 	
`(config)# router ospf 123`
`(config-rtr)# area 0 authentication`
`message-digest`
	authentication message-digest: Enable MD5 authentication for the OSPF process.
	
	`(config)# router ospf core`
	`(config-ospf)# router-id 192.168.1.1`
	`(config-ospf)# authentication message-`
	`digest`

No directly comparable command exists in IOS 12.0S.	**message-digest-key**: Configure the MD5 authentication key for the OSPF process.
	
	`(config)# router ospf core`
	`(config-ospf)# router-id 192.168.1.1`
	`(config-ospf)# message-digest-key 18`
	`key s3cr3ts`
	`(config-ospf)# area 0`
	`(config-ospf-ar)# interface`
	`POS0/0/0/0`

OSPF Interface Authentication Commands	—

ip ospf message-digest-key key-id encryption-type md5: Enable OSPF MD5 authentication on the interface.
 	
`(config)# interface POS0/0`
`(config-if)# ip ospf message-digest-`
`key 1 md5 s3cr3ts`
	No directly comparable interface configuration command exists in IOS XR. All authentication commands are applied within the routing protocol configuration. (See the **message-digest-key** command above.)

EIGRP Security-Related Commands	
EIGRP Interface Authentication Commands	—
ip authentication mode eigrp {*ASN*} **md5**: Enable EIGRP MD5 authentication.	EIGRP authentication is not supported in IOS XR at the time of this writing.

Table C-2 *Control Plane Security Commands (Continued)*

IOS 12.0S	IOS XR

ip authentication key-chain eigrp {*ASN*} {*keychain*}: Specify the key chain for use in EIGRP MD5 authentication.
 	
`(config)# interface POS0/0`
`(config-if)# ip address 10.10.10.1`
`255.255.255.252`
`(config-if)# ip authentication mode`
`eigrp 10 md5`
`(config-if)# ip authentication`
`key-chain 10 s3cr3ts`	

RIPv2 Security-Related Commands	
RIPv2 Interface Authentication Commands	—
ip rip authentication mode md5: Enable RIPv2 MD5 authentication. **ip rip authentication key-chain** {*keychain*}: Specify the key chain for use in RIPv2 MD5 authentication.	RIP authentication is not supported in IOS XR at the time of this writing.

`(config)# interface Serial0`
`(config-if)# ip address 10.10.10.1`
`255.255.255.252`
`(config-if)# ip rip authentication`
`mode md5`
`(config-if)# ip rip authentication`
`key-chain s3cr3ts`	

LDP Security-Related Commands	
LDP Session Protection	LDP Session Protection

mpls ldp session protection [**vrf** {*vpn-name*}] [**for** {*acl*}] [**duration** {*seconds*}]: Enable LDP sessions to be protected during a link failure. By default, the command protects all LDP sessions. The command has several options that enable you to specify which LDP sessions to protect. The **vrf** keyword lets you protect LDP sessions for a specified VRF. The **for** keyword lets you specify a standard IP ACL of prefixes that should be protected.
 	
`(config)# mpls ldp session protection`
`for 1 duration 60`
	session protection for {*acl*} **duration** {*seconds*}: Configure LDP session protection for peers specified by *acl* with a maximum duration specified in seconds.
	
	`(config)# mpls ldp`
	`(config-ldp)# session protection for`
	`peer_acl_1 duration 60`

continues

Table C-2   *Control Plane Security Commands (Continued)*

IOS 12.0S	IOS XR
LDP Authentication Commands	LDP Authentication Commands

mpls ldp neighbor {*ip-address*} **password** {*password*}: Configure a TCP MD5 authentication key for the given LDP neighbor.
 	
`(config)# mpls label protocol ldp`
`(config)# mpls ldp neighbor 10.1.1.1`
`password s3cr3ts`
	neighbor {*ip-address*} **password** [**encryption**] {*password*}: Configure a TCP MD5 authentication key for the given LDP neighbor.
	
	`(config)# mpls ldp`
	`(config-ldp)# neighbor 192.168.1.1`
	`password s3cr3ts`

<td colspan="2" align="center">**RSVP Security-Related Commands**</td>	
—	RSVP Global Authentication Commands
No directly comparable commands exists in IOS 12.0S.	**rsvp authentication**: Enter RSVP authentication mode. **key-source key-chain** {*key-chain-name*}: Specify the source of the key information to authenticate RSVP signaling messages.

	life-time {*seconds*}: Control how long RSVP maintains security associations with RSVP neighbors.
	
	window-size {*n*}: Specify the maximum number of authenticated messages that can be received out of order.
	
	`(config)# rsvp authentication`
	`(config-rsvp-auth)# key-source key-chain`
	`RSVP_KEY`
	`(config-rsvp-auth)# life-time 2000`
	`(config-rsvp-auth)# window-size 2`

RSVP Interface Authentication Commands	RSVP Interface Authentication Commands
ip rsvp authentication type [md5 | sha-1]: Select either the MD5 or SHA-1 hash algorithm for RSVP authentication. **ip rsvp authentication key** {*keystring*}: Specify the data string (key) for the authentication algorithm. **ip rsvp authentication challenge**: Configure RSVP to perform a challenge-response handshake when RSVP learns about any new challenge-capable neighbors on a network.	**rsvp interface**: Enter RSVP interface mode. **authentication**: Enter RSVP authentication mode. **key-source key-chain** {*key-chain-name*}: Specify the source of the key information to authenticate RSVP signaling messages. **life-time** {*seconds*}: Control how long RSVP maintains security associations with RSVP neighbors.

Table C-2   *Control Plane Security Commands (Continued)*

IOS 12.0S	IOS XR
ip rsvp authentication lifetime {*hh:mm:ss*}: Control how long RSVP maintains security associations with RSVP neighbors. **ip rsvp authentication window-size** {*n*}: Specify the maximum number of authenticated messages that can be received out of order. **ip rsvp authentication**: Activate RSVP cryptographic authentication.	**window-size** {*n*}: Specify the maximum number of authenticated messages that can be received out of order. `(config)# `**`rsvp interface POS0/0/0/0`** `(config-rsvp-if)# `**`authentication`** `(config-rsvp-if-auth)# `**`key-source key-`** **`chain RSVP_KEY`** `(config-rsvp-if-auth)# `**`life-time 2000`** `(config-rsvp-if-auth)# `**`window-size 2`**
`(config)# `**`interface POS0/0`** `(config-if)# `**`ip rsvp bandwidth 7500`** **`7500`** `(config-if)# `**`ip rsvp authentication`** **`type sha-1`** `(config-if)# `**`ip rsvp authentication`** **`key 11223344`** `(config-if)# `**`ip rsvp authentication`** **`challenge`** `(config-if)# `**`ip rsvp authentication`** **`lifetime 00:30:05`** `(config-if)# `**`ip rsvp authentication`** **`window-size 2`** `(config-if)# `**`ip rsvp authentication`**	
—	RSVP Neighbor Authentication Commands
No directly comparable command exists in IOS 12.0S.	**rsvp neighbor** {*IP address*} **authentication**: Enter RSVP neighbor authentication mode. **key-source key-chain** {*key-chain-name*}: Specify the source of the key information to authenticate RSVP signaling messages. **life-time** {*seconds*}: Control how long RSVP maintains security associations with RSVP neighbors. **window-size** {*n*}: Specify the maximum number of authenticated messages that can be received out of order. `(config)# `**`rsvp neighbor 192.168.1.1`** **`authentication`** `(config-rsvp-nbor-auth)# `**`key-source key-`** **`chain RSVP_KEY`** `(config-rsvp-nbor-auth)# `**`life-time 2000`** `(config-rsvp-nbor-auth)# `**`window-size 2`**

continues

Table C-2 *Control Plane Security Commands (Continued)*

IOS 12.0S	IOS XR
PIM Commands	
ip pim neighbor-filter: Filter PIM neighbor messages from specific IP addresses.	**neighbor-filter**: Filter PIM neighbor messages from specific IP addresses.

`(config)# access-list 1 deny`
`192.168.1.1`
`(config)# interface POS0/0`
`(config-if)# ip pim neighbor-filter 1`
	`(config)# ipv4 access-list 1`
	`(config-ipv4-acl)# deny 192.168.1.1`
	`(config)# router pim address-family ipv4`
	`(config-pim-ipv4)# neighbor-filter 1`

IGMP Commands	
ip igmp access-group: Set limits for multicast group join requests by hosts on the subnet serviced by the interface.	**access-group**: Set limits for multicast group join requests by hosts on the subnet serviced by the interface.

`(config)# access-list 1 permit`
`225.2.2.2 0.0.0.0`
`(config)# interface Ethernet 0`
`(config-if)# ip igmp access-group 1`
	`(config)# ipv4 access-list mygroup permit`
	`225.2.2.2 0.0.0.0`
	`(config)# router igmp`
	`(config-igmp)# interfacePOS0/1/0/1`
	`(config-igmp-if)# access-group mygroup`

ICMP Control	
IP ICMP Rate-Limit Command	ICMP Rate-Limit Command
ip icmp rate-limit unreachables {*rate*}: Configure the rate at which ICMP Destination Unreachable messages are generated (in milliseconds).	**icmp ipv4 rate-limit unreachable** {*rate*}: Configure the rate at which ICMP Destination Unreachable messages are generated (in milliseconds).
`(config)# ip icmp rate-limit` `unreachables 10`	`(config)# icmp ipv4 rate-limit` `unreachables 10`
IP Redirects Command	IP Redirects Command
no ip redirects: Disable sending ICMP Redirect messages on the interface. (Generated by default.)	**no ipv4 redirects**: Disable sending ICMP Redirect messages on the interface. (Disabled by default.)
`(config-if)# no ip redirects`	`(config-if)# no ipv4 redirects`
IP Unreachables Command	IP Unreachables Command
no ip unreachables: Disable the sending of ICMP Destination Unreachable messages on the interface. (Generated by default.)	**ipv4 unreachables disable**: Disable sending ICMP Destination Unreachable messages on the interface. (Generated by default.)
`(config-if)# no ip unreachables`	`(config-if)# ipv4 unreachables disable`

Table C-2   *Control Plane Security Commands (Continued)*

IOS 12.0S	IOS XR
IP Mask Reply	IP Mask Reply
no ip mask-reply: Disable the sending of ICMP Mask Reply messages in response to ICMP Address Mask Request messages on the interface. (Not sent by default.) `(config-if)# no ip mask-reply`	**no ipv4 mask-reply**: Disables the sending ICMP Mask Reply messages in response to ICMP Address Mask Request messages on the interface. (Not sent by default.) `(config-if)# no ipv4 mask-reply`
IP Information Reply	IP Information Reply
no ip information-reply: Disable the sending of ICMP Information Reply messages on the interface. (Not sent by default.) `(config-if)# no ip information-reply`	**no ip information-reply**: Disable the sending of ICMP Information Reply messages on the interface. (Not sent by default.) `(config-if)# no ip information-reply`
Proxy ARP Control	
IP Proxy ARP	Proxy ARP
no ip proxy-arp: Disable proxy ARP on the interface. (Enabled by default.) `(config-if)# no ip proxy-arp`	**no proxy-arp**: Disable proxy ARP on the interface. (Disabled by default.) `(config-if)# no proxy-arp`
Key Chain Commands	
Key Chain Commands	Key Chain Commands

key chain {*name*}: Configure the key chain(s) used by routing protocol authentication mechanisms (protocol independent).
 	
`(config)# key chain s3cr3ts`
`(config-keychain)# key 18`
`(config-keychain-key)# key-string t0ugh`
`(config-keychain-key)# accept-lifetime 08:00:00 Jan 1 2007 infinite`
`(config-keychain-key)# send-lifetime 08:00:00 Jan 1 2007 infinite`
 	
At the time of this writing, IOS 12.0S supports the use of key chains for the following protocols: IS-IS, EIGRP, RIP, and RSVP.
	key chain {*name*}: Configure the key chain(s) used by routing protocol authentication mechanisms (protocol independent).
	
	`(config)# key chain s3cr3ts`
	`(config-s3cr3ts)# key 18`
	`(config-s3cr3ts-0x12)# key-string t0ugh`
	`(config-s3cr3ts-0x12)# accept-lifetime 08:00:00 Jan 1 2007 infinite`
	`(config-s3cr3ts-0x12)# send-lifetime 08:00:00 Jan 1 2007 infinite`
	`(config-s3cr3ts-0x12)# cryptographic-algorithm MD5`
	
	At the time of this writing, IOS XR supports the use of key chains for the following protocols: BGP, OSPF, and RSVP.

Management Plane Security Commands

Management plane security commands refer to those commands that configure, directly or indirectly, security features within management plane functions such as SNMP, syslog, SSH, NetFlow, and many others. Table C-3 lists Cisco IOS commands and their Cisco IOS XR counterparts, if any, along with a short example of how each command is used. In addition, best common practice (BCP) configurations are also included in Table C-3. BCP commands configure, directly or indirectly, security features for the routing platform itself. Generally, this includes commands that enable or disable specific functions or features that make the router more secure or more resilient, such as password encryption, and many others.

Table C-3 *Management Plane Security Commands*

IOS 12.0S	IOS XR
SNMP Support	
SNMP Server Commands	SNMP Server Commands

snmp-server: Configure various SNMP attributes.
 	
`(config)# snmp-server community s3cr3t RO 4`
`(config)# snmp-server community s3cr3t view NOC RO 123`
`(config)# snmp-server view NOC ciscoPingMIB included`
`(config)# snmp-server view NOC interfaces included`
`(config)# snmp-server view NOC sysUpTime included`
`(config)# snmp-server view NOC ifXEntry included`
`(config)# snmp-server trap-source Loopback0`
`(config)# snmp-server host 10.1.1.1 p433w0rd`
	snmp-server: Configure various SNMP attributes.
	
	`(config)# snmp-server community s3cr3t RO SystemOwner 4`
	`(config)# snmp-server community s3cr3t view NOC RO LROwner 123`
	`(config)# snmp-server view NOC ciscoPingMIB included`
	`(config)# snmp-server view NOC interfaces included`
	`(config)# snmp-server view NOC sysUpTime included`
	`(config)# snmp-server view NOC ifXEntry included`
	`(config)# snmp-server host 10.1.1.1 traps version  2c s3cr3t`
	`(config)# snmp-server traps fabric plane`
	`(config)# snmp-server traps fabric bundle link`
	`(config)# snmp-server traps fabric bundle state`
	`(config)# snmp-server trap link ietf`
	`(config)# snmp-server traps snmp`
	`(config)# snmp trap-source Loopback 0`

Table C-3   *Management Plane Security Commands (Continued)*

IOS 12.0S	IOS XR
AAA Support	
AAA Commands	AAA Commands

aaa: Configure various AAA attributes.
 	
`(config)# aaa new-model`
`(config)# aaa authentication login`
`default tacacs+ enable`
`(config)# aaa authorization exec`
`default tacacs+ none`
`(config)# aaa authorization commands 1`
`default tacacs+ none`
`(config)# aaa authorization commands`
`15 default tacacs+ none`
`(config)# aaa accounting send stop-`
`record authentication failure`
`(config)# aaa accounting exec default`
`start-stop tacacs+`
`(config)# aaa accounting commands 1`
`default start-stop tacacs+`
`(config)# aaa accounting commands 15`
`default start-stop tacacs+`
`(config)# aaa accounting system`
`default start-stop tacacs+0`
	aaa: Configure various AAA attributes.
	
	`(config)# aaa authentication login default`
	`group tacacs+ local`
	`(config)# aaa authorization exec default`
	`group tacacs+ none`
	`(config)# aaa authorization commands`
	`default group tacacs+ none`
	`(config)# aaa accounting exec default`
	`start-stop group tacacs+`
	`(config)# aaa accounting system default`
	`start-stop group tacacs+`
	`(config)# aaa accounting commands default`
	`start-stop group tacacs+`
	
	Note: There is no **aaa new-model** command within IOS XR.

TACACS+ Support	
TACACS Server Commands	TACACS Server Commands

tacacs-server: Configure various TACACS+ server attributes.
 	
`(config)# tacacs-server host 10.1.1.1`
`(config)# tacacs-server key s3cr3t`
`(config)# tacacs-server timeout 2`
`(config)# no tacacs-server directed-`
`request`
`(config)# tacacs source-interface`
`Loopback0`
	tacacs-server: Configure various TACACS+ server attributes.
	
	`(config)# tacacs-server host 10.1.1.1 port`
	`49`
	`(config-tacacs-host)# timeout 2`
	`(config-tacacs-host)# key s3cr3t`
	`(config-tacacs-host)# exit`
	`(config)# tacacs source-interface`
	`Loopback0`

continues

Table C-3 *Management Plane Security Commands (Continued)*

IOS 12.0S	IOS XR
NTP Support	
NTP Commands	NTP Commands

ntp: Configure various NTP attributes.
 	
```(config)# ntp source Loopback0```
```(config)# ntp update-calendar```
```(config)# ntp authenticate```
```(config)# ntp authentication-key 1```
```md5 ntpk3y```
```(config)# ntp trusted-key 1```
```(config)# ntp server 10.1.1.1```
```key 1```
```(config)# ntp peer 10.2.2.2 key 1```
```(config)# ntp peer 10.3.3.3 key 1```
 	
Note that NTP packets can be rejected on a per-interface basis.
 	
```(config-if)# ntp disable```
	ntp: Enter NTP configuration mode, and configure various NTP attributes.
	
	```(config)# ntp```
	```(config-ntp)# source Loopback 0```
	```(config-ntp)# update-calendar```
	```(config-ntp)# authenticate```
	```(config-ntp)# authentication-key 1 md5```
	```clear ntpk3y```
	```(config-ntp)# trusted-key 1```
	```(config-ntp)# server 10.1.1.1 key 1```
	```(config-ntp)# peer 10.2.2.2 key 1```
	```(config-ntp)# peer 10.3.3.3 key 1```
	
	Note that NTP packets can be rejected on a per-interface basis.
	
	```(config)# ntp```
	```(config-ntp)# interface POS0/0/0/1 disable```

User/Account Support	
Enable Password/Secret Commands	—

enable password: Configure the password that grants privileged administrative access to the IOS system using the **enable password** protection mode. The use of the **enable password** protection mode is considered insecure because it is either stored as plain text or, when the **service password-encryption** command is also issued, stored using a weak encryption algorithm.
 	
```(config)# enable password s3cr3t```
 	
enable secret: Configure the password that grants privileged administrative access to the IOS system using the **enable secret** protection mode. The use of the **enable secret** protection mode is considered more secure because the password is stored using an MD5-based password hashing mechanism.
 	
```(config)# enable secret s3cr3t```
	No such configuration.
	
	You must have a username. The password for enable privileges is defined within the username and taskgroup set of commands.

Table C-3   *Management Plane Security Commands (Continued)*

IOS 12.0S	IOS XR
—	Task Group Commands

No directly comparable command exists in IOS 12.0S.	**taskgroup** {*taskgroup*}: Configure various taskgroup attributes.
	
	`(config)# taskgroup mgmt`
	`(config-tg)# description backbone support functions`
	`(config-tg)# inherit taskgroup sysadmin`
	`(config-tg)# task read bgp`
	`(config-tg)# commit`

—	User Group Commands

No directly comparable command exists in IOS 12.0S.	**usergroup** {*usergroup*}: Configure various usergroup attributes.
	
	`(config)# usergroup NOC_Ops`
	`(config-ug)# description NOC users`
	`(config-ug)# taskgroup mgmt`
	`(config-ug)# commit`

Username Commands	Username Commands

username: Configures various username attributes.
 	
`(config)# username Bob password s3cr3t`
`(config)# username Bob privilege 10 password h4rd0n3`
	username: Configure various username attributes.
	
	`(config)# username Bob`
	`(config-un)# password s3cr3t`
	`(config-un)# group root-system`
	`(config-un)# exit`
	`(config)# username Joe`
	`(config-un)# password pa33w0rd`
	`(config-un)# group NOC_Ops`
	`(config-un)# group operator`
	`(config-un)# commit`

Privilege Commands	—

privilege {*mode*}: Configure various privilege attributes.
 	
`(config)# privilege exec level 10 show ip route`
`(config)# privilege exec level 10 show ip interface`
	No directly comparable command exists in IOS XR. This functionality is provided in IOS XR via the **taskgroup** command.

continues

Table C-3 *Management Plane Security Commands (Continued)*

IOS 12.0S	IOS XR
Syslog Support	
Logging Commands	Logging Commands

logging: Configure various syslog attributes.
 	
`(config)# logging 10.1.1.1`
`(config)# logging facility local7`
`(config)# logging buffered debug`
`(config)# logging buffered 64000`
`(config)# no logging console`
`(config)# logging source-interface`
`Loopback0`
	logging: Configure various syslog attributes.
	
	`(config)# logging buffered 2000000`
	`(config)# logging buffered debug`
	`(config)# logging 10.1.1.1`
	`(config)# logging facility local7`
	`(config)# logging source-interface`
	`Loopback0`
	`(config)# logging trap debugging`
	`(config)# logging hostname prefix`
	`ThisRouter`
	`(config)# logging history warning`
	`(config)# logging history size 2`
	`(config)# logging console disable`

bgp log-neighbor-changes: Enable logging of BGP neighbor status changes (up or down) and resets.
 	
`(config)# router bgp 65001`
`(config-router)# bgp log-neighbor-`
`changes`
	bgp log neighbor changes: Enable logging of BGP neighbor status changes (up or down) and resets.
	
	`(config)# router bgp 65001`
	`(config-bgp)# no bgp log neighbor changes`
	`disable`
	
	Note that the default is to log BGP neighbor changes. If logging is disabled, it may be re-enabled as shown here.

log-adjacency-changes: Enable logging of IS-IS adjacency change events and other non-IIH events.
 	
`(config)# router is-is Core`
`(config-router)# log-adjacency-`
`changes`
	log adjacency changes: Configure the generation of a log message when an IS-IS adjacency states change (up or down).
	
	`(config)# router is-is Core`
	`(config-is-is)# log adjacency changes`

—	Logging Correlator Commands

No directly comparable command exists in IOS 12.0S.	**logging correlator**: Configure various logging correlation rules.
	
	`(config)# logging events threshold 10`
	`(config)# logging events buffer-size 10000`
	`(config)# logging events level errors`
	`(config)# logging correlator rule alarm1`
	`timeout 600000 PKT_INFRA LINK UPDOWN L2`
	`SONET ALARM`
	`(config)# logging correlator apply-rule`
	`alarm1 location all-of-router`

Table C-3   *Management Plane Security Commands (Continued)*

IOS 12.0S	IOS XR
TCP Support	
Services Commands	—
service nagle: Enable the Nagle congestion control algorithm. `(config)# service nagle`	No directly comparable command exists in IOS XR. Nagle is turned on by default (on a per-service basis) within IOS XR and is not user-configurable.

service tcp-keepalive [**in** | **out**]: Enable TCP keepalives.
 	
`(config)# service tcp-keepalives in`
`(config)# service tcp-keepalives out`
	No directly comparable command exists in IOS XR. In Cisco IOS XR, each application decides whether to use keepalives or not. This is not user-configurable. The Telnet server sends keepalives every 5 minutes. The Telnet client does not send them. Other TCP-based protocols (BGP, SSH, etc.) have similar built-in keepalive values.

IP TCP Commands	TCP Commands

ip tcp: Configure various TCP attributes.
 	
`(config)# ip tcp path-mtu-discovery`
`age-timer 30`
`(config)# ip tcp window-size 32768`
`(config)# ip tcp synwait-time 5`
	tcp: Configure various TCP attributes.
	
	`(config)# tcp path-mtu-discovery age-timer`
	`30`
	`(config)# tcp window-size 32768`
	`(config)# tcp synwait-time 5`

SSH Support	
IP SSH Commands	SSH Commands

ip ssh: Configure various SSH attributes.
 	
`(config)# ip ssh time-out 20`
`(config)# ip ssh authentication-`
`retries 3`
`(config)# ip ssh version 2`
`(config)# ip ssh source-interface`
`Loopback0`
 	
To configure a router for SSH, a host name and domain name must first be specified. In addition, an RSA key pair must be generated.
 	
`(config)# hostname RouterA`
`(config)# ip domain-name cisco.com`
`(config)# crypto key generate rsa`
	ssh: Configure various SSH attributes.
	
	`(config)# ssh server v2`
	`(config)# ssh timeout 20`
	`(config)# ssh client source-interface`
	`Loopback0`
	`(config)# ssh client`
	
	SSH Version 2 (SSHv2) uses Digital Signature Algorithm (DSA) keys. To configure a router for SSH, a host name and domain name must first be specified. In addition, a DSA key pair must be generated.
	
	`(config)# hostname RouterA`
	`(config)# domain-name cisco.com`
	`(config)# exit`
	`# crypto key generate dsa`

continues

Table C-3 *Management Plane Security Commands (Continued)*

IOS 12.0S	IOS XR
HTTP/HTTPS Support	
IP HTTP Commands	HTTP Commands

ip http: Configure various HTTP server attributes. IOS 12.0S does not support running HTTP over SSL.
 	
`(config)# ip http access-class 10`
`(config)# ip http authentication tacacs`
`(config)# ip http port 8088`
`(config)# ip http server`
	http server: Configure various HTTP server attributes. IOS XR supports running HTTP over SSL when enabled.
	
	`(config)# http server ssl access-group NOC`

FTP/TFTP/SCP/SFTP/rcmd Support	
IP FTP Commands	FTP Commands

ip ftp: Configure various FTP client attributes.
 	
`(config)# ip ftp source-interface Loopback0`
`(config)# ip ftp username ftpsess`
`(config)# ip ftp password s3cr3t`
 	
Note that the FTP feature is being removed from IOS 12.0S and the above functionality should be replaced by the Secure Copy (SCP) feature.
	ftp: Configure various FTP attributes.
	
	`(config)# ftp client anonymous-password s3cr3t`
	`(config)# ftp client source-interface Loopback0`

IP TFTP Commands	TFTP Commands

ip tftp source-interface: Configure a TFTP source interface.
 	
`(config)# ip tftp source-interface Loopback0`
	tftp: Configure various TFTP attributes.
	
	`(config)# tftp ipv4 server access-list NOC homedir disk0`
	`(config)# tftp client source-interface Loopback0`

IP SCP Commands	SFTP Commands
ip scp server enable: Configure the Secure Copy functionality. `(config)# ip scp server enable` Before enabling SCP, you must correctly configure SSH, authentication, and authorization on the router.	SFTP is a feature that provides a secure and authenticated method for copying router configuration or router image files. The SFTP client functionality is provided as part of the SSH component and is always enabled on the router. No additional configurations are required beyond SSH, authentication, and authorization in order to use SFTP services.

Table C-3   *Management Plane Security Commands (Continued)*

IOS 12.0S	IOS XR
IP RCMD Commands	RCP Commands

ip rcmd source-interface: Configure rcmd source interface.
 	
`(config)# ip rcmd source-interface Loopback0`
	rcp: Configure various rcp attributes.
	
	`(config)# rcp client source-interface Loopback0`
	`(config)# rcp client username netadmin1`

VTY/Console/Aux Line Support	
Line Console Commands	Line Console Commands

line con 0: Configure various console line attributes.
 	
`(config)# line con 0`
`(config-line)# access-class 10 in`
`(config-line)# exec-timeout 60 0`
`(config-line)# password s3cr3t`
	line console: Configure various console line attributes.
	
	`(config)# line console`
	`(config-line)# access-class 10 in`
	`(config-line)# exec-timeout 60 0`
	`(config-line)# password s3cr3t`

Line VTY Commands	Line Default Commands

line vty 0 4: Configure various terminal line attributes.
 	
`(config)# line vty 0 4`
`(config-line)# access-class 10 in`
`(config-line)# exec-timeout 60 0`
`(config-line)# password s3cr3t`
`(config-line)# transport preferred ssh`
	line default: Configure various terminal (VTY) line attributes.
	
	`(config)# line default`
	`(config-line)# access-class 20 in`
	`(config-line)# exec-timeout 60 0`
	`(config-line)# password s3cr3t`
	`(config-line)# transport preferred ssh`

Line Auxiliary Port Commands	Line Template Commands

line aux 0: Configure various auxiliary port attributes.
 	
`(config)# line aux 0`
`(config-line)# access-class 10 in`
`(config-line)# exec-timeout 60 0`
`(config-line)# password s3cr3t`
	line template: Configure various auxiliary port attributes.
	
	`(config)# line template Use-for-Aux`
	`(config-line)# exec-time-out 60 0`
	`(config-line)# password s3cr3t`
	
	Note that the **line template** command replaces the deprecated **aux** command.

continues

Table C-3 *Management Plane Security Commands (Continued)*

IOS 12.0S	IOS XR
Banner Support	
Banner Commands	Banner Commands
banner exec: Define a customized banner that is displayed whenever the EXEC process is initiated.	**banner exec**: Define a customized banner that is displayed whenever the EXEC process is initiated.
banner incoming: Define a customized banner that is displayed when there is an incoming connection to a terminal line from a host on the network.	**banner incoming**: Define a customized banner that is displayed when there is an incoming connection to a terminal line from a host on the network.
banner login: Define a customized banner that is displayed before the username and password login prompts.	**banner login**: Define a customized banner that is displayed before the username and password login prompts.
banner motd: Define a customized message-of-the-day banner.	**banner motd**: Define a customized message-of-the-day banner.

`(config)# banner motd "`
 	
`Unauthorized Access Is Prohibited`
`Contact support: 800.555.1212`
`"`
	banner prompt-timeout: Define a customized banner that is displayed when there is a login timeout.

	`(config)# banner motd "`
	
	`Unauthorized Access Is Prohibited`
	`Contact support: 800.555.1212`
	`"`

Table C-3   *Management Plane Security Commands (Continued)*

IOS 12.0S	IOS XR
NetFlow Support	
IP Flow Commands	Global Flow Commands

ip [flow-export | flow-sampling-mode]: Configure various NetFlow attributes.
 	
`(config)# ip flow-export version 9`
`(config)# ip flow-export destination 10.10.10.1 9999`
`(config)# ip flow-sampling-mode packet-interval 100`
	flow: Configure various NetFlow attributes.
	
	`(config)# sampler-map Sample1`
	`(config-sm)# random 1 out-of 1`
	`(config-sm)# exit`
	`(config)# flow exporter-map FlowEx1`
	`(config-fem)# version v9`
	`(config-fem-ver)# options interface-table timeout 120`
	`(config-fem-ver)# options sampler-table timeout 120`
	`(config-fem-ver)# template timeout 30`
	`(config-fem-ver)# template data timeout 30`
	`(config-fem-ver)# template options timeout 30`
	`(config-fem-ver)# exit`
	`(config-fem)# transport udp 9999`
	`(config-fem)# source TenGigE0/2/0/0`
	`(config-fem)# destination 10.10.10.1`
	`(config-fem)# exit`
	`(config)# flow monitor-map FlowMon1`
	`(config-fmm)# cache permanent`
	`(config-fmm)# record ipv4-raw`
	`(config-fmm)# exporter FlowEx1`
	`(config-fmm)# exit`

IP Route-Cache Commands	Interface Flow Commands

ip route-cache flow [input | output | sampled]: Configure NetFlow on the selected interface.
 	
`(config)# interface POS0/0`
`(config-if)# ip route-cache flow input sampled`
	flow: Configure NetFlow on the selected interface.
	
	`(config)# interface POS0/0/0/0`
	`(config-if)# flow ipv4 monitor FlowMon1 sampler Sample1 ingress`
	`(config-if)# exit`

continues

Table C-3 *Management Plane Security Commands (Continued)*

IOS 12.0S	IOS XR
Fault Services Support	
Embedded Event Manager Commands	Fault Manager Commands

event manager: Configure various Embedded Event Manager (EEM) attributes.
 	
`(config)# event manager applet linkfail`
`(config-applet)# event syslog pattern ".*UPDOWN.*"`
`(config-applet)# action 1.0 syslog priority warnings msg`
`    "FLIPFLOP: $_syslog_msg"`
 	
`# show logging`
 	
`-- <output skipped> --`
 	
`4w3d: %HA_EM-5-LOG: linkfail:`
`FLIPFLOP: 4w3d: %LINEPROTO-5-UPDOWN:`
`Line protocol on Interface Loopback10,`
`changed state to down`
	fault manager: Configure various Fault Manager attributes.
	
	`(config)# fault manager environment _cron_entry 0-59/2 0-23/1 * * 0-7`
	`(config)# fault manager environment _email_server alpha@cisco.com`
	`(config)# fault manager environment _email_from beta@cisco.com`
	`(config)# fault manager environment _email_to beta@cisco.com`
	
	`(config)# fault manager environment _email_cc`
	`(config)# fault manager user-policy-directory disk1:user_policy_dir`
	`(config)# fault manager policy gw2_proc_avail.tcl username Bob`
	`(config)# fault manager policy term0_diag_cmds.tcl username Bob`

IP Source Tracker	
IP Source Tracker	—

ip source-track: Gather information about traffic flows *to* a host that is suspected of being under attack.
 	
`(config)# ip source-track address-limit 2`
`! configure syslog interval (minutes)`
`(config)# ip source-track syslog-interval 2`
`! configure export interval (seconds)`
`(config)# ip source-track export-interval 5`
`! configure victim ip address`
`(config)# ip source-track 192.168.0.10`
 	
`# show ip source-track 192.168.0.10 summary`
`# execute slot 0 show ip source-track cache`
`# show ip source-track export flows`
 	
Caveat: IP Source Tracker supports native IPv4 packets only, not MPLS encapsulated IPv4 packets.
	No directly comparable command exists in IOS XR. IP Source Tracker is not available in IOS XR at the time of this writing. Similar capabilities are provided by telemetry-based instrumentation such as NetFlow data export and other management plane tools.

Table C-3   *Management Plane Security Commands (Continued)*

IOS 12.0S	IOS XR
Global Process Controls	
Scheduler Allocate Command	—
scheduler allocate {*interrupt-time*} {*process-time*}: Configure guaranteed CPU time for processes (in microseconds). (config)# `scheduler allocate 4000 400`	There is no equivalent configuration in IOS XR. IOS XR uses a microkernel architecture and underlying Real Time Operating System (RTOS) design that is preemptive, and the scheduler is priority based. This ensures that context switching between processes is very fast, and the highest-priority threads always have access to CPU when required.
Boot System Commands	—
boot system flash : Specify the system image to boot at startup. (config)# `boot system flash disk0:gsr-k4p-mz.120-27.S5.bin`	There is no equivalent configuration in IOS XR.
Memory Free Command	—
memory free low-watermark processor {*threshold*}: Configure a router to issue a syslog message when available memory falls below the specified threshold. (config)# `memory free low-watermark processor 100000`	No directly comparable command exists in IOS XR. Similar functionality is accomplished with IOS XR Fault Manager.
Process CPU Threshold Command	—
process cpu threshold : Configure the router to issue a syslog message when configured CPU utilization thresholds are crossed. (config)# `process cpu threshold type total rising 30 interval 5 falling 20 interval 5`	No directly comparable command exists in IOS XR. Similar functionality is accomplished with IOS XR Fault Manager.

continues

Table C-3 *Management Plane Security Commands (Continued)*

IOS 12.0S	IOS XR
Service Commands	
Service Password Command	—
service password-encryption: Enable encrypted password storage. (config)# `service password-encryption`	No such configuration. Passwords are always encrypted in IOS XR.
Service Compress Config Command	—
service compress-config: Compress startup configuration files. (config)# `service compress-config`	No such configuration. IOS XR has a different configuration file management model.
Service PAD Command	—
no service pad: Disable the X.25 packet assembler/disassembler (PAD) service. (Enabled by default.) (config)# `no service pad`	No such configuration. IOS XR does not support PAD.
Service tcp-small-servers Command	Service ipv4 tcp-small-servers Command
no service tcp-small-servers: Disable the minor TCP servers for Echo, Discard, Chargen, and Daytime services. When disabled, IOS discards the initial incoming packet (TCP SYN request) and sends a TCP RST packet to the source. (Enabled by default,) (config)# `no service tcp-small-servers`	**no service ipv4 tcp-small-servers**: Disable the minor TCP servers for Echo, Discard, and Chargen services. TCP small-servers are disabled by default. (config)# `no service ipv4 tcp-small-servers`
Service udp-small-servers Command	Service ipv4 udp-small-servers Command

Table C-3   *Management Plane Security Commands (Continued)*

IOS 12.0S	IOS XR
no service udp-small-servers: Disable the minor UDP servers for Echo, Discard, and Chargen services. When disabled, IOS discards the initial incoming packet and sends an ICMP Port Unreachable message (Type 3, Code 3) to the source. (Enabled by default.) `(config)#` `no service udp-small-servers`	**no service ipv4 udp-small-servers**: Disables the minor UDP servers for Echo, Discard, and Chargen services. UDP small-servers are disabled by default. `(config)#` `no service ipv4 udp-small-servers`
Service Timestamp Commands	Service Timestamp Commands
service timestamps debug : Configure the system to apply a time stamp to debugging messages. `(config)#` `service timestamp debug datetime msec localtime`	**service timestamps debug**: Configure the system to apply a time stamp to debugging messages. `(config)#` `service timestamp debug datetime msec localtime`
service timestamps log : Configure the system to apply a time stamp to system logging messages. `(config)#` `service timestamp log datetime msec localtime`	**service timestamps log**: Configure the system to apply a time stamp to system logging messages. `(config)#` `service timestamp log datetime msec localtime`
Other Global Security Best Practices	
IP Finger Command	—

no ip finger: Disable the finger protocol. (Disabled by default.)
 	
`(config)#` `no ip finger`
 	
no service finger: Newer versions of IOS 12.0S may also use this form of the command to disable the finger service.
 	
`(config)#` `no service finger`
	No such configuration is available or required. IOS XR does not support the finger service.

continues

Table C-3   *Management Plane Security Commands (Continued)*

IOS 12.0S	IOS XR
IP Bootp Command	—
no ip bootp server: Disable the Bootstrap Protocol (BOOTP) service. (Enabled by default.) (config)# `no ip bootp server`	No such configuration. IOS XR does not support the BOOTP service.
Logging Console Command	Logging Console Command
no logging console: Disable the logging of messages to the console terminal. (config)# `no logging console`	**logging console disable**: Disable the logging of messages to the console terminal. (config)# `logging console disable`
CDP Command	CDP Command
no cdp run: Disable Cisco Discovery Protocol (CDP) globally. (Enabled by default.) (config)# `no cdp run` CDP can also be disabled on a per-interface basis. (config)# `interfacePOS0/0` (config-if)# `no cdp enable`	**no cdp**: Disable CDP globally. (Disabled by default.) (config)# `no cdp` CDP can also be disabled on a per-interface basis. (config)# `interface POS0/0/0/0` (config-if)# `no cdp`
IP Domain-Name Command	Domain Lookup Command
no ip domain-lookup: Disable Domain Name System hostname translation. (config)# `no ip domain-lookup`	**domain lookup disable**: Disable Domain Name System hostname translation. (config)# `domain lookup disable`

Services Plane Security Commands

Services plane–specific commands refer to those commands that configure, directly or indirectly, security features within services plane functions such as MPLS VPN TTL propagation, VRF maximum prefix limits, and many others. Obviously, it is not possible to list every services plane command here. Only those used within this book are included, but many others exit. Table C-4 lists Cisco IOS commands and their Cisco IOS XR counterparts, if any, along with a short example of how each command is used.

Table C-4 *Services Plane Security Commands*

IOS 12.0S	IOS XR
MPLS-Related Commands	
VRF Maximum Route Command	VRF Maximum Prefix Command
maximum routes {*limit*} {*warn-threshold* | **warn-only**}: Configure limits on the maximum number of routes that a VRF instance can import to prevent a PE router from exhausting memory resources. The optional *threshold* value specifies the percentage of the maximum argument value at which an SNMP trap is generated. (config)# **ip vrf Customer-A** (config-vrf)# **maximum routes 5000 80** (config-vrf)#	**maximum prefix** {*limit*} {*threshold*}: Configure limits on the maximum nuber of prefixes that a VRF instance can import. The optional *threshold* value specifies the percentage of the maximum argument value at which an SNMP trap is generated. (config)# **vrf Customer-A** (config-vrf)# **address-family ipv4 unicast** (config-vrf-af)# **maximum prefix 10000 80** (config-vrf-af)#
MPLS TTL Propagate Command	MPLS TTL Propagate Command
no mpls ip propagate-ttl [forwarded]: Disable the propagation (copying) of the IP TTL into the MPLS label header. Instead, set the initial MPLS TTL value to 255. By default, the IP TTL value is propagated to the MPLS header TTL field when IP packets enter the MPLS domain. Within the MPLS domain, the MPLS TTL is decremented at each MPLS hop. When an MPLS encapsulated IP packet exits the MPLS domain, the MPLS TTL is propagated to the IP header if (and only if) the MPLS TTL is less than the IP TTL. When propagation is disabled, the MPLS TTL is set to 255 during label imposition and the IP TTL is not altered. (config)# **no mpls ip propagate-ttl forwarded**	**mpls ip-ttl-propagate disable**: Disable the propagation (copying) of the IP TTL into the MPLS label header. Instead, set the initial MPLS TTL value to 255. By default, the IP TTL is propagated to the MPLS header TTL field when IP packets enter the MPLS domain. Within the MPLS domain, the MPLS TTL is decremented at each MPLS hop. When an MPLS encapsulated IP packet exits the MPLS domain, the MPLS TTL is propagated to the IP header if (and only if) the MPLS TTL is less than the IP TTL. When propagation is disabled, the MPLS TTL is set to 255 during label imposition and the IP TTL is not altered. (config)# **mpls ip-ttl-propagate disable**
MPLS Label Commands	MPLS Label Commands

continues

Table C-4   *Services Plane Security Commands (Continued)*

IOS 12.0S	IOS XR

mpls ldp advertise-labels: Control the distribution of locally assigned (incoming) labels by means of label distribution protocol (LDP).
 	
`(config)# ip access-list standard pfx-`
`filter`
`(config-std-nacl)# permit 10.101.0.0`
`0.0.255.255`
`(config-std-nacl)# permit 10.221.0.0`
`0.0.255.255`
`(config-std-nacl)# exit`
`(config)# mpls ldp advertise-labels for`
`pfx-filter`
	label advertise: Control the distribution of locally assigned (incoming) labels by means of LDP.
	
	`(config)# ipv4 access-list pfx_acl_1`
	`(config-ipv4-acl)# permit 10.101.0.0`
	`(config-ipv4-acl)# permit 10.221.0.0`
	
	`(config)# mpls ldp`
	`(config-ldp)# label advertise`
	`(config-ldp-lbl-advt)# disable`
	`(config-ldp-lbl-advt)# for pfx_acl_1`

mpls ldp neighbor labels accept: Configure a label switching router (LSR) to filter LDP inbound label bindings from a particular LDP peer.
 	
`(config)# mpls ldp neighbor vrf vpn1`
`19.19.19.19 label accept 1`
	label accept for {prefix-acl} from {ip-address}: Control the receipt of labels (remote bindings) for a set of prefixes from a peer.
	
	`(config)# mpls ldp`
	`(config-ldp)# label accept`
	`(config-ldp-lbl-acpt)# for pfx_acl_1`
	`from 1.1.1.1`
	`(config-ldp-lbl-acpt)# for pfx_acl_2`
	`from 2.2.2.2`
	`(config-ldp-lbl-acpt)# for pfx_acl_3`
	`from 3.3.3.3`

Interface MTU-Related Commands	
Interface MTU Command	Interface MTU Command

mtu {*value*}: Configure the interface Layer 2 MTU value. This Layer 2 command applies to any upper-layer protocols transmitted on the interface (such as IP, MPLS, ARP, and so on).
 	
`(config)# interface POS0/0`
`(config-if)# mtu 4474`
	mtu {*value*}: Configure the interface Layer 2 MTU value. This Layer 2 command applies to any upper-layer protocols transmitted on the interface (such as IP, MPLS, ARP, and so on).
	
	`(config)# interface POS0/0/0/0`
	`(config-if)# mtu 4474`

ip mtu {*value*}: Configure the maximum transmission unit (MTU) size of IP packets (only) sent on an interface. The maximum MTU size that can be set on an interface depends on the interface medium. The router will fragment any IP packet that exceeds the MTU set for the interface.
 	
`(config)# interface POS0/0`
`(config-if)# ip mtu 1300`
	ipv4 mtu {*value*}: Configure the MTU size of IPv4 packets sent on an interface. The maximum MTU size that can be set on an interface depends on the interface medium. The router will fragment any IPv4 packet that exceeds the MTU set for the interface.
	
	`(config)# interface POS0/0/0/0`
	`(config-if)# ipv4 mtu 1300`

Further Reading

Converting Cisco IOS Configurations to Cisco IOS XR Configurations, Release 3.4. Cisco Documentation. http://www.cisco.com/en/US/products/ps5845/ products_technical_reference_book09186a00806b9204.html.

Cisco IOS XR Security Configuration Guide, Release 3.4. Cisco Documentation. http://www.cisco.com/en/US/products/ps5845/ products_configuration_guide_book09186a00806b66d2.html.

Cisco IOS XR Software Command References. Cisco Documentation. http://www.cisco.com/en/US/products/ps5845/prod_command_reference_list.html.

Cisco IOS XR Software Configuration Guides. Cisco Documentation. http://www.cisco.com/en/US/partner/products/ps5845/ products_installation_and_configuration_guides_list.html.

Converting Cisco IOS Configurations to Cisco IOS XR Configurations, Release 3.4. Cisco Documentation. http://www.cisco.com/en/US/partner/products/ps5845/ products_technical_reference_book09186a00806b9204.html.

Security Incident Handling

Chapter 2 outlined many threats against IP (and L2 Ethernet) networks. Chapters 4 through 7 described a wide variety of techniques available to mitigate these threats. Although this book focuses on IP network traffic plane security, many other threats exist that aim to exploit vulnerabilities in host operating systems and application software. Hence, network operational security must consider both network-based attacks and host-based attacks.

This appendix focuses on security incident handling; that is, the method by which you prepare for and respond to active host-based or network-based attacks. The industry best common practice (BCP) for incident response handling includes a six-phase approach, which is described here. In addition, this appendix provides a brief summary of Cisco product security and several industry incident response teams and network operators' groups.

Security operators are also recommended to consider building their own security operations center (SOC). This appendix does not cover SOC designs or operations. More information on this topic can be found in the Cisco white paper "How to Build a Cisco Security Operations Center," available on Cisco.com. For more information on security incident handling, see the "Further Reading" list at the end of the appendix.

Six Phases of Incident Response

Malware, including viruses, worms, and distributed DoS attacks, may adversely impact legitimate traffic flows and network infrastructure, including the wider Internet, within minutes or even seconds. Consequently, the speed with which you recognize and respond to attacks is critical to minimizing the impact of an attack. When an effective incident response plan is not available, networks are at increased risk.

To reduce incident response times, you must proactively establish incident response procedures within an operational security framework, as opposed to simply *reacting* to events. This also requires monitoring for security events so that attacks can be quickly detected. The industry BCP for incident response handling includes a six-phase approach, which is illustrated in Figure D-1. In adopting these phases (or steps) within your security operations framework, you may significantly reduce response times and improve the mitigation effectiveness against attacks. In addition, this six-phase approach has proven capable of serving well for addressing both existing and emerging threats.

Figure D-1   *Six Phases of Incident Response*

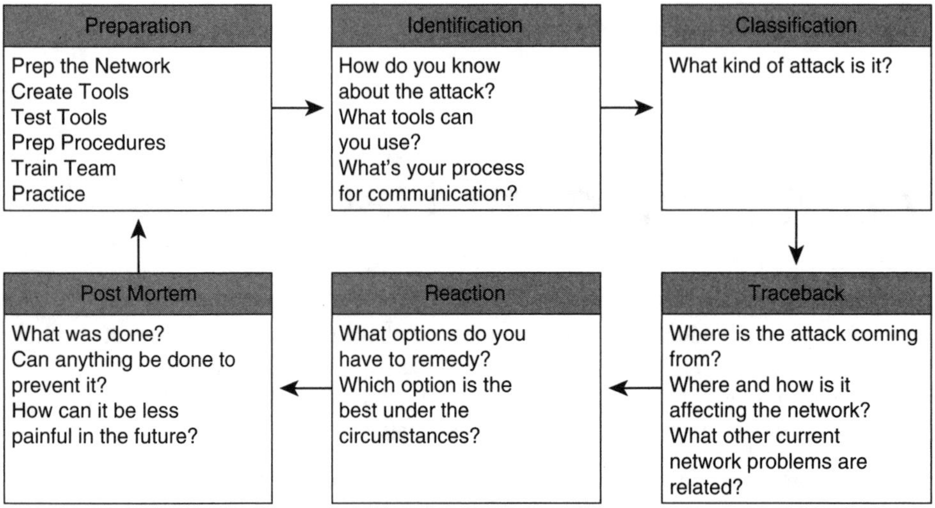

Preparation	Identification	Classification
Prep the Network Create Tools Test Tools Prep Procedures Train Team Practice	How do you know about the attack? What tools can you use? What's your process for communication?	What kind of attack is it?
Post Mortem	**Reaction**	**Traceback**
What was done? Can anything be done to prevent it? How can it be less painful in the future?	What options do you have to remedy? Which option is the best under the circumstances?	Where is the attack coming from? Where and how is it affecting the network? What other current network problems are related?

Let's review each of these six phases.

Preparation

Being prepared significantly improves your ability to respond to attacks and, therefore, improves response time, improves mitigation effectiveness, and reduces network downtime. Without preparation, you are often left to employ highly reactive and perhaps misguided actions in the event of an attack. Preparation is considered the most difficult and costly phase of the six-phase approach, yet it represents the most important of the six phases because it lays the foundation for the remaining phases. The preparation phase involves a number of distinct components, which are described next.

Understand the Threats

As outlined in Chapter 2, there are a variety of methods by which attackers may target IP networks and devices. Further, threats may differ due to the variety of IP networks deployed, including product mix, network topology, traffic behavior, and organizational mission (for example, SP versus enterprise). Understanding the threats against your specific network will help you to assess your risk, mitigate the risk to acceptable levels, and classify attacks once detected.

Deploy Defense in Depth and Breadth Security Strategies

IP routers and network devices today support a wide variety of security mechanisms to detect, prevent, and mitigate attacks, as outlined in Chapters 4 through 7. These mechanisms must be proactively deployed, however, because implementing them in the midst of an attack may place the network at even greater risk given the potential for unintended consequences such as misconfiguration errors and collateral damage. For example, implementing certain features may cause router performance degradation. When this is not well understood, implementing a feature in the midst of an attack without prior understanding of feature impact can cause more problems than the attack itself.

Performance impacts, if any, depend on different factors, as outlined in Chapters 1 and 3. Therefore, to harden the network infrastructure and minimize the risk of an attack (as well as harmful side effects resulting from reactive configuration changes), defense in depth and breadth strategies should be proactively deployed. An example of where this is critical is preprovisioning, testing, and establishing a usage procedure for the mechanisms required to implement remotely triggered black hole (RTBH) filtering (such as deploying a static route to Null0 on all edge routers and deploying a BGP trigger router as described in Chapter 4). Deploying up-to-date software versions that include fixes for disclosed security vulnerabilities is another proactive step you should take to mitigate the risk of known vulnerabilities.

When emergency software upgrades are required, understanding available flash and dynamic memory as well as having prepared procedures for performing upgrades reduces the risk of errors and collateral damage. Understandably, deploying infrastructure security can be difficult because it affects many network devices, each of which potentially has its own limitations and platform-specific dependencies. Further, there is a cost associated with deploying security measures, which may include administrative overhead, operational inconvenience, and router scale and performance impacts. The cost of applying security measures needs to be weighed against the potential risks. Organizations (not just security operators) must understand the risks and the cost of applying security measures to mitigate the risk to acceptable levels.

Establish Well-Defined Incident Response Procedures

As previously described, you should prepare the network in advance with any preconfigurations necessary for attack mitigation, as opposed to configuring in real time during an incident. Once you have done so, it is then imperative that you establish a *playbook* that defines the roles and responsibilities of everyone on the incident response team. Well-defined procedures must be established and training drills must be conducted. This not only helps people understand their roles, but brings to light any areas of question, allowing for procedural modifications where required. Further, these incident response procedures must consider the associated performance impact, if any, of enabling a security feature for all applicable network equipment before deploying it. Without knowing the performance impacts, if any, applying a mitigation technique such as an ACL, for example, may actually have a more adverse impact on the network than the attack itself. The established incident response procedures must take these factors into consideration as previously stated.

Establish an Incident Response Team

Because security attacks threaten network availability, the incident response team should include both network and security operators. They must be well trained and versed in their roles during times of attack. Once attacks occur, it is too late to begin identifying who is doing what, where, and when. The incident response team owns the six phases of incident response and is responsible for executing against each of them. Further, the incident response team should also maintain contact information for all external network peers. Many attacks are sourced from external networks. Hence, it is important to maintain emergency contact information and understand how they may be able to assist in attack mitigation. For SPs, an Inter-NOC (INOC) Dial-By-ASN (DBA) Hotline is also available to facilitate real-time communication among the SP community. For more information, refer to http://www.pch.net/inoc-dba/ and http://www.pch.net/technology/operations.php#3.

Identification

In order to mitigate an attack, it must first be detected and identified. Detection requires visibility into network activity, threats, and traffic patterns. Without such network visibility, you are left with an incomplete view of network traffic and events. This significantly increases the time to repair (or mitigate) depending upon the root cause diagnosis. As stated in the previous section, detection time is critical to containing the impact of an attack. IP routers support a wide variety of tools that provide network visibility and anomaly detection, as outlined in Chapter 6. These include but are not limited to SNMP polling and traps, syslog messaging, NetFlow telemetry, and various other router health statistics such as those related to CPU and memory utilization and feature performance. Such network telemetry is considered a network security best practice and should be defined and deployed as part of the preparation phase previously outlined.

Further, to detect network anomalies and potential security events, you must first understand the baseline network activity and traffic patterns during normal network operating conditions. The comparison of real-time network conditions against the established baseline is the very nature of the identification phase. For more information on network telemetry and event identification, refer to the Cisco Networkers 2005 session SEC-2102 entitled "Detection and Classification of Network Traffic."

Classification

Classification provides the context for further action (in other words, the traceback and reaction phases, discussed next) once a network fault or anomaly is identified. Network events may be caused by any number of sources, as outlined in Chapter 2, including both intentional and unintentional threats. Classification is about diagnosing the problem cause, severity, and scope of the threat. For example, does the threat affect a single device or the wider network infrastructure, and what damage is it causing? Classification also relies on network telemetry to gain network visibility. Whereas the previous identification phase collects and establishes trends for network activity and traffic patterns, the classification phase correlates the observed network activity and events in order to isolate problem cause and determine a root cause.

Traceback

After an attack has been detected and classified, you need to identify and locate the source(s) of the attack. Attacks that use spoofed IP source addresses are the most difficult to trace back to their origin. Source traceback for spoofed attacks can be arduous. Deploying antispoofing protection as part of the preparation phase minimizes such threats and can significantly reduce the associated operational expenses of dealing with such attacks.

IP routers support a wide variety of tools that facilitate source identification and traceback of an attack, including but not limited to classification ACLs, NetFlow, IP Source Tracker, and the ICMP backscatter traceback technique. If an attack originates externally, then it must be traced back to the point(s) of ingress at the network edge. Once it has been traced back to your network edge, the pre-established contacts with your peer networks (as discussed earlier in the section "Establish an Incident Response Team") become useful for gaining mitigation support from external peer networks. Traceback must also consider whether multiple paths exist to the external peer from which the attack originates.

Reaction

Once an attack has been identified, classified, and traced back to the source(s), you may need to explicitly mitigate it. If the attack is insignificant or inconsequential, you may decide not to do anything. Chapters 4 through 7 describe a variety of mechanisms to protect and mitigate attacks against IP networks and IP routers. No single technique can be identified as *the best approach* to mitigate all of the many different threats. The effectiveness of each technique is dependent on specific network environments such as product mix, network topology, traffic behavior, and organizational mission. Nevertheless, you should avoid deploying techniques that have not been previously defined within the established incident response procedures documented during the preparation phase previously described. Without understanding the potential impacts, if any, applying a mitigation technique may make the problem worse. Further, attacks should be mitigated as close to the source or ingress point(s) as possible. Otherwise, a mitigated attack may still have the potential to cause collateral damage on intermediate network devices.

Post-Mortem Analysis

After the dust settles, your incident response team should analyze the root causes of the incident, and fine-tune existing incident response procedures. This should result in changes to incident response procedures, where required, and potential changes in the baseline network security configuration. In this way, the incident response team and procedures are continuously evolving and providing greater resistance to known and emerging threats.

Cisco Product Security

The Cisco Product Security Incident Response Team (PSIRT) is a dedicated, global team that manages the receipt, investigation, and public reporting of security vulnerability-related information, related to Cisco products and networks. PSIRT works with Cisco customers, independent security researchers, consultants, industry organizations, and other vendors to identify possible security issues with Cisco products and networks. Responses can range from Release Note Enclosures (RNE), which are visible to customers via BugToolkit on Cisco.com, to Security Advisories, depending upon a number of factors.

Anyone who has a product security issue is strongly encouraged to contact PSIRT directly. To report security-related bugs in Cisco products, or to get assistance with security incidents involving Cisco products, send an e-mail to psirt@cisco.com for nonemergency issues or security-alert@cisco.com for urgent matters. Cisco PSIRT may also be contacted via the PSIRT Security Hotline by dialing 877 228-7302 or 408 525-6532. Alternatively, if you are under active security attack or have more general security concerns about your Cisco network, you can contact the Cisco Technical Assistance Center at 408 526-7209, 800 553-2447, or by locating country-specific contact information. Cisco worldwide contact information is available at http://www.cisco.com/warp/public/687/Directory/DirTAC.shtml. The technical support agents will escalate to the proper PSIRT personnel to assist you. For more information, refer to the following section, "Cisco Security Vulnerability Policy."

Cisco Security Advisories are available via the following methods:

- Cisco's Internet web portal at http://www.cisco.com/en/US/products/products_security_advisories_listing.html.

- E-mail via cust-security-announce@cisco.com. Anyone interested may subscribe to this e-mail list using the procedures described in the "Subscribing to the Customer Security Announce Mailing List" section of the Cisco Security Vulnerability Policy, described in the following section.

- PSIRT RSS feeds available via Cisco.com. These feeds are free and do not require any active Cisco.com registration. Information for subscribing to RSS feeds is found at http://www.cisco.com/en/US/products/products_psirt_rss_feed.html.

Major Cisco Security Announcements are also available at http://www.cisco.com/security/announcements.html.

Cisco Security Vulnerability Policy

Cisco's policy for receiving and responding to products and services security vulnerabilities is posted at http://www.cisco.com/en/US/products/products_security_vulnerability_policy.html.

Cisco Computer and Network Security

If you want to report a computer or network security-related incident involving the Cisco corporate network, please contact the Cisco Computer Security Incident Response Team (CSIRT) by sending an e-mail to infosec@cisco.com.

Cisco Safety and Security

To report an issue or inquire about Cisco's safety and physical security program, including the protection of company employees, property, and information, please call 408 525-1111 or send an e-mail to safetyandsecurity@cisco.com.

Cisco IPS Signature Pack Updates and Archives

Cisco IPS Active Update Bulletins are posted at http://www.cisco.com/security.

Cisco Security Center

Visit the Cisco Security Center site for information on emerging threats and the Cisco network IPS signatures available to protect your network. The Cisco Security Center is available at http://www.cisco.com/security/center/home.x.

You can also find Cisco Applied Intelligence Response documents at the Cisco Security Center site. Cisco Applied Intelligence Responses (AIRs) provide identification and mitigation techniques that can be deployed on Cisco network devices. As applicable, Cisco IOS access control lists, Cisco Intrusion Prevention System (IPS) signatures, Control Plane Policing, and firewall rules are among the techniques discussed in the AIR.

Cisco IntelliShield Alert Manager Service

Cisco Security IntelliShield Alert Manager Service provides a comprehensive, cost-effective solution for delivering the intelligence that organizations need to identify, prevent, and quickly mitigate IT attacks. IntelliShield Alert Manager Service is a customizable, web-based threat and vulnerability alert service that allows security staff to easily access timely, accurate, and credible information about vulnerabilities that may affect their environments, without conducting time-consuming research. Registration is required. For more information, refer to http://www.cisco.com/en/US/products/ps6834/serv_group_home.html.

Cisco Software Center

The latest Cisco software is posted to the Cisco Software Center at http://www.cisco.com/kobayashi/sw-center/. Access requires a Cisco.com username and password.

Industry Security Organizations

There are a number of leading industry and government security organizations that help the industry and Internet community deal effectively with emerging security threats. Contact information for Computer Security Incident Response Teams (CSIRT) that have responsibility for an economy or country is available at http://www.cert.org/csirts/national/contact.html. An interactive map is also available at http://www.cert.org/csirts/national/ to locate CSIRTs around the world with national responsibility.

Industry forums include but are not limited to the following:

- CERT/CC (Computer Emergency Readiness Team/Coordination Center)
  http://www.cert.org/

- Cisco PSIRT (Product Security Incident Response Team)
  http://www.cisco.com/go/psirt

- FIRST (Forum of Incident Response and Security Teams)
  http://www.first.org/

- IETF OPSEC (Operational Security Capabilities for IP Network Infrastructure)
  http://www.ietf.org/html.charters/opsec-charter.html

- SANS Internet Storm Center
  http://isc.sans.org/

- IT-ISAC (Information Technology – Information Sharing and Analysis Center)
  https://www.it-isac.org/

- ITU Cybersecurity Gateway
  http://www.itu.int/cybersecurity/itu_activities.html

- NSP-SEC Forum
  http://puck.nether.net/mailman/listinfo/nsp-security

- SANS (SysAdmin, Audit, Network, Security) Institute
  http://www.sans.org/
- TERENA (Trans-European Research and Education Networking Association)
  TF-CERT
  http://www.terena.nl/tech/task-forces/tf-csirt/
- US-CERT
  http://www.uscert.gov/
- World Wide ISAC (Information Sharing and Analysis Center)
  http://www.wwisac.com

Regional Network Operators Groups

In addition to the industry security associations, a number of leading industry operator forums help the industry and regional Internet communities to effectively deal with network operational issues, including operational security (OPSEC). Many have regular meeting forums, Internet portals, and e-mail mailing lists that offer open participation to all interested parties.

- AFNOG (African Network Operators' Group)
  http://www.afnog.org/
- APRICOT (Asia Pacific Regional Internet Conference on Operational Technologies)
  http://www.apricot.net/
- APOPS (Asia Pacific Operators Forum)
  http://www.apops.net/
- CNNOG (China Network Operators' Group)
  http://www.cnnog.org/index-e.html
- FRnOG (French Network Operators Group)
  http://www.frnog.org/
- DENOG (German Network Operators Group)
  http://www.denog.de/
- IE-NOG (Irish Network Operators Group)
  http://www.ienog.org/
- JANOG (Japan Network Operators' Group)
  http://www.janog.gr.jp/index-e.html

- MENOG (Middle East Network Operators Group)
  http://www.ripe.net/meetings/menog/
- NANOG (North American Network Operators' Group)
  http://www.nanog.org/
- NAPLA (Latin America NAP Regional Interconnection Forum)
  http://lacnic.net/en/eventos/lacnicx/napla.html
- NZNOG (New Zealand Network Operators Group)
  http://www.nznog.org/
- PacNOG (Pacific Network Operators Group)
  http://www.pacnog.org/
- RIPE NCC (Réseaux IP Européens Network Coordination Centre)
  http://www.ripe.net

Note   RIPE also hosts the European Operators Forum (EOF) as part of the
RIPE meetings.

- SANOG (South Asian Network Operators Group)
  http://www.sanog.org/
- SwiNOG (Swiss Network Operators Group)
  http://www.swinog.ch/
- UKNOF (UK Network Operators' Forum)
  http://www.uknof.org.uk/

Further Reading

Dobbins, R. "Detection and Classification of Network Traffic." Session SEC-2102. Cisco Networkers 2005. June 2005.

Gemberling, B., C. Morrow, and B. Greene. "ISP Security – Real World Techniques: Remote Triggered Black Hole Filtering and Backscatter Traceback." NANOG. http://www.nanog.org/mtg-0110/greene.html.

Greene, B., and R. Dobbins. "ISP Security 101 Primer." NANOG. http://www.nanog.org/mtg-0602/greene.html.

Kaeo, M. "Current Operational Security Practices in Internet Service Provider Environments." RFC 4778. IETF, Jan. 2007. http://www.ietf.org/rfc/rfc4778.txt

Morrow, C., and B. Gemberling. "How to Track a DoS Attack." NANOG. http://www.secsup.org/Tracking/.

Parmakovic, D. "Service Provider Security." Cisco white paper. http://www.cisco.com/web/about/security/intelligence/sp_infrastruct_scty.html.

Stewart, J. "Vulnerability Disclosure." Cisco Executive Thought Leadership Research Perspective. http://tools.cisco.com/dlls/tln/page/media/perspectives/detail/ep/2006/john-stewart-01.

"How to Build a Security Operations Center." Cisco white paper. http://www.cisco.com/en/US/netsol/ns341/ns121/ns310/networking_solutions_white_paper0900aecd80598c16.shtml.

"ISACs." Cisco Incident Response Support. http://www.cisco.com/web/about/security/security_services/ciag/incident_response_support/ISACs.html.

"NANOG Security Curriculum." NANOG. http://www.nanog.org/ispsecurity.html.

"New Rapid Response Strategy Helps Security Services Firm Block Emerging Network." Cisco Case Study. http://www.cisco.com/en/US/products/ps6542/products_case_study0900aecd803fc82a.shtml.

INDEX

Numerics

10MQC, rate limiting, 173
3DES (Triple DES), 378
802.1Q (IEEE)
double encapsulation attacks, 92
headers, 543–550

A

AAA (authentication, authorization, and accounting), 326–329, 422, 439
IPsec VPN case study, 462
MPLS VPN case study, 479
commands
aaa accounting command, 328
aaa authentication command, 328
aaa authorization command, 328
aaa command, 579
aaa new-model command, 322, 328
aaa new-model configuration, 422, 439
access
case studies, 406
HTTPS, 439
Internet case study, 444–455
intranets, 465
IPsec VPN control, 391–393
MPLS VPNs, 426
passwords, 303–306
remote terminal access security, 309–311
role-based CLI, 320–324
access control entries. *See* **ACE**
access control lists. *See* **ACLs**
access mode, 210
access-class {access-list} in command, 309
access-group command, 576
accounting policies, BGP, 331
ACEs (access control entries), 235
ACK flags, 513
acknowledgment numbers, 512
ACLs (access control lists), 558, 563
antispoofing, 419
commands, 558
community strings (SNMP), 307

crypto, 392
filters, 75, 277–279
iACLs, 40, 366
interfaces, 222, 418, 435
CsC, 373
data plane security, 147–156
IKE, 387
IPsec VPN access control, 393
MPLS VPN case study, 481
IP options, filtering, 177
packets, defining classification, 244–247
PACLs, 212
rACLs, 230, 366–367, 563
control plane security, 230–232
deploying, 232–241
IPsec VPN case study, 459
MPLS VPN case study, 475
types of, 148
uRPF, applying, 157
VACLs, 211
aCoPP (aggregate CoPP) deployment, 260–261, 564
activation of rACLs, 233–234
Address Resolution Protocol. *See* **ARP**
addresses, 545, 548
attacks, 76
bogon, 161
broadcast, 231
destination, 508
limiting, 239–240
trigger routers, 196
feasible uRPF, 167
loose mode uRPF, 161–163
MAC, 545
dynamically, 208
static, 208
sticky, 208
traffic blocking, 209
Martian, 76, 162
NAT, data plane security, 201–203
networks, 231
next-hop Layer 2, 39
private networks, 76, 162
reflectors, 74
source, 507, 545, 548
limiting, 237–239

B